Fr Oscar Wilde
posing Somdomite
Marquis of Queensberry.

A

ABOVE Lord Queensberry's card, with his inscription, "For Oscar Wilde posing as a somdomite [*sic*]," and marked Exhibit "A"

LEFT Wilde's letter to the London *Evening News* (see page 223), jotted down by Robert Ross on two envelopes, saying: "I am determined . . . to bear on my own shoulders whatever ignominy and shame might result from my prosecuting Lord Queensberry"

Oscar Wilde

Books by H. Montgomery Hyde

HENRY JAMES AT HOME

THE RISE OF CASTLEREAGH

THE EMPRESS CATHERINE AND PRINCESS DASHKOV

THE TRIALS OF OSCAR WILDE

MR AND MRS BEETON

CASES THAT CHANGED THE LAW

CARSON

THE TRIAL OF CRAIG AND BENTLEY

THE STRANGE DEATH OF LORD CASTLEREAGH

THE TRIAL OF SIR ROGER CASEMENT

SIR PATRICK HASTINGS: HIS LIFE AND CASES

AN INTERNATIONAL CASE BOOK OF CRIME

ROOM 3603: THE BRITISH INTELLIGENCE CENTER IN NEW YORK

OSCAR WILDE: THE AFTERMATH

CYNTHIA

LORD READING

STRONG FOR SERVICE: THE LIFE OF LORD NATHAN OF CHURT

STALIN

Oscar Wilde

A BIOGRAPHY BY

H. Montgomery Hyde

FARRAR, STRAUS AND GIROUX

NEW YORK

Library of Congress Cataloging in Publication Data
Hyde, Harford Montgomery.
  Oscar Wilde.
  Bibliography: p. 391
  Includes index.
  1. Wilde, Oscar, 1854–1900—Biography.   I. Title.
PR5823.H88   828'.8'09 [B]   75-22439

To the Memory of Sir Peter Daubeny

Contents

Illustrations

16 Tite Street
From Lord Alfred Douglas, Oscar Wilde and Myself, *London, 1914*

Constance Wilde
Photo: courtesy of the late Vyvyan Holland

Cyril Wilde

Vyvyan Wilde
Photos: courtesy of the late Vyvyan Holland

Oscar Wilde and Lord Alfred Douglas
*Photo taken in Oxford in 1893: courtesy of the William Andrews Clark
Library, UCLA*

Robert Ross and Reginald Turner
Photo: courtesy of Giles Robertson

William Rothenstein and Max Beerbohm
as undergraduates at Oxford
Photo: courtesy of Sir Rupert Hart-Davis

Robert Sherard
Photo: courtesy of Mrs Muriel Sherard

Richard Le Gallienne
Engraving: courtesy of the Mansell Collection

Oscar Wilde. By William Rothenstein
Pen and ink drawing: courtesy of Sir John Rothenstein

Oscar Wilde. By Max Beerbohm
*Pen and ink drawing: courtesy of Sir John Rothenstein and
Mrs Eva Reichmann*

George Alexander and Allan Aynsworth
in *The Importance of Being Earnest*
*Photo: Gabrielle Enthoven Collection, courtesy of the Victoria and
Albert Museum*

The Importance of Being Earnest
Photo: author's collection

Oscar Wilde at the height of his success, 1894
Photo: Ellis & Walery, London

The Marquess of Queensberry
Photo: Radio Times Hulton Picture Library

Edward Carson. By Julia Folkard
Portrait: courtesy of the owner, the Hon. Edward Carson

Sir Edward Clarke. By "Spy" (Leslie Ward)
in *Vanity Fair*
Cartoon: author's collection

Acknowledgements

First of all, I wish to thank the late Mr Vyvyan Holland, younger son of Oscar Wilde, and Rupert Hart-Davis Ltd. (now part of Granada Publishing Ltd.) and Harcourt Brace Jovanovich, Inc., the publishers of *The Letters of Oscar Wilde,* edited by Sir Rupert Hart-Davis, for permission to quote from Wilde's letters, which are still in copyright.

For her unfailing help and interest in this work, I am under a great debt of gratitude to Mary Hyde, who, with her husband, the late Donald F. Hyde, has formed the finest and most comprehensive collection of Wildeana, Wilde manuscripts, original editions, and association copies of his books existing today in private hands.

To Dr Lawrence Clarke Powell and Mrs Edna C. Davis, late librarian and associate librarian of the William Andrews Clark Memorial Library, University of California, Los Angeles, I would like to express my warm thanks for the many kindnesses I have received from them in facilitating my researches in the great Wilde collection of which they were the custodians. Other institutions from which I have similarly benefited are the Bodleian Library and Magdalen College library in Oxford; the British Museum, the Home Office, and the Public Record Office in London; the library of Trinity College, Dublin; and the New York Public Library. To those in charge of the relevant departments of these institutions I am particularly grateful.

I am likewise indebted to the following for their help in various ways: Judge Edward Clarke, Mr Rupert Croft-Cooke, Mr John Cullen of Eyre Methuen Ltd., Professor Richard Ellmann, Sir Rupert Hart-Davis, Mrs Vyvyan Holland and Mr Merlin Holland, Mr Felix Hope-Nicholson, Mr Percy Muir, Sir John Rothenstein, Mr Martin Secker, Mr George Sims, Mr Timothy d'Arch Smith, Mr Stanley Weintraub, and Mrs Guy Wyndham.

In addition to Mr Vyvyan Holland, I have been fortunate during the past thirty-five years in having met and known various people who knew or remembered Oscar Wilde, and I think I ought to take this opportunity of recording my sense of obligation to them for having communicated their recollections of him to me—namely, Mr Allan Aynsworth, Sir Max Beerbohm, Lord Alfred Douglas, Mr Franklin Dyall, Mr Richard Le Gallienne, Sir Seymour Hicks, Sir Travers Humphreys, Sir Albion Richardson, Alice Lady Rothenstein, and Mr W. B. Yeats.

Others no longer alive who contributed to the making of this book, and whose contributions I am glad to acknowledge, are Lord Burnham, Mr Percy Colson, Sir Lionel Fox, Mr Hugh Kingsmill, Sir Shane Leslie, Sir Compton Mackenzie, Mr Cecil Palmer, Mr Hesketh Pearson, Mr Frederick Peters, Francis Marquess of Queensberry, Sir Arthur Quiller-Couch, Mr Arthur Ransome, Mrs Margery Ross, M. Guillot de Saix, Mrs Robert Sherard, Lord Tenby and Mr Louis Wilkinson.

Finally, this book could not have been produced without the active co-operation of my wife, and I thank her for her constant patience and understanding while she typed the manuscript. In these difficult times for authors, this one is indeed fortunate in having such an able and willing partner.

H.M.H.

Westwell House
Tenterden
Kent

"Would you like to know the great drama of my life? It's that I've put my genius into my life; I've put only my talent into my works."

Oscar Wilde in conversation with André Gide (1895)

PART ONE

Success

1 / *Ireland and Oxford*

I

Oscar Wilde's parents, Sir William and Lady Wilde, were remarkable and unusual people with strong literary tastes, which Oscar and his elder brother Willie both inherited. Sir William's father, Thomas Wills Wilde, was a country doctor from Castlerea in County Roscommon; he was greatly beloved in that part of Ireland, since he would ride the length and breadth of the county on horseback in all weather to visit an ailing patient. Thomas's father, Ralph Wilde, farmed the land near Castlerea and also managed the property of the local landowner, Lord Mount Sandford, as his agent. Ralph Wilde seems to have prospered since, besides sending his second son, Thomas, to complete his medical studies in England, he put his eldest son, Ralph, through Trinity College, Dublin, so that he could enter the church, and he sent his third son, William, to seek his fortune in the sugar plantations of Jamaica.

According to the hitherto accepted account by Oscar Wilde's biographers and those of his parents, Ralph Wilde's father was a builder who came from Wolsingham, a village near Durham, in the north-east of England, and crossed the Irish Sea during the earlier part of the eighteenth century to follow his trade in Dublin. But this was not so. Ralph Wilde was descended, not from the Wildes of Wolsingham, but from Colonel de Wilde, a Dutch army officer who accompanied King William of Orange to Ireland after the "Glorious Revolution" and for his services was granted lands in Connaught, where he married an Irishwoman and subsequently dropped the "de" from his name. Pronounced "de Vilde," it would have sounded to local ears very much like "the builder," which is a possible explanation of the confusion.

On the other hand, Oscar's son Vyvyan, whom the present writer knew well, thought that his grandmother Lady Wilde may well have invented the story of the builder from Durham since, as a fervent Irish patriot, she had every reason to conceal her husband's family connection with William of Orange. Although Oscar himself acknowledged it, Vincent O'Sullivan, the American writer who befriended him during his last years in Paris, noted that "he did not seem particularly proud of this; at least he liked to say that he took after his mother's family which, it seems, was pure Irish, more than his father's."

William Ralph Wills Wilde, Oscar's father, was a successful eye and ear surgeon in Dublin, and he founded a hospital there in 1853, a year before Oscar was born; his work gained for him the honorary appointment of Surgeon Oculist in Ordinary to the Queen, a post which was specially created for him. Eleven years later he was knighted, largely in recognition of his work on the medical statistics of the Irish census. Sir William Wilde was also interested in natural history and ethnology—his three-volume catalogue of the contents of the Royal Irish Academy has been described as a monumental work of archaeological erudition and insight—and he published in all twenty books, including two excellent works of Irish antiquarian topography, *The Beauties of the Boyne and the Blackwater* (1849) and *Lough Corrib and Lough Mask* (1867), which can still be read with advantage by visitors to the west of Ireland. He also attempted to prove, in a short and most readable narrative, that Dean Swift was not mad in his last days. For many years his *Aural Surgery* (1853) was the standard textbook on the subject on both sides of the Irish Sea.

Besides these achievements, Oscar's father exercised a powerful fascination upon women, whom he used to pursue with vigour. In addition to the legitimate offspring of his marriage, he had several natural children, including a son named Henry Wilson and two daughters, Emily and Mary, who took their father's surname. Henry became a popular Dublin oculist like his father, whom he helped with his professional practice. Sir William Wilde was good company, and surprising as it may appear in view of his personal habits, he was generally liked by his female patients, although he was alleged to have criminally assaulted one of them, Mary Josephine Travers, having first given her a whiff of chloroform to make her submit more easily to his will. This forced Sir William to sue Miss Travers for libel and it became the most sensational scandal of the sixties in Dublin. In the end she was awarded one farthing damages with costs. But although the jury rated her chastity at the lowest coin in the realm, the elder Wilde's reputation never fully recovered from the case.

He was also slovenly in his dress and dirty in physical appearance. "Why are Sir William Wilde's nails black?" was a popular conundrum of the day in Dublin. The answer was: "Because he scratches himself." No wonder the Viceroy's wife, Lady Spencer, refused the soup one evening when dining at the Wildes' house in Merrion Square after she had seen her host put his thumb in the tureen.

To his many poor patients, Sir William Wilde willingly gave his professional services free. He earned an unusually large income, which he spent lavishly on himself and his family and in the cause of science and archaeology. His wife, who was reputed to turn a blind eye to her husband's amorous exploits, had a great admiration for him as a scholar. "There was probably no man of his generation more versed in our national literature, in all that concerned the land and the people, the arts, architecture, topography, statistics, and even the legends of the country," she wrote after his death, "but above all in his favourite department, the descriptive illustration of Ireland, past and present, in historic and prehistoric times, he has justly gained a wide reputation as one of the most popular writers of the age on Irish subjects."

Some years younger than her husband, Jane Francesca Agnes Lady Wilde, known as "Speranza," had become celebrated in Ireland for her passionate nationalist outpourings in verse and prose. Like her husband, she was also an enthusiastic collector of Irish folklore and was active in the women's rights movement of the time. Her father, Charles Elgee, was a country solicitor from Wexford, while her grandfather, Archdeacon John Elgee, also of Wexford, was a scholarly and benevolent Church of Ireland clergyman, so popular in his parish that the local rebels spared his life during the rising of 1798. According to one account, which Speranza herself accepted, the family originally came from Florence, the name Elgee being a Hibernian version of Algiati, which in turn was a corruption of Alighieri; she liked to think that she had some remote kinship with the great Dante and indeed boasted of it. Her immediate ancestry is easier to establish. Her mother, Sarah Kingsbury, was the daughter of Dr. Thomas Kingsbury, a Commissioner of Bankruptcy in Ireland and the owner of Lisle House, one of the finest Dublin mansions of the period. She was also a grandniece of the Rev. Charles Maturin, the romantic novelist who flourished in the early years of the nineteenth century and whose *Melmoth the Wanderer* was later to prompt her son Oscar to use the pseudonym Sebastian Melmoth, under which he lived out his last years as an exile on the Continent. As a young girl, Jane Elgee became an ardent Irish nationalist, contributing both verse and prose to the revolutionary patriot weekly *The Nation* under the penname Speranza. It was an inflammatory article in which she appealed to the young men of Ireland to take up arms in defence of their country's liberties, in the revolutionary year 1848 that led to the suppression of *The Nation* and the prosecution of its editor, Charles Gavan Duffy, for sedition. For her part in the affair, she became a national figure in Ireland overnight. In fact, at the time of her marriage to William Wilde three years later, she was much better known throughout the country than her husband. Thirty years afterwards, her son Oscar was to write: "I don't think that age has dimmed the fire and enthusiasm of that pen which set the Young Irelanders in a blaze."

Oscar Fingal O'Flahertie Wills Wilde was born at 21 Westland Row,

Dublin, on 16 October 1854.[1] He was the second son, his elder brother, William Charles Kingsbury Wills ("Willie"), having been born two years previously. Victorian children were often given long strings of names, which they would mostly discard in later life; Oscar dropped all of his except the first soon after leaving Oxford. The choice of Oscar as the first of his Christian names was long believed in Dublin to have been dictated by the fact that Sir William Wilde had professionally attended King Oscar I of Sweden, on whom he performed a successful operation for cataract and who became his second son's godfather. But the name is more likely to have been chosen by Speranza on account of its association, like that of Fingal, with legendary Celtic history. At that period there was a great vogue for the poems, popularized by Macpherson's translation, of Ossian, or Oisin, the ancient Irish warrior-bard whose father, Fingal, had saved Erin from her enemies and whose chivalrous son Oscar was slain in battle at an early age. "He is to be called Oscar Fingal Wilde," she told a friend when the baby was a month old.[2] "Is not that grand, misty and Ossianic?" As for O'Flahertie, this addition may be traced to some real or supposed family connection with the "ferocious O'Flaherties of Galway," in whose country Sir William Wilde had a holiday house and also a fishing lodge. Wills was a somewhat later addition and was adopted by both brothers in their youth out of respect for their Wills cousins, who were landowners in County Roscommon and included James Wills the poet and W. G. Wills the dramatist. Sir William Wilde, who also adopted the name Wills, as did his father, was proud of his "county" relatives.

It has been said that Lady Wilde longed for a girl, and when her second child turned out to be a boy, she insisted on dressing him in girl's clothes. (This will be considered in discussing the problem of Oscar Wilde's sexual inversion.) Lady Wilde's third and last child was a daughter who was born in 1858 and named Isola Francesca. Unfortunately, this daughter died young, in her ninth year, and Oscar, who was then a dreamy-eyed schoolboy of twelve and appears to have been devoted to his sister, is said to have vented his "lonely and inconsolable

[1] Several biographies and encyclopedia articles, including the *Dictionary of National Biography,* wrongly state that Oscar Wilde was born at 1 Merrion Square, Dublin, on 16 October 1856. The error as to his birthday seems to have arisen from his vanity in habitually understating his age, a foible which was to cause him some embarrassment at the first of his trials. Although the registration of births in Ireland did not become legally compulsory until 1867, the date of Oscar Wilde's birth has been placed beyond doubt by his baptismal record, which is still in existence. For a facsimile of the baptismal entry, see article by Dr. T. G. Wilson ("Oscar Wilde at Trinity College, Dublin") in *The Practitioner,* vol CLXXIII, pp. 473–80 (October 1954). There is no doubt, too, that his parents were living at 21 Westland Row at this time and did not move to the better-known house in Merrion Square until about a year later. A plaque commemorating the fact of Oscar Wilde's birth was erected and unveiled by the Irish dramatist Lennox Robinson in the front of the house in Westland Row in 1954.

[2] Oscar Wilde was not baptized until more than two months after his birth. The ceremony took place in St Mark's Church, Dublin, on 26 April 1855, and was performed by his uncle, the Rev. Ralph Wilde, Vicar of Kilsallaghan.

grief" in long and frequent visits to her grave.[3] Some years later he was to perpetuate her memory in the poem which he called "Requiescat," which has been included in numerous anthologies of verse; it has even been set to music and sung at concerts. It is perhaps the most often quoted of all Wilde's poems, with the exception of *The Ballad of Reading Gaol,* although its author never regarded it, as he told his fellow countryman and poet W. B. Yeats, as being "very typical of my work." Written while Wilde was an undergraduate at Oxford, it owes something at least in metre to Hood. The first two of its five stanzas run as follows:

> Tread lightly, she is near
> Under the snow,
> Speak lightly, she can hear
> The daisies grow.
>
> All her bright golden hair
> Tarnished with rust
> She that was young and fair,
> Fallen to dust.[4]

Lady Wilde never ceased to mourn Isola's loss. Two years after the girl's death she was still writing on black-edged paper. "A sadness is on me for life—a bitter sorrow that can never be healed," she wrote to a Swedish friend. And when in 1875 the same friend herself suffered a family loss, Lady Wilde wrote in sympathy: *"Eight years* have passed since I, too, stood by a grave—but the sorrow knows no change and sometimes it deepens with the bitterness of despair." She may also have been affected when two of her husband's illegitimate daughters, Emily and Mary Wilde, lost their lives in a tragic accident in November 1871. The two girls, aged twenty-four and twenty-two respectively at the time of their death, lived in County Monaghan with their uncle the Rev. Ralph Wilde, Sir William's eldest brother, by whom they were brought up. Emily's dress was suddenly enveloped by flames when she was dancing near a coal fire at a local ball at Drumaconnor House near Drumsnatt, in Monaghan. Mary went to help her sister and her dress also caught fire. Although both girls were rushed out of the house by their host and rolled in the snow outside, they were too badly burned to survive. Both were buried in Drumsnatt churchyard under a headstone

---

[3] Isola Francesca Wilde died on 23 February 1867, at The Glebe, Edgworthstown, Co. Longford, when staying with her aunt (her father's only sister), who was married to the rector, the Rev. William Noble.

[4] Although included in the anthology of Dublin University undergraduate verse, *Echoes of Kottabos* (1906), "Requiescat" was not originally published in the undergraduate journal *Kottabos,* and it is not known whether it ever appeared before its publication in the first edition of Wilde's *Poems* in 1881. George Augustus Sala pointed out at the time of the latter publication that golden hair does not tarnish in the tomb, citing Emile Zola's *Nana* in support of his statement: See Stuart Mason, *Bibliography of Oscar Wilde* (1914), pp. 295–6.

inscribed with a quotation from the Book of Samuel: "They were lovely and pleasant in their lives and in their death they were not divided."

Once a year a woman in black used to come by train from Dublin to Monaghan, where she hired a car to drive her to the graveyard. This pilgrimage went on for twenty years, but the only admission she made to the sexton was that the two dead girls "were very dear to me." The sexton was never able to discover whether the anonymous visitor was Lady Wilde or the girls' mother.

When Willie and Oscar were quite young, their mother used to take them to stay during the summer months at a farmhouse in the vale of Glencree about fifteen miles from Dublin. During one of these visits, she is stated to have met a Catholic priest, Father Lawrence Fox, who used to celebrate Mass on Sundays in the chapel of a nearby reformatory for boys. According to Father Fox, Speranza asked if she could bring the two children to Mass, and he readily agreed. "After a few weeks I baptized these two children, Lady Wilde herself being present on the occasion," Father Fox was to write many years later, after all three were dead. "At her request I called on their father, and told him what I had done, his sole remark being that he did not care what they were so long as they became as good as their mother."

This curious story has received no direct corroboration, although, according to his bibliographer, Stuart Mason, Oscar Wilde declared more than once to intimate friends in later years that he had a distinct recollection as a child of being christened in a Catholic church.[5] One of these occasions is said to have been when he was writing his last play, *The Importance of Being Earnest,* which contains an allusion to christening in Act II, when Algernon Moncrieffe and Jack Worthing both express "a desire for immediate baptism" in order that each may take the name of Ernest.

However, although he was to be strongly attracted by Roman Catholicism during his adolescent years, Oscar was not to be formally received into the Catholic Church until he was on his deathbed.

2

In 1864, the year of the sensational libel trial in which he figured so prominently and embarrassingly, Sir William Wilde built Moytura House, a comfortable villa of no particular architectural distinction (except for its fine Italian marble fireplaces) about two miles from Cong near the mouth of Lough Corrib. It was designed primarily for a holiday home, but in fact Sir William was to spend most of his time there until his death a dozen years later, since the disgrace which he felt he had incurred as a result of the trial prompted him to give up the greater part of his medical practice and concentrate on his literary work. As Oscar went to boarding school for the first time in the year Moytura was completed, it was an ideal place for the holidays, "situated," so Oscar described it at

---

[5] Mason, p. 118, citing Father Fox's account.

the time, "in the most romantic scenery in Ireland." One feature of the place which the boy particularly remembered was "the melancholy carp," which swam close to the shore in the expectation of titbits of food from the Wilde children. Sir William also had a fishing lodge at Illaunroe, about twenty miles from Moytura on Lough Fee in Connemara; in due course, this served to make the young Oscar a proficient and enthusiastic angler.

When he was eleven, Oscar joined his elder brother as a boarder at Portora Royal School, which had been founded by King Charles II on a hill overlooking the waters of Lough Erne and the ancient Ulster town of Enniskillen. Portora had a high reputation among the relatively few Irish public schools, as indeed it still has. Moreover, the fees were modest—only £17 10s a term, "a considerable reduction being made in the case of brothers"—which may explain why it catered largely to the sons of Church of Ireland clergymen and other professional people who hoped to go on to Dublin University. Indeed, the headmaster was himself a clergyman, the Rev. William Steele, D.D., and "religious training" was regarded as of supreme importance according to the school prospectus. ("The boarders are regularly instructed in Divinity, and on Sundays attend the respective Protestant churches in charge of responsible masters.") Compulsory churchgoing was not a regimen calculated to appeal to either of the Wilde boys, and in Oscar's case it was to turn him permanently away from the Protestant faith. Although well versed in the scriptures and in church matters generally, it is significant that when he went on to Trinity College, Dublin, where attendance at divine service was voluntary, there is no record of his ever having partaken of holy communion in the college chapel.

A copy of part of only one letter which Oscar wrote home from Portora has survived. It is typical of any schoolboy. "Darling Mama," he wrote on 8 September 1868. "The Hamper came today. I never got such a jolly surprise, many thanks for it, it was more than kind of you to send it." Oscar's career at Portora was not noticeably distinguished, except in his final year. Willie Wilde was already there when he arrived and seems to have considerably outshone his younger brother at lessons. It was only in his last year that Oscar began to show signs of promise, when he won the school prize for Greek Testament, a Gold Medal in Classics, and an entrance scholarship to Trinity College, Dublin. But even then, Dr Steele, the headmaster, in calling him into his study to tell him the news of the scholarship, clearly showed which of the two brothers was his favourite. "The doctor wound up, I remember," Oscar recalled long afterwards, "by assuring me that if I went on studying as I had been studying during the last year I might yet do as well as my brother Willie, and be as great an honour to the school and everybody connected with it as he had been." While the elder boy carefully studied the prescribed textbooks and excelled at both work and games, Oscar was inclined to confine his reading to what pleased him. Nor did he care for either cricket or football—"I never liked to kick or be kicked"—

although he was certainly no milksop, in spite of the fact that he wore his hair quite long like a girl's. "Nearly everyone went in for athletics—running and jumping and so forth," he added. "No one appeared to care for sex. We were healthy young barbarians and that was all."

> Until the last year of my school life at Portora, I had nothing like the reputation of my brother Willie. I read too many English novels, too much poetry, dreamed away too much time to master school tasks. Knowledge came to me through pleasure, as it always comes, I imagine . . . I was nearly sixteen when the wonder and beauty of the old Greek life began to dawn upon me . . . I began to read Greek eagerly, and the more I read the more I was enthralled.

A schoolboy contemporary who remembered Oscar at Portora has recorded that he was an excellent talker, his descriptive powers being far above the average: his exaggerations of school occurrences were always highly amusing. A favourite place for the boys to sit and gossip in the late afternoon in wintertime was a stove which stood in the Stone Hall. Here Oscar was at his best. His friend Edward Sullivan, who was a son of the Lord Chancellor of Ireland, has recalled that at one of these gatherings a discussion took place about an ecclesiastical prosecution which was making a considerable stir at the time. Oscar seemed to know all about the Court of Arches and showed great interest in the case. Indeed, he made a remark of curious prophetic insight. "He told us there was nothing he would like better in after life than to be the hero of such a *cause célèbre* and to go down to posterity as the defendant in such a case as *Regina* versus *Wilde*." [6]

3

It was taken for granted that Oscar should follow his elder brother by going to Dublin University. Accordingly, on 10 October 1871, he matriculated at Trinity College. In the entrance examination for Junior Freshmen (as the first-year students were called), for which he sat on the same day, his best marks were for Greek, Latin, and history; he did worst in arithmetic, as might be expected from his record at school, where a class fellow described him as "absolutely incapable of mathematics." In the aggregate of marks, another Portora contemporary, Louis Claude Purser, an outstanding classical scholar, subsequently Professor of Latin and Vice-Provost of Trinity, came first, while Oscar Wilde secured the second place. A few weeks later Oscar was elected to a scholarship by examination, in addition to his entrance scholarship from Portora. He was to continue this auspicious start to his university career throughout the next three years at Trinity.

Within its gracious compass Dublin's three-century-old university

[6] Sir Edward Sullivan, 2nd Bart, published a number of books, including a fine edition of *The Book of Kells* (1918), a descriptive account of the greatest treasure in the library of Trinity College, Dublin, where he was also Wilde's contemporary. He also edited (with Professor R. Y. Tyrrell) *Echoes from Kottabos* (1906), mentioned above.

embodied both academic distinction and architectural charm. Situated in the middle of the city, with the clatter of traffic at its gates, it was in some ways more in touch with contemporary happenings and influences than the older foundations of learning at Oxford and Cambridge. It was a largely Protestant society, although Catholics were never unwelcome within its walls. For long "T.C.D." had enjoyed a high reputation for classical scholarship, and this reputation was enhanced by the election two years before Oscar Wilde's arrival of the Rev. Dr John Pentland Mahaffy to the chair of ancient history. Mahaffy, who was only thirty at this time, was already an accomplished man of the world, with an encyclopedic knowledge extending from Greek poetry and Egyptian papyri to snipe shooting and the cultivation of wines. He was also a great talker, and something of a snob; he was to write a book on *The Principles and Art of Conversation,* among upwards of forty works on a wide variety of subjects. Oscar was fortunate in having him as his tutor. Another brilliant classicist was Robert Yelverton Tyrrell, who had just become university professor of Latin at the early age of twenty-six and whose lectures Oscar was to attend with profit to himself. Tyrrell was probably unique in successively holding the chairs of Latin, Greek, and ancient history in the university. A better scholar than Mahaffy, Tyrrell was also more of a humanitarian, as will be seen from his reaction when Oscar was in serious trouble.

For his first year at Trinity, Oscar lived with his parents in the large house in Merrion Square where his father had his surgery and his mother kept a weekly *salon,* which was a popular centre of the capital's intellectual life. ("Come home with me," Oscar is stated to have said to a college friend. "My mother and I have formed a society for the suppression of virtue.") For his second and third years, he moved into college, where he and Willie shared rooms—believed to have been on the first floor of No. 18—in the block known as Botany Bay to the north of Library Square, so called because the lecturers in botany formerly grew their specimens there, according to one explanation; according to another, it got its name from the notorious convict settlement in Australia where the Irish political prisoners had staged a celebrated mutiny in 1801, and being furthest removed from official college eyes, its residents had the reputation for being noisier and less disciplined than most of their fellow students, who lived nearer the centre of authority.

Edward Sullivan, Oscar's contemporary at Portora and Trinity, states that his rooms in Botany Bay were exceedingly grimy and ill-kept, and that he never entertained there. On the rare occasions when visitors were admitted, an unfinished landscape in oils would be seen on an easel in a prominent place in the sitting-room. Oscar would claim this to be his own work—which may well have been so—adding, in allusion to Whistler's characteristic signature, that he had "just put in a butterfly." It is not generally known that Oscar was something of a draughtsman and painter in his youth.

His college life was mainly devoted to reading and preparing for the various examinations and university prizes which he was to take with such distinction. According to Sullivan, he was an intense admirer of Swinburne and constantly reading his poems; John Addington Symonds's works too, particularly on the Greek authors, were often in his hands. Although Sullivan noted that he never expressed any pronounced views on the social, religious, and political questions of the day, which exercised the minds of other students, there is no doubt that he shared his mother's nationalist views. Like his brother he joined the two major college societies, the College Historical Society, which regularly held debates, and the University Philosophical Society, where papers were read and discussions took place on literary and scientific subjects. But oratory appealed to Oscar less than to his elder brother, who had decided to go to the Irish Bar.

On one occasion, Sir William Wilde presided as guest chairman at a meeting of "The Phil" and the question of national morality was the topic for discussion. If Oscar was present, as he may well have been, he remained silent. However, Willie delivered an impassioned speech in defence of prostitutes, a subject on which both he and his father were reputed to possess firsthand knowledge. On another occasion, Sir William accidentally opened a letter intended for his elder son, in which Willie was accused of having made a girl pregnant. "Here is a most disgraceful letter," said the elder Wilde as he handed it over to his son. "Yes, sir," replied Willie with a serious air when he had read it, promptly assuming that it was intended for his father. "What are you going to do about it?"

What he called "coarse *amours* among barmaids and women of the streets," in which many of his fellow students at Trinity indulged, had no attractions for Oscar. He preferred the society of intellectual companions like Edward Sullivan and teachers like Mahaffy and Tyrrell, as he was to recall in later years:

I got my love of the Greek ideal and my intimate knowledge of the language at Trinity from Mahaffy and Tyrrell; they were Trinity to me; Mahaffy was especially valuable to me at that time. Though not so good a scholar as Tyrrell, he had been in Greece, had lived there and saturated himself with Greek thought and Greek feeling. Besides he took deliberately the artistic standpoint towards everything, which was coming more and more to be my standpoint. He was a delightful talker, too, a really great talker in a certain way—an artist in vivid words and eloquent pauses. Tyrrell, too, was very kind to me—intensely sympathetic and crammed with knowledge.

Although he did not form a high opinion of most of his classmates— "their highest idea of humour was an obscene story," he once said—Oscar seems to have been generally popular. "He was a good-natured man and most amusing," one of them recalled in later life. "Everyone liked him." This statement was not quite true. There was at least one exception to it, in the person of a certain plodding student whom the more brilliant Oscar left far behind in the university examinations. His name was Edward Carson, and his path was destined to cross Oscar Wilde's with tragic effect at the most dramatic period in the latter's career. But at Trinity, although they knew each other and were on speaking terms, Edward Carson and Oscar Wilde were never intimate friends, as has sometimes been supposed. Indeed, Carson disliked the long-haired student genius and distrusted what he considered to be his flippant approach to life. Yet, even at this early period, Wilde did not fail to recognize the latent ability of this particular classmate. "There goes a man destined to reach the very top of affairs," he remarked to a young lady, as they were walking across the Front Square in college and chanced to pass Carson. "Yes," agreed Wilde's companion, adding with a touch of feminine malice: "And one who will not hesitate to trample on his friends in getting there."

Oscar Wilde's academic career at Trinity was a series of unbroken successes, as it was later largely to be at Oxford. He was twice placed in the First Class in the university examinations, he won a Composition Prize for Greek Verse, he was elected to a Foundation Scholarship in Classics in addition to the two entrance scholarships which he already held, and in February 1874, when in his third year, he carried off the coveted Berkeley Gold Medal for Greek. This last distinction gave his father particular pleasure, and the elder Wilde wrote to Sir John Gilbert, the president of the Royal Irish Academy, inviting him to celebrate the event in Merrion Square: "We are asking a few old friends upon Moytura cheer [i.e., to drink whiskey or poteen] on Thursday, and also to cheer dear old Oscar on having obtained the Berkeley Gold Medal last week with great honour. You were always a favourite of his, and he hopes you will come."

The medal was competed for annually and presented from a fund left for the purpose by Dr George Berkeley, the eighteenth-century Irish philosopher-bishop who denied the existence of matter and of whom Byron later remarked that "when he said that there was no matter it really was no matter what he said." The subject for 1874 was *The Fragments of the Greek Comic Poets,* as edited by the German scholar Johann Meineke. Wilde was specially coached for the examination by a knowledgeable but somewhat broken-down and penurious classical teacher named John Townsend Mills, from whom (according to Edward Sullivan) the candidate contrived to get a good deal of amusement in the course of his studies.[7] For instance, he once expressed sympathy for Mills on seeing him come into his rooms in Botany Bay wearing a tall hat completely covered in crape. "Mills, however, replied with a smile, that no one was dead—it was only the evil condition of his hat that had made him assume so mournful a disguise." Sullivan thought afterwards that the incident was still fresh in his friend's mind when he introduced

[7] An exercise book in Wilde's handwriting dated Michaelmas 1873 and containing various Greek proverbs collected from fragments of the Greek comic poets, used by Wilde when preparing for the Berkeley Medal examination, fetched £100 at an auction in Dulau's sale rooms in London in 1928. It was bought by the American collector William Andrews Clark, and is now in the Clark Library at the University of California, Los Angeles. It is the first known Wilde manuscript to have survived.

the character of John Worthing in Act II of *The Importance of Being Earnest* in mourning for the loss of his fictitious friend Bunbury.

The Berkeley Gold Medal was the highest award for classics at Trinity, and Oscar was justly proud of having obtained it, particularly since it had been awarded to his great-uncle Ralph Wilde a century earlier. Later it was to serve a practical purpose. He was to pawn it on more than one occasion when he was short of money, and once, in 1883, he had to swear a statutory declaration before a London magistrate that he had lost the pawnbroker's ticket to enable him to redeem his property. When he died, another such ticket was found among his few personal belongings by his friend and literary executor, Robert Ross.

In June 1874, Wilde crowned his brilliant academic record at Trinity by winning a Classical Demyship, or scholarship, to Magdalen College, Oxford. "My dear Oscar," Mahaffy is said to have remarked to his star pupil at this time, "you are not clever enough for us in Dublin. You had better run over to Oxford."

Had Oscar stayed on at Trinity for a fourth year and taken his degree there, as his brother had already done, he would have had a strong claim to be elected to a college fellowship, seeing that in the immediately following years some seven Berkeley medallists, including the great classical scholar and historian J. B. Bury, all became fellows of T.C.D. His decision to try for an entrance scholarship to Oxford at the end of his third year was certainly encouraged if not actually inspired by "that dear Mahaffy," as Oscar called his tutor in a contemporary letter. "He has a charming house by the sea here, on a place called the Hill of Howth (one of the crescent horns that shuts in the Bay of Dublin), the only place near town with fields of yellow gorse, and stretches of wild myrtle, red heather and ferns." Oscar was a frequent visitor to this seaside house, and he seems to have spent much of the summer of 1874 there, before he went up to Oxford, working on the proofs of Mahaffy's *Social Life in Greece from Homer to Menander,* which came out later the same year with a grateful acknowledgement to "Mr Oscar Wilde of Magdalen College, Oxford" for "having made improvements and corrections all through the book." Incidentally, this work contained a notably frank discussion of the prevalence of homosexuality among the ancient Greeks.

As noted above, in later years Oscar Wilde used to assert that he had been greatly influenced by his old Trinity tutor's conversational talents as well as by what he called his "Hellenism." To what extent this was so, it is impossible to say with any degree of certainty. The Irish writer Sir Shane Leslie and others have suggested that phrases like "Poets are born, not paid," "All art is perfectly useless," and "It is the spectator and not life that art mirrors," which have always been attributed to Oscar Wilde, were originally Mahaffy's. On the other hand, there are some passages in *Social Life in Greece* which might well have been written by Wilde, perhaps the result of the "improvements" for which the pupil was thanked by the author in the preface. The following is an example:

Thus it came to pass that Homer, in one sense "the idle singer of an empty day,"—because he sought no other object than the clear and deep delineation of human character and human passion—was degraded . . . into a moral teacher and accredited with definite theories of life and of duty. It was the same *sort* of blunder that we should make were we to dilate on the moral purposes of Shelley and Keats, and insist upon classing them with the school of Mr Tupper and Dr Watts.

As Mahaffy's biographers have pointed out, the phrase "degraded . . . into a moral teacher" was an extraordinary one for a young clerical don to use, and it comes very close to the amorality of art for art's sake, a Wildean doctrine which Mahaffy later rejected emphatically. The whole passage certainly bears the hallmark of Wilde's personality and what he considered, and was to proclaim in his writings, to be the role of the artist in society.

Although Mahaffy had been careful to stigmatize the homosexual aspect of Greek social life in his book as a "strange and to us revolting perversion," his frank discussion of the subject caused some hostile criticism, and most of the matter objected to was omitted from the second and subsequent editions of the work. The references to Greek homosexuality in Mahaffy's *Social Life* seem to have been Wilde's first introduction to the subject, which hitherto was regarded as unmentionable, at least in polite print. This is confirmed by the fact that on going up to Oxford, his Balliol contemporary J. E. C. Bodley, the future historian of France, noted his "chaffable innocence" about the subject. Twenty years later, when the storm of scandal burst on Wilde's head, Mahaffy professed to be horrified at the accusations brought against his former pupil. "Were they young boys?" he asked. Having been told that, broadly speaking, they were, Mahaffy declared that he hoped he would never hear Wilde's name again. It is a sad reflection that he should have later described his one-time pupil as "the one blot of my tutorship." And whenever any acquaintance happened to mention him, the reverend professor would fix the inquirer with a stony stare and observe ponderously: "We no longer speak of Mr Oscar Wilde."

4

"I was the happiest man in the world when I entered Magdalen for the first time," Wilde was to recall years later. With its spacious grounds, which included a deer park, and its noble tower, from the top of which the choristers intoned a Latin hymn on May Day, Magdalen was considered by many to be the university's loveliest college. It was the college of Addison, Gibbon, and Charles Reade, and Addison's memory was kept alive there by "Addison's Walk," on which the essayist and poet was said to have planted some trees. As for Oxford itself, the mere word to the newly arrived demy was "full of an inexpressible, an incommunicable charm."

Oxford—the home of lost causes and impossible ideals; Matthew Arnold's Oxford—with its dreaming spires and grey colleges, set in velvet lawns and hidden away among the trees, and about it the beautiful fields, all starred with cowslips and fritillaries . . . Oxford was paradise to me . . . the enchanted valley, holding in its flowerlet cup all the idealism of the Middle Ages.

Wilde's demyship carried with it an annual "stipend" of £95 and was tenable for five years. In Wilde's case it was supplemented by an allowance from his father and a legacy of some £300 from the estate of one of his mother's relatives.[8] Thus he found himself reasonably well off as an Oxford undergraduate. On 17 October 1874, the day after his twentieth birthday, he duly matriculated before the Vice-Chancellor, the Rev. J. E. Sewell, Warden of New College. The rooms which he was allocated for his first year were near the Entrance Lodge—Chaplain's Quad 1, 2 pair right; for his second year he moved to Cloisters VIII, ground floor right; and for the following two years he occupied the fine set of oak-panelled rooms commonly associated with his name on the first floor of the Kitchen Staircase overlooking the Cherwell River and Magdalen Bridge.

The head of the college, who had occupied the President's Lodgings for the past nineteen years, was the sedate and courteous Dr Frederic Bulley, a conservative ruler who had shown himself little more amenable to change than his famous predecessor, Dr Martin Joseph Routh, who wore an eighteenth-century wig to the day of his death, which took place in 1854, the hundredth year of his life and the sixty-fourth of his reign. Like Routh, Bulley did not welcome the legislative reforms which were designed to improve the level of studies and degrees and remove such anomalies as the automatic right of a demy to become a fellow of the college, which ensured him a comfortable berth for life provided he did not marry. Greek was still compulsory—no problem for Wilde—and dissenters had been admitted to the degree of M.A. only in 1871. Indeed, conditions in the college had changed little since Gibbon's time in the 1750's, when the historian of the later Roman Empire described the college fellows as "decent men who supinely enjoyed the gifts of the founder."

Their days were filled by a series of uniform employments; the chapel and the hall, the coffee-house, and the common room, till they retired, weary and well satisfied, to a long slumber . . . Their conversation stagnated in a round of college business, Tory politics, personal anecdotes, and private scandal; their dull and deep potations excused the brisk intemperance of youth.

It was to remain for Herbert Warren, who became a fellow and tutor in classics during Wilde's fourth year, and president seven years later at the unusually early age of thirty-two, to pull the college finally out of the

[8] Probably Vice-Admiral Sir Robert McClure, discoverer of the North-West Passage and a cousin of Speranza's, who had died in 1873.

eighteenth century. When Wilde first appeared there, there were fewer than seventy undergraduates in the college.

"The two great turning points in my life were when my father sent me to Oxford, and when society sent me to prison." Thus Oscar Wilde was to write more than thirty years later in the solitude of a cell in Reading Gaol: "I will not say that prison is the best thing that could have happened to me, for that phrase would savour of too great bitterness towards myself. I would sooner say, or hear it said of me, that I was so typical a child of my age, that in my perversity, and for that perversity's sake, I turned the good things of my life to evil, and the evil things of my life to good."

At Oxford, where he was to repeat on an extended scale his earlier scholastic successes, Wilde confined his perversity largely if not entirely to the intellectual field. Thus, the trait found expression in his inclination to oppose by his behaviour the accepted conventional standards of the day. However, the poses which he originally affected to draw attention to himself gradually became a habit and, as will be seen, were to lead to perverse behaviour of a more dangerous kind. For the time being, however, he contented himself with concealing his industry with his books while secretly reading hard, by a blasé veneer of assumed idleness, by trying to "live up" to the blue china with which he filled his rooms, and by attending Ruskin's crowded lectures on *The Aesthetic and Mathematical Schools of Florence,* which the celebrated Slade Professor of Fine Arts would sometimes suddenly interrupt to exhort his listeners male and female to fall in love with each other.

"Oscar is now a scholar at Oxford and resides there in the very focus of intellect," his mother wrote to a friend during his first year. "Ruskin had him to breakfast and Max Müller loves him . . . ." Ruskin's breakfast invitation was the usual reward for those undergraduates who helped "the Master" to maintain the dignity of manual labour with his celebrated road-making experiment at Hinksey. Max Müller was Professor of Comparative Philology and a leading authority on Sanskrit, to whose lectures, like those of John Ruskin and Walter Pater, Wilde was strongly drawn.

On one occasion he was "ragged" by some fellow members of the college, but the popular version of this ragging is almost certainly apocryphal. According to it, he was waylaid while out walking, bound with cords, and dragged to the top of a nearby hill, where he is supposed to have simply flicked the dirt from his coat with the air of a Regency beau and, looking round, exclaimed, "Yes, the view from this hill is really very charming." The real story of the ragging is somewhat different. According to the actor-manager Sir Frank Benson, who was up at Oxford at the same time, several "hearty" characters invaded his rooms with the intention of breaking up his furniture. Wilde was ready for them. He threw three of them down the stairs, propelling the first with a hefty kick. He then picked up the largest of the invading gang and carried him off to his own rooms, where he proceeded to bury him under a heap of his own furniture. "When the débris of tables, sofas, chairs and pictures had been raised to the height of a respectable mausoleum, Wilde invited the now admiring crowd to sample the victim's cellar." No second invitation was necessary, and the recumbent and parsimonious victim was soothed by "the gurgle of expensive liqueurs and choice vintages pouring down the throats of his uninvited guests." After this incident it was hardly surprising that Wilde should have been left alone.

Wilde's particular undergraduate friends at Magdalen were Reginald Harding, William Ward, and David Hunter Blair.[9] The latter two afterwards recorded their memories of Wilde at Oxford. Those of another college contemporary, G. T. Atkinson, have also been drawn on in the narrative, in addition to the letters Wilde wrote to Ward and Harding. Nicknames, which were much in fashion, frequently appear in this correspondence—Wilde himself was known as "Hoskie," presumably a diminutive of Oscar; Hunter Blair was "Dunskie," from Dunskey, his family home in Scotland; while Ward was "Bouncer," from Cuthbert Bede's comic novel of Oxford life *Little Mr Bouncer and His Friend Verdant Green,* first published in 1875. Harding answered to "Kitten," evidently suggested by a popular music-hall song of the time which began:

> Beg your parding, Mrs Harding,
> Is my kitting in your garding?

According to Bouncer Ward, who had the fine rooms on Kitchen Staircase which Wilde took over when Ward went down in 1876, Oscar Wilde was his "most intimate" friend during Ward's final year at Oxford.[10]

How brilliant and radiant he could be! How playful and charming! How his moods varied and how he revelled in inconsistency! The whim of the moment was his acknowledged dictator. One can see now, reading his character by the light of his later life, the beginnings of those tendencies which led to his destruction. There was the love of pose, the desire for self-realisation, the egotism, but they seemed foibles rather than faults, and his frank regret or laugh at his own expense robbed them of blame and took away offence.

[9] David Hunter Blair (1853–1939) became a Roman Catholic convert in 1875 and three years later entered the Benedictine Order. He was afterwards Abbot of Fort Augustus. He succeeded to his father's baronetcy in 1896.

[10] When the present writer occupied these rooms in 1929–30, a drawing of "Little Mr Bouncer," which Wilde had scratched on one of the windowpanes, was still plainly visible. The pane is no longer there, having been smashed in the course of some college festivity. Also, the oak-panelled sitting-room has changed out of all recognition, since the panelling developed dry rot and had to be removed shortly after the last war. The manuscript of Ward's "Oscar Wilde: An Oxford Reminiscence," together with Wilde's letters to him at this period, were presented by his daughter Miss Cecil Ward to Magdalen College Library and have since been published by Vyvyan Holland in his *Son of Oscar Wilde* (1954).

I daresay we were a little dazzled by his directness and surprised by the unexpected angle from which he looked at things. There was something foreign to us, and inconsequential, in his modes of thought, just as there was a suspicion of a brogue in his pronunciation, and an unfamiliar turn in his phrasing. His qualities were not ordinary and we, his intimate friends, did not judge him by the ordinary standards. Of course there were many who disliked him, those whom he naturally offended by his unconventionality and whom he did not attempt to conciliate. But, speaking generally, I would say that during my last year at Magdalen he had gained a much larger amount of popularity than might have been expected. This, I think, may be accounted for partly by the fact that at that little College more importance was attached to social ability than to individual or athletic superiority. And certainly Oscar Wilde was socially distinguished. It was impossible to overlook him in any company of College men. He might be disliked by some as a poseur and as being conceited and affected, but he was a brilliant talker and said clever things and could, if he tried, make himself a pleasant companion to the ordinary undergraduate, and he had a reputation of being something out of the common . . .

One dim morning I remember well in my rooms at Magdalen when he and I and Hunter Blair, a new and eager convert to Roman Catholicism, a man of singular enthusiasm and vivacity, had talked through the short summer night till there was the sound of waking birds in the trees that fringe the Cherwell, and Oscar had hung, poised in a paradox, between doubt and dogma—I remember that Hunter Blair suddenly hit him on the head and exclaimed: "You will be damned, you will be damned, for you see the light and will not follow it!"

That Wilde had become strongly attracted to Roman Catholicism by this time is confirmed by an entry in the diary of Lord Ronald Gower for 4 June 1876:

By early train to Oxford with F. Miles . . . There I made the acquaintance of young Oscar Wilde, a friend of Miles's. A pleasant cheerful fellow but with his long-haired head full of nonsense regarding the Church of Rome. His room filled with photographs of the Pope and Cardinal Manning.

Frank Miles, two years older than Wilde, was a budding artist with homosexual inclinations who belonged to a wealthy Bristol family. His father, the Rev. Robert Miles, was Rector of Bingham in Nottinghamshire and a Prebendary of Lincoln. Shortly afterwards Wilde was a guest at the rectory with young Miles and his friend Gower, the younger son of the second Duke of Sutherland and then aged thirty-one. "Mr Miles *père* is a very advanced Anglican and a great friend of Newman, Pusey, Manning, Gladstone and all English theologians," Wilde wrote after this visit. "He is very clever and interesting: I have learned a lot from him." As for Lord Ronald Gower, he was to achieve a reputation as a sculptor and art critic as well as a highly cultivated "queer" with a host of friends. He always managed to steer clear of the criminal law and was eventually to publish a volume of respectable memoirs, from which the above extract from his diary is taken. Wilde was to base the character of the cynically decadent Lord Henry Wotton in *The Picture of Dorian Gray* on this Scottish aristocrat.

Wilde spent most of the first summer vacation in 1875 travelling in northern Italy with Mahaffy and a Cambridge undergraduate from Ireland named William Goulding, later a baronet and privy councillor; apparently he went by sea to Leghorn and visited Florence, Bologna, Venice, Padua, Verona, Milan, and Lake Maggiore. The tour inspired him to write two poems which he called *"Graffiti d'Italia,"* which were later published in *The Dublin University Magazine* and *The Month and Catholic Review* respectively. The first was composed on 15 June after visiting the Franciscan monastery of San Miniato on the hill to the south-east of Florence, with its marble façade and admirably proportioned church and fine mosaics; the second, which incidentally was to win high praise from Cardinal Newman, was composed on 10 July at Arona, about forty miles from Milan at the southern end of Lake Maggiore. Both were to be subsequently revised and reprinted in the collected *Poems,* the second under the title "Rome Unvisited." It should be explained that lack of funds prevented him from going on to Rome, which he very much wished to do.

> The corn has turned from grey to red
>   Since first my spirit wandered forth,
>   From the drear cities of the North,
> And to Italia's mountains fled.
>
> And here I set my face towards home,
>   Alas! my pilgrimage is done—
>   Although, methinks, yon bloodred sun
> Marshals the way to Holy Rome . . .
>
> O joy to see before I die
>   The only God-anointed King,
>   And hear the silver trumpets ring
> A triumph as He passeth by.

He wrote dutifully and at length to his parents describing his travels in more restrained language than he was accustomed to use in correspondence with his college friends—to his mother he would refer to his father as "Sir William" and embellish his letters with lively drawings. On the morning of his visit to San Miniato, he went first to see San Lorenzo, one of the most ancient churches in Italy, with architectural additions by Michelangelo.

Then to the Biblioteca Laurenziana in the cloisters of San Lorenzo, where I was shown wonderfully illuminated missals and unreadable manuscripts and autographs. I remarked the extreme clearness of the initial letters in the Italian missals and bibles, so different from those in the Book of Kells, etc., which might stand for anything. The early illuminations are very beautiful in design and sentiment, but the later are mere mechanical *tours de force* of geometrical scroll-work and absurd designs . . .

In the evening I dined at a restaurant on top of San Miniato, air delightfully clear and cool after the thunderstorm. Coming back I met just opposite the Pitti Palace a wonderful funeral; a long procession of monks bearing torches, all in white and wearing a long linen veil over their faces—only their eyes can be seen. They bore two coffins and looked like those awful monks you see in pictures of the Inquisition.

"After marriage the Italian women degenerate awfully, but the boys and girls are beautiful," he told his mother in one letter. Venice, where he stayed in a hotel on the Piazza San Marco, he found even more thrilling than Florence. "Believe me, Venice in beauty of architecture and colour is beyond description. It is the meeting place of the Byzantine and Italian art—a city belonging to the *East* as much as to the West."

In Milan he made a point of going to the Biblioteca Ambrosiana to see among other treasures the Antiphonary of Bangor, perhaps the oldest known Irish manuscript, which (as he reminded his mother) had been collated by two Trinity scholars, J. H. Todd and Whitley Stokes. "Milan is a second Paris," he wrote. "Wonderful arcades and galleries; all the town white stone and gilding."

"I wrote this at Arona on the Lago Maggiore, a beautiful spot," he added in a postscript. "Mahaffy and young Goulding I left at Milan and they will go on to Genoa. As I had no money I was obliged to leave them and feel very lonely. We have had a delightful tour."

After he had paid thirty-eight Swiss francs for the eighteen-hour journey by *diligence* from Milan over the Simplon Pass to Lausanne, he found he had only £2 left to take him on to Paris. "If there is no money at Paris for me, I will not know what to do," he wrote in desperation to his mother, "but I feel sure there will be the genial £5." No doubt there was.

5

G. T. Atkinson was to look back more than half a century later when he wrote:

Oscar Fingal O'Flahertie Wills Wilde, as he signed himself in early days and filled two lines of paper in doing it, was a personality even in 1874 [11] . . .

Wilde was a personality from the first. His hair was much too long, sometimes parted in the middle, sometimes at the side, and he tossed it off his face with much the same gesture used by the flapper of today. His face was colourless, "moonlike," with heavy eyes and thick lips; he had a perpetual simper and a convulsive laugh. He swayed as he walked, and lolled when at table. I never saw him run . . .

His writing was huge and sprawling—somewhat like himself. When sit-

[11] Wilde wrote to Ward in September 1876: "I like signing my name as if it was to some document of great importance as 'Send two bags of gold by bearer' or 'Let the Duke be slain tomorrow and the Duchess await me at the hostelry!' "

ting for his demyship he consumed reams of foolscap . . . Four words to a
line was his normal allowance, and he took no notice of lines. One wonders
if examiners ever mark by weight . . .

In Hall he was a clever talker of the monopolist type. He wanted to have
all the factory chimneys and vulgar workshops herded together in some out-
of-the-way island. He would give Manchester back to the shepherds and
Leeds to the stock farmers and make England beautiful again. Dining in ordinary clothes was one of his abominations. "If I were alone, marooned in a
desert island and had my things with me, I should dress for dinner every
evening." Of course men laughed, but he was quite serious over it . . .[12]

Atkinson has recalled several incidents involving Wilde which he witnessed. One occurred in the college chapel when Prince Leopold of
Belgium, accompanied by Mrs Liddell, the wife of Canon Liddell, Dean
of Christ Church, and Miss Alice Liddell, the Alice of *Alice in Wonderland,* came to hear the choir singing under Sir William Parratt's expert direction. It was Wilde's duty to read the First Lesson. He went up
to the lectern, turned over the pages, and began in a languorous voice to
recite The Song of Solomon. The Dean of Arts, the Rev. Henry Bram-
ley, promptly swooped down from his stall and, thrusting his beard into
the reader's face, exclaimed in a tone of concern, "You have the wrong
lesson, Mr Wilde. It is Deuteronomy XVI." Atkinson's comment on the
incident was characteristic. "Poor Oscar! he was so thoroughly enjoying
himself."

Wilde and Atkinson were both induced to come down to the college
barge on the Isis, where they were "tubbed" by a very unaesthetic
coach—"A Philistine of the Philistines"—as potential candidates for the
Torpids races on the river. Their progress was not noticeably inspiring.
One day, as the Varsity Eight was coming downstream and heading for
their boat, the two oarsmen were told to put their backs into it and pull
to the side. Wilde, who was stroking the boat, took no notice, observing after some uncomplimentary remarks from the Varsity cox and his
own that "he saw no *a priori* reason for rowing with a straight back and
did not believe that the Greeks did so at Salamis." Needless to add, that
was the last of his efforts as a college oar.

Oscar's spring vacation studies in 1876 were interrupted by the news
that his father was seriously ill in his Merrion Square house in Dublin,
and he hurried home just in time to see him alive. The fact that three of
his son's poems had recently been published in *The Dublin University
Magazine* had given the elder Wilde considerable pleasure.[13] The third,
which had been written at San Miniato the previous year, appeared in
the March issue. When it arrived in Merrion Square, "Sir W. carried it

[12] George Thomas Atkinson was a year younger than Wilde and had been at St Paul's
School. Like Wilde, he got a First in "Mods," but unlike him only a Third in "Greats."
On going down he became a schoolmaster, being Assistant Master at Highgate School
and subsequently Headmaster of Durlston Court, Swanage. He retired in 1928 and in
the following year wrote "Oscar Wilde at Oxford" for the *Cornhill.* He died in 1938.

[13] The earliest of Wilde's known published writings was an English-verse rendering of
the chorus of cloud maidens in *The Clouds* of Aristophanes, which appeared in *The Dublin
University Magazine* for November 1875.

off," wrote Speranza. It was one of his last conscious acts, since he died on 19 April, barely sixty years of age. A few days later Lady Wilde wrote:

> His health was failing in the winter—no actual complaint—except bronchial attacks, and we hoped for spring—but spring brought no strength. He faded away gently before our eyes—still trying to work, almost to the last, going down to attend to professional duties. Then he became weaker and for the last six weeks never left his bed. He himself still planning and hoping and planning as usual for his loved Moytura, but still he grew weaker day by day, no pain, thank God, no suffering—the last few days he was almost unconscious, quiet and still and at the last passed away like one sleeping—gently and softly—no struggle—with his hand in mine and his two sons beside him . . .
>
> For us the loss is one that plunges our life into darkness. I feel like one shipwrecked. A wife feels the position more fatally than all the others—a broken desolate life, a changed fortune, and in the midst of grief, the necessity coming for all the exertion that legal affairs demand. It is a sad sorrow to me to leave this house, yet it must be done. A married man lives on day by day and cannot think of the morrow. Probably at least £3,000 a year goes down in to the grave with him. This forces a sad change in a family. Happily my sons are of age. They will be self-supporting soon, I trust . . .

Sir William Wilde was buried in the family vault in Mount Jerome cemetery, Dublin. Besides his three sons—Willie, Oscar, and Henry Wilson—the funeral was attended by a distinguished gathering, which shows that the elder Wilde was held in considerable esteem in spite of his "peculiarities." Those present, according to the newspapers, included the Lord Mayor of Dublin, the Lord Chancellor of Ireland, the Lord Chief Justice, the president of the Royal Irish Academy, Professor Mahaffy and other Fellows of Trinity, and various Church dignitaries and Members of Parliament. It was certainly not the funeral of a forgotten man.

Oscar returned to Oxford for the summer term and "Mods," after which he went to stay with his uncle the Rev. Ralph Wilde, who now had a living in Lincolnshire and to whom Oscar proposed himself by sending a telegram for which the vicar of West Ashby had to pay half-a-crown for special delivery. "Dear me, now," he kept saying to his nephew throughout the visit, "wouldn't you have found the penny post more convenient than a telegram?"

Besides the usual *viva voce* for "Mods," for which Wilde went back to Oxford in July, he also had to take the oral examination in Divinity then obligatory for all undergraduates. He was in bed in college reading Swinburne when he was suddenly roused by the Clerk of the Schools, who told him that the Divinity exam was on and that he should go up to the Schools immediately. When he arrived, he was asked by the Rev. William Spooner, one of the examiners, why he was late. The fact was that he had mistaken the day, but he answered with his usual air of bravado, "You must excuse me. I have no experience of these pass examinations!"

Annoyed by this impertinence, the examiners gave him a Greek Testament and told him to make a written translation of the long twenty-seventh chapter of Acts, which describes how St Paul was shipwrecked while a prisoner on his way to Rome. He translated it so industriously that after a while he was told that he need not translate any more. But he continued for another half hour, after which Spooner asked him, "Didn't you hear us tell you, Mr Wilde, that you needn't copy out any more?"

"Oh, yes," Wilde replied. "I heard you, but I was so interested in what I was copying that I could not leave off. It was all about a man named Paul, who went on a voyage and was caught in a terrible storm, and I was afraid that he would be drowned. But, do you know, Mr Spooner, he was saved? And when I found out that he was saved, I thought of coming to tell you."

Since Spooner was a university lecturer in divinity and in addition was a nephew by marriage of the Archbishop of Canterbury, he not unnaturally felt this further impertinence could not be overlooked. Consequently, he failed the audacious candidate on the spot. "In Divinity I was ploughed of course," Wilde wrote to his friend Harding.

The "Mods" *viva* followed immediately. "I was rather afraid of being put on in Catullus, but got a delightful exam from a delightful man," he added, "first in the *Odyssey,* where we discussed epic poetry in general, dogs, and women. Then in Aeschylus where we talked of Shakespeare, Walt Whitman and the *Poetics.* He had a long discussion about my essay on Poetry in the Aristotle paper and altogether was delightful. Of course I knew I had got a First . . ."

Indeed, Wilde refused to go up to the Schools when he heard the results were out the following evening, infuriating the men with whom he happened to be dining by saying "it was a bore" and that he knew he was in the First Class. It was not until the following morning towards noon, when he was breakfasting in the Mitre Hotel, that he learned the result from *The Times.* "Altogether I swaggered horribly, but am really pleased with myself," he wrote in conveying the news to Bouncer Ward. However, for the first time there is a note of despondency in his otherwise cheerful letters:

My mother is in great delight and I was overwhelmed with telegrams on Thursday from everyone I know. My father would have been so pleased about it. I think God has dealt very hardly with us. It has robbed me of any real pleasure in my First, and I have not sufficient faith in Providence to believe it is all for the best—I know it is not. I feel an awful dread of going home to our old house, with everything filled with memories.

6

When he returned to Dublin for the summer vacation in 1876, Oscar made the unpleasant discovery that his father had been living largely on capital. His will was sworn at under £7,000 and he left a load of debts which had to be paid, so that Speranza became largely dependent upon her two sons, with barely enough to keep her in a state of genteel poverty. Oscar was left a half-share, with Henry Wilson, in the fishing lodge in Connemara, together with some house property at Bray by the sea in County Wicklow. Willie got the Dublin house, while Speranza's jointure was inadequately charged on Moytura. All the houses were mortgaged, so that the outlook was bleak. "It is so new to me to *beg,*" she told Oscar. Nevertheless, she moved some friends to apply for a civil list pension on her behalf. "We could not keep up this house [in Merrion Square] and the female servants, fires, gas, food, rent—there is a mortgage—under £500 a year. Nothing is to be had out of *wretched Moytura.* I am in a very distracted state of mind. What is to be done?"

Fortunately, her late husband's natural son Henry Wilson came to the rescue with an offer of £2,500 for No. 1 Merrion Square which, after the mortgage had been paid off, left Willie with £1,500. Henry also allowed his stepmother and half-brother to continue to live there, and after his sudden death in the following year, the house was left to Willie.

Frank Miles stayed with Oscar that summer at Moytura and also at Illaunroe, where Oscar tried to make his guest land a salmon and kill a brace of grouse, though Frank had never fired a gun in his life and said he did not want to. "I have only got one salmon as yet but have had heaps of sea trout which give great play," Oscar wrote to Ward from Connemara. "I have not had a blank day yet. Grouse are few but I have got a lot of hares so have had a capital time of it. I hope next year that you and the Kitten will come and stay a (lunar) month with me. I am sure you would like this wild mountainous country, close to the Atlantic and teeming with sport of all kinds. It is in every way magnificent and makes me years younger than actual history records."

These letters show a very different man from the emerging homosexual and namby-pamby aesthete of popular tradition. His sexual tastes were quite normal and he fell in love with at least two girls at this time. "I am just going out to bring an *exquisitely pretty girl* to afternoon service in the Cathedral," he wrote to Kitten Harding from Merrion Square one Sunday in August 1876. "She is just seventeen with the *most perfectly beautiful face I ever saw and not a sixpence of money.* I will show you her photograph when I see you next." (Wilde's italics.) The teenage beauty, whose name was Florence ("Florrie") Balcombe, was Wilde's first love, and he was never to forget her. Her father was a retired army officer, and she lived with her parents at Clontarf, near Dublin.

As for homosexual behaviour, Oscar found this mildly shocking, if one can judge from what he wrote on the same day to Ward about a Magdalen contemporary named Charles Todd, whom Oscar had seen with a Magdalen chorister named Ward—no relation of Bouncer's—in a Dublin theatre.

> I want to ask your opinion on this psychological question. In our friend Todd's ethical barometer, at what height is his moral quicksilver? Last night I strolled into the theatre about ten o'clock and to my surprise saw Todd and

young Ward the quire [sic] boy in a private box together, Todd very much in the background. He saw me so I went round to speak to him for a few minutes . . . I wonder what young Ward is doing with him. Myself I believe that Todd is extremely moral and only mentally spoons the boy, but I think he is foolish to go about with one, if he *is* bringing this boy about with him.

You are the only one I would tell about it, as you have a philosophical mind, but *don't tell anyone about it like a good boy—it would do neither us nor Todd any good.*

He [Todd] looked awfully nervous and uncomfortable.[14]

Oscar had made tentative plans for a "pilgrimage to Rome" with Miles and Ronald Gower before going up to Oxford for his third year, but he eventually dropped them. "We would have been a great Trinity," he wrote to Ward in September. "But at the last hour Ronald couldn't get time so I am staying in Dublin to the 20th, when I go down to Longford [for the partridge shooting] and hope to have good sport."

He returned to Oxford for the Michaelmas term in 1877 to begin reading for the Literae Humaniores, the examination known as "Greats," for which he would have to sit eighteen months later. Meanwhile, he took over his friend Bouncer Ward's rooms on Kitchen Staircase in College ("I am awfully pleased about it"). At the same time, he complained to his mother about being hard up and even contemplated an advantageous marriage as a way out of his financial difficulties. Speranza was not sympathetic. "I should be sorry that you had to seek the marriage situation and give up the chance of a Fellowship," she wrote, "but I do not see that your so [impoverished] state is one that demands pity or commiseration. From May last—just five months—you have received in cash and for your own private personal expenses £145, and the rents of Bray and the sale of your furniture may bring you over the year till Spring when you can sell your houses for £3,000, £2,000 of which will give you £200 for ten years—a very ample provision to my way of thinking. I wish I could have £200 a year for ten years."

Before joining his family firm of solicitors in Bristol, Bouncer Ward spent several months in Italy. He was there when Wilde wrote to him at the end of February 1877, giving him some of the college gossip and complaining that the undergraduate talk was mostly "nonsense and smut":

I would give worlds to be in Rome with you and Dunskie. I know I would enjoy it awfully but I don't know if I can manage it. You would be a safeguard against Dunskie's attacks.

I am in for the "Ireland" on Monday [5 March 1877].[15] God! how I have wasted my life up here. I look back on weeks and months of extravagance, trivial talk, utter vacancy of employment, *with feelings so bitter that I have lost faith in myself.* I am too ridiculously easily led astray. So I have idled and

---

[14] Todd later took orders and served as Chaplain to the Royal Navy from 1881 to 1909. He died in 1939.

[15] The Ireland Scholarship in "classical learnings and taste," competed for annually.

won't get it and will be wretched in consequence. I feel that if I had read I would have done well up here but I have not.

I enjoy your rooms awfully. The inner room is filled with china, pictures, a portfolio and a piano—and a grey carpet with stained floor. The whole get-up is much admired and a little made fun of on Sunday evenings. They are more delightful than I ever expected—the sunshine, the cawing rooks and waving tree-branches and the breeze at the window are too charming.

I do nothing but write sonnets and scribble poetry—some of which I send you—though to send anything of mine to Rome is an awful impertinence, but you always took an interest in my attempts to ride Pegasus . . .

Your letters are charming and the one from Sicily came with a scent of olive-gardens, blue skies and orange trees, that was like reading Theocritus in this grey climate. Goodbye.

Ever, dear boy, your affectionate friend

OSCAR WILDE [16]

"I have been in for 'the Ireland' and of course lost it," he wrote in his next letter to Ward. "On six weeks reading I could not expect to get a prize for which men work two and three years. What stumped me was Philology of which they gave us a long paper: otherwise I did rather well: it is horrid receiving the awkward commiserations of most of the College. I shall not be sorry when term ends: though I have only a year for Greats work, still I intend to reform and read hard, if possible."

A characteristic example of Wilde's perverse delight in shocking his elders occurred at the college ceremony known as "Collections," at the end of the Hilary term in 1877, at which the president and Fellows used to meet the undergraduate members of the college in Hall and hear the tutorial progress reports. On this particular occasion the high table was filled with dons. The president, Dr Bulley, called up Atkinson and Wilde together.

"How do you find Mr Wilde's work, Mr Allen?" the president asked Wilde's tutor.

"Mr Wilde absents himself without apology from my lectures," replied the tutor with an aggrieved air. "His work is most unsatisfactory."

"That is hardly the way to treat a gentleman," Dr Bulley remarked to the delinquent in his usual courtly manner.

"But, Mr President, Mr Allen is *not* a gentleman." [17]

Amazement followed this sally, and Wilde was told to leave the hall. No doubt he apologized with his customary charm, but the incident was not exactly calculated to endear him to the college authorities, least of all Mr Allen, whom his mother hoped would appoint him to a Fellowship if he got a First in Greats.

At first Wilde did not think he could afford to go to Rome for Easter as he had planned to, since he had been elected somewhat earlier than he had expected to the St Stephen's Club in London and had to produce

[16] Wilde had recently dropped the middle names in his signature and adopted the style which he was to use for the rest of his life.

[17] The Rev. W. D. Allen was a Fellow of the College and Classical Tutor from 1873 to 1881, when he became Vicar of Findon, Sussex.

£42 to cover the entrance fee and annual subscription. That he was able to do so was due to Hunter Blair, who wrote to him from Monte Carlo on his way to Rome that he would have luck at the Casino if it was heaven's wish that Oscar should join him and Ward there. Dunskie was successful and sent Oscar £60 from his winnings so that he could make the journey. Thus Oscar was able to tell Harding that he hoped "to see the golden dome of St Peter's and the Eternal City" by Easter Day and would "burn a candle" for him at the shrine of Our Lady. "This is an era in my life, a crisis," he wrote on the eve of his departure. "I wish I could look into the seeds of time and see what is coming." (It was just as well that he could not.)

He did not travel direct to Rome as he originally intended. "I never went to Rome at all!" he wrote from Corfu to Harding on Easter Monday. "What a changeable fellow you must think me, but Mahaffy my old tutor carried me off to Greece with him to see Mycenae and Athens." Besides Mahaffy, the party included William Goulding and George Macmillan, a member of the publishing family and one of the founders a few years later of the Hellenic Society.

> We came first to Genoa, which is a beautiful marble city of palaces over the sea, and then to Ravenna which is extremely interesting on account of the old Christian churches in it of enormous age and the magnificent mosaics of the *fourth century*. These mosaics are very remarkable as they contained two figures of the Madonna enthroned and receiving adoration; they completely upset the ordinary Protestant idea that the worship of the Virgin did not come in till late in the history of the Church.

From Ravenna they went to Brindisi, whence they caught the boat to Corfu and thence to Zante. To the present-day generation of travellers, accustomed to comfortable "package" tours of Greece and the Greek islands, the excitement shown at the prospect of their visit by Wilde and his companions, who rose to get their first glimpse of the mainland at dawn, may seem surprising. But a century ago a journey through Greece by British tourists was relatively uncommon, since the roads were bad, brigands infested the byways, and visitors who strayed from the main carriage ways were liable to be kidnapped. Shelley and Swinburne, who owed much to Greece, never got beyond Italy, while Ruskin was deterred from visiting the country by what he had heard of its dangers. Indeed, only a few years previously four well-known English travellers had been held ransom and murdered when the ransom was not forthcoming. Consequently, Mahaffy and his party all carried firearms on their journey. They disembarked at Katakolo (where Wilde immediately wrote a sonnet) in the company of Dr Hirschfield, the director of the German excavation at Olympia, where many fine sculptures and fragments, since removed, lay near their places of discovery.

Next day Oscar and his companions found horses and set off, full of enthusiasm, to ride across the Peloponnese, which took them a week. No bandits appeared, and the only danger came from the owner of the horses, who accompanied them on foot for part of the way as guide. He objected to any pace faster than a walk, not because of his inability to keep up with the travellers, but because he believed that anything more than a gentle amble was bad for the horses. Weary of such slow progress, the travellers urged their mounts to a trot and finally to a gallop. At this the hot-tempered guide, losing control of himself, seized Wilde's mount by the bridle and drew his knife. Oscar, with what Macmillan described as "great presence of mind," promptly drew the revolver he was carrying and pointed it at the guide, who thereupon replaced his knife in his belt and melodramatically bared his breast "as if to invite destruction." Oscar then replaced his own weapon and rode on, without further ado. They reached Mycenae and Epidaurus in safety, whence they sailed to the Piraeus, and so to Athens.[18]

They returned by way of Rome, where Oscar met Ward and Hunter Blair and visited Keats's grave with them, an experience which inspired him to compose another sonnet. "As I stood beside the mean grave of this divine boy," he wrote in an introductory article, "I thought of him as a Priest of Beauty slain before his time."[19]

"The chance of seeing such great places—and in such good company—was too great for me," he wrote to the Dean at Magdalen, explaining why he was unable to be back at the beginning of the summer term.

> I hope you will not mind if I miss ten days at the beginning: seeing Greece is really a great education for anyone and will I think benefit me greatly, and Mr Mahaffy is such a clever man that it is quite as good as going to lectures to be in his society.

This excuse did not satisfy the college authorities, and on his return to Oxford he was fined the sum of £47 10s, being half the amount of his demyship for the year, and in addition was "rusticated," that is, sent down, for the remainder of the term. Years later he was reported as saying: "I was sent down from Oxford for being the first undergraduate to visit Olympia." So after "a delightful time in town with Frank Miles and a lot of friends," he went home to Dublin, early in May, where he again wrote to Harding:

> My mother was of course awfully astonished to hear my news and very disgusted with the wretched stupidity of the college dons, while Mahaffy is *raging!* I never saw him so indignantly angry: he looks on it as an insult to himself.
> The weather is charming, Florrie more lovely than ever, and I am going to give two lectures on Greece to the Alexandra College girls here, so I am rapidly forgetting the Boeotian *anaesthesia* of Allen and the wretched timeserving of that old woman in petticoats, the Dean.
> As I expected, all my friends here refuse to believe my story, and my brother who is down at Moytura at present writes me a letter marked *"Pri-*

[18] Mahaffy subsequently described the journey in his *Rambles and Studies in Greece;* see 3rd edition (1887), chapter XI.

[19] The article and sonnet appeared in the *Irish Monthly* for July 1877.

vate" to ask "what it *really* is all about and *why* I have been rusticated," treating my explanations as mere child's play.

I hope you will write and tell me all about the College, who is desecrating my rooms and what is the latest scandal.

A week or two later he was writing to the ex-Liberal Prime Minister Mr Gladstone, sending him a sonnet inspired by "your noble and impassioned protests, both written and spoken, against the massacres of the Christians in Bulgaria." He described himself as "little more than a boy," with "no literary interest in London," adding that if "perhaps *you* saw any good stuff in the lines I send you, some editor (of the *Nineteenth Century* perhaps or the *Spectator*) might publish them: and I feel sure that you can appreciate the very great longing that one has when young to have words of one's own published for men to read."

Gladstone sent a courteous reply to the effect that he "saw some promise" in the verses and advising Wilde to try *The Spectator*. Wilde was delighted and responded in kind. "The idea of *your* reading anything of mine has so delighted me, that I cannot help sending you a second sonnet. I am afraid you will think it a poor return for your courtesy to repeat the offence, but perhaps you may see some beauty in it." Gladstone was to preserve Wilde's letters carefully, as he was also to do the first collection of his *Poems,* which the author sent him when it appeared four years later.[20]

If Wilde had to wait for a while before the sonnets were published, *The Dublin University Magazine* immediately accepted an article which he had written on the first exhibition in the Grosvenor Gallery in London, which opened at the beginning of May and which Wilde had seen on his way home from Oxford. The gallery had been established by a wealthy banker and art lover, Sir Coutts Lindsay, for the exhibition of paintings by contemporary artists, in opposition to the more conventional Royal Academy. Incidentally, the exhibition contained Whistler's "Nocturne in Black and Gold," usually known as "The Falling Rocket," which was so fiercely criticized by Ruskin that the artist sued him for libel. Wilde was more complimentary in his notice, which attracted the favourable comment of the aesthetic Walter Pater at Oxford. "Your excellent article . . . shows that you possess some beautiful, and, for your age, quite exceptionally cultivated tastes: and a considerable knowledge too of many beautiful things," wrote Pater. "I hope you will write a great deal in time to come."

This budding literary success was clouded by a shock which Wilde received in mid-June. "I am very much down in spirits and depressed," he wrote to Harding. "A cousin of ours to whom we were all very much attached has just died—quite suddenly from some chill caught riding. I dined with him on Saturday and he was dead on Wednesday." The

[20] The subject of the second sonnet was "Easter Day in Rome." Neither appeared in *The Spectator,* which presumably rejected them, but the second was published in *Waifs and Strays* for June 1879. Both subsequently appeared with slight revisions in the *Poems* (1881).

"cousin" was in fact Wilde's half-brother Henry Wilson, who contracted pneumonia with fatal results at the age of thirty-nine.

My brother and I were supposed to be his heirs but his will was an unpleasant surprise, like most wills. He leaves my father's hospital £8,000, my brother £2,000 and me £100 on condition of my being a Protestant!

He was, poor fellow, bigotedly intolerant of the Catholics and seeing me "on the brink" struck me out of his will. It is a terrible disappointment to me; you see I suffer a good deal from my Romish leanings, in pocket and mind.

My father had given him a share in my fishing lodge in Connemara, which of course ought to have reverted to me on his death; well, even this I lose "if I become a Roman Catholic for five years" which is very infamous.

Fancy a man going before "God and the Eternal Silences" with his wretched Protestant prejudices and bigotry clinging still to him.

However, the testator need have had no fears. The pagan influences which he absorbed during his tour of Greece with Mahaffy was to postpone Oscar Wilde's conversion to the Roman Catholic Church until he was on his deathbed. "Religion does not help me," he was to write in *De Profundis:* "The faith that others give to what is unseen I give to what one can touch and look at. My gods dwell in temples made with hands . . . . When I think about religion at all I feel as if I would like to found an order for those *who cannot* believe: the Confraternity of the Faithless one might call it."

He seems to have got over his disappointment quite quickly, as he went down to fish at Illaunroe in the following month and was soon writing his usual cheery letters to Harding and Ward. He tried without success to persuade the latter to join him there, promising him, in addition to fishing, "scenery, sunsets, bathing, heather, mountains, lakes, whiskey and salmon to eat." At the same time he asked Ward for "the name and address of Miss Fletcher whom I rode with at Rome, and of her step-father. I have never sent her some articles of Pater's I promised her." This was Constance Fletcher, an aspiring young novelist who was then engaged in writing a three-volume novel called *The Mirage,* in which Wilde appears as the thinly disguised character Claude Davenant, and which was to be published some months later under the pseudonym George Fleming. Wilde heard from her in due course. "She sends her best wishes to you of course, and writes as cleverly as she talks," he told Ward. "I am much attracted to her in every way." [21]

Wilde confessed to Ward that while at Illaunroe he spent his evenings playing pool or écarté and drinking "potheen punch." "I wish you had

[21] Constance Fletcher, who was twenty when Wilde first met her, never married. She had private means and lived for many years with her mother and stepfather, a painter named Eugene Benson in the Palazzo Capello on the Rio Marin in Venice, which Henry James, with whom she was friendly, had in mind when he wrote *The Aspern Papers.* As she grew older, she became very stout, and on one occasion while staying with Henry James in Lamb House, Rye, caused some embarrassment by getting stuck in the narrow bath. She was decorated for her work for the Italian Red Cross during the First World War. She died in 1938.

come; one requires sympathy to read," he added. "I am however in the midst of two articles, one on Greece, the other on Art, which keep me thinking if not writing.[22] But of Greats work I have done nothing. After all there are more profitable studies, I suppose, than the Greats course: still I would like a good Class awfully and want you to lend me your notes on Philosophy . . . And also *give me advice*—a thing I can't stand from my elders because it's like preaching, but I think I would like some from you 'who have passed through the fire.' "

Before returning to Oxford for his last year, Wilde spent a few days as usual in London. A sudden impulse took him to Brompton Oratory, where he made his confession to Father Sebastian Bowden. Afterwards Father Bowden wrote to him:

> Whatever your first purpose may have been in your visit yesterday, there is no doubt that as a fact you did freely and entirely lay open to me your life's history and your soul's state. And it was God's grace which made you do so.
>
> You would not have spoken of your aimlessness and misery or of your temporal misfortune to a priest in a first interview unless you hoped that I should have some remedy to suggest, and that not of man's making. Be true to yourself then, it was no power or influence of mine (which it is nonsense to speak of) but the voice of your own conscience urging you to make a new start and escape from your present unhappy self, which provoked your confession . . .
>
> On the other hand, God in His mercy has not left you to remain contented in this state. He has proved to you the hollowness of this world in the unexpected loss of your fortune and has removed thereby a great obstacle to your conversion; He allowed you to feel the sting of conscience and the yearnings for a holy pure and earnest life. It depends therefore on your own free will which life you lead. As God calls you, He is bound, remember, to give you the means to obey the call . . . I trust then you will come on Thursday and have another talk; you may be quite sure I shall urge you to do nothing but what your conscience dictates. In the meantime pray hard and talk little.

Wilde had now to some extent reacted against Mahaffy's "paganism" and he was of two minds as to whether he should join the Church of Rome. One thing held him back, apart from the prospect of losing his late half-brother's share in the family fishing lodge. This was the fact that he had recently become a Freemason.[23] "I have got rather keen on Masonry and believe in it awfully," he wrote to Bouncer Ward at this time, "—in fact would be awfully sorry to have to give it up in case I secede from the Protestant Heresy . . . I have dreams of a visit to New-

---

[22] The article on Greece entitled "Hellenism" was never published. The first half of the MS, which formerly belonged to me, is now in the collection of Mrs Donald F. Hyde of Somerville, New Jersey. The second half is in the Clark Library, as is also the article on art, which Wilde used for his lectures "Art and the Handicraftman" in Philadelphia in 1882 and "A Lecture to Art Students" in London in 1883.

[23] He was admitted to the thirty-third degree of the Scottish Masonic rite at the Oxford University chapter on 27 November 1876. His certificate of admission is now in the Donald F. Hyde collection.

man, of the holy sacrament in a new Church, and of quiet and peace afterwards in my soul. I need not say, though, that I shift with every breath of thought and am weaker and more self-deceiving than ever."

7

"I am reading hard for a Fourth in Greats," Oscar wrote on arriving in Oxford to begin his last year. "How are the mighty fallen!!" Indeed, he worked so hard that he came near to a nervous breakdown during the following Easter vacation, for which he had stayed up, and in consequence had to go off to the Royal Bath Hotel in Bournemouth "to try and get some ozone." At the same time, he was busy scribbling verses. One of his poems, a sonnet which appeared in the T.C.D. magazine *Kottabos* for Michaelmas Term 1877, was called "Wasted Days" and is perhaps the first example of the author's writing of youthful male physical qualities in a manner which was to be subsequently used with damaging effect against him, although in this instance the subject was not taken from real life but from a small painting of a youth in medieval dress by a girl acquaintance.[24]

> A fair slim boy not made for this world's pain,
>   With hair of gold thick clustering round his ears,
>   And longing eyes half-veil'd by foolish tears
> Like bluest water seen through mists of rain,
> Pale cheeks whereon no kiss hath left its stain,
>   Red under-lip drawn in for fear of Love,
>   And white throat whiter than the breast of dove—
> Alas! Alas! if all should be in vain.

Another poem, more conventional in character, "Magdalen Walks," was published in the *Irish Monthly* for April 1878, and was later to be set to music by a composer called Kurt Schindler in New York under the title "Early Spring." Wilde also decided to compete for the Newdigate Prize, which was offered annually "for the best composition in English verse, not limited to Fifty Lines, by any Undergraduate who on the day above specified [31 March 1878] shall not have exceeded *four* years from his Matriculation." The prize, of an annual value of £21, which had been founded by the antiquarian Sir Roger Newdigate in 1805, had originally been limited to fifty lines on a theme of Greek or Roman antiquity, but this provision was subsequently modified when the requirement was added that the poem should be in heroic couplets. The judges included the current Professor of Poetry and the Public Orator, who were not to know the winner's identity until after they had

---

[24] The painting on a tile six inches square was the work of Violet Troubridge (later Mrs Walter Gurney); it is reproduced as being "From a Painting by Miss V.T." in Stuart Mason's *Bibliography of Oscar Wilde,* facing p. 96. Wilde rewrote the sonnet for the first collected edition of his poems (1881), calling it "Madonna Mia" and making the subject "a lily white girl" instead of "a fair, slim boy."

made their decision. By an extraordinary piece of luck for Wilde, the subject for the year 1878 had been announced as "Ravenna" sometime after his visit to Italy and Greece the previous spring.

On 18 June, it was announced in the *Oxford University Gazette* that the judges had awarded the Newdigate Prize to Oscar O'Flahertie Wilde, Demy of Magdalen College. To Father Mathew Russell, S.J., the editor of the *Irish Monthly* who had asked for some particulars which he could publish in the next issue, Wilde wrote about "my recent success":

> The subject is given out at the June Encaenia and is the same for all. There is besides the *kudos* a prize of twenty guineas. It was originally limited to fifty lines, and the subject used to be necessarily taken from some *classical* subject, either Greek or Latin, and generally a work of art. The metre is heroic couplets, but as you have seen perhaps from my poem, of late years laxity is allowed from the horrid Popeian jingle of regular heroics, and *now* the subject may be taken from any country or time and there is no limit to the length . . . There is a picture of the Founder hanging in the dining hall of University College, Oxford . . . Besides I have an idea that Ruskin and Dean Stanley got it . . .[25]

> There was a strange coincidence about my getting it. On the 31st March 1877 (long before the subject was given out) I entered Ravenna on my way to Greece, and on 31st March 1878 I had to hand my poem in. It is quite the blue ribbon of the Varsity and my college presented me with a marble bust of "young Augustus" which had been bequeathed by an old Fellow of Magdalen, Dr Daubeny, to the first undergraduate [of the college] who should get the Newdigate.

In accordance with tradition, the winner walked in procession with the Vice-Chancellor, heads of colleges, and other university dignitaries, attended by the proctors, to the Sheldonian Theatre, where, after the usual formalities had been completed, he recited parts of the prize poem, which on this occasion, so we are informed, were "listened to with rapt attention and frequently applauded." No doubt the loudest applause was reserved for the allusions to another poet, Lord Byron, who had spent two years in Ravenna, which he preferred to all the other towns of Italy, influenced in some measure as he undoubtedly was by his mistress the young Countess Teresa Guiccioli, a member of a local family noted for its liberal principles.

> And Greece stood up to fight for Liberty,
> And called him from Ravenna, never knight
> Rode forth more nobly to wild scenes of fight! . . .
>
> For as the olive-garland of the race,
> Which lights with joy each eager runner's face,
> As the red cross which saveth men in war,
> As a flame-bearded beacon seen from far
> By mariners upon a storm-tossed sea,—
> Such as his love for Greece and Liberty!

[25] Wilde was correct. Stanley won it in 1837 and Ruskin in 1839.

Byron, thy crowns are ever fresh and green:
Red leaves of rose from Sapphic Mitylene
Shall bind thy brows; the myrtle blooms for thee,
In hidden glades by lonely Castaly;
The Laurels want thy coming: all are thine,
   And round thy head one perfect wreath will twine.

The Professor of Poetry at this time was John Campbell Shairp, a somewhat unsympathetic Scot who had himself won the Newdigate—in 1842, with a poem on Charles XII of Sweden. One of the professor's duties was to suggest textual improvements to the winning composition before it was published, and these were usually accepted with gratitude by the winner. But Oscar Wilde was an exception. He is said to have listened to Shairp's many proposed amendments with courtesy and even to have taken notes of these, afterwards going away and having his prize poem printed without a single alteration.

Ravenna was published by Thomas Shrimpton and Son, Broad Street, Oxford, with grey paper wrappers printed in black on a single sheet of laid paper folded into eight leaves and sewn in pamphlet form, thus forming sixteen pages and retailing at the price of 1s 6d. Below the author's name on the front cover and title page was a design of the university arms, while on the third page the dedication read: "To My Friend George Fleming, author of *A Nile Novel* and *Mirage.*" [26]

One friend who received an inscribed copy of *Ravenna* was Harold Boulton, then an undergraduate at Balliol. Boulton, who was to come second in the Newdigate in 1881 and afterwards to write many lyrics including the "Skye Boat Song" and "Glorious Devon," also edited the Oxford poetry magazine *Waifs and Strays,* to which Wilde contributed at this time, including a sonnet composed on disembarking upon "the strand of Greece at last" at Katakolo in April 1877.

Meanwhile, Wilde had sat for the final "Greats" examination, and after a brief visit to London to see Frank Miles, he returned to Oxford in the middle of July for the *viva.* The results were announced on 19 July, and as in "Mods" Wilde's name appeared in the First Class. He immediately wrote to Bouncer Ward, who had telegraphed his congratulations:

It is too delightful altogether this display of fireworks at the end of my career. I cannot understand my First except for the essays which I was fairly good in. I got a very complimentary *viva voce.*

The dons are "astonished" beyond words—the Bad Boy doing so well in the end! They made me stay up for the Gaudy [27] and said nice things about me. I am on the best of terms with everyone including *Allen* who I think is remorseful of his treatment of me!

---

[26] It is now a valuable collector's item. A later version, in the form of an attempted facsimile, was published by a piratical bookseller in 1904. It can be distinguished from the genuine article, since it lacks the university arms on the cover and title page.

[27] The annual college dinner for graduates, who were not usually invited until they had been "down" for some years.

Then I rowed to Pangbourne with Frank Miles in a birchbark canoe and shot rapids and did wonders everywhere—it was delightful!

Besides inviting him to the Gaudy, the college authorities remitted the amount they had fined him when he was rusticated for being late for term after his trip to Greece with Mahaffy the previous year. They also confirmed his demyship for a fifth year, so that he could come up again if he wished and read for the Chancellor's English Essay Prize which he had formed the intention of doing when he learned that the subject for 1879 was "Historical Criticism among the Ancients." This was a prize normally competed for by postgraduates, since it was confined to members of the university who had exceeded four years but had not exceeded seven from their matriculation.

Bouncer Ward had asked his friend to go yachting with him, but Wilde had to decline and return to Dublin to help in settling his father's confused affairs. He had sold the Bray house for something less than £3,000, but had been involved in a lawsuit resulting from too many agents and a conflict of contracts and, although he won the case, he had to pay his untaxed costs, which when the mortgage had also been discharged left him with but little. Willie did somewhat better on his second sale of the Merrion Square house, as appears from a letter from Speranza to a friend at this period:

We have arranged to leave Ireland, and this is my last note from the old family mansion in Merrion Square. Both my sons prefer residing in London, the focus of light, progress and intellect, and we have taken a house there, and disposed of this on very good terms. It belongs to my son and he gets £3,500 for it.

But Speranza gave a grander impression than the real facts. What she had in fact taken were lodgings in Kensington. Oscar was never to live with her there, although her elder son, who had given up the Irish Bar for journalism, was to do so.

Oscar spent most of the late summer and autumn fishing in the west of Ireland. "I am resting here in the mountains," he wrote to Father Russell from Illaunroe, "—great peace and quiet everywhere—and I hope to send you a sonnet as the result."

November found him back in Merrion Square, somewhat hurt to learn that his old flame Florence Balcombe was engaged to be married and, as he reproached her, had not thought it worthwhile to let him know of her approaching marriage. Her fiancé was a young Irish civil servant named Bram Stoker, who is chiefly remembered as the author of the horrific novel *Dracula*. "As I shall be going back to England, probably for good, in a few days," Oscar wrote to her with his wishes that she might be happy, "I should like to bring with me the little gold cross I gave you one Christmas morning long ago . . . We stand apart now, but the little cross will serve to remind me of the bygone days, and though we shall never meet again, after I leave Ireland, still I shall always remember you at prayer." As the cross had his name on it, this "of course would have prevented you from wearing it ever."

Instead of suggesting that Oscar should come out to her home at Clontarf, Florrie somewhat thoughtlessly suggested they might meet in the house of her future husband's brother Thornley, later a distinguished surgeon, in the middle of Dublin. But Oscar turned this down in reproving terms:

> As you expressed a wish to see me I thought that *your mother's house* would be the only suitable place, and that we should part where we first met. As for my calling at Harcourt Street, you know, my dear Florence, that such a thing is quite out of the question: it would have been unfair to you, and me, and to the man you are going to marry, had we met anywhere else but under your mother's roof, and with your mother's sanction. I am sure that you will see this yourself on reflection; as a man of honour I could not have met you without the full sanction of your parents and in their house . . .
>
> Goodbye, and believe me yours very truly
>
> OSCAR WILDE

Oscar left Dublin before the wedding, which took place early in December 1878, and he returned to Oxford to satisfy the examiners in the "rudiments of religion," the examination for which he had been ploughed two years previously, and afterwards to take his degree as Bachelor of Arts, which he did on 28 November. Apart from two brief visits to lecture and incidentally to become engaged himself to another Irish girl, he was never to return to Ireland. If he sometimes felt he was an expatriate, he certainly never admitted it. Nevertheless, as Bernard Shaw was to remark of his fellow countryman, "it must not be forgotten that though by culture Wilde was a citizen of all civilised capitals, he was at root a very Irish Irishman, and as such, a foreigner everywhere but in Ireland."

2 / London and America

In the year Oscar Wilde graduated from Oxford, his friend Hunter Blair asked him what his real ambition in life was. "God knows!" Wilde replied. "I won't be a dried-up Oxford don, anyhow." He went on:

I'll be a poet, a writer, a dramatist. Somehow or other I'll be famous, and if not famous, I'll be notorious. Or perhaps I'll lead the *bios apolaustikos* [life of pleasure] for a time and then—who knows?—rest and do nothing. What does Plato say is the highest end that man can attain here below? To sit down and contemplate the good. Perhaps that will be the end of me too. These things are on the knees of the gods. What will be, will be.

Viewed in retrospect, it was a remarkable prophecy.

The earlier months of 1879 Wilde seems to have divided between London and Oxford, working on his entry for the Chancellor's English Essay Prize. In March he had a letter from George Macmillan, telling him of the foundation of the Society for the Promotion of Hellenic Studies, of which Macmillan became the first honorary secretary. Macmillan had also just been made a partner in the family publishing business, and he was determined to promote and extend the firm's interest in Greek and Latin classics, art and archaeology; indeed, it was to be due to his activities in this field that the firm was able to secure the works of such scholars as Mahaffy, Bury, Bryce, and Frazer for its publishing list. In this context Macmillan asked Wilde if he would like to do some translating and editing of the Greek classical writers.

"Nothing would please me more than to engage in literary work for your house," Wilde replied from the St Stephen's Club on 22 March 1899. "I have looked forward to this opportunity for some time." Selections from Herodotus, he went on, he would like to translate "very much indeed," since he felt sure that "the wonderful picturesqueness of his writings, as well as the pathos and tenderness of some of his stories, would command a great many readers." He also suggested editing some of the plays of Euripides, "with which I am well acquainted."

Apparently Macmillan was agreeable, but Wilde did not follow up the idea. He might have done so, had he been elected to a Fellowship at Magdalen, as his mother fondly hoped. But the College Fellows did not invite him to join their body, no doubt considering that he would not fit into their tight little community particularly well. Had they offered him a Fellowship in Classics, Wilde might well have accepted in spite of his admission to Hunter Blair already quoted, since it would have given him an assured income for some years, provided he did not marry. Another reason why his enthusiasm for the classics may have waned at this time and induced him to direct his attention from classical to modern art was probably his failure to secure the Chancellor's English Essay Prize. No award was made for that year, only the second time that this had happened since the prize was founded in 1768. The judges were the same as for the Newdigate and it may well be that Professor Shairpe was getting his own back on Wilde for having declined to take advantage of his suggested improvements to *Ravenna*.[1]

Sometime in the latter part of 1879, Oscar Wilde took rooms in Thames House, Salisbury Street, between the Strand and the Embankment, which he shared with his artist friend Frank Miles. The house, which no longer exists, was said to have once been occupied by Count Alfred d'Orsay, the French dandy and wit who married Lord Blessington's daughter and later lived with her socially gifted authoress stepmother.[2]

"I very often have beautiful people to tea, and will always be very glad to see you and introduce you to them," Wilde wrote to Harold Boulton shortly after he had moved in. "Any night you like to go to the

[1] The complete work was never published in England during the author's lifetime and did not appear until 1909, when Wilde's literary executor, Robert Ross, included it in Wilde's *Essays and Lectures* under the title "The Rise of Historical Criticism." Ross sent the proofs for correction to Professor J. W. Mackail, then Professor of Poetry at Oxford and one of the judges for the current entries. "The essay, young as it is, is quite up to the general level of that sort of thing and I do not know why the prize was not awarded," Mackail replied when he returned the proofs. "It would be interesting to find out . . . what the essays were in that year." Unfortunately, this was not possible, since all the essays had been returned to their authors. The original MS consisted of three parts and was contained in three morocco-bound quarto exercise books. Part I disappeared at the time of the sale of Wilde's effects at his house in Tite Street in April 1895, presumably either sold or stolen. It later turned up in America, where it was sold for $275 by a rare-book dealer and published by the Sherwood Press, Hartford, Connecticut, in a privately printed edition stated to be limited to 225 numbered copies. Parts II and III were subsequently discovered by Robert Ross, who published the whole work for the first time as stated above. The MS of Parts II and III was bought by William Andrews Clark, who also acquired Part I. The three parts of the MS were thus reunited and are now in the Clark Library at the University of California, Los Angeles.

[2] The houses in Salisbury Street and the neighbouring Cecil Street belonged to the Marquess of Salisbury. They were pulled down when Lord Salisbury sold the property in 1888 for development. The Hotel Cecil, now Shell-Mex House, was built on the site.

theatre I will give you a bed with great pleasure in this untidy and romantic house."

The "beautiful people" included Lillie Langtry and Gladys Lonsdale, then both in their twenties and recently married. Mrs Langtry, known as "the Jersey Lily," from Millais's famous portrait of her, and the first openly recognized mistress of the Prince of Wales, was considered the most beautiful woman of her generation. She was shortly to make her debut on the London stage. Wilde had just written a poem to her entitled "The New Helen" for *Time,* a new monthly edited by Edmund Yates. Soon he was acting as her unpaid secretary and teaching her Latin as well as advising her on other matters. Once, after calling at Thames House and finding him out, she wrote to him from Plymouth, "I wanted to ask you how I should go to a fancy ball here, but I chose a soft black Greek dress with a fringe of silver crescents and stars, and diamond ones in my hair and on my neck, and called it Queen of the Night. I made it myself." Evidently she liked her "kind tutor," as she called him. For his part, he played up to her, and when his *Poems,* which included "The New Helen," came out a year or so later, he sent her a copy inscribed, "To Helen, formerly of Troy, now of London." He was never to lose his affectionate regard for "the adored and adorable Lily," as he called her. In 1899, the year before his death, he was recorded as saying: "The three women I have most admired are Queen Victoria, Sarah Bernhardt, and Lillie Langtry. I would have married any one of them with pleasure. The first had great dignity, the second a lovely voice, the third a perfect figure."

Gladys Countess of Lonsdale, later Countess de Grey and Marchioness of Ripon, was a pleasure-loving and discreetly amorous beauty, tall and dark, who, according to a contemporary, "made any woman near her look pale." Wilde remained in her good graces for many years, and he was to dedicate the published version of his play *A Woman of No Importance* to her. In 1882, she was in Monte Carlo enjoying herself when her husband died suddenly, not in his usual abode in Carlton House Terrace, but in a house near the Marble Arch which, according to an entry in Lord Rosebery's diary, "he took to give actresses supper in," his body subsequently being smuggled home in a cab. Speranza had a fleeting hope that Oscar would marry the widowed Lady Lonsdale, who had been born Gladys Herbert and was a sister of Lord Pembroke, but she preferred to stay with the peerage and married Lord de Grey.

Others who came to the tea parties in Thames House, at which, incidentally, Oscar's mother was usually present to act as chaperone, were the novelist Mrs Alfred Hunt, the original of Tennyson's "Margaret," her daughter Violet, also the author of many novels—"the sweetest Violet in England, I think her"—Laura Troubridge, later Mrs Adrian Hope, whose father, Sir Thomas Troubridge, was an A.D.C. to Queen Victoria, the actresses Helena Modjeska, Ellen Terry, and Genevieve Ward, and Nellie Sickert, the teenage sister of the artist Walter Sickert; as Mrs H. M. Swanwick she was to become known as a writer and lecturer and untiring advocate of women's rights. At this time Nellie Sickert was about to go up to Cambridge and Wilde told her he hoped she would accept a volume of poems by "a purely Oxford poet," namely Matthew Arnold. She did so gratefully after Wilde had "marked just a few of the things" he liked best in the collection, "in the hope that we may agree about them," such as "Sohrab and Rustum" and "The Scholar Gypsy." They also used to go skating together and take lessons at the rink. "Some future day I hope you will teach me skating," he told her at this time, "and a great many other things."

Laura Troubridge first met Oscar with her younger sister Violet, whose picture had inspired the poet's sonnet "Wasted Days." On 30 June 1879, she wrote in her diary that "both fell awfully in love with him, thought him quite delightful." A week or two later her cousin Charles Orde took her to tea in Thames House—"great fun, lots of vague 'intense' men, such duffers, who amused us awfully," she noted at the time. "The room was a mass of white lilies, photos of Mrs Langtry, peacock feather screens and coloured pots, pictures of various merit."

Then there was Helena Modjeska, the Polish actress who had scored a success in America, and had come to London to make her debut in *Heartsease,* an adaptation of the younger Dumas's *La Dame aux Camelias,* at which the Prince of Wales was present on the first night. Wilde, who hoped she might agree to appear in a play he was writing called *Vera,* also invited her to tea. But Madame Modjeska replied that she felt "it would be unwise to visit so young a man, even for tea." A little later she came to Salisbury Street with Lillie Langtry and the artist Louise Jopling. "When we three women left," Miss Jopling recalled afterwards, "Oscar, with great ceremony, presented us each with a single long-stalked Annunciation lily."

Apparently *Vera* did not appeal to Helena Modjeska. However, she gave Wilde a poem which she had written in Polish with a rough English translation, which he later polished up and sent to Clement Scott, the dramatic critic and editor of Routledge's Christmas annual *The Green Room.* Scott accepted it and in due course it appeared under the title "Sen Artysty; or the Artist's Dream," and as having been "translated from the Polish by Oscar Wilde." This gave Wilde "very great pleasure," as he told the editor at the time, though he was careful to give the actress due credit for her part. "Whatever beauty is in the poem is due to the graceful and passionate artistic nature of Madame Modjeska," he wrote to Scott. "I am really only the reed through which her sweet notes have been blown." [3]

Meanwhile, his passion for the theatre was growing, and while he danced attendance on actresses like Lillie Langtry and Ellen Terry, composing sonnets in praise of their beauty, Frank Miles would make sketches of them for the magazines. When the "divine" Sarah Bernhardt arrived from Paris for a season. Oscar met her as she stepped off the boat

[3] The poem was reprinted in *Poems* (1908).

at Folkestone and flung an armful of lilies at her feet; soon he was working as her unpaid secretary too. Ellen Terry had recently begun her
brilliantly successful association with Henry Irving at the Lyceum Theatre, of which Oscar was not slow to take advantage. On 28 November
1879, he wrote to Kitten Harding: "I am going with Ruskin to see Irving as Shylock, and afterwards to the Millais ball. How odd it is." [4]

Instead of giving what *Vanity Fair* called "that most tiresome of all
things, a wedding breakfast, they did much better by giving in its stead
a ball in the evening . . . . There were notable artists (with their wives
in Grosvenor Gallery dresses), notable actors and actresses and notable
persons of the smarter sort, all met together like a happy family." In *The
Merchant of Venice* at the Lyceum, Ellen Terry played Portia, which
inspired another sonnet from Wilde, who was also a guest at the Lyceum
banquet to celebrate the play's hundredth performance on 14 February
1880.

Wilde's interest in the theatre extended beyond the London stage,
since he was in Cambridge at this time for a performance by the Cambridge Amateur Dramatic Club. On this occasion Wilde stayed with
Oscar Browning, then a don at King's; Browning had previously been a
housemaster at Eton, from which he had been dismissed ostensibly for
slackness in the running of his house but in reality for his homosexual
proclivities and undue familiarity with some of the boys in his charge,
including the future statesman George Nathaniel Curzon. Browning
first met Wilde at Oxford with Walter Pater. In Cambridge they went
up to the A.D.C. performance together, and afterwards Browning gave a
supper party in his rooms at King's at which most of the cast were
present. Browning noted Wilde's "affectation" during the evening—he
was "really very clever and amusing and full of interesting conversation." However, on the occasion of another visit some years later,
Browning recorded that his guest had "lost a lot of his affectation and is
much improved." Wilde always found his host "everything that is kind
and pleasant."

After his first visit, Wilde wrote to his friend Harding: "I was only in
Cambridge for the night with Oscar Browning (I wish he was *not* called
Oscar) and left the next morning for the Hicks-Beach's in Hampshire to
kill time and pheasants and the *ennui* of not having set the world quite
on fire as yet." Money was beginning to run short, and he was having
difficulty letting the fishing lodge in Connemara. Hence his appeal to
Oscar Browning in an attempt to get a job, although unfortunately
nothing came of it.

Will you do me a good service, and write me a testimonial of what you
think my ability for a position in the Education Office or School Inspec-

---

[4] Ruskin had previously been married to Mrs Millais, and after the marriage had been
annulled, she had married the painter John Millais; they had a daughter who became the
wife of Captain W. C. James of the Scots Greys in November 1879. Their son, Admiral
Sir William James, who died in 1973, aged ninety-one, sat for his grandfather Millais
when he was about four for the famous picture "Bubbles," which became an advertisement for Pears soap.

torship would be? Rents being as extinct in Ireland as the dodo or moly, I want to get a position with an assured income, and any Education work would be very congenial to me, and I have here good opportunity of studying the systems of France and Germany. I think your name would carry a good deal of weight with it in a matter of this kind. The Duke of Richmond is the President of the Council in whose hands the appointments rest.

Sometime during the summer of 1880, Wilde and Miles gave up their rooms in Salisbury Street and moved to Chelsea, where a brilliant and now largely forgotten architect named Edward William Godwin had designed a studio house for Miles at the southern end of Tite Street. Another house belonging to a Miss Skeates had formerly occupied the site and been called Skeates's House, by which name Godwin's new house also came to be known locally. "The address is *horrid* but the house is very pretty," Wilde told Mrs Alfred Hunt at the time. "It is much nearer you than my old house, so I hope we shall often, if you let me, have 'dishes of tea' at one another's houses." Wilde's poetic imagination immediately caused him to drop the initial letter, so that he was henceforth to call it Keats House. It was to be his address until he parted company with Frank Miles and left the house eighteen months later for America.[5] Another reason for the name may have been that round the corner on the Chelsea Embankment there was a Shelley House, which had recently been built by the poet's son, Sir Percy Shelley, for himself.

Wilde's previous biographers have constantly represented the move from Salisbury Street to Chelsea as the result of a desire on the part of Wilde and Miles to look for cheaper lodgings in a less centrally situated locality. This was not so. On the contrary, it was a step up from bachelor rooms off the Strand to a specially built house in what was becoming quite a chic neighbourhood in spite of Wilde's jocular description of the address. Miles was making a good income as an artist at this time, and with his moneyed family background he also possessed private means, so that he could easily afford a studio house built to his own specifications, where there would also be room for his friend, with whom he may well have already established some kind of homosexual relationship. Godwin had already designed a house on the other side of the street for another artist, James McNeill Whistler, which may have encouraged Miles to go to the same architect. The original designs for the Whistler house were considered too revolutionary by the Metropolitan Board of Works, the authority from which planning permission had to be obtained in those days, and the exterior design had consequently to be modified. The design for Keats House was similarly rejected, the architect to the Board exclaiming when he first saw it, "Why this is worse than Whistler's!" Accordingly, the plans were also modified. The construction then went ahead, largely in the form in which the house exists today; this has been described as a composition of interlocking rectangles, the windows being

---

[5] Miles continued to live in the house until 1887, when, at the height of his career as an established and successful artist, he became mentally ill and was removed to an asylum near Bristol, where he died four years later at the age of thirty-nine.

embellished with balconies, with green slates on the roof and alternating red and pale yellow brickwork. "I introduced a number of reminiscences of a visit to Holland," Godwin remarked at the time, "and the whole thing was pronounced charming." Though no longer revolutionary, it was still a sophisticated and original design, while inside there was a delicate, elegant staircase and an attractive inglenook off the studio.

At the time of his move to Keats House, Wilde was working on his four-act play with a prologue which, when it was finished, he called *Vera: or, the Nihilists*. The Russian Nihilists were much in the news at this period by reason of their terrorist activities, and the author made them the subject of this immature melodrama. Nevertheless, the work showed signs of promise and contained several characteristic epigrams destined to reappear in his later and more successful dramatic productions. ("Experience, the name men give to their mistakes" is a typical example.) Wilde had a few copies privately printed at his own expense, which he sent to several friends in the theatre in the hope of enlisting their interest and getting it produced.

"Will you accept the first copy of my first play, a drama on modern Russia?" he wrote to Ellen Terry about September 1880. "Perhaps some day I shall be fortunate enough to write something worthy of your playing." [6] The American actress Clara Morris, to whom he wrote at the suggestion of "my friend Dion Boucicault," the Irish actor-dramatist, likewise received a complimentary copy, which Wilde sent her in New York in the hope that she would accept it "as a homage to your genius," even if she did not think it suitable for dramatic production in America.

On account of its avowedly republican sentiments I have not been able to get permission to have it brought out here, but with you there is more freedom, and though democracy is the note through which the play is expressed, yet the tragedy is an entirely human one.

"In case you approve of the play," Wilde added in a postscript, "I shall be so happy to correspond on the subject."

Finally, in October 1880, the eager author sent a copy to Hermann Vezin, an American actor who played mostly in England and is said to have introduced greasepaint into the English theatre. As a sideline Vezin taught elocution, and he had been coaching Wilde, who had read him parts of *Vera*. "Any suggestions about situations or dialogue I should be so glad to get from such an experienced artist as yourself," Wilde wrote in his accompanying letter. "I have just found out what a difficult craft playwriting is."

[6] This copy, which Wilde had specially bound in dark red leather with Ellen Terry's name stamped in gold on the binding, was inscribed, "From her sincere admirer the Author." It is now in the Ellen Terry Museum at Smallhythe, near Tenterden, Kent. Only two other copies are known, one in the Clark Library and the other in Mrs Donald Hyde's collection in New Jersey. The latter was similarly inscribed to Genevieve Ward, the cover with its inscription having been reproduced by Stuart Mason in his *Bibliography of Oscar Wilde* (1914), with the recipient's name omitted, doubtless at her request; see Mason, p. 250.

2

At this time Wilde became friendly with Norman Forbes-Robertson, a young actor who belonged to a well-known theatrical family and was just starting in the profession as Norman Forbes. Wilde found him a sympathetic listener to his "life and troubles," and from time to time seems to have poured out his heart to him. "I am not yet finished furnishing my room, and have spent all my money over it already," he wrote to Norman in the autumn of 1880, "so if no manager gives me gold for *The Nihilists* I don't know what I shall do; but then I couldn't really have anything but Chippendale and satinwood. I shouldn't have been able to write . . . As for me I am lonely, *désolé* and wretched. I feel burned out."

He soon perked up, due to an invitation he received from a fellow poet and future diplomat, James Rennell Rodd, who had won the Newdigate earlier in the same year with a poem on Sir Walter Raleigh, to accompany him on a trip to France. The acquaintance began when a mutual friend brought Wilde to Rodd's rooms in Balliol; they met again when Rodd came to what he called Wilde's "old world apartment" in Salisbury Street. "What was less appreciated then as now," Rodd was to recall forty years later, "was his really genial and kindly nature which seemed at times in strident contrast with his egotism, self-assertion and incorrigible love of notoriety. No one was more ready than he was at that time to accept the laugh against himself, and no one could be more generous in acknowledging the qualities and gifts of his friends. Of that unhappy madness which many years afterwards made havoc of a gifted life, we saw no premonition in those London days."

Wilde wrote of his French tour at the time:

I had a very charming time in France, and travelled among beautiful vineyards down the Loire, one of the most wonderful rivers in the world, mirroring from sea to source a hundred cities and five hundred towers. I was with a delightful Oxford friend and, as we did not wish to be known, he travelled under the name of Sir Smith, and I was Lord Robinson.

The move to Tite Street with Frank Miles made Wilde a neighbour and at first the admiring friend of the artist Whistler. At the same time Wilde went the rounds of the picture galleries and wrote articles of art criticism as well as pouring out streams of verse. Soon he became a regular diner-out and was much in demand by hostesses for his witty conversation. In refusing an invitation from Mrs Alfred Hunt, he wrote: "On Wednesday the 2nd [March 1881] I have a long-standing engagement with Sir Charles Dilke, a lion who has clipped his radical claws and only roars through the medium of a quarterly review now—a harmless way of roaring. So I cannot come to you, which *makes me very sad.*" And to the Hon. Mrs Stanley, later Lady St Helier, he had to write: "The fates are always against me! And on the night when the only place in London worth going to is your brilliant salon I find myself so engaged that I cannot escape."

In spite of his intermittent shortages of cash, Wilde had become a familiar figure at all the fashionable gatherings by the beginning of the London season in 1881. This is evident from W. P. Frith's picture "Varnishing Day at the Royal Academy," in which Wilde can be seen smartly dressed in top hat and frock coat and holding a catalogue in his hand. On the other hand, as a so-called "Professor of Aesthetics and Art Critic," he, in common with other followers of the gospel of beauty, which Ruskin and Pater had been preaching at Oxford, was already being caricatured and lampooned in the pages of *Punch*. This began when Frank Burnand took over the editorship in 1880 and enlisted the cartoonist George du Maurier to poke fun at two typical "aesthetes" whom he dubbed Postlethwaite and Maudle; their behaviour was exemplified in their manner of dress and other forms of affectation, particularly their fondness for lilies and sunflowers. Thus, Wilde was not the founder of the aesthetic movement or, as some people preferred to call it, the aesthetic craze, which had begun before he descended on London and took a hand in it. What he did was to constitute himself a convenient vehicle for its advertisement, which was considerably promoted by *Punch*'s somewhat ponderous brand of humour. Of this humour Wilde was largely the butt, but he took it all in good part, and indeed seemed to relish it, as it undoubtedly kept him in the public eye.

During his last term at Oxford, Wilde had gone to a fancy-dress ball given by Mrs Frederic Morrell at her house on Headington Hill in the character of Prince Rupert. For this he was dressed in a velvet coat edged with braid, knee-breeches, buckle shoes, a soft silk shirt with a wide turn-down collar, and a large flowing green tie. He would appear from time to time in this garb in London, usually in the evenings, with the object of drawing attention to himself, jokingly declaring that reformation of dress was more important than reformation of religion. At the same time two plays were produced in the West End in which Beerbohm Tree played parts burlesquing Wilde—Scott Ramsey in *Where's the Cat?* by James Albery, and Lambert Streyke in *The Colonel* by Frank Burnand, the *Punch* editor. The first opened on 20 November 1880 at the Criterion Theatre and the second on 2 February 1881 at the Prince of Wales's; both had good runs, and *The Colonel* was revived in 1887. Wilde certainly bore the actor no malice, since they subsequently became great friends and Tree was to play the lead in Wilde's own play *A Woman of No Importance*.

However, the theatrical production that brought Wilde most into the public eye at this period was the Gilbert and Sullivan "aesthetic opera" *Patience*, which cleverly satirized the "excesses" of the aesthetic movement. The producer, Richard D'Oyly Carte, described the purpose of the work in these words:

> The "movement" in the direction of a more artistic feeling, which had its commencement some time since in the works of Mr Ruskin and his supporters, doubtless did much to render our everyday existence more pleasant

and more beautiful. Latterly, however, their pure and healthy teaching has given place to the outpourings of a clique of professors of ultra-refinement, who preach the gospel of morbid languor and sickly sensuousness, which is half real and half affected by its high priests for the purpose of gaining social notoriety. Generally speaking the new school is distinguished by an eccentricity of taste tending to an unhealthy admiration for exhaustion, corruption and decay. In satirising the excesses of these (so-called) aesthetes the authors of *Patience* have not desired to cast ridicule on the true aesthetic spirit, but only to attack the unmanly oddities which masquerade in its likeness. In doing so, they have succeeded in producing one of the prettiest and most diverting musical pleasantries of the day.

"Wilde is slightly sensitive although I don't think appallingly so," wrote Carte at this time. "I, however, suggested to him that it would be a good boom for him if he were to go one evening to see *Patience* and were to let it be known beforehand, and he would probably be recognised. This idea he quite took to."

Patience opened at the old Opera Comique Theatre on 23 April 1881 and received eight encores on the first night. It was an immediate success and ran in London for more than a year before going on tour in the provinces; it was also to be produced with considerable success in America and Australia.[7] Wilde is said to have been greatly amused when he saw it at Carte's invitation. But neither of the two principal characters, Reginald Bunthorne, the "fleshly poet," and Archibald Grosvenor, the "idyllic poet," was expressly based on Wilde, although some of his peculiarities were portrayed by each of them. For instance, it is Grosvenor who says "I am aesthetic and poetic" and "I am a very narcissus" as he gazes admiringly at himself in a looking-glass. But it is Bunthorne who sings,

> Though the Philistines may jostle, you may rank as an
> apostle in the high aesthetic band,
> If you walk down Piccadilly with a poppy or a lily in
> your medieval hand.

Contrary to the general opinion at the time, Wilde never walked down Piccadilly thus adorned. "Anyone could have done that," he used to say. "The difficult thing to achieve was to make people think that I had done it."

By this date Wilde had written enough verse to make a volume of his collected poems. He therefore wrote to a publisher named David Bogue who had an office off Trafalgar Square, with a view to their immediate publication. "Possibly my name requires no introduction," he added. The publisher, who was to go bankrupt two years later and to be found dead on the beach at Folkestone, agreed to bring out the work on a commission of 10 percent of the sale price to the trade, provided that the au-

---

[7] In November 1881, it was transferred to the Savoy Theatre, which D'Oyly Carte had just completed. The Savoy was the first London theatre to be furnished with electric light.

thor paid the estimated cost within two months of publication. The work was put in hand immediately, and the first edition of 250 copies was announced at the end of June 1881 at the retail price of half a guinea a copy, "printed on Dutch handmade paper and handsomely bound in parchment." [8] Among those who received complimentary copies from the author were Matthew Arnold, Robert Browning, and Mr Gladstone, all of whom Wilde particularly admired. Gladstone, who had recently become Prime Minister for the second time, was asked by the author in the letter which accompanied the volume to accept it "as a very small token of my deep admiration and loyalty to one who has always loved what is beautiful and noble and true in life and art, and is the mirror of the Greek ideal of the statesman." The Prime Minister duly accepted the gift which the author had inscribed, "To William Ewart Gladstone, in deep and sincere admiration from Oscar Wilde," and put it on the shelves of his library at Hawarden. [9]

Oscar Browning was sent a review copy with a request for a notice, which he was obligingly to write for *The Academy*. "Books so often fall into ignorant and illiterate hands that I am anxious to be really criticised," Wilde told Oscar Browning at the time: "ignorant praise or blame is so insulting." On the whole, the *Poems* met with a mixed reception from the reviewers, *Punch* naturally being in the vanguard of the hostile critics. ("Mr Wilde may be aesthetic, but he is not original. This is a volume of echoes, it is Swinburne and water.") At the same time, *Punch* published a cartoon of the poet peering out of the heart of a sunflower and surrounded by a vase of lilies, an open cigarette case, and a wastepaper basket. It was accompanied by the following verse:

> Aesthete of aesthetes
> What's in a name?
> The poet is Wilde
> But his poetry's tame. [10]

No doubt the reviews, whether friendly or hostile, were useful publicity, since the first edition quickly sold out, to be followed by four more editions of 250 copies each during the next eighteen months. A little later, in the summer of 1881, an authorized American edition appeared under the imprint of Roberts Brothers of Boston, who confidently announced that "the great merit of these poems, and the notoriety of their author, who is today the most talked-about man in London literary

---

[8] On his bankruptcy, Bogue's stock was taken over by Chatto & Windus, then of Piccadilly.

[9] After Wilde's conviction and imprisonment, Gladstone did not destroy or deface the volume as some other recipients of the author's presentation copies did. Gladstone's copy remained in the Hawarden Library until 1967, when I happened to see it on a visit and was able to acquire it from the late Sir Charles Gladstone, the statesman's grandson, who was then living at Hawarden.

[10] *Punch*, 25 June 1881.

circles, will surely cause a demand for the book." The American publication inspired one of the best reviews, from *The New York Times*, which wrote:

> In Wilde England has a new poet who, if not of the first order of power, is so true a poet underneath whatever eccentricity of conduct or cant of school that his further persecution in the press must be held contemptible. It will only be on a par with the infatuation some people have to vilify what is really best in their own country.

Unhappily, he had a less favourable reaction from the Oxford Union, the famous university debating society to which he had belonged in his undergraduate days and to which he sent an inscribed presentation copy for the library. When the librarian announced the gift to a crowded house one evening, an undergraduate named Oliver Elton rose to object. "It is not that these poems are thin, and they are thin," he said; "it is not that they are immoral, and they are immoral; it is not that they are this or that, and they are this or that; it is that they are for the most part not by their putative father at all, but by a number of better-known and more deservedly reputed authors. They are in fact by William Shakespeare, by Philip Sidney, by John Donne, by Lord Byron, by William Morris, by Algernon Swinburne, and by sixty more, whose works have furnished the list of passages which I hold in my hand at this moment." Here Mr Elton displayed the offending volume, and continued: "The Union Library already contains better and fuller editions of all these poets. The volume which we are offered is theirs, not Mr Wilde's: and I move that it be not accepted."

The librarian and his supporters naturally opposed this motion, which they conceived to have been brought forward in a spirit of undergraduate banter. But Mr Elton was serious, and he insisted that his motion should be put to the vote. It was so put—and it was carried. Thus, for the first and only time in the history of the Oxford Union, an author's presentation copy of his work was returned to him.[11] No doubt Mr Elton was unduly severe. Wilde was certainly not a conscious plagiarist, although he had steeped himself in the works of at least some of the poets to whom Mr Elton alluded.[12]

Willie Wilde was now a regular contributor to *The World*, a weekly society magazine which Edmund Yates edited, as well as the monthly *Time*, and which had published Oscar's sonnets to Sarah Bernhardt and Ellen Terry as well as "Ave Imperatrix! A Poem on England," inspired by the Afghan War, which had led to the British occupation of Kandahar and control of the Khyber Pass. Through the magazine's gossip column, Willie puffed his brother and his achievements whenever he could. One such paragraph for which Willie was responsible was to the

[11] The rejected copy, which was inscribed in Wilde's hand, "To the Library of the Oxford Union my first volume of Poems, Oscar Wilde, Oct. 27, '81," is now in the Donald F. Hyde collection in New Jersey.

[12] Oliver Elton (1861–1945) was later Professor of English at Liverpool University.

effect that, owing to the "astonishing success" of his *Poems,* Oscar had been invited to lecture in America. According to Oscar's friend and biographer, Frank Harris, who is not always to be trusted, the idea originated with Oscar. However that may be, Oscar had received no such invitation at the date the paragraph appeared. But it may have contributed to the dispatch of a cable which Oscar received from Colonel W. F. Morse in D'Oyly Carte's New York office shortly after *Patience* opened there on 22 September.

> Responsible agent asks me to inquire if you will consider offer he makes by letter for fifty readings beginning November first. This is confidential. Answer.

Wilde immediately replied: "Yes, if offer good."

Helen Lenoir, who ran Carte's New York office with Colonel Morse, had asked an American friend "how the New York public could be brought to understand the aesthetic craze" and so better appreciate the subtle humour of *Patience.* This friend subsequently told Oscar Wilde: "I suggested that you should be hired to give a course of lectures over here in the costume of an aesthete, with a sunflower in your buttonhole and a poppy or a lily in your medieval hand. She cabled that evening to D'Oyly Carte." The English impresario approved of the idea as a means of boosting the New York production, and Morse was authorized to go ahead and book a hall if Wilde was agreeable.

The offer, which Wilde accepted after some negotiation, was for a single lecture in New York to be given in January 1882 and to be followed by a tour of the country, if the initial lecture proved a success, the lecturer to have all his expenses paid and one third of the receipts. For his part, Wilde was quite attracted by the prospect of addressing an American audience, even if he had to do so in velvet jacket and knee-breeches. "I told him he must not mind my using a little bunkum to push him in America," D'Oyly Carte wrote to Helen Lenoir after he had booked Wilde's passage. "You must deal with it when he arrives." He added that there had been some "stupid paragraphs" in *The Sporting Times,* one saying that he was sending Wilde out as a sandwich man for *Patience,* and another one afterwards stating that he was not going after all, as "D'Oyly Carte found that he could get sandwich men in America with longer hair for half the money."

Another inducement which Wilde had for going to New York was the possibility of his being able to arrange for the production of *Vera* there. His efforts to have the play produced in London got no further than persuading the management of the Adelphi Theatre to agree to put it on for a single performance one Saturday morning in December 1881 with Mrs Bernard Beere in the name part. However, about three weeks before the agreed date, it was announced that, "considering the present state of political feeling in England," the author had decided to postpone the production. ("Vera is about Nihilism," *Punch* remarked facetiously on learning the news; "this looks as if there were nothing in it.")

The fact was that the Czar Alexander II had recently been assassinated by Nihilist revolutionaries, and the new Czar's Danish wife was a sister of the Princess of Wales, later Queen Alexandra. No doubt it was to avoid giving offence to her as well as to the Prince, whom Wilde had already met and who had been amused by him—the Prince had been in Keats House on the occasion of a spiritualist séance—that the author agreed to abandon the production.

On Christmas Eve, 1881, Oscar Wilde sailed from Liverpool on board the Cunard liner *Arizona* bound for New York. Richard D'Oyly Carte wished him luck before he left and undertook to follow him in a fortnight's time.

3

The S.S. *Arizona* dropped anchor in the bay of New York late in the afternoon of 2 January 1882. The medical officers who came on board to clear her from quarantine were accompanied by a swarm of reporters. One of them spotted Wilde coming out of the captain's cabin and noted that he looked more like an athlete than a du Maurier model—"Instead of having a small, delicate hand only fit to caress a lily, his fingers are long and when doubled up would form a fist that would hit a hard knock." In a few moments he was the centre of a crowd of newsmen.

"What did you come to America for, Mr Wilde?" asked one.

"To lecture at Chickering Hall and elsewhere, if the public approve of my philosophy," replied Wilde. "Also to produce a play on Nihilism." He went on to say something about his philosophy being compounded of aestheticism.

"And what are aesthetics?"

"Aesthetics is the science of the beautiful," Wilde laughingly answered his questioner. "In this modern movement there is search after the true, you know. Aestheticism is a sort of correlation of all the arts." It had begun with Keats, he went on, and there were other contributors, such as Burne-Jones, Rossetti, William Morris, and Swinburne, whose names the reporters scribbled down assiduously if not with invariable accuracy.

More intimate personal questions followed, some of which Wilde considered downright impudent. For instance, at what temperature did he like his bath? And was it true that he always had the water lightly coloured with triple essence of verbena?

Asked about the voyage, he admitted that the Atlantic had been "a disappointment." A passenger, similarly interrogated, said that Mr Wilde had talked of how much he admired a Roumanian gypsy girl among the immigrants below and that he sometimes wished he were a gypsy. On the other hand, the captain had not liked him. Indeed, he said, "I wish I had that man lashed to the bowsprit on the windward side."

The reporters went ashore to file their stories for the morning papers, but the passengers had to remain on board overnight until the quarantine formalities had been completed and the ship was allowed to proceed to her berth in the North River. On the way she got stuck in the mud, and before she could be got off, more newspapermen came aboard, along with Colonel Morse from D'Oyly Carte's office. Wilde was now getting used to the native style of questioning. "Man is hungry for beauty and must be filled," he told the reporters. "There is a void. Nature will fill it."

"What about that grain elevator over there, Jersey side?" he was asked.

Wilde replied that he was too nearsighted to make it out, but he would examine it later. By this time the *Arizona* was approaching the dock, and in a short time Wilde stepped onto American soil to face the customs officers. Apparently the story had got about that he slept in gorgeous lace nightgowns, so that he was asked to open his luggage. But no lace nightgowns were there.

"Have you anything to declare?" asked the customs inspector.

"Nothing," said Wilde. "Nothing but my genius!"

After breakfasting at Delmonico's, Colonel Morse took him to the Grand Hotel at Thirty-first Street and Broadway, where a two-room suite had been reserved for him. He was thus able to relax for the next few days and see something of New York, since he was not due to give his first lecture until 7 January. "The first thing that struck me on landing in America," he was to say on his return to England, "was that if the Americans are not the best dressed people in the world, they are the most comfortably dressed . . . There is an air of comfort in the appearance of the people which is a marked contrast to that seen in this country, where, too often, people are seen in close contact with rags." Obviously he had not been taken to the East Side with its swarms of immigrants jammed into shabby tenements nor to some other poor districts of New York. Then there was the constant bustle and noise. Everybody seemed to be in a hurry to catch a train. As for the noise, "one is waked up in the morning, not by the singing of the nightingale, but by the steam whistle. It is surprising that the sound practical sense of the Americans does not reduce this intolerable noise. All Art depends upon exquisite and delicate sensibility, and such continual turmoil must ultimately be destructive of the musical faculty."

From the beginning the American press found him newsworthy, and he was frequently interviewed, sketched, and photographed, even before he mounted the lecture platform.

"What are your politics, Liberal or Conservative, Mr Wilde?" asked a reporter from the *Philadelphia Press* who had been specially sent by his paper to interview the visitor.

"Oh, do you know," answered Wilde, "those matters are of no interest to me. I know only two terms—civilization and barbarism; and I am on the side of civilization. It is very strange that in the House of Commons you never hear the word 'civilization.' They spend night after night squabbling over petty things, when they ought to be working against barbarism. Then, in our country, there is seldom a piece of legislation that does not benefit one class more than another; and that perhaps makes the wretched party spirit more bitter." But, he added, Mr Gladstone, the present occupant of No. 10 Downing Street, was "the greatest Prime Minister England had ever had."

The night before the lecture, Colonel Morse took a party including Wilde to the Standard Theatre, where *Patience* was running. As he entered the box which had been reserved for them, Oscar was seen to be wearing his velvet coat and waistcoat, from which a red silk handkerchief protruded conspicuously. A few minutes later Bunthorne came on stage similarly clad and singing:

> Though my book I seem to scan,
> In a rapt ecstatic way . . .

From the way in which all eyes in the auditorium now turned towards the box where Oscar was lolling beside Mrs Morse, it was clear that the audience believed that the character of Bunthorne was based upon him. The guest of the evening quickly perceived this, as he leaned across to the lady beside him and observed: "Caricature is the tribute which mediocrity pays to genius." He was to repeat the epigram in his lecture. At the end of the first act, the host led the party backstage, where Oscar appeared at his most affable and congratulated the company on their performance. After the show was over, about fifty people waited in the theatre foyer hoping for a glimpse of the aesthete they had all read or heard about. But they were disappointed. Oscar and the rest of the party left by a side exit.

Chickering Hall was filled to capacity next evening in spite of a rival attraction in the shape of the high society Patriarch's Ball at Delmonico's. Colonel Morse led the way onto the platform and briefly introduced the lecturer, who for this occasion wore tails besides his knee-breeches and buckled shoes. After the colonel had announced the title of the lecture as "The English Renaissance of Art," the lecturer, blushing and for once looking a little sheepish, advanced to the reading desk, on which he placed his manuscript. No doubt some of the effect of the lecture was lost by reason of his reading it. In spite of the elocution lessons he had had from Hermann Vezin before leaving London, Oscar showed that he was no orator, at least on this occasion, though he was to show a marked improvement in subsequent lectures. To some of the reporters present, his voice sounded unnatural and even "sepulchral."

At first he was heard in what the newspapers called "grim silence," but gradually the audience warmed to him, noticeably after he raised a laugh when he said, "Since you have all heard of *Patience,* which has been given for so many nights, you might listen to me for at least one evening." Thus encouraged, he went on: "You must not judge our aestheticism by the satire of Mr Gilbert any more than you can judge of the strength and splendour of the sun or sea by the dust that dances in the beam or the bubble that breaks upon the wave."

One remark not included in the version eventually published in England was loudly applauded. But the applause was believed to have come from the Irish members of the audience. That was when he said, "There can be no great sculpture, no great drama, without a noble national life. The commercial spirit of England has killed that."

Several members of the audience showed signs of restlessness and left before the end. Those who did so missed the concluding passages of the lecture, which Wilde had evidently prepared with some care and which were perhaps the best in it.

> You have heard, I think, a few of you, of two flowers connected with the aesthetic movement in England, and said—I assure you erroneously—to be the food of some aesthetic young men. Well, let me tell you that the reason we love the lily and the sunflower, in spite of what Mr Gilbert may tell you, is not for any vegetable fashion at all. It is because these two lovely flowers are in England the two most perfect models of design, the most naturally adapted for decorative art—the gaudy leonine beauty of the one and the precious loveliness of the other giving to the artist the most entire and perfect joy. And so with you: let there be no flower in your meadows that does not wreathe its tendrils around your pillows, no little leaf in your Titan forests that does not lend its form to design, no curving spray of wild rose or brier that does not live for ever in carven arch or window or marble, no bird in your air that is not giving the iridescent wonder of its colour, the exquisite curves of its wings in flight, to make more precious the preciousness of simple adornment. For the voices that have their dwelling in sea and mountain are not the chosen music of liberty only. Other messages are there in the wonder of wind-swept heights and the majesty of silent deep—messages that, if you will listen to them, will give you the wonder of all new imagination, the treasure of all new beauty.
>
> We spend our days, each one of us, in looking for the secret of life. Well, the secret of life is in art.

After the lecture a New York society hostess, Mrs John Mack, who was a friend of Lady Wilde's, gave a reception and supper in honour of the lecturer in her home. The fact that the guests included the president of Columbia College and his wife was apparently important enough for the newspapers to give a list of all of them next day. The New York *Herald* reported:

> Mrs John Bigelow, who entertained the poet at dinner on Sunday evening, was the first to congratulate him on his success as a lecturer. Mr Wilde showed remarkable self-possession. Scores upon scores of beautiful and elegantly dressed society belles crowded each other in their efforts to grasp his hand, and yet he met them all with a conventional welcome. Any ordinary young man would have been nervous from the outset.

Besides the Bigelows—John Bigelow had been U.S. Ambassador in Paris and was an authority on Benjamin Franklin—Wilde was also entertained by Sam Ward, the financier and gastronome, known popularly as "Uncle Sam." He was a brother of Julia Ward Howe, who wrote "The Battle Hymn of the Republic," and he was to provide Wilde with an introduction to her when the lecturer later visited Boston. "You are a magician and a master of all things, from finance to a dinner, and from lyrics to medicine," Wilde told him after they became friends. Finally, there was Mrs Frank Leslie, a rich American widow who owned *Leslie's Illustrated Newspaper* and may have originally suggested to Helen Lenoir the idea of Wilde's lecture tour. Her paper consistently puffed the visiting lecturer throughout his tour. She was later to marry Oscar's elder brother, Willie.

The national publicity which Wilde received was tremendous, as accounts of his inaugural lecture were relayed by wire to cities across the country. Comment was not invariably flattering. "Oscar has come in search of the secret of life," remarked the Chicago *Daily News*. "It is ten chances to one he will be in search of the secrets of life along a lunch-route of his own discovery before long." Another Chicago paper described him as "a twittering sparrow come to fill his maw with insects," while the Cincinnati *Commercial* gave him an invitation: "If Mr Wilde will leave the lilies and daffodils and come west to Cincinnati, we will undertake to show him how to deprive thirty hogs of their intestines in one minute." At the same time, *The Nation,* edited by the Ulster-Scot Edwin Godkin, wrote in its editorial column:

> Mr Wilde is essentially a foreign product and can hardly succeed in this country. What he has to say is not new, and his extravagance is not extravagant enough to amuse the average American audience. His knee breeches and long hair are good as far as they go, but Bunthorne has really spoiled the public for Wilde.

Nevertheless, D'Oyly Carte, who arrived a few days later and was asked by newsmen when he disembarked what he thought of his "Bunthorne in the flesh," realized that he had made a shrewd investment in sending Wilde to lecture on aesthetics. "A clever young man" was how the impresario described him. "I think I shall take him around the country."

"You will be glad to hear that *Patience* is still running here, doing now a fair jogtrot business," Carte wrote shortly afterwards to Arthur Sullivan, the opera's composer, in London. "The receipts had gone down, but inscrutable are the ways of the American public, and absurd as it may appear it seems that Oscar Wilde's advent here, which has caused a regular 'craze,' has given the business a fillip up."

Well might D'Oyly Carte and Colonel Morse be pleased, since the lecture at Chickering Hall had netted $1,000 in takings at the ticket office, an amount exceeded only by such veteran lecturers as Henry Ward Beecher, Ralph G. Ingersoll, and Wendell Phillips. Meanwhile, Wilde was evidently enjoying the attention he received, as the *Herald* put it, "even if there is a managerial collar around his neck." Before leaving New York on 15 January for Philadelphia, where Morse had arranged for him to give his next lecture, Wilde wrote from his hotel to Mrs George Lewis, wife of a well-known London solicitor who had given him introductions to their American friends:

> I am sure you have been pleased at my success! The hall had an audience larger and more wonderful than even Dickens had. I was recalled and applauded and am now treated like the Royal Boy.[13] I have several "Harry Tyrwhitts" as secretaries.[14] One writes my autographs all day for admirers, the other receives the flowers that are left really every ten minutes. A third whose hair resembles mine is obliged to send off locks of his own hair to the myriad maidens of the city, and so is rapidly becoming bald.
>
> I stand at the top of the reception rooms when I go out, and for two hours they defile past for introduction. I bow graciously and sometimes honour them with a royal observation, which appears next day in all the newspapers. When I go to the theatre the manager bows me in with lighted candles and the audience rise. Yesterday I had to leave by a private door, the mob was so great. Loving virtuous obscurity as much as I do, you can judge how much I dislike this lionising, which is worse than that given to Sarah Bernhardt I hear.
>
> For this, and indeed for nearly all my successes, I have to thank your dear husband.

He told his friend Norman Forbes-Robertson that he also had "a black servant, who is my slave—in a free country one cannot live without a slave," and also a carriage and a "black tiger" or Negro groom in livery. "I give sittings to artists," he added, "and generally behave as I have always behaved—'dreadfully.' "

4

Wilde was accompanied on the trip to Philadelphia by Colonel Morse and a reporter from the *Philadelphia Press* whom that journal had dispatched to New York for the purpose of recording his sayings en route. In those days Pennsylvania Station was not in Manhattan but on the New Jersey side of the Hudson, so that Wilde had to cross the river by ferry to Jersey City, where a small crowd was waiting at the dock. "There he is," someone exclaimed. "See him, that's Oscar Wilde!" On disembarking, Wilde went straight to the smoking compartment in the Pullman car which had been reserved for him. There he lit a cigarette and settled down to read Ruskin's *Fors Clavigera* and *The Poetry of Architecture*. "I hate to fly through a country at this rate," he remarked as the train gathered speed. "The only true way, you know, to see a country is to ride on horseback. I long to ride through New Mexico and Colorado and California. There are such beautiful flowers there, such quantities of lilies and, I am told, whole fields of sunflowers."

"Do you not hope to bring back picturesque dressing as one of the forms in which the spirit of your art will work itself out?"

---

[13] The Prince of Wales, later King Edward VII.
[14] The Hon. Henry Tyrwhitt, the Prince's equerry.

"All that must take time," Wilde replied to the reporter's question. "Prejudice cannot be carried by storm. And, by the way, one of the most delightful things I find in America is meeting a people without prejudice—everywhere open to the truth. We have nothing like it in England . . . *Patience,* by the way, has done our cause no harm—I enjoyed it very much. The music is delightful, and that is certainly on our side, even if the words are not."

Wilde paused to take a puff or two on his cigarette. "I am charmed with American beauty," he continued. "American women possess a certain delicacy of outline surpassing English women . . . But the colour of English women is richer and warmer, I think. I saw Clara Morris on the stage in New York one evening, and I was delighted with her as with Sarah Bernhardt, who had told me very much about her charm; and I have met many surprisingly beautiful young ladies since my arrival."

His questioner now changed the subject and asked him which poet he most admired in American literature.

"I think that Walt Whitman and Emerson have given the world more than anyone else," Wilde replied after a few moments' thought. "I do so hope to meet Mr Whitman. Perhaps he is not widely read in England, but England never appreciates a poet until he is dead . . . There is something so Greek and sane about his poetry. It is so universal, so comprehensive."

His first night in Philadelphia was spent at a large reception given for him by a local magazine publisher and art collector named Robert Stewart Davis, who had sent out over three hundred invitations, including one to President Chester Arthur at the White House. The President did not appear nor did Walt Whitman, whom Wilde so admired.

Mr Davis was about to bring out a new illustrated weekly called *Our Continent,* to which he had invited Wilde by cable before he left England to contribute a poem, "twenty lines, terms guinea a line: subject— *sunflower or lily* to be delivered on arrival" in America. Wilde obliged and on the way over wrote two poems under the general title "Impressions," of which the first (*"Le Jardin"*) described both the lily and the "gaudy leonine sunflower" and the second (*"La Mer"*) his impressions of the voyage. The poems duly appeared in the first issue of the new magazine (15 February 1882) and were later set to music by a composer named H. V. Jervis-Read. Wilde seems to have been particularly pleased with one verse in the second poem, since he inscribed it on the flyleaf of a copy of the American edition of his *Poems,* which he was to present to an admirer a few weeks later in Chicago.[15]

> The muffled steersman at the wheel
> Is but a shadow in the gloom;—
> And in the throbbing engine room
> Leap the long rods of polished steel.

[15] This copy was recently sold by an antiquarian bookdealer in California for $1,500.

The morning after Davis's party, the lecturer rested in his hotel, while, according to one account, a Negro stood outside his door telling callers, "Massa Wilde is too busy to recept today." That evening Wilde lectured in Philadelphia's Horticultural Hall. Most of the thousand seats were filled at a dollar a ticket, so that the takings were almost as much as those for his first lecture in New York. But Wilde found the audience unresponsive to the aesthetic theme. Afterwards he told a reporter: "My hearers were so cold I several times thought of stopping and saying, 'You don't like this, and there is no use of my going on.' " From the hall he was taken to North Nineteenth Street, where a reception was given in his honour by J. M. Stoddart, a local publisher who had acquired the American publishing rights to the Gilbert and Sullivan operas. Indeed, Stoddart took charge of his programme for the remainder of his brief visit to the Quaker City. Next morning they went to a breakfast party given by one of the professors of the University of Pennsylvania, after which Stoddart took the visitor to see the Women's School of Design, where he met a number of distinctly unaesthetic maidens. One of them, who noticed the green overcoat he was wearing, asked pointedly whether the colour extended "all the way through"!

In the afternoon Stoddart and Wilde crossed the Delaware River to the working-class town of Camden to call on Walt Whitman, who had been living there for the past nine years. Fortunately they found the poet at home. "I took him up to my den where we had a jolly good time," said the author of *Leaves of Grass* afterwards. "I think he was glad to get away from lecturing and fashionable society, and spend a time with an old rough. I think him genuine, honest and manly. I was glad to have him with me, for his youthful health, enthusiasm, and buoyancy are refreshing. He was in his best mood and I imagine he laid aside any affectation he is said to have. He talked freely about the London literati and gave me many inside glimpses into the life and doings of Swinburne, Dante Gabriel Rossetti, Morris, Tennyson and Browning."

At the outset of their talk, the American poet told his visitor that he would like to call him by his first name. "I should like that so much," answered Oscar, laying his hand on the older man's knee. Later Whitman made him a glass of milk punch, and "he tossed it off and away he went." They had earlier drunk a bottle of wine together. "Goodbye, Oscar. God bless you" was the American poet's farewell. Afterwards, on the ride back to Philadelphia, Wilde spoke admiringly of Walt Whitman as that "grand old man" and of his struggles and triumphs.

Since the Philadelphia lecture had been favourably reported in the *Philadelphia Press* and *The New York Times,* Wilde asked Stoddart to send copies to various friends in England, and this was accordingly done. Besides Wilde's mother and brother, the recipients included Whistler, Lillie Langtry, Mrs Millais, Philip Burne-Jones, Edmund Yates, George Curzon, Oscar Browning, Rennell Rodd, Herbert Warren, and the Junior Common Room at Magdalen.

Like Wilde, young Rennell Rodd had recently had his first volume of poems published by David Bogue in England under the title *Songs in the South,* which he dedicated to his father, and he was anxious that they should be brought out in America. Before Wilde left England, his friend asked him if he would try to arrange this with an American publisher. Accordingly, Wilde showed Stoddart a copy of *Songs in the South* which the author had inscribed to him and suggested that Stoddart should publish the American edition. On looking through the poems, Stoddart agreed, provided that Wilde would write an introduction. Wilde undertook to do this and they then discussed the format of the projected volume. As the publisher afterwards confessed, this owed more to Stoddart than to Wilde: an edition *de luxe* was printed in brown ink on green paper from David Rittenhouse's mill near Philadelphia, reputedly the first papermill in the country; the paper was originally intended to be used for U.S. banknotes. Two editions were published by Stoddart later in 1882 under the title *Rose Leaf and Apple Leaf,* which Wilde had suggested. The dedication read:

TO

OSCAR WILDE—

"HEART'S BROTHER"—

THESE FEW SONGS AND MANY SONGS TO COME.

Needless to add, the author was considerably upset by this dedication, for which Wilde was responsible on his own initiative. Rodd protested to Stoddart that it was "too effusive" and that if he had been sent a proof he would not have allowed it to stand. He asked that it should be removed from any copies sent out in the future, but this could not be done, since no further edition was called for. He wrote to Wilde in the same sense and the incident ended their friendship. (Wilde later described the author as "the true poet and the false friend.") Rodd was about to enter the diplomatic service and realized that, if the dedication came to the notice of the Foreign Office, it might jeopardize his career. It did not do so, since he was to rise to ambassadorial rank and to be created Lord Rennell on his retirement from the service.

On 15 January 1882, the *Philadelphia Press* announced that Mr Oscar Wilde would leave the city two days later with a party of friends, including D'Oyly Carte, Helen Lenoir, and Archibald Forbes, a well-known British war correspondent of the time, for Baltimore, where Wilde would attend a lecture by Forbes that evening and then depart for Washington, where "The English Renaissance" was to have its third reading. Exactly what happened after the party boarded the train on 17 January is not clear. Forbes was also on a lecture tour of the United States at this time and used to appear on the platform wearing all his medals. He was an extremely tough man who had easily outpaced the official dispatch rider in the recent Zulu war, which he covered. He had little sympathy with Wilde's ideas on aesthetics and dress reform, and had made a point of saying that while reporting the fighting in Bulgaria he "did not look much like an art object," having just ridden 150 miles and not changed his clothes for a fortnight. He did not have his knee-breeches and his velvet coat with him, he added facetiously, while his black silk stockings were full of holes. "Neither was the wild, barren waste of Bulgaria congenial to the growth of sunflowers and lilies."

According to one version, Wilde was shown a report of what Forbes had said at his expense, and it appears that words passed between them. Anyhow, Wilde did not get off the train at Baltimore and went on to Washington. A heated exchange of letters followed between him and Forbes, who refused to omit the offensive references to Wilde in subsequent lectures. Eventually Forbes agreed to do so after George Lewis, the London solicitor, had cabled him: LIKE A GOOD FELLOW DON'T ATTACK WILDE. I ASK THIS PERSONAL FAVOUR TO ME.

As regards my motive for coming to America [Wilde wrote to Forbes] I should be very disappointed if when I left for Europe I had not influenced in *however* slight a way the growing spirit of art in this country, very disappointed if I had not out of the many who listen to me made one person love beautiful things a little more, and very disappointed if in return for the dreadfully hard work of lecturing—hard to me who am inexperienced—I did not earn enough money to give myself an autumn at Venice, a winter at Rome, and a spring at Athens; but all these things are perhaps dreams.

In Washington the lecturer was entertained and shown the sights by a wealthy Republican member of the House of Representatives, George Maxwell Robeson, and his handsome, ambitious wife. Congressman Robeson had been Secretary of the Navy in President Grant's Administration and was now chairman of the Republican caucus; he was so impressed by his guest's aesthetic taste that he announced that he would put gilded sunflowers on the lightning conductors of the new house he was building. Wilde did not ask to meet President Arthur, although Robeson could easily have arranged this. Nor did Wilde show any interest in the trial, then in its concluding stages in Washington, of Charles Guiteau for the murder of Arthur's predecessor President Garfield. But at a dance at the smart Bachelors' Club, to which the Robesons took him, he did meet Abraham Lincoln's only surviving son, Robert, Secretary of War in President Arthur's Cabinet.

Henry James, the novelist and critic, also happened to be on a visit to Washington at this time. Learning that Wilde had described him and his friend W. D. Howells as the only American writers worth reading, he called on Wilde at his hotel to thank him. Their meeting was hardly felicitous. James, who was eleven years older than Wilde and a model of social decorum, disliked the younger man's flippancy, although he was later to appropriate as his own Wilde's saying that "Washington has too many bronze generals." When Henry told the apostle of the aesthetic movement that he was homesick for London, Oscar hinted that this was rather provincial of him ("Really, you care for *places?* The world is my home"). "Oscar Wilde is here—an unclean beast," James wrote to Godkin of *The Nation.* He was also to refer to him as "a fatuous fool" and "a tenth-rate cad."

Frankly Wilde did not much care for the nation's capital, particularly after *The Washington Post* published a cartoon in doubtful taste comparing him to "The Wild Man of Borneo," which Morse protested in a letter to the paper was "a senseless exhibition of gratuitous malice." Wilde found Morse's intervention equally annoying. "I regard all caricature and satire as absolutely beneath notice," he subsequently wrote to the Colonel. "You, without consulting me, wrote a letter in which . . . you said it was an insult to Mr Carte to caricature anyone under his management. I regret you took any notice. The matter was mine and should have been left for me to decide on." Unfortunately too, Morse had to leave Wilde in Washington, presumably to accompany D'Oyly Carte, who went on to Florida. Wilde thereupon complained to Carte about the substitute who had been provided in Morse's place to look after him in Baltimore, which was his next stop.

Another such fiasco as the Baltimore business and I think I would stop lecturing. The little wretched clerk or office boy you sent to me in Colonel Morse's place is a fool and an idiot.

Do let us be quite frank with one another. I must have, according to our agreement, Morse or some responsible experienced man always with me. This is for your advantage as well as mine. I will not go about with a young office boy, who has not even the civility to come and see what I want. He was here for five minutes yesterday, went away promising to return at eleven o'clock a.m. and I have not seen him since. I had nine reporters, seven or eight telegrams, eighteen letters to answer and this young scoundrel amusing himself about the town. I must never be left again, and please do not expose me to the really brutal attacks of the papers. The whole tide of feeling is turned by Morse's stupidity.

I know you have been ill, and that it has not been your doing; but we must be very careful for the future.

After Baltimore came Albany, the New York State capital, where Wilde spoke to a somewhat sparsely attended gathering in the town's Music Hall, but as before he was besieged by autograph hunters. "I hope that I am obliging beautiful young ladies," he told them, "for I make it a point to grant my autograph to no others." Then on by the 2 a.m. train to Boston, where he was accommodated in the Vendôme Hotel. Here he breakfasted with the Irish actor-dramatist Dion Boucicault before meeting Oliver Wendell Holmes, who invited him to dinner, and Julia Ward Howe. She was later to come to his defence in print when some of his poems had been denounced for their "immorality" by Colonel Thomas Higginson, who suggested that Wilde should be socially ostracized because of them. "If one wants to realize what English Puritanism is," Wilde said after his return to England, "much can be found about Boston and Massachusetts. We have got rid of it. America still preserves it, to be, I hope, a short-lived curiosity."

He also breakfasted with America's most popular poet, Henry Wadsworth Longfellow, and lunched with Wendell Phillips, the reformer and slavery abolitionist. Longfellow was in poor health and for this reason declined the honour when Wilde sent word that he would like to call on him. However, Wilde turned up next morning in a snowstorm and was invited to stay to breakfast.

"How do you like Browning?" asked Wilde.

"I like him well," replied Longfellow gravely, adding, after a moment or two's pause, "what I can understand of him."

"Capital! Capital!" was his guest's reaction, clapping his hands. "I must remember that to repeat."

Eventually "that lovely old man," as Wilde later called him, summoned his daughters to come and relieve him of the burden of further entertaining the visitor. He was indeed tired, for he died within a matter of weeks. "Longfellow was himself a beautiful poem," Wilde exclaimed when he heard the news, "more beautiful than anything he ever wrote."

In spite of his success, Wilde was worried about the tour, and before the lecture he went to see his friend Dion Boucicault, to whom he poured out his heart. Next day Boucicault wrote to their mutual friend Mrs George Lewis:

> I am sure you will be gratified to hear about Oscar Wilde—his doings here and his progress. He has been much distressed and came to see me last night looking worn and thin.
>
> Mr Carte has not behaved well, and Mr Forbes—well, I do not wish to trust myself with an expression of opinion. But I cannot help feeling that so long as Carte and Forbes thought Oscar was only a puppet—a butt—a means of advertising the Opera Comique of *Patience*—they were charming; but when Oscar's reception and success threw Forbes into the shade, Forbes went into an ecstasy of rage, and "went back" on Wilde, behaving more like a wild bull than a gentleman. Carte escaped all responsibility, turned Oscar over to a subordinate and left him at the mercy of the Press, making a market of their caricatures to advertise him in connection with *Patience* and Bunthorne . . .
>
> Oscar is helpless because he is not a practical man of business, so when I advised him to throw over Carte, and offered to see him through financially if he did so, he was afraid. I offered him a thousand pounds or two if he required it, but he says he will play out his contract to April . . .
>
> There is a future for him here, but he *wants management*.
>
> Carte thought he had got hold of a popular fool. When he found that he was astride of a wild animal instead of a wooden toy, he was taken aback.

The Boston Music Hall was filled for the lecture. Tickets for the first few rows accommodating sixty people had been bought by Harvard undergraduates, who all turned up in velvet coats and knee-breeches in imitation of the lecturer, but Wilde, who got wind of their intention beforehand, surprised everyone by appearing on the platform in conventional evening dress, white tie and tails. The lecture on the whole went down well, particularly an impromptu reference which Wilde introduced into the prepared script on the subject of Ruskin's road-building operations at Oxford, in which he had himself participated.

"Our enemies and our friends came out and mocked us at our work," he said, "but we didn't care much then, and we don't care at all now!" He paused, and then with a sweep of his arm indicated the rows of Harvard students directly in front of him and continued: "These charming young men might be inclined to follow our example. The work would be good for them, though I do not believe they could build so good a road!"

It so happened that his next lecturing engagement was at New Haven on 1 February. On this occasion, two hundred Yale undergraduates, hoping to outdo their contemporaries at Harvard, appeared wearing red neckties and yellow sunflowers in their buttonholes. But the jest failed to attract much newspaper attention, so that the boys of Temple College in Hartford, where Wilde repeated his lecture the following evening, abandoned their plans for a similar demonstration.

At Brooklyn, where he spoke on 3 February, a reporter asked him about his reaction to the behaviour of the Harvard men. "Oh, I could sympathize with them," he replied, "because I thought to myself that when I was in my first year at Oxford I would have been apt to do the same. But, as they put their head into the lion's mouth, I thought they deserved a little bite."

The reporter also asked him whether it was true that the D'Oyly Carte office had found so much interest in him that a Western tour had been arranged, extending as far as St Louis. Wilde agreed that it was.

> I suppose I shall lecture in the West, if there is anything left of me. I like the excitement of lecturing, and when one gets an interested audience it is a pleasure. But I hate travelling, I hate punctuality, and I hate time-tables. The railroads are all alike to me. One is simply intolerable; another is simply unbearable.

5

Wilde's next lecture billings were in upstate New York, at Utica, Rochester, and Buffalo respectively. For these and his tour to the West, Carte and Morse were anxious that Wilde should be happy, and Morse accordingly employed a competent manager named J. H. Vale to accompany the lecturer, together with a Negro valet. The only trouble occurred in Rochester, where some of the lads from the local university tried to break up the lecture with the aid of a coloured buffoon dressed as Bunthorne who paraded up the central aisle with a bouquet of flowers to take a conspicuous seat in the front row. This was the signal for an outburst of jeering, catcalls, and ironic applause. Eventually the police were called in to eject the disturbers of the peace, after which, in the words of the New York *Herald* correspondent, "a general melée ensued, which was made more interesting by the turning off of the gas. More police were sent for, but before they arrived most of the undergraduates departed together with many of the rest of the audience," leaving the lecturer to conclude his discourse to "a few people who had remained more to see the fun than to hear the lecturer."

This unseemly affair drew a letter of sympathy from the American poet Joaquin Miller, who had lectured in London in cowboy clothes and who posed as something of a literary backwoodsman. He invited Wilde to stay at his father's house in Oregon, where he assured him he would be welcomed and "loved as a brother" should his tour take him so far west.

> And bear this in mind, my dear boy, the more you are abused the more welcome you will be. For I remember how kind your country was to me; and at your age I had not done one-tenth of your work. May my right hand fail me when I forget this . . .
>
> But don't lose heart and come to dislike America. For whatever is said and done the real heart of this strong young world demands, and will have, fair play for all. This sentiment is deep and substantial and will show itself when appealed to.
>
> So go ahead, my brave youth, and say your say if you choose. My heart is with you; and so are the hearts of the best of America's millions.
>
> Thine for the Beautiful and True
>
> JOAQUIN MILLER

Wilde thanked the so-called "American Byron" for his "chivalrous and courteous letter," which Miller had already sent to the New York *World,* where it duly appeared on 10 February under the heading THE SINGER OF THE SIERRAS SMITES THE PHILISTINES. "For myself and the cause I represent I have no fear as regards the future," wrote Wilde in his letter of thanks. "Slander and folly have their way for a season, but for a season only; while, as touching either the few provincial newspapers which have so vainly assailed me, or that ignorant and itinerant libeller of New England who goes lecturing from village to village in such open and ostentatious isolation [Colonel Higginson], be sure I have no time to waste on them."

By contrast with Rochester, Wilde had a quiet reception in Buffalo, and after his lecture there he took an evening train to Niagara, where he spent a couple of restful days, sightseeing and catching up with his correspondence. From Prospect House, the hotel on the Canadian side where he and his new manager stayed, Wilde wrote to George Lewis:

> Things are going on very well, and you were very kind about answering my telegrams. Carte blundered in leaving me without a manager, and Forbes through the most foolish and mad jealousy tried to lure me into a newspaper correspondence. His attack on me, entirely unprovoked, was one of the most filthy and scurrilous things I ever read—so much so that Boucicault and [W. H.] Hurlbert [editor-in-chief] of the [New York] *World* both entreated me to publish it, as it would have brought people over to my side, but I thought it wiser to avoid the garbage of a dirty-water-throwing in public. It was merely on Forbes's part that the whole thing began, I really declining always to enter into any disquisition. I will show you his letter—it was infamous. He has been a dreadful failure this year and thought he would lure me on to a public quarrel.
>
> I am hard at work, and I think making money, but the expenses seem very heavy. I hope to go back with a £1,000: if I do it will be delightful.

Wilde and Vale put on oilskins to go under the falls at Table Rock, although the former is said to have refused at first on aesthetic grounds and only to have agreed when he was told that Sarah Bernhardt had worn them. "The sight was far beyond what I had ever seen in Europe," he told the Niagara Falls *Gazette*. Afterwards he inscribed a strikingly republican sentiment in the hotel visitors' book: "The roar of these waters is like the roar when the mighty wave of democracy breaks on shores where kings lie couched in ease." But on the whole he professed himself disappointed with Niagara. "Most people must be disappointed with Niagara," he said afterwards. "Every American bride is taken there, and the sight of the stupendous waterfall must be one of the earliest, if not the keenest, disappointments in American married life."

A day's journey brought him to Chicago, where he spent the best part of a week. Asked what he thought of the metropolis of the Middle West, he replied that the number of telephones impressed him, and he told his questioner how a fellow Briton, doing business in America, had said that the comparatively undeveloped device had saved him $8,000 a year, not to speak of time and worry. He liked the city's parks but the architecture depressed him. "Why don't you get some good public dwellings?" he asked his hosts, who proceeded to explain that after the great fire of 1871 innumerable five- and six-storey buildings had been erected with a plethora of fire escapes, which largely accounted for their ugliness. Then he looked up a young Irish sculptor he had heard about named John Donaghue, whom he found working in "a bare little room at the top of a great building." From him he commissioned a bas-relief of a young girl in pensive mood, which was suggested by Wilde's poem "Requiescat" and which Wilde was later to have inlaid in the mantelpiece of his drawing room in Chelsea after he got married.

From the Grand Pacific Hotel in Chicago, he wrote to Mrs George Lewis, from whom he had heard that his American visit was being decried by some sections of the English press:

> The English papers are too ridiculous. You know the Americans—they don't spend their money without a return. For lecturing in Chicago I received before I stepped on the platform a fee of 1,000 dollars—£200: for one hour's work—that is answer enough. Of course in smaller places I get less, but never less than £40. Here I get £200 as at Boston. I could lecture from now till day of doom if I had strength and time to do it . . .

> I lecture again at New York, Boston, Philadelphia and other cities, so you see they understand and like me. All this sounds egotistical, but I do not like my friends in England to be ignorant of the success of one they have been so kind and loyal to.

To "My dear George Curzon," who was still up at Oxford, he wrote a similarly enthusiastic account of his progress:

> The excitement of a sane strong people over the colour of my necktie, the fear of the eagle that I have come to cut his barbaric claws with the scissors of culture, the impotent rage of the ink-stained, the noble and glorious homage of the respectable—you shall know it all . . .

Well, it's really wonderful, my audience are enormous. In Chicago I lectured last Monday to 2,500 people! This is of course nothing to anyone who has spoken at the Union [16]—but to me it was delightful—a great sympathetic electric people who cheered and applauded and gave me a sense of serene power that even being abused by the *Saturday Review* never gave me.

I lecture four times a week, and the people are delightful and lionise one to a curious extent. But they follow me and start schools of design when I visit their town—at Philadelphia the school is called after me and they really are beginning to love and know beautiful art.

As for myself, I feel like Tancred or Lothair, I travel in such state; for in a *free* country one cannot live without slaves, and I have slaves, black, yellow and white.

After repeating his lecture at a number of places between Fort Wayne, Indiana, and St. Louis, Missouri, he returned to Chicago and on 28 February again wrote to Mrs Lewis:

I send you a line to say that since Chicago I have had two great successes: Cincinnati where I have been invited to lecture a second time—this time to the workmen, on the handicraftsmen—and St. Louis. Tomorrow I start to lecture eleven consecutive nights at eleven different cities, and return here on Saturday week for a second lecture. I go to Canada then, and also return to New England to lecture.

Of course I have much to bear—I have always had that—but still as regards my practical influence I have succeeded beyond my wildest hope. In every city they start schools of decorative art after my visit, and set on foot public museums, getting my advice about the choice of objects and the nature of the building. And the artists treat me like a god. But of this I suppose little reaches England.

The lecture to the workers of Cincinnati was later published as "Art and the Handicraftsman" and that at Chicago as "House Decoration." When he reached Omaha, Nebraska, he found a letter from Colonel Morse saying he was arranging for a three-week extension of his tour to California, returning by way of Kansas City. The terms proposed were 60 percent of the gross takings, a guarantee of $200 a night, and return fares for himself, Vale, and the valet. Although "the business of last week was bad as the smaller towns are of no use," wrote Morse, nevertheless "everything is being done that can be done to make the tour a success." [17]

"Six lectures a week for three weeks seem to be enormous," Wilde answered by return. "I do not know whether I can stand it. You should have communicated with me first. However I will do my best, and if I feel Titan-like will do matinées, but I do not think that possible: it depends of course on the distances. I am very tired and worn out." Later, after thinking it over, he added a postscript: "I will lecture as long as the public stands being lectured." Morse's proposal also meant

[16] Curzon had been president of the Oxford Union in 1880.

[17] This letter and a considerable amount of other correspondence concerning the lecture tour, formerly in the possession of Robert Ross, were sold at auction in 1928 after Ross's death for £55 5s to William Andrews Clark and are now in the Clark Library.

that he would have to prepare a fourth lecture for delivery in San Francisco to suit the largely Irish-American audience that was expected there.

The rail journey to San Francisco took four days, "racing along tied to an ugly tin-kettle of a steam engine." In the course of it the traveller realized that the works of English writers originally published in England enjoyed no copyright protection in the United States.

I found but poor consolation for this journey in the fact that the boys who infest the cars and sell everything that one can eat—or should not eat—were selling editions of my poems vilely printed on a kind of grey blotting paper, for the low price of ten cents. Calling these boys on one side I told them that though poets like to be popular they desire to be paid, and selling editions of my poems without giving me a profit is dealing a blow at literature which must have a disastrous effect on poetical aspirants. The invariable reply that they made was that they themselves made a profit out of the transaction and that was all they cared about.

California, with its "groves of orange trees in fruit and flower, green fields and purple hills," struck him at first sight as "a very Italy, without its art." He described his arrival in San Francisco and his initial impressions in a letter to Norman Forbes-Robertson:

There were 4,000 people waiting at the "depot" to see me, open carriage, four horses, an audience at my lecture of the most cultivated people in 'Frisco, charming folk. I lecture again here tonight, also twice next week; as you see I am really appreciated—by the cultured classes. The railway have offered me a special train and private car to go down the coast to Los Angeles, a sort of Naples here, and I am fêted and entertained to my heart's content . . .
The women here are beautiful. Tonight I am escorted by the Mayor of the city through the Chinese quarter, to their theatre and joss houses and rooms, which will be most interesting. They have "houses" [brothels] and "persons" [prostitutes].

The Chinese quarter, "peopled by Chinese labourers," he later described as "the most artistic town I have ever come across:"

The people—strange melancholy Orientals, whom many people would call common, and they are certainly very poor—have determined that they will have nothing about them that is not beautiful. In the Chinese restaurant, where these navvies meet to have supper every evening, I found them drinking tea out of china cups as delicate as the petals of a rose-leaf, whereas at the gaudy hotels I was supplied with a delft cup an inch and a half thick. When the Chinese bill was presented it was made out on rice paper, the account being done in Indian ink as fantastically as if an artist had been etching little birds on a fan.

Wilde lectured five times in San Francisco. His final lecture, "The Irish Poets of '48," was at Platt's Hall on 5 April, the only occasion on which he spoke on this subject throughout his tour. Although he stirred the local Irish patriots by tributes to Daniel O'Connel and quoted the

"Liberator's" poem "Feelings of an Irish Exile," it was to his mother that he gave pride of place. Indeed, his references to Speranza and his reading of two of her poems drew great applause from the audience and caused a young lady to rush up to the platform with a fragrant bouquet of violets for the lecturer, "whereat," so we are told in a contemporary newspaper account, "the audience again applauded and Oscar bowed his thanks." [18]

Since this lecture is not generally known and has not been included in any of the various collected editions of Wilde's works, it may be of interest to quote some extracts:

As regards the men of '48, I look on their work with peculiar reverence and love, for I was indeed trained by my mother to love and reverence them as a Catholic child is the saints of the calendar, and I have seen many of them also. The earliest hero of my childhood was Smith O'Brien, whom I remember so well, tall and stately, with the dignity of one who has failed—such failures are at least often grander than a hundred victories. [19] John Mitchel too I saw on his return to Ireland at my father's table, with his eagle eye and impassioned manner, [20] John Savage I met in New York, [21] Charles Gavan Duffy is one of my friends in London . . . [22]

Of the quality of Speranza's poems perhaps I should not speak—for criticism is disarmed before love—but I am content to abide by the verdict of the nation which has so welcomed her genius and understood the song, notable for its strength and simplicity that ballad of my mother's on the trial of the Brothers Sheares in '98, and that passionate and lofty lyric written in the year of the revolution called 'Courage,' [23] I would like to linger on her work

[18] *The Call,* 6 April 1882. The original MS of this lecture, written by Wilde in two exercise books and consisting of thirty-four folios, is now in the Donald F. Hyde collection. It is not mentioned by Mason in his bibliography, although at one time Mason seems to have considered publishing it, since he sent the MS, which formerly belonged to Robert Ross, to W. B. Yeats for editorial advice. It has recently been published in a limited edition by the Book Club of California as *Irish Poets and Poetry of the Nineteenth Century* (San Francisco, 1972), edited with an introduction and biographical notes by Robert D. Pepper.

[19] William Smith O'Brien (1803–64), one of the leaders of the abortive rising of 1848, was convicted of high treason and sentenced to be hanged, drawn, and quartered. The sentence was commuted to transportation, which he served in Tasmania. He was eventually pardoned and returned to Ireland in 1854, where he spent most of the remaining ten years of his life but took no further part in politics.

[20] John Mitchel (1815–75) was sentenced to fourteen years' transportation for treason-felony in 1848, but after five years in Tasmania he succeeded in escaping to America. He returned to Ireland in 1872 and was elected Nationalist M.P. for Tipperary but was held ineligible to take his seat. His finely-written *Jail Journal,* first published in New York in 1854, is a classic work of penology.

[21] John Savage (1828–88) was an Irish poet who was active in the 1848 rising. He escaped to America, where he spent the rest of his life in New York as a journalist and an organizer of the Fenian movement there.

[22] Sir Charles Gavan Duffy (1816–1903) was editor of *The Nation* at the time of its suppression in 1848 on account of an allegedly seditious article by Speranza entitled *"Jacta Alea Est."* Between July 1846 and April 1849 he was tried five times and eventually discharged, as no jury would convict him. In 1855 he emigrated to Australia, where he rose to be Prime Minister of Victoria, and was knighted in 1873. He returned to Europe in 1880 and devoted the remainder of his life to literary work.

[23] The poem "Courage," beginning "Lift up your pale faces, ye children of sorrow," is entitled "The Year of Revolutions" in the edition of Lady Wilde's poems.

longer, I acknowledge, but I think you all know it, and it is enough for me to have had once the privilege of speaking about my mother to the race she loves so well . . .

Indeed the poetic genius of the Celtic race never flags or wearies. It is as sweet by the groves of California as by the groves of Ireland, as strong in foreign lands as in the land which gave it birth. And indeed I do not know anything more wonderful, or more characteristic of the Celtic genius, than the quick artistic spirit in which we adapted ourselves to the English tongue. The Saxon took our lands from us and left them desolate—we took their language and added new beauties to it.

Wilde's next public appearance was at the Opera House in Salt Lake City, where he lectured to the Mormon community there. "The President, a nice old man, sat with five wives in the stage box," Wilde wrote to Mrs Bernard Beere describing the Opera House as "an enormous affair about the size of Covent Garden," which "holds with ease fourteen [Mormon] families." Incidentally, John Taylor, the British-born president of the Church of Jesus Christ of Latter-Day Saints, had seven wives, who bore him thirty-four children. According to Wilde, when Brigham Young, who founded Salt Lake City and lived in the presidential palace (called "Amelia" after one of his wives), died in 1877, Taylor "stood up in the Tabernacle and said that it had been revealed to him that he was to have the Amelia Palace, and that on this subject there were to be no more revelations of any kind!"

Wilde also lectured to the silver miners at Leadville, near Denver, in the Rocky Mountains, which it took him a whole day to reach by a narrow-gauge railway at a height of fourteen thousand feet. According to Wilde, Leadville had the reputation of being the richest city in the world. It also had the reputation of being the roughest, and every man carried a gun. "I was told that if I went there they would be sure to shoot me or my travelling manager," Wilde afterwards recalled. "I wrote and told them that nothing that they could do to my travelling manager would intimidate me." [24]

On going to the local theatre to give his lecture, he was told that a short time before two men had been seized for committing a murder, that they had been brought onto the stage at eight o'clock in the evening, and then and there tried and executed before a crowded audience. "But I found these miners very charming and not at all rough."

> I read them passages from the autobiography of Benvenuto Cellini and they seemed much delighted. I was reproved by my hearers for not having brought him with me. I explained that he had been dead for some little time which elicited the inquiry, "Who shot him?"

They afterwards took him to a dance saloon where he saw what he called "the only rational method of art criticism I have ever come across." This took the form of a printed notice above the piano:

[24] This remark was appropriated by Wilde from the Irish landlord the Marquess of Clanricarde, who during the agrarian troubles declared that he would not be intimidated by the threats to shoot his agent.

PLEASE DO NOT SHOOT THE PIANIST
HE IS DOING HIS BEST

"The mortality among pianists in that place is marvellous," Wilde also commented. "Then they asked me to supper, and having accepted, I had to descend a mine in a rickety bucket in which it was impossible to be graceful. Having got into the heart of the mountain I had supper, the first course being whiskey, the second whiskey and the third whiskey."

The amazement of the miners when they saw that art and appetite could go hand in hand knew no bounds [he wrote to Mrs. Bernard Beere]; when I lit a long cigar, they cheered till the silver fell in dust from the roof on our plates; and when I quaffed a cocktail without flinching, they unanimously pronounced me in their grand simple way "a bully boy with no glass eye"— artless and spontaneous praise which touched me more than the pompous panegyrics of literary critics ever did or could.

Then I had to open a new vein, or lode, which with a silver drill I brilliantly performed, amid unanimous applause. The silver drill was presented to me and the lode named "The Oscar." I had hoped that in their simple way they would have offered me shares in "The Oscar" but in their artless untutored fashion they did not. Only the silver drill remains as a memory of my night at Leadville.

"I have had a delightful time all through California and Colorado," Wilde concluded, "and am now returning home twice as affected as ever, my dear Bernie." Nevertheless he was to admit when he got home that the knowledge of art west of the Rocky Mountains, he had found "infinitesimal"—so infinitesimal in fact that "an art patron—one who in his day had been a miner—actually sued the railroad company because the plaster cast of Venus de Milo, which he had imported from Paris, had been delivered minus the arms. And, what is more surprising still, he gained his case and the damages."

6

On his way back to New York, Wilde spent a week lecturing in Kansas and Missouri. A town in Kansas called Griggsville was not on the itinerary, but when the local notables heard he was in the neighbourhood they sent him a telegram asking him to come and talk to them about aesthetics. There was no time for more than a passing glance at Griggsville, so the lecturer contented himself by cabling in reply to the invitation: BEGIN BY CHANGING THE NAME OF YOUR TOWN.

"The summer is just breaking in Kansas, and everything looks lovely," he wrote after his arrival in Topeka. "I took a long drive by myself yesterday afternoon and had a delightful time in what they call a 'spider buggy and a fly-up trotter.' No one knows the pleasure of driving till one drives an American trotter. They are absolutely perfect!" Here the local poet called on him "with his masterpiece," which he evidently thought Wilde might get published for him. It was "a sanguinary lyric of 3,000 lines on the Civil War," of which "the most impassioned part" began thus:

> Here Mayor Simpson battled bravely with
> his Fifteenth Kansas Cavalry.

"What am I to do?" asked Wilde in despair at the request.

When he reached St Joseph, Missouri, the lecturer found there was a rival attraction, as he explained to Nellie Sickert:

> At St Joseph the great desperado of Kansas, Jesse James, had just been killed by one of his followers, and the whole town was mourning over him and buying relics of his house. His door-knocker and dust-bin went for fabulous prices, two speculators absolutely came to pistol shots as to who was to have his hearth brush, the unsuccessful one being, however, consoled by being allowed to purchase the water butt, for the income of an English bishop, while his sole work of art, a chromo-lithograph of the most dreadful kind, of course was sold at a price which in Europe only a Mantegna or an undoubted Titian can command!
>
> Last night I lectured at Lincoln, Nebraska, and in the morning gave an address to the undergraduates of the State University there: charming audience—young men and women all together in the same college, attending lectures and the like, and many young admirers and followers among them.
>
> They drove me out to see the great prison afterwards! Poor odd types of humanity in hideous striped dresses making bricks in the sun, and all mean looking, which consoled me, for I should hate to see a criminal with a noble face. Little whitewashed cells, so tragically tidy, but with books in them. In one I found a translation of Dante, and a Shelley. Strange and beautiful it seemed to me that the sorrow of a single Florentine in exile should, hundreds of years afterwards, lighten the sorrow of some common prisoner in a modern gaol, and one murderer with melancholy eyes—to be hung they told me in three weeks—spending that interval in reading novels, a bad preparation for facing either God or Nothing.
>
> So every day I see something curious and new, and now think of going to Japan and wish Walter [Sickert] would come with me.

A day or two after he reached New York at the beginning of May, Wilde read with horror in the newspapers of the assassination by Irish terrorists in Dublin of the newly installed Chief Secretary for Ireland, Lord Frederick Cavendish, and the Under-Secretary, T. H. Burke, while they were walking together in Phoenix Park. Incidentally, Burke, who was a Catholic and a nephew of Cardinal Wiseman, had been trying to get a civil list pension for Speranza. Wilde was immediately asked by a newspaper reporter how he felt about the news of what came to be known as the Phoenix Park murders. "When liberty comes with hands dabbled in blood it is hard to shake hands with her," he replied. But, no doubt remembering the large number of Irish in New York, he added: "We forget how much England is to blame. She is reaping the fruit of seven centuries of injustice." This sentiment caused the *Philadelphia Press* to come out with the comment: "After all the silly twaddle we have heard from Oscar Wilde, it is both surprising and refreshing to hear him utter these sensible words."

D'Oyly Carte had intended that Wilde's tour should finish in New York with one final lecture in which the lecturer should sum up what he had seen and what he thought of art in the parts of the country he had visited. However, the box office receipts showed that as an attraction he was far from exhausted, with the result that he was persuaded to postpone his return home and instead to continue the tour, first to Canada, since *Patience* had done well there, and then to the Southern states for three weeks. So, after giving a couple of lectures in New York, he was dispatched to Montreal.

From his room in the Windsor Hotel he could see his name in huge letters on a poster in the square below advertising his next public appearance. On 12 May he wrote to Norman Forbes-Robertson, who was planning a visit with a theatrical company, welcoming the prospect of seeing him and drinking champagne with him and watching "the large posters with our names."

> I am now six feet high (my name on the placards), printed it is true in those primary colours against which I pass my life protesting, but still it is fame, and anything is better than virtuous obscurity, even one's own name in alternate colours of Albert blue and magenta six feet high . . . I feel I have not lived in vain.
>
> My second lecture in New York was a brilliant success. I lectured at Wallack's theatre in the afternoon, *not an empty seat,* and I have greatly improved in speaking and in gesture. I am really quite eloquent—at times. I was greatly congratulated.

He asked one of the reporters about the Canadian universities. "I take great interest in universities everywhere," he explained. When he had been given some information on this subject, he observed: "It is better for the country to have a good general standard of education than to have, as we have in England, a few desperately overeducated, and the remainder ignorant. One of the things that delighted me most in America was that the universities reached a class that we in Oxford have never been able to reach—the sons of the farmers and people of moderate means."

From Montreal, Wilde went to Ottawa, as he put it, "to lecture Lorne on dadoes." The Duke of Argyll's son, the Marquess of Lorne, who had married Queen Victoria's fourth daughter, Princess Louise, was Governor-General of Canada at this time, and he was hospitable enough to accommodate Wilde at Government House when he lectured on the subject of "The House Beautiful" in the Canadian capital. It was in this lecture that Wilde declared that he regarded Whistler's famous Peacock Room as "the finest thing in colour and art decoration which the world has known since Correggio painted that wonderful room in Italy where the little children are dancing on the walls." [25]

[25] Whistler had designed the Peacock Room for Frederick Leyland, a wealthy art collector who lived in Prince's Gate, London. In 1904, the American collector Charles L. Freer bought the panelled room, and it is now in the Freer Gallery of Art, Washington,

While staying at Government House, Ottawa, Wilde met a young Canadian woman artist about his own age named Frances Richards, who asked him to sign her birthday book, which he did, and also to provide her with a few lines of introduction to Whistler, as she was shortly leaving for London. "You will appreciate him, and he you," he told her when he sent the introduction. "I wish I could be in London to show you a few houses and a few men and women, but I will be in Japan, sitting under an almond tree, drinking amber-coloured tea out of a blue and white cup, and contemplating a decorative landscape." (He never did get to Japan, although he fully intended to do so.) "I must go to Japan," he told Norman Forbes-Robertson at this time, "and live there with sweet little Japanese girls." Indeed, he tried to persuade Whistler to join forces with him there. "Fancy the book, I to write it, you to illustrate it. We would be rich."

The letter of introduction was in character:

My dearest Jimmy,

I want you to know, and to know is to delight in, Miss Richards, who is an artist, and a little oasis of culture in Canada. She does really good work and has already civilised the Marquis of Lorne.

She is already devoted to your pictures, or rather to my descriptions of them, which are just as good, I often think better. She is quite worthy of your blue and white china, so I send her to you with this letter: I know you will be charming to her. *Toujours*

OSCAR

P.S. I have already civilised America—*il reste seulement le ciel!*

Nor did he forget others at home. He sent his mother a cheque for $400 from his earnings, and to Mrs. George Lewis, whose husband had been so helpful with introductions, he dispatched "an Indian fan, made by a Canadian tribe I visited in Canada." He described it as "a fanciful thing of feathers," which, being yellow, he thought would "go delightfully" with the sunflowers at the top of her garden walk outside her cottage at Walton-on-Thames. "I have just lectured here again," he wrote to her from Boston, "and am now going to New Orleans. They talk about yellow fever, but I think that one who has survived the newspapers is impregnable."

On his way to the South, Wilde stopped at Cincinnati to deliver what was advertised as "a farewell lecture on the decorative arts." He also attended a meeting of the local Musical Club, where a Dr Forcheimer read a paper on "Our Musical State," after which the chairman called on Wilde to come up to the platform and say a few words. Although taken by surprise, Wilde rose to the occasion and for the next ten minutes attacked American outdoor advertising, told the story of his whiskey supper in the Leadville mine, described how in the Mormon country he had

---

D.C. The room in Italy to which Wilde compared the Peacock Room was the Camera di San Paolo in the monastery of San Lodovico at Parma, where in 1519 Correggio painted the frescoes constituting "Diana Returning from the Chase" with auxiliary groups of attractive and vivacious boys.

realized polygamy was "most prosaic," how "much more poetic it was to marry one and love many," and how "no living English novelist can be named with Henry James and Howells."

It was hardly the best time for a British lecturer to discourse on art in the South, since the old plantation owners who might best have been expected to appreciate him were dispirited and impoverished, and many of them had been forced to part with their estates as the result of the prolonged slump in cotton prices. However, he was heartily applauded when he spoke on "Decorative Art" at the Grand Opera House in New Orleans, before an audience described in the *Daily Picayune* as "select, large, and brilliant." And when it became known that General Beauregard, the local Confederate military leader, had called at the lecturer's hotel and taken him for a drive, visiting the Catholic Cathedral on their way, Wilde's social stature increased considerably; Creole by blood and Catholic by faith, the handsome Pierre Beauregard was generally believed in Louisiana to have been held back in the campaign by the bigoted Protestants of Richmond.

Jefferson Davis was then living in retirement at Beauvoir, on the Gulf of Mexico between New Orleans and Mobile. It was rumoured that Wilde wished to meet him, and when a reporter from the *Picayune* called at the St Charles Hotel and asked Wilde if it was true, he agreed it was:

I have an intense admiration for the chief of the Southern Confederacy. I have never seen him, but I have followed his career with much attention. His fall, after such an able and gallant pleading of his own cause, must necessarily arouse sympathy, no matter what might be the merits of his pleas. The head may approve the success of the winners, but the heart is sure to be with the fallen.

The case of the South in the Civil War is to my mind much like that of Ireland today. [In Ireland] it is not a struggle to see the empire dismembered, but only to see the Irish people free, and Ireland still as a willing and integral part of the British Empire. To dismember a great empire in this age of vast armies and overweening ambition on the part of other nations is to consign the peoples of the broken country to weak and insignificant places in the panorama of the nations, but people must have freedom and autonomy before they are capable of their greatest results in the cause of progress. This is my feeling about the Southern people as it is about my own people, the Irish.

Wilde's meeting with the seventy-four-year-old Jeff Davis took place at Beauvoir on 27 June, and he was invited to stay the night. Asked to comment on his visit when he reached Atlanta, Georgia, Wilde had this to say:

He lives in a very beautiful house by the sea amid lovely trees. He impressed me very much as a man of the keenest intellect, and a man fairly to be a leader of men on account of a personality that is as simple as it is strong, and an enthusiasm that is as fervent as it is faultless. We in Ireland are fighting for the principle of autonomy against empire, for independence against centralisation, for the principles for which the South fought.

So it was a matter of immense interest and pleasure for me to meet the leader of such a great cause. Because, although there may be a failure in fact, in ideas there is no failure possible. The principles for which Mr Davis and the South went to war cannot suffer defeat.

However, he was later to comment on what he called the "melancholy tendency" he found among the more elderly inhabitants of the South to date every event of importance by the Civil War. "How beautiful the moon is tonight," he recalled having remarked to a gentleman who was standing next to him. "Yes" was his reply, "but you should have seen it before the war!"

It was natural that Wilde should play up to his Southern hosts and flatter their vanity. Just as he had told them in the North that the best American poet was Whitman, so he declared that "the South has produced the best poet in America—Edgar Allan Poe." In the same vein he proclaimed that "the very physique in the South is far finer than that in the North, and its temperament infinitely more susceptible to the influences of beauty."

Wilde was in Atlanta, Georgia, for Independence Day. When a reporter from the Atlanta *Constitution* called on him in his rooms at the Markham Hotel, the bangs of firecrackers and the yells of the happy crowd in the street outside came through the open window. Wilde, who was evidently conscious of the noise as well as the heat, exclaimed with a note of irritation in his voice as he slammed down the window, "Oh, the patriots! The patriots!"

"This the first Fourth of July you ever saw in America?" asked the reporter. Wilde agreed that it was. Asked what he thought of it, Wilde answered frankly: "I don't think that anything so fine as the Declaration of Independence should be celebrated at all if it cannot be celebrated in a very noble manner. Amongst the most artistic things that any city can do is to celebrate by pageant any great eras in its history. Why shouldn't the Fourth of July pageant in Atlanta be as fine as the Mardi Gras carnival in New Orleans? Indeed, the pageant is the most perfect school of art for a people."

As the result of following Wilde to the railroad station, where the lecturer, along with his manager, Mr Vale, and his Negro valet, were due to take the night train for Savannah, the reporter witnessed an incident which he later described. At the booking office, Vale asked for three first-class tickets for Savannah and three sleeping-car tickets. On learning that one set of tickets was required for Wilde's Negro valet, the station-master informed Wilde's manager that it was against the rules of the company to sell sleeping-car tickets to Negroes and requested the return of the ticket, promising to refund the money. When the manager refused, the station-master went to the sleeping-car and repeated his request to Wilde and the valet, but Wilde supported his manager and said that "he had never been interfered with before" in this way. Seeing that further argument was useless, the station-master then asked the help of the station porter. The porter thereupon "went to Mr Wilde's valet and told him the train would soon pass through Jonesboro, and if the people saw a Negro in the sleeper they would mob him. This had the desired effect; in a short time the sleeping-car ticket was returned and Mr Wilde's valet had vacated the berth."

Attendance at the lectures began to show a considerable falling off, owing no doubt to the hot weather and to the fact that many people who had been expected to come were away on holiday at the seaside or in the mountains. "It is very annoying to me to find that my Southern tour extends beyond the three weeks you spoke of," Wilde wrote to Colonel Morse at this time. "It is now three weeks since I left New York, and I am informed I have two weeks more. Five weeks for sixteen lectures— nothing could be worse in every way. It is quite stupid and gross and will do me much harm." Indeed, the turnout at the lectures was very disappointing after Atlanta, notably at Augusta, Savannah, Charleston, Wilmington, and Norfolk and Richmond, Virginia, where the tour ended on 11 July.

Wilde had accepted an invitation to spend a few days with Mrs Julia Ward Howe at her summer home in Newport, Rhode Island, and in the letter he wrote confirming this from Augusta, Georgia, he summed up his impressions of the Southern states:

> I write to you from the beautiful, passionate, ruined South, the land of magnolias and music, of roses and romance: picturesque too in her failure to keep pace with your keen northern pushing intellect; living chiefly on credit, and on the memory of some crushing defeats. And I have been to Texas, right to the heart of it, and stayed with Jeff Davis at his plantation (how fascinating all failures are!) and seen Savannah, and the Georgia forests, and bathed in the Gulf of Mexico, and engaged in voodoo rites with the Negroes, and am dreadfully tired and longing for an idle day which we will have in Newport.

7

By the time he had delivered his final lecture at Richmond, Wilde had netted rather more than $6,000 (£1,200) for approximately six months' work after all expenses had been paid, and this placed him high in the ranks of foreigners lecturing in America. As events turned out, it would have been better for him to have finished then and there, and after two or three weeks' holiday at Newport to have left for home, perhaps by way of Japan, which he still wished to see. On his arrival in Newport, he asked Charles Eliot Norton, Professor of Art at Harvard, to give him an introduction to one of his opposite numbers in Japan, which would enable him to see the Japanese method of studying art, their schools of design, and the like. "I have just returned from the South," he added, "and have a three weeks' holiday now before Japan, and so find it not unpleasant to be in this little island where idleness ranks as a virtue." But his plans were suddenly changed by the D'Oyly Carte office in New York.

Why not work Wilde through the summer resorts on an easy schedule? There might be some money in that, Morse suggested to Carte, who agreed, as did the lecturer. And so Wilde found himself at various places in Long Island, in Saratoga, Pawtucket, and Bangor, Maine, and back again at Boston. He then agreed to return to Canada, since further engagements had been made for him in New Brunswick and Nova Scotia. Another reason keeping him in America was that he had begun to sketch out the scenario for a blank-verse tragedy called *The Duchess of Padua,* which he thought might suit the young American actress Mary Anderson, whom he had met and who had greatly impressed him. Also, Lillie Langtry was coming to New York in late October and he decided to stay to welcome her. "I am off to Nova Scotia and will be back in three weeks," he wrote to Sam Ward towards the end of September from Boston. "Your idea of a dinner to Mrs Langtry is charming, but then everything you do from poetry to menus is perfect. You are the great authority on lyrics and Lafite."

"The Jersey Lily" was the subject of a question put to Wilde by a reporter from the *Morning Herald* when he arrived in Halifax. "I believe you discovered Mrs Langtry?"

"I would rather have discovered Mrs Langtry than have discovered America" was his reply. "Her beauty is in outline perfectly moulded. She will be a beauty at eighty-five. Yes, it was for such ladies that Troy was destroyed, and well might Troy be destroyed by such a woman."

By this time Wilde was accepting much smaller fees than he had been paid earlier in the year. Indeed, he was prepared to take as little as $75 (£15) to lecture to the Young Men's Christian Association in Moncton, New Brunswick. This came to light when his manager accepted another engagement for the same night, at a presumably bigger fee, from another body in the town. This resulted in the Y.M.C.A. issuing a writ, claiming $200 damages from the lecturer for breach of contract. A settlement was reached, the details of which were not disclosed. Nevertheless, the incident caused some talk at the time. "The action of the Y.M.C.A. is generally condemned in the colony" ran one account, "both by the very pious, who lift up their eyes and hands in pious horror at one who attempts to raise the love of Art and beauty into a kind of religious worship; and by the ungodly, who see that the Y.M.C.A. merely sought to fill its coffers out of the attraction of the Arch Prophet, irrespective of his teachings, and failing that, feed their revenge by attempts to levy blackmail." What is noteworthy is that Wilde should have been willing to lecture for so little and under the auspices of the Y.M.C.A., an organization with which he cannot have had very much sympathy.

Wilde was back in New York in time to welcome Lillie Langtry with a huge bunch of lilies when she arrived on the *Arizona,* the same ship that had brought him over. In England her social and financial position had recently been undermined by her husband's bankruptcy and the birth of a child, of whom Edward Langtry was commonly said not to be the father; also by rumours of a pending divorce involving her in scandalous details. Consequently, she resolved to embark on a theatrical career, since she had some talent for acting, and this was facilitated by the Prince of Wales, who procured an opening for her with the London actor-manager Squire Bancroft. Her successful debut early in 1882 as the heroine in *Ours,* a comedy about the Crimean War by Tom Taylor, had led to an invitation to her to star in another play by the same author in New York in the autumn.

For the next few weeks her old admirer was seldom far from her side. "Ever since Mrs Langtry arrived," wrote the Broadway correspondent of the Chicago *Daily News,* a fortnight or so later, "Wilde clung to her skirts." Another correspondent wrote in the same paper shortly afterwards: "As for love-smitten Oscar Wilde, he is head over heels in love with the much-discussed grass widow, Mrs Langtry." The photographer Sarony secured the exclusive rights to take pictures of her for a reputed $5,000, and when he showed her a proof of the first effort, she handed it back to him with a remark which everyone took to have been inspired by Wilde: "You have made me pretty—I am beautiful." After she had insisted on visiting Niagara against his advice, Wilde remarked, "She was photographed at Niagara, with the falls as an insignificant background." He was often with her in her hotel room when she was being interviewed by the press. On one occasion a reporter heard Wilde tell her he was thinking of visiting Australia next. The actress asked him why. "Well, do you know," replied Wilde with a laugh, "when I look at the map and see what an awfully ugly-looking country Australia is, I feel as if I want to go there to see if it cannot be changed into a more beautiful form." It was clear from the way that Lillie Langtry joined in the laughter that she was not averse to Wilde's ostentatious devotion.

Mrs Langtry's first professional engagement was to play Hester Grazebrook in *An Unequal Match* by Tom Taylor. The show opened on 6 November at Wallack's Theatre; Wilde was in the audience, having been invited by his friend Hurlbert, the editor of the New York *World,* to be guest dramatic critic on this occasion. After adding his personal congratulations to those of others in the star's crowded dressing-room, Wilde went off to the *World*'s offices, where he dashed off his copy for the morning edition

> It is only the best Greek gems, on the silver coins of Syracuse, or among the marble figures of the Parthenon frieze that one can find the ideal representation of the marvellous beauty of that face which laughed through the leaves last night as Hester Grazebrook. Pure Greek it is, with the grave, low forehead, the exquisitely arched brow, the noble chiseling of the mouth shaped as if it were the mouthpiece of an instrument of music.

Thus the review began, and continued in the same strain for several columns of print, being an unrelieved paean in praise of the star's beauty. He said little or nothing of her acting, which he dismissed as "the mingling of classic grace with absolute reality, which is the secret of all beautiful art." On the other hand, her dresses lived up to her beauty in the critic's opinion, especially the one in the last act which he described as "a symphony in silver-grey and pink, a pure melody of colour which I feel sure Whistler would have called a scherzo." Only the scenery was painful, the cottage setting having "roses dreadfully out of tone and badly grouped." But in the end the beauty of Hester Graze-brook had "survived the crude roses and the mauve tablecloth triumphantly," and "that it is a beauty that will be appreciated to the full in America I do not doubt for a moment . . ."

Notwithstanding this praise, Wilde could not compete with some of Lillie Langtry's American admirers. Soon tongues were wagging, and the New York *Tribune* commented disapprovingly on "her indiscretion in accepting attentions from certain wealthy and reckless young men who are conspicuous members of our 'fast set.' " One of these was a millionaire playboy named Freddie Gebhardt, who lavished expensive presents on her, including flowers to the value of $950; he also put at her disposal a house on Twenty-third Street where she could entertain. And when her New York engagement ended early in December and she went on tour to Boston and other cities, young Gebhardt accompanied her. However, Freddie gave a good deal of trouble during the tour, and eventually her manager had to order him peremptorily to return to New York, which he did. Oscar Wilde felt that somehow "The New Helen" had let him down:

> Lily of love, pure and inviolate!
> Tower of ivory! red rose of fire!

There was nothing except the question of his own plays *Vera* and *The Duchess of Padua,* of which he had sketched out the scenario, to keep Wilde any longer in America. The idea of going to Australia originated with D'Oyly Carte's New York office, since *Patience* was shortly to be staged in Sydney and it was thought that Wilde might be able to lecture there. "If Mary Anderson takes my play I could not go," Wilde had written to Colonel Morse in October. "This time of year would be better, or in March, but I would sooner go this time of year." Meanwhile, in order to secure American copyright for *Vera,* he had about twenty-five copies printed, which could also serve as an acting edition, and one of the copies was sent to Miss Anderson. "*Vera* charms me; it is very mournful" was her first reaction on reading it. "I think I should like to play the part." However, she eventually turned it down on the advice of her manager-stepfather, Hamilton Griffin. Wilde thereupon began negotiations with another actress, Marie Prescott. Nevertheless, Mary Anderson did agree to play in *The Duchess of Padua* if she liked the work, and a contract was prepared by Griffin by which Wilde was to get $1,000 on signature and a further $4,000 on acceptance, the work to be completed on or before 1 March 1883. "I am glad to think that things are settled," Wilde wrote to her during the negotiations. "How long it seems to take one to get any business done! You and I could have done it all in five minutes." Since Wilde agreed to waive any claim to author's royalties, he asked for the additional $4,000 also to be paid in advance and the play to be put on within twelve months. But to this Griffin demurred. "I am willing to risk the thousand dollars, so strongly do I believe in your ability to write a superb play," he told Wilde, "but I will not agree to pay the four thousand and to play the piece within a year unless it suits Miss Anderson." The contract was signed by both parties early in December, and the author received the $1,000 down as agreed.

Wilde did no more lecturing after his return to New York from Nova Scotia towards the end of October 1882. While his theatrical negotiations were going on, he took furnished rooms first at the south-west corner of Irving Place and Seventeenth Street, next to the house once occupied by Washington Irving, and then at 48 West Eleventh Street in Greenwich Village, where he remained until he sailed for home two days after Christmas. One acquaintance he made at this time was the American poet and novelist Theodore Tilton, whose lawsuit against the Brooklyn preacher Henry Ward Beecher for alienating his wife's affections had been a sensation some years previously. The jury was unable to agree that Mrs Tilton had committed adultery with her favourite preacher, and Tilton lost his case. But none of the parties really succeeded in living down the scandal, and Tilton, who had in the meantime left his wife, was planning to settle in France when Wilde met him. He presented Wilde with a copy of his poems, which, among others, contained a verse translation of a poem by Théophile Gautier which caught Wilde's fancy. ("It is a little masterpiece, and there are very few who can pour the wine of song from the golden to the silver chalice, as you have done, without spilling a drop.") One Friday in November, Tilton took Wilde to see the room where Poe wrote *The Raven*. In the copy of Tilton's poems which the author had given him, Wilde noted: "An old wooden house over the Hudson, low rooms, fine chimney piece, very dull Corot day, clergyman with reminiscences about Poe, about chickens."

By this time, since he was no longer lecturing, the newspapers had largely lost interest in Wilde. However, he was to provide one further piece of copy as the result of a chance meeting with a young man who accosted him as he was walking up Fifth Avenue, near Seventeenth Street. "Excuse me, Mr Wilde. You remember me, the son of Anthony J. Drexel?" Wilde had no recollection of meeting the youth, although he had been to Morgan's banking house where the senior Drexel was a partner. As the youth was hungry, Wilde gave him lunch, after which the youth took him to a house between Second and Third Avenues where gentlemen were shaking dice for large stakes, the pretext for the visit being that the supposed Drexel Junior had won a lottery prize which he had to collect. Soon Wilde was induced to play, and in a short time he had lost all the cash in his pockets, about $60. However, on learning that cheques were acceptable, he went on playing, no doubt hoping to recover his losses, and eventually signed cheques totalling $1,200.

By this time Wilde realized that he had been the victim of a bunch of crooks. On leaving the house, he took a cab to his bank, where he stopped payment on the cheques and then drove up to the Thirtieth Street Police Station, where he gave the station captain an account of what had happened. "Well, I declare," said Wilde, as he picked one out of a number of pictures he was shown, "that's young Drexel, without a doubt."

The captain quickly disabused him. It was not young Drexel, but "Hungry Joe" Sellick, one of the cleverest "bunco-steerers" in town. Wilde should prosecute, advised the police officer. But, as *The New York Times* subsequently put it, "Wilde said he had been advertised enough, and didn't want the American public to know he had been taken in by a shark."

Four days later, Wilde was asked to call at the police station, where he was handed back his cheques, which he tore up. It took a little longer for the story to "break" in the newspapers. Wilde was sitting smoking a cigarette at Delmonico's on Christmas Eve when a reporter approached him and asked him to confirm the story. Wilde was noncommittal. "I should object to losing $1,000," he said, as he blew smoke rings at the ceiling. "But I should not object to have it known if I had done so."

Three days later, Oscar Wilde drove up to the Cunard dock and embarked on board the S.S. *Bothnia,* stepping out of a carriage driven by a coachman in a dark green livery and accompanied by two friends who had come to see him off—perhaps Colonel Morse and Theodore Tilton. "This is the end of the aesthetic movement," remarked one paper, while the New York *Tribune* stated that before his departure Wilde had "confessed" that "his mission to our barbaric shores had been substantially a failure." In so far as he had not changed America in any appreciable measure, this was no doubt true. On the other hand, America had certainly changed him, in that his tour had provided him with valuable experience and had weaned him from such affectations as his velvet coat and knee-breeches. As Mrs Frank Leslie saw him when he said goodbye to her, he was returning to England "as the conventional nineteenth century gentleman, quiet in dress and reserved in manner."

On the homeward voyage he had time to ruminate on his impressions of America and the Americans. "I fear I cannot picture America as altogether an Elysium—perhaps, from the ordinary standpoint, I know but little about the country. I cannot give its latitude or longitude; I cannot compute the value of its dry goods, and I have no very close acquaintance with its politics." The American woman he liked, but the American man, being "entirely given to business," did not appeal to him so much. ("For him Art has no marvel, and Beauty no meaning, and the Past no message.") His summing-up was brief and to the point: "America is a land of unmatched vitality and vulgarity, a people who care not at all about values other than their own, and who, when they make up their minds, love you and hate you with a passionate zeal."

3 / *Marriage and*
The Woman's World

Since he had given up his rooms at Keats House and had parted on none too friendly terms from Frank Miles, with whom he had shared them, Wilde went to his mother's on reaching London early in January 1883. She had recently moved from Kensington and taken a house with Willie, 116 Park Street, off Grosvenor Square. Here Speranza was to succeed in establishing a literary *salon* on much the same lines as she had in Dublin, helped financially as well as socially by her two sons, since she had not yet received the civil list pension for which she had applied and was not to do so for some years. "She is always glad to see my friends," Oscar had written shortly after her arrival in London, "and usually some good literary and artistic people take tea with her." After a fortnight or so with her, during which he looked up some old friends, like Whistler, he crossed over to Paris, where he planned to spend the next three months writing and living on what remained from his American earnings.

From the luxurious Hôtel Continental in the Rue Castiglione, where he first stayed, he wrote to the American sculptor Waldo Story:

> I saw a great deal of Jimmy [Whistler] in London *en passant*. He has just finished a second series of Venice etchings—such water-painting as the gods never beheld. His exhibition opens in a fortnight in a yellow and white room (decorated by the master of colour) and with a catalogue which is amazing. He spoke of your art with more enthusiasm than I ever heard him speak of any modern work. For which accept my warm congratulations: praise from him is something.[1]

[1] Whistler's exhibition "Arrangement in Yellow and White" had its private view at the Fine Art Society's Rooms on 17 February 1883. It created a sensation, since the walls were yellow, the assistants' neckties were yellow, and Whistler wore yellow socks. After each item in the catalogue the artist printed a quotation from past critics, and on the title-page, "Out of their own mouths shall ye judge them."

Wilde soon left the Continental for a comfortable but less expensive hotel on the Left Bank, the Hôtel Voltaire, Quai Voltaire, described by Alphonse Daudet as "the writer's true quarter in Paris." Certainly the Quai Voltaire had great literary and artistic associations which Wilde must have appreciated. Voltaire died in the hotel when it belonged to the Marquis de Villette; the painter Ingres lived at No. 11, where he also died; the painters Delacroix and Corot lived at No. 13; and the writer Alfred de Musset spent a year or so at No. 23. Wilde had a suite of rooms on the second floor, with a fine view over the Seine and of the Louvre. But to a friend who happened to remark upon its beauty, Wilde pretended to be unimpressed. "Oh," he said with a sweep of his hand, "that is altogether immaterial, except to the *hôtelier,* who of course charges for it in the bill. A gentleman never looks out of the window."

Wilde had had his long hair cut off in London. He now had what remained of his locks curled in imitation of the Roman Emperor Nero's coiffure, which he saw on a bust in the Louvre. At the same time he put aside his knee-breeches for good and began to dress as a fashionable man-about-town, carrying an ivory walking-stick copied from Balzac's. Indeed, he professed a strong admiration for Balzac, and when working in the Hôtel Voltaire he wore a white dressing gown fashioned after the monk's cowl that Balzac used to wear at his writing table. With the help of introductions, which he had brought with him, Wilde had no difficulty in securing an entrée to the literary and artistic society of Paris, which welcomed him with the respect due to a foreign poet. French writers he met ranged from Victor Hugo, Edmond de Goncourt, Alphonse Daudet, and Paul Bourget, to Émile Zola, Maurice Rollinat, and Paul Verlaine, while the artists whose acquaintance he made included the French Impressionists Edgar Degas and Camille Pissarro, the Italian painter and engraver Giuseppe de Nittis, and the French portrait painter Jacques-Émile Blanche. He also met the American virtuoso John Sargent, who was then studying art in Paris, as well as a young English journalist named Robert Sherard, with whom he was to form a close friendship and who was to become the first and most devoted of his biographers.

Sherard, who was a great-grandson of Wordsworth, first met Wilde at a dinner party given by a beautiful Greek lady and began by disliking him. He showed his dislike towards the end of the meal when Wilde was holding forth on the subject of the Venus de Milo in the Louvre and "the sheer physical delight" which the famous statue had produced in him. "I have never been to the Louvre," Sherard interrupted rudely. "When that name is mentioned, I always think of the Grands Magasins du Louvre, where I can get the cheapest ties in Paris." But instead of taking offence, Wilde exclaimed, "I like that—that is very fine!" After dinner Sherard was charmed by Wilde's talk, they left the house together, and the night ended with Sherard accepting an invitation to dine with Wilde the next evening.

They dined in luxury at Foyot's in the Rue de Tournon. At the outset of the dinner, as Sherard afterwards recalled, they agreed that "one should speak of yellow wine, not white." There was something of the philistine in Sherard, who was at times apt to be a bore, and on this occasion he showed a little impatience with Wilde's raptures on the aesthetic theme. Stubbing out his cigar in the dregs of his coffee, Sherard asked him bluntly if he saw any beauty in the mess before him. "Oh, yes," said Wilde pleasantly enough. "It makes quite an effective brown." Nevertheless, Sherard thought he detected a glint of ill-humour in Wilde's eyes and he resolved to be more careful in future.

Sherard also noted that his host addressed him by his first name from the very beginning of their friendship and asked Sherard to do the same with him. Because of his fairly formal upbringing—his father was a wealthy clergyman called Sherard Kennedy, whose surname the son dropped for some reason—young Sherard admitted he had some difficulty at first in meeting Wilde's request, but was prepared to settle simply for "Wilde" as a mode of address. The other quickly corrected him. "You mustn't call me Wilde," he said. "If I am your friend, my name to you is Oscar. If we are only strangers, I am Mr Wilde."

At this time Sherard was living in a cottage in a remote part of suburban Passy. Wilde visited his friend there only once and refused to go there again. "Passy is a dreadful place to get to," he told Sherard. "It is so far off that one's cabman keeps getting down off his box to ask something on account of his *pourboire!*" Also, Sherard kept dogs, which Wilde could not abide. "Dogs are so fussy that they become tedious," he used to say. It was an aversion which he shared with Alphonse Daudet.

Together they explored Paris, usually on foot, while Wilde would talk about literature and art and occasionally history. Once, when they were passing the remains of the dismantled Tuileries palace, Wilde remarked, "There is not there one little blackened stone which is not to me a chapter in the Bible of Democracy." They frequented the cafés in the Latin Quarter, particularly Lavenue's, near the Gare Montparnasse, a popular meeting-place for artists, where John Sargent once sketched them together with Paul Bourget for the album which was one of the curiosities of the place. Wilde and his new-found friend were both interested in the eccentric *feuilletoniste* Gérard de Nerval, who spent some time in the mental asylum at Passy run by Jacques-Émile Blanche's father and eventually hanged himself from the grille of a disreputable inn in a sinister little alley called the Rue de la Vieille Lanterne. Wilde was pleased to have found the place, which exercised an almost morbid fascination for him. Afterwards he searched the bookshops for a rare book on the unhappy man of letters, for which he had to pay an expectedly high price when he found it, as a present for Sherard. "Literary men in England often talk about Gérard de Nerval," he remarked as he handed it to his friend, "but nobody really knows anything about him. With this little book you will be able to write an article which will be welcomed, and which may help your reputation."

The spectacle of the poets Verlaine and Rollinat slowly killing themselves, the first with absinthe and the second with drugs, did not move Wilde to take any action with the object of halting their course of self-destruction. This somewhat shocked Sherard. "If you saw a man throw himself into the river here," he asked as they were crossing the Pont des Arts, "would you go after him?"

"I should consider it an act of gross impertinence to do so," replied Wilde. "His suicide would be a perfectly thought-out act, the definite result of a scientific process, with which I should have no right whatever to interfere."

Among the Parisian literary figures to whom he sent complimentary copies of his poems, a supply of which he had brought with him, was the diarist and *boulevardier* Edmond de Goncourt. Wilde expressed the hope, in an accompanying letter in carefully studied French, that the volume (*"mes premières fleurs de poésies"*) might find a place beside the owner's Watteaus and Bouchers and other treasures in his famous art collection. They met one evening shortly afterwards when Wilde told him that the only Englishman who had read Balzac was Swinburne. According to the Goncourt journal, *"le Poète anglais Wilde"* proceeded to denounce Swinburne for posing as a homosexual, which he was not, *"un fanfaron du vice, qui avait tout fait pour faire croire ses concitoyens à sa pédérastie, à sa bestialité, sans être le moins du monde pédéraste ni bestialitaire."* Goncourt does not record where this took place. It may well have been at Victor Hugo's house, since Sherard has recalled how Wilde discoursed on Swinburne one evening there to an eager group while Victor Hugo was asleep by the fire.

A few weeks later, Edmond de Goncourt met Wilde again at a dinner given by the Italian painter de Nittis, where the diarist had an opportunity of studying his subject closely. The description of him which he recorded was far from flattering—*"cet individu au sexe douteux, au langage de cabotin, aux récits blagueurs."* On this occasion Wilde regaled the company with his recollections of the Leadville miners, embellishing his tale with an account of how he had seen one man who was being hanged at the local theatre clinging to the uprights in the wings while the audience fired at him from their seats.

Goncourt was no stranger to the Paris brothels, as his journals show, but he did not suggest taking his new acquaintance to any of them. However, Wilde was to spend at least one night with a local prostitute, as he was afterwards to admit to Sherard. The experience may well have suggested "The Harlot's House," a poem which Wilde is known to have written at this time, although it was not published until two years later.[2]

> We caught the tread of dancing feet,
> We loitered down the moonlit street,
> And stopped beneath the harlot's house

[2] *The Dramatic Review*, 11 April 1885; reprinted in *Poems* (1908).

Inside, above the din and fray,
We heard the loud musicians play
The "Treues Liebes Herz" of Strauss.

Like strange mechanical grotesques,
Making fantastic arabesques,
The shadows raced across the blind.

We watched the ghostly dancers spin
To sound of horn and violin,
Like black leaves wheeling in the wind . . .

Then turning to my love, I said,
"The dead are dancing with the dead,
The dust is whirling with the dust"

But she—she heard the violin,
And left my side and entered in:
Love passed into the house of lust.

Then suddenly the tune went false,
The dancers wearied of the waltz,
The shadows ceased to wheel and whirl.

And down the long and silent street,
The dawn, with silver-sandalled feet,
Crept like a frightened girl.

Wilde certainly worked hard during his three months in Paris. Besides "The Harlot's House," he completed "The Sphinx," a long poem he had begun at Oxford. He also finished *The Duchess of Padua* and made further revisions to *Vera*. A friend of his mother's named Clarissa Moore, who lived in Rome, invited him to visit her there at this time. "Were I less busy, it would give me great pleasure to accept," he wrote back. "But at present I am deep in literary work, and cannot stir from my little rooms over the Seine till I have finished two plays. This sounds ambitious, but we live in an age of inordinate personal ambition and I am determined that the world shall understand me, so I will now, along with my art work, devote to the drama a great deal of my time. The drama seems to me to be the meeting place of art and life."

Wilde wrote the last lines of *The Duchess of Padua* on 15 March 1882 and he immediately sent off the manuscript to Mary Anderson in New York. At the same time, he managed to have a few copies privately printed, the work being described on the title page as "Op. II"—presumably *Vera* was Op. I—and "A Tragedy of the XVI Century . . . Written in the XIX Century." [3]

"I have no hesitation in saying that it is the masterpiece of all my lit-

---

[3] Only five copies of this edition are known to be extant. One containing the author's manuscript corrections, which was used for the version published in Methuen's collected edition of Wilde's works in 1908, is now in the British Museum, having been presented by Wilde's literary executor, Robert Ross. Another is in the Bodleian Library, and a third is in the Donald F. Hyde collection.

erary work, the chef d'oeuvre of my youth," he wrote to Mary Anderson. Robert Sherard was with him for much of the time that he was working on this stark tragedy in blank verse, and used to recall how agreeably the author was taken with the sound of some of the lines which he would quote to his friend, such as

Am I not Duchess here in Padua?

It is true that the author tried to relieve the melodrama by introducing some comedy on the Shakesperian model which, so he assured Miss Anderson, "never fails to raise laughter." But it was heavy-handed stuff and it is hard to believe that it is the work of the man who was to write plays like *Salomé* and *Lady Windermere's Fan* less than ten years later.

It was hardly surprising that Mary Anderson, no doubt prompted by Hamilton Griffin, who was very jealous of her success, should have turned it down. Impatient to have her decision, Wilde cabled her one morning, and her reply came while he and Sherard were talking together after lunch in the Hôtel Voltaire. Sherard recalls how Wilde managed to conceal his disappointment, tearing a little piece off the blue telegram and rolling it up into a pellet and putting it in his mouth. All he said, as he passed the telegram over to his friend, was, "This, Robert, is rather tedious."

He had better luck with *Vera,* as Marie Prescott accepted the play, offering him $1,000 down and a royalty of $50 for every performance. She assured him that Dion Boucicault never got more than a $25 royalty per performance, "and now he's glad to get ten dollars a performance." Wilde gladly accepted. "What we want to do is to have *all* the real conditions of success in our hands," he wrote to her.

The actress agreed. "Between us we will create the conditions," she replied, "and of course we'll get the result."

2

There being nothing further to keep him in Paris, and having used up his American earnings, Wilde returned to London in the middle of May 1883. "I am hard at work being idle; late nights and famishing morrows follow one another," he wrote to Sherard after he had established himself in lodgings near his mother's house. "I wish I was back in Paris, where I did such good work. However society must be amazed, and my Neronian coiffure has amazed it. Nobody recognises me, and everybody tells me I look young: that is delightful, of course." His rooms, where he was to live for the remainder of his bachelor days, were in an old house kept by a retired butler and his wife in Charles Street (later renamed Carlos Street), off Grosvenor Square. Wilde had an oak-panelled sitting-room and bedroom on the third floor; the food, which was cooked by the butler's wife, was excellent, and the lodger was made most comfortable by these servants of the old school. There was also a spare bedroom on the ground floor, where guests like Robert Sherard were put up from time to time.[4]

Since he had been away from London for so long, Wilde spent a good deal of his time renewing his former contacts in the art world, such as Whistler and Millais. Hence, he solicited an invitation to the latter's "Academy soirée" and also asked for the former's help with a lecture he had been invited to give to the Academy art students at their club in Golden Square. Whistler responded by telling him what he thought Wilde should say to the students, and in adopting much of what Whistler had told him, Wilde repaid him by a flattering compliment when he came to speak at the club, which he did on 30 June.

> To paint what you see is a good rule in art, but to see what is worth painting is better. See life under pictorial conditions. It is better to live in a city of changeable weather than in a city of lovely surroundings.
> Now, having seen what makes the artist, and what the artist makes, who is *the* artist? There is a man living amongst us who unites in himself all the qualities of the noblest art, whose work is a joy for all time, who is, himself, a master of all time. That man is Mr Whistler.

A few weeks after his lecture to the art students, Wilde met Laura Troubridge at a tea party given by a mutual friend. It was four years since she had last seen him, and she thought he had changed considerably. "He is grown enormously fat with a huge face and tight curls all over his head—not at all the aesthetic he used to look," she noted in her diary on 25 July 1883. "He was very amusing and talked cleverly, but it was all monologue and not conversation. He is vulgar, I think, and lolls about in, I suppose, poetic attitudes with crumpled shirt cuffs turned back over his coat sleeves."

At this time Wilde was introduced to Wilfrid Scawen Blunt, who was married to Byron's granddaughter Lady Anne Noel and wrote poetry and bred Arab horses at Crabbet Park, his Sussex estate, besides championing the Irish nationalist cause, for which he was later to be imprisoned. ("It will give me great pleasure to come down to you on Saturday week, and look at your horses, and talk about sonnets.") He also looked up George Curzon, who, like Blunt, had developed a taste for Oriental travel; he had just returned from the Levant and was reading hard for a Fellowship at All Souls, which he was to win, although he had got only a Second in "Greats." ("I will come round one morning and smoke a cigarette with you. You must tell me about the East. I hope you have brought back strange carpets and stranger gods.")

Meanwhile, in New York, Marie Prescott had begun to advertise the forthcoming production of *Vera,* which she planned to open with herself in the title part at the Union Square Theatre on 20 August. According to the advertisement, "the interior of the Czar's palace represented in this play will be the most gorgeous piece of stage setting ever seen in this country." When he learned of the production details, the author

---

[4] The house, 7 Charles Street, has since been pulled down.

wrote enthusiastically to Miss Prescott, informing her that he would come over for the opening.

It is with great pride and pleasure that I look forward to seeing you in the character of the heroine of my play—a character which I entrust to you with the most absolute confidence, for the first night I saw you act I recognised in you a great artist . . .

As regards the play itself, I have tried to express within the limits of art that Titan cry of the peoples for liberty, which in the Europe of our day is threatening thrones, and making governments unstable from Spain to Russia, and from north to southern seas. But it is a play not of politics but of passion. It deals with no theories of government, but with men and women simply; and modern Nihilistic Russia, with all the terror of its tyranny and the marvel of its martyrdoms, is merely the fiery and fervent background in front of which the persons of my dream live and love. With this feeling was the play written, and with this aim should the play be acted . . .

I look forward with much interest to a second visit to America, and to having the privilege of presenting to the American people *my first drama.* There is, I think, no country in the world where there are such appreciative audiences as I saw in the United States.

Wilde sailed from Liverpool on the R.M.S. *Britannic* on 2 August 1883 and arrived in New York nine days later. "Oscar Wilde has been the life and soul of the voyage," his fellow passenger St John Brodrick, then a budding young Conservative M.P., later Lord Midleton, wrote to Curzon:

He has showered good stories and bon mots, paradoxes and epigrams upon me all the way, while he certainly has a never failing bonhomie, which makes him roar with laughter over his own absurd theories and strange conceits. Of course you know all this—but I don't know that I have ever laughed so much as with him and at him all through the voyage.

Wilde attended the rehearsals of *Vera* and was present on the first night, when he took a curtain call at the end of the performance and made a short speech. During the last act there were some catcalls and booing, after which the critics went back to their offices to write generally hostile notices of the play. The three principal dailies were devastating—"a foolish, highly peppered story of love, intrigue, and politics" (New York *Tribune*); "unreal, long-winded, and wearisome" (*The New York Times*); "long drawn, dramatic rot, a series of disconnected essays and sickening rant, with a coarse and common kind of cleverness" (New York *Herald*). Only the weekly New York *Mirror* had a good word to say for it, and it went to the other extreme in calling it "the noblest contribution to its literature the stage has received in many years."

It was hardly surprising in the light of this reception that the play should close after only a week. Miss Prescott was to take it on tour some months later, opening in the Detroit Opera House on 28 December; but it was never subsequently revived and was never to be played in England. When the news of the failure of *Vera* reached that country, a theatrical journal published a cartoon showing the author dressed in the knee-breeches and buckle shoes which he had by this time discarded, being consoled by his brother Willie, who remarks, as the aesthetic emblem the sunflower falls to the ground: "Never mind, Oscar; other great men have had their dramatic failures!" [5]

Before leaving England, Wilde had met Colonel Morse, who had come over to London and was now European manager for the Philadelphia publisher J. M. Stoddart's publications and the Encyclopedia Americana. He suggested to Wilde that he should undertake a lecture tour of the British Isles during the autumn and winter, although he could not promise as high fees as Wilde had earned in America. "I can foresee a good season's work and fair prices—not large," Morse wrote to him while he was in New York. "From ten to twenty-five guineas per night is all they will pay." Wilde, who needed the money, was agreeable. A few days after his return to England, he started off in Wandsworth Town Hall on 24 September with "Impressions of America." During the succeeding eighteen months, he was to repeat that lecture and "The House Beautiful" at various centres in England, Scotland, and Ireland. The lecture which he gave at Oxford, soon after Wandsworth, resulted in his being attacked by an undergraduate in the course of a debate at the Union. It so happened that Curzon was present, and as an ex-president he made an intervention which earned him a characteristic expression of gratitude from Wilde, who had not forgotten how the presentation of his *Poems* had been rejected by the famous debating society.

You are a brick! and I thank you very much for your chivalrous defence of me in the Union. So much of what is best in England passes through Oxford that I should have been sorry to think that discourtesy so gross and narrowmindedness so evil could have been suffered to exist without some voice of scorn being raised against them.

Our sweet city with its dreaming towers must not be given entirely over to the Philistine. They have Gath and Ekron and Ashdod and many other cities of dirt and dread and despair and we must not give them the quiet cloisters of Magdalen to crawl in or the windows of Merton to peer from.

During the last week of November, he lectured twice at the Gaiety Theatre in Dublin, and on this occasion he renewed his acquaintance with Constance Lloyd, a beautiful and gentle girl of twenty-six. Her father, Horatio Lloyd, and her grandfather, John Lloyd, had both practised at the English Bar and become Queen's Counsel, but Horatio Lloyd, whose only daughter she was, had died comparatively young and her mother had married again.[6] Constance lived in London with her Lloyd grandfather and an aunt ("Aunt Emily") at their house in Lancaster Gate, and from time to time would go over to Dublin to stay with her maternal grandparents, Captain John Atkinson of the 60th Rifles and his wife Mary, in their fine Georgian house in Ely Place.

[5] *The Entr'Acte*, 1 September 1883.
[6] Mrs Lloyd's second husband was named King.

Constance Lloyd had originally met Oscar Wilde two years previously in London, probably through his mother, who knew the Atkinsons in Dublin, and particularly Mrs Atkinson's brother Serjeant Hemphill, later Lord Hemphill, a leading member of the Irish Bar who also lived in Merrion Square. In 1881, when Constance first met Oscar, who had known her brother Otho at Oxford, she told Otho that she could not help liking Oscar "because when he's talking to me alone he's never a bit affected, and speaks naturally, excepting that he uses better language than most people." A year or so later, when Oscar was either in America or in Paris, Speranza wrote telling him that Serjeant Hemphill, who happened to be on a visit to London, had called on her in Park Street. "He praised Constance immensely. I had nearly in mind to say I would like her for a daughter-in-law, but I did not. It was Constance who told him where we lived."

Constance and her cousin Stanhope Hemphill, the Serjeant's son, on learning that Oscar was staying at the Shelbourne Hotel while in Dublin for his lectures, left a note for him there asking him to call at Ely Place. "He accordingly did," wrote Constance afterwards, "and though decidedly extra affected, he made himself very pleasant . . . He was dining with the Fellows of Trinity College at six o'clock." Constance went to both his lectures with Stanhope Hemphill, but did not think that "Impressions of America" was so interesting as "The House Beautiful." "They all think him so improved in appearance," she added. "Stanhope has started on a new tack and chaffs my life out of me about O.W., such stupid nonsense!"

Constance's next letter to her brother, written three days later from Ely Place, contained a surprise for him:

Prepare yourself for an astounding piece of news! I am engaged to Oscar Wilde and perfectly and insanely happy. I am sure you will be glad because you like him, and I want you now to do what has hitherto been my part for you, and make it all right. Grandpapa [Lloyd] will, I know, be nice, as he is always so pleased to see Oscar. The only one I am afraid of is Aunt Emily.

Oscar will write to Grandpapa and to Mama when he arrives at Shrewsbury today, and probably to you at the same time, and he will call next Sunday (he is going up to town on purpose) so you must be at home and be nice to him. I shall probably be there myself, but I shall let you know in a day or two about that. I want to go because otherwise I shall not see him until Christmas . . .

Now that he is gone, I am so dreadfully nervous over my family; they are so cold and practical. Everyone in this house is quite charmed, especially Mama Mary [Mrs Atkinson] who considers me very lucky.

Mind you write to me soon, dear old boy, and congratulate me. I am longing to know how you will all take it. I won't stand opposition, so I hope they won't try it.

"I am pleased indeed," Otho Lloyd wrote to his prospective brother-in-law, in reply to Oscar's letter confirming the news. "If Constance makes as good a wife as she has been a good sister to me, your happiness is certain; she is staunch and true." [7] Unfortunately, other members of the Lloyd family, particularly Constance's mother, Mrs King, and Aunt Emily, were far from enthusiastic, "considering that he was not good enough for her," according to Oscar's son Vyvyan Holland.[8] On the other hand, Lady Wilde was delighted and wrote to her son:

> You both have been true and constant, and a blessing will come on all true feeling. I would like you to have a small house in London, and live the literary life and teach Constance to correct proofs, and eventually go into Parliament.

If he took such a house, she thought "all the relations will furnish it." It was just the settled life she wished for Oscar. "Literature and lectures and Parliament, receptions etc. for the world and small dinners for genius and culture—at 8 o'clock. Charming this life, begin it at once." That Speranza thought Oscar should get into Parliament is noteworthy, since she appreciated his sympathy with her Irish nationalist aspirations, which she considered he ought to be able to further in this way. But as has already been seen, he had no interest in English party politics or parliamentary life. As he was to put it in his essay *The Soul of Man under Socialism,* "The Lords Temporal say nothing, the Lords Spiritual have nothing to say, and the House of Commons has nothing to say and says it."

In giving the news of his engagement to Lillie Langtry, who was still in America, Oscar described Constance as "a beautiful girl" and "a grave, slight, violet-eyed little Atemis, with great coils of heavy brown hair which make her flower-like head droop like a blossom, and wonderful ivory hands which draw music from the piano so sweet that the birds stop singing to listen to her." Besides these admirable qualities, Constance Lloyd had a little money of her own, eventually amounting to some £800 a year when she came into her inheritance from her grandfather provided for in her marriage settlement. Oscar told the American sculptor Waldo Story that she was "quite perfect except that she does not think Jimmy [Whistler] the only painter that ever existed: she would like to bring Titian or somebody in by the back door; however, she knows I am the greatest poet, so in literature she is all right."

> We are, of course, desperately in love. I have been obliged to be away nearly all the time since our engagement, civilising the provinces with my remarkable lectures, but we telegraph to each other twice a day, and the telegraph clerks have become quite romantic in consequence. I hand in my messages, however, very sternly, and try to look as if "love" was a cryptogram for "buy Grand Trunks" and "darling" a cypher for "sell out at par." I am sure it succeeds.

[7] Otho Holland Lloyd (1856–1943) was Constance's only brother. A non-practising barrister and translator of the classics, he was twice married. He died as the result of a fall in the "blackout" during the war.

[8] "They were incurably middle-class and lived their lives by the strictest conventional code, so that my father's notoriety and flamboyance must have offended all their instincts, particularly as my parents were married when the aesthetic period was at its height." Vyvyan Holland, *Son of Oscar Wilde* (1954), p. 33.

"I am with Oscar when he is in town, and I am too miserable to do anything when he is away," wrote Constance on 21 December 1883. "He and I are going to Norwood to lunch today as he lectures at the Crystal Palace, and after that he has a week's holiday, which will be a joy for me." On 26 December, *The World* reported that "Mr Whistler's last Sunday breakfast of the year was given in honour of two happy couples, Lord Garmoyle and his fairy queen, and Oscar and the lady whom he has chosen to be the *châtelaine* of the House Beautiful." [9]

Oscar Wilde and Constance Lloyd were married by special licence at St James's Church, Sussex Gardens, by the vicar, the Rev. Walter Abbot, on 29 May 1884. The witnesses who signed the register, in which the bridegroom's rank or profession was given as "Gentleman," were his mother, Lady Wilde, the bride's great-uncle Serjeant Hemphill, her mother Mrs King, and the bridegroom's brother Willie. Constance's wedding dress, which Oscar had specially chosen for her, was "of a delicate cowslip hue," while "the bodice, cut square and somewhat low in front, was finished with a high Medici collar; the ample sleeves were puffed"; and "the skirt, made plain, was gathered by a silver girdle of beautiful workmanship," the gift of the bridegroom. In her hair was a wreath of myrtle leaves, and she was attended by six bridesmaids, who were her cousins. Lady Wilde appeared in a somewhat startling get-up of grey satin with "a luxuriant plume of ostrich feathers," and one of the other ladies present wore what was described as "a very aesthetic costume." Admission to the church was by ticket only on the bridegroom's orders, with the result, according to the *Irish Times*, that "parishioners complained, and seatholders protested against a stranger presuming to shut the doors of the church, until, after half an hour of angry remonstrance with the officials by a number of residents in the immediate vicinity of the church, the order was revoked, and about fifty people, besides the guests, took seats in the pews." In addition, a considerable crowd waited outside the church to see the happy couple leave for a small reception at Lancaster Gate after the service, since old John Lloyd was in poor health and could not stand the strain of a large wedding breakfast. (Willie Wilde used to say that "old Lloyd was dying but the news of the marriage revived him and he took on a new lease of life.") Later the bridal couple were seen off by their friends at Charing Cross on the boat-train for Paris, where they planned to spend the first part of their honeymoon.

A few days later, Constance wrote to her brother from the Hôtel Wagram in the Rue de Rivoli:

Today we had a young Mr Sherard here to breakfast; he has a romantic story and a romantic face: I thought Chatterton was walking in when he ap-

---

[9] Viscount Garmoyle was the son of the ex-Lord Chancellor Earl Cairns, whom he succeeded in the title in 1885. Garmoyle broke off his engagement to his "fairy queen" and in the resulting action for breach of promise, which she brought against him, she was awarded £10,000, a record sum in an action of this kind hitherto. She was an actress named Emily Finney, whose stage name was Fortescue. Garmoyle subsequently married a clergyman's daughter, and died of pneumonia in 1890, aged twenty-eight.

peared. When I knew him a little I remarked on this resemblance and he told me he had so many traits of character like him. His father is a millionaire (English) and he starves here in a garret and lives in dreamland always: he interests me. Very different but also interesting is the young sculptor Donaghue whom I have seen several times, very handsome Roman face but with Irish blue eyes . . .

We have an *appartement* here of three rooms, twenty francs a day: not dear for a Paris hotel: we are *au quatrième* and have a lovely view over the gardens of the Tuileries: the ruins of the palace are, alas, no more.[10]

Of course I need not tell you that I am very happy, enjoying my liberty enormously.

While Constance was writing this letter, her husband had gone for a walk with Sherard, who afterwards recalled that Oscar had told him that "marriage was indeed wonderful." Oscar then proceeded to expatiate upon the physical joys of wedlock in such detail that Sherard felt quite embarrassed. "We were passing through the Marché St Honoré at the time," wrote Sherard, "and here he stopped and rifled a flower-stall of its loveliest blossoms and sent them, with a word of love on his card, to the bride whom he had quitted but a moment before."

The lovers roamed the Paris streets together and went to the theatres and picture galleries. Sarah Bernhardt in *Macbeth* Constance considered "the most splendid acting I ever saw . . . she simply stormed the part." John Donaghue, the young American sculptor whom Oscar had met in Chicago, was now working in Paris and had done "a lovely bronze bas-relief for the Salon, a seraph: a nude figure full profile of a boy playing a harp, perfectly simple and quite exquisite in line and expression. Everything else in the Salon horrid except, of course, Mr Whistler's two pictures, one very interesting, the Carlyle that Boehm copied for his statue, and which I have only seen before in a print." [11] One night they gave a dinner in the hotel, to which they invited Paul Bourget, John Sargent, John Donaghue, and Henrietta Reubell, a wealthy American whom Henry James called "the shepherdess of the studios," on account of the help she gave struggling artists. "As everything is sure to go well in a hotel," noted Constance a little naïvely, "I am rather looking forward to it."

Oscar and Constance finished their honeymoon in Dieppe and came back to London, having been away for nearly a month. On 25 June, Constance wrote from the Brunswick Hotel in Jermyn Street to her brother, who had also just got married and was spending his honeymoon on the Continent:

We came back yesterday, arrived at 5:30 and came here for the night, the only place that Willie [Wilde] could find for us, London is so crammed. It is

[10] The ruins, which her husband had seen the previous year, had recently been removed.

[11] Whistler's well-known engraved portrait of Thomas Carlyle ("Arrangement in Grey and Black, No. 2") is now in the Glasgow Art Gallery. Sir Edgar Boehm's statue stands on the Chelsea Embankment.

two guineas a day for rooms, scarcely suitable for our purse, so we went and dined at Lancaster Gate and gave them hints to ask us there, which they did not take, so I had to ask Auntie if we might! However she met my suggestion half way and suggested our staying for a few days till we found lodgings. London seems very horrid after Dieppe where we spent a delightful week . . .

Look out for squalls at the Custom House when you return: they were brutal to us, wanted to make me pay for the silver fittings of my dressing case, bagged all Oscar's Tauchnitz which they had to give back because none of them were copyright.[12] They turned over everything and I am sure they have ruined my clothes. They might at least have clean hands if they insist on rummaging one's things . . .

P.S. Oscar is out, and I never send imaginary messages from people.

3

While they were looking round for a house, Oscar and Constance lived in Charles Street, Grosvenor Square, where Oscar's old bachelor rooms were temporarily available. For much of the time, however, he was away lecturing. Sometime during the summer of 1884, they found a house in Chelsea, 16 (now 34) Tite Street, five houses up the street from Keats House, and they were able to take a lease of it with the aid of Constance's dowry, which had been provided by her grandfather Lloyd. While its exterior was that of an ordinary mid-Victorian terrace dwelling-house—it was one of a row of undistinguished examples of contemporary speculative housing—its new tenants planned to convert its interior into something extraordinary and quite unlike the interior of the average domestic building of the period. For this purpose Wilde secured the services of E. W. Godwin, who had designed the house in the same street occupied by Whistler and Frank Miles. Godwin devised and carried out the original and, as some visitors to the "House Beautiful" considered, bizarre scheme of interior decoration of 16 Tite Street in addition to designing most of the furniture. In this work he is said to have had some help from Whistler, with whom he and his wife were on the friendliest terms. Indeed, when Godwin died two years later, his widow promptly married Whistler.

Godwin is said to have been "a singularly attractive man to the ladies" and to have had "many adventures." After the death of his first wife, he had set up house in Hertfordshire with the twenty-one-year-old Ellen Terry, whose child-marriage with the painter G. F. Watts had recently ended in separation and who in the six years that she lived with Godwin bore him two children, Gordon and Edith Craig. Their *ménage* broke up when Ellen Terry decided to return to the stage and Godwin married another young girl, Beatrix Phillip, the daughter of the sculptor J. B. Phillip, who was responsible for the frieze on the Albert Memorial.

---

[12] Bernhard Tauchnitz was a Leipzig publisher who published paperback editions of British authors. Works in copyright were not permitted to be imported into England.

There is no doubt that Edward Godwin was an outstandingly gifted individual, and his contributions to architecture and the sister arts were remarkable for their extensive range and variety. The son of a decorator in Bristol, where he was born in 1833, Godwin had by the time he was twenty-five won first prize in an open competition for the design of Northampton Town Hall. The succeeding quarter of a century showed that he was much more than an accomplished draughtsman. He became an acknowledged authority on theatrical costume—amongst others, he dressed all Henry Irving's plays at the Lyceum; he lectured on dress in relation to health—this particularly endeared him to Wilde; he designed fine furniture as well as theatrical costumes; he was in the forefront of the aesthetic movement; and he was the principal founder of the Fine Arts Society, at one of whose functions he had first made Wilde's acquaintance. For many years he was Whistler's staunchest defender in print, and when the artist decided to settle in Tite Street some years before Wilde's first arrival there, it was Godwin who, as has been seen, designed the building which was to become well known as "The White House." Shortly afterwards Whistler went bankrupt, following the libel action he brought against Ruskin; and when he shut the front door for the last time, Whistler left a notice on the door which read: "Except the Lord build the house, they labour in vain that built it. E. W. Godwin, F.S.A., built this one."

Number 16 Tite Street was a four-storey dwelling with a basement. To the right of the entrance hall was a panelled room facing the street, known as the library, which had a strikingly carved wooden mantelpiece and surround to the fireplace.[13] Here Wilde was to do most of his work on a writing-table which had once belonged to Carlyle. The motif of this room was blue and golden brown. On a column in the corner, Wilde placed a plaster cast of the Hermes of Praxiteles, and on the walls he hung a few favourite pictures—a Simeon Solomon, a Monticelli, and a drawing of the actress Mrs Patrick Campbell by Aubrey Beardsley. To the right of the fireplace there was a large glass-fronted bookcase, full of copies of the Greek classics and other books. Also on the ground floor, leading off the hall at the foot of the staircase and giving on to the garden at the back, was the dining-room: here the prevailing colours were white and grey.

The whole of the first floor was taken up by a large drawing-room which was divided in two by folding doors, the front portion above his study being earmarked by Wilde as a smoking-room when the doors were closed. Heavy curtains draped the windows, "giving the room a rather mysterious look," as Oscar's son Vyvyan was to recall. "The walls were lined with a peculiar embossed paper called lincrusta-walton, with a William Morris pattern of dark red and dull gold. The general decor was a mixture of the Far East and Morocco, with divans and a glass bead curtain before the door." The main attraction of the other half of the

---

[13] The mantelpiece now belongs to Sir Peter Daubeny.

drawing-room was the ceiling, designed by Whistler, into which pea-
cocks' feathers had been inserted. A painted grand piano, on which Constance would occasionally play, stood in one corner of the room, occupy-
ing a disproportionately large part of it. Opposite the fireplace to the
right of the door hung a large painting of Wilde by an American admirer, Harper Pennington.[14] There were two bedrooms on the second
floor, and another on the third. The master bedroom, which Oscar and
his wife occupied, was the second floor front. Looking out over the back
garden on the third floor was a large room, originally intended as a
study for Oscar, but he was to use it seldom, preferring the library on
the ground floor for such work as he did at home; it was later to be converted into a day nursery for the two Wilde children. The top floor consisted of the servants' quarters.

Several of Godwin's drawings for the drawing-room have survived.[15]
One of them shows the elaborate overmantel into which was to be set
John Donaghue's bronze bas-relief of the scene suggested by Wilde's
poem "Requiescat." Godwin also prepared sketches showing how several
of Whistler's etchings—Venetian studies presented to Oscar and Constance by the artist—and a few drawings by Edward Burne-Jones could
best be arranged along the walls so as to form a deep frieze against a
background of dull gold. For the dining-room furniture Godwin designed a suite in white, and also a sideboard, with both of which he took
particular pains. The chairs for this room were modelled in various
Grecian styles, while round the walls there was a strip of shelving
designed to serve for tea parties and buffet suppers—"a sort of Japanese
arrangement of shelves—but very tiny," Wilde called it. "By this arrangement," as one visitor was to remark, "the centre of the room was
an open space instead of being absorbed by the customary huge table
laden with refreshment, and gave an impression of greater size and
lightness to the room." Godwin was also responsible for the soft fur-
nishings, and even for such aids to ablutions as were procurable in those
days. "I should be very glad," wrote Constance to the architect, "if a
bath of any artistic shape could be found for my room."

Another novel feature of the house was that all the doors were removed, except the folding-doors in the drawing-room, and the pictures
were protected by curtains. Some members of the public, usually those
who had not been inside, stigmatized the interior decoration as bizarre
and vulgar, even vaguely sinful. "Vulgarity is the conduct of others" was
Wilde's characteristic comment.

Like all newly-wed couples who are waiting to get into their matrimonial home, Oscar and Constance were consumed by impatience at the
leisurely pace with which British workmen usually seem to proceed with
their building operations. And so it happened that one day in July 1884
Wilde called on the architect at his office in Westminster in the hopes of

[14] This is now in the Clark Library in Los Angeles.
[15] Godwin's plans and drawings of the whole house, together with Wilde's letters
to him, are now in the Donald F. Hyde collection.

hurrying on the work. But Godwin was not in. In fact, he was busily engaged with Lady Archibald Campbell in directing an open-air performance of *As You Like It* on the grounds of Dr McGeagh's hydropathic establishment at Coombe Wood, near Kingston. Wilde scribbled a note on a sheet of Godwin's paper. "I suppose you are busy as you like it (or don't like it)! When can I see you Monday at Tite Street? I want to press on the laggards . . ."

According to Whistler's biographers, Godwin had a habit of invariably making his estimates lower than the actual cost, and then siding with the builders in case of disagreements or misunderstandings. That, they allege, was the way the crash came which obliged Whistler to leave the White House. In the case of 16 Tite Street, it would appear that something of this kind happened. The original building contractor, a man named Green, was already under contract to the landlord to carry out certain work of which the landlord was willing to give the benefit to the incoming tenant. To facilitate this arrangement, Green apparently allowed Wilde to deduct so much from his account in respect of the work which had already been contracted for. Unfortunately, a difference of opinion arose between them as to the amount with which Wilde was to be credited. It was also suggested that Green had skimped some parts of the work besides failing to carry out his instructions with regard to others. The result was that Wilde dismissed Green and declined to pay his account when it was rendered. He then hurried off again to the provinces to go on with his lecturing, but before leaving he asked Godwin to employ another contractor. This the architect undertook to do, and he got hold of a contractor named Sharpe.

On 14 October, Wilde wrote to Godwin from Bristol ("your own city") to tell him that the surveyor employed by Wilde when he took the house had estimated the work done by Green at £72. "Amazing" was Wilde's comment. "Now let us for heaven's sake [get a] move on. Is Sharpe in? And can I see you on Friday anywhere: it is my first day in town. I want if possible Sharpe to be in and doing. I am so overwhelmed with expenses." There were some more expenses to come, since on the same day as Wilde wrote to Godwin the architect approved the new contractor's estimate of the work to be done at a cost of £110.

When Wilde got back to town, an unwelcome surprise awaited him in the shape of a writ from the old contractor claiming the amount of his account. "What shall I do about Green?" Wilde asked the architect. "He is too horrid." Godwin advised his client to defend the action, and apparently he also recommended a firm of City solicitors, Messrs George and William Webb of 11 Austin Friars, whom Wilde instructed to enter an appearance on his behalf. This meant interviews, affidavits, and other tiresome legal documents, not to mention costs and a sum of money which the solicitors felt they must pay into court. Of particular importance were the details of the oral agreement which Wilde alleged Green had made with him; on this subject the solicitors were quite explicit. "For greater caution," they wrote to Godwin, "we ought to see

Mr Wilde and examine him as he would be examined before a Master, because of course 'understandings' won't do; we have to go upon arrangements."

Meanwhile, furniture began to arrive ("the Japanese couch is exquisite"), only to be appropriated by the indefatigable Green. On 3 November, Wilde wrote as he was again on the point of leaving London:

> Don't you think a vermilion band in the front room—ground floor—in the recess—to continue the moulding would do for the present—till the bookcase is arranged?
> I am in much distress over Green seizing the furniture—you alone can comfort me.

And again, a month later, as he was on the point of returning to town:

> I wish you would choose the colours—the red for the drawing-room—as the thing is at a standstill. Is it to be vermilion? Is it not?
> The universe pauses for an answer! Don't keep it waiting!

Later in December, Wilde was again away lecturing, this time in Scotland, when the new contractor's bill, amounting in all to £227 17s, arrived as a further unpleasant surprise.

> The Balmoral,
> Edinburgh
>
> [December 17, 1884]
>
> My dear Godwin,
>   I cannot understand Sharpe's account—enclosed—what is (1) extra painting? What is (2) 14 gas brackets—what is deal shelf overmantel and case in Dining room—etc? Sharpe has been paid first £40 for the overmantel in bedroom and drawing-room, and the sideboard—which by the by I thought very dear—then £120 for his contract—but this new £100 takes me by surprise—I thought the £120 was for everything—surely Green fixed the gas stoves? I may be wrong, but would you look over it again?
>   I hope you have been able to choose the stuffs—I don't think the oriental blue and red hanging is big enough for two curtains on landing at drawing-room—would you choose something for that place—and see my wife about them? I do hope to see things nearly ready when I come home—the coverings for settees especially.
>   I wish you were in Edinboro' with me—it is quite lovely—bits of it.
>   The house must be a success—do just add the bloom of colour to it in curtains and cushions.
>
> Ever yours,
> OSCAR

Godwin had little difficulty in explaining how "this new £100" was made up. Extra painting throughout the house accounted for £32; four coats of paint, with labour, to the outside cost a further £21. Then there were such items as "Japan gold paper" for the drawing-room, the study, and the bathroom (£12), "putting Mr Green's mistake right" (£12 17s) and the services of a night watchman (£5). Unfortunately for Wilde, there was worse to come, since the contractor sent in a further account shortly afterwards. "I am aghast at Sharpe's bill," Wilde expostulated. "His charges are worse than Green's. £3.9s for a screen of iron piping! £3.6s for hanging lamps!!! £9 for the man who [put up] an array of shelves which is ridiculous. Sharpe told me he had not made much over the furniture in Constance's room. It is clear what he is doing—over-claiming on other things."

Despite his grumbling about the expense, Wilde was far from ungrateful to the architect. "You have had a great deal of trouble over the house," he told him, "for which I thank you very much, and must insist on your honorarium being not ten but fifteen guineas at least." A few weeks later, he wrote again:

> I enclose a cheque and thank you very much for the beautiful designs of the furniture. Each chair is a sonnet in ivory, and the table is a masterpiece in pearl.
> Will you let me know what I owe you for the plan of the new room? I fear I cannot build it yet—money is as scarce as sunlight—but when I do I will look for your aid.

Unfortunately, Godwin was suffering from inflammation of the bladder, and he now retired to the country in the hope of effecting a cure. In April 1885, Wilde wrote to "Dear Godwino":

> I am glad you are resting—nature is a foolish place to look for inspiration in, but a charming one in which to forget one ever had any. Of course we miss you, but the white furniture reminds us of you daily, and we find a rose leaf can be laid on the ivory table without scratching it.
> We look forward to seeing you robust, and full of vigour. My wife sends her best wishes for your health.

But "Godwino" never recovered his health, although he submitted to the painful operation of lithotomy. A few months later he was dead. For Wilde he remained in the perspective of memory as the creator of his "house beautiful," the only home Wilde was ever able to call his own.

Meanwhile, the court proceedings initiated by Green had dragged their way through the usual interlocutory stages of a legal action. Eventually the plaintiff took out a summons to refer the matter to an arbitrator; this was agreed to, and the reference was set down for hearing in the Law Courts towards the end of May 1885. Unfortunately, when the time came, Godwin felt too ill to give evidence, but Wilde's solicitors, who were also Godwin's, begged him to attend for a few minutes so as to explain this to the arbitrator and ask for an adjournment. The result was that the hearing was adjourned for a month, and during this period Green's solicitors opened negotiations for a settlement.

Wilde left a note for Godwin at his club which the architect received on 22 June:

> There is a compromise proposed—but it means my paying £215! I cannot do that: but am ill with apprehension. It really rests on your evidence. If you cannot come my case is lost.

When this note was found among Godwin's papers after his death, it was seen to have been endorsed by the architect with these words: "Answered that my evidence was his always."

However, on the day before the adjourned hearing, the parties succeeded in coming to terms, so that Godwin did not have to go into the witness box after all. No record of the details has been discovered, although it is known that the settlement was based on the report of an independent surveyor. But assuming that Wilde had to pay the plaintiff's costs in addition to his own, he must have been out of pocket to the extent of at least £250.

So ended a protracted and irritating dispute. It was Wilde's first but not his last experience of the workings of the English law.

4

That Oscar and Constance Wilde were deeply in love with each other at the time of their marriage and for some years afterwards, certainly until after the birth of their second child in November 1886, is beyond dispute. Frank Harris in his controversial biography has described Constance as "a lady without particular qualities or beauty." This is demonstrably untrue, and is contradicted by her husband and also by others who knew her. She had received a good conventional education and could read and speak French and Italian fluently, besides which she was musical (which Oscar was not) and played the piano *con spirito*. She had literary interests too, and in the early days of their marriage she helped her husband with his journalistic work, as Speranza hoped she would. "I am thinking of becoming a correspondent to some paper, or else of going on the stage, *qu'en pensez-vous?*" she wrote to her brother shortly after the honeymoon. "I want to make some money: perhaps a novel would be better. At present I am deep in *Les Misérables,* which is wonderful."

Some of Oscar's biographers and others who have written about him, taking their cue from Frank Harris, have dwelt on her alleged stupidity. It would be fairer to say that as time went on she failed to keep pace with her husband's changing personality and that she was unable, in the popular word, to "cope." She had little if any sense of humour, and she neither appreciated nor in some instances understood her husband's brilliant and amusing talk.

"Mr and Mrs Oscar Wilde to tea," noted Laura Troubridge in her diary for 8 July 1884, "she dressed for the part in limp white muslin, with absolutely *no* bustle, saffron coloured silk swathed about her shoulders, a huge cartwheel Gainsborough hat, white and bright yellow stockings and shoes—she looked too hopeless and we thought her shy and dull. He was amusing of course."

According to Richard Le Gallienne, then a young poet whose acquaintance Wilde made while lecturing in Birkenhead and who was later to be a frequent guest in Tite Street, Constance was "evangelically religious" as well as humourless, and shared a particular interest in missionaries with her friend Lady Sandhurst, a prominent church worker of the period.

"Missionaries, my dear!" Wilde once remarked at a dinner party in Tite Street, as Le Gallienne has recalled, when the subject happened to come up. "Don't you realise that missionaries are the divinely provided food for destitute and under-fed cannibals? Whenever they are on the brink of starvation, Heaven, in its infinite mercy, sends them a nice plump missionary."

Upon which Constance exclaimed with a shocked expression, "Oh, Oscar! You cannot surely be in earnest. You can only be joking." It is less easy to accept the story, for which Hesketh Pearson is the authority, that on a similar occasion Constance interrupted one of her husband's characteristic monologues at table by asking, "Oh, Oscar, *did* you remember to call for Cyril's boots?" Their other son Vyvyan's comment on this unlikely tale is worth recalling: "In those days, no man of fashion would dream of being seen carrying a parcel through the streets of London, and furthermore no lady of the period would have thought of saddling her husband with such a domestic detail, when every middle-class household boasted at least two servants to fetch and carry . . . It is quite possible that, as is the habit of women, she interrupted a diatribe of which she did not wholly grasp the import, but it was certainly not *à propos de bottes.*"

The words used about Constance Wilde by Arthur Ransome, who wrote the first serious critical study of her husband, are a severe but not unjust judgment; there is no doubt that they precisely reflect the opinion of Robert Ross, who had plenty of opportunities for observing Constance at close quarters in Tite Street, and subsequently supplied Ransome with biographical material.

> She was sentimental, pretty, well-meaning and inefficient. She would have been very happy as the wife of an ornamental minor poet, and it is possible that in marrying Wilde she mistook him for such a character, It must be remembered that she married the author of *Poems* and the lecturer on the asethetic movement. His development puzzled her, made her feel inadequate, and so increased her inadequacy. She became more a spectacle for Wilde than an influence upon him, and was without the strength that might have prevented the disasters that were to fall through him on herself. She had a passion for leaving things alone, broken only by moments of interference badly timed. She became one of those women whose Christian names their husbands, without malice, preface with the epithets "poor dear." Her married life was no less ineffectual than unhappy.

For the first year of their marriage, little money came into Tite Street for housekeeping, since Oscar was almost entirely dependent upon his meagre fees from lecturing. Indeed, Constance was known to borrow occasionally from neighbours. In the second year Oscar was able to supplement his income by regular reviewing for *The Pall Mall Gazette,* with which he established a connection as the result of a letter he sent this journal for publication on the subject of women's dress. For the next two years he was to contribute an average of a review a month, mainly hack work which appeared anonymously and cannot have given Wilde much pleasure to produce. It was not until Constance came into her inheritance under her grandfather's will some years later that the family finances were more than marginally eased.

On 15 March 1885, Adrian Hope went to lunch at 16 Tite Street and afterwards described the house and its occupants in a letter to his fiancée Laura Troubridge:

> Through a thick fog I found my way to Tite Street and looked for a white door—which being opened let me into a very ordinary Hall passage painted white. Going up a staircase, also white, and covered with a whitish sort of matting, I found the whole of the landing cut off by a dark curtain from the staircase, leaving just room to turn round if you were going higher. I, however, went through the curtain and found rooms to the right and left of the little ante-rooms thus formed. The little man-servant showed me into the room on the left looking out across Tite Street on to the garden of the Victoria Hospital for Children. No fire and a look as if the furniture had been cleared out for a dance for which the matting did not look inviting. The walls, all white, the ceiling like yours a little (gold) but with two lovely dragons painted in the opposite corners of it. On either side of the fireplace, filling up the corners of the room, were two three-cornered divans, very low, with cushions, one tiny round Chippendale table, one arm-chair and three stiff other chairs, also covered with a sort of white lacquer. The arm-chair was a sort of curule chair and very comfy to sit on. This is the summer parlour. Nothing on the walls so as not to break the lines. Certainly a cool-looking room and ought to be seen in the long dog days. Effect on the whole better than it sounds.
>
> All the white paint (as indeed all the paint used about the house) has a high polish like Japanese lacquer work, which has great charm for one who hates paper on walls as much as I do.
>
> The room at the back has a very distinctly Turkish note. No chairs at all. A divan on two sides of the room, very low, with those queer little Eastern inlaid tables in front. A dark dado, but of what colour I know not, as the window, looking on a slum, they have entirely covered with a wooden grating on the inside copied from a Cairo pattern which considerably reduced the little light there was today. A gorgeous ceiling and a fire quite made me fall in love with this room and I thought how lovely someone would look sitting on the divan with her legs crossed and with a faithful slave kissing her pretty bare feet. Here Oscar joined me and presently appeared Constance with her brother and his wife. Lunch was in the dining room at the back on the ground floor . . . A cream coloured room with what Oscar assured me was the only sideboard in England, viz. a board running the whole length of the room and about nine inches wide at the height of the top of the wainscoting. Table of a dirty brown with a strange device: maroon napkins, like some rough bath towels, with deep fringes. Quaint glass and nice food made up a singularly picturesque table.
>
> Afterwards we went upstairs to see where the great Oscar sleeps. This room had nothing particular but hers was too delightful. You open the door only to find yourself about to walk through the opening in a wall apparently

three feet thick. When you get into the room you find that on the one side of the door, forming a side of the doorway, is an ideal wardrobe with every kind of drawer and hanging cupboard for dresses. Next to this again and between it and the corner of the room is a book-case and a writing table. All this is white and delightfully clean and fresh besides taking so little room. The writing-table is fixed to the book-case with kneehole, solid part drawers. The bed looked very soft and nice.

Upstairs again Oscar had knocked the garrets into one delightful room for himself in which he had his bath as well. The doors and woodwork of this room were vermilion with a dado of gold leaves on a vermilion ground giving a delicious effect of colour which I revelled in. Here I sat talking till half-past six and listening to Oscar who, dressed in a grey velvet Norfolk shooting jacket and looking fatter than ever, harangued away in a most amusing way.

The domestic expenses increased with the birth of their first child. " 'My wife has a cold' but in about a month will be over it," Oscar wrote to Godwin on 20 May 1885. "I hope it is a boy cold, but will love whatever the gods send." His hope was fulfilled a fortnight later, more quickly than he anticipated. Among those who wrote to congratulate the proud parents was a young man named Edward Heron-Allen, who dabbled in astrology and had recently written a book on violin-making which he sent Wilde. "Will you cast the child's horoscope for us?" Wilde replied to Heron-Allen's congratulations. "It was born [in Tite Street] at a quarter to eleven last Friday morning [5 June 1885]. My wife is very anxious to know its fate, and has begged me to ask you to search the stars."

"The baby is wonderful," wrote the father at the same time to his old friend Norman Forbes-Robertson; "it has a bridge to its nose! which the nurse says is a proof of genius! It also has a superb voice, which it freely exercises: its style is essentially Wagnerian. Constance is doing capitally and is in excellent spirits." The boy's birth was duly registered in the name of Cyril Wilde. No doubt Heron-Allen did cast the baby's horoscope, but the details have not survived. (Cyril was fated to be killed in action when barely thirty years old during the First World War.) Meanwhile, by a curious twist of fate, Heron-Allen, who was attracted by Constance Wilde, was to fall in love with her, while Wilde was attracted by Heron-Allen's youthful beauty and was to fall in love with him.

"Did you see the Wildes have a boy, I rather pity the infant, don't you?" Adrian Hope wrote to Laura Troubridge. The latter had not heard of the infant's arrival, and she replied: "I agree that it is much to be pitied. Will it be swathed in artistic baby clothes? Sage green bibs and tuckers, I suppose, and a peacock blue robe."

As godfather to Cyril his parents made what appears at first sight to be a rather curious choice in Walter Harris, a young man still up at Cambridge who had developed a strong passion for the Moslem countries and was to become *The Times* correspondent in Morocco, as well as an intrepid explorer of Arabia and the Sahara and other remote places. He seems to have been responsible for the Oriental decor of the smoking-room in Tite Street, with its divans, ottomans, Moorish hangings, and glass beads. He was eventually to settle in Tangier, where he shared a house for a time with R. B. Cunninghame Graham, and to adopt the Moslem faith, speaking Arabic fluently, wearing Moorish dress, dying his skin brown, and passing for a native. He told his godson, when Cyril was still quite a small boy, that he had once unwittingly attended a cannibal feast and had partaken of the fare, which he described as being "rather like a suckling-pig, but more delicate in flavour." Oscar probably met Walter Harris through Constance, since the Harris family seems to have been friendly with the Lloyds.

"Believe me it is impossible to live by literature," Wilde wrote at this time to a young unidentified correspondent who had sought his help in launching himself upon a career of letters. "By journalism you may make an income, but rarely by pure literary work . . . The best work in literature is always done by those who do not depend upon it for their daily bread, and the highest form of literature, poetry, brings no wealth to the singer. For producing your best work also you will require some leisure and freedom from sordid care."

Suiting his action to his words in his own case, since with the arrival of a child his household expenses were rising, Wilde's thoughts turned again to the post he had sought to obtain through the aid of Oscar Browning without success five years previously. This time he wrote to George Curzon, who had recently made his political debut by being adopted as a Conservative candidate for Parliament:

> I want to be one of Her Majesty's Inspectors of Schools! This is ambition—however, I want it, and want it very much, and I hope you will help me. Edward Stanhope has the giving away and, as a contemporary of mine at Oxford, you could give me great help by writing him a letter to say (if you think it) that I am a man of some brains. I won't trouble you with the reasons which make me ask for this post—but I want it and could do the work, I fancy, well . . .
>
> I hope to get this and to get it with your approval and your good word. I don't know Stanhope personally and am afraid he may take the popular view of me as a real idler. Will you tell him it is not so?

Curzon did as he was asked, although he was busy contesting his seat in the General Election. "I hope you will be successful," wrote Wilde in thanking him for his trouble. "Though I believe I am a Radical I should be sorry not to see Coningsby in the House." Wilde also enlisted the support of Mahaffy in Dublin; but, though he was put on the so-called "Education List" of candidates for a School Inspectorship, he was never appointed to one of these posts, possibly on account of the "popular view" he had indicated in his letter to Curzon. In fact, as has been seen, he was capable of sustained work when it was required. Unfortunately, he could never completely rid himself of the impression of dilettantism he had given in his aesthetic period.

Meanwhile, Constance Wilde was again pregnant. Her second child, another boy, was born in November 1886. The infant's father is said to have been disappointed, as he hoped for a girl, whom he intended to call Isola Deirdre after his dead sister, for whom he had entertained such a strong affection. The boy was named Vyvyan Oscar Beresford. His birth was not registered for several weeks, apparently as his father and mother each thought that the other had seen to it. When it was registered by Constance, neither parent could remember the exact date of birth, but both were sure that it was during the first five days of November. Thus the third was chosen as a happy medium. However, Vyvyan's uncle Otho Lloyd later told him that the real reason for "the apparent confusion" was that he was actually born on 5 November, "but that this fact was suppressed in order to avoid any possible connection between the Aesthetic Movement and Guy Fawkes Day."

Although Cyril and Vyvyan were never to see their father after 1895, their childhood memories of him were very happy. The younger son has left a vivid picture of him playing with his children.

> He was a real companion to us, and we always looked forward eagerly to his frequent visits to our nursery. Most parents in those days were far too solemn and pompous with their children, insisting on a vast amount of usually undeserved respect. My own father was quite different; he had so much of the child in his own nature that he delighted in playing our games. He would go down on all fours on the nursery floor, being in turn a lion, a wolf, a horse, caring nothing for his usually immaculate appearance. And there was nothing half-hearted in his methods of play. One day he arrived with a toy milk-cart drawn by a horse with real hair on it. All the harness undid and took off, and the churns with which the cart was filled could be removed and opened. When my father discovered this he immediately went downstairs and came back with a jug of milk with which he proceeded to fill up the churns. We then all tore round the nursery table, slopping milk all over the place, until the arrival of our nurse put an end to that game.
>
> Like other fathers he mended our toys; he spent most of one afternoon repairing a wooden fort that had come to pieces in the course of various wars, and when he had finished he insisted upon everyone in the house coming to see how well he had done it and to give him a little praise . . .
>
> When he grew tired of playing he would keep us quiet by telling us fairy stories, or tales of adventure, of which he had a never-ending supply. He was a great admirer of Jules Verne and Stevenson, and of Kipling in his more imaginative vein. The last present he gave me was *The Jungle Book;* he had already given me *Treasure Island* and Jules Verne's *Five Weeks in a Balloon,* which were the first books I read through entirely by myself. He told all his own written fairy stories suitably adapted for our young minds, and a great many others as well . . . Cyril once asked him why he had tears in his eyes when he told us the story of "The Selfish Giant," and he replied that really beautiful things always made him cry.

Richard Le Gallienne happened to be talking to Wilde in the drawing-room of his house in Tite Street one day when the two boys were also present. The forthcoming publication of *The Happy Prince and Other Tales,* which includes "The Selfish Giant," prompted Wilde to bring up the subject of fairy tales, as Le Gallienne was afterwards to recall.[16]

"It is the duty of every father," he said with great gravity, "to write fairy tales for his children. But the mind of a child is a great mystery. It is incalculable, and who shall divine it, or bring to it his own peculiar delights? You humbly spread before it the treasures of your imagination, and they are as dross. For example, a day or two ago, Cyril yonder came to me with the question, 'Father, do you ever dream?' 'Why of course, my darling. It is the first duty of a gentleman to dream.' 'And what do you dream of?' asked Cyril, with a child's disgusting appetite for facts. Then I, believing, of course, that something picturesque would be expected of me, spoke of magnificent things: 'What do I dream of? Oh, I dream of dragons with gold and silver scales, and scarlet things coming out of their mouths, of eagles with eyes made of diamonds that can see over the whole world at once, of lions with yellow manes, and voices like thunder, of elephants with little houses on their backs, and tigers and zebras with barred and spotted coats . . .' So I laboured on with my fancy, till, observing that Cyril was entirely unimpressed, and indeed quite undisguisedly bored, I came to a humiliating stop, and, turning to my son there, I said: 'But tell me, what do you dream of, Cyril?' His answer was like a divine revelation: 'I dream of *pigs,*' he said."

Wilde would also tell his children about Moytura, the family house on Lough Corrib, and of the "great melancholy carp" that never moved from the bottom of the lough unless he called them with the Irish songs he had learned from his father. He would sing these songs to the children. Vyvyan did not think he sang very well, but to both boys he had the most beautiful voice in the world. There was one song in particular he remembered, beginning *"Atha me in mu codladh, is na duishe me,"* and meaning, "I am asleep, do not wake me." Vyvyan was to come across it again when in later years he was trying to learn the Irish language himself. In addition, Wilde would recite what his younger son called "poems in prose." Many of these were never published. However, Wilde would also tell them to other children and their elders, one of whom subsequently wrote down several as she remembered them and gave them to Vyvyan.[17]

"My father lived in a world of his own" was his younger son's summing-up; "an artificial world, perhaps, but a world in which the only things that really mattered were art and beauty in all their forms. This gave him that horror of conventionality which destroyed him in the end."

[16] *The Happy Prince and Other Tales,* with illustrations by Walter Crane and Jacob Hood, was published by David Nutt. It consisted of an ordinary edition and a large paper edition limited to seventy-five numbered copies, each signed by the author and the publisher. Wilde's own copy (No. 2) from which he used to read to his children, was bought by a bookdealer at the sheriff's sale of Wilde's effects in April 1895. It is now in the Donald F. Hyde collection in New Jersey.

[17] "The Poet," "The Actress," "Simon of Cyrene," and "Jezebel" were subsequently published by Vyvyan Holland in his autobiography, *Son of Oscar Wilde* (1954), pp. 257–64.

5

In April 1887, Oscar Wilde at last found a means of supplementing his income from journalism when he accepted an offer from the publishing house of Cassell to become the editor of a new magazine. The periodical had been launched the previous November under the title *The Lady's World* as a shilling monthly "Magazine of Fashion and Society," with the expressed object of giving its readers details of the latest "Dress and Fashion of the highest class" as well as "the doings of Society at Home and Abroad," fully illustrated and "thus affording a mirror of English Society at the present day in its most attractive aspects" and describing "ladies of position, with a pictorial account of their homes and surroundings." The offer was conveyed to Wilde by Cassell's general manager Thomas Wemyss Reid, who sent Wilde several issues and at the same time asked him how he thought its style and quality might be improved. This suggests that the initial venture had not proved as successful as the publishers had hoped—hence the engagement of a new and more original editor.

Wilde replied tactfully that he "would be very glad to join with" Wemyss Reid in "the work of editing and to some extent reconstructing" *The Lady's World.*

> It seems to me that at present it is too feminine, and not sufficiently womanly. No one appreciates more fully than I do the value and importance of Dress, in its relation to good taste and good health: indeed the subject is one that I have constantly lectured on before Institutes and Societies of various kinds, but it seems to me that . . . the field of mere millinery and trimmings is to some extent already occupied by such papers as *The Queen* and *The Lady's Pictorial,* and that we should take a wider range, as well as a high standpoint, and deal not merely with what women wear, but with what they think, and what they feel. *The Lady's World* should be made the recognised organ for the expression of women's opinions on all subjects of literature, art, and modern life, and yet it should be a magazine that men could read with pleasure, and consider it a privilege to contribute to.

"All women are flattered by being asked to write," the editor-designate told Wemyss Reid. Accordingly, with the help of his friend Mrs Jeune, he compiled a list of potential contributors ranging from Princess Christian of Schleswig-Holstein and the Queen of Roumania to professionals like Olive Schreiner, Marie Corelli, "Ouida," Constance Fletcher ("George Fleming"), and Mrs Alfred Hunt, all of whom he proposed to ask for contributions. "Literary criticism I think might be done in the form of paragraphs," he went on; "that is to say, not from the standpoint of the scholar or the pedant, but from the standpoint of what is pleasant to read: if a book is dull, let us say nothing about it, if it is bright let us review it." There should also be news from the women's colleges at Oxford and Cambridge. ("We must have the Universities on our side.") For instance, "the wife of the young President of Magdalen, Oxford [Mrs Herbert Warren] might write on her own college, or, say on the attitude of Universities towards women from the earliest times down to the present—a subject never fully treated of." Finally, the magazine should have a new cover, since "the present one is not satisfactory."

With a new cover we should start our new names, and try and give the magazine a *cachet* at once: let dress have the end of the magazine; literature, art, travel and social studies the beginning. Music in a magazine is somewhat dull, no one wants it; a children's column would be much more popular. A popular serial story is absolutely necessary for the start. It need not be by a woman, and should be exciting but not tragic.

Although the first number of the magazine with its new look was not planned to appear until November, there was plenty of preliminary work to be done, so that Wilde was engaged from the beginning of May at a salary of six pounds a week. "It is absolutely necessary to start at once," he told Reid, "and I have already devoted a great deal of time to devising the scheme, and having interviews with people of position and importance." He certainly earned his salary at the start, as he wrote scores of letters to women he thought might provide articles; he also made trips to Paris to engage a local correspondent and to the women's colleges at Oxford and Cambridge. "The magazine will try to be representative of the thought and culture of the women of this century," he explained to Nellie Sickert, "and I am very anxious that those who have had university training, like yourself, should have an organ through which they can express their views on life and things." He added that the honorarium was a guinea a page, "which is the same as *The Nineteenth Century* pays, and more than most of the magazines." He suggested that she might write an article on "the value of Political Economy in education," and if she was interested she should come with her mother to one of Constance's Thursday "At Homes" to talk over the matter. Miss Nellie did as she was asked and produced an article described by the editor as "brightly and pleasantly written" and eventually published as "The Evolution of Economics."

Shortly before the first issue went to press, Wilde begged Cassell's directors to change the title from *The Lady's World* to *The Woman's World*. "The present name of the magazine has a certain taint of vulgarity about it that will always militate against the success of the new issue and is also extremely misleading," he wrote to Reid. "It is quite applicable to the magazine in its present state; it will not be applicable to a magazine that aims at being the organ of women of intellect, culture and position." The directors were agreeable and the first issue of *The Woman's World,* with a new cover decorated in pink and printed in dark red, with Wilde's name as editor on the title page, duly went on sale towards the end of November 1887.[18]

[18] The change in the title had been suggested to Wilde by Mrs Craik, the author of the best-selling novel *John Halifax Gentleman.* Wilde hoped she would be a regular contributor, but her sudden death at the age of fifty-one prevented her from writing more than one article. This was on Miss Mary Anderson in *The Winter's Tale* and appeared posthumously in the December issue. Mrs Craik, born Dinah Mullock, was married to

The initial reception of the new periodical was encouraging, and for a time the editor was warmly congratulated on his journalistic venture. As his mother's friend Anna Comtesse de Brémont put it, "He was at once a man of importance in the eyes of all those ladies who adopted a literary role as a pleasant pastime or a means of local celebrity. There was a flutter in the boudoirs of Mayfair and Belgravia when *The Woman's World* appeared. Lady Wilde's Saturdays were thronged. Ladies of high degree and ladies of no degree—poets and painters, artists and art critics, writers and scribblers, all eager to attain a place in the pages of the new magazine." In short, Society began to take Oscar Wilde seriously for the first time.

The Times went out of its way to be gracious, declaring that *The Woman's World,* "gracefully got up as it is in every respect, has taken a high place among the illustrated magazines." The larger engravings were singled out for particular praise. Also, "Mr Wilde has been fortunate in securing the assistance of the best known lady authors of the day. He has the honour by the way of numbering Princess Christian among his contributors, and she writes with knowledge and sympathy on nursing the sick." The editor himself wrote the "Literary and Other Notes," including the book reviews. The Princess Christian had recently translated *The Memoirs of Wilhelmine Margravine of Bayreuth* from the German, and it was not surprising that Wilde should have led off with a flattering review of "a most delightful and fascinating book," drawing special attention to the literary Princess's "admirably written introduction," in which she had pointed out that the Margravine and her brother King Frederick the Great of Prussia were "among the first of those questioning minds that strove after spiritual freedom" in the eighteenth century.

The second number contained a characteristic review of *Gossips with Girls and Maidens,* a highly moral work by a certain Lady Bellairs on women's mental and physical training. Under the heading "What to Avoid" were "Sudden exclamations of annoyance, surprise and joy— often dangerously approaching to 'female swearing'—as 'Bother!' 'Gracious!' 'How jolly!' " and "Entertaining wild flights of the imagination, or empty idealistic aspirations." On this the reviewer wrote:

> I am afraid that I have a good deal of sympathy with what are called "empty idealistic aspirations"; and "wild flights of imagination" are so extremely rare in the nineteenth century that they seem to me deserving rather of praise than of censure. The exclamation "Bother," also, though certainly lacking in beauty, might, I think, be permitted under circumstances of extreme aggravation, such as, for instance, the rejection of a manuscript by the editor of a magazine; but in all other respects the list seems to me to be quite excellent.

G. L. Craik, a partner in Macmillan & Co., the publishers. "Few women have enjoyed a greater popularity than Mrs Craik, or have better deserved it," wrote Wilde in the obituary tribute in *The Woman's World* (November 1887). "It is sometimes said that John Halifax is not a real man, but only a woman's ideal of a man. Well, let us be grateful for such ideals. No one can read the story of which John Halifax is the hero without being the better for it."

At first Wilde carried out his editorial duties with marked zest, continuing to write to contributors and suggesting subjects for articles from cookery to corsets and from shorthand to servants. Greatly daring, he wrote to Queen Victoria asking whether she had any early verses of her own which he might publish. His letter has not survived, but the Queen's reaction to the request has been preserved in the form of a minute in her own hand:

> Really what will people not say and invent? Never c[oul]d the Queen in her whole life write *one line* of *poetry* serious or comic or make a *Rhyme* even. This is therefore all *invention* & *a myth.*

Lady Wilde contributed five "Irish Peasant Tales," while Constance wrote an illustrated article on women's muffs, obtaining the historical background from the British Museum. A number of male writers, including Oscar Browning, Gleeson White, and Arthur Symons, also contributed articles.

On the days that he went to Cassell's editorial offices in La Belle Sauvage Yard, off Ludgate Hill, usually thrice a week, Wilde would walk from Tite Street to Sloane Square underground station, take the Inner Circle line to Charing Cross, and continue his walk along Fleet Street past Ludgate Circus. But after a time his enthusiasm showed signs of waning, particularly as Cassell's did not allow smoking in their offices and Wilde had by this time developed a strong liking for Turkish cigarettes. Arthur Fish, his assistant editor, was to recall:

> At first the work was taken quite seriously and 11 o'clock on his appointed morning saw the poet entering the dingy portals of "the Yard," but after a few months his arrival became later and his departure earlier, until at times his visit was little more than a call. After a very short time in my association with him I could tell by the sound of his approach along the resounding corridor whether the necessary work to be done would be met cheerfully or postponed to a more congenial period. In the latter case he would sink with a sigh into his chair, carelessly glance at his letters, give a perfunctory look at proofs or make-up, ask "Is it necessary to settle anything today?", put on his hat, and, with a sad "Good-morning," depart again.
>
> On his cheerful days, however, everything was different. These were fairly constant in the spring days of the year: there would be a smiling entrance, letters would be answered with epigrammatic brightness, there would be a cheery interval of talk when the work was accomplished, and the dull room would brighten under the influence of his great personality.

For Arthur Fish, who was to spend the whole of his working life with Casssell's and eventually to become chief editor of their publications, Wilde developed a strong affection. He was especially touched when Fish remembered his birthday after he had ceased to edit *The Woman's World.* Fish had recently got married, and Wilde wrote to him: "Though we see each other so rarely, I always think of you as one of my real friends, as I hope you will always think of me . . . How happy you must be in your little house; there are only two things in the world of any importance, Love and Art; you have both; they must never leave you."

During his time at Cassell's, Fish could remember only a single occasion when Wilde's temper was roused. That was when John Williams, who was then chief editor, read Wilde a passage from a book entitled *People I've Smiled With* by M. P. Wilder, an American author, which Cassell's was thinking of bringing out in an English edition.

The first time I saw Oscar he wore his hair long and his breeches short; now, I believe, he wears his hair short and his trousers long.

Wilde was furious. "Monstrous! Perfectly monstrous!" he exclaimed as he strode up and down the room. Accordingly, the offending reference was deleted.

Another story about Wilde at this period concerns the poet W. E. Henley, who edited the *Magazine of Art,* another of Cassell's publications. Edwin Bale, the painter who managed the firm's art department, admired both Wilde and Henley, although he realized that they were mutually opposed in their habits and attitudes towards the aesthetic movement. He determined to bring them together, and for this purpose invited them both to dine at his house along with some others. "Wilde completely won over Henley, the latter insisting that Wilde should drive home with him to Chiswick, and at three in the morning they left together in a hansom cab," Bale afterwards recalled. "I saw Wilde next day and he told me that they had 'sat and babbled' at Chiswick till nine o'clock."

Henley next invited Wilde to lunch with him at the Savile Club, and offered to propose him for membership. "That is of course one of your merry jests," wrote Wilde in accepting the invitation. Nevertheless, Wilde was anxious to join the club and a few weeks later his name appeared in the Candidates' Book. But, although his candidature was supported by more than thirty members besides Henley, including Henry James, Edmund Gosse, Rider Haggard, Walter Besant, Herbert Warren, George Macmillan, and J. W. Mackail, he was never elected. It is not the practice in the Savile Club to "blackball" a candidate whose election has encountered opposition. His proposer simply withdraws his name and the election is not proceeded with. This is what happened in Wilde's case. It would appear to show that, in spite of his strong support from so many distinguished members, he already had powerful enemies who were determined not to have him among them.

Another visit to Chiswick on a Saturday night had to be postponed as Henley's mother was very seriously ill. "I am so sorry to hear about your trouble," Wilde wrote to him. "All poets love their mothers, and as I worship mine I can understand how you feel." At this time Wilde was getting up a memorial to obtain a government pension for his mother. "I am trying to get her name added to the civil list, and have some hopes of success," he told Edward Dowden, Professor of English Literature at Trinity College, Dublin, at this time. Gladstone, whom he approached, felt unable to sign the memorial as so many similar demands were made upon him, but others of influence did so, including the Trinity historian W. E. H. Lecky and the Hon. David Plunket, later Lord Rathmore, who was M.P. for Dublin University and a member of the government. Eventually, in 1890, Speranza was awarded a civil list pension of £70 a year. From time to time Oscar would also give her money, sometimes champagne as well. "Best and kindest of sons," she called him. "My best aid and comforter . . . Good and kind and generous you are . . . All my help comes from you ever since you began an income in America."

After the first five numbers of *The Woman's World,* the editor ceased to write any further "Literary and Other Notes," and for the next eight months no contributions from his pen appeared in the journal. When eventually taken to task by the directors, he complained that he did not feel qualified to write on current topics. "There are many things in which women are interested about which a man really cannot write," he told Wemyss Reid, and suggested that some well-known woman should be engaged for this purpose. As for his literary criticism, he felt this should be anonymous. "Literary subjects are the only subjects on which I care to write," he added, "and even in this sphere I have felt myself hampered by my name being attached." But Cassell's were paying for his name and the directors refused to allow his literary notes to appear anonymously, although they excused him from continuing to write on the other topics, of which the following example taken from the issue of March 1888 is a typical example:

> Miss May Morris, whose exquisite needlework is well known, has just completed a pair of curtains for a house in Boston. They are the most perfect specimens of modern embroidery that I have seen, and are from Miss Morris's own design. I am glad to hear that Miss Morris has determined to give lessons in embroidery. She has a thorough knowledge of the art, her sense of beauty is as rare as it is refined, and her power of design is quite remarkable.[19]

Wilde was aware, as were the directors, that circulation was falling. Hence he urged that the price should be reduced to sixpence or sevenpence. ("At present it is too dear.") But again the directors would not agree. Their remedy to boost sales was what Wilde considered a retrograde step, namely that more space should be given to dress and fashion, and an announcement to this effect was duly made. At the same time Wilde evidently promised to mend his ways. He put on a sudden spurt, since the December number for 1888 contained two contributions from him. The first was a long review of a French book on the history of embroidery and lace, on which incidentally he was to draw for the description of embroideries in *The Picture of Dorian Gray.* The other review was of

[19] May Morris (1862–1938) was a younger daughter of the poet and artist William Morris, whose life she wrote. She was an expert embroiderer, and Bernard Shaw is said to have been in love with her at one time. She also collected autographs, and Wilde sent her those of Henry Irving and Ellen Terry among others.

the published verses of "Some Modern Poets," including Henley. ("If he took himself more seriously, his work would become trivial.") Then, for the first six numbers of 1889, he contributed "Some Literary Notes." But by March the directors had already had enough of him, and he was given six months' notice terminating his editorship of *The Woman's World*. Yet he was generally liked in the office even by the directors who sacked him. Henley's services were also dispensed with at this time, but for a different reason. Talking to the Irish poet W. B. Yeats about the relative merits of Henley and Wilde as editors, a senior member of the Cassell's staff blamed Henley, who was "no use except under control," while praising Wilde, "so indolent but such a genius."

Incidentally, Yeats, who was then twenty-three years old, had recently come to London and had first met Wilde in Henley's house. In December 1888, as he was at a loose end for Christmas, Wilde invited him to eat his Christmas dinner in Tite Street, which the young poet was glad to do. "I was delighted by his pretty wife and children, and his beautiful house designed by Godwin," Yeats afterwards recalled. "He had a white dining room, the first I had seen, chairs, walls, cushions all white, but in the middle of the table a red cloth table-centre with a red terracotta statue and above it a red hanging lamp. I have never and shall never meet conversation that could match his. Perplexed by my own shapelessness, my lack of self-possession and of easy courtesy, I was astonished by this scholar who as a man of the world was so perfect."

Wilde had just written an essay, "The Decay of Lying," subsequently reprinted in his *Intentions*, for the following month's *Nineteenth Century* and he was correcting the proofs, from which he read extracts to his guest. "Ah, Yeats," he said when he finished, "we Irish are too poetical to be poets; we are a nation of brilliant failures." In this context he admired Smith O'Brien, Daniel O'Connel, and Charles Stewart Parnell, and he praised Balzac for placing O'Connel among the three principal figures of the first half of the nineteenth century.

Unlike Yeats, however, Wilde has sometimes been blamed for "not putting Irish things into his writings, for not making them definitely Irish," as his Irish-American contemporary Vincent O'Sullivan has put it. But there have been writers in all countries whose writings bear no trace of geographic or ethnic accidents. As for Wilde, he wrote largely in a vacuum. "His works have value not as pictures of a life in a given place, but as pictures of ideas. The ideas are not always first-rate; but what of that? It is not the idea in itself which counts, but the power which lies within it to excite and inspire. It was as alien to his genius as to the genius of Watteau to give realistic pictures of life in Ireland or anywhere."

To return to Henley and *The Woman's World*. Henley now went off to Edinburgh to become editor of *The Scots Observer*. Before he left the Belle Sauvage, he asked Wilde, "How often do you go to the office?"

"I used to go three times a week for an hour a day," replied Wilde, "but I have since struck off one of the days."

"My God!" exclaimed Henley. "I went five times a week for five hours a day, and when I wanted to strike off a day they had a special committee meeting."

"Furthermore," continued Wilde, "I never answered their letters. I have known men come to London full of bright prospects and seen them complete wrecks in a few months through a habit of answering letters."

One letter addressed to him at the office which Wilde did answer at this time was a final demand from the local Inspector of Taxes, and even here his habitual sense of humour did not desert him. He began by pointing out to this importunate official that it had been arranged in the previous year that he should send in his income tax return from Chelsea, where he lived, and as he was "resigning" his position and would not be with Messrs Cassell after August, he thought it would be better to continue that arrangement. "I wish your notices were not so agitating and did not hold out such dreadful threats," he added. "A penalty of fifty pounds sounds like a relic of mediaeval torture."

In July 1889, shortly before Wilde left Cassell's, *Blackwood's Edinburgh Magazine,* commonly called "Maga," published an ingenious piece of Shakespearian research by Wilde entitled "The Portrait of Mr W.H.," in which the author advanced the theory that the "Mr W.H.," for whom the poet wrote his sonnets, was not William Herbert, Earl of Pembroke, as has generally been supposed, but a boy actor named Willie Hughes.[20] In an unsigned notice, *The Scots Observer* remarked: "With the exception of one article which is out of place in *Maga*—or, indeed, in any popular magazine—the July number of *Blackwood* is particularly good." This reference prompted Wilde to write in his usual bantering mood to Henley:

> To be exiled to Scotland to edit a Tory paper in the wilderness is bad enough, but not to see the wonder and beauty of my discovery of the real Mr W.H. is absolutely dreadful. I sympathise deeply with you, and can only beg you to return to London where you will be able to appreciate a real work of art.
>
> The Philistines in their vilest form have seized on you. I am so disappointed.
>
> Still, when you return you will be welcome; all is not lost.

With the exception of Wilde, the tradition of editorial anonymity had always prevailed at Cassell's—not even Henley had his name on the cover of his magazine. With Wilde's departure, the directors reverted to tradition in *The Woman's World,* with a new anonymous editor who was probably Arthur Fish. But the revival of the old "fashion and society" features failed to stop the rot, and *The Woman's World* ceased publication in the autumn of 1890. The truth was that the magazine had been too ambitious—and also too highbrow, as was *The Paris Mode and*

[20] Subsequently reprinted in *Lord Arthur Savile's Crime and Other Prose Pieces* (1908). Wilde later expanded the essay with a view to separate publication by John Lane. On the history of the manuscript, which was lost for many years, see below pp. 233–4. It was eventually published in a limited edition in 1921, and has since been republished.

Woman's Journal, which succeeded it. This was killed by the new type of woman's journal, like *Home Chat,* brought out by a brilliant young man in Fleet Street named Alfred Harmsworth, who formed a company in 1891 for the publication of women's magazines. While *The Woman's World* was a signal failure, the "bittier" *Home Chat* was to prove a gold mine, one of many, for the future Lord Northcliffe.

6

"The basis of literary friendship is mixing the poisoned bowl," Wilde remarked to his fellow countryman W. B. Yeats when they met in 1888 for the first time in Henley's house. Soon, as Yeats observed, Henley began mixing the poisoned bowl for Wilde. Whistler had been doing this for several years. His mixture was prompted by his resentment at Wilde continuing to lecture on art, a subject on which Whistler considered that Wilde was not really qualified to speak with authority, although it will be remembered that the painter had supplied Wilde with some notes for the lecture he gave to an audience of London art students shortly after his return from America. Although Wilde cut down his lectures after contracting a severe chill "caught by lecturing in a Lincolnshire snowstorm" at the beginning of 1885, and with his increasing journalistic commitments he soon stopped lecturing altogether, Whistler kept up his sniping. The famous "Ten O'Clock Lecture" which Whistler gave on art, and in which he referred to Benjamin West and Paul Delaroche, prompted Wilde, besides reviewing it for *The Pall Mall Gazette,* to write to "Dear Butterfly" with the information that with the aid of a biographical dictionary he had discovered there were once two painters of those names "who recklessly took to lecturing on art."

> As of their works nothing at all remains, I conclude that they explained themselves away. Be warned in time, James; and remain, as I do, incomprehensible. To be great is to be misunderstood.

In November 1886, Whistler wrote to the committee of the National Art Exhibition, castigating them for listening to Wilde and so bringing on themselves "the scorn and ridicule of your *confrères* in Europe." He continued:

> What has Oscar in common with Art? except that he dines at our tables and picks from our platters the plums for the pudding he peddles in the provinces.
> Oscar—the amiable, irresponsible, esurient Oscar—with no more sense of a picture than of the fit of a coat, has the courage of the opinions . . . of others!

And again:

> Oscar went forth as my St John, but, forgetting that humility should be his chief characteristic and unable to withstand the unaccustomed respect with which his utterances were received, he not only trifled with my shoe but bolted with the latchet!

"With our James 'vulgarity begins at home' and should be allowed to stay there," Wilde replied. To this Whistler retorted: " 'A poor thing,' Oscar!—but, for once, I suppose, 'your own.' "

Many of the exchanges which passed between Wilde and Whistler were published at the time by Edmund Yates in *The World*. But when Whistler reprinted them a few years later in *The Gentle Art of Making Enemies* (1890), the two men were no longer on speaking terms. The final breach was caused by Wilde's appropriation of Whistler's phrase about his having the courage of the opinions of others in "The Decay of Lying." Some months later, after his attention had been drawn to this by a writer named Herbert Vivian, Whistler sent a letter to *Truth,* which was published, accusing Wilde of plagiarism. In this Whistler behaved "with both venom and vulgarity," as Wilde described the "impertinence" of the painter's attack upon him. Wilde continued with what was to be his last word on "The Butterfly":

> The definition of a disciple as one who has the courage of the opinions of his master is really too old even for Mr Whistler to be allowed to claim it, and as for borrowing Mr Whistler's ideas about art, the only thoroughly original ideas I have ever heard him express have had reference to his own superiority over painters greater than himself.

Later in 1890, Wilde's sense of professional pride was perhaps more deeply wounded by an anonymous attack upon his work published in Henley's paper *The Scots Observer,* since this called in question his whole conception of the relationship of art and morality. On leaving *The Woman's World* Wilde had written a novel, his only one, *The Picture of Dorian Gray;* he is stated to have received £200 for the serial rights in it. The original version appeared in *Lippincott's Monthly Magazine* for July 1890, published in Philadelphia; it came out in the same month under the London imprint of Ward, Lock & Co., which later published the work as a book after the author had made certain changes in the text and added six new chapters. The attack in *The Scots Observer* was written by Charles Whibley, a journalist who assisted Henley on the paper and shared his high Tory views on literature and art. Although Henley may not have directly inspired the attack, it was certainly made with his approval, and Wilde was deeply hurt by the attitude of a man whose colleague he had been at Cassell's, who had supported his candidature for election to the Savile Club, and whom he regarded as his friend.

Whibley's notice appeared under the heading "Reviews and Magazines" in *The Scots Observer* on 5 July 1890 in the following terms:

> Why go grubbing in muck heaps? The world is fair, and the proportion of healthy-minded men and honest women to those that are foul, fallen and unnatural, is great. Mr Oscar Wilde has again been writing stuff that were better unwritten; and while "The Picture of Dorian Gray," which he contributes to *Lippincott's* is ingenious, interesting, full of cleverness, and plainly the work of a man of letters, it is false art—for its interest is medico-legal; it is false to human nature—for its hero is a devil; it is false to morality—for it is not made sufficiently clear that the writer does not prefer a course of un-

natural iniquity to a life of cleanliness, health and sanity. The story—which deals with matters fitted only for the Criminal Investigation Department or a hearing *in camera*—is discreditable alike to author and editor. Mr Wilde has brains, and art, and style; but if he can write for none but outlawed noblemen and perverted telegraph-boys, the sooner he takes to tailoring (or some other decent trade) the better for his own reputation and the public morals.

The reference to the noblemen and the telegraph-boys, concerned in the so-called Cleveland Street scandal, was particularly offensive. The scandal involved two ducal offspring, Lord Arthur Somerset and the Earl of Euston, who were said to have frequented a homosexual brothel off the Tottenham Court Road, where telegraph-boys from the General Post Office were able to earn additional money by going to bed with the Cleveland Street establishment's aristocratic customers.[21] There is no evidence that Wilde ever went to the house in Cleveland Street, but Henley may have thought that he did so or at least had been active in a homosexual circle, since the editor, who had evidently heard some gossip, is on record as having asked Whibley what was the nature of "this dreadful scandal about Mr Oscar Wilde."

So far as Whibley's notice was concerned, Wilde made a calm and dignified rejoinder in the form of a letter which the editor published the following week:

> Your reviewer suggests that I do not make it sufficiently clear whether I prefer virtue to wickedness or wickedness to virtue. An artist, sir, has no ethical sympathies at all. Virtue and wickedness are to him simply what the colours on his palette are to the painter. They are no more, and they are no less. He sees that by their means a certain artistic effect can be produced and he produces it. Iago may be morally horrible and Imogen stainlessly pure. Shakespeare, as Keats said, had as much delight in creating the one as he had in creating the other.
>
> It was necessary, sir, for the dramatic development of this story to surround Dorian Gray with an atmosphere of moral corruption. Otherwise the story would have had no meaning and the plot no issue. To keep this atmosphere vague and indeterminate and wonderful was the aim of the artist who wrote the story. I claim, sir, that he has succeeded. Each man sees his own sin in Dorian Gray. What Dorian Gray's sins are no one knows. He who finds them has brought them.

Henley added a brief editorial comment on Wilde's letter which was designed to lower the temperature and to take the argument into a less perilous arena:

> It was not to be expected that Mr Wilde would agree with his reviewer as to the artistic merits of his booklet. Let it be conceded to him that he has succeeded in surrounding his hero with such an atmosphere as he describes. That is his reward. It is none the less legitimate for a critic to hold and express the opinion that no treatment, however skilful, can make the atmo-

---

[21] For the details of the Cleveland Street scandal, see the present writer's *Their Good Names* (1970), pp. 94–120; also his forthcoming work on the scandal based on official and other papers which have recently become available.

sphere tolerable to his readers. That is his punishment. No doubt it is the artist's privilege to be nasty; but he must exercise that privilege at his peril.

In fact, Henley had not read the story. "I wish I had," he admitted to Whibley; "for if he keeps us to our first utterance, he has us in a tight place. Our second has *him*, I think; but he's a dexterous and a slippery bitch." The editor may well have been afraid that Whibley had gone too far and that if Wilde chose to sue for libel a defence of fair comment would not succeed. Five years later, when Wilde prosecuted Lord Queensberry on a charge of criminal libel, the defence at the outset sought to justify the libellous statement that Wilde was posing as a homosexual by quoting extracts from the magazine version of *Dorian Gray;* in the absence of the damning evidence which came into the possession of Queensberry's solicitors, after Wilde had begun his proceedings, it is doubtful whether Queensberry could have proved his case to the satisfaction of the jury on the basis of these extracts alone.

The result of Whibley's and other hostile reviews was that W. H. Smith & Son, the retail newsagents and booksellers, informed Ward, Lock, the publishers and distributors, that the story "having been characterised by the press as a filthy one," they were compelled to withdraw the July issue of *Lippincott's Magazine* from their bookstalls. "We need not say that this is a serious matter for us," Ward, Lock wrote to Wilde informing him of this on 10 July 1890. "If you are in the City during the next day or two, we should be glad if you could give us a call." [22]

Among Wilde's friends who complimented him on the book was Arthur Fish, who had been his assistant editor on *The Woman's World* and was now about to get married. "Lord Henry Wotton's views on marriage are quite monstrous, and I highly disapprove of them," wrote Wilde to Fish. "I am delighted you like *Dorian Gray*—it has been attacked on ridiculous grounds, but I think it will be ultimately recognised as a real work of art with a strong ethical lesson inherent in it. Where are you going for your honeymoon?" Later in the same year Wilde again wrote to Fish, telling him about the production of *Dorian Gray* in book form. "Ricketts has just done for me a lovely cover for *Dorian Gray*—grey pastel-paper with a white back and tiny gold marigolds. When it appears I will send you a copy."

The critics were kinder when the book came out the following spring. "*Dorian Gray,* with all its faults, is a wonderful book," wrote W. B. Yeats, while Walter Pater praised it in a long review in *The Bookman* under the heading "A Novel by Mr Oscar Wilde." In this the author of *Marius the Epicurean* observed:

> There is always something of an excellent talker about the writing of Mr Oscar Wilde; and in his hands, as happens so rarely with those who practise

[22] A copy of Ward, Lock's letter subsequently came into Queensberry's hands and enabled Edward Carson, his counsel in the first trial, to strengthen the case against Wilde for allegedly "posing as a sodomite," when Carson came to cross-examine him on *Dorian Gray* and his other writings.

it, the form of dialogue is justified by its being really alive. His genial, laughter-loving sense of life and its enjoyable intercourse, goes far to obviate any crudity there may be in the paradox, with which, as with the bright and shining truth which often underlies it, Mr Wilde, startling his "countrymen," carries on, more perhaps than any other writer, the brilliant critical work of Matthew Arnold . . .

Dorian himself, though certainly a quite unsuccessful experiment in Epicureanism, in life as a fine art, is (till his inward spoiling takes visible effect suddenly, and in a moment, at the end of his story) a beautiful creation. But his story is also a vivid, though carefully considered, exposure of the corruption of a soul, with a very plain moral pushed home, to the effect that vice and crime make people coarse and ugly.

The story of Dorian Gray and his picture suggested itself to Wilde quite by chance. Frances Richards, the young Canadian artist whom he had met in Ottawa and introduced to Whistler, had studied art in Paris and later came back to London to get married and settle in England. When she met Wilde again, she asked if she could paint a portrait of him. After the sittings were over, he looked at the result and exclaimed, "What a tragic thing it is! The portrait will never grow older, and I shall. If it was only the other way!"

7

At this time Miss Richards, later Mrs W. E. Rowley, was friendly with a fellow Canadian and widow named Augusta Ross, then living in London with her children. Mrs Ross, who was a daughter of Robert Baldwin, the first Premier of Upper Canada under responsible government, had married John Ross, Q.C., an Ulsterman who had emigrated to Canada with his parents as a child and who was Attorney-General in her father's government. When John Ross died in 1869, shortly after the birth of his third son, Robert Baldwin Ross, he left instructions that his children were to be brought up in Europe. Mrs Ross, who had been left quite comfortably off, consequently took them to London. It is quite likely that it was through Frances Richards that Wilde made the acquaintance of the Ross family, notably Robert and his elder brother Alexander ("Alec"). The first meeting with Robert, known as "Bobbie" and later "Robbie," is said to have taken place in 1886 in Oxford, where young Robert may have been having some private tutoring to prepare him for the university. The following year he stayed in Tite Street with the Wildes for two months, possibly as a paying guest, while his mother was abroad, as she liked to spend the winters in the south of France. Oscar Wilde and Robert Ross, who was thirteen years younger, were to become close friends, and eventually Ross was to become the elder man's literary executor. No more may be noted on the nature of their relations at this point than that Ross was homosexual and that, as will be seen, there are strong grounds for believing that it was with him that Wilde first deliberately experimented in homosexual practices.

"I congratulate you," Wilde wrote to Robert Ross in October 1888 on learning that he was going up to King's College, Cambridge. "University life will suit you admirably, though I shall miss you in town . . . Are you in College or lodgings? I hope in College; it is much nicer. Do you know Oscar Browning? You will find him everything that is nice and pleasant." He added that he had just been to Stratford-upon-Avon, where he had proposed the health of his old friend Lord Ronald Gower at the unveiling of Gower's statue of Shakespeare in the gardens of the Memorial Theatre, but "in spite of that" had enjoyed himself immensely. "My reception was semi-royal, and the volunteers played God Save the Queen in my honour."

Ross's university career was brief and came to an abrupt and unhappy end. He was ducked in the Fountain at King's by some of the college "hearties" for being an "aesthete," and this despite the fact that he had rowed in the college boat, which contrary to the traditions of King's rowing had gone up two places on the river. In March 1889, Oscar Browning wrote to his mother:

> Poor dear Ross has been seized with a violent brain attack, the result of the outrage preying upon his mind. He was taken suddenly ill on Friday night and was so bad that I was not allowed to see him. They were afraid that he would kill himself. However his brother came down and was able to take him to London. Poor fellow! I was afraid that something of the kind would happen. He is terribly sensitive, and though he bore the thing itself bravely, yet it was always preying upon his mind. I do not know what will become of him. I cannot tell you how distressed we all are about it. His friends are devoted to him.

Although those who were responsible for the incident expressed their regret, the victim did not return to Cambridge. Instead, he turned to journalism and art criticism, and with the help of his brother Alec, who was friendly with Henley, he began to work for *The Scots Observer,* becoming its London representative and "devilling" generally for the editor.

When "The Portrait of Mr W.H." appeared in *Blackwood's* in July 1889, Ross sent Wilde a congratulatory telegram. "It was really sweet of you to send it," Wilde replied. "For indeed the story is half yours, and but for you would not have been written . . . Now that Willie Hughes has been revealed to the world, we must have another secret." Wilde was also pleased by his young friend's appreciation of his short story "The Birthday of the Infanta," which had recently appeared in *Paris Illustré,* and later the same month he wrote again to Ross from Kreuznach, the Rhineland watering place near Bingen.

> Dear Bobbie, I am actually in Germany! I had an invitation to come here to see somebody about a play, and I thought it would be a superb opportunity for forgetting the language. So I arrived on Saturday after a day's journey from Cologne by steamer.
> The Rhine is of course tedious, the vineyards are formal and dull, and as far as I can judge the inhabitants of Germany are American.

I return this week, via Wiesbaden and Ostend. Somebody I used to like is at Ostend, and I have promised to stay a day.

I am charmed with what you say about the little Princess—the Infanta: in style (in *mere* style as honest Besant would say) it is my best story. The *Guardian* on Mr W.H. you must send me at Tite Street. Write to me there: I shall be home on Saturday. And oh! Bobbie, let us have an evening together. What ages since we had a talk! Yours, with much love

OSCAR

The friendship ripened during the ensuing months, and Ross would send Wilde any literary gossip he managed to pick up from his clubs and the Society of Authors, of which his brother Alec was secretary.

Sir William Rothenstein's portrait of Robert Ross, painted a few years later, shows a good-looking young man with dark hair, fine sensitive eyes, and rather sensuous lips. Although not himself "a creative person," as this artist put it, Ross had what Rothenstein called "a genius for friendship." "No man had a wider circle of friends than he," wrote Rothenstein in his *Men and Memories*. "He had a delightful nature, was an admirable story-teller, and a wit; above all he was able to get the best out of those he admired. Oscar Wilde was never wittier than when at Ross's parties; the same was true of Aubrey Beardsley and Max Beerbohm."

In this context Rothenstein recalled an incident which shows that Wilde was beginning to be regarded even by some members of what was primarily an artists' club in none too flattering a light.

Ross was a member of the Hogarth Club. On one occasion he had been entertaining a party, one of which was Oscar Wilde. After dinner we adjourned to the Hogarth Club. As we entered the room an old member of the Club, ostentatiously staring at Wilde, rose from his chair and made for the door. One or two other members also got up. Everyone felt uncomfortable. Wilde, aware of what was happening, strode up to the member who was about to leave, and haughtily exclaimed: "How dare you insult a member of your own club! I am Mr Ross's guest, and an insult to me is an insult to him. I insist upon your apologising to Mr Ross." The member addressed had nothing to do but to pretend very lamely that no insult had been intended, and he and the others returned to their seats. I thought this showed great pluck on Oscar's part.

In July 1890, in which month the first part of Wilde's long essay "The Critic as Artist" appeared in *Nineteenth Century,* in addition to "The Picture of Dorian Gray" in *Lippincott's,* Ross wrote to the author: "Even in the precincts of the Savile nothing but praise of Dorian Gray, though of course it is said to be very dangerous. I heard a clergyman extolling it, he only regretted some of the sentiments of Lord Henry as apt to lead people astray." He had also heard on good authority that the current number of *Lippincott's* was having "a phenomenal sale," eighty copies having been sold in one day at a bookseller's in the Strand, which normally averaged only three copies of the magazine. "Your article in the *Nineteenth Century* if possible eclipses 'The Decay of Lying,'" he added, "but it seems a pity it should have come out in the same month as Dorian Gray. Perhaps it is as well that you should be in every magazine to correct the note of tediousness in all the other articles. Will you come to dinner some night this week?"

The dinner duly took place, and as might be expected, *Dorian Gray* formed the chief topic of conversation. As a result, Wilde sent a further open letter to the editor of *The Scots Observer* with the object of closing the correspondence on his controversial publication, although it was to be continued by others for three more weeks. In this letter he wrote:

It has been suggested to me by a great friend of mine, who is a charming and distinguished man of letters, and not unknown to you personally, that there have been really only two people engaged in this terrible controversy, and that these two people are the editor of *The Scots Observer* and the author of *Dorian Gray*. At dinner this evening, over some excellent Chianti, my friend insisted that under an assumed and mysterious name you had simply given dramatic expression to the views of some of the semi-educated classes in our community . . . Well, sir, if it be so—and my friend is strong upon the point—allow me to congratulate you most sincerely on the cleverness with which you have reproduced that lack of literary style which is, I am told, essential for any dramatic and life-like characterisation.

Shortly afterwards the title of *The Scots Observer* was changed to the *National Observer* and its headquarters were moved to London, continuing under Henley's editorship until the proprietor was eventually obliged to get rid of the editor after the journal had been steadily losing money for some time. When Wilde was negotiating with the publisher John Lane in 1892 to bring out his poem *The Sphinx* with "decorations" by Charles Ricketts, he made it clear that the selection of journals to which the work should be sent for review must be a matter of mutual arrangement. "A book of this kind—very rare and curious—must not be thrown into the gutter of English journalism," he told Lane at the time. "No book of mine, for instance, ever goes to the *National Observer*. I wrote to Henley to tell him so, two years ago. He is too coarse, too offensive, too personal to be sent any book of mine."

Yet when Henley's six-year-old daughter died of meningitis eighteen months later and it was rumoured in Fleet Street that he was on the way out, Wilde sent him a touching letter of sympathy, just as he had written to the boisterous editor when his mother was dying five years before.

I am very sorry to hear of your great loss. I hope you will let me come down quietly to you one evening and over our cigarettes we will talk of the bitter ways of fortune, and the hard ways of life.

But, my dear Henley, to work, to work; that is your duty; that is what remains for natures like ours. Work never seems to me a reality, but a way of getting rid of reality.

In the matter of literary activity, the year 1891 was Wilde's busiest, marking as it did the height of his output combined with published work. One play was performed on the stage, he wrote two more, and he published three volumes of essays and short stories, besides elaborating at length in *The Fortnightly Review* his views on how socialism should work for the benefit of the artist in society.

On 21 January 1891, *The Duchess of Padua,* which had been retitled *Guido Farranti* and described in the advertisements as "a new Italian Love Tragedy," opened at the Broadway Theatre, New York, under the production of Lawrence Barrett, who also took the name part, with Minna Gale in the role of the Duchess which Wilde had originally designed for Mary Anderson. "The name of the author was kept a dead secret and indeed not revealed till yesterday when at Barrett's request I acknowledged the authorship by cable," Wilde wrote a few days after the opening to the English actor-manager George Alexander. "Barrett wires me that it was a huge success, and that he is going to run it for his season. He seems to be in great delight over it."

The reviews were scarcely enthusiastic, including that in the New York *Tribune,* which disclosed the identity of the author before his cable arrived. The play was withdrawn on 14 February after twenty-one performances. Later in the year, Miss Gale took it on tour in a repertory of five other plays, reverting to the original title but not giving it as often as the others. This annoyed Wilde, who protested to his agent: "It was in order to have my play played, not in order to have my play suppressed, that I assigned my American rights to Miss Gale . . . My play should be the opening production in each important city. To keep it for the last night is to show a want of recognition of the value and importance of the play."

He had already made up his mind to write a modern comedy, and George Alexander, who had just become the lessee of the St James's Theatre, London, had given him £50 for an option on such a play. Wilde set to work, but at first he found the going so hard that he despaired and even thought of abandoning it altogether and returning Alexander's £50. On 2 February 1891, he wrote to Alexander:

I am not satisfied with myself or my work. I can't get a grip of the play yet: I can't get my people real. The fact is I worked on it when I was not in the mood for work, and must forget it, and then go back quite fresh to it. I am very sorry, but artistic work can't be done unless one is in the mood; certainly my work can't. Sometimes I spend months over a thing, and don't do any good; at other times I write a thing in a fortnight . . .

With regard to the cheque for £50 you gave me, shall I return you the money, and end the agreement, or keep it, and when the play is written let you have the rights and refusal of it? This will be just as you wish.

No doubt Alexander encouraged him to persevere; at all events he would not hear of getting his money back. His confidence in Wilde was fully justified. Later in the year Wilde brought him the finished play, which he proposed eventually to call *Lady Windermere's Fan*—it was provisionally entitled *A Good Woman*—and read it to him. Alexander was so pleased that he immediately offered the author £1,000 for the rights.

"Do you really mean to say that you will give me a thousand pounds for it?" Wilde asked.

"I will, certainly," said Alexander.

"Then, my dear Aleck, as I have such complete faith in your judgment, I will *not take it*—I will take a good percentage instead." And this was precisely what he did, by agreement with Alexander.

To the February issue of *The Fortnightly Review,* then being edited by Frank Harris, Wilde contributed an essay entitled "The Soul of Man under Socialism." The subject is said by Robert Ross to have been suggested by a lecture on Fabian socialism given some months before in Westminster by Bernard Shaw, at which Wilde turned up and spoke, somewhat to Shaw's surprise. However that may be, the heterodox views expressed in the essay were calculated to upset what has come to be called the Establishment. "The article, if serious, would be thoroughly unhealthy," wrote the Tory *Spectator,* "but it leaves on us the impression of being written merely to startle and to excite talk." On the contrary, the author was deadly serious. "The chief advantage that would result from the establishment of Socialism," he wrote, "is, undoubtedly, the fact that Socialism would relieve us from the sordid necessity of living for others which, in the present condition of things, presses so hardly upon almost everybody." He then proceeded to elaborate this thesis to the extent of some fourteen thousand words.[23]

Wilde followed up this stimulating exercise in social polemics by writing a preface to *Dorian Gray* for the next issue of the *Fortnightly.* It consisted of twenty-three aphorisms, some of which were subsequently to be brought up against him at his trials. ("There is no such thing as a moral or an immoral book. Books are well written, or badly written. That is all.") In July, *The Picture of Dorian Gray* was published as a book by Ward, Lock, with certain textual differences which were to

---

[23] Here are some typical extracts:

The true perfection of man lies, not in what man has, but in what man is. Private property has crushed true Individualism, and set up an Individualism that is false. It has debarred one part of the community from being individual by starving them. It has debarred the other part of the community by putting them on the wrong road, and encumbering them. Indeed, so completely has man's personality been absorbed by his possessions that the English law has always treated offences against a man's property with far more severity than offences against his person, and property is still the test of complete citizenship . . .

High hopes were once formed of democracy; but democracy means simply the bludgeoning of the people by the people for the people. It has been found out. I must say that it was high time, for all authority is quite degrading. It degrades those who exercise it, and degrades those over whom it is exercised . . .

With authority, punishment will pass away. This will be a great gain—a gain, in fact, of incalculable value. As one reads history, not in the expurgated editions written for school-boys and passmen, but in the original authorities of each time, one is absolutely sickened, not by the crimes that the wicked have committed, but by the punishments that the good have inflicted . . .

be noted in the context of the author's first trial. In the same month, *Lord Arthur Savile's Crime and Other Stories* appeared under the imprint of James R. Osgood, McIlvaine & Co., which had brought out Wilde's essays *Intentions* two months previously and were also to publish *A House of Pomegranates,* his second book of fairy tales, later in the year.

Osgood, McIlvaine, were a relatively new firm which made a point in all their advertisements that their books were "published simultaneously in London and New York," in both of which cities they had offices. It was a good point, since without more or less simultaneous publication in England and the United States there was a danger that copyright might be lost in one country or the other. One morning Richard Le Gallienne happened to meet Wilde in Piccadilly, and later recalled what Wilde said as an example of "that skill which gave his wit so incomparable a levity."

> After our first greetings, he assumed an air of deep grief: "Did you see in the papers this morning," he said, "that Osgood is dead?" He paused for a moment, his manner deepening in solemnity, and continued: "Poor Osgood! He is a great loss to us! However," he added, as with consolatory cheerfulness, "I suppose they will bury him simultaneously in London and New York!" [24]

8

A House of Pomegranates, with illustrations by Charles Ricketts and C. H. Shannon, was dedicated to "Constance Mary Wilde," while each of the four stories it contained carried a separate dedication to young society women of the author's acquaintance who were interested in literature and the arts. Thus, "The Young King" was dedicated to Lady Brooke, Ranee of Sarawak and the wife of the "White Rajah"; "The Birthday of the Infanta" to Mrs Grenfell, later Lady Desborough; "The Fisherman and His Soul" to Princess Alice of Monaco; and "The Star-Child" to Miss Margot Tennant, later Mrs Asquith, whose politician husband was shortly to become Liberal Home Secretary and later Prime Minister.

As he did with all his books, Wilde sent his mother a copy of *A House of Pomegranates.* By this date she had moved to a house in Oakley Street in Chelsea so as to be nearer her son. The last of the four stories deeply affected her, as she was to write to Oscar when describing how an Irish woman named Bessie Byrne, who may have been a domestic "daily," suddenly appeared in Oakley Street:

> Who should come in but Bessie Byrne, all in a flutter. "Oh Lady Wilde, I have come to borrow thirty shillings. Can you give it to me at once?" Well, to lend Bessie Byrne was not to be thought of, and so I *set my face hard,* but then thought of the Star Child and how he gave the whole gold piece to the

---

[24] Shortly after Osgood's death, his partner Clarence McIlvaine amalgamated the firm with Harper Brothers of New York.

leper and my heart melted and actually—yes, actually, I drew the £1 10s 0d from my purse and handed it to Bessie Byrne! Think of that. All your doing, and, of course, I shall never hope to see my £1 10s 0d again. But see what you can do! Now, is this not a beautiful comment on your style?

She also wrote to her son when she received her copy:

December 1st, '91
146 Oakley St. Chelsea

Caro Figlio Mio,

Your book is beautiful, most beautiful! Jewels of thought set in the fine gold of the most exquisite words. And yet it all seems written with the most unconscious grace, without strain or effort, and no matter how strange and fantastic the incidents, yet the pathos, the human pathos is always real . . .

Constance is looking well, and is much pleased at the dedication to her, and the other ladies are named prettily.

You have quite taught this age the meaning of a really beautiful book. Ever so many thanks for so kindly sending it to me.

Yours ever lovingly,
LA MADRE

The book contained four full-page "delicate and lovely illustrations" by Shannon. Unfortunately, after the book had been printed and bound, it was discovered that a dusty deposit had formed on each plate, which, incidentally, had been made in Paris by some "improved" process; this was probably due to the presence of a chemical impurity either in the printer's ink or in the chalky paper used. To remove this deposit each plate was rubbed with soft flannel, which removed the surface and left the reproductions faint and in some cases almost obliterated. This may well have had an adverse effect upon the sales, since at a guinea the book was relatively highly priced for those days. (*The Happy Prince,* his earlier book of fairy stories, which also carried illustrations, sold for five shillings in the bookshops.) At all events, the fact remains that *A House of Pomegranates* was the only one of Wilde's works to appear during his lifetime which was not a commercial success on its first publication.[25]

By the autumn, Wilde had completed the draft of what he publicly called *A Good Woman,* as he wished to keep the real title a secret. He also had hopes that the play might be produced in New York as well as London, and so he showed it to Augustin Daly, the American impresario, who had taken the Lyceum for a season with a company which included Ada Rehan; Daly was eventually to have his own theatre named after him in both cities. "I should so much like you to read it and let Miss Rehan see it also," Wilde wrote in a covering note to Daly. "I would sooner see her play the part of Mrs Erlynne than any English speaking actress, or French actress for that matter."

He then went to Paris, leaving Constance and the children behind in Tite Street. He now planned to spend a couple of months in the French

[25] One thousand copies were printed. Shortly after Wilde's death the book was remaindered and copies were obtainable for a few shillings. Today they fetch over £100 with antiquarian bookdealers.

capital completing another play which he had already begun to write, and which was to be based on the story of Herod and Salomé. Before leaving London, he breakfasted with George Curzon and Wilfrid Scawen Blunt; Blunt noted that the play was to be in French, and according to Blunt, Wilde hoped that it would be performed at the Comédie Française. "He is ambitious of becoming a French Academician," noted Blunt at the time. "We promised to go to the first representation, George Curzon as Prime Minister."

Earlier in the year Wilde had spent a week in Paris, possibly to arrange for the printing of the ill-fated illustrations for *A House of Pomegranates*. On that occasion he had stayed in the Hôtel de l'Athenée in the Rue Scribe, whence he had written to his elder son, the only letter of its kind to have survived: "I go every day and drive in a beautiful forest called the Bois de Boulogne, and in the evening I dine with my friend, and sit out afterwards at little tables and see the carriages drive by. Tonight I go to visit a great poet [Stéphane Mallarmé] who has given me a wonderful book about a Raven." [26]

At the British embassy, Wilde met Caton Woodville, an artist who had recently painted a portrait of Queen Victoria at her Golden Jubilee Service in Westminster Abbey. The Queen asked to see it and the painter duly arrived at Windsor with his canvas, which was displayed in a cold anteroom. After he had waited in this near-freezing atmosphere for about an hour, the Queen entered, glanced at the picture, and remarked as she swept out, "We are redder than that." Wilde was entranced by this story. "Dear wonderful Queen," he is said to have commented, "she is so pleased that I have come here to put right the little differences with France."

On his return to Paris, Wilde again sought out Mallarmé, to whom he presented a copy of *Dorian Gray*, *"comme témoignage de mon admiration pour votre noble et sévère art,"* adding a further studied piece of flattery in the letter which accompanied the gift: *"En France la poésie a beaucoup de laquais mais un seul maître."* Other French writers and poets whom he met at this time included Pierre Louÿs, Adolphe Retté, Marcel Schwob, Stuart Merrill, Remy de Gourmont, Catulle Mendès, Jean Moréas, and André Gide. Gide, a twenty-one-year-old homosexual who had started to keep a diary in which Wilde figured prominently, was introduced to Wilde by Louÿs. Afterwards Gide recalled their first meeting:

> In Paris, no sooner did Wilde arrive, than his name was on everybody's lips . . . I had heard him spoken of at Mallarmé's: he was a brilliant talker and I wished to know him, though I had no hope of managing to do so. A happy chance, or rather a friend, to whom I had communicated my desire, arranged it for me. Wilde was invited to dinner. It was at a restaurant. There were four of us but Wilde was the only one who talked.
>
> Wilde did not converse: he narrated. Throughout almost the whole of the meal he did not stop narrating. He narrated gently, slowly; his very voice

---

[26] Mallarmé had published a remarkable translation of Edgar Allan Poe's poems, including "The Raven," with illustrations by Manet.

was wonderful. He knew French admirably, but he pretended to hunt about a bit for the words which he wished to keep in reserve. He had almost no accent, or at least only such as it pleased him to retain and which might give his words a strange novelty. For instance, he was fond of pronouncing *scepticisme* as "skepticisme." . . .

After the meal, as they were walking back to Wilde's hotel, Wilde took Gide aside and said to him, "You listen with your eyes. That is why I am going to tell you this story." When he had finished, he gave a strange laugh, so Gide thought. "That is called 'The Disciple,' " he said.[27] He then asked Gide to meet him again, which Gide did almost every day until Wilde left Paris towards the end of December. "Gide is in love with Oscar Wilde," noted one of Gide's acquaintances after he had noticed a photograph of Wilde on Marcel Schwob's mantelpiece.

Wilde was introduced to another young homosexual writer, Marcel Proust, by the portrait painter Jacques-Émile Blanche. Impressed by Proust's interest in English literature and by the questions he asked about Ruskin and George Eliot, Wilde willingly accepted Proust's invitation to dinner at his home in the Boulevard Haussmann. Unfortunately, Proust was held up and arrived a few minutes late, somewhat out of breath. "Is the English gentleman here?" he asked the servant. "Yes, sir" was the reply. "He arrived five minutes ago, but hardly had he gone into the drawing-room than he asked for the bathroom, and has not come out of it."

Proust ran to the end of the passage and shouted through the bathroom door, "Mr Wilde, are you ill?"

A moment or two later the door opened and Wilde made a majestic appearance. "Ah, there you are, Monsieur Proust," he greeted his host. "No, I am not in the least ill. I thought I was to have the pleasure of dining with you alone. But when I was shown into the drawing-room and saw your parents there, my courage failed me. Goodbye, dear Monsieur Proust, goodbye!" With that he left the house, refusing young Proust's repeated invitation to stay to dinner.

Will Rothenstein and Charles Conder, struggling to make their names as artists, both had studios in Paris at this time, and Wilde saw something of them as well as the French writers. Rothenstein was doing

---

[27] "The Disciple" was one of Wilde's so-called *Poems in Prose:*

When Narcissus died the pool of his pleasure changed from a cup of sweet waters into a cup of salt tears, and the Oreads came weeping through the woodland that they might sing to the pool and give it comfort.

And when they saw that the pool had changed from a cup of sweet waters into a cup of salt tears, they loosened the green tresses of their hair and cried to the pool and said, "We do not wonder that you should mourn in this manner for Narcissus, so beautiful was he."

"But was Narcissus beautiful?" said the pool.

"Who should know better than you?" answered the Oreads. "Us did he ever pass by, but you sought he for, and would lie on your banks and look down at you, and in the mirror of your waters he would mirror his own beauty."

And the pool answered, "But I loved Narcissus because, as he lay on my banks and looked down at me, in the mirror of his eyes I saw ever my own beauty mirrored."

some sketches of the elder Coquelin at the Comédie Française and introduced Wilde to the great actor. Wilde talked to Coquelin about who might translate *Lady Windermere's Fan* into French, and when Coquelin intimated that the most convenient time for Wilde to call upon him to discuss the matter further would be nine o'clock, Wilde took this to be nine o'clock at night and was surprised to be told that it was in the morning. He jokingly told Coquelin that he never went to bed before 4 or 5 a.m. (*"Je suis beaucoup plus bourgeois que vous."*) But Coquelin did not see the joke and, according to Rothenstein, stared blankly at Wilde. However, Wilde did turn up one morning at nine-thirty and Coquelin recommended the dramatist and poet Paul Delair, who had translated *The Taming of the Shrew;* Coquelin was currently playing in the French version at the Comédie Française. Shortly afterwards Wilde met Delair and outlined the story of his play. "He is fascinated by the plot," Wilde told Princess Alice of Monaco, who was on a visit to Paris at this time, "but I don't know if he understands *society*-English sufficiently well. I mean the English of the salon and the boudoir, the English one talks. I am sending him the manuscript tomorrow."

Besides Coquelin, Rothenstein did a pastel portrait of Wilde, for which Wilde sat in a red waistcoat, which he wore, according to Rothenstein, "doubtless in imitation of Théophile Gautier."

> The pastel I made was exhibited at the small exhibition I held with Conder. I think it was rather more frank than he liked—only its colour pleased him, the red waistcoat and gold background. "It is a lovely landscape, my dear Will; when I sit to you again you must do a real portrait." Nevertheless, he acquired the pastel and used to take it about with him. It was stolen from him a few years afterwards in Naples, and has never been traced.

Rothenstein has also recalled that he used to go with Wilde to the Café d'Harcourt, in the Boulevard St Michel, where Jean Moréas "reigned over a *cénacle* of noisy poets,[and] propounded rich and complex theories on the art of poetry which found an enthusiastic response from Stuart Merrill, his disciple Raymonde de la Tailhade, and other poets of the École Romaine." They would recite laudatory sonnets and odes to Moréas after Wilde had asked Moréas to recite something and the poet had refused, a practice which eventually caused Wilde to pick up his hat and coat and go off into the night. On another occasion, Wilde accompanied Rothenstein, Merrill, and Robert Sherard to the Château Rouge, a notorious night-haunt of the Paris underworld which they all disliked. Sherard made matters worse by shouting that anyone who meddled with his friend Oscar Wilde would soon be sorry for himself. "Robert," Wilde protested with little effect, "you are defending us at the risk of our lives!"

Wilde also lunched at the British embassy. The Ambassador was then Lord Lytton, formerly Viceroy of India, who had published a good deal of verse under the name "Owen Meredith," and Wilde had been friendly with him for some time. It would seem that besides the Ambassador and his family only Wilde was present, since the Ambassador was in failing health and indeed was to die very shortly afterwards. His seventeen-year-old daughter, later Lady Emily Lutyens, wrote to a friend next day:

> Oscar Wilde came here to luncheon yesterday and we all thought him very amusing and not so odious as we expected, though he is evidently fearfully conceited. He talked chiefly about his own health and his books, but he was very amusing. He has just written a play which he wants to have translated into French and acted at the Française; nothing less would be good enough for him.

Lytton had been reading "The Decay of Lying," and he told his daughter after the guest had left that "he thought still more highly of it than before and that it was very true and wonderfully done." But it made a different impression on the young and unsophisticated Emily. "Taken seriously, it is an absurd statement that there can be no such thing as art without lies, and there is no fun in it, taken as a joke."

Wilde was in Paris when Lytton died very suddenly and unexpectedly in the embassy on 24 November, a fortnight after his sixtieth birthday; he had been composing poetry all day and was actually writing when he suffered a fatal coronary attack. Wilde went to what he called "the hideous Protestant service" for him in the embassy church, relieved by a single laurel wreath on the purple-coloured coffin and the gorgeous uniforms of the diplomatic corps. "We had become during the last year very great friends," he wrote to Lady Dorothy Nevill, "and I had seen him only a few days before he died, lying in Pauline Borghese's lovely room at the Embassy, and full of charm and grace and tenderness . . . He was a man of real artistic temperament. I had grown to be very fond of him, and he was most kind always to me."

In spite of his busy social round, Wilde worked hard at *Salomé* and actually completed three drafts or versions of the play during his two months in Paris. Years later he told the Irish-American poet and novelist Vincent O'Sullivan how he began to write it. He had been lunching with a party of young French writers including André Gide, and he told them the story of the play he had been thinking about for some weeks, inventing and filling in as he talked. Then after a prolonged lunch he returned to his lodgings in the Boulevard des Capucines. He was alone, and it was getting dusk. A blank notebook, which he had bought some time before at a local stationer's was lying on the table. It now occurred to him to write down what he had just been "narrating," to use Gide's word. "If the blank book had not been there on the table, I should never have dreamed of doing it," he told O'Sullivan. "I should not have sent out to buy one."

He wrote and wrote. Finally he looked at the clock. It was between ten and eleven at night, and he felt he could not go on any longer without getting something to eat. So he went over to the Grand Café, on the corner of the Boulevard des Capucines and the Rue Scribe. After he had ordered some food, he beckoned the leader of the Tziganer orchestra across to where he was sitting and said to him: "I am writing a play about a woman dancing with her bare feet in the blood of a man she has craved for and slain. I want you to play something in harmony with my thoughts."

The orchestra leader, an accomplished musician, who incidentally later ran away with the Princesse de Chimay, proceeded, in Wilde's words, to play "such wild and terrible music that those who were there ceased their talk and looked at each other with blanched faces." Then, he said, he went back and finished *Salomé*. Although O'Sullivan in recalling the incident was inclined to doubt whether the customers of the Grand Café at supper would have been so profoundly affected by the music as Wilde had indicated, he accepted the rest of the story as corresponding with what he knew of Wilde's habits.

Since some confusion exists about whether Wilde wrote *Salomé* in English or French, it is as well to set the record straight. Lord Alfred Douglas, who was later to translate the French text into English at Wilde's request, has stated his belief that Wilde "originally wrote the play in English and translated it into French with the assistance of Pierre Louÿs and André Gide, since he did not know French well enough to write a play in that language." This is not correct.[28] The facts have been stated by Stuart Merrill, who was personally involved:

> So as to put an end to inaccurate statements it will be of advantage to repeat that *Salomé* was written in French by Wilde, then revised and corrected by me, Retté and Pierre Louÿs in that order, but solely from the point of view of the language. Schwob corrected the proofs. Wilde was thus the sole author of *Salomé*, any corrections that were made being only for the purpose of drawing attention to the faults in his French.[29]

According to Merrill, who was bilingual in English and French, Wilde wrote French as he spoke it, and Merrill realized that, however lively it might be in table talk, "it would produce a deplorable impression in the theatre." Most of the characters began their speeches with the colloquial expletive *"enfin"* and Merrill struck these out for a start. But he did not find it easy to persuade Wilde to accept his corrections; hence he suggested that the symbolist writer Retté should also look over the text. However, as Wilde seemed equally doubtful about his judgment, Retté proposed Louÿs as the final arbiter. It was the third of the three manuscript versions of the play that Louÿs perused, since unlike the other two, which are lightly corrected in Wilde's hand, the third contains Louÿ's interlinear corrections and suggestions. In so far as these were concerned with points of grammar, Wilde accepted them, but most of Louÿs's other remarks he either deleted or ignored. It was from this version, thus amended, that the ultimately published text was taken.[30]

[28] Nor does Douglas's statement that Gide told him subsequently that "Oscar's first draft was a mass of blunders and misspelling" square with Gide's statement quoted above that Wilde "knew French admirably."

[29] From the original manuscript in French, which I have translated. This MS of Merrill's recollections of Wilde was formerly in Pierre Louÿ's library and is now in the Donald F. Hyde collection.

[30] The first of the three MSS is in the Bodmer Library at Cologny, Geneva, and the second, which is dated "Paris November '91," is in the University of Texas. Both are in

Wilde's name remained "on everybody's lips," certainly in the Paris literary world, to the end of his stay. Before he left so as to be home by Christmas, he received a final piece of publicity. Extracts from Edmond de Goncourt's journals were being published in the *Écho de Paris,* and on 17 December part of the entry for 21 April 1883 appeared in which the diarist described Wilde's speaking of Swinburne as "a braggart in the matter of vice who had done everything he could to convince his fellow citizens of his pederasty and bestiality, without being in the least addicted to either." Wilde immediately wrote to Goncourt a letter in French plainly intended for publication, protesting in restrained and dignified language at this breach of confidence which, besides giving pain to himself, was bound to offend Swinburne, who was in fact now "living a very austere life in the country, entirely consecrated to art and literature." Undoubtedly he had been at fault, Wilde admitted, but he pleaded that what he had said might have been misunderstood owing to his lack of knowledge of precise French. "One can adore a tongue without speaking it well, just as one can love a woman without knowing her," he added by way of explanation. "French by sympathy, I am Irish by race, and the English have condemned me to speak the language of Shakespeare." Wilde sent the letter to the *Écho de Paris,* which published it next day with an editorial note describing it as *"très curieuse"* and adding that although Wilde pleaded ignorance of colloquial French it would at least be seen that he had written his letter *"en toute élégance."*

It was now high time for him to return home. "Constance was here last evening," wrote his mother on 3 December. "She is so nice always to me. I am very fond of her. *Do* come home. She is very lonely and mourns for you." However, Speranza added, "all the papers mention your play you are writing. In fact you are the leading man of England as Willie is of New York." [31]

Certainly Wilde could look back upon the year 1891 with a sense of satisfaction with what he had achieved. Nevertheless, if it marked the height of his literary output and established his position as a successful writer on both sides of the English Channel, it also contained the seeds of misfortune. For it was in that year that he first met Lord Alfred Douglas, the handsome Oxford undergraduate who was to ruin his career and to have such a baneful influence on his life.

---

notebooks bearing the ticket of a stationer in the Boulevard des Capucines. The third, with Louÿs's corrections, is in the Rosenbach Museum in Philadelphia.

[31] Willie Wilde had thrown up his job of leader-writer on the *Daily Telegraph* to marry the wealthy American Mrs Frank Leslie, who owned *Leslie's Illustrated Newspaper.* Mrs Leslie offered her mother-in-law £400 a year, which Lady Wilde refused, though she eventually accepted £100, which she felt she could justify by letting the couple use the house in Oakley Street, the rent of which incidentally Oscar paid, when they were in London. However, Willie's marriage was not a success. A divorce followed after two years and Willie returned to London, where he took to alcohol. He later married Sophie (Lily) Lees; she bore him a daughter, Dorothy Ierne (Dolly), who lived in Paris for many years and was a friend of Natalie Clifford Barney and her circle. Dolly Wilde died in 1941. After Willie Wilde's death in 1898, his widow married Alexander Texeira de Mattos, the Anglo-Dutch translator of Maeterlinck and other Continental writers.

4 / *Prelude to Disaster*

I

In January 1892, *Lady Windermere's Fan,* which the author had provisionally called *A Good Woman,* by which title it was to be known for the purpose of advance publicity until within a few days of its opening, went into rehearsal at the St James's Theatre. Alexander cast himself in the part of Lord Windermere, the other leads being taken by Marion Terry (Mrs Erlynne), Lily Hanbury (Lady Windermere), and Nutcombe Gould (Lord Darlington). Briefly, the story of the play centres round Mrs Erlynne, a woman with an unfortunate past who is struggling to get back into society; she deliberately ruins her reputation in order to save that of her daughter, Lady Windermere, who is unaware of the relationship between them, and, suspecting that her husband is unfaithful to her, plans to elope with Lord Darlington.

Soon Wilde was at loggerheads with the producer, who wished to make changes in the script which Wilde resisted. For instance, Alexander felt Act II should end on a note of comedy after Mrs Erlynne has told her suitor, Lord Augustus Lorton, to keep Lord Windermere engaged on some pretext or other at his club so that she can go to Lord Darlington's rooms, where Lady Windermere is waiting for her prospective lover, and persuade her to leave and return to her home and her husband, who is under the mistaken impression that she has gone to bed early. After considerable argument by Alexander—"I have pointed this out to you at almost every rehearsal but you only received my suggestion with contempt"—Wilde reluctantly agreed. He concluded the act with an admirable curtain, when Lord Augustus, left alone for a few moments on the stage, comments wryly on what Mrs Erlynne has just asked him to do.

LORD AUGUSTUS   Well, really, I might be her husband already. Positively I might. (*Follows her in a bewildered manner.*)

Again, Wilde was anxious not to let the audience into the secret of Mrs Erlynne's relationship with Lady Windermere until the last act. In the story, Lord Windermere had been helping Mrs Erlynne financially, a fact Lady Windermere accidentally discovered when she looked through her husband's bank book, which he had left open on his writing table. However, Alexander, with his fine sense of stagecraft, felt that "for the good of the play" the audience should know very early in Act II, or at any rate at the end of it, that Mrs Erlynne was the mother. "This too I have impressed upon you over and over again, but you have refused even to discuss it," Alexander remonstrated with the author. "The interest would be increased by this knowledge, and Mrs Erlynne and Lord Windermere would not be in a false position." But Wilde could not see it in that light, and he wrote petulantly from the Hotel Albemarle, where he had taken a room so as to be nearer the theatre than Tite Street:

> An equally good play could be written in which the audience would know beforehand who Mrs Erlynne really was, but it would require completely different dialogue, and completely different situations. I have built my house on a certain foundation, and this foundation cannot be altered. I can say no more.
>
> With regard to matters personal between us, I trust that tonight will be quite harmonious and peaceful. After the play is produced and before I leave for the South of France where I am obliged to go for my health, it might be wise for us to have at any rate one meeting for the purpose of explanation.

A rumour of the differences which had arisen between Oscar and the producer evidently reached the ears of Lady Wilde, who feared that he might go off to the Riviera before the first night. She had also read in a Sunday newspaper that Oscar was calling his play *A Good Woman*. "I do not like it," she wrote to him on 8 February. "It is mawkish. No one cares for a good woman. *A Noble Woman* would be better." She went on to give her son some shrewd advice:

> Also do try to be *present yourself at the first performance*. It would be right and proper and Constance would like it. Do not leave her all alone. Then you might be of real use if any hint were wanting behind the scenes to the actors. And it is really better and *more dignified* for you to be present. It would give courage to everyone.
>
> And I advise you to keep on good cordial terms with Mr Alexander. If you go away it will look cowardly, as if you feared to be present. But above all remember that Constance would like to be there . . . so do make up your mind to be present.
>
> I have just been writing to Willie and telling him when your play is to appear. I am very anxious about it, and for you, and for Constance, whose whole heart is in the success, and I have every hope it *will be a success*.
>
> I believe in you and your genius.

Described in the theatre programme as "A New and Original Play, in four acts, by Oscar Wilde," *Lady Windermere's Fan* had its first night on 20 February 1892. The date fell on a Saturday and the auditorium was filled with fashionable society theatregoers, for the habit of spending the weekend in the country, at least when Parliament was sitting, had not yet caught on. The audience received the play with great enthusiasm, and the author, who had reserved a box for himself and his wife, whom he had made a point of bringing to witness his first theatrical triumph, was highly elated. Constance, we are told, "looked charming in her pale brocaded gown made after the fashion of Charles I's time, with its long tabbed bodice, slashed sleeves, and garniture of old lace and pearls." Oscar's old flame Florrie Balcombe, carrying "a wonderful evening wrap of striped brocade," came with her husband, Bram Stoker, who now managed the Lyceum for Irving. The stage was also represented by Lillie Langtry, Julia Neilson, Florence Terry, Mrs A. W. Pinero, Mrs Charles Hare, Squire Bancroft, and Norman Forbes-Robertson, among others. Painters included Luke Fildes and Louise Jopling (Mrs Jopling-Rowe), "becomingly arrayed in shrimp-pink, lightly accented with black." Among the various recipients of complimentary tickets were Richard Le Gallienne and his wife ("Dear Poet, Here are two stalls for my play. Come, and bring your poem to sit beside you"); also Pierre Louÿs, who travelled over from Paris—he found himself sitting beside a young friend of Wilde's, Edward Shelley, who worked in the publishing offices of Elkin Mathews and John Lane; the latter were about to bring out a new edition of Wilde's *Poems*, with an ornately designed title page by Charles Shannon. As will be seen, Shelley's name was to figure prominently in the trials. Another youngster present whose name was to be similarly mentioned along with that of Shelley was Maurice Schwabe, a nephew by marriage of Frank Lockwood, Q.C., M.P., who as Solicitor-General was to prosecute Wilde in his last trial. Young Schwabe had been introduced to Wilde by Robert Ross, who came to the first night with his friend and later business partner William More Adey. Also present were Lord Alfred Douglas and Reginald ("Reggie") Turner, always a faithful friend of Wilde's; he was an illegitimate son of Edward Levy-Lawson, later Lord Burnham, the proprietor of the *Daily Telegraph*, where he was employed to write a gossip column.

During one of the intervals between the acts, Le Gallienne looked round for the author and found him in the theatre bar, the centre of a circle of youthful admirers, which included Shelley, Schwabe, Reggie Turner, and Robbie Ross. When he saw his fellow poet, Wilde immediately left them and came over to his friend.

"My dear Richard, where have you been?" asked Wilde, who planned to have a little fun at his expense. "It seems as if we hadn't met for years. Now tell me what you have been doing." But before Le Gallienne could answer, Wilde assumed an air of concern. "Oh, yes!" he said. "I remember. I have a crow to pick with you . . . Yes, you recently published a book called *The Religion of a Literary Man*."

Le Gallienne nodded, and Wilde went on: "Well, you were very unkind to me in that book"—here he put on an air of deep grievance—"most unkind."

"I, unkind to you?" said Le Gallienne, looking puzzled.

"Most unkind. I could not believe it of you—so unkind to so true a friend."

"Why, Oscar," the other stammered after pondering the matter for some moments. "I don't know what you mean by being unkind to you in *The Religion of a Literary Man*. Why I can't remember that I even mentioned your name in it."

"Ah, Richard," said Wilde, greatly enjoying his little joke. "That was just it!"

Relaxing over drinks at the bar, Wilde resumed, "Do tell me, what else have you been writing?" Le Gallienne replied that he had been writing an essay on loving his enemies. "That's a great theme," said Wilde. "I should like to write on that, too. For, do you know, all my life I have been looking for twelve men who didn't believe in me." He paused for a moment, and went on, "And, so far, I have only found eleven."

Le Gallienne was to recall this remark when three years later a friend brought him the news of Wilde's sentence at the end of his last trial. "Poor Oscar!" he remarked. "He has found his twelfth man."

Wilde responded to the shouts for the author when the curtain fell at the end of the last act by coming on stage smoking a cigarette and delivering a short speech. Conflicting accounts of what he said were subsequently published and the author himself was wont to embroider upon them. However, his words were taken down in shorthand by a member of the theatre staff, so that George Alexander was subsequently able to tell Wilde's biographer Hesketh Pearson not only what Wilde had said but the very words he stressed.

Ladies and Gentlemen, I have enjoyed this evening *immensely*. The actors have given us a *charming* rendering of a *delightful* play, and your appreciation has been most intelligent. I congratulate you on the *great* success of your performance, which persuades me that you think *almost* as highly of the play as I do myself.

After the show, Constance went home to Tite Street, while her husband took Robbie Ross, More Adey, Reggie Turner, Maurice Schwabe, Lord Alfred Douglas, and several other young men on to supper at Willis's, then a favourite after-theatre resort. Here they discussed the play and its merits until the small hours of the following morning.

"The man or woman who does not chuckle with delight at the good things which abound in *Lady Windermere's Fan* should consult a physician at once." Thus wrote A. B. Walkley, one of the leading drama critics of the day. He was an exception. Most of the other critics were unkind, particularly Clement Scott, who denounced the author's "insolent effrontery" in coming onto the stage smoking a cigarette. ("People of birth and breeding don't do such things.") Even brother Willie, who had returned from New York, wrote a disparaging notice. But the author dismissed it with good-humoured tolerance. "After a good dinner one can forgive anybody, even one's own relations."

"You have had a splendid success and I am very happy and very proud of you," his mother wrote to him at this time.

I have been so busy collecting and sending all the notices to Willie that I had no time to write before. I thought the *World* very good, and the *St. James's* [*Gazette*], and *Observer;* only the *Referee* was *bad* and *spiteful,* and the *D[aily] T[elegraph]* was *mean* and *poor.* I sent all to Willie, except the *Referee*—that I threw in the fire . . .

I hope you will have time to come and see me and tell me all about it. I thought *The Times* had some good criticism, and it was not rude like the *Referee.* I sent it to Willie . . .

God bless you and keep your intellect in the best working order.

For the first few performances the secret of Mrs. Erlynne's relationship with Lady Windermere was not revealed until the last act. However, about the fourth or fifth night, the change which Alexander had demanded was made, and the fact that Lady Windermere was Mrs Erlynne's illegitimate daughter, which had been hinted at in the first act, was disclosed to the audience in the second. One London evening paper (*The St James's Gazette*) suggested on 26 February that the change was due to what some of the drama critics had written. In a letter which the paper published the following day, Wilde described this statement as "entirely untrue, and grossly ridiculous."

The facts are as follows: On last Saturday night, after the play was over, and the author, cigarette in hand, had delivered a delightful and immortal speech, I had the pleasure of entertaining at supper a small number of personal friends: and, as none of them was older than myself, I naturally listened to their artistic views with attention and pleasure. The opinions of the old on matters of Art are, of course, of no value whatsoever. The artistic instincts of the young are invariably fascinating; and I am bound to state that all my friends, without exception, were of opinion that the psychological interest of the second act would be greatly increased by the disclosure of the actual relationship between Lady Windermere and Mrs Erlynne—an opinion, I may add, that had previously been strongly held and urged by Mr Alexander. As to those of us who do not look on a play as a mere question of pantomime and clowning, I determined consequently to make a change in the precise moment of revelation. This determination, however, was entered into long before I had the opportunity of studying the culture, courtesy and critical faculty displayed in such papers as the *Referee, Reynolds,* and the *Sunday Sun.*

The hostile reviews did not deter the public from flocking to the St James's Theatre. An acquaintance stopped Wilde in the street and asked him how the play was going. "Capitally," he replied. "I am told that Royalty is turned away nightly." It was temporarily taken off at the end of July for a provincial tour and then brought back to the St James's at the end of October. How right Wilde was in refusing Alexander's original offer and insisting on a "good percentage" is shown by the fact that from this first production alone he received £7,000 in royalties, at a time when income tax was eighteenpence in the pound and the purchasing power of money three or four times what the equivalent amount commands today.

"I suppose there are wittier men than the author of *Lady Windermere's*

Fan," quipped Wilde at this time, "but if so I have never met one." After the play had been running for some weeks, the author heard that the actor Charles Brookfield and Jimmy Glover, a fellow Irishman, who was director of music at the Drury Lane Theatre, had composed a musical skit on the successful play for which they had applied to the Lord Chamberlain for a licence for its public performance under the title *The Poet and the Puppets*. As the poet was called Oscar in the work, the real Oscar appealed to the Lord Chamberlain and insisted that Brookfield should read the libretto to him. This was agreed, and with his customary good humour, Wilde punctuated the reading with such exclamations as "Delightful!" "Charming, my old friends!" "Exquisite!" and the like. The only change he asked to be made was in the poet's name. He objected to Oscar, he said, but he had no objection to O'Flaherty. "I feel," he told Brookfield as he showed him out at the end of the reading, "that I have been—well—what is the thing you call in your delightfully epigrammatic stage English?— Oh, yes—delightfully spoofed!"

The Poet and the Puppets, advertised as "a travestie of *Lady Windermere's Fan*" by Charles Brookfield, with music by J. M. Glover, opened at the Comedy Theatre on 19 May under the direction of the actor-manager Charles Hawtrey, who played the name part of the poet. But, despite Hawtrey's talented acting, it was not a success and was taken off after a few weeks. Nevertheless, it has earned a place in the list of "notable productions" in *Who's Who in the Theatre*, and though it lampooned Wilde mercilessly, it served to give him and his play some additional gratuitous publicity.

Lady Windermere's Fan ended its successful run after 156 performances. It was later published in book form by Elkin Mathews and John Lane "at the Sign of the Bodley Head," with decorative devices by Charles Shannon in an ordinary and large paper edition. Both editions were dedicated by the author "to the dear Memory of Robert Earl of Lytton in Affection and Admiration." For Speranza he inscribed a copy of the large paper edition, "To my dear wonderful mother, with my love Oscar Wilde '93." [1]

Wilde's assumption of Queen Victoria's interest in him, which he had jokingly expressed during his visit to Paris the previous year, was indirectly realized at this time. Like her sister Violet, Laura Troubridge, who was now married to Adrian Hope and living a few houses away from the Wildes in Tite Street, possessed some skill as an artist.[2] She had recently finished a portrait in pastels of Wilde's elder son. "I am deep in a portrait of Cyril Wilde, who is awfully picturesque and nice to do," she wrote on 14 November 1891. Her next portrait was of her cousin Minnie Cochrane, who was Lady-in-Waiting to the Queen's daughter Princess Beatrice of Battenburg. The Princess sat while Laura

---

[1] This copy is now in the University of Texas Library.

[2] When he married Laura Troubridge in 1888, Adrian Hope bought More House (52 Tite Street), which had been built a few years previously for the artist John Collier and which the latter decided to sell after his first wife's death in 1887.

Hope was on a visit to her great-aunt Lady Cochrane in the Isle of Wight. Queen Victoria, who was in residence at Osborne, heard about it and asked to see a finished example of the artist's work. Laura accordingly wired to Constance, asking her to give the portrait of Cyril to her husband to bring down to the Isle of Wight. This was done, with the result that the Queen was so impressed by the portrait that she commissioned Laura Hope to do similar portraits of various members of the Royal Family, beginning with her granddaughter Princess Ena, later Queen of Spain.

"It was Cyril Wilde's portrait that made the Queen so keen about Princess Ena who they say is very pretty," wrote Laura to her husband at the time. "She is to be done in the same style as they all like it so much." A day or two later, Adrian Hope replied to his wife: "Have just met Oscar who was killing about the picture of Cyril for which he said he expected a knighthood."

Soon Wilde was again in the news. He had met Sarah Bernhardt at a party given by Henry Irving. The French actress told him that she had heard about *Salomé* and asked him to read it to her. "I did so," Wilde stated shortly afterwards, "and she expressed a wish to play the title role." Since she had no other theatrical engagements in the immediate future, she collected an all-French cast, which included Albert Darmont as Herod, and *Salomé* accordingly went into rehearsal at the Palace Theatre, London, with stage costumes designed by Graham Robertson. The author was delighted that Sarah Bernhardt, whom he regarded as "undoubtedly the greatest artist on any stage," should have been so "charmed and fascinated by my play" that she should have wished to act in it. "Every rehearsal has been a source of intense pleasure to me," he said. "To hear my own words spoken by the most beautiful voice in the world has been the greatest artistic joy that it has been possible to experience."

Then the blow fell. It did not come altogether as a surprise, as Wilde had learned, when the play was submitted to the Lord Chamberlain's office for licensing, that it was unlikely to be passed for public performance on the ground that it portrayed biblical characters whose representation on the stage was forbidden under an old rule dating from the time of the Protestant Reformation in England.[3] Wilde's immediate reaction was expressed in a press interview he gave at the time.

If the Censor refuses *Salomé*, I shall leave England and settle in France where I will take out letters of naturalisation. I will not consent to call myself a citizen of a country which shows such narrowness in its artistic judgment. I am not English. I am Irish—which is quite another thing.

In another interview, which he gave to the London correspondent of the Paris journal *Le Gaulois* after the Lord Chamberlain had formally

---

[3] The object of the rule was not any fear of blasphemy or sacrilege, but to suppress the old Catholic "Mystery Plays." However justified it may have been during the Reformation, the veto had long since become completely futile and outmoded.

banned the play, Wilde pointed out the absurdity of the veto, which also prevented English audiences from seeing such operatic productions as Saint-Saëns's *Samson and Delilah* and Massenet's *Herodiade*. He repeated that he would transfer himself to another fatherland of which he had long been enamoured. "There is but one Paris, *voyez-vous,* and Paris is France. It is the abode of artists; nay, it is *la ville artiste.* I adore Paris. I also adore your language . . ."

No doubt I have English friends to whom I am deeply attached; but as to the English, I do not love them. There is a great deal of hypocrisy in England which you in France very justly find fault with.

The typical Briton is Tartuffe seated in his shop behind the counter. There are numerous exceptions, but they only prove the rule.

"Isn't it killing also about Oscar's *Salomé* being interdicted by the Lord Chamberlain?" the budding young caricaturist Max Beerbohm, still an Oxford undergraduate, wrote to Reggie Turner. "I have designed a great picture in which King Bull makes a great feast and when they have feasted the daughter of Mrs Grundy dances before them and pleases the King—insomuch that he promises her whatever she shall desire. After consultation with her mother she demands that 'they bring unto her by and by the head of Oscar the Poetaster on a charger.' The picture—which will be called 'The Modern Salomé'—represents Lord Lathom [the Lord Chamberlain] holding the charger."

Wilde's declared intention of crossing the Channel and changing his nationality provided the English press with some fun at the outraged author's expense. For instance, *Punch* came out with an amusing cartoon by Bernard Partridge showing Wilde as a conscript *poilu* with a copy of *Salomé* protruding from his knapsack; above the caption: "A Wilde Idea. Or, More Injustice to Ireland!" William Watson, whose poetry was greatly admired by Gladstone and who was to be seriously considered for the office of poet laureate, wrote some rather tepid verses which the *Spectator* published and which caused Wilde to comment that "there is not enough fire in William Watson's poetry to boil a tea-kettle." It began and continued in the same strain for four more stanzas:

> And wilt thou, Oscar, from us flee,
>   And must we, henceforth, wholly sever?
> Shall thy laborious *jeu-d'esprit*
>   Sadden our lives no more for ever?

"I do not know exactly what course Oscar will take," wrote Max Beerbohm when he heard this further news, "but inasmuch as French naturalisation entails a period of service in the French army, I fancy that his house in Tite Street will not be in the hands of an agent." Max was quite right. The fact that the "essentially anti-artistic and narrow-minded" English were still flocking to see *Lady Windermere's Fan* months later also induced Wilde to have second thoughts about becoming a French citizen. Instead, he went off to take the cure at Homburg, a watering place then much in fashion with well-to-do English visitors; his trip was undertaken apparently at the suggestion of his new-found young friend Lord Alfred Douglas, who was going there with his grandfather Alfred Montgomery. But the Lord Chamberlain's action still rankled, since among other results Sarah Bernhardt was understandably annoyed at having wasted a considerable amount of time and money to no purpose. In July, Wilde wrote to Will Rothenstein from 51 Kaiser-Friedrich Promenade, the Homburg address which he shared with Douglas and his grandfather:

> . . . The licenser of plays is nominally the Lord Chamberlain, but really a commonplace official—in the present case a Mr Pigott, who panders to the vulgarity and hypocrisy of the English people, by licensing every low farce and vulgar melodrama.[4] He even allows the stage to be used for the purpose of the caricaturing of the personalities of artists, and at the same moment when he prohibited *Salomé*, he licensed a burlesque of *Lady Windermere's Fan* in which an actor dressed up like me and imitated my voice and manner!!!
>
> The curious thing is this: all the arts are free in England, except the actor's art; it is held by the Censor that the stage degrades and that actors desecrate fine subjects, so the Censor prohibits not the publication of *Salomé* but its production. Yet not one single actor has protested against this insult to the stage—not even Irving, who is always prating about the Art of the Actor. This shows how few actors are artists. All the *dramatic* critics, except Archer of *The World*, agree with the Censor that there should be a censorship over actors and acting! This shows how bad our stage must be, and also shows how Philistine the English journalists are.
>
> I am very ill, dear Will, and can't write any more.

At the same time, Constance wrote from London to her brother Otho Lloyd: "Oscar is at Homburg under a regime, getting up at 7:30, going to bed at 10:30, smoking hardly any cigarettes and being massaged, and of course drinking waters. I only wish I was there to see it."

2

Alfred Bruce Douglas was a younger son of a well-known sporting peer, the eighth Marquess of Queensberry, and as such enjoyed the courtesy title of "Lord." At the time of his first meeting with Oscar Wilde, in the summer of 1891, he had just completed his second year as an undergraduate of Wilde's old college at Oxford. Gifted with fine poetic talents as well as extraordinary good looks, he was known to his friends as "Bosie," a contraction of "Boysie," which he had been called from childhood by his beautiful and indulgent mother, who had recently divorced his father on the grounds of adultery and cruelty. His striking good looks, which no doubt he inherited from his mother, née Sybil Montgomery, a granddaughter of the first Lord Leconfield, were to last well into middle age and in many ways to prove a curse rather than a

---

[4] E. F. Smyth Pigott was Examiner of Plays in the Lord Chamberlain's office from 1875 to 1895. After his death Bernard Shaw described him as "a walking compendium of vulgar insular prejudice."

blessing. As Bernard Shaw afterwards remarked to Douglas, "That flower-like sort of beauty must have been a horrible handicap to you; it was probably nature's reaction against the ultra-hickory type in your father."

Among Douglas's friends at Oxford was another slightly older poet, Lionel Johnson, a homosexual who already knew Wilde, and was to die a few years later of drink. He offered to introduce his friend to the older man, and Douglas, who had read some of Wilde's poems, was curious to meet him. So far as it is possible to determine, this meeting took place early in the summer vacation towards the end of June or the beginning of July 1891, when Johnson called for Douglas in a hansom cab one afternoon at his mother's house in Cadogan Place and took him on to Tite Street, where Wilde had invited them both to tea. They had tea in Wilde's book-lined study on the ground floor. In his "life and confessions" of Oscar Wilde, Frank Harris has given a highly coloured account of this first meeting, in which Douglas is stated to have "hung upon his [Wilde's] lips with his soul in his eyes." ("Before he had listened long, I have been told, the youth declared his admiration passionately.") This was subsequently denied by Douglas. "What really happened, of course, at that interview was just the ordinary exchange of courtesies," he wrote in his autobiography. "Wilde was very agreeable and talked a great deal, I was very much impressed, and before I left, Wilde had asked me to lunch or to dinner at his club, and I had accepted his invitation." After tea Wilde brought Douglas upstairs and introduced him to Constance.

His impressions of Constance, which he afterwards recorded, are worth noting:

> I liked her and she liked me. She told me, about a year after I first met her, that she liked me better than any of Oscar's other friends. She frequently came to my mother's house and was present at a dance which my mother gave during the first year of my acquaintance with her husband. After the *débacle* I never saw her again, and I do not doubt that Ross and others succeeded in poisoning her mind against me, but up to the very last day of our acquaintance, we were the best of friends . . .
>
> Honesty compels me to say that Oscar during the time I knew him was not very kind to his wife. He certainly had been (as he often told me) very much in love with her, and the marriage was purely a love match. At the time when I first met him he was still fond of her, but he was often impatient with her, and sometimes snubbed her, and he resented, and showed that he resented, the attitude of slight disapproval she often adopted towards him.

What impressed Douglas about Wilde from the beginning, as it did many others, was the magical quality of his conversation. "I have never known anyone to come anywhere near him," Douglas told the present writer, looking back more than thirty years after Wilde's death. "He did succeed in weaving spells. One sat and listened to him enthralled. It all appeared to be wisdom and power and beauty and enchantment." Or, as Douglas put it in his well-known sonnet "The Dead Poet":

And as of old in music measureless
I heard his golden voice, and marked him trace
Under the common thing the hidden grace,
And conjure wonder out of emptiness,
Till mean things put on Beauty like a dress
And all the World was an enchanted place.

A few years after their first meeting, Wilde and Douglas dined at the Albemarle Club, a mixed club in Albemarle Street to which Wilde and his wife both belonged. Soon they were on "Oscar" and "Bosie" terms. Douglas found in the elder man a most entertaining companion, and it flattered his vanity to be seen in Wilde's company, particularly after the resounding success of *Lady Windermere's Fan*. Wilde, for his part, was drawn to Douglas's poetic feeling and his gifts as a writer of sonnets, a form which particularly appealed to Wilde, and no doubt he was also influenced by the fact—for like many Irishmen there was a vein of snobbery in his makeup—that his latest young friend was a lord whose family on both sides occupied a distinguished place in Debrett. By the time they had known each other for a year, Wilde had become infatuated with the younger man. In a candid note to Ross, undated but almost certainly written in May or June 1892, shortly after Douglas had yielded to Wilde's homosexual advances, "as the result of a long, patient and strenuous siege on his part," Wilde described how they stayed together in the Royal Palace Hotel, Kensington: "Bosie has insisted on stopping here for sandwiches. He is quite like a narcissus—so white and gold . . . Bosie is so tired: he lies like a hyacinth on the sofa, and I worship him."

This is confirmed by Douglas, who has recounted how from an early stage in their association Wilde "made up" to him in every possible way:

He was continually asking me to lunch or dine with him, and sending me letters, notes and telegrams. He flattered me, gave me presents, and made much of me in every way. He gave me copies of all his books with inscriptions in them.[5] He wrote a sonnet to me, and gave it to me at dinner one night in a restaurant. That was after I had known him about six months. It is in the Methuen complete edition, and it begins: "The sin was mine, I did not understand." Anyone who takes the trouble to read it carefully will see that it shows clearly that the "familiarities" (to use [Frank] Harris's word) had not then begun.

Douglas does not seem to have been aware that Wilde had in fact written the sonnet some years previously and it had already been published, so that it would have been more accurate to state that Wilde had adapted it rather than written it specially for Douglas. (The latter was to

[5] A copy of the so-called "author's edition" of his *Poems*, published by Elkin Mathews and John Lane in May 1892, was given by the author to Douglas shortly after publication when Wilde was staying with him at Oxford. It is inscribed: "From Oscar to the gilt-mailed Boy, at Oxford, in the heart of June," and is now in the Robert H. Taylor collection.

publish it as "The New Remorse" in *The Spirit Lamp*, the Oxford under-graduate magazine with a homosexual slant which he edited.[6])

Douglas soon fell completely under the spell of Wilde's peculiar charm. "He is the most chivalrous friend in the world," he wrote after they had known each other for about two years; "he is the only man I know who would have the courage to put his arm on the shoulder of an ex-convict and walk down Piccadilly with him and combine with that the wit and personality to carry it off so well that nobody would mind." Looking back at the time he wrote his autobiography with the advantage of hindsight, Douglas was anxious not to make him appear responsible for what he called "corrupting" him more than he did.

> All the same, I must say that it strikes me now that the difference be-tween us was this: that I was at that time a frank and natural pagan, and that he was a man who believed in sin and yet deliberately committed it, thereby obtaining a doubly perverse pleasure. I was a boy and he was a *blasé* and very intellectual and brilliant man who had immense experience of life. Inevitably I assimilated his views to a great extent . . . Long after Wilde was dead, and after I was married and had utterly got away from the Wilde cult and tradition, I went on subconsciously believing that he was, more or less, a prophet and that his views about morals, whether one liked them or not, were based on abstract truth and were unanswerable and irrefutable. It was not till after Wilde had been dead at least eight years, and while I was still devoted to his memory, that it first occurred to me that he really was a very wicked man, quite apart from his sexual aberrations. I was then gradu-ally getting towards a comprehension of the Christian system of ethics which I had so long scorned.

Because of the evidence given at his trials by a series of juvenile delinquents with whom Wilde was proved to have been on terms of criminal intimacy, it was generally assumed at the time—and also later—that Douglas was an accomplice in these practices. The foreman of the jury in the last trial actually asked the judge whether a warrant had been issued for Lord Alfred's arrest. In his autobiography, which was published in 1929, Lord Alfred Douglas confessed that for a short time there did occur between them certain "familiarities" of the kind which not infrequently take place among boys at English public schools; but, he went on, "of the sin which takes its name from one of the cities of the Plain there never was the slightest question. I give this as my sol-emn word before God, as I hope to be saved."

Douglas reiterated these remarks in a conversation the present writer had with him shortly after the publication of his autobiography. He ad-mitted that when he first met Wilde he was not any more innocent than other boys of his age:

> From the second time he saw me, [Douglas said] when he gave me a copy of *Dorian Gray* which I took with me to Oxford, he made overtures to me. It was not until I had known him for at least six months and he had twice

[6] Originally published as *"Un Amant de nos Jours"* in *The Court and Society Review*, 13 December 1887; republished in *The Spirit Lamp*, 6 December 1892.

stayed with me in Oxford, that I gave in to him. I did with him and allowed him to do what was done among boys at Winchester and Oxford . . . Sodomy never took place between us, nor was it attempted or dreamed of . . . I never liked this part of the business. It was dead against my sexual instincts, which were all for youth and beauty and softness. After a time he tumbled to the fact that I did not like it at all and only consented to it to oblige him, and he very soon cut it out altogether. For at least six months before he went to prison no such thing happened between us, nor was it as much as hinted at after he came out two years later when I met him again.

Wilde returned from Homburg about the end of July 1892, looking considerably fitter and thinner than when he had left London. For the summer holidays he had taken a farmhouse (Grove Farm, Felbrigg) near Cromer, where he immediately started work on a new play, while his wife played with the children on the nearby beach. The play, which he had provisionally called *Mrs Arbuthnot* but which was eventually to be known as *A Woman of No Importance,* he had agreed to write for the actor-manager Herbert Beerbohm Tree, who was the lessee of the Theatre Royal, Haymarket, and an elder brother of Max Beerbohm. "I have written two acts, and had them set up by the typewriter," he wrote to Tree early in September. "The third is nearly done, and I hope to have it all ready in ten days or a fortnight at most. I am very pleased with it so far . . . If you would send me your dates I would read it to you somewhere about the end of this month." He added as an after-thought: "I find Cromer excellent for writing, and golf still better." Bosie Douglas was invited to stay, and he spent about ten days in the farmhouse making himself an agreeable guest. Edward Shelley was also asked to come down and Wilde gave him £3 for his railway fare; but Shelley did not come to Cromer, possibly because his father had begun to object to his friendship with the dramatist. Afterwards Wilde told him he did not want the money back.

Tree was on tour with the Haymarket company and reached Glasgow by the end of September, when Wilde arrived to read his play. In many ways the two men were alike. They both enjoyed life and good food and wine, and they were both full of fun and good humour, laughing at their own jokes as much as those of others, particularly when the jokes were against themselves. Consequently, there was plenty of gaiety at Glasgow's sombre Central Station Hotel, where Wilde spent three days with Tree and his company and read *Mrs Arbuthnot* to him. Tree was delighted with the play, or what he heard of it, as there was still another act to be written, describing it afterwards as "a great modern play" and complimenting the author on the development of the plot. But Wilde loftily brushed this aside. "Plots are tedious," he told the actor-manager. "Anyone can invent them. Life is full of them. Indeed one has to elbow one's way through them as they crowd across one's path. I took the plot of this play from *The Family Herald,* which took it—wisely I feel—from my novel *The Picture of Dorian Gray.* People love a wicked aristocrat who seduces a virtuous maiden, and they love a virtuous maiden for being seduced by a wicked aristocrat. I have given them what they like, so that they may learn to appreciate what I like to give them." The part of the wicked aristocrat, originally called Lord Brancaster and later changed to Lord Illingworth, Beerbohm Tree proposed to play himself. In this context it may be noted that Wilde often gave his characters the names of places near where he was staying at the time he was working on a play, and such place names as Brancaster, Illingworth, and Hunstanton were adopted by him for the purpose of *A Woman of No Importance*.

On his return to London, Wilde found it difficult to settle down to further writing. After a week or so, he also felt unwell and went off, apparently alone, to the Royal Bath Hotel at Bournemouth, where he had enjoyed the recuperative air for a break when he had been overworking at Oxford fifteen years before. The new term had already begun at the university and Alfred Douglas was now in his third year. Wilde sent him a present in the form of a silver card case and yearned to see him again. "Oxford is quite impossible in winter," he contented himself with writing to him. "I go to Paris next week—for ten days or so . . . I should awfully like to go away with you somewhere where it is hot and coloured." He ended on an ominous note: "I am terribly busy in town— Tree running up to see me on all occasions, also strange and troubling personalities walking in painted pageants." The "personalities" were youths whom Wilde met at this time and to whom he gave presents of money, cigarette cases, and the like in return for their homosexual favours. One of them was a billiard marker who also acted as a bookmaker's tout named Fred Atkins, whom he had met through Maurice Schwabe. He took Atkins with him nominally as his private secretary on the trip to Paris, where he went for the purpose of arranging for the publication of *Salomé*. They stayed in the rooms in the Boulevard des Capucines, a kind of private hotel, where Wilde had written the play a year previously.

Constance also hankered for a change with the children at this time. It so happened that Babbacombe Cliff, the Dowager Lady Mount Temple's house near Torquay, was available for the winter. Constance, to whom she was distantly related, had stayed there and liked it, and when she offered it to her and her husband, they gratefully accepted. Apparently Lady Mount Temple was willing to let them live there rent-free while she presumably went abroad, but Wilde insisted on paying her £100 for the three months, extended for an additional fortnight or so until early in March 1893. So it was arranged, and the family moved in towards the middle of November.

"I want to write two plays, one in blank verse," Wilde told Lady Mount Temple at the time, "and I know the peace and beauty of your home will set me in tune, so that I can hear things that the ear cannot hear and see invisible things."

3

Babbacombe Cliff, which overlooked the sea at Babbacombe, about two miles from Torquay, was a large, rambling house, following no particular style of architecture; it had been designed for the Dowager Lady Mount Temple with interior decorations by William Morris and Edward Burne-Jones, since the owner was a great friend and patron of the Pre-Raphaelites, as had been her late husband, the politician heir of Lord Melbourne and Lord Palmerston. Pictures by Burne-Jones and Rossetti hung in the various rooms, notably in Lady Mount Temple's large boudoir, which was at the end of the house, part of which was over an archway in the carriage drive.[7] This room, which had three windows which caught the sun all day, was known as "Wonderland," having originally been decorated with scenes from *Alice in Wonderland*. This "lovely house in a glen over the sea," as its tenant called it, was probably as congenial as any country house could be to Wilde. According to his son Vyvyan, the house was the first in the west country to have central heating installed. "This was confined to the corridors and landings, where it was really needed in the cold weather; everyone was frightened of it, as well they might be. It was a very primitive affair, with no safety devices of any kind, and it was always either freezing or blowing up." The wooded garden, which went halfway down the cliff side to the sea, made a perfect playground for children, since it was full of hiding places, and, possessing little beyond woodland flowers, there was nothing in it to spoil. In sending Lady Mount Temple a cheque for the first half of the rent "with many thanks for allowing us to enjoy your lovely place," Wilde added: "The last few days have been wonderfully bright and sunny, and the children are so well and happy here."

During his stay at Babbacombe, Wilde completed *A Woman of No Importance* and also wrote most of the blank-verse play he had in mind, *A Florentine Tragedy*, as well as beginning work on another historical drama in the vein of *Salomé*, which he proposed to call *La Sainte Courtisane*. He also supervised some rehearsals of a production of *Lady Windermere's Fan*, which opened at the Theatre Royal, Torquay, on 2 January 1893. It was largely an amateur production, directed by the local Mayoress, who played Mrs Erlynne, but reinforced by two professionals, Nutcombe Gould and Lily Hanbury, who were in the original cast. But he was unable to attend the opening, "as an east wind, not knowing, I suppose, who I was, has given me a cold."

Douglas, who spent the time that he should have devoted to his studies writing poetry, had failed in one of the examinations necessary to qualify for the bachelor of arts degree, probably "Pass Mods," and he had been rusticated for a term. His mother, who was staying in her house in the Cathedral Close in Salisbury, looked round for a tutor to

[7] The pictures, left to the nation in Lady Mount Temple's will, are now in the Tate Gallery.

coach him, and eventually found a suitable person in Campbell Dodgson, a scholar of Winchester and New College who had been recommended by Lionel Johnson, and who agreed to come to Salisbury. Meanwhile, Bosie was "gadding about" in London, from which he dispatched a sonnet he had written entitled "In Sarum Close" to his friend at Babbacombe. Wilde acknowledged its arrival in these terms:

> My Own Boy, Your sonnet is quite lovely, and it is a marvel that those red rose-leaf lips of yours should have been made no less for music of song than for madness of kisses. Your slim gilt soul walks between passion and poetry. I know Hyacinthus, whom Apollo loved so madly, was you in Greek days.
>
> Why are you alone in London, and when do you go to Salisbury? Do go there to cool your hands in the grey twilight of Gothic things and come here whenever you like. It is a lovely place, and only lacks you; but go to Salisbury first.
>
> Always, with undying love, yours
>
> OSCAR

When he had read it, Douglas put this letter in his pocket and forgot about it, with unfortunate results for himself and Wilde, as will be seen. Shortly afterwards he went off to Salisbury, where his mother and the tutor were waiting for him. He arrived in the evening, according to Dodgson, "with a flutter of telegrams about him, and dishevelled locks, and plunged at once into editorial correspondence" about *The Spirit Lamp.*

> The next day [Dodgson wrote to Lionel Johnson] Bosie read Plato with zeal for one and a half hours. He then quietly informed me at lunch that we were going to Torquay that afternoon to stay with Oscar Wilde! I gasped amazed, but I am phlegmatic and have a strong constitution, so I bore the shock well, and resignedly spent the whole afternoon in repacking the portmanteau which I had just unpacked. Our departure was dramatic; Bosie was as usual in a whirl; he had no book, no money, no cigarettes and had omitted to send many telegrams of the first importance. Then, with a minimum of minutes in which to catch our train, we were required to overload a small pony chaise with a vast amount of trunks while I was charged with a fox terrier and a scarlet morocco dispatch-box, a gorgeous and beautiful gift from Oscar. After hurried farewells to the ladies, we started on a wild career, Bosie driving. I expected only to drag my shattered limbs to the Salisbury infirmary, but we arrived whole at the station.

Since Douglas had forgotten to warn Wilde that they were coming, "a vast telegram" was dispatched from Exeter. Finally they arrived at Babbacombe at nine o'clock and "dined luxuriously" with their host, but without his wife, who had gone off to stay with friends in Florence. Next day Wilde wrote to Lady Mount Temple with the balance of the rent due:

> As I suppose Constance has told you, I have returned to your lovely house in order to be with the children while she is away, and if you will still allow me I will gladly and gratefully accept your kind invitation to stay on for a couple of weeks more—till March 1st if it will not inconvenience you, as I

find the peace and beauty here so good for troubled nerves, and so suggestive for new work.

Indeed, Babbacombe Cliff has become a kind of college or school, for Cyril studies French in the nursery, and I write my new play in Wonderland and in the drawing-room Lord Alfred Douglas—one of Lady Queensberry's sons—studies Plato with his tutor for his degree at Oxford in June. He and his tutor are staying with me for a few days, so I am not lonely in the evenings.

Constance seems very happy in Florence. No doubt you hear from her.

I venture to enclose the formal tribute due to the Lady of The Manor . . .

Campbell Dodgson described the regime at Babbacombe to Lionel Johnson in less formal language:

Our life is lazy and luxurious; our moral principles are lax. We argue for hours in favour of different interpretations of Platonism. Oscar implores me, with outspread arms and tears in his eyes, to let my soul alone and cultivate my body for six weeks. Bosie is beautiful and fascinating, but quite wicked. He is enchanted with Plato's sketch of democratic man, and no arguments of mine will induce him to believe in any absolute standards of ethics or of anything else. We do no logic, no history, but play with pigeons and children and drive by the sea.

Oscar sits in the most artistic of all the rooms called "Wonderland," and meditates on his next play. I think him perfectly delightful with the firmest conviction that his morals are detestable. He professes to have discovered that mine are as bad. His command of language is extraordinary, so at least it seems to me who am inarticulate, and worship Irishmen who are not. I am going back on Saturday. I shall probably leave all that remains of my religion and my morals behind me.

The tutor had to leave at the end of the week, as he was unexpectedly called to London to sit the entrance examination to the British Museum, for which, incidentally, he was successful, eventually becoming Keeper of Prints and Drawings. "I am still conducting the establishment on the old lines," Wilde wrote to Dodgson shortly after he had left, "and really think I have succeeded in combining the advantages of a public school with those of a private lunatic asylum, which, as you know, was my aim. Bosie is very gilt-haired and I have bound *Salomé* in purple to suit him. That tragic daughter of passion appeared on Thursday last, and is now dancing for the head of the English public . . . All the boys of the school send their best love, and kindest wishes."

Wilde drew up a set of rules for "Babbacombe School" which have survived:

Headmaster — Mr Oscar Wilde
Second Master — Mr Campbell Dodgson
Boys — Lord Alfred Douglas

Rules.

Tea for masters and boys at 9:30 a.m.
Breakfast at 10:30.

Work. 11:30—12:30.

At 12:30 Sherry and biscuits for headmaster and boys (the second master objects to this).

12:40—1:30. Work.

1:30. Lunch.

2:30—4:30. Compulsory hide-and-seek for headmaster.

5. Tea for headmaster and second master, brandy and soda (not to exceed seven) for boys.

6—7. Work.

7:30. Dinner, with compulsory champagne.

8:30—12. Écarté, limited to five-guinea points.

12—1:30. Compulsory reading in bed. Any boy found disobeying this rule will be immediately woken up.

At the conclusion of the term the headmaster will be presented with a silver inkstand, the second master with a pencil-case, as a token of esteem, by the boys.

Salomé was published on 22 February 1893 jointly by the Librairie de l'Art Indépendant in Paris, and Elkin Mathews and John Lane in London, being printed in Paris and copies imported into England for distribution by the English publishers. It was dedicated *"A mon ami Pierre Louÿs"* and the edition consisted of six hundred copies on ordinary paper and fifty on special handmade paper. Although he had refused to license the play for public performance, the Lord Chamberlain was powerless to prevent its publication in book form. Wilde made a point of sending complimentary copies to William Archer and Bernard Shaw, as being the only critics of note who had "upheld me at all against the Censorship." To Shaw he wrote:

> You have written well and wisely and with sound wit on the ridiculous institution of a stage censorship . . .
> England is the land of intellectual fogs but you have done much to clear the air. We are both Celtic, and I like to think that we are friends. For these and many other reasons Salomé presents herself to you in purple raiment.

"I wonder how *Salomé* will be received," wrote Speranza to her son. "It is so audacious a thing to write in French. I hope you sent a copy to *Swinburne.*"

Wilde was annoyed by the review in *The Times*, which described *Salomé* as "the play, written for Mme Sarah Bernhardt, which the Lord Chamberlain declined to license for performance in this country." ("As a whole it does credit to Mr Wilde's command of the French language, but we must say that the opening scene reads very much like a page from one of Ollendorf's exercises.") In a letter commenting upon the review the paper published, Wilde wrote of the pleasure which "the greatest tragic actress of any stage now living" had given him by lending the work "the glamour of her personality" and "the music of her flute-like voice," and that he looked forward to seeing her present the play in Paris, "that vivid centre of art, where religious dramas are often performed." But the play was in no sense of the word written for her. He added, momentarily forgetting about *The Duchess of Padua* and Mary Anderson, "I have never written a play for any actor or actress, nor shall I ever do so. Such work is for the artisan in literature, not for the artist." [8]

He was also upset by a cryptic telegram from Pierre Louÿs, to whom he had dedicated the published version of *Salomé*. "I cannot tell you how hurt I am," he wrote to him in English.

> Those to whom I merely gave copies have written me charming letters coloured with delicate appreciation of my work. You alone—you whose name I have written in gold on purple—you say nothing, and I don't understand what your telegram means; some trivial jest I suppose; a drop of froth without wine. How you disappoint me! Had you wired *"Je vous remercie"* it would have been enough.
>
> It is new to me to think that friendship is more brittle than love is.

It was apparently about this time, when Constance was still abroad, that Oscar spent a few days with her friends the Walter Palmers at their house at Frognal. Others staying there included George Meredith, H. B. Irving (Henry Irving's criminologist son), the actor-manager Johnston Forbes-Robertson, and the painter Louise Jopling. According to the latter, it was the first time that Wilde had met George Meredith, whom he had once called "a prose Browning," and they got on well together, which is not always the case with rival authors in the public esteem. One afternoon he read the party the last act of *A Woman of No Importance*, which greatly moved his listeners until he repeated what he had already told Beerbohm Tree—the scene in which Mrs Arbuthnot strikes Lord Illingworth across the face with her glove he had taken from *The Family Herald*.

As usual on these occasions, the party was photographed by a professional photographer for the hostess's album. After the conventional picture had been taken, Louise Jopling turned to the others and said, "Oh, do let us get up a scene! I will make love to Oscar, and you must all be shocked!"

When Constance called to see Louise Jopling shortly afterwards, she was shown the second photograph with the painter's arms round his neck in an affectionate pose. Her only comment, after looking at it for about a minute, was "Poor Oscar!"

Constance Wilde had the reputation of not possessing much of a sense of humour, but Louise Jopling thought that this incident showed that she had it in a subtle degree. She certainly needed it with a husband who believed, like Lord Henry Wotton in *The Picture of Dorian Gray*, that "the one charm of marriage is that it makes a life of deception absolutely necessary for both parties."

Constance herself was incapable of deceiving anyone. But she did suspect Oscar of having a love affair, not with Alfred Douglas, but with an actress. On one occasion, when the actress, possibly Ellen Terry or Lillie

[8] *The Times,* 2 March 1893.

Langtry, was touring the provinces, Oscar supposedly spent a week as a guest at a country house party like the one at Frognal. On his return to Tite Street, he described the party with such particularity that Constance's suspicions were aroused and she interrupted him with the query, "And did she act well, Oscar?"

It must be admitted that he was a better father than husband. Although he loved his two children dearly, his wife began to bore him and he tended to leave her more and more to her own devices. This did not go unnoticed by her friends. Once when he ran into one of them, their neighbour Adrian Hope, in Tite Street, he seems to have had a slightly guilty conscience, judging by his remark, "I know what you're thinking —there goes that horrid Mr Wilde leaving Constance alone again!" For his part, Adrian Hope described Wilde on meeting him at the Lyric Club at this time as "fat and greasy as ever and looking particularly revolting in huge white kid gloves."

For a while Wilde explained his absence to his wife by saying he had taken up golf, and she actually believed him.

<h1 style="text-align:center">4</h1>

Apparently, while Campbell Dodgson was still at Babbacombe, Wilde and Douglas had a violent lovers' quarrel about some unknown but probably quite trivial matter, and Douglas left the house in a huff the next morning. Four years later Wilde was to recall what happened when he wrote to Douglas from prison:

> When at the end of March '93,[9] you left my house at Torquay I had determined never to speak to you again, or to allow you under any circumstances to be with me, so revolting had been the scene you had made the night before your departure. You wrote and telegraphed from Bristol to beg me to forgive and meet you. Your tutor, who had stayed behind, told me that he thought at times you were quite irresponsible for what you said and did, and that most, if not all, of the men at Magdalen were of the same opinion. I consented to meet you, and of course I forgave you. On the way up to town you begged me to take you to the Savoy. That was indeed a fatal visit to me.

Wilde accordingly engaged a suite at the Savoy, consisting of two bedrooms and a sitting-room. As will be seen, there is some evidence that one or other or both of them entertained boys in these rooms. According to Henri de Régnier, who passed on this juicy piece of gossip to Edmond de Goncourt, a friend of his who went to see Wilde in the hotel told de Régnier afterwards that "there was only one bed in the room, with two pillows, and that while he was there Wilde's wife, who brings him his post every morning, arrived in tears."

No doubt Wilde's excuse to his wife for staying in the Savoy was that it was necessary to be near the Haymarket theatre, where Beerbohm Tree was casting his play and preparing to rehearse it. After a week or

[9] This must be a slip for February.

so, Douglas left, possibly as the result of another quarrel, and returned for a short time to his mother's house in Salisbury. Evidently he wrote to Wilde from there, as his letter produced the following reply:

Savoy Hotel
Victoria Embankment
London

Dearest of all Boys,

Your letter was delightful, red and yellow wine to me; but I am sad and out of sorts. Bosie, you must not make scenes with me. They kill me, they wreck the loveliness of life. I cannot see you, so Greek and gracious, distorted with passion. I cannot listen to your curved lips saying hideous things to me. I would sooner be blackmailed by every renter [10] in London than have you bitter, unjust, hating.

I must see you soon. You are the divine thing I want, the thing of grace and beauty; but I don't know how to do it. Shall I come to Salisbury?

My bill here is £49 for a week. I have also got a new sitting-room over the Thames. Why are you not here, my dear, my wonderful boy? I fear I must leave—no money, no credit, and a heart of lead.

Your own,
OSCAR

Unfortunately for himself, as it was to turn out, Wilde did not leave the Savoy immediately but stayed on for some time longer, since it was to emerge two years later at his trial that he twice took a youth named Charles Parker late at night to his room in the hotel. This "renter" had been introduced to him by Alfred Taylor, a young man of his acquaintance, who was eventually to stand beside him in the dock at the Old Bailey. Meanwhile, Douglas had left his mother's and gone off for some unknown reason to an old town with Lutheran associations in central Germany, where he was in correspondence with the elderly consumptive homosexual scholar John Addington Symonds, who had written an article on Beethoven for *The Spirit Lamp*. "I daresay it is rather dreadful for you at Klein Schmalkalden," Symonds wrote to him on 30 March. "But you'll shake down. You can't always be pampered in the Savoy. It was very pleasant for Oscar pampering you, I doubt not. I wish you would come and see how I can make you comfortable, and feed your soul on honey of sweet-bitter thoughts—in Italy—in Switzerland—it is all the same."

By the time Douglas was back in London in mid-April, the rehearsals of *A Woman of No Importance* were in full swing. "We have only just finished Act 2!!" Wilde scribbled in a hurried note sent round by hand to Douglas, who was expecting to have lunch with him. "Order, of course, what you want. Lunch 1:30 tomorrow: at Albemarle. I do not rehearse tomorrow at all." Beerbohm Tree, according to his biographer Hesketh Pearson, always thought that authors should attend rehearsals solely for the pleasure of seeing how perfectly he produced their plays. Like Alexander, Tree would have much preferred Wilde to have stayed away, particularly as he had been pestering him to give the juvenile lead

---

[10] "Renter" was current slang for a homosexual who received money for his services.

to a young actor named Sydney Barraclough, to whom he had taken a fancy. "You know you are my ideal Gerald, as you are my ideal friend," he told Barraclough. "It is absurd that I can't have the boy I want in the part, and there is no one but you." But Tree, whom Wilde called "foolish" and "slippery and deceptive," had to consider the stock members of his company first, and the part of Gerald Arbuthnot went to Fred Terry, brother of Marion, who had played Mrs Erlynne in *Lady Windermere's Fan*. The title role was played by Mrs Bernard Beere and the other leads by Henry Kemble and Tree himself.

Asked by his biographer if he had produced the play "with the assistance of Wilde," Tree replied that he had done so "with the interference of Wilde." This is borne out in the script used by the author at rehearsals which contains such jottings as "Tree's question far too theatrical" (when Tree, who was playing Lord Illingworth, asks Mrs Allonby how long she gives him to convert the Puritan), "Don't like your false exit" (Illingworth's at the end of Act 2), and "Tree not emphasise this" (Illingworth's speech on youth at the beginning of Act 3). In the latter speech, as originally written, Illingworth denounces Puritanism in favour of profligacy to his natural son, Gerald Arbuthnot. The speech begins:

> My dear boy, the real enemy of modern life, of everything that makes life lovely and joyous and coloured for us, is Puritanism, and the Puritan spirit. *There* is the danger that lies ahead of the age, and most of all in England. Every now and then this England of ours finds that one of its sores shows through its rags and shrieks for the nonconformists. Caliban for nine months of the year, it is Tartuffe for the other three. Do you despise a creed that starves the body, and does not feed the soul?
>
> Why, I tell you, Gerald, that the profligate, the wildest profligate who spills his life in folly, has a better, saner, finer philosophy of life than the Puritan has. He, at any rate, knows that the aim of life is the pleasure of living, and does in some way realise himself, be himself . . .

Tree considered that a diatribe against Puritanism was out of place in a scene in which the principal character is delivering a series of worldly-wise epigrams, and he wanted the speech to be cut completely. Wilde tried to compromise by cutting the latter part and substituting for it another epigram—"Puritanism is not a theory of life. It is an explanation of the English middle classes, that is all." But Tree was insistent, and in the end Wilde gave way. The whole of the speech was cut and none of it appeared in the published version of the play. At the same time, when a further portion of the script needed revision, Tree was enthusiastic in his admiration for the author who "retired into a corner of the theatre and shortly emerged with a completely new scene bristling with wit and epigram."

Tree was excellent in the part of the wicked Lord Illingworth, a character into which Wilde had put much of himself and his hedonist outlook. Indeed, the actor-manager liked it so much that he used to throw off his own witticisms in the style of Lord Illingworth. "Ah," commented Wilde, "every day dear Herbert becomes *de plus Oscarisé*,—it is a wonderful case of Nature imitating Art!" On the other hand, Wilde's addiction to the profligate way of life which he had propounded through the mouth of Lord Illingworth was becoming more and more evident in himself. Max Beerbohm, who was down from Oxford for the Easter vacation and attended several rehearsals at his brother's invitation, wrote to Reggie Turner a week before the opening:

> I am sorry to say that Oscar drinks far more than he ought: indeed the first time I saw him, after all that long period of distant adoration and reverence, he was in a hopeless state of intoxication. He has deteriorated very much in appearance, his cheeks being quite a dark purple and fat to a fault. I think he will die of apoplexy on the first night of the play.

While the rehearsals were in progress, Beerbohm Tree received a disturbing communication about the author and Douglas, which he immediately took up with Wilde. It came about in this way. Before his recent trip abroad, Douglas had given an old suit of his clothes to an unemployed clerk named Wood, whom he had befriended at Oxford. In the pockets he had left several letters which Wilde had written to him and which he unfortunately forgot to remove. Wood, working in conjunction with two professional blackmailers named Allen and Clibborn, now proceeded to use them as a means of extorting money from Wilde. Copies of the more seemingly compromising epistles were made by the blackmailers, and one such copy was sent to Beerbohm Tree. This was the letter beginning "My own Boy, your sonnet is quite lovely," which Wilde had written from Babbacombe. Tree immediately handed the copy to Wilde, remarking as he did so that its sentiments were open to misconstruction. Wilde airily explained that it was really a "prose poem" and that if put into verse it might be printed in such a respectable anthology as *The Golden Treasury*. A rendering of it in French verse was in fact made shortly afterwards by the French poet Pierre Louÿs, and this version was published in *The Spirit Lamp* on 4 May 1893.

A little later Wood succeeded in extorting £35 from Wilde in return for a bundle of his letters to Douglas, which he alleged had been stolen from him by Allen and which he had recovered with the aid of a detective. The money was good-humouredly handed over on the pretext of enabling Wood to start a new life in America. But Wood did not remain in America for long. He was soon back in London, and he was to give evidence against his benefactor at the Old Bailey. What is more, on examining the letters more closely after Wood had gone, Wilde discovered that the original of the one sent to Tree was not among them.

In due course, Allen turned up at Wilde's house. "I suppose you have come about my beautiful letter to Lord Alfred Douglas," Wilde said to him. "If you had not been so foolish as to send a copy of it to Mr Beerbohm Tree, I would gladly have paid you a very large sum of money for the letter, as I consider it to be a work of art."

"A very curious construction can be put on that letter," the blackmailer murmured.

"Art is rarely intelligible to the criminal classes," rejoined Wilde. "A man has offered me £60 for it."

"If you will take my advice, you will go to that man and sell my letter to him for £60. I myself have never received so large a sum for any prose work of that length: but I am glad to find that there is someone in England who considers a letter of mine worth £60."

Allen now looked somewhat taken aback. On recovering his composure he said, "The man is out of town."

"He is sure to come back," answered Wilde, who repeated his advice.

The would-be blackmailer changed his tone and admitted that he was in urgent need of money and had been trying to find Wilde for some time. Wilde said he could not guarantee him his cab expenses, but that he would gladly give him half a sovereign. As Allen pocketed the money, Wilde remarked, "The letter is a prose poem, will shortly be published in sonnet form in a delightful magazine, and I will send you a copy of it."

Five minutes later Clibborn, the third blackmailer, rang the bell of the house in Tite Street. By this time Wilde was getting somewhat tired. "I cannot bother any more about this matter," he said on going out to him.

To Wilde's surprise, the caller produced the original letter from his pocket and said, "Allen has asked me to give it back to you."

Wilde did not take it immediately but asked, "Why does Allen give me back this letter?"

"Well, he says you were kind to him, and there is no use trying to rent you, as you only laugh at us."

"I will accept it back," Wilde now declared, taking the letter, "and you can thank Allen from me for all the anxiety he has shown about it."

Then, looking at the letter and seeing that it had become badly soiled, Wilde went on in his customary vein of banter, "I think it quite unpardonable that better care was not taken of this original manuscript of mine."

At this Clibborn expressed regret, but pointed out it had been in so many hands.

Wilde thereupon gave him half a sovereign likewise for his pains, saying as he did so, "I am afraid you are leading a wonderfully wicked life."

"There is good and bad in every one of us," said Clibborn.

"You are a born philosopher," Wilde told him. And on this note they parted.

Unfortunately for Wilde, a copy had fallen into Lord Queensberry's hands. And Queensberry did not see the matter in the same light as Beerbohm Tree had done.

5

A Woman of No Importance opened as planned at the Theatre Royal, Haymarket, on Wednesday, 19 April 1893. The author always made a point of paying for complimentary tickets for himself and his friends on the first night, and he insisted on special cardboard vouchers being written out for this purpose. "If I go to Charing Cross Station and pay a penny to go to Westminster," he told Tree, "I get a nicer ticket than if I bought one of your ten-and-sixpenny stalls." On this occasion the demand was considerable, and among others he could send only one to Graham Robertson. "I wish I could send another for your mother," he wrote to him, "but the rush for seats has been so enormous, and for my friends I have only had a very few stalls, and have been obliged to refuse many dear and delightful people." Pierre Louÿs, who had been forgiven for his telegram, got a seat in the dress circle ("I think the best in the house"), also the publisher John Lane. "Next to you," he told Lane, "you will find Pierre Louÿs, the young poet to whom I dedicated *Salomé*. Pray introduce yourself to him. He is a perfect English scholar." Lane received his ticket by special messenger on the day of the opening, with a note written by Wilde from the Albemarle Hotel, where he and Douglas were staying.

The first-night audience, which included several prominent politicians such as A. J. Balfour and Joseph Chamberlain, responded as enthusiastically as it had done to *Lady Windermere's Fan*. But this time Wilde did not take a curtain call on the stage smoking a cigarette. Instead, he replied to the shouts of "Author" by standing up in his box in full view of the audience and announcing in ringing tones: "Ladies and gentlemen, I regret to inform you that Mr Oscar Wilde is not in the house." Immediately afterwards Wilde went before the curtain to "make his bow," as Max Beerbohm noted, and "there was a slight mingling of hoots and hisses, though he looked very sweet in a new white waistcoat and a large bunch of little lilies in his coat. He then went to Tree's crowded dressing-room to congratulate him on the production and also on his performance as Lord Illingworth.

"I shall always regard you as the best critic of my plays," Wilde added.

"But I have never criticized your plays," replied Tree.

"That's why," said the happy author, as he and Tree joined in the general laughter.

"How the critics attack gentle Oscar," wrote Max Beerbohm to Reggie Turner; "have you, though, read Archer's very true and just critique? [11] Walkley also is to the point, but the rest have scarcely tried to write on the play at all. They have simply abused Oscar." Nevertheless, the notices were better than Max had expected. "The piece is sure of a long, a very long run, despite all that the critics may say in its favour," he again wrote to Turner after the second night.

[11] William Archer wrote in *The World* (26 April 1893): "It is not his wit, then, and still less his knack of paradox-twisting that makes me claim for him a place apart among living dramatists. It is the keenness of his intellect, the individuality of his point of view, the excellence of his verbal style, and above all the genuinely dramatic quality of his inspirations. I do not hesitate to call the scene between Lord Illingworth and Mrs Arbuthnot at the end of the second act of this play the most virile and intelligent—yes, I mean it, the most intelligent—piece of English dramatic writing of our day."

Last night I went again: the Prince [of Wales] also there. He had command of the Royal Box (is it not the irony of fate?) just after it had been allotted to Mrs Langtry. I believe she suggested they should share it but the prince was adamant. After the play I supped with Oscar and Alfred Douglas (who is staying with him) and my brother at the Albemarle. Oscar talked a great deal about my article—said he knew no other undergraduate who could have written it, that I had a marvellous intuition and sense of the phrase, that I must take to literature alone, and that my style was like a silver dagger.[12] I am becoming vainer than ever.

He has told us one lovely thing. A little journalist who had several times attacked him vulgarly came up to him in the street the other day and cordially accosted him. Oscar stared at him and said after a moment or two: "You will pardon me: I remember your name but I can't recall your face."

"You had a brilliant success!" his mother wrote to him a few days later, "and I am so happy. I receive many notes of congratulation. The Prince [of Wales] was very nice, and you ought really to go to the Levée." Speranza lovingly cut out all the notices from the newspapers which she had read, burning one particularly unfavourable one and sending her son the rest. "They all want *more plot* and more human feelings," she went on, "so in your next [play] strengthen the plot and heighten the human interest."

I had a crowd here on Saturday; many had seen the play and nothing else was talked of.

When you have leisure come and see me—some evening . . . I would so like to see you. You are now the great sensation of London and I am very proud of you. You have made your name and taken your place and now take a distinguished place in the circle of intellects. *That* all your critics acknowledge, tho' they are a little sharp on some points.

Take care of yourself and of your health and keep clear of suppers and late hours and champagne. Your health and calm of mind is most important.

No doubt he saw that his mother was informed of his answer to the critics. "English critics always confuse the action of a play with the incidents of a melodrama," he told them in characteristic vein. "I wrote the first act of *A Woman of No Importance* in answer to the critics who said that *Lady Windermere's Fan* lacked action. In the act in question there is absolutely no action at all. It is a perfect act."

A Woman of No Importance ran for 118 nights in London, thirty-eight fewer than *Lady Windermere's Fan*. Wilde was at the final performance with Alfred Douglas, Robert Ross, and Aubrey Beardsley. "The last of these had forgotten to put vine-leaves in his hair, but the others wore rich clusters—especially poor Robbie," wrote Max Beerbohm, describing the occasion to Reggie Turner. ". . . Nor have I ever seen Oscar so fatuous: he called Mrs Beere 'juno-like' and Kemble 'Olympic quite' and waved his cigarette round and round his head. Of course I would rather

---

[12] Max Beerbohm had just written an article on Wilde, his first published, for the *Anglo-American Times*, which Beerbohm described as "a very good paper of recent birth." In it he wrote that "a more complete figure than Oscar Wilde has not been known since the days of Byron." The article has been reprinted by Sir Rupert Hart-Davis as an appendix to his edition of Max Beerbohm's *Letters to Reggie Turner* (1964).

see Oscar free than sober, but still, suddenly meeting him after my simple and lovely little ways of life . . . I felt quite repelled."

Tree then sent the play on tour in the provinces, with Lewis Waller in the part of Lord Illingworth, as Tree had to supervise a new production at the Haymarket. Waller was a robust actor of the heroic romantic school and gave superb renderings of Shakespearian characters like Hotspur and Henry V, but he was new to the sophisticated society role which had been assigned to him. At his urgent request Wilde attended a rehearsal. Many years later Waller told Hesketh Pearson what had happened between him and Wilde after the rehearsal:

> After it was over and Wilde had complimented the entire company, Waller, who did not feel at all happy in his part, took him aside and asked:
> "Have you any criticism to make?"
> "None, my dear Lewis, none."
> "I mean about any individual performance?"
> "Why cavil at a part when the whole is so charming?" countered Wilde.
> "Any criticism at all would be helpful."
> "Nothing I might say could possibly improve such a finished representation."
> "That may be taken in two ways," objected Waller.
> "I won't quarrel over the number."
> "Am I good in my part?" asked Waller desperately.
> "Admirable."
> "But does the part suit me?"
> "You make it suit you."
> "Please tell me what you think. I shall be grateful, and I can stand anything."
> "I think you are so good," replied Wilde, "that no one except myself will know that the part was not written for you . . . But between ourselves, my dear fellow, I long to see you as Milton's Samson Agonistes . . . Now come and have supper with me. I long for that too."

A *Woman of No Importance* is the most definitely dated of Wilde's comedies. Apart from such sentimental lines as "Child of shame, be still the child of my shame!" which would make a present-day audience laugh, the ending has become anachronistic: Mrs Arbuthnot's refusal to marry Lord Illingworth, the father of her illegitimate son Gerald, to show her contempt for him, would today deprive her son of becoming the legitimate heir to his father's title, which few modern mothers would turn down. Consequently, unless played strictly as a period piece, revivals of this play have invariably proved a failure.[13]

6

The summer term began at Oxford in the week following the opening of A *Woman of No Importance,* and Douglas was allowed to go up again

[13] It was first published by John Lane in October 1894 and dedicated to Gladys Countess de Grey. The manuscript was subsequently presented by Robert Ross to the British Museum.

for what was to be his last term. Wilde went along with him and stayed in the lodgings which Douglas had at No. 34 The High, where Max Beerbohm, who was at Merton, saw something of them. Douglas, he told Reggie Turner, was "a very pretty reflection of Oscar—and we get on very nicely . . . Oscar came to see me the other day with Douglas (at whose house he was staying) . . . he behaved quite quietly and gentlemanly and the visit was quite a success." On one point he was able to reassure Turner. "You need not, by the way, be jealous of Alfred Douglas as he does not peculiarly fascinate me: he is for one thing obviously mad (like all his family I believe) and though he is pretty and clever and nice I never judge my friends from an Aesthetic, an Intellectual or an Ethical standpoint: I simply like them or dislike them: that is all. You are fortunate to have fallen into the former category." A few days later he wrote to tell Turner that he had been to a dinner given by Denis Browne, a relative of the Marquess of Sligo, "to meet the Divinity Oscar." Douglas and his friend Lord Encombe, who had had Wilde's old rooms at Magdalen, were there too; also the Earl of Kerry and Lord Basil Blackwood—"quite a peers' dinner: at any rate as regards aristocracy of intellect as represented by me and the Divinity. He was in a very nice mood—young and schweet [sic] and most amusing."

Wilde had commissioned Rothenstein to do a drawing of Douglas, which the artist did. Entitled "The Editor of *The Spirit Lamp* at Work," it showed Douglas in profile, wearing flannels and lying back in an armchair. He now wrote to Rothenstein from his friend's lodgings, asking for it to be put in a black and white frame and enclosing a cheque:

> The lovely drawing is complete in itself. It is a great delight to me to have so exquisite a portrait of a friend done by a friend also . . .
>
> Enclosed is an absurdly coloured thing which foolish bankers take in exchange and for which they give, in reckless moments, gold, both yellow and red.

Another subject of Rothenstein's pencil, whose acquaintance Wilde made at this time, was an eccentric first-year undergraduate named Trelawny Backhouse, a homosexual with a passion for jewels who ran up enormous debts at Oxford; he was to leave the university without a degree, like Douglas, and eventually to become a world-renowned Chinese scholar and intimate friend of the famous Empress Dowager Tzu Hsi in Peking.[14] According to Backhouse, who was in the same college as

---

[14] Sir Edmund Trelawny Backhouse, Bart (1873–1944), who succeeded to his father's baronetcy in 1913, left England for China in 1898 and spent almost the whole of the remainder of his life in Peking, where he was successively a student interpreter at the British Legation, professor at the University, and a collector of Chinese manuscripts, many of which he presented to the Bodleian Library in Oxford. His best-known works, which he wrote in collaboration with J. O. P. Bland, the *Times* correspondent in China, are *China under the Empress Dowager* (1910) and *Annals and Memoirs of the Court of Peking* (1914). In his old age he wrote two volumes of scandalous memoirs, of which the first, entitled *The Dead Past*, covers his life down to the time of his departure for China and contains some candid references to Wilde and his contemporaries. The manuscript of this work is also in the Bodleian.

Max Beerbohm, he frequently dined with Beerbohm, Douglas, and Wilde at this time. He has also recalled, with what truth it is impossible to say, since the evidence has, not surprisingly, disappeared, that "Max Beerbohm produced a cartoon of Oscar and Bosie copulating, the expression on the former's face resembling the goat of Pompeii, while Douglas the willing pathic was deliciously satirised."

It was probably on the occasion of this visit to Oxford that Wilde and Douglas called on Dr Herbert Warren, the president of Magdalen, in the President's Lodging in college. In the course of conversation Wilde remarked casually, "I am thinking of presenting a statue of myself to the college." For a few moments Warren appeared horrified. Then his look changed to one of relief as Wilde went on: "Yes, to stand in the 'quad' here," pointing out of the window, "a colossal equestrian statue!" He was in equally bantering mood when he turned down a proposal that the sculptor Henry Texeira de Mattos should do a bust of him for the theatre. "There are difficulties about the bust being placed in the Haymarket," he wrote to the sculptor's brother Alexander, who was later to marry Mrs Willie Wilde. "In the daytime there are the middle classes crowding in, who might break it; in the evening there are the aristocracy crowding out, who might steal it."

Douglas went down from Oxford for good at the end of the term, presumably because he could not or would not pass any further degree examinations. Wilde remarked that this was like Swinburne, who had determined to remain an undergraduate all his life. But both Lord and Lady Queensberry were far from pleased that their son had left Oxford without a degree. Then, to please him, Wilde took a place called "The Cottage" on the river at Goring, to which Douglas quickly moved.[15] Constance was already there with Cyril and Vyvyan, but after a short while she took the children off to Dinard in Brittany, so that they could have a seaside holiday, leaving her husband behind with Douglas. They were ostensibly working, Douglas on *Salomé*, which Wilde had given him to translate into English, and Wilde on his next play, to be called *An Ideal Husband*—as Wilde put it, "divided in interest between paddling a canoe and planning a comedy—and finding that life in a meadow and stream is far more complex than is life in streets and salons."

"I have done no work here," Wilde wrote after a few weeks at Goring to Charles Ricketts, who was designing elaborate decorations for *The Sphinx*, his long poem which he had begun years before at Oxford, continued in Paris, and finally completed for publication by Elkin Mathews and John Lane. "The river-gods have lured me to devote myself to a Canadian canoe, in which I paddle about. It is curved like a flower."

It was at this time that he began to correspond with Mrs Ada Leverson, the novelist and contributor to *Punch*, whom he nicknamed "The Sphinx." ("The author of *The Sphinx* will on Wednesday at two eat pomegranates with the Sphinx of Modern Life.") It was while he was at

[15] Subsequently enlarged, it is now known as The Ferry House and belongs to Marshal of the Royal Air Force Sir Arthur Harris.

Goring that Lady Randolph Churchill, mother of Winston, had been accused of misquoting a line from *A Woman of No Importance* and had had a bet with a friend that she had quoted it correctly. She promised to present Wilde with "a beautiful penholder" if she was right. Wilde replied:

"The only difference between the saint and the sinner is that every saint has a past, and every sinner has a future!" That, of course, is the quotation. How dull men are! They should listen to brilliant women, and look at beautiful ones, and when, as in the present case, a woman is both beautiful and brilliant, they might have the ordinary common sense to admit that she is verbally inspired.

I trust your bet will be promptly paid, as I want to begin writing my new comedy, and have no pen!

The local vicar is said to have been rather shocked when he called and found Wilde and Douglas lying in the garden draped in bath towels and drying off after they had turned the garden hose on each other. "I am delighted to see you," Wilde is supposed to have said, "you have come just in time to enjoy a perfectly Greek scene." But, according to Frank Harris, who states that Wilde told him about it shortly afterwards, the scene was too much for the vicar, who "got very red, gave a gasp and fled from the place," after which Wilde laughed heartily and subsided into his chair. Less amusing was the same kind of row as occurred at Babbacombe, as Wilde was to remind Douglas bitterly in *De Profundis:*

Some of your Oxford friends come to stay from a Saturday to Monday. The morning of the day they went away you made a scene so dreadful, so distressing that I told you that we must part. I remember quite well, as we stood on the level croquet-ground with the pretty lawn all round us, pointing out to you that we were spoiling each other's lives, that you were absolutely ruining mine and that I evidently was not making you really happy, and that an irrevocable parting, a complete separation was the one wise philosophic thing to do. You went sullenly after luncheon, leaving one of your most offensive letters behind with the butler to be handed to me after your departure. Before three days had elapsed you were telegraphing from London to beg to be forgiven and allowed to return. I had engaged your own servants at your request. I was always terribly sorry for the hideous temper to which you were really a prey. I was fond of you. So I let you come back and forgave you . . .

When after leaving Goring I went to Dinard for a fortnight you were extremely angry with me for not taking you with me, and, before my departure there, made some very unpleasant scenes on the subject at the Albemarle Hotel, and sent me some equally unpleasant telegrams to a country house I was staying at for a few days. I told you, I remember, that I thought it was your duty to be with your own people for a little, as you had passed the whole season away from them. But in reality, to be perfectly frank with you, I could not under any circumstances have let you be with me. We had been together for nearly twelve weeks. I required rest and freedom from the terrible strain of your companionship. It was necessary for me to be a little by myself. It was intellectually necessary.

Wilde returned from Dinard to London by way of Jersey, where he stopped to see *A Woman of No Importance,* which was being given by Tree's touring company. "It was rather good, and I had a great reception from a crowded house," he wrote from the Albemarle Hotel to Douglas, with whom he had patched things up. "I entertained the actors afterwards at supper. I am off to Goring now, to try and settle up things. I don't know what to do about the place—whether to stay there or not—and the servants are a worry." In fact, the Goring establishment proved expensive as well as unproductive, and for this Douglas was largely responsible, since the expenses of the place including the rent for the three months amounted to £1,340, an enormous sum for those days, when food and drink were relatively cheap.[16]

They had another row when Wilde pointed out to Douglas "the schoolboy faults of your attempted translation of *Salomé,*" as he afterwards reminded him. Aubrey Beardsley, a brilliant young artist in black and white, had been engaged by John Lane, the publisher, to do the illustrations for the book, and became involved in the arguments between Wilde and the publisher, because several of his illustrations were considered indecent. "I can tell you I had a warm time of it between Lane and Oscar and Co.," Beardsley wrote in November to Robert Ross, with whom he had become friendly. "For one week the numbers of telegraph and messenger boys who came to the door was simply scandalous. I really don't quite know how the matter really stands now. Anyhow Bosie's name is not to turn up on the title. The book will be out soon after Xmas. I have withdrawn three of the illustrations and supplied their places with three new ones (simply beautiful and quite irrelevant)."

In the same month Wilde wrote to Lady Queensberry, who had consulted him on more than one occasion about her third son:

> Bosie seems to me to be in a very bad state of health. He is sleepless, nervous, and rather hysterical. He seems to me quite altered.
>
> He is doing nothing in town. He translated my French play last August. Since then he has really done nothing intellectual. He seems to me to have lost, for the moment only I trust, his interest even in literature. He does absolutely nothing, and is quite astray in life, and may, unless you or Drumlanrig,[17] do something, come to grief of some kind. His life seems to me aimless, unhappy and absurd.
>
> All this is a great grief and disappointment to me, but he is very young, and terribly young in temperament. Why not try and make arrangements of some kind for him to go abroad for four or five months, to the Cromers in Egypt if that could be managed, where he would have new surroundings, proper friends, and a different atmosphere? I think that if he stays in London he will not come to any good, and may spoil his young life irretrievably,

[16] Wilde's account book with a Chelsea firm of grocers for the period 1892–5, now in the Donald F. Hyde collection, reveals that he paid 3d for a loaf, 1s 3d for a dozen eggs, 2s per lb. for tea, 3s 6d for a bottle of whisky, 3s 8d for a jar of caviar, 5s 6d for a quart of champagne, and 18s for a dozen claret. Judging by the quantities ordered, his favourite drink seems to have been hock (at 39s a dozen) and seltzer water.

[17] Francis Archibald Douglas Viscount Drumlanrig was Lady Queensberry's eldest son.

quite irretrievably. Of course it will cost money no doubt, but here is the life of one of your sons—going quite astray, being quite ruined.

I like to think myself his greatest friend—he, at any rate, makes me think so—so I write to you quite frankly to ask you to send him abroad to better surroundings. It would save him, I feel sure. At present his life seems to be tragic and pathetic in its foolish aimlessness.

Lady Queensberry took Wilde's advice and immediately wrote to her friend Lady Cromer, whose husband was British Agent and Consul-General in Cairo. The result was that Douglas was invited to spend the winter with the Cromers in the Residency and to Wilde's immediate relief sailed for Egypt towards the end of the year, having first made it up once more with his friend. Meanwhile, Wilde had taken rooms in a private hotel in St James's Place so as to work undisturbed on *An Ideal Husband* and incidentally to entertain other young men, whom he felt to be necessary for his existence. "My dearest Boy," he wrote to Douglas as he was on the point of leaving, "I am overwhelmed by the wings of vulture creditors, and out of sorts, but I am happy in the knowledge that we are friends again, and that our love has passed through the shadow and night of estrangement and sorrow and come out rose-crowned as of old. Let us always be infinitely dear to each other, as indeed we have been always." He added that John Hare, the actor-manager for whom he was writing *An Ideal Husband,* was returning to town shortly. "I am going to make an effort to induce him to see that my new play is a masterpiece, but I have grave doubts."

Looking back afterwards, Wilde was to remind Douglas of his behaviour before he left for Cairo when Wilde was using the rooms he had taken in St James's Place:

> During the first week you kept away. We had, not unnaturally indeed, differed on the question of the artistic value of your translation of *Salomé,* so you contented yourself with sending me foolish letters on the subject. In that week I wrote and completed in every detail, as it was ultimately performed, the first act of *An Ideal Husband.* The second week you returned and my work practically had to be given up. I arrived at St James's Place every morning at 11:30, in order to have the opportunity of thinking and writing without the interruptions inseparable from my own household, quiet and peaceful as that household was. But the attempt was vain. At twelve o'clock you drove up, and stayed smoking cigarettes and chattering till 1:30, when I had to take you out to luncheon at the Café Royal or the Berkeley. Luncheon with its *liqueurs* lasted usually till 3:30. For an hour you retired to White's. At tea-time you appeared again, and stayed till it was time to dress for dinner. You dined with me either at the Savoy or at Tite Street. We did not separate as a rule till after midnight, as supper at Willis's had to wind up the entrancing day. That was my life for those three months, every single day, except during the four days when you went abroad. I then, of course, had to go over to Calais to fetch you back. For one of my nature and temperament it was a position at once grotesque and tragic.

Douglas was already in Cairo when the English version of *Salomé* was published, on 9 February 1894, with a cover design and eleven pictures by Beardsley. It is not known exactly how much Douglas contributed to the translation, but his name did not appear on the title page. However, the dedication read:

TO MY FRIEND
LORD ALFRED BRUCE DOUGLAS
THE TRANSLATOR OF
MY PLAY

In addition to the ordinary edition, of which five hundred copies were printed for sale at 15s, there was a large paper edition limited to one hundred copies, bound in green silk and sold at 30s each.

A few nights after the publication of *Salomé,* Wilde took a box at the St James's Theatre, where A. W. Pinero's *The Second Mrs Tanqueray* was being played to crowded houses with Mrs Patrick Campbell in the name part. The successful production of this work by George Alexander began the vogue for so-called problem plays; it also established the renown of Mrs Campbell as an actress as well as that of the author. Since the play was very much the talk of the town, Wilde was naturally keen to see it and he invited Beardsley to share the box in the theatre with him as his guest. During one of the intervals he procured a sheet of paper on which he addressed a note to the actress and sent it round to her dressing room backstage.

"Dear Mrs Campbell," Wilde wrote from Box F, "Mr Aubrey Beardsley, a very brilliant and wonderful young artist, and like all artists a great admirer of the wonder and charm of your art, says that he must once have the honour of being presented to you, if you will allow it. So, with your gracious sanction, I will come round after Act III with him, and you would gratify and honour him much if you would let him bow his compliments to you. He has just illustrated my play of *Salomé* for me, and has a copy of the *édition de luxe* which he wishes to lay at your feet. His drawings are quite wonderful."

"This seems to me the perfect letter with which to introduce a young genius," Sir Sacheverell Sitwell has aptly commented upon it. "And what more absolute instance of that than the young Beardsley; then not quite twenty-two years old (his birthday was in the next month)?"

The meeting led to the artist doing a drawing of the actress in profile which appeared shortly afterwards in the first number of *The Yellow Book,* the avant-garde journal launched by Elkin Mathews and John Lane with Beardsley as art editor in April 1894: The original was presented by the artist to Wilde, who hung it in his library-study on the ground floor of his house in Tite Street.

At the same time Wilde gave Beardsley a complimentary copy of *Salomé,* which he inscribed: "For the only artist who, besides myself, knows what the dance of the seven veils is, and can see that invisible dance." [18]

[18] This copy is now in the Sterling Library of the University of London. After the forced sale of Wilde's effects in April 1895, Beardsley's drawing of Mrs Campbell somehow found its way to the National Gallery of Modern Pictures in Berlin.

7

According to Wilde, Douglas wrote to him by every post from Egypt, and he ignored his communications until Douglas was on his way home in March 1894. None of these communications has survived. However, Douglas's letters to his mother at this time certainly show how he felt. "You cannot do anything against the power of my affection for Oscar Wilde and his for me," he wrote to his mother.

> I am passionately fond of him and he of me . . . There is nothing I would not do for him and if he dies before I do I shall not care to live any longer. Surely there is nothing but what is fine and beautiful in such a love as that of two people for one another, the love of the disciple and the philosopher . . . There is no good in saying any more, except that while I perhaps have no right to say that Oscar Wilde is a good man, neither you nor anyone else has the right to say that he is a bad man. A really bad man I might admire .intellectually but I could never love, and what is still more he could never love anyone faithfully, loyally, devotedly, unselfishly and purely as Oscar loves me.

Through the influence of Lord Cromer and partly through his grandfather, Alfred Montgomery, Douglas was offered and accepted the post of honorary attaché at the British embassy in Constantinople. But instead of proceeding direct from Cairo to take up this appointment, Douglas set off for Paris, beseeching Wilde to meet him there. Wilde eventually consented to do so after repeated entreaties, culminating in a telegram to Constance Wilde in which Douglas begged her to use her influence with her husband to get him to write to him. According to Wilde, he (Wilde) at first refused, but eventually agreed to join Douglas in Paris, after a series of further telegrams including one eleven pages long from Paris addressed to Tite Street. A sentimental reunion took place in circumstances of which Wilde was later to remind the younger man:

> When I arrived in Paris, your tears, breaking out again and again all through the evening, and falling over your cheeks like rain as we sat, at dinner first at Voisin's, at supper at Paillard's afterwards: the unfeigned joy you evinced at seeing me, holding my hand whenever you could, as though you were a gentle and penitent child: your contrition, so simple and sincere, at the moment: made me consent to renew our friendship.
> Two days after we had returned to London, your father saw you having luncheon with me at the Café Royal, joined my table, drank of my wine, and that afternoon, through a letter addressed to you, began his first attack on me.

The eight days they spent in Paris cost Wilde nearly £150, as, in addition to Douglas, Wilde had to pay for the accommodation of the Italian servant Douglas had brought with him—Paillard's restaurant alone accounting for £85. "At the rate at which you wished to live," Wilde afterwards pointed out to his friend, "your entire income for a whole year, if you had taken your meals alone, and been especially economical in the cheaper form of pleasures, would hardly have lasted you for three weeks." Douglas had an allowance of £250 a year from his father, which he now told Queensberry he would rather give up than sever his friendship with Wilde, and eventually did so. Then, as Wilde reminded him, "the fact that in what was merely a pretence of bravado you had surrendered your allowance, such as it was, gave you at least a plausible reason for your claim to live at my expense, or what you thought a plausible reason: and on many occasions you seriously availed yourself of it, and gave the very fullest expression to it . . ."

News of Douglas's meeting with Wilde in Paris reached the ears of Lord Currie, the British ambassador in Constantinople, and he consequently cancelled his appointment as attaché, much to his grandfather Montgomery's annoyance. Douglas subsequently wrote of the incident in his autobiography:

> If Lord Currie—who, to quote Wilde, did not "rise from the ranks of the aristocracy but was born in the purple of commerce"—had been a little more *grand seigneur* than he was he would not have made such a ridiculous fuss, and it would not have occurred to him (he was a newly created peer) that any assault on his dignity had been so much as dreamed of. However, there was the end of my "diplomatic career," and I was in disgrace with my grandfather Alfred Montgomery, and once more exposed to the mad-dog threats of my father, who had then already for some time past been threatening Wilde and me because of our association and our being constantly in each other's company in public places.

In order to get her son away from Wilde, Lady Queensberry now gave Bosie some money and sent him off to Florence, which he had always wished to see and where there was an expatriate English colony, including several homosexuals, like the poet and songwriter Lord Henry Somerset, whose brother Arthur had been involved in the Cleveland Street scandal. "I miss you so much," wrote Wilde in reply to a telegram from Douglas announcing his arrival in Florence.

> The gay, gilt and gracious lad has gone away—and I hate everyone else they are tedious. Also I am in the purple valleys of despair, and no gold coins are dropping down from heaven to gladden me. London is very dangerous: writters come out at night and writ one, the roaring of creditors towards dawn is frightful, and solicitors are getting rabies and biting people.

It had been a year since Wilde had had a play produced, and little money was coming into the Tite Street household apart from his wife's income. In fact, Wilde was distinctly hard up, and he continued to be subjected to demands for money from various sources. In his next letter to Douglas, he volunteered the information that he had received "a frantic telegram from Edward Shelley, of all people!" asking to see him. "When he came he was of course in trouble for money," having apparently lost his job with Elkin Mathews and John Lane because of his carrying on a correspondence with Wilde. "As he betrayed me grossly, I of course gave him money and was kind to him. I find that forgiving one's enemies is a most curious morbid pleasure: perhaps I should check it."

However short of money he may have been at this time, Wilde managed to raise enough to join Douglas in Florence, where he took an apartment for a month. This seems to have been a quiet and not unproductive period in their relations, as Douglas wrote some poetry there and Wilde worked on his play *A Florentine Tragedy*. They both saw something of Lord Henry Somerset and also of André Gide, who was also on a visit to Florence. Gide thought that Wilde looked "old and ugly" but still excelled as a raconteur. He and Douglas did not apparently spend the whole month that had been intended in the apartment, as they left to return to London after about two weeks and Wilde offered the apartment to Gide, who also noted that Wilde had not been pleased to see him as he "thought he was incognito."

Back in London, Wilde had an idea for another play, quite different from *A Florentine Tragedy*. This was to be *The Importance of Being Earnest*, and he put it to George Alexander:

> The real charm of the play, if it is to have a charm, must be in the dialogue. The plot is slight, but, I think, adequate . . '. Well, I think an amusing thing with lots of wit and fun might be made. If you think so too, and care to have the refusal of it do let me know, and send me £150. If when the play is finished, you think it too slight—not serious enough—of course you can have the £150 back. I want to go away and write it, and it could be ready in October, as I have nothing else to do . . .
>
> In the meanwhile, my dear Aleck, I am so pressed for money that I don't know what to do. Of course I am extravagant. You have always been a good wise friend to me, so think what you can do.

Alexander did produce some money, but apparently not straightaway, as Wilde was still very hard up when he wrote to Douglas about the end of July; he was being pressed by creditors and also chased by Queensberry.

> I am overdrawn £41 at the bank: it really is intolerable the want of money. I have not a penny. I can't stand it any longer, and don't know what to do. I go down to Worthing tomorrow. I hope to do work there. The house, I hear, is very small, and I have no writing room. However, anything is better than London . . .

Fortunately, he was able to escape from London, as Constance had taken a seaside house on the Esplanade at Worthing for the children's holidays, and he invited Douglas to visit them:

> When you come to Worthing, of course all things will be done for your honour and joy, but I fear you may find the meals, etc. tedious. But you will come, won't you? at any rate for a short time—till you are bored . . .
>
> What purple valleys of despair one goes through! Fortunately there is one person in the world to love.

After a few days at Worthing, Wilde wrote again to Douglas, telling him he should not come. "A horrid ugly Swiss governess has, I find, been looking after Cyril and Vyvyan for a year. She is quite impossible. Also, children at meals are tedious. Also, you the gilt and graceful boy would be bored. Don't come here. I will come to you." However, Douglas did come and stayed a day or two in a hotel, long enough to meet three boys, Percy and Stephen, and a third called Alphonse Conway; the last sold newspapers and Wilde had first become acquainted with him on the beach at Worthing.

After Douglas had left, Wilde sent him an account of how he had been spending his time.

> I have been doing nothing here but bathing and playwriting. My play is really very funny: I am delighted with it. But it is not shaped yet. It lies in Sibylline leaves about the room, and Arthur [the servant] has twice made a chaos of it by "tidying up." The result, however, was rather dramatic. I am inclined to think that Chaos is a stronger evidence for an Intelligent Creator than Kosmos is; the view might be expanded.
>
> Percy left the day after you did. He spoke much of you. Alphonso is still in favour. He is my only companion, along with Stephen. Alphonso always alludes to you as "the Lord," which however gives you, I think, a Biblical Hebraic dignity that gracious Greek boys should *not* have. He also says, from time to time, "Percy was the Lord's favourite," which makes me think of Percy as the infant Samuel—an inaccurate reminiscence, as Percy was Hellenic.
>
> Yesterday (Sunday) Alphonso, Stephen, and I sailed to Littlehampton in the morning, bathing on the way. We took five hours in an awful gale to come back! did not reach the pier till eleven o'clock at night, pitch dark all the way, and a fearful sea. I was drenched, but was Viking-like and daring. It was, however, quite a dangerous adventure. All the fishermen were waiting for us. I flew to the hotel for hot brandy and water, on landing with my companions, and found a letter for you from dear Henry,[19] which I send you: they had forgotten to forward it. As it was past *ten* o'clock on a Sunday night the proprietor could not *sell* us any brandy or spirits of any kind! So he had to *give* it to us. The result was not displeasing, but what laws! A hotel proprietor is not allowed to sell "necessary harmless" alcohol to three shipwrecked mariners, wet to the skin, because it is Sunday! Both Alphonso and Stephen are now anarchists, I need hardly say . . .
>
> Dear, dear boy, you are more to me than any one of them has any idea; you are the atmosphere of beauty through which I see life; you are the incarnation of all lovely things. When we are out of tune, all colour goes from things for me, but we are never really out of tune. I think of you day and night.

Wilde and Douglas were also together in London, where they met Max Beerbohm, who had just come down from Oxford. "Oscar and Bosie lunched with me today in the Royal Coffee House [i.e., the Café Royal] and were very charming," Max wrote to Reggie Turner on 7 August. "Oscar was just in the mood I like him—very 1880 and withal brimful of intellectual theories and anecdotes of dear Lady Dorothy Nevill and other whores. Bosie came in a Homburg hat—dove-coloured—and wearing a *very* sweet present from you in his shirt-cuffs . . . Oscar was also all admiration and said he supposed that 'dear Reg's present to him was in some way delayed.' "

---

[19] Possibly Lord Henry Somerset.

"I went yesterday up to town for the afternoon," Wilde wrote to Douglas early in September, "lunched with George Alexander at the Garrick, got a little money from him, and returned by the 4:30 for dinner, so I can pay my rent, and Cyril's (little wretch and darling) school-fees." He added that he dared not lodge the money in the bank on account of being overdrawn, "but I think of hiding gold in the garden." Douglas had sent him a "sweet letter" and a "delightful telegram" which had cheered him and, now that he had some money, was more than eager to see him again. "What do you think of three days in Dieppe? I have a sort of longing for France, and with you, if you can manage to come (I could only manage three days, as I am so busy)." The Dieppe excursion does not seem to have materialized, as there is no further mention of it. But Douglas did turn up at Worthing shortly afterwards and asked Wilde to take him for a few days to the luxury Metropole Hotel in Brighton. As the house at Worthing was being given up and Constance and the children were returning to Tite Street, Wilde agreed to go to Brighton and come on to London later. Unfortunately, Douglas went down with influenza the night they arrived at the Metropole. "I sit by his side and read him passages from his own life," Wilde wrote to Ada Leverson. "They fill him with surprise. Everyone should keep someone else's diary; I sometimes suspect you of keeping mine."

When Douglas was better, they moved into rooms, where Wilde hoped to put the finishing touches to *The Importance of Being Earnest*. But by the morning after they were installed, he had caught influenza from Douglas. The latter had to go up to London on business, where he spent a couple of days, and when he returned there was an ugly scene in which Wilde reproached him bitterly for his neglect.

Wilde's chagrin promptly turned to sympathy when he heard that Lord Drumlanrig, Douglas's eldest brother and the heir to the Queensberry titles, had been killed in a shooting accident, supposedly by the accidental explosion of his own gun. "It is a great blow to Bosie," Wilde noted at the time; "the first noble sorrow of his boyish life: the wings of the angel of Death have almost touched him . . ." The "accident" took place on 18 October 1894 while Lord Drumlanrig was a guest at a shooting party in Somerset. A verdict of "accidental death" was returned at the coroner's inquest. However, the late Lord Queensberry (Francis 11th Marquess) told the present writer that he was positive his uncle Drumlanrig had taken his own life in the shadow of a suppressed scandal. Drumlanrig was a junior minister in Gladstone's government, a post he had secured through the influence of Lord Rosebery, whose private secretary he had been. He was rumored to have been implicated in a homosexual affair with Rosebery and, if Drumlanrig's father the Marquess of Queensberry knew or thought his eldest son had committed suicide under these circumstances, his violent reaction to his younger son's relationship with Wilde had greater grounds than were previously suspected.

Meanwhile, John Hare had rejected *An Ideal Husband* on the basis of the last act's weakness; he thought it had too many entrances and exits. So Wilde again turned to Tree at the Haymarket. Tree liked *An Ideal Husband,* but he explained to Wilde that he could neither produce it nor act in it himself, as he had arranged an American tour for the 1895 season and was handing over the running of the Haymarket theatre to Lewis Waller and H. H. Morrell, son of the throat specialist Sir Morrell Mackenzie. Waller and Morrell agreed to produce the play as the first in the new season and to open after Christmas. Accordingly, it went into rehearsal in the second half of December, with Lewis Waller as Sir Robert Chiltern, Charles Hawtrey as Lord Goring, Julia Neilson as Lady Chiltern, and Florence West as Mrs Cheveley. Charles Brookfield, who had written the spiteful skit on *Lady Windermere's Fan,* had no objection to playing the small part of Lord Goring's servant, nor did Wilde take this amiss.[20]

Much to the annoyance of the actors, Wilde insisted on having a rehearsal on Christmas Day, and they were further incensed when the author kept them standing about the cold stage for an hour before appearing. Brookfield alone was moved to protest.

"Don't you keep Christmas, Oscar?" he asked.

"No, Brookfield," Wilde replied blandly. "The only festival of the Church I keep is Septuagesima. Do you keep Septuagesima, Brookfield?"

"Not since I was a boy."

"Ah, be a boy again!"

An Ideal Husband opened at the Theatre Royal, Haymarket, on 3 January 1895 and was an immediate success. The play showed a considerable advance in construction and characterization over the author's two previous comedies, in spite of the weak fourth act, and foreshadowed the satirical nonsense of his next and most famous play. "In a certain sense Mr Wilde is to me our only thorough playwright," wrote Bernard Shaw in *The Sketch.* "He plays with everything: with wit, with philosophy, with drama, with actors and audiences, with the whole theatre."

The Prince of Wales occupied the Royal Box for the opening night and sent for Wilde after the last act to congratulate him. The flattered author remarked that he would have to cut some of the scenes, as the performance was too long. But the Prince would not hear of this. "Pray do not take out a single word," he said. It was a command which Wilde was only too pleased to obey.

8

While he was at Worthing, Wilde had dashed off the scenario of another play which he thought might suit Alexander, the underlying theme being "a sheer flame of love between a man and a woman," and which he later provisionally entitled *Mr and Mrs Daventry* but which he

[20] The MS draft of *An Ideal Husband* and the typescript corrected in the author's hand are in the Clark Library of the University of California at Los Angeles.

really intended to call *Constance* after his wife, who was an essentially
"good woman" like the Mrs Daventry in the projected play. He now
sent Alexander the scenario, which he had hurriedly sketched out in a
letter. Towards the end of October, when he had returned to London
after his bout of what he called "a sort of malarial fever," he again wrote
to Alexander at the St. James's Theatre:

> I am quite well now, and, as you wished to see my somewhat farcical com-
> edy, I send you the first copy of it. It is called *Lady Lancing* on the cover: but
> the real title is *The Importance of Being Earnest*. When you read the play, you
> will see the punning title's meaning. Of course, the play is not suitable to
> you at all: you are a romantic actor: the people it wants are actors like
> Wyndham and Hawtrey. Also, I would be sorry if you altered the definite
> artistic line of progress you have always followed at the St James's. But, of
> course, read it, and let me know what you think about it. I have very good
> offers from America for it.

However, George Alexander returned the script of *The Importance of
Being Earnest* to the author, either because he thought the play was too
slight or because Wilde thought that the actor-manager and his company would be too serious in the parts. It was then sent to Charles
Wyndham, a producer as well as the best light-comedy actor of the day.
Alexander had put on Henry James's play *Guy Domville* at the St James's
two days after *An Ideal Husband* had opened at the Haymarket. *Guy
Domville* was a failure and he saw that it would have to be taken off very
soon. He thereupon asked Wyndham to return *The Importance of Being
Earnest*. Wyndham, in no immediate need of a play, agreed on condition
that Wilde should write another play for him prior to the one for which
Wilde had sketched out a scenario for Alexander.

The Importance of Being Earnest went into rehearsal, with Alexander
playing John Worthing, Allan ("Tony") Aynsworth in the role of Algernon Moncrieffe, Irene Vanbrugh as Gwendolen Fairfax, Rose Leclercq as
Lady Bracknell, and Franklin Dyall as Merriman, the butler in Worthing's country house. Incidentally, Wilde called Jack Worthing's manser-
vant Lane, after his publisher, to whom he had taken a strong dislike.
Elkin Mathews and John Lane had severed their partnership, and Lane
had taken over Wilde as one of his authors.

For many years—at least half a century after the original production—it was not generally known that Wilde had originally written *The
Importance of Being Earnest* in four acts, which included an amusing scene
in which Algernon is arrested for debt. Alexander felt that as it stood
the play was too long and that Acts II and III should be compressed into
a single act, which involved cutting this particular scene.[21]

---

[21] The MSS of Acts I and II are in the Arents collection in the New York City Public
Library, and those of Acts III and IV are in the British Museum. A German translation
of the original four-act version was published in Germany as *Ernst Sein* in 1903. The
complete English text, with facsimile reproductions of the MS of Act II and the type-
scripts of Acts I, III, and IV with the author's corrections, was first published in two
volumes by the New York Public Library in 1956.

"Do you realize, Aleck, what you are asking me to sacrifice?" the author asked the producer.

"You will be able to use it in another play," replied Alexander.

"It may not fit into another play."

"What does it matter? You are clever enough to think of a hundred things just as good."

"Of course I am," Wilde retorted. "A thousand if need be—but that is not the point. This scene you feel is superfluous cost me terrible exhausting labour and heart-rending nerve-wracking strain. You may not believe me, but I assure you on my honour that it must have taken fully five minutes to write!"

In the scene in question a solicitor named Gribsby appears at Jack Worthing's country house to serve a writ of attachment at the suit of the Savoy Hotel Co. for £762 14s 2d on his imaginary brother Ernest, in reality Algernon, who has just arrived. The solicitor explains that as he has written to the debtor no less than thirteen times he has no option but to remove him to London under a committal order.

ALGERNON   If you imagine I am going up to town the moment I arrive you are extremely mistaken.

GRIBSBY   I am merely a solicitor myself. I do not employ personal violence of any kind. The officer of the court whose function it is to seize the person of the debtor is waiting in the fly outside. He has considerable experience in these matters. In point of fact he has arrested in the course of his duties nearly all the younger sons of the aristocracy, as well as several eldest sons, besides of course a good many members of the House of Lords. His style and manner are considered extremely good. Indeed he looks more like a betting man than a court official. That is why we always employ him. But no doubt you will prefer to pay the bill.

ALGERNON   Pay it? How on earth am I going to do that? You don't suppose I have got any money. How perfectly silly you are. No gentleman ever has any money.

GRIBSBY   My experience is that it is usually relatives who pay.

After some further discussion, during which Jack Worthing peruses the bill and shows it to Dr Chasuble, who remarks that "it is certainly a painful proof of the disgraceful luxury of the age" and that "we are far away from Wordsworth's plain living and high thinking," Gribsby pulls out his watch.

GRIBSBY   I am sorry to disturb this pleasant family meeting, but time presses. We have to be at Holloway not later than four o'clock; otherwise it is difficult to obtain admission. The rules are very strict.

ALGERNON   Holloway!

GRIBSBY   It is at Holloway that detentions of this character take place always.

ALGERNON   Well, I really am not going to be imprisoned in the suburbs for having dined in the West End. It is perfectly ridiculous.

GRIBSBY   The bill is for suppers, not for dinners.

ALGERNON   I really don't care. All I say is that I am not going to be
            imprisoned in the suburbs.
GRIBSBY   The surroundings, I admit, are middle class; but the gaol itself is
            fashionable and well-aired, and there are ample opportunities for
            taking exercise at certain stated hours of the day. In the case of a
            medical certificate, which is always easy to obtain, the hours can
            be extended.
ALGERNON   Exercise! Good God! No gentleman ever takes exercise. You
            don't seem to understand what a gentleman is.
GRIBSBY   I have met so many of them, sir, that I am afraid I don't. There
            are the most curious varieties of them. Will you kindly come now,
            sir, if it will not be inconvenient to you.

Alexander knew his business as a producer and he eventually convinced Wilde of the necessity of cutting this scene, as well as making
other cuts, so as to bring the play within the normal duration of a three-
act play. But Wilde continued to be difficult at rehearsals and his inter-
ruptions were so frequent that Alexander feared that they would never be
ready for the opening on 14 February. Eventually he took Wilde aside
and said, "We know now everything you want and if you'll leave us
alone to get on with the rehearsals, we shall try our best to give it to
you. But if you don't, we shall never be ready. So I'll send you a box for
the first night and see you again after the performance."

Wilde was taken aback for a few moments. Then he assumed a solemn
air. "My dear Aleck," he said, "I have still one more thing to say to you
and Tony Aynsworth. So if you will both of you come and have supper
with me tonight at the Albemarle Club, I shall not trouble you again."

To humour him, Alexander and Aynsworth agreed, but they both
wondered what on earth Wilde had on his mind to tell them as they
walked up St James's Street from the theatre after a long day's rehearsal.
When they reached the club, Wilde was waiting for them in full evening dress. "My dear Aleck and my dear Tony," he said as he laid a
friendly hand on the shoulder of each of them, "I have only one thing to
say to you. You are neither of you my favourite actor. We will now go
in to supper."

Wilde left London about the middle of January immediately after this
meeting. A rumour had reached Ada Leverson as to where he was going
and with whom. "Yes," he wrote her, "I fly to Algiers with Bosie tomorrow. I begged him to let me stay to rehearse, but so beautiful is his
nature that he declined at once."

On the eve of his departure he was interviewed by a representative of
the *St James's Gazette,* then a Conservative evening paper of considerable
influence to which Wilde used to contribute book reviews and which
had later attacked *The Picture of Dorian Gray* when it first appeared in
serial form. The interviewer found him reading "of course nothing so
obvious as a timetable, but a French newspaper which contained an account of the first night of *An Ideal Husband* and its author's appearance
after the play." The interview, published on 18 January 1895 after
Wilde had left for Algiers with Douglas, continued:

"How well the French appreciate these brilliant wilful moments in an artist's life," remarked Mr Wilde, handing me the article as if he considered the interview already at an end.

"Does it give you any pleasure," I inquired, "to appear before the curtain after the production of your plays?"

"None whatsoever. No artist finds any interest in seeing the public. The public is very much interested in seeing an artist. Personally, I prefer the French custom, according to which the name of the dramatist is announced to the public by the oldest actor in the piece."

"Would you advocate," I asked, "this custom in England?"

"Certainly. The more the public is interested in artists, the less it is interested in art. The personality of the artist is not a thing the public should know anything about. It is too accidental." Then, after a pause—

"It might be more interesting if the name of the author were announced by the *youngest* actor present."

"It is only in deference, then, to the imperious mandate of the public that you have appeared before the curtain?"

"Yes; I have always been very good-natured about that. The public has always been so appreciative of my work I felt it would be a pity to spoil its evening."

"I notice some people have found fault with the character of your speeches."

"Yes, the old-fashioned idea was that the dramatist should appear and merely thank his kind friends for their patronage and presence. I am glad to say I have altered all that. The artist cannot be degraded into the servant of the public. While I have always recognized the cultured appreciation that actors and audience have shown for my work, I have equally recognized that humility is for the hypocrite, modesty for the incompetent. Assertion is at once the duty and privilege of the artist."

Wilde went on to air his views on stage censorship in the context of the banning of *Salomé,* and the difference in France and England between dramatic critics and actors. "The English critics should be pensioned off," said Wilde, "and only allowed to write on politics or theology or bimetallism, or some subject easier than art." Asked about his favourite dramatists, he admitted that only two in the present century had interested him—Victor Hugo and Maeterlinck. "Setting aside the prose and poetry of Greek and Latin authors," he added, "the only writers who have influenced me are Keats, Flaubert, and Walter Pater; and before I came across them I had already gone more than half-way to meet them. Style must be in one's soul before one can recognise it in others."

"And do you consider *An Ideal Husband* the best of your plays?" queried the interviewer.

A charming smile crossed Mr Wilde's face.

"Have you forgotten my classical expression—that only mediocrities improve? My three plays are to each other, as a wonderful young poet has beautifully said,

—as one white rose
On one green stalk to another one.

They form a perfect cycle, and in their delicate sphere complete both life and art."

"Do you think that the critics will understand your new play, which Mr George Alexander has secured?"

"I hope not."

"I dare not ask, I suppose, if it will please the public?"

"When a play that is a work of art is produced on the stage what is being tested is not the play, but the stage; when a play that is *not* a work of art is produced on the stage what is being tested is not the play, but the public."

"What sort of play are we to expect?"

"It is exquisitely trivial, a delicate bubble of fancy, and it has its philosophy!"

"Its philosophy?"

"That we should treat all the trivial things of life very seriously, and all the serious things of life with sincere and studied triviality."

"You have no leanings towards realism?"

"None whatever. Realism is only a background; it cannot form an artistic motive for a play that is to be a work of art."

"Still I have heard you congratulated on your pictures of London society."

"If Robert Chiltern, the Ideal Husband, were a common clerk, the humanity of his tragedy would be none the less poignant. I have placed him in the higher ranks of life merely because that is the side of social life with which I am best acquainted. In a play dealing with actualities to write with ease one must write with knowledge."

"Then you see nothing suggestive of treatment in the tragedies of everyday existence?"

"If a journalist is run over by a four-wheeler in the Strand, an incident I regret to say I have never witnessed, it suggests nothing to me from a dramatic point of view. Perhaps I am wrong; but the artist must have his limitations."

"Well," I said, rising to go, "I have enjoyed myself immensely."

"I was sure you would," said Mr Wilde. "But tell me how you manage your interviews."

"Oh, Pitman," I said carelessly.

"Is that your name? It's not a very *nice* name."

Then I left.

Robert Ross forwarded a copy of the journal containing the interview together with Wilde's mail to Algiers. "The interview is most brilliant and delightful, and your forwarding my letters really most sweet of you," Wilde wrote back from the Hôtel de l'Europe.

There is a great deal of beauty here. The Kabyle boys are quite lovely. At first we had some difficulty in procuring a proper civilised guide. But now it is all right, and Bosie and I have taken to hashish: it is quite exquisite: three puffs of smoke and then peace and love. Bosie wakes up at night and cries like a child for the best hashish.

We have been on an excursion into the mountains of Kabylia—full of villages peopled by fauns. Several shepherds fluted on reeds for us. We were followed by lovely brown things from forest to forest. The beggars here have profiles, so the problem of poverty is easily solved.

You are a great dear over my letters. Bosie sends his love, so do I.

Ever yours
OSCAR

> The most beautiful boy in Algiers is said by the guide to be "deceitful":
> isn't it sad? Bosie and I are awfully upset about it.

Wilde returned to London in time for the dress rehearsal of *The Importance of Being Earnest* on 12 February, when he staggered the company by telling Alexander that he supposed "we must start rehearsals for the play on Monday." Asked by a press reporter next day whether he thought the play would be a success, he replied, "My dear fellow, you have got it wrong. The play *is* a success. The only question is whether the first night's audience will be one." As will be seen, it was.

Wilde's wit as a playwright reached its height in *The Importance of Being Earnest,* generally regarded as one of the finest light comedies in the English language and the only one of Wilde's plays thoroughly to stand the test of time. Yet the wit as exemplified in this and the other comedies is only a pale reflection of what his friends and acquaintances have recalled of him as a conversationalist. "He was without exception the most brilliant talker I have ever come across, the most ready, the most witty, the most audacious," Wilfrid Scawen Blunt noted in his diary when Wilde died. "Nobody could pretend to outshine him, or even to shine at all in his company." This has been confirmed by Max Beerbohm, among others. "Oscar was always a good host and always in excellent form," Beerbohm told the present writer at the time of Wilde's centenary in 1954.

> Some people are off their form sometimes, but Oscar was always at the top
> of his form all the time. He was helped by his rich, melodious voice which
> added effect to his conversation. As I said in my message for the centenary,
> he was the best talker I have ever heard. He was charming too with young
> people and would always try to bring them into the conversation. Not that
> the really intelligent ones wanted very much to be brought into the conver-
> sation. They were quite content to listen.

According to Robert Ross, when he was staying with Wilde in Tite Street in 1887, he wrote down all the witty things his host said to him and later gave his notes to Wilde, who used them for *The Importance of Being Earnest* when he was writing the play as quickly as he could—it was completed in three weeks—because he needed money.

It was the rapidity and spontaneity of his repartee, combined with characteristic amiability, that made such an unforgettable impression upon those who remembered him. For example, he once greeted a new arrival at a reception given by his friend Lady de Grey with the words: "Oh, I'm so glad you've come! There are a hundred things I want not to say to you." On another occasion at a lunch party given by the same hostess, an argument arose between him and Lord Ribblesdale about after-dinner speeches. Lady Randolph Churchill was also present and she later recalled how Wilde declared that there was no subject on which he could not speak at a moment's notice.

Taking him at his word, Lord Ribblesdale raised his glass and said, "The Queen."

"She is not a subject," answered Wilde, quick as lightning.

Again a youth was being told by one of his elders and so-called betters that, like everyone else, he must begin at the bottom of the ladder. "No, begin at the top and sit upon it," was Wilde's advice. When the lad said that he was going to Sandhurst, Wilde urged him to go to Oxford instead. "But I am going to be a soldier," he pointed out. Upon which Wilde replied, "If you took a degree at Oxford, they would make you a colonel at once—at any rate in a West Indian regiment."

Having seen Ellen Terry's performance as Lady Macbeth, in which she wore a magnificent green robe upon which Oriental beetles' wings glittered like emeralds and in which she was later painted by Sargent in a celebrated portrait, Wilde remarked to Graham Robertson: "Judging from the banquet, Lady Macbeth seems an economical housekeeper and evidently patronizes local industries for her husband's clothes and the servants' liveries, but she takes care to do all her own shopping in Byzantium."

Incidentally, Sargent's studio was on the opposite side of Tite Street to No. 16, and Ellen Terry used to drive there in her exotic stage costume for the sittings for her portrait. This prompted Wilde to declare to her: "The street that on a wet and dreary morning has vouchsafed the vision of Lady Macbeth, in full regalia magnificently seated in a four-wheeler, can never again be as other streets; it must always be full of wonderful possibilities."

Shortly after the birth of his second son, Wilde happened to meet Adrian Hope and his fiancée Laura Troubridge. They congratulated him and asked what the latest arrival was going to be called. "We think of calling him 'Nothing' " was the reply, "as then it can be said that he is nothing Wild(e)."

On another occasion, Wilde was holding forth on the great suicides of history and claimed that all of them had taken their own lives in the grand manner. "What about Judas?" asked someone. "Oh, Judas! I don't count him. After all he was merely a *nouveau riche!*"

"Surely you remember knowing me in Manchester?" said a man whom Wilde had failed to recognize. "Very possibly in Manchester I may know you again" was Wilde's reply. And when he accidentally cut an old acquaintance, his apology was, "I'm sorry I didn't recognize you—I've changed a lot." To a request that he should compile a list of his hundred favourite books, he answered, "I fear that would be impossible." Asked why: "Because I have written only five."

One day, as he stood outside the front door of his house in Tite Street, about to insert the latchkey, he was approached by a little man who respectfully informed him that he had called about the taxes.

"Taxes!" said Wilde, looking down from the door steps. "Why should I pay taxes?"

"But, sir," said the little man, "you are the householder, are you not? You live here—you sleep here?"

"Ah, yes," replied Wilde with mock solemnity, "but then, you see, I sleep so badly."

On another occasion, as he was walking in the Haymarket, a beggar in rags came up to him and asked him for a little money. He said he had no work to do and no bread to eat.

"Work!" exclaimed Wilde, affecting surprise. "Why should you want to work? And bread? Why should you eat bread?"

Then, after an elaborate pause, he put his hand on the poor man's shoulder and said, "Now, if you had come to me and said that you had work to do, but you couldn't dream of working, and that you had bread to eat, but couldn't think of eating bread—I would have given you half-a-crown." He paused again, and then went on, "As it is, I give you two shillings."

These and other stories were repeated to the present writer by Wilde's contemporary Richard Le Gallienne, who knew Wilde well and was proud to have been his friend. "He has become the symbolic figure of his age," remarked Le Gallienne, looking back thirty years later. "He made dying Victorianism laugh at itself, and what serious reformers had laboured for years to accomplish he did in a moment with the flash of an epigram; gaily, with humour and wit for his weapons." Apart from the plays, this was particularly true of *The Soul of Man under Socialism,* which originally appeared in *Blackwood's* and was republished as *The Soul of Man* in 1895 by Arthur Humphreys, who managed Hatchard's bookshop in Piccadilly. Earlier in the same year, Humphreys brought out a selection of Wilde's epigrams which had been made by Constance Wilde under the title *Oscariana.* In gratitude Wilde sent him a stall for the first night of *The Importance of Being Earnest*—"the last to be got!" he told him. "I hope you will enjoy my 'trivial' play. It is written by a butterfly for butterflies."

When it was clear towards the end of the first night that the play was a roaring success, Wilde spoke to Franklin Dyall about himself and his greatest theatrical triumph. "I don't think I shall take a call tonight," he said. "I took one only last month at the Haymarket, and one feels so much like a German band!" Now Wilde had two huge successes running in London's West End—but, alas, not for long. The Damoclean sword which had been hanging over him in the shape of the near-insane Marquess of Queensberry was about to fall upon him.

9

In considering Wilde as a pathological case study, there is first the question of heredity and early environment. He was the child of parents of marked eccentricity as well as of exceptional ability; both qualities became concentrated in him to a striking degree. They help to explain his congenital antipathy for the ordinary and commonplace, his natural love of paradox, and his aestheticism, all of which he sought to express in his conversation and writings. Sir William Wilde, moreover, was a man of abnormal sexual drive: as we have seen, he was a notorious runner after women; he had illegitimate offspring; and he figured in a sensational trial in Dublin in which he was accused of having violated a woman patient. Lady Wilde, on the other hand, exhibited certain peculiar physical characteristics due to the excessive development of her pituitary gland, which were reproduced in her second son. This excess appeared in general physical overgrowth. For instance, Bernard Shaw recalled that her hands were enormous "and the gigantic splaying of her palm was reproduced in her lumbar region." To Shaw, Oscar Wilde also appeared as an overgrown individual with something not quite normal about his bigness. To people like Lady Colin Campbell who were repelled by his physical appearance, he was "that great white caterpillar." Undoubtedly there was some truth in his fellow Irishman's diagnosis. "I have always maintained that Oscar was a giant in the pathological sense," wrote Shaw, "and that this explains a good deal of his weakness."

It has been said that Speranza was disappointed that her son Oscar was not a girl, and a good deal has been made of the fact that she dressed him in girl's clothes during his childhood days, decking him out with jewels, which made him look like "a little Hindu idol." But this treatment has probably little, if any, pathological significance in Wilde's case. Victorian mothers were accustomed to dress their children of either sex in petticoats and skirts until they were six or seven years old. And to this day, as T. G. Wilson, the biographer of Wilde's father, has pointed out, little boys are dressed as girls in parts of rural Ireland, lest the fairies should steal them, "for, of course, the fairies are interested only in little boys."

Havelock Ellis has expressed the opinion that homosexuality was latent in Wilde's constitution from the beginning, although it did not become active until he was in his early thirties. It is certain that Wilde betrayed no signs of it in adolescence and early manhood; on the contrary, his inclinations seem to have been decidedly heterosexual. While an undergraduate at Oxford, or shortly after coming down, he contracted syphilis as the result of a casual connection with a female prostitute. In those days the recognized treatment for this venereal disease was mercury. In Wilde's case this treatment undoubtedly produced the discolouration and decay in his teeth, which remained a permanent feature of his appearance for the rest of his life and added to the general impression of physical overgrowth and ugliness which his person presented. Nor, it may be added, was there the slightest suggestion of effeminacy about him, either at Oxford or at any subsequent period. If somewhat ungainly in movement, he was endowed with an abundant measure of manly strength, as a number of his college contemporaries discovered to their cost.

While at Oxford he seems to have fallen in love, or at least seriously flirted, with several "respectable" girls, if we may judge from an indignant outburst from the mother of one of them when he had followed up a vacation visit to her home by inviting the daughter to meet him in Dublin. ("I was very much pained the last time I was at your house when I went into the drawing-room and saw Fidelia sitting on your knee. Young as she is, she ought to have had—and so I told her—the instinctive delicacy that would have shrunk from it. But, oh, Oscar, the thing was neither right, nor manly, nor gentlemanlike in you! You have disappointed me—nay, so low and vulgar was it that I could not have believed anyone of refined mind capable of such a thing.") The mother was particularly upset by Oscar's leaving her to open the front door for herself, while he stayed behind in the hall to steal a surreptitious kiss from the apparently by no means unwilling Fidelia. This conduct incurred a further reproach. ("Do you think for a moment that I was so supremely stupid as not to know that you always kissed Fidelia when you met her, if you had an opportunity?")

His first serious love affair during this early period, as we have seen, was with Florence Balcombe, a girl four years younger than himself. Oscar's passion for Florrie lasted two years—"the sweetest of all the years of my youth," so he told her afterwards—and no doubt he wished to marry her. But she turned him down in favour of Bram Stoker. It took some years for the wound to heal. In 1881, when Florrie got her first stage part, a walk-on, in Henry Irving's production of Tennyson's verse play *The Cup,* Wilde wrote to Ellen Terry, who had a leading part, and sent her a crown of flowers, which he asked the great actress to give the beginner without revealing its origin. ("I shall like to think she was wearing something of mine the first night she comes on the stage, that anything of mine should touch her . . . She thinks I never loved her, thinks I forget. My God, how could I?") Certainly Wilde never forgot his first true love. A dozen years later we find him sending her a copy of *Salomé*—"my strange venture in a tongue that is not my own, but that I love as one loves an instrument on which one has not played before"— and subscribing himself, "Always your sincere friend Oscar Wilde."

Wilde's emerging interest in male physical beauty, as exemplified in some of his early poems, has already been noticed. He may well have been unaware of its significance at the same time as his inclinations gradually became bisexual. Before his marriage he certainly had recourse to prostitutes. Besides the professional prostitute at Oxford, known among the undergraduate community as "Old Jess," from whom he may have received his first dose of venereal disease, we know on the authority of his friend Robert Sherard that he had connections of this kind in Paris and New York, as well as in London. He once told Sherard how surprised he was during his first American visit, when he had just finished a rhapsodical discourse, on the beauties of English art, by the matter-of-fact way in which some of the young men in the lecture hall approached him with some such words as: "And now, Oscar, after all that soulthrob, of course you feel like a bit of skirt"—and took him straight off to a brothel. Sherard also records how Wilde, while staying in Paris in 1883, confessed to him one evening that "Priapus was calling" and thereupon departed by himself for The Eden, a music hall, which was the place in which to pick up the better-class whores in the town. There, according to Sherard, he picked up and spent the night with Marie Aguétant, a well-known *demi-mondaine.* (She was afterwards murdered by one of her lovers, Prado, the illegitimate son of the President of Peru, and a notorious *maquereau* and *homme-à-femmes,* who in a fit of jealous rage "cut her throat from ear to ear while the lady was astride the *bidet.*") Next morning, Wilde was "in great form" when he met Sherard. The first thing he said to him was, "What animals we are, Robert!" Sherard's chief care was to make sure that his friend had not been robbed, to which Wilde replied, "One gives them all in one's pockets."

Although he played up to women and flattered their vanity, which no doubt explains why he was generally liked by them, Oscar Wilde had no illusions whatever about female virtue. He considered women as being prompted mainly, if not solely, by the sexual urge, and he regarded many of them as devoid of what is commonly called "morality." On one occasion, he happened to meet Sherard in a London hotel. Sherard was accompanied by a lady with whom he had eloped from Paris and for whom he had taken a separate room in the hotel, pending arrangements for marrying her. "Act dishonourably, Robert," Wilde said to his friend. "Act dishonourably. It is what sooner or later she'll certainly do to you!" Whether Sherard took this advice is not known, but we do know for certain that he did marry his companion, and also that in the process of time Wilde's prediction came true. So did a similar prophecy with regard to Wilde's elder brother, Willie. At the time of Willie's marriage to the wealthy American, Mrs Frank Leslie, Oscar blamed his brother for not having got a good financial settlement from her beforehand. "When she has glutted her lust on him and used him up," he told Sherard, "she'll pitch him his hat and coat and by means of an American divorce get rid of him legally and let him starve to death for all she'll care." Which is precisely what did happen, the lady in question telling the reporters after they had parted that "he was of no use to me either by day or by night."

Wilde thought that there were barely 5 percent of English husbands who had not been deceived by their wives. Sherard relates that he once asked Wilde how a husband should act when he discovered that his wife had a lover. "Pretend to ignore the liaison and delight in watching them" was the reply. "It will get so interesting as the time gets near for his departure, when you three have been spending the evening together. You show yourself more and more marital and you close the séance by giving him his congé with some such remark as 'Well, so long! We young married folks, you know?' And to the adulterous wife: 'Au lit, darling, au lit!' The touching scene ends with the husband later going in his pyjamas to the window, while the disconsolate lover stands on the other side of the road gazing up towards 'the place where Cressid lay' and sighing. There you attract his attention and wave your hand towards him to imply that he must be on his way, while you hasten to the matrimonial delights that are awaiting you."

On the other hand, we know that at the outset of their married life Wilde was deeply in love with his wife and that they experienced normal sexual intercourse, which resulted in the birth of their two sons. Indeed, he seems to have been an enthusiastic lover. To Sherard, whom he chanced to meet during the honeymoon in Paris, he spontaneously expatiated upon the physical joys of wedlock. And on the occasion of his first separation from his wife, some months later, when he was lecturing in Edinburgh, he wrote to her:

> Here am I; and you at the Antipodes: O execrable fates that keep our lips from kissing, though our souls are one . . . The messages of the gods to each other travel not by pen and ink, and indeed your bodily presence here would not make you more real: for I feel your fingers in my hair and your cheek brushing mine. The air is full of the music of your voice, my soul and body seem no longer mine, but mingled in some exquisite ecstasy with yours. I feel incomplete without you.[22]

Before proposing to his wife, Wilde had been to consult a doctor in London, who had assured him that he was completely cured of his youthful malady. On the strength of this assurance, he got married. About two years later he discovered to his dismay that all traces of syphilis had not been eradicated from his system; on the contrary, the spirochetes were quite active. It was this unpleasant discovery which obliged him to discontinue physical relations with his wife. As a result, *inter alia,* he turned towards homosexuality.[23]

At first Wilde developed what was merely an inquisitive interest in sexual inversion. Such an inquisitive interest, as Havelock Ellis has observed, is sometimes the sign of an emerging homosexual impulse. According to his contemporary André Raffalovich, he liked to discuss the subject with his friends.[24] "I do not think," he used to tell them, "that the people who do these things derive as much pleasure as I do from talking about them." Prominent homosexual characters in history began to attract him. He was fascinated by the story of King James I's favourite, Robert Carr, Earl of Somerset, who on the eve of his trial for the murder of Sir Thomas Overbury threatened to reveal publicly that "the King had slept with him"—with the result that two men in long robes were posted on either side of the accused in court with instructions literally to stifle any attempted incrimination of His Majesty. In this context Wilde studied the lives of Plato and Michelangelo, and as has already been seen, he conducted a piece of ingenious research into the origins of Shakespeare's sonnets to "W.H.," whom he thought to be a boy actor named Willie Hughes. Wilde is also stated by Raffalovich to have

[22] Apart from a few brief notes, this letter (now in the Pierpont Morgan Library, New York) is the only one from Wilde to his wife that is known to have survived.

[23] Sherard has confirmed this in his unpublished (and unpublishable) letters to A. J. A. Symons, now in the Donald F. Hyde collection. The fact that Wilde was syphilitic was first made publicly known by Arthur Ransome, who got his facts from Robert Ross. See Ransome, *Oscar Wilde* (1912), p. 199.

[24] Marc-André Raffalovich (1865–1934), psychologist and writer, became an authority on this aspect of Wilde's life. He belonged to a wealthy family of Russian Jewish bankers in Paris; his sister married William O'Brien, the Irish Nationalist leader. At this time he was living in London and was a friend, among others, of Aubrey Beardsley, becoming the anonymous recipient of *The Last Letters of Aubrey Beardsley* (1904). His study of male homosexuality, *Uranisme et Unisexualité,* which was published in France the year after Wilde's conviction, contained the first full, though not noticeably sympathetic, account of the Wilde trials and their background to appear in any language, besides a great deal of curious material on the history and prevalence of male inversion in England.

shown an increased interest in the subject as the result of reading *Monsieur Venus,* the extraordinary novel by "Rachilde" on the theme of male homosexuality which created such a sensation on its first appearance in 1889.

Indeed, sin in all its aspects became a preoccupation with Wilde amounting almost to an obsession. This is evident in such of his writings as *Intentions, Lord Arthur Savile's Crime,* and *Salomé.* In *The Picture of Dorian Gray,* in which the character of the cynically decadent Lord Henry Wotton was largely based on the real-life Lord Ronald Gower, there is a pervading atmosphere of homosexuality. John Addington Symonds, though himself a homosexual, resented what he called "the unhealthy, scented, mystic, congested touch which a man of this sort has on moral problems," and described the work on its original appearance in *Lippincott's* as "an odd and very audacious production, unwholesome in tone, but artistically and psychologically interesting," adding that "if the British public will stand this, they can stand anything."

It is likely that Wilde first became a practising homosexual in 1886 as the result of his meeting Robert Ross; the latter subsequently admitted to Frank Harris that he was "the first boy Oscar ever had," and there seems no reason to doubt this statement, confirmed by a similar admission to Arthur Ransome.

Later in the 'eighties, after he had met Ross, some curious evidence of Wilde's tastes came to light. A French bookseller named Charles Hirsch came over from Paris to London and opened a bookshop, the Librairie Française in Coventry Street, for the sale of French publications. Among his first customers was Oscar Wilde, who used to buy the works of the leading French authors of the day, such as Zola and Maupassant. After a while, when he got to know the bookseller better and had taken him into his confidence, Wilde would order "certain licentious works of a special *genre,*" which he euphemistically described as "socratic" and which the bookseller was able to obtain not without difficulty.

One day, in 1890, Wilde came into the bookshop carrying a small package, which was carefully wrapped up and sealed. "A friend of mine will call for this manuscript and will show you my card," he told the Frenchman, to whom he also gave the name of the prospective caller. Some few days later, a young man whom the bookseller had previously seen in Wilde's company appeared and took the package away. After a while, he came back with it, saying in turn, "Please give this to one of our friends who will call for it on behalf of the same person."

The procedure was repeated three times. The last borrower, who was not so careful as the others, returned the manuscript unwrapped and simply tied round with a piece of ribbon. The temptation to open it and read it was too great for M. Hirsch to resist. On the greyish paper cover which held together the pages of the MS there was a single word, "Teleny." The same evening the bookseller read through the whole of the MS, which proved to be the story in the form of an erotic novel of a well-to-do Parisian called Des Grieux—the author had given his hero the same surname as Manon Lescaut's lover—and his love for a young male pianist named Teleny. What particularly struck the bookseller about the MS was the extraordinary mixture of different handwriting, erasures, interlineations, corrections, and additions obviously made by different hands. "It was evident to me," M. Hirsch noted at the time, "that several writers of unequal literary merit had collaborated on this anonymous but profoundly interesting work." The bookseller subsequently told C. R. Dawes, the English authority on erotic literature, that in his opinion *Teleny* was mainly the work of various friends of Wilde, who had himself looked over and corrected the MS, adding touches of his own here and there. Dawes subsequently admitted that *Teleny* was "better written than most English erotic books" but that if Wilde really had a hand in it, as apparently he must have done, "perhaps it may be regarded as an outlet for the worst and most sensational side of Wilde's artistic nature." [25]

If Wilde had been content to confine his homosexual relations to Robert Ross, and even to Lord Alfred Douglas, it is extremely unlikely that his conduct in this respect would ever have come to the notice of the Director of Public Prosecutions. Unfortunately for him, he made the fatal mistake of extending the range of his homosexual acquaintances to such individuals as a groom, an unemployed clerk, and a newspaper boy. In this, of course, Wilde acted with a reckless disregard of his personal safety, since he exposed himself as a victim to blackmailers. Most of these youths were procured for him by Alfred Taylor. Although Wilde probably did not meet Taylor on more than half a dozen occasions, usually in Taylor's exotically furnished rooms in Little College Street, Westminster, Alfred Taylor was to play a significant part in Wilde's undoing and eventually to stand beside him in the dock at the Old Bailey.

Wilde's association with Alfred Taylor was particularly unfortunate for the playwright, since Taylor was a homosexual with transvestite inclinations who had already come up against the law in the course of his association with Wilde. As the result of a midnight raid by the police on a house in Fitzroy Street in the Bloomsbury district of London in August 1894, eighteen men were taken into custody, among them Taylor and an unemployed valet named Charles Parker, who had been introduced to Wilde by Taylor and who was to be the first of the string of Crown witnesses to testify against Wilde at his trials. After a week's remand, five of those charged were bound over to be of good behaviour, and the remainder, including Taylor and Parker, were discharged unconditionally. In announcing his decision, the magistrate stated that he had had a number of letters informing him that many of the men were of "the vilest possible character," but no one had come forward to give evidence to that effect, although most of those charged were said to be al-

---

[25] *Teleny, or The Reverse of the Medal,* was published under an anonymous imprint in 1893 by Wilde's latter-day publisher Leonard Smithers, who ran a profitable sideline in erotica. "It is a book which will rank as the chief of its class," wrote Smithers in advertising it, "and it may truthfully be said to make a new departure in English amatory literature." Hirsch brought out a French translation in 1934. The original English text with some omissions and an introduction by the present writer was published by Icon Books in London in 1966.

ready known to the police. "Poor Alfred Taylor," wrote Wilde at the time. "It is a dreadful piece of bad luck."

This incident prompted Max Beerbohm to make a jocular but uncannily accurate prophecy to Reggie Turner. "Oscar has been arrested for certain kinds of crime," he wrote on the same day as the police raid had taken place in Fitzroy Square. "He was taken in the Café Royal (lower room). Bosie escaped, being an excellent runner, but Oscar was less nimble."

The precise mode in which Wilde's peculiar inverted instincts found satisfaction is of interest from the medico-legal standpoint. His conduct with the various youths whom he met, or who were procured for him by the obliging Taylor, usually began with close physical contact and fondling. This would be followed by some form of mutual masturbation or intercrural intercourse. (Amongst the articles of clothing found in Taylor's room were several pairs of trousers with slits or vents in place of pockets, a feature plainly designed to facilitate masturbation.) Finally oral copulation would be practised, with Wilde as the active agent, though this role was occasionally reversed. It gave him inspiration, he said. He is also stated, on the questionable authority of Trelawny Backhouse, to have sometimes indulged in anal penetration, although it was suggested by only one of the witnesses who gave evidence at his trials that Wilde had actually committed sodomy. (This may have been due to a misunderstanding by the witness of the precise meaning of the word.) Nor indeed was Wilde ever charged with this graver offence, which carried the maximum penalty of life imprisonment.

With his literary friends in Paris, Wilde was particularly candid. "He makes no secret of it," Henri de Régnier told Edmond de Goncourt. "He admits that he's a homosexual." Meanwhile, Wilde's relations with a series of characters in London's homosexual underworld, out-of-work stable boys, clerks, domestic servants, and the like, proceeded with an increasing and almost unbelievable recklessness. "The Treasury will always give me twenty-four hours to leave the country just as they did in Lord Arthur Somerset's case," he said when warned by Robert Ross and other friends of the risks he was running. It seems to have been only the fact that he was regarded as a great poseur, which indeed in many respects he was, that postponed the day of reckoning for so long. He habitually wore in his buttonhole a carnation artificially coloured green, an emblem which he knew to be the distinguishing mark of homosexuals in Paris, and this was speedily imitated by his youthful admirers on the other side of the Channel. Indeed, the cult of the green carnation led the novelist Robert Hichens to write an amusing skit in which the two chief characters were admittedly based on Wilde and Douglas. And as late as the autumn of 1894, when *The Green Carnation* made its original anonymous appearance, people were still saying: "It's only Oscar. He likes to talk about it, but he doesn't do anything." Yet he had already done a great deal, for which he was soon to be called upon to answer at the Old Bailey.

As Trelawny Backhouse later wrote in his scabrous memoirs, "Wilde's reckless publicity and flaunting his predilection, more particularly with the *canaille,* lackeys, grooms and professional blackmailers, was drawing him to the abyss: incidents repeated themselves when he left behind ocular proofs of his orgies in hotel bedrooms: horrible proofs of a most painstaking *pedicatio* [anal penetration] were found on the sheets and meticulously preserved by the management to be produced in due course at the third *procès,* with the medical analysis of human semen, human excrement *et de la vaseline,* like Messalina (except for the homosexuality)." According to Aubrey Beardsley, so states Backhouse, one night at the Savoy, "when a lot of us were having an after-theatre supper," Wilde boasted of having had five love affairs with telegraph and district messenger boys in a single night. ("I kissed each one of them in every part of their bodies: they were all dirty and appealed to me just for that reason.") Backhouse has also recalled that he happened to be staying in the Hôtel des Deux Mondes in the Avenue de l'Opéra in Paris with a homosexual actor named Henry Stanford in May 1894, when Wilde and Douglas were stopping in the same hotel, presumably on their way back to London from Florence. "The unbiassed reader will not be astonished to hear that sexual relations were frequently commemorated between us," Backhouse wrote afterwards, "although Oscar admitted to me that he derived greater pleasure from association with the type of *laquais, la canaille et la lie du peuple,* 'because their passion was all body and no soul!' "

Among the young men whom Wilde met through Taylor was one called Charles Spurrier Mason, with whom Taylor was said to have gone through a ceremony of "marriage." Wilde wrote to him from Worthing for news of how Taylor had taken the police raid. "When I come back to town, do come and dine," he added. "What fun our dinners were in the old days! I hope marriage has not made you too serious? It has never had that effect on me." It was a subject on which Wilde could speak from personal experience. "I've been married three times in my life," he confessed to another acquaintance at this period, "once to a woman and twice to men."

After Nemesis had overtaken him, Wilde had plenty of time for reflection. In a petition which he addressed to the Home Secretary in 1896, when he had served a little more than half his prison sentence, he wrote:

> The Petitioner is now keenly conscious of the fact that while the three years preceding his arrest were from the intellectual point of view the most brilliant years of his life (four plays from his pen having been produced on the stage with immense success, and plays not merely in England, America and Australia, but in almost every European capital, and many books that excited much interest at home and abroad having been published), still that during the entire time he was suffering from the most horrible form of erotomania, which made him forget his wife and children, his high social position in London and Paris, his European distinction as an artist, the honour of his name and family, his very humanity itself, and left him the helpless prey of the most revolting passions, and of a gang of people who for their own profit ministered to them, and then drove him to his hideous ruin.

PART TWO
Nemesis

5 / The First Trial

John Sholto Douglas, eighth Marquess of Queensberry, was an extremely eccentric Scottish nobleman. To judge from his recorded actions and utterances, he may be taken to have been mentally unbalanced. His principal preoccupations were sport and atheism, and he knew much more about his horses and dogs than about the human members of his family. He had, however, proved himself a successful steeplechaser and an efficient Master of Hounds, and he had also been an amateur lightweight boxing champion. Apart from his ill-fated quarrel with Wilde, he is chiefly remembered as the author of the rules which govern amateur boxing and which bear his name. But his professions of atheism had already won for him a contemporary notoriety. As a representative peer of Scotland he had refused to take the oath in the House of Lords on the ground that this necessary preliminary was a mere "Christian tomfoolery." In his private life he bullied his wife, who subsequently divorced him, and neglected his children, preferring instead the society of his mistresses and his sporting cronies. He was arrogant, vain, conceited, and ill-tempered.[1] His fury at his eldest son, Lord Drumlanrig (Lord Rosebery's private secretary), being created an English peer led to a ridiculous scene at Homburg: the irate Marquess pursued the Foreign Secretary (as Rosebery then was) there with a dog whip. Peace was preserved only as the result of the personal intervention of the Prince of Wales.[2]

Not long afterward the eccentric Marquess learned of his third son being seen about with "this man Wilde," as he was in the habit of describing Alfred's friend. Eventually Queensberry told his son that he

---

[1] In 1887 he was divorced by his wife for adultery and cruelty; he married again a few years later and this marriage ended in an annulment after a few months.

[2] Queensberry's fury was caused in part by the fact that since 1880 his own election as a representative peer had not been renewed.

must give up knowing Wilde, as he was not a fit man to associate with. Alfred Douglas refused; the Marquess got angry and threatened to cut his allowance.

One day, toward the end of 1892, Wilde and Douglas happened to be lunching together in the Café Royal and noticed Queensberry glowering at them from an adjoining table. At Wilde's prompting, Douglas got up and went over to his father, who somewhat reluctantly consented to be introduced to Wilde, and the three men sat down and finished their lunch together. In a very short time Queensberry was completely captivated by Wilde's charm of manner and conversation, the lunch was prolonged over liqueurs and cigars, and about three o'clock Douglas left them in an animated discussion of Christianity and atheism. Immediately after this, Queensberry wrote to his son saying that he took back everything he had previously said about Wilde, whom he considered charming and extremely clever. Their next meeting took place eighteen months later, shortly after Alfred Douglas had returned from Egypt, again in the Café Royal. This encounter was also quite friendly.

Unfortunately the calm was short-lived. Soon Queensberry was writing his son abusive letters threatening once more to cut him off if he did not drop Wilde. This correspondence culminated in a most insulting missive, which Queensberry wrote on 1 April 1894 and which contained the following extract:

> Your intimacy with this man Wilde must either cease or I will disown you and stop all money supplies. I am not going to try and analyse this intimacy, and I make no charge; but to my mind to pose as a thing is as bad as to be it. With my own eyes I saw you both in the most loathsome and disgusting relationship, as expressed by your manner and expression. Never in my experience have I seen such a sight as that in your horrible features. No wonder people are talking as they are. Also I now hear on good authority, but this may be false, that his wife is petitioning to divorce him for sodomy and other crimes. Is this true, or do you not know of it? If I thought the actual thing was true, and it became public property, I should be quite justified in shooting him at sight.

To this amazing effusion Alfred Douglas replied in a celebrated telegram: WHAT A FUNNY LITTLE MAN YOU ARE. Queensberry was now bordering on frenzy, and he threatened to give his impertinent young jackanapes of a son "the thrashing you deserve," should he send any similar communication in future. "If I catch you again with that man," he went on, "I will make a public scandal in a way you little dream of; it is already a suppressed one. I prefer an open one, and at any rate I shall not be blamed for allowing such things to go on."

He then proceeded to visit the various restaurants frequented by Wilde and his son, warning the managers and maîtres d'hôtel that he would thrash them both if he discovered them together on the premises. Douglas reacted to these tactics by making a point of going to these restaurants, writing to his father with details of time and place, and inviting him to come along and "see what happened to him" if he started any of his "ruffianly tricks."

Wilde was now beginning to feel worried by these unwelcome attentions on Queensberry's part. For one thing, they interfered with his professional work and they disturbed the peace of mind he needed as a writer. On the advice apparently of Robert Ross, he consulted the well-known firm of solicitors C. O. Humphreys, Son & Kershaw, as to whether the letter about him and his wife was actionable and whether anything could be done to restrain Queensberry's violent and offensive behaviour. He discussed the matter with the senior partner, Charles Octavius Humphreys, a most experienced criminal lawyer, who in fact was to represent Wilde in the subsequent proceedings against Queensberry. Wilde was eventually dissuaded from taking the matter further by Alfred Douglas's cousin, George Wyndham, M.P., who was prompted to intervene by his natural desire to avert a family scandal. It was agreed between them that Wilde was at least entitled to an apology, and that Humphreys should write to the Marquess and demand one. This was accordingly done, but Queensberry flatly refused to make any amends. "I certainly shall not tender to Mr Oscar Wilde any apology for letters I have written to my son," he wrote back to Humphreys.

Had Wilde prosecuted Queensberry for criminal libel at the time of this interview—May 1894—instead of waiting for nearly twelve months, by which time more damning evidence against himself had become available, it is quite possible that Queensberry would have been convicted and silenced. That Wilde regretted this is apparent from a letter he wrote Douglas almost immediately afterwards. "Your father is on the rampage again—been to the Café Royal to inquire after us—with threats, etc., I think now it would have been better for me to have had him bound over to keep the peace. But what a scandal! Still, it is intolerable to be dogged by a maniac."

One afternoon in June 1894, the "scarlet Marquess," as Wilde called him, presented himself at Wilde's house in Chelsea without any previous warning. He was accompanied, to quote Wilde again, "by a gentleman with whom I was not acquainted"—in fact, a prize-fighter. The interview took place in the library.

"Sit down," said the Marquess, as Wilde walked over to the fireplace.

Wilde turned on him. "I do not allow anyone to talk like that to me in my house or anywhere else." He continued, "I suppose you have come to apologise for the statement you made about my wife and myself in letters you wrote to your son. I should have the right any day I chose to prosecute you for writing such a letter."

"The letter was privileged," interrupted Queensberry, "as it was written to my son."

This time it was Wilde's turn to be angry. "How dare you say such things to me about your son and me?"

Queensberry went on, seemingly unabashed. "You were both kicked out of the Savoy Hotel at a moment's notice for your disgusting conduct."

"That is a lie."

"You have taken furnished rooms for him in Piccadilly."

"Somebody has been telling you an absurd set of lies about your son and me. I have not done anything of the kind."

"I hear you were thoroughly well blackmailed for a disgusting letter you wrote to my son."

Again Wilde protested. "The letter was a beautiful letter, and I never write except for publication."

Wilde thereupon changed his tone to one of the utmost seriousness. "Lord Queensberry," he asked his embarrassing caller, "do you seriously accuse your son and me of improper conduct?"

Queensberry thought for a moment. "I do not say you are it," he said, "but you look it, and you pose as it, which is just as bad. If I catch you and my son together in any public restaurant, I will thrash you."

Although thus confronted with a bully and a bruiser, Wilde did not betray the slightest fear. "I do not know what the Queensberry rules are," he told his unwelcome guest, "but the Oscar Wilde rule is to shoot at sight."

With this, Wilde requested Queensberry to leave the house. Queensberry refused, whereupon Wilde threatened to call the police and have him put out.

"It's a disgusting scandal," foamed the Marquess, as he made for the hallway.

"If it is so," retorted Wilde, "you are the author of the scandal and no one else."

Then, following his visitors into the hall, he pointed out the Marquess to the servant who was waiting there to show them out. "This is the Marquess of Queensberry, the most infamous brute in London. You are never to allow him to enter my house again."

It was now a fight to the finish, and no punches were to be pulled, to use a metaphor from the Marquess's favourite sport. Queensberry had already stopped his son's allowance, and he now directed his venom towards the boy's mother, his own divorced wife, whom he accused of interfering in the quarrel. He wrote to her father, Alfred Montgomery:

> Your daughter is the person who is supporting my son to defy me . . .
> She evidently wants to make out that I want to make out a case against my
> son. It is nothing of the kind. I have made out a case against Oscar Wilde
> and I have to his face accused him of it. If I was quite certain of the thing, I
> would shoot the fellow at sight, but I can only accuse him of posing. It now
> lies in the hands of the two whether they will further defy me. Your daugh-
> ter appears now to be encouraging them, although she can hardly intend
> this. I don't believe Wilde will now dare defy me. He plainly showed the
> white feather the other day when I tackled him—damned cur and coward of
> the Rosebery type. As for this so-called son of mine, he is no son of mine,
> and I will have nothing to do with him. He may starve as far as I am con-
> cerned after his behaviour to me.

At the same time, Queensberry wrote to Alfred Douglas, who had been sending his father postcards, since his letters were now returned to him unopened. Queensberry told him that all future cards would go into the fire unread. He then repeated the threat of a thrashing. "You reptile," concluded this paternal epistle. "You are no son of mine, and I never thought you were."

Douglas promptly replied that he treated his father's absurd threats with absolute indifference and that he was making a point of being seen with Wilde in as many public restaurants as possible. He went on:

> If O.W. was to prosecute you in the criminal courts for libel you would get seven years' penal servitude for your outrageous libels. Much as I detest you, I am anxious to avoid this for the sake of the family; but if you try to assault me I shall defend myself with a loaded revolver which I always carry, and if I shoot you, or he shoots you, we would be completely justified, as we should be acting in self-defence against a violent and dangerous rough, and I think if you were dead not many people would miss you.

Queensberry was fully determined not to let the matter rest, but for a time his prey eluded him. Having finished *The Importance of Being Earnest,* and the play having gone into rehearsal in January 1895, Wilde went abroad to Algiers with Douglas, as has already been noted, where he continued to be pursued by Queensberry's threats and gibes.

In Algiers they fell in with the French writer André Gide, who like them had come to amuse himself with the local Arab boys. They began to discuss Wilde's work, and the Frenchman asked the dramatist why he failed to put the best of himself into his plays.

"Would you like to know the great drama of my life?" Wilde exclaimed. "It is that I have put my genius into my life—I have put only my talent into my works."

According to Gide, whose testimony on this occasion there is no reason to doubt, Wilde went on to speak of returning to London as a well-known peer was insulting him, challenging him, and taunting him with running away.

"But if you go back, what will happen?" asked Gide. "Do you know the risk you are running?"

"It is best never to know," answered Wilde. "My friends are extraordinary. They beg me to be careful. Careful? But how can I be careful? That would be a backward step. I must go on as far as possible. I cannot go much further. Something is bound to happen . . . something else."

At this point Wilde broke off the conversation, as if he had a premonition of approaching disaster. On the following day he set out for England.

2

Meanwhile, Queensberry had planned to create a scene on the opening night of *The Importance of Being Earnest* (14 February 1895) at the St James's Theatre and to harangue the audience. However, he unwisely made known his plan beforehand, so that it reached the ears of the author, who had the theatre surrounded by police. The "scarlet Marquess" duly arrived with his prize-fighting attendant and, finding himself unable to obtain admission to the theatre at any of the entrances, prowled about for three hours, and finally left "chattering," said Wilde, "like a monstrous ape," having first deposited at the stage door a "grotesque bouquet of vegetables" addressed to the object of his enmity. "This, of course," as Wilde told Douglas, "makes his conduct idiotic—robs it of dignity."

Although he had a box, Wilde spent most of the first night in the wings or at the back of the stage, since it was anticipated that Queensberry might attempt to gain admission by way of the stage door disguised as a policeman. However, the weather was not favourable to a further assault upon the theatre, since it was snowing hard outside, and the baffled Marquess accordingly withdrew to plan the next step in his campaign. Meanwhile, the reception accorded to the play inside the theatre was phenomenal. "In my fifty-three years of acting," Allan Aynsworth was to recall when he was an old man, "I never remember a greater triumph than the first night of *The Importance of Being Earnest*. The audience rose in their seats and cheered again and again." When Wilde went into Alexander's dressing room to congratulate him, he did so with characteristic panache. "My dear Alec, it was charming, quite charming," he said, as the actor-manager purred with pleasure. "And, do you know, from time to time I was reminded of a play I once wrote myself called *The Importance of Being Earnest*." But afterwards he admitted that it had been "delightfully acted," which indeed it had.

Four days later—about 4:30 p.m. on 18 February—Queensberry called at the Albemarle Club in Albemarle Street, to which Wilde and his wife both belonged, and left his visiting card with the hall porter. "Give that to Oscar Wilde," he said. On the card he had written: "For Oscar Wilde posing as somdomite," the latter word being thus misspelled in his fury. The porter looked at the card, but he did not quite understand the meaning of the words; he thought Queensberry had written "ponce" instead of "posing." After noting on the back the time and date on which he had received it ("4:30. 18-2-95"), he put it in an envelope, to be given to Wilde when he was next in the club. As it happened, nearly a fortnight elapsed before the club porter saw Wilde.

About a year previously, Wilde had revised and expanded *The Portrait of Mr W.H.*, which Elkin Mathews and John Lane had accepted for publication, the typography to be selected by Charles Ricketts, while C. H. Shannon was to be responsible for the art work and illustrations. However, Ricketts, who was supposed to send the manuscript to the printers, had not done so, and during the afternoon of 28 February, Wilde went along to the studio which Ricketts and Shannon shared in The Vale, Chelsea, to find out what had happened. Shannon was out, but he found Ricketts at home, and they spoke about the manuscript. Ricketts said he would send it to the printers in due course, and his dilatoriness seems to have displeased Wilde, as he left shortly afterwards, bidding Ricketts a somewhat frosty goodbye. A little later

Shannon returned. "I have just met Oscar in the King's Road," he told his friend. "He stopped me and said charming things about you and about your publishing *Mr W.H.* I thought he looked tired and preoccupied. We waited in the fog for a hansom to pass, near a shop with sausage rolls and pork pies lit by gas. Wilde became quite funny and said suddenly, 'What curious things people will sometimes eat . . . I suppose they must be hungry.' A cab passed and, hailing it, he named a club near Piccadilly."

The club was the Albemarle, and as soon as Wilde entered the building, the porter handed him an open envelope containing Queensberry's offensive enclosure, saying as he did so, "Lord Queensberry desired me, sir, to hand this to you when you came into the club." When Wilde read what Queensberry had written on the card, he went back to the hotel in Piccadilly where Douglas had been staying with him but which he had now left. He then wrote to Douglas and Ross asking them to come and see him urgently. This is what he wrote to Ross the same evening:

> Since I saw you something has happened. Bosie's father has left a card at my club with hideous words on it. I don't see anything now but a criminal prosecution. My whole life seems ruined by this man. The tower of ivory is assailed by the foul thing. On the sand is my life spilt.
>
> I don't know what to do. If you could come here at 11.30 please do so tonight. I mar your life by trespassing ever on your love and kindness. I have asked Bosie to come tomorrow.

Ross came to the hotel as requested, and the two men discussed the business into the small hours. Ross advised Wilde once again to see his solicitor and this time to get him to apply for a warrant for the arrest of his tormentor. This is in fact what happened. Next day, which was a Friday, Lord Alfred Douglas arrived, and all three together went to see Humphreys. The solicitor, who recalled his previous meeting with Wilde ten months before, was amazed when he heard the details of Queensberry's recent conduct. He asked Wilde point-blank on his solemn oath whether there was any truth in the libel. Wilde solemnly assured him that he was absolutely innocent. "If you are innocent," said Humphreys, "you should succeed." On the strength of this assurance, Humphreys agreed to apply for a warrant for Queensberry's arrest.

One important question which arose during the momentous conference in the solicitor's office was the cost of the contemplated proceedings against the obnoxious Marquess. At this time Wilde was considerably in debt. He therefore told Humphreys that he had no funds immediately available and that he doubted whether he could afford the "terrible expense" involved in prosecuting Queensberry. At this point, according to Wilde, Lord Alfred Douglas interposed. Douglas said that his own family "would be only too delighted to pay the necessary costs," that his father "had been an incubus to them all," that they "had often discussed the possibility of getting him put into a lunatic asylum so as to keep him out of the way," and that he was "a daily source of annoyance and distress" to his divorced wife and to everybody else. So far as the immediate proceedings against Queensberry were concerned, Wilde was able to borrow £500 from his friend Ernest Leverson, while Alfred Douglas came to the rescue as well. The young man scraped up all the ready cash he could—about £360—which he handed over to his friend on the day of his father's arrest.

Another curious but little-known fact which has emerged is that, had Wilde not been in such acute financial embarrassment at the time, he might have gone abroad on the very day that he called at his club and so might have missed receiving the Marquess's card—at any rate until the lapse of time had either rendered it innocuous or else dictated a different course of action. During most of the preceding fortnight he had been staying at the Avondale Hotel, along with Lord Alfred Douglas and a friend of the latter, both of whom Wilde had regarded as his guests. The total bill for the three of them for ten days was £140. As soon as the other two had left the hotel, Wilde had been hoping to go over to France on a fairly long visit, but the hotel proprietor refused to allow his luggage to be moved until the bill had been paid.

> Had it not been for the hotel bill, I would have gone to Paris on Thursday morning [Wilde afterwards reminded Douglas]. On that fatal Friday, instead of being in Humphreys's office weakly consenting to my ruin, I would have been happy and free in France, away from you and your father, unconscious of his loathsome card and indifferent to your letters, if I had been able to leave the Avondale Hotel. But the hotel people absolutely refused to let me go . . . That is what kept me in London.

Since Wilde had previously been in consultation with Mr Humphreys, as we have seen, about Lord Queensberry, it was quite natural for this solicitor to be consulted again on the subject. It is worth noting, however, that Alfred Douglas wished Wilde to go to Sir George Lewis. This was Wilde's old friend, the first Sir George Lewis, head of the well-known firm of Lewis & Lewis, and a shrewd lawyer who had a great reputation for settling awkward society cases out of court. Now Lewis knew a good deal more about the background of Wilde's private life at this time than Humphreys did, and it is quite possible that, if he had been professionally or even privately consulted, he would have taken a different view of Wilde's protestation of innocence and would have told his client to tear up the Marquess's card and do nothing more about it. As it happened, Sir George Lewis was instructed by Queensberry himself.

Lord Queensberry was staying at Carter's Hotel in Albemarle Street, and it was here that he was arrested on Saturday morning, 2 March. "I have been wanting to find Mr Oscar Wilde for nine or ten days," he said to the police officer when the warrant was produced. "This thing has been going on for about two years." The Marquess was taken to Vine Street Police Station, where he was formally charged, and thence he was immediately conveyed to the court in Great Marlborough Street and there brought up before the sitting magistrate.

After hearing formal evidence, the magistrate adjourned the case for a week and released Queensberry on bail. Although Sir George Lewis appeared for his client at this hearing, he told him immediately afterwards that he could no longer act for him. Apparently this was because Lewis knew Wilde socially and was unwilling to appear in a sensational case involving a man at whose house he had been a guest. Lewis returned his instructions and Queensberry had to obtain the services of another solicitor. The only offices which he was able to find open were those of Day & Russell in Norfolk Street. It was as the result of this accident of being in his office on a Saturday afternoon that Charles Russell, Jr, was entrusted with the conduct of this remarkable case, in which, after consulting with his father, he decided to brief Edward Carson, Q.C., M.P.[3]

Carson disliked the idea of appearing against a fellow classmate, although he had never been friendly with Wilde at Trinity, and in fact since their college days in Dublin they had not set eyes on each other until a chance meeting a few months before Lord Queensberry left his offensive visiting card in the Albemarle Club. One day Carson happened to be crossing the Strand, having just left his chambers for the Law Courts, when a fine carriage drawn by two spanking horses drove past him, splashing him with mud and nearly knocking him down. The carriage stopped and out of it stepped the slightly overdressed person of Oscar Wilde. He seemed prosperous, but had put on a lot of weight since Carson had last seen him, and his features bore unmistakeable signs of self-indulgence and good living. He wore a white flower in his buttonhole. So did his coachman. "Hullo, Ned Carson, how are you?" said Oscar, holding out his hand, which Carson took. He went on in a tone of friendly and good-humoured banter: "Fancy you being a Tory and Arthur Balfour's right-hand man! You're coming along, Ned." The conversation ended with Wilde inviting Carson to his house in Chelsea. "Come and dine with me one day in Tite Street," he said, getting back into his carriage and driving off.

Like many invitations extended at chance meetings, this one was not intended to be taken seriously by either party, neither of whom in this instance had much in common with the other. Carson was as little attracted to his fellow Irishman as he had been in their college days, while Wilde's political sympathies were with Carson's Nationalist opponents in the House of Commons. Yet if Carson had somehow been induced to go to Tite Street, Wilde's eventual fate might have been different, since the advocate made it a strict rule never to appear against anyone whose hospitality he had received. As it was, Carson did return the brief, telling Russell that in the circumstances he felt he could not undertake such a case.

Russell was now in a quandary. To establish a successful defence to a

[3] Russell's father was Lord Russell of Killowen, then Lord Chief Justice of England.

charge of criminal libel, his client had to prove to the jury's satisfaction that the words he had written were true and that they were "published" for the public benefit. The law required that the substance of this defence be embodied in a written plea of justification, a copy of which had to be delivered to the prosecutor before the trial. Russell realised that on the evidence available it would be far from easy for Queensberry to justify the libel. So far, this consisted of the two letters to Lord Alfred Douglas and Wilde's published writings, so that the ability to prove immoral tendencies would indeed be formidable. It is true that there were ugly rumours going round London about Wilde's private life and for some time past Queensberry had been employing a private detective in an attempt to discover evidence of practices which would show that Wilde had gone far beyond mere "posing." These inquiries had led the detectives to the rooms of young Alfred Taylor, which, it appeared, were the centre of an extensive homosexual circle. It transpired that Wilde had been in the habit of visiting these rooms, but as yet there was no evidence linking him criminally with any of the young men, mostly in the humbler walks of life, who were also known to frequent them. Nevertheless, Russell considered that if only one of the youths whose names were found there could be induced to come forward, evidence incriminating Wilde was bound to be forthcoming. He felt that this development justified his asking Carson to reconsider his decision, and accordingly he went round to Carson's chambers in the Temple again.

Carson still hesitated, and it was not until he had consulted that eminent jurist and former Lord Chancellor, Lord Halsbury, that he finally agreed to take the brief. "The great thing," Halsbury told him, "is to arrive at justice, and it is you, I believe, who can best do it." In fact, the dossier against Wilde does not seem to have been completed until sometime later, but whatever it was that Carson learned during his second consultation with Russell, it was sufficient in his own mind to justify his appearance at the adjourned hearing before the Great Marlborough Street magistrate on 9 March. He had with him, as junior counsel, Charles Gill, a hard-working as well as hard-headed Irishman who probably possessed the largest practice of any man in those days at the criminal bar. It is said that at this consultation Carson had been strongly inclined to advise his client to plead guilty but that he changed his mind at the last moment before leaving his chambers for Great Marlborough Street, on being informed that Russell had obtained, or was about to obtain, a statement incriminating Wilde from a youth named Charles Parker. Parker, who was to be the first Crown witness called in the subsequent proceedings against Wilde, was then serving as a gunner in the Royal Artillery, and Russell had considerable difficulty in persuading him to come forward, since, of course, the solicitor was not instructed by the Crown and consequently could not confer immunity on a witness whose testimony, being that of an accomplice, might lead to his own prosecution. Russell is believed to have been put in touch with

Parker by a source in the Savoy Hotel, where, as Parker was later to admit, "indecencies" had taken place between Wilde and himself.

The launching of such a libel prosecution by a successful and popular dramatist against a well-known peer and sporting character was bound to create widespread public interest. It was hardly surprising that the small court in Great Marlborough Street should have been packed with inquisitive spectators at the adjourned hearing. Incidentally, they included, in spite of their previous estrangement, Willie Wilde, who had written to tell his brother that he would be present "in order to show the world that the family think no evil of you." When the case was called shortly after eleven-thirty on the morning of 9 March, there was hardly even standing room, and numbers of prominent people who had endeavoured to obtain seats beside the magistrate on the Bench were disappointed. Wilde, who had driven up to the court in a carriage and pair and was accompanied by the defendant's two sons, Lord Alfred Douglas and Lord Douglas of Hawick, had considerable difficulty in obtaining seats; while Humphreys, who again appeared for Wilde, was obliged to apply to the magistrate before accommodation could be found for his clerk. As soon as his name was called, Queensberry entered the dock, but the magistrate ordered a chair to be placed for his convenience outside the rails, and he was later allowed to sit behind his counsel. On looking round, the magistrate then recognized Lord Alfred Douglas and directed him to leave the court at once. Lord Alfred accordingly withdrew.

Formal evidence not given at the first hearing was now taken, this time Wilde himself as prosecutor taking the stand. Wilde's examination, however, proceeded slowly, since it was necessary that his testimony should be recorded by the clerk of the court in longhand. Wilde could not resist the temptation to show off, a temptation which was later to prove damaging when he was in the box at the Old Bailey. Almost his very first answer called down a mild reproof from the Bench. To his solicitor's question, "Are you a dramatist and author?" Wilde replied "I believe I am well known in that capacity."

"Only answer the questions, please," the magistrate interrupted.

In his examination-in-chief Wilde recalled the two occasions on which he and Alfred Douglas had met the latter's father at the Café Royal, and which he described, as already noted. The examination concluded with evidence of Wilde's receipt of the libellous card, which, with the accompanying envelope, was produced and passed up to him for identification, being marked "A" as the first exhibit in the case.

It was his first appearance at the Albemarle Club since his return from Algiers, said Wilde. He confirmed that the hall porter had handed him an open envelope with his name on the outside and the card inside, with the date and time of Queensberry's visit written on the back and what the porter had said to him as he did so.

"Did you read what was on the card?"

"Yes."

"Did you immediately communicate with your solicitor and have an interview the following day with him?"

"Yes. And on that day also I applied, through my solicitor, for a warrant for Lord Queensberry's apprehension."

On Carson rising to cross-examine, some legal argument took place on the scope of his proposed questions. Carson was, of course, entitled to cross-examine, but not as to the truth of the libel, since there was no such issue before the court. What he proposed to show was why the defendant sent the letters he did—in other words, that "Lord Queensberry thought it was well for the morality of his son to put a stop to the relations between the parties." However, the magistrate ruled that this would amount to quasi-justification and was accordingly not admissible then. Carson thereupon resumed his seat.

The case for the prosecution thus being closed, Wilde's depositions were read over to him by the clerk of the court. He made one slight correction and was about to affix his signature when he suddenly asked to have a certain portion read a second time. "If you would just attend," exclaimed the magistrate testily, "this would not have happened." However, the privilege was accorded, and after a whisper from the usher, "Initials will do," in reply to whether he should sign in full, Wilde without removing his gloves took up a quill pen and appended his initials to the documents.

The magistrate then turned to the defendant and asked him whether, having heard the charge, he had anything to say in answer to it.

"I have simply, your worship, to say this," replied Queensberry, who appeared a diminutive figure as he stood up behind his tall counsel. "I wrote that card simply with the intention of bringing matters to a head, having been unable to meet Mr Wilde otherwise, and to save my son, and I abide by what I wrote."

"Then," said the magistrate, "you are committed for trial and the same bail will be allowed you as before."

3

The next Old Bailey sessions were due to open in less than three weeks from the date of Queensberry's committal, so that neither side had much time to lose before the trial. For the role of leading counsel for the prosecution, Humphreys determined to cast one who was at the top of his profession and would in every way be a match for Carson. Accordingly, within the next few days, the solicitor went along to the Temple and offered the brief to Sir Edward Clarke, Q.C., M.P. Then in his early fifties, Clarke was a veritable titan at the Bar, a former Law Officer of the Crown and a man of the highest personal integrity as well as great forensic ability. His conduct of the defence in two celebrated murder trials—the Penge case and the trial of Mrs Bartlett—had long since established him in the foremost rank of English advocates, while his efforts on behalf of Sir William Gordon-Cumming in the more recent "Baccarat case," when he examined the Prince of Wales, had shown courage in his client's interest when battling against strong Court and society prejudices.

Unlike Sir Frank Lockwood, the Solicitor-General who had enjoyed some measure of Wilde's friendship and hospitality and was ultimately to appear as his leading prosecutor in the last trial, Clarke had never met Wilde before he was instructed in this case. All he knew about him was what was common knowledge among theatregoers, namely, that he was a brilliant playwright who had two successes running at the same time in the West End. Nevertheless, the case was not one which on the face of it appealed to him. Indeed, he hesitated before accepting the brief, just as Carson had done with his, though for a different reason. He asked the solicitor if he might first see his prospective client.

Next day Humphreys brought Wilde to Clarke's chambers, and after some conversation a remarkable scene took place between them. "I can only accept this brief, Mr Wilde," said Clarke, "if you can assure me on your honour as an English gentleman that there is not and never has been any foundation for the charges that are made against you." The fact, apparently overlooked by Clarke in the gravity of the moment, that he was an Irishman did not deter Wilde from standing up and solemnly declaring on his honour that the charges were "absolutely false and groundless." It should perhaps be pointed out here that, since his client was technically the prosecutor in this case, Clarke was justified in putting this question to him. Of course, had Wilde been facing a criminal charge himself at this stage, Clarke would obviously not have done so, it being contrary to professional etiquette and the tradition of the Bar for counsel to make his client's declaration of his innocence a condition of defending him.

It was on the strength of this assurance, so solemnly and emphatically given, that Clarke consented to appear against Queensberry. As events were to show, the further the case proceeded, the less Clarke relished it. In after years he preferred to forget about it, and it is significant that there is no mention of it in his published memoirs. He did, however, place on record his personal attitude in the case. From the notes discovered among his papers after his death, it is clear that he simply did what he conceived to be his duty towards the client who must have assuredly been one of the most embarrassing he had to represent in the whole course of his career. "I need hardly say," he wrote, "I had nothing to do with the institution of that prosecution." But once briefed, the great leader turned all his attention and energies into the case, along with the two junior counsel instructed with him. These were Willie Mathews, a most experienced criminal practitioner who had appeared with Clarke in many previous cases, and Travers Humphreys, son of Wilde's solicitor, then a young barrister making his way at the English Criminal Bar and later a well-known judge.

Meanwhile, in the nearby solicitors' offices of Day & Russell, the defence was busily building up a formidable case against Wilde. For some time past Queensberry had been employing private detectives to collect discreditable evidence of Wilde's private life, hitherto with little success. It is a curious fact, which does not seem to be generally known, that the most damning clues were provided by an entirely voluntary agent who received no fee for his services. This was Charles Brookfield, an actor and writer who had conceived a violent hatred of Wilde, although at this time he had a part in Wilde's play *An Ideal Husband* at the Haymarket theatre. It is all the more surprising since Brookfield was a man of cultured upbringing who had benefited in various ways from Wilde's theatrical successes. He had written a number of plays and short stories which, though greatly inferior to Wilde's productions, had attracted a certain amount of attention. It seems likely that Brookfield became jealous of Wilde's success. As has already been noted, he had parodied *Lady Windermere's Fan*. The good-natured tolerance with which Wilde regarded this effort only served to fan the flames of Brookfield's hatred, which had by this time developed into a positive obsession with Brookfield. Consequently, when the Queensberry storm broke, he went round London getting up opposition wherever he could. He induced the commissionaire at the Haymarket theatre to supply the defence with the names and addresses of Wood and the other blackmailers who, as we have seen, had acquired various letters from Wilde to Douglas and had sent a copy of one of them to Beerbohm Tree, the theatre's manager. He also put Inspector Littlechild, one of the detectives employed by Queensberry, in touch with a prostitute whom he knew to possess information about Wilde and his disreputable male associates. This woman frankly attributed the falling off in her business to the unfair competition promoted by Oscar Wilde and his like. Pressed for further details, the prostitute told the detective that he only had to visit the rooms of a man named Taylor in a certain house in Chelsea and he would find all the evidence he needed. The detective immediately hastened to 3 Chapel Street, and pushing past the caretaker, who vainly tried to prevent his entrance, he found a kind of post-box which contained the names and addresses of numbers of young male homosexuals, mostly in the humbler walks of life, as well as other documents linking them with Wilde. These damning particulars were forwarded to the defendant's solicitors, who now proceeded to amend their client's plea of justification accordingly.

For the time being, Wilde, who had gone off with Lord Alfred Douglas to the south of France to enjoy a short breathing space before the trial, remained ignorant of how the shades of the prison house were beginning to close round him. Nor when the full extent of Brookfield's malevolence was brought home to him some years later by his friend Robert Ross, after he had come out of prison, did he feel the least vindictive. All he said was, "How absurd of Brookfield!"

An incident now occurred which caused perhaps the greatest sensation abroad of the whole case. Since it involved a name far more illustrious than Wilde's—that of Lord Rosebery, now Prime Minister—it was destined at a later stage to result in a critical misfortune for Wilde as prosecutor of Lord Queensberry. As a further necessary preliminary to his appearance in the dock at the Old Bailey, English criminal procedure then required the charge which had been brought against the Marquess to be considered by a grand jury. Grand jurors were usually well-to-do men with substantial property qualifications. On this occasion a distinguished French journalist who had lived in England for many years was empanelled in error. He went down to the Old Bailey intending to excuse himself from attendance on the ground of his French citizenship; but, when he found that Oscar Wilde's prosecution of Lord Queensberry for criminal libel was among the bills before the jury, he decided to remain and say nothing. In due course, a true bill was returned on the strength of evidence, which included, *inter alia,* Queensberry's insulting letters to his son, which Wilde's solicitor had referred to in the Police Court proceedings but had not read, but which mentioned the name of Lord Rosebery, against whom, it will be remembered, the defendant had conceived almost as violent an antipathy as he had expressed against Wilde.

A grand jury's deliberations were invariably private and its findings never reported in the newspapers. The French press, however, fully acquainted its readers with what had happened on this occasion, and the information thus imparted was not only spread throughout the Continent but was openly discussed in London bars and clubs. Brookfield and his friends were incited to fresh efforts in the cause of public morality. The fact that the Prime Minister's name had been mentioned in connection with the case was all the stronger reason that nothing should be hushed up. Hostile feeling about Wilde was increasing, and it seems to have reached as far as the south of France, since Wilde and Douglas were refused admission by the manager of one hotel in Monaco.

Afterwards, writing from prison to Lord Alfred Douglas, Wilde made the following comments on this interlude:

> The warrant once granted, your will, of course, directed everything. At a time when I should have been in London taking wise counsel and calmly considering the hideous trap in which I had allowed myself to be caught—the booby trap, as your father calls it to the present day—you insisted on my taking you to Monte Carlo, of all revolting places on God's earth, that all day and all night as well you might gamble as long as the Casino remained open. As for me—baccarat having no charms for me—I was left alone outside to myself. You refused to discuss even for five minutes the position to which you and your father had brought me. . . .
>
> On our return to London those of my friends who really desired my welfare, implored me to retire abroad, and not to face an impossible trial. You imparted mean motives to them for giving such advice and cowardice to me for listening to it. You forced me to stay, to brazen it out, if possible, in the box by absurd and silly perjuries. At the end, of course, I was arrested, and your father became the hero of the hour.

The precise circumstances of their visit to Monte Carlo together are obscure, but what happened when the two men returned to London is fairly clear. They arrived about a week before the Old Bailey proceedings were due to begin. A consultation was immediately held in Clarke's chambers, at which Wilde and Douglas were both present, in addition to solicitor and counsel; and the opportunity was taken of going through all the particulars of Queensberry's amended plea of justification. In spite of all this new evidence for the defence—the truth of which he persisted in denying—which must have come as an unpleasant surprise to him, Wilde remained outwardly unmoved.

Thanks to the activities of Brookfield and the rest of Queensberry's eager band of assistants, much of this evidence was already common knowledge in London, with the result that during the next few days Wilde was besought by his friends on all sides to leave the country. But to all their entreaties he turned a deaf ear, and in this course he needed no prompting from Douglas. A perverse and foolish sense of obstinacy, amounting indeed to bravado, induced him to stay at all costs to himself and see the thing through. This is amply confirmed by the testimony of a number of independent witnesses.

For instance, two nights before the trial opened, he took his wife and Douglas to a box at the St James's Theatre, where *The Importance of Being Earnest* was playing to crowded houses. In the interval between the acts he went backstage to see George Alexander, the theatre's manager, who was also acting the lead part in the play. Alexander reproached him for coming to the theatre at such a time, as people would be sure to consider it "in bad taste." Wilde laughingly replied that he might as well accuse every member of the audience of bad taste in coming to see the play. "I would consider it in bad taste," he added, "if they went to see anyone else's play."

Alexander then proffered this piece of advice: "Why don't you withdraw from this case and go abroad?"

"Everyone wants me to go abroad," replied Oscar in the same jesting mood. "I have just been abroad, and now I have come home again. One can't keep on going abroad, unless one is a missionary or, what comes to the same thing, a commercial traveller."

It was the last occasion on which Douglas saw Constance Wilde. "She was very much agitated," he recalled, looking back long afterwards, "and when I said good-night to her at the door of the theatre she had tears in her eyes. I felt dreadfully sorry for her for, though I then believed that Oscar would beat my father, and had not the slightest anticipation of the frightful catastrophe that was imminent, I knew that at the very best the whole business must be a terrible ordeal for her."

About this time, possibly earlier that same day, Wilde had received similar advice to Alexander's from Frank Harris, formerly editor of *The Fortnightly Review,* to which Wilde had been a contributor. He asked Harris if he would be a witness for him at the trial and testify that in his opinion *The Picture of Dorian Gray,* one of the works which had been singled out for attack by Queensberry in his plea of justification, was a moral story. Harris declined, urging his friend to flee, but on being implored to reconsider his decision, he asked Wilde to join him next day at the Café Royal, where he had a luncheon engagement with Bernard Shaw. The story of this celebrated encounter has been told by Harris, Shaw, and Douglas (who was also present), and though they differ as to minor details, they are agreed on the main outlines.

First of all [argued Harris] we start with the assumption that you are going to lose the case against Queensberry. You don't realise what is going to happen to you. It is not going to be a matter of clever talk about your books. They are going to bring up a string of witnesses that will put art and literature out of the question. Clarke will throw up his brief . . . You should go abroad and, as ace of trumps, you should take your wife with you. Now for the excuse. I would sit down and write such a letter as you alone can write to *The Times*. You should set forth how you have been insulted by the Marquess of Queensberry and how you went naturally to the Courts for a remedy, but you found out very soon that this was a mistake. No jury would give a verdict against a father, however mistaken he might be. The only thing for you to do, therefore, is to go abroad, and leave the whole ring with its gloves and ropes, its sponges and pails to Lord Queensberry. You are a maker of beautiful things, you should say, and not a fighter, whereas the Marquess of Queensberry takes joy only in fighting. You should refuse to fight with a father under these circumstances . . . But don't stay here clutching at straws like testimonials to *Dorian Gray*. . . . I know what is going to happen. . . . I know what evidence they have got. You must go.

Shaw, when appealed to, agreed with the force of this argument, and like Harris he was surprised at the attitude of sulky intransigence which it provoked on the part of the other two. "Your telling him to run away shows that you are no friend of Oscar's," said Douglas, getting up from the table. "It is not friendly of you, Frank," added Wilde, as he followed the younger man out of the restaurant.

There can be no doubt that their line of conduct was reckless in the extreme. Although neither Harris nor Shaw was aware of it, both Wilde and Douglas had already seen Queensberry's amended plea of justification and must have realised that the defendant's tactics at the trial would take the court far beyond the relatively innocent realm of the prosecutor's published writings. The only possible explanation has been given by Douglas himself. He was most anxious that the case against his father should proceed and resented any arguments in favour of its abandonment. During the meeting in the Café Royal, he was, as he put it in a letter which he wrote to Harris many years later (1925), "terribly afraid that Oscar would weaken and throw up the sponge." Hence his desire to get him out of the restaurant as soon as possible. "I did not tell you our case for fear I might not convince you," he continued in this letter, "and that you and Shaw might, even after hearing it, argue Wilde out of the state of mind I had got him into."

What Douglas described as "our case" was really his private case against his father, and he failed to see, at this stage or at any time, that the evidence he wished to give would not be admissible in any English court of law. It rested on the mistaken belief that Sir Edward Clarke would begin by launching a violent attack against Queensberry. In later years Douglas liked to assert that he had obtained a promise from Clarke that he would put him into the witness box to prove his father's true character—a claim emphatically denied by Sir Edward Clarke. ("I made no such agreement or promise.") Douglas certainly appears to have expected that he would be allowed to depict Queensberry as outwardly pretending to be a solicitous father trying to save his son, whereas in fact he had behaved like an inhuman brute towards every member of his family. Douglas did not appreciate—indeed he never grasped the point as long as he lived—that such evidence as this had nothing to do with the issue to be decided at the trial, and that, even if he did go into the witness box, he would never be permitted to give it. "The question of Lord Queensberry's character was quite irrelevant to the case, and was never mentioned in my instructions or in consultation," wrote Sir Edward Clarke in answer to a correspondent who raised the point when Douglas's autobiography was published in 1929; "and if an attempt had been made to give such evidence, the judge would of course have peremptorily stopped it."

The sole issue which the jury would have to decide was a simple one of fact. Did Oscar Wilde pose as a sodomite? If the jury found that he did not, then Queensberry was guilty of libel. On the other hand, if they found that he did, Queensberry was not guilty.

4

The trial of Lord Queensberry on a charge of criminally libelling Oscar Wilde opened at the Old Bailey on 3 April 1895, before Mr Justice Henn Collins, an excellent criminal judge, later Lord Collins of Kensington.[4] Like Oscar Wilde and Edward Carson, who were in reality the principal protagonists in the case, Henn Collins was an Irishman and had been educated at the University of Dublin. The trial took place, not in the commodious building which houses the present Central Criminal Court, but in the dingy courtroom, the scene of so many grim tragedies in the past, which was pulled down with the surrounding structure a few years later. The prosecution was represented by Sir Edward Clarke, Q.C., M.P., Willie Mathews, and Travers Humphreys, while Edward Carson, Q.C., M.P., along with Charles Gill and Arthur Gill, appeared for the defence. Edward Besley, Q.C., and J. L. Monckton held watching briefs for Lord Alfred Douglas and Lord Douglas of Hawick.[5]

---

[4] The account of this and the two subsequent trials given here is necessarily condensed. For a more detailed narrative together with a full transcript of the court proceedings, the reader is referred to *The Trials of Oscar Wilde* by the present writer, with a foreword by Sir Travers Humphreys (1948; revised editions, 1962 and 1973).

[5] Percy Lord Douglas of Hawick, elder brother of Lord Alfred Douglas and heir to the Marquessate of Queensberry since Lord Drumlanrig's death, had become acquainted with one of the youths mentioned in the defendant's plea of justification—Ernest Scarfe—whom he had first met on his way to Australia in 1893. For this reason it was considered desirable for him to be legally represented.

The court began to fill up long before the judge was due to take his seat on the Bench. Someone made a joke about "the importance of being early," which raised a laugh. Soon there was not a seat or corner to be had, while the gangways and gallery were crowded with curious spectators. It was observed, however, that no ladies were present. First of the parties to arrive was Lord Queensberry. He came in alone and stood beside the dock, an unaristocratic-looking figure with a drooping lower lip and red whiskers, set off by the Cambridge blue hunting stock which he wore instead of the more usual collar and necktie. He was followed some time later by Wilde, who immediately sat down in front of his counsel and began to talk to them in animated tones. Wilde was smartly dressed in a frock-coat, and a flower decorated his buttonhole. He is said to have smiled at Carson, who looked coldly past him. Actually, Queensberry's leading counsel, who was suffering from an extremely bad cold, was feeling far from well that morning. In the seats reserved for the defendant's solicitors, Charles Russell was seen to be in conversation with Inspector Littlechild, the private detective who had been instrumental in procuring the evidence on which the defendant was relying to complete his plea of justification. Meanwhile, in another room in the building, carefully guarded from further contamination by the outside world, a wretched band of youths was waiting to substantiate the evidence, laughing together and smoking cigarettes.

The judge was a little late but, when he arrived, no time was wasted in preliminaries. First, the jury took their place in the box and were sworn. Then, in answer to the usual question put to him by the Clerk of Arraigns, the defendant, speaking in a clear voice, pleaded not guilty and that the words complained of were true and "published" for the public benefit. As he did so, he cast a glance of undisguised contempt in the direction of Wilde.

By the time the hands of the clock in the courtroom pointed to eleven o'clock, Sir Edward Clarke had begun his opening speech for the prosecution. Short, stout, and bewhiskered, he looked more like an old-fashioned parson than a successful Queen's Counsel. On this occasion he was at his best, although in its studied moderation his speech did not commend itself to Lord Alfred Douglas, who had been hoping for an all-out attack on his father. "I never heard anything to equal it in all my life," said Carson afterwards to a friend in the House of Commons. "Both matter and manner were superb."

At the outset Sir Edward Clarke emphasized that the words of the libel were not directly an accusation of the gravest offence but that the person of whom they were written had "posed" as a person guilty of or inclined to the commission of the gravest offence. He then went on to point out that in Lord Queensberry's written plea of justification, which had been considerably expanded beyond its original form, the names of various persons were mentioned, it being alleged that Wilde had solicited them to commit the gravest offence with him and that he had been guilty with each and all of them of indecent practices. Having outlined Wilde's career and described the course of his association with Lord

Alfred Douglas, Sir Edward related the story of the unsuccessful attempts to blackmail Wilde on account of his letters to Douglas, quoting the first of these letters, already mentioned above. The text of that letter, he told the jury, to the amusement of the spectators in court, might "appear extravagant to those in the habit of writing commercial correspondence," but Mr Wilde was a poet, the letter was considered by him a "prose sonnet," and he was not ashamed to produce it anywhere as the expression of true poetic feeling, and with no relation to the hateful and repulsive suggestion put upon it by Lord Queensberry.

Finally, he dealt with the literary part of the case. The defendant had alleged that *The Picture of Dorian Gray* as well as Wilde's "Phrases and Philosophies for the Use of the Young," which appeared as an introduction to this work but were originally published separately as a contribution to an undergraduate magazine called *The Chameleon,* were calculated to subvert morality and encourage unnatural vice. As for the epigrammatical "Phrases and Philosophies," Wilde's counsel remarked that they gave brilliancy and effect to dialogue and even supplied wisdom in a witty form. As for *Dorian Gray,* Sir Edward went on, "I shall be surprised if my learned friend can pitch on any passage in that book which does more than describe, as novelists and dramatists may—nay, must—describe, the passions and fashions of life."

After the Albemarle Club porter had formally proved "publication" of the libel, Wilde himself went into the box. He answered his counsel's questions with an easy assurance, and was in fact an excellent witness, being quite clear and definite in his evidence. However, the statement that his age was thirty-nine caused Carson to sit up suddenly and make a note. When the witness was on the subject of his first meeting with Lord Alfred Douglas, Queensberry asked for writing materials and from his place in the dock proceeded to scribble furiously, the result ultimately being handed down to Carson by one of the ushers.

Sir Edward Clarke sat down shortly before the luncheon adjournment, and his opponent rose to face his former classmate. When Wilde had first learned, through his junior counsel Travers Humphreys, that Carson was to cross-examine him at this trial, he had said, "Then I am sure he will do so with all the added bitterness of an old friend!" In fact, as we have seen, Carson and Wilde were never friends at any time, even at college, otherwise Carson would never have consented to appear against him. On the other hand, there seems little doubt that Wilde seriously underestimated Carson's skill as a cross-examiner, which in fact was revealed by the very first question he put to him. Carson always attached prime importance to the opening question, but when he went into court on that April morning in this case, he had no idea what it would be. Wilde's statement about his age gave him his cue.

"You stated that your age was thirty-nine. I think you are over forty? You were born on the sixteenth October 1854?" Carson emphasized the point of the question by holding up a copy of Wilde's birth certificate.

Wilde appeared unconcerned. "I have no wish to pose as being

young," he said. A titter ran round the court. "I am thirty-nine or forty.
You have my certificate and that settles the matter."

"But being born in 1854 makes you more than forty?" Wilde paused
for a moment, as if to congratulate Carson on a remarkable feat of mathematics. He then gave a long-drawn-out "Ah! Very well."

It was a small point, but at the very outset Wilde had been detected
in a stupid lie. The effect of this was not lost upon the jury, particularly
when Carson followed it up by contrasting Wilde's true age with that of
the twenty-four-year-old Lord Alfred Douglas, with whom the witness
admitted to have stayed at many places both in England and on the Continent. The damaging effect of these admissions, however, was to some
extent offset by Wilde's sparkling answers to the questions put to him
about *Dorian Gray* and his other writings. Here Wilde scored off Carson heavily, and soon had the whole court in fits of laughter.

Carson mentioned a highly improper story called "The Priest and the
Acolyte," which had appeared in the same issue of *The Chameleon* as
Wilde's "Phrases and Philosophies for the Use of the Young."

"You are of opinion, I believe, that there is no such thing as an immoral book?"

"Yes."

"May I take it that you think 'The Priest and the Acolyte' was not
immoral?"

"It was worse. It was badly written."

Questioning Wilde about a sentence in *Dorian Gray*, "I quite admit
that I adored you madly," Carson asked, "What do you say to that?
Have you ever adored a young man madly?"

"No, not madly," Wilde replied. "I prefer love—that is a higher
form."

"Never mind about that. Let us keep down to the level we are at
now."

"I have never given adoration to anybody except myself." Carson felt
nettled by the mirth which this answer caused. "I suppose you think
that a very smart thing?" "Not at all," replied Wilde blandly.

Carson quoted another passage from *Dorian Gray*—"I have adored you
extravagantly"—which he put to the witness.

"Do you mean financially?" countered Wilde.

"Oh, yes, financially," remarked Carson in tones of deepest sarcasm.
"Do you think we are talking about finance?"

"I don't know what you are talking about," answered Wilde.

For a moment Carson fixed the witness with a steely stare. He looked
grim. "Don't you?" he said. "Well, I hope I shall make myself very
plain before I have done."

" 'I was jealous of every one to whom you spoke,' " Carson went on
reading. "Have you ever been jealous of a young man?"

"Never in my life."

" 'I wanted to have you all to myself.' Did you ever have that feeling?"

"No. I should consider it an intense nuisance, an intense bore."

" 'I grew afraid that the world would know of my idolatry.' Why should he grow afraid that the world should know of it?"

"Because there are people in the world who cannot understand the intense devotion, affection, and admiration that an artist can feel for a wonderful and beautiful personality. These are the conditions under which we live, I regret them."

"These unfortunate people that have not the high understanding that you have might put it down to something wrong?"

Carson's sarcasm left Wilde unmoved. "Undoubtedly," he agreed with his cross-examiner; "to any point they chose. I am not concerned with the ignorance of others."

Carson then mentioned a certain book in the story which Dorian Gray had received. "Was the book to which you refer a moral book?"

"Not well written, but it gave me an idea."

"Was not the book you had in mind of a certain tendency?"

"I decline to be cross-examined upon the work of another artist. It is an impertinence and a vulgarity."

On being further pressed on the point, Wilde admitted that the book he had in mind in the particular passage was the French novel by J. K. Huysmans entitled *A Rebours*. But when Carson persisted in his attempts to elicit the witness's view as to the morality of this work, Sir Edward Clarke appealed to the judge, who ruled against any further reference to it.

The last passage which Carson read from Wilde's book described the painter's remonstration with Dorian Gray about his "infamous reputation" and the fact that he had ruined the lives of several other men, including one who had committed suicide, and another who had been obliged to leave England "with a tarnished name." Carson then asked Wilde whether this passage did not suggest a charge of "unnatural vice." Wilde admitted that it described Dorian Gray as a man of very corrupt influence. "But as a matter of fact," he added, "I do not think that one person influences another, nor do I think there is any bad influence in the world."

"A man never corrupts a youth?"

"I think not."

"Nothing could corrupt him?"

"If you are talking of separate ages—"

"No, sir," Carson broke in harshly. "I am talking common sense."

Wilde kept his temper as he replied, "I do not think one person influences another."

"You don't think flattering a young man, making love to him, in fact, would be likely to corrupt him?"

"No," Wilde replied emphatically.

5

Having covered Wilde's published writings, Carson moved on to the allegedly compromising letters Wilde had written to Lord Alfred Douglas, of which one, the so-called "prose poem" letter, had already been read aloud by Wilde's counsel. In answer to Carson's questions, Wilde explained that this particular letter had been written while Douglas was staying at the Savoy Hotel in London and Wilde was at Babbacombe. The letter was in answer to a poem Douglas had sent him.

"Why should a man of your age address a boy nearly twenty years younger as 'My own Boy'?"

"I was fond of him. I have always been fond of him."

"Do you adore him?"

"No, but I have always liked him." Wilde then went on to elaborate upon the letter. "I think it is a beautiful letter. It is a poem. I was not writing an ordinary letter. You might as well cross-examine me as to whether *King Lear* or a sonnet of Shakespeare was proper."

"Apart from art, Mr Wilde?"

"I cannot answer apart from art."

"Suppose a man who was not an artist had written this letter, would you say it was a proper letter?"

"A man who was not an artist could not have written that letter."

"Why?"

"Because nobody but an artist could write it. He certainly could not write the language unless he were a man of letters."

"I can suggest, for the sake of your reputation, that there is nothing very wonderful in this 'red rose-leaf lips of yours.'"

"A great deal depends on the way it is read."

" 'Your slim gilt soul walks between passion and poetry,' " Carson continued. "Is that a beautiful phrase?"

"Not as you read it, Mr Carson. You read it very badly."

It was now Carson's turn to be nettled. "I do not profess to be an artist," he exclaimed, "and when I hear you give evidence, I am glad I am not."

These words immediately brought Sir Edward Clarke to his feet. "I don't think my learned friend should talk like that," he observed. Then, turning towards his client in the witness box, he added, "Pray do not criticize my learned friend's reading again."

This clash caused a buzz of excitement in the courtroom. When it had died down, Carson went on with his cross-examination, indicating the document he was holding in his hand. "Is not that an exceptional letter?"

"It is unique, I should say." Wilde's answer produced loud laughter in court, which was still largely on the side of the witness.

"Was that the ordinary way in which you carried on your correspondence?"

"No. But I have often written to Lord Alfred Douglas, though I never wrote to another young man in the same way."

"Have you often written letters in the same style as this?"

"I don't repeat myself in style."

Carson held out another sheet of paper. "Here is another letter which I believe you also wrote to Lord Alfred Douglas. Will you read it?" It was the letter he had written from the Savoy Hotel in March 1893.

Wilde refused this invitation. "I don't see why I should," he said.

"Then I will," retorted Carson

"Is that an ordinary letter?" Carson asked, when he had finished reading it.

"Everything I wrote is extraordinary," Wilde answered with a show of impatience. "I do not pose as being ordinary, great heavens! Ask me any question you like about it."

Carson had only one question to ask about this letter, but its effect was deadly. "Is it the kind of letter a man writes to another?"

Wilde replied as best he could: "It was a tender expression of my great admiration for Lord Alfred Douglas. It was not, like the other, a prose poem." He added that he had been in the Savoy for about a month, while he also had his house in Tite Street, and that Douglas had been staying with him at the Savoy immediately before he wrote the letter.

So long as he remained on literary ground, even when questioned about his seemingly, equivocal letters to Lord Alfred Douglas, Wilde more than held his own in the duel of wits with his fellow countryman. But when Carson moved on to the witness's relations with certain other named individuals, which he did later in the afternoon, Wilde began to be less sure of himself, although he maintained his brilliant flow of repartee. The mention of the name of Alfred Wood, followed by the names of other blackmailers, introduced an ominous note into the cross-examination.

Carson next proceeded to question the witness about the specific occasions on which Queensberry had alleged in his plea of justification that Wilde had committed sodomy or acts of indecency with certain named individuals. The first such occasion was said to be in February 1892 at the Albemarle Hotel, where Wilde admitted that he had stayed on the date in question.

"At that time were Messrs Elkin Mathews and John Lane, of Vigo Street, your publishers?"

"Yes."

"Did you become fond of their office boy?"

This question made Wilde extremely indignant. "I really do not think that is the proper form for the question to be addressed to me in," he said, his voice quivering with anger. "I deny that was the position of Mr Edward Shelley, to whom you are referring. I object to your description."

Carson allowed this outburst to pass without comment. He merely asked, "What age was Mr Shelley?"

"I should think about twenty," said Wilde. He added that he had first met him the previous October when arranging for the publication of his books. He had later asked him to dinner at the Albemarle Hotel, when he was staying there.

"Was that for the purpose of having an intellectual treat?" asked Carson in tones of undisguised contempt.

"Well, for him, yes," Wilde answered good-humouredly. "We dined in my own sitting-room, and there was one other gentleman there."

At this point Carson caused some surprise by telling the witness that he need not mention this gentleman's name; it would be sufficient if he wrote it down. This Wilde did from his place in the witness box on a sheet of paper, which was then handed to counsel by the court usher. (The name was that of Maurice Schwabe, who was a nephew of Lady Lockwood, wife of the Solicitor-General Sir Frank Lockwood.)

"On that occasion did you have a room leading into a bedroom?"

"Yes."

"Did you give him whiskey-and-sodas?"

"I suppose he had whatever he wanted. I do not remember."

Questioned as to what happened later, Wilde stoutly denied that any improper conduct had taken place between them. "He did not stay all night, nor did I embrace him," he added. Replying to further questions about his association with Shelley, Wilde said that he had invited him to his house and that he had dined with him and his wife. ("He expressed great admiration for my works.") The witness admitted that he had taken him to the Earl's Court exhibition, to the Café Royal, and to Kettner's, as well as to the theatre and the Lyric Club. Had he ever given him any money? Yes, on three occasions: the first time £4, the second time £3, and the third time £5. The £3 was for his railway fare to Cromer, where Wilde and his family were staying, but Shelley did not come and Wilde wrote to him saying he was not to send back the money.

Wilde also agreed that he had given young Shelley two books. One was a signed copy of the first edition of *The Picture of Dorian Gray*. The other was a novel entitled *The Sinner's Comedy* and inscribed "From the Author to dear Edward Shelley." On being handed the work in question, Wilde admitted that the inscription was in his handwriting. He added, "That was purely a piece of nonsense. I was not the author of the book." [6]

"Did you think this young man of eighteen was a proper or natural companion for you?"

"Certainly."

Carson's last question before the court rose for the day concerned

[6] The author of *The Sinner's Comedy* was John Oliver Hobbes (Mrs Craigie), a popular novelist of the day. It was published in 1892.

Alphonse Conway, the lad at Worthing with whom Wilde and Douglas used to go sailing. "Did he not sell newspapers at the kiosk on the pier?" "No," said Wilde, "it is the first I have heard of his connection with literature."

Wilde was at his best in this kind of sparring, and the court rocked with laughter. Carson, with a look of dogged determination, put more questions about this youth.

"What was he?"

"He led a happy, idle life."

"He was a loafer, in fact?"

"He seemed to me to be just enjoying life."

"Was his conversation literary?"

"On the contrary, quite simple and easily understood. He had been to school, where naturally he had not learned much."

This was all very amusing, and the witness seemed to be enjoying it as much as the spectators, but the jurymen did not appear to be so amused. One or two of them seemed slightly shocked at the account they heard of Wilde's association with these youths. Then, had not Wilde given them presents? Yes, he had. Suddenly, to the general astonishment, Carson produced a signed photograph of Wilde, a cigarette case, and a silver-mounted walking-stick, which Master Conway had accepted from him.

"Did you take the lad to Brighton?"

"Yes."

"And provide him with a suit of blue serge?"

"Yes."

"And a straw hat with a band of red and blue?"

"That, I think, was his unfortunate selection."

"You dressed this newsboy up to take him to Brighton?"

"I did not want him to be ashamed of his shabby clothes."

"In order that he might look more like an equal?"

"Oh, no, he could not look like that."

What had they done in Brighton? They had dined at a restaurant and stayed the night at the Albany Hotel, where Wilde had taken a sitting-room and two bedrooms.

Wilde looked rather less sure of himself now. So did the jury. Nevertheless, he was still confident that he could explain all these matters to their satisfaction.

6

Next morning Wilde again took his place in the witness box. But his air was not so jaunty: indeed, he appeared considerably more subdued than on the first day. However, his repartee was still in characteristic vein.

Carson questioned him about Alfred Taylor, about the youths he had met in Taylor's rooms, and about the mode of Taylor's life.

"Did he use to do his own cooking?"

"I don't know. I don't think he did anything wrong."

"I have not suggested that he did."

"Well, cooking is an art."

"Another art?" queried Carson. This time the laughter was against the witness.

It appeared that Taylor's rooms were exotically furnished and artificially lighted, the curtains drawn tight across the windows, through which the daylight seldom if ever penetrated. The faces of the middle-class jury looked solemn as they listened to Wilde's description of an establishment so different from their own homes. And what about these youths, whose names rolled so uncompromisingly from Carson's lips? Wood, Mavor, Atkins, Parker . . . Did Taylor introduce him to Charles Parker? Yes. And did they become friends? Yes. Was Wilde aware that Taylor and Parker had both been arrested in a police raid in a house in Fitzroy Square? Yes.

"Did you know that Parker was a gentleman's servant out of employment?"

"No."

"But if he were, you would still have become friendly with him?"

"Yes. I could become friendly with any human being I liked."

"How old was he?"

"Really, I do not keep a census."

"Never mind about a census," said Carson sharply. "Tell me how old he was."

"I should say he was about twenty," replied Wilde with an air of bored resignation. "He was young and that was one of his attractions."

"Was he a literary character?"

"Oh, no."

To further questions as to whether Parker was intellectual and an educated man, Wilde was forced to admit that "culture was not his strong point." Nor was he an artist. But then, Wilde explained, education depends on what one's standard is.

Had Wilde also been introduced to Parker's brother? Yes. Did he become friendly with him too? Yes. In fact, he became friendly with him at their first meeting, when he had invited them to a birthday dinner he gave at Kettner's for Taylor.

"Did you know that Parker was a gentleman's valet and the other a groom?"

"I did not know it, but if I had I should not have cared. I didn't care twopence what they were. I liked them. I have a passion to civilize the community."

"What enjoyment was it to you to entertain grooms and coachmen?"

"The pleasure to me was being with those who are young, bright, happy, careless, and free. I do not like the sensible and I do not like the old."

Carson asked about the dinner, which was in a private room. "Was it a good dinner?"

"Kettner's is not so gorgeous as some restaurants," was Wilde's answer, "but it was Kettner at his best."

"Was there plenty of champagne?"

"Well, I did not press wine upon them."

"You did not stint them?" went on Carson.

"What gentleman would stint his guests?" Wilde asked the advocate.

Carson looked at Wilde contemptuously. "What gentleman would stint the valet and the groom?"

Both Wilde and his counsel protested at this remark. Carson took no notice, but went on with his cross-examination.

"Do you drink champagne yourself?" he asked.

"Yes," replied Wilde. "Iced champagne is a favourite drink of mine—strongly against my doctor's orders."

"Never mind your doctor's orders, sir," said Carson sternly.

"I never do," said Wilde, as the court laughed loudly.

The court laughed once more with the witness. It was when he was asked whether Parker's rooms were about ten minutes' walk from Tite Street. "I don't know," said Wilde. "I never walk." "I suppose when you pay visits you always take a cab?" "Always." "And if you visited you would leave the cab outside?" "Yes, if it were a good cab."

By this time Carson had led Wilde onto very dangerous ground. The questions now had a particularity about them which made Sir Edward Clarke distinctly uneasy. Parker, Atkins, Scarfe . . . Introduced to Wilde like others by the obliging Taylor, these youths were either grooms or valets or else out of employment. What could a man like Wilde have in common with them? Yet he admitted that he had given them all money or presents, having received nothing in return except the pleasure of their company. The witness, now obviously nettled, reiterated his delight in the society of people much younger than himself, those who might be called idle or careless. "I recognize no social distinctions of any kind," he added by way of explanation, "and to me youth, the mere fact of youth, is so wonderful that I would sooner talk to a young man for half an hour than"—here Wilde paused for a moment and then ended with a smile—"than be cross-examined in court."

It was the last time Wilde scored in this remarkable cross-examination. A few minutes later everyone sat up in court when Carson asked Wilde about a letter he had received from Charles Parker. It was merely a note asking whether he might have the pleasure of dining with him one evening, but it led to a significant piece of information on Carson's part. Carson had the letter in his hand. "I should like to see the handwriting," said Sir Edward Clarke. Carson looked grimmer than ever. "We will see all about that," he said. "Parker himself will be here, which is better."

No wonder everyone looked surprised, since it seemed incredible that an accomplice, on whom no immunity had been conferred, since he was not technically a Crown witness, was willing to come forward and supply testimony which would almost certainly incriminate himself. But there it was. Carson had the evidence after all to substantiate his line of cross-examination.

The climax to this sensational cross-examination came shortly afterwards when Wilde was asked about a boy named Grainger, who was a servant in Lord Alfred Douglas's rooms in Oxford.

"Did you kiss him?" asked Carson.

For a moment, a fatal moment, Wilde was off his guard. "Oh, dear no," he replied unthinkingly. "He was a peculiarly plain boy. He was, unfortunately, extremely ugly. I pitied him for it."

Quick as lightning Carson pressed home his advantage. Was that the reason Wilde had never kissed him? "Oh, Mr Carson, you are pertinently insolent." Why had he mentioned his ugliness? "I do not know why I mentioned he was ugly," said Wilde, now on the verge of breaking down, "except that I was stung by the insolent question you put to me and the way you have insulted me throughout this hearing."

But Carson continued remorselessly in a sharp staccato repetition: "Why? Why? Why did you add that?" Wilde began several answers almost inarticulately. At last he managed to stammer out: "You sting me and insult me and try to unnerve me, and at times one says things flippantly when one ought to speak more seriously. I admit it."

A few more questions on minor matters and Carson gathered up his papers and sat down, to the witness's intense relief. Sir Edward Clarke then began his re-examination, first of all putting to his client the letters written by Lord Queensberry to his son containing statements about Wilde which the witness swore were quite unfounded. Clarke also sought to show that Wilde's association with Taylor and the various youths whose names had been mentioned was perfectly innocent. But it was too late. The damage had been done, and the foolish slip about the boy Grainger which caused it could not be covered up.

At this point the court adjourned for luncheon. As they were leaving the building, Clarke explained to his client that his introduction of fresh evidence in the shape of Queensberry's letters gave Carson the right to cross-examine further and that Wilde might therefore have to undergo another ordeal in the witness box. "Can they examine me about anything and everything they choose?" Wilde asked his leading counsel. Clarke replied that this was so, and that Carson need not necessarily confine himself to Queensberry's letters, provided the judge had no objection. Wilde went on to inquire whether "they" could question him about an incident which had not been mentioned at all. "Certainly," rejoined the advocate. "What is it that is in your mind?" "Well," said Wilde, "some time ago I was turned out of the Albemarle Hotel in the middle of the night and a boy was with me. It might be awkward if they found out about that!"

Sir Edward Clarke said nothing, but what his client told him worried him considerably. Could there be some foundation for Queensberry's allegations after all? Yet his client had solemnly assured him that they were absolutely false.

When the court reassembled after the luncheon adjournment, Wilde was not in his place in the witness box, and the rumour quickly went round the Old Bailey that Wilde had thrown up the case and was fleeing abroad rather than face Carson again. But the rumour turned out to be false, for about fifteen minutes later Wilde hurriedly appeared and apologized to the Bench for being late, explaining that the clock in the restaurant where he had been lunching was slow.

As soon as Wilde's re-examination was concluded, his counsel declared that the case against Lord Queensberry was closed. Carson did not ask to cross-examine further but proceeded to his opening speech on behalf of his client. This he did in his most effective manner. He made it clear that the defendant adhered to all the charges he had put forward against the prosecutor, and he called upon the jury as fathers to say whether Lord Queensberry was not justified in endeavouring by every means in his power to rescue his son from Mr Wilde's baneful domination. He then went on to say that he was proposing to put into the witness box the various young men with whom Wilde had been criminally associated and most of whom had been introduced to him by Taylor. And where was Taylor? Why had he not given evidence? Because he was "a most notorious character," who "occupied rooms which were nothing more or less than a shameful den." Then there was the blackmailer Wood. No wonder Wilde was so anxious to ship him off to America, where no doubt he hoped he would remain for good. "But as a matter of fact," announced Carson, "Wood is here and will be examined before the jury." A gasp of amazement went round the court at these words.

Carson had been on his feet for about an hour when the court rose for the day, and Sir Edward Clarke went back to the Temple to consider what should be done in the light of his opponent's imminent disclosures. That evening he considered the situation very carefully. In view particularly of what his client had told him earlier in the day, during the luncheon adjournment, Carson's speech had already assumed a very serious aspect, and there would be more to come on the following day. Wilde's counsel had appointed a consultation before the sitting of the court next morning. That night he made up his mind to tell Wilde frankly, when he met him with his solicitor and junior counsel, that in view of the way the case had gone the jury must be expected to acquit Lord Queensberry. In these circumstances he thought it best for his client to withdraw from the prosecution and allow him to make a statement to the court, consenting to a verdict as regards the charge of "posing." By thus admitting the lesser charge, which in fact had not been made out by the defence, Clarke hoped to prevent the intervention of the Public Prosecutor, a development which might lead to Wilde's arrest in open court if the case were allowed to continue. Mathews, who was one of the two junior counsel, was for fighting the case to a finish, since, as he pointed out, the witnesses whom Carson had indicated his intention of calling were all self-confessed accomplices and themselves criminals whose testimony might well be discredited, and he regarded the case as far from lost. However, Clarke's advice prevailed and his client agreed with it.

When I saw Mr Wilde [Clarke subsequently wrote in his unpublished recollections of the trial], I told him that it was almost impossible in view of all the circumstances to induce a jury to convict of a criminal offence a father who was endeavouring to save his son from what he believed to be an evil companionship. I said that upon full consideration I advised him in his own interest to allow me to make that statement to the Court, and to withdraw from the prosecution; and I said that, if the case went to its end and the jury found that the accusations were justified, the judge would unquestionably order his arrest. He listened quietly and gravely, and then thanked me for my advice and said he was prepared to act upon it. I then told him that there was no necessity for his presence in Court while the announcement was being made. I hoped and expected that he would take the opportunity of escaping from the country, and I believe he would have found no difficulty in doing so.

Next morning, the third day of the trial, Carson continued his remorseless haranguing. Charles Parker, counsel estimated, would also go into the witness box, albeit reluctantly. "Parker will tell you that when he went to the Savoy with Mr Wilde," said Carson to the jury, "he had whiskey-and-sodas and iced champagne—that iced champagne in which Mr Wilde indulged contrary to his doctor's orders. Parker will furthermore tell you of the shocking acts he was led by Mr Wilde to perpetrate on that occasion." Counsel would also call the hotel masseur and other servants to prove the character of Mr Wilde's relations with his visitors. Was there any wonder that reports of scandal should have reached Lord Queensberry, whose son was living a portion of the time at this hotel? "The wonder is not that the gossip reached Lord Queensberry," Carson went on, "but that, after it was known, this man Wilde should have been tolerated in society in London for the length of time he has."

Carson next proceeded to deal with the lad Conway, who, he observed, had not been procured by Taylor but by Wilde himself. Had there ever been confessed in a court of justice a more audacious story than that confessed to by Wilde in relation to this lad? Wilde had got the boy a suit of clothes to dress him up like a gentleman's son, put some public-school colours on his hat, and generally let him look like a lad fit and proper to associate with Mr Wilde. The whole thing in its audacity was almost past belief. Why did Wilde dress him up? "If Mr Wilde were really anxious to assist Conway, the very worst thing he could have done was to take the lad out of his proper sphere, to begin by giving him champagne luncheons, taking him to his hotel, and treating him in a manner in which the boy could never in the future expect to live."

At this point Sir Edward Clarke, who had left the court for a short time with Willie Mathews, was seen to return and pluck Carson by the gown. He whispered into Carson's ear that he had been in consultation with his client and his instructions were now to withdraw from the prosecution. After a few moments Carson resumed his seat and Clarke addressed the judge. He spoke under the obvious strain of great emotion.

"I think," said Clarke, "it must have been present to your Lordship's mind that those who represent Mr Wilde in this case have before them a very terrible anxiety." He and his colleagues, he went on to explain, felt that what had already been admitted "might not improbably induce the jury to say that Lord Queensberry in using the word 'posing' was using a word for which there was sufficient justification" to entitle him to take the action he had. Consequently, if the case were to continue, as he could not expect a verdict for his client, "we should be going through, day after day, investigation of matters of the most appalling character." In these circumstances he was prepared to accept a verdict of not guilty—not guilty having reference to the word "posing." "I trust," he concluded, "that this may make an end of the case."

"I can only say, as far as Lord Queensberry is concerned," observed Carson, "that if there is a plea of not guilty, a plea that he has succeeded in his plea of justification, I am quite satisfied." With this remark the judge agreed.

After consulting together for a few moments without leaving the jury box, the jury returned a verdict of "Not guilty," thus finding that the plea of justification had been proved and that the defendant's words were published for the public benefit. A prolonged outburst of cheering amongst the onlookers in court, which the ushers made little attempt to suppress, followed the declaration of this verdict. Soon the news spread to the crowds in the street outside the Old Bailey. Before leaving the Bench, the judge awarded the defendant his costs and also ordered his discharge. Queensberry at once stepped out of the dock and joined his solicitor in the well of the court. His formal discharge, which immediately followed, was accompanied by renewed applause from the spectators in the public gallery.

When Mr Justice Collins reached the judge's room, he sat down and penned a note to Queensberry's leading counsel. "I never heard a more powerful speech or a more searching cross-exam," he wrote. "I congratulate you on having escaped most of the filth."

By this time Wilde had left the building by a side door, and so he avoided the ribald scenes which met the eyes of Clarke and Carson when they emerged together shortly afterwards. Prostitutes were dancing on the pavement. "What a filthy business!" Clarke exclaimed in disgust. "I shall not feel clean for weeks."

As soon as he had been released from court, the victorious defendant sent a characteristic message to his unsuccessful adversary, on whom the tables were now to be savagely turned. "If the country allows you to leave, all the better for the country!" said Queensberry. "But if you take my son with you, I will follow you wherever you go and shoot you!"

6 / The Second Trial

t was towards noon on the morning of 5 April when Oscar Wilde
left the Old Bailey. He was accompanied by Lord Alfred Douglas
and Robert Ross, who remained in court throughout the trial.
Together they drove to the nearby Holborn Viaduct hotel, where
Wilde wrote the following letter to the editor of the *Evening News:*

5 April 1895

Sir,

It would have been impossible for me to have proved my case without
putting Lord Alfred Douglas in the witness box against his father. Lord
Alfred Douglas was extremely anxious to go into the box, but I would not
let him do so. Rather than put him into so painful a position I determined
to retire from the case, and to bear on my own shoulders whatever ignominy
and shame might result from my prosecuting Lord Queensberry.

Yours, etc.,

OSCAR WILDE [1]

At the same time he sent his wife an urgent note telling her to see no
one but her friends and not to let anyone into his bedroom or sitting-
room in Tite Street except the servants.

Wilde dispatched these letters and lunched in the hotel with Douglas,
while Ross went off to cash a cheque for Wilde for £200. They then
went on to call at the offices of Messrs Lewis & Lewis, solicitors, in Ely
Place. There they saw Sir George Lewis and asked him if he could

[1] This letter, of which the original is in the Donald F. Hyde collection, was jotted
down by Ross on the back of two hotel envelopes and signed by Wilde after consulting
his solicitor. It was then apparently given to a reporter to take to the newspaper offices,
so that it could appear in the afternoon editions. The *Evening News,* once edited by Frank
Harris, had recently been acquired by Alfred Harmsworth, later Lord Northcliffe, and
was on its way to becoming the most popular and widely read London evening paper.

suggest anything. "What is the good of coming to me now?" exclaimed this shrewd old lawyer. "I am powerless to do anything. If you had had the sense to bring Lord Queensberry's card to me in the first place, I would have torn it up and thrown it in the fire and told you not to make a fool of yourself."

But even before this discussion took place, Queensberry's solicitor had written to the Director of Public Prosecutions.

37 Norfolk Street
Strand WC
5 April 1895

Hon. Hamilton Cuffe
Director of Public Prosecutions

RE OSCAR WILDE

Dear Sir,

In order that there may be no miscarriage of justice, I think it my duty at once to send you a copy of all our witnesses' statements together with a copy of the shorthand notes of the trial.

Yours faithfully,
CHARLES RUSSELL

In those days the Director of Public Prosecutions had his office in the Treasury building in Whitehall, and it was here that the decision was taken to apply for a warrant for Wilde's arrest after the director had examined the papers he had received from Russell in the course of the morning, and after he had had an opportunity of speaking to Russell in person about an hour later.[2] Particulars were also dispatched by hand to the House of Commons, where they were placed before the Home Secretary, Mr Asquith, and the Law Officers, Sir Robert Reid and Sir Frank Lockwood. It was at once agreed that a warrant should be applied for, and the Home Secretary gave instructions that wherever Wilde might be found he should be stopped. A little later, about 3:30 p.m., Detective-Inspector Brockwell of Scotland Yard, accompanied by one of the Treasury lawyers, appeared before Sir John Bridge, the Bow Street magistrate, to apply for the warrant. The magistrate did not immediately grant the application, but adjourned the court for over an hour and a

---

[2] Hamilton Cuffe, who was a son of the 3rd Earl of Desart, succeeded to the title, which was an Irish one, on his elder brother's death in 1898. On his retirement as Director of Public Prosecutions in 1909, he was created a peer of the United Kingdom, which entitled him to sit in the House of Lords, which his Irish peerage did not. On 15 April 1921, Desart spoke strongly in the Lords against a clause in the new Criminal Law Amendment Bill which had somewhat surprisingly been passed by the Commons and which would have made homosexual acts between women a criminal offence, even when committed in private. In his speech on this occasion, he referred to the Wilde case and its effect on the country at large. "At that time," said Desart, "I had access to the Chief Constable's reports of all the counties and towns in England. After that prosecution there was for about eighteen months, according to my recollection, a perfect outburst of that offence all through the country . . . I am sure that a prosecution [for lesbian acts] would really be a very great public danger." Largely as the result of his opposition, the clause was defeated by the House of Lords and allowed to drop by the Commons. Lord Desart died in 1934 without heirs and all his titles became extinct.

half. Whether this was to enable Wilde to catch the last train for the Continent, or because he wished to have time to read the documents forwarded by Charles Russell to Hamilton Cuffe, is not clear. It has been said that the magistrate was careful to inquire the time of the boat-train's departure from the clerk of the court and, on receiving this information, to have fixed the time of the application a quarter of an hour later. The fact remains that it was not until past five o'clock, by which time the train had left, that Sir John Bridge actually signed the warrant for Wilde's arrest.

Meanwhile, Wilde had gone to the Cadogan Hotel in Sloane Street, where Alfred Douglas was staying. Robert Ross, who arrived there soon after lunch, advised him to proceed immediately to Dover and thence try to get over to France. Other friends apparently repeated this advice in the course of the afternoon. Even Wilde's wife, when Ross went to tell her what had happened at the Old Bailey, said between sobs, "I hope Oscar is going away abroad." But unfortunately Wilde could not make up his mind what to do until it was made up for him by the force of events. He remained in a pathetic state of indecision, lamenting that "the train has gone" and that "it is too late." Soon after five o'clock Thomas Marlowe, later editor of the *Daily Mail,* who was then a reporter on the *Star,* called at the hotel and asked to see Wilde. Wilde refused to see him, but sent Ross instead. The journalist then declared that he had just seen a message come through on the tape to the effect that the warrant had already been issued. Ross immediately went into the other room and gave the news to Wilde, who went "very grey in the face." Shortly before this, Douglas, who could stand the tension no longer, had gone off to the House of Commons to see his cousin George Wyndham and find out whether a prosecution was inevitable. Oscar sat on with his two friends, Robert Ross and Reginald Turner, glumly waiting for the blow to fall and drinking glass after glass of hock and seltzer in an endeavour to steady his nerves.

About half-past six there was a knock on the door of room 53. Two men entered. "Mr Wilde, I believe?" said one of them. "Yes? Yes?" replied Wilde, who was seated in an armchair by the fireplace, smoking a cigarette. His two companions were seated by a table on which stood some half-empty glasses. On the floor lay copies of the evening papers, which had evidently been scanned in haste and thrown aside. "We are police officers," said one of the visitors, "and hold a warrant for your arrest on a charge of committing indecent acts." The speaker was Inspector Richards of Scotland Yard, and he immediately added, "I must ask you to accompany me to the police station."

"Where shall I be taken to?" Wilde then asked.

"You will have to go to Scotland Yard with me and then to Bow Street."

"Can I have bail?"

"I don't think you can," replied the detective-inspector. "But that is a matter for the magistrate to decide."

"Well," said Wilde, "if I must go, I will give you the least possible trouble."

Before accompanying the detectives to Scotland Yard, Wilde asked if he might write a few lines to leave for Lord Alfred Douglas, and permission was granted. In the letter which he now wrote under the eyes of the detectives and which he began "My dear Bosie," he asked his friend to ask his brother Percy (Lord Douglas of Hawick) and also the theatrical managers George Alexander and Lewis Waller, at whose theatres Wilde's plays had been running, to attend to give bail at Bow Street Police Court. He also asked him to send a telegram to Humphreys, his solicitor, asking him to appear for him in court. "Also," he added, "come to see me."

As he struggled into his overcoat and picked up his gloves and a novel which he had been reading, the effects of the hock and seltzer which he had been imbibing throughout the afternoon were plainly noticeable. He was allowed to take the book with him.[3]

At Scotland Yard the warrant upon which Wilde had been arrested was read to him. It charged him with committing acts of gross indecency with various male persons. Wilde put out his hand and asked to be allowed to read it. This he was not permitted to do. He then asked, "What are the mentioned dates?" To this the inspector in charge replied, "On the twentieth March 1893, and divers other dates." Prisoner and escort then continued their journey to Bow Street Police Station, where the prisoner was booked in. In accordance with the current regulations, he was searched, a proceeding which revealed £200 in £5 Bank of England notes, also several writs and a letter from Taylor. Taylor's letter showed that he (Taylor) knew he was being watched by Inspector Littlechild and that the detective had searched his room during his absence. The writs had been issued by various firms for money owing in respect of cigarette cases, jewellery, and other goods supplied by them to the prisoner. When these formalities were completed, Wilde was conducted to one of the cells, where he was locked up for the night.

At the time of his arrest, Wilde had asked Robert Ross to go along to his house in Tite Street and collect some clothes and other necessaries which he would require when in custody. In due course Ross arrived at Bow Street, but he was allowed neither to see the prisoner nor to leave

---

[3] Next morning the newspapers came out with the headlines: ARREST OF OSCAR WILDE. YELLOW BOOK UNDER HIS ARM. This gave rise to the erroneous impression, widely believed at the time and subsequently repeated by R. H. Sherard, Frank Harris, and others of Wilde's biographers, that the work which Wilde had been reading at the time of his arrest was *The Yellow Book,* the famous contemporary periodical. This was published by John Lane (The Bodley Head), who was also Wilde's publisher. Actually, the book in question was *Aphrodite,* a novel by Wilde's friend Pierre Louÿs, and it happened to have a yellow cover. That the contrary impression prevailed at the time is evidenced by the fact that an angry crowd demonstrated outside the offices of The Bodley Head in Vigo Street and broke the windows. "It killed *The Yellow Book,*" John Lane used to say, "and it nearly killed me." Though popularly identified with this publication, Wilde never contributed to its pages and had no connection whatever with *The Yellow Book.*

the dressing-case which he had brought with him. A little later Alfred Douglas appeared. He had succeeded in seeing his cousin George Wyndham in the lobby of the House of Commons, only to be told on the authority of the Attorney-General that his friend was to be prosecuted. Returning to the Cadogan Hotel, he found Wilde's letter with the news of his arrest, and so he had hurried off in a cab to Bow Street. He hoped somehow that he might be able to bail him out, and was much distressed when informed by the inspector on duty that on no consideration could his application be entertained. He was also told that, even if bail were subsequently granted by the magistrate, other sureties besides himself would certainly be required. Douglas then went on, at Wilde's previous suggestion, to the Haymarket and St James's theatres, and asked their respective managers, Lewis Waller and George Alexander, if they would be prepared to go bail for the author. Both refused, as did Adrian Hope next day.[4]

That evening the sensational developments of the day were being discussed in hundreds of bars and clubs and homes throughout the country, and pundits of the I-told-you-so type were sanctimoniously holding forth on the dangers of art and literature, at least when pursued by Oscar Wilde. To their discredit, the newspapers surpassed themselves in their vulgar gloating. "And so a most miserable case is ended," wrote the *Echo*, a London evening paper of the period. "Lord Queensberry is triumphant, and Mr Oscar Wilde is 'damned and done for.' He may now change places with Lord Queensberry and go into the dock himself. He appears to have illustrated in his life the beauty and truthfulness of his teachings. He said, in cross-examination, that he considered there was no such thing as morality, and he seems to have harmonised his practice with his theory. The counsel for the prosecution, the judge, and jury are entitled to public thanks for abruptly terminating the trial, and so preventing the publication of probably revolting revelations."

But this desire on the part of the *Echo* to spare its readers' feelings was only a sham. Next day it did not hesitate to print what it called a "detailed report" of the proceedings at Bow Street Police Court, where the magistrate heard the first part of the evidence on which he ultimately committed Wilde for trial.

The *National Observer* also published a leading article, probably written by Charles Whibley, strongly attacking the unsuccessful prosecutor in the Queensberry trial.

There is not a man or woman in the English-speaking world possessed of the treasure of a wholesome mind who is not under a deep debt of gratitude to the Marquess of Queensberry for destroying the High Priest of the Deca-

---

[4] The following entries appear in Mrs Adrian Hope's diary: "April 5th. A most trying visit from Mrs William Napier [daughter of J. H. Lloyd] in a most frantic state about her poor niece Constance Wilde as the whole verdict has gone against her monstrous husband—the whole episode most terrible."

"April 6th. Adrian had a most painful interview with Lord Alfred Douglas, who came to implore him to go bail for that fiend O.W. which was of course impossible."

dents. The obscene imposter, whose prominence has been a social outrage ever since he transferred from Trinity Dublin to Oxford his vices, his follies, and his vanities, has been exposed, and that thoroughly at last. But to the exposure there must be legal and social sequels. There must be another trial at the Old Bailey, or a coroner's inquest—the latter for choice; and of the Decadents, of their hideous conceptions of the meaning of Art, of their worse than Eleusinian mysteries, there must be an absolute end.

Meanwhile, messages of congratulation were pouring in to Queensberry. On being informed by one of the Sunday newspapers that a further pile of messages was waiting for him, the delighted Marquess said, "You know, I have not much to do with distinguished people, but I had a very nice letter from Lord Claud Hamilton, and a kind telegram from Mr Charles Danby, the actor, with 'Hearty Congratulations,' et cetera. Various clubs have telegraphed also. Here is a message: 'Every man in the City is with you. Kill the bugger!' "

2

Before his committal for trial on 19 April, Wilde was twice remanded in custody, since Charles Gill, who appeared for the prosecution, required three hearings before asking for a committal. On each occasion Wilde's defending counsel Travers Humphreys applied for bail, saying that sureties could be offered to any amount and pointing out that the prisoner had made no attempt to get away, although he knew for many hours prior to his arrest that a warrant might be issued. "You can understand," urged Travers Humphreys on the third occasion, "that there are witnesses to be obtained for the defence, and it is very difficult for Mr Wilde to communicate with persons and prepare his defence unless he is to have the facilities of a man at liberty." But the magistrate persisted in his refusal, both in respect of Wilde and also of Alfred Taylor, who had also been arrested. "In deciding what to do with a case of this kind," declared Sir John Bridge from the Bench, "I have to use my discretion according—in the words of a great judge—to the evidence given and the gravity of the accusation. With regard to the gravity of the case, I think there is no worse crime than that with which the prisoners are charged. As to the evidence, all I shall say is that I do not think it slight, and I shall therefore refuse bail."

In the first part of this declaration, the magistrate seems to have allowed his sense of righteous indignation to get the better of him, since he momentarily overlooked the fact that murder, rape, and a good many other offences are unquestionably more serious than the misdemeanours with which Wilde and his fellow prisoner were charged. So far as the evidence went, however, the magistrate was on surer ground. The blackmailer Wood, the youth Charles Parker, and the bookmaker's tout Fred Atkins all deposed to have been introduced to Wilde for immoral purposes, and each swore that misconduct had taken place between himself and Wilde at various times and in various places. Their statements were corroborated generally by two witnesses, a masseur and a chambermaid respectively, who swore that in March 1893 they had seen Wilde in bed with a young man in the Savoy Hotel.

The Police Court proceedings, which began on 6 April, continued on 11 April, and concluded on 19 April, were on the whole unspectacular. In reporting them, the daily press displayed the utmost animosity against Wilde, referring to him as "described as a gentleman," and so on.[5] At one point the magistrate, who, like the newspapers, seems to have had some difficulty in restraining his feelings, gave a remarkable example of judicial ignorance when he inquired what Kettner's was. It is scarcely credible that Sir John Bridge, who had sat as a magistrate for many years, should not have known of this celebrated restaurant, which was situated barely a mile distant from his own court. Taylor, whose role as co-defendant was to be particularly unfortunate for Wilde, was brought into the dock when Gill was in the middle of examining one of his witnesses on the first day. He was a dark, clean-shaven man in his early thirties who appeared well-dressed and greeted his fellow prisoner with a bow.[6]

Perhaps the most sensational moment, although its full implication was not generally realized until the trial, was when Atkins, in describing a visit he had made to Paris with Wilde, stated that, on his return from the theatre one night to the hotel where they were staying, he found someone else in bed with Wilde. "That was Schwabe," he added in a low, hesitating tone. "Leave that for the moment," hurriedly interposed Gill. Reference had been made to a certain Maurice Schwabe during the Queensberry trial, as we have seen, but his name had been written down on a piece of paper and handed up to the judge without actually being mentioned.

While Wilde was making his first appearance before the Bow Street magistrate, Sir Edward Clarke went into his room in the Law Courts and wrote the following letter to the solicitor who had instructed him in the Queensberry case.

Royal Courts of Justice
6 April 1895

Dear Sir,

Having regard to the events of yesterday, I think it right to say that if Mr Oscar Wilde would like me to defend him at his trial my services shall be at his disposal, and in respect of services so offered I, of course, shall not accept

---

[5] With the exception of one daily and one weekly journal, the *Daily Chronicle* and *Reynold's Newspaper* respectively, the whole of the London press was uniformly hostile to Wilde. Lord Alfred Douglas protested publicly against this unfair attitude of the newspapers, writing to the *Star* on 10 April 1895: "I submit that Mr Oscar Wilde has been tried by the newspapers before he has been tried by a jury, that his case has been almost hopelessly prejudiced in the eyes of the public from whom the jury who must try the case will be drawn, and that he is practically delivered over to the fury of a cowardly and brutal mob."

[6] Taylor had been offered his liberty if he would turn Queen's Evidence and testify against Wilde, but he refused.

any fees. Will you kindly communicate with Mr Oscar Wilde and ascertain his wishes.

Faithfully yours,
EDWARD CLARKE

C. O. Humphreys Esq.

The solicitor replied the same day that he had seen his client, "who wishes me to express to you his deepest gratitude for your very kind offer, which he most gladly accepts." This magnanimous gesture, which also involved the gratuitous services of the two junior counsel who had been with him in the first trial, Willie Mathews and Travers Humphreys, was fully in keeping with Clarke's reputation for personal integrity and his lofty conception of a barrister's duty. "It was upon these terms," he modestly noted afterwards, "that I appeared in all subsequent proceedings." Needless to say, he was thoroughly reviled in certain quarters for this action in defending such a man as Wilde, although he was content to leave his client's interests in the Bow Street proceedings largely in the hands of his able junior Travers Humphreys.[7]

When Gill had concluded his examination-in-chief of Charles Parker, the first of the Crown witnesses at Bow Street on 6 April, Humphreys announced that he intended to defend, but that the charge had taken his client "by surprise" and that consequently he was not prepared to cross-examine Parker. The magistrate accordingly allowed the cross-examination of all the Crown witnesses to be postponed. On the resumption of the hearing on 11 April, Clarke—whose offer to defend Wilde without fee had in the meantime been accepted—came into court and informed the magistrate that he had decided not to cross-examine any of these witnesses, "as probably no cross-examination could affect the result as far as this court is concerned, and so far as your action in the matter is concerned"; he also wished to shorten the Police Court proceedings as much as possible. Douglas subsequently blamed Clarke for his failure to cross-examine the Crown witnesses at Bow Street, which he said had resulted in Wilde and Taylor being committed for trial. He even went so far as to assert in his autobiography that, if he had known as much about the law as he did at the time he wrote, he would have urged Wilde to request Clarke to retire from the case and let someone else—"even any smart junior"—take over and cross-examine these witnesses. But this only shows how completely ignorant of the English criminal law Lord Alfred Douglas was. The depositions sworn by the Crown witnesses at Bow Street were so strong that committal in the case of both Wilde and Taylor was inevitable, as Clarke rightly realized, and there was nothing to be gained in unnecessarily prolonging the proceedings.

It was widely thought that Alfred Douglas would also be arrested. But the authorities had no evidence against the younger man, a fact

---

[7] Even the reputable *Law Journal* (13 April 1895) censured Clarke for defending Wilde without fee, although it later modified its attitude and sought to justify Clarke's conduct of the defence generally.

revealed in an interesting letter written by George Wyndham, M.P., to his father within forty-eight hours of Wilde's arrest.

Sunday, 7 April 1895

. . . I ought to tell you that I know on the authority of Arthur Balfour, who has been told the case by the lawyers who had all the papers, that W[ilde] is certain to be condemned, and that the case is in every way a very serious one, involving the systematic ruin of a number of young men.[8] Public feeling is fiercely hostile to him, among all classes.

There is no case against Bosie, but he has associated himself with W[ilde] up to the last moment; and is spoken of as having known the witnesses who will be called. Men like Arthur [Balfour] and Lord Houghton, who have spoken to me, speak in kind terms of him; but are unanimous in saying that he had better go abroad for a year or two.

Bosie took it very well. He thought I was going to ask him to go at once, and began by saying that nothing on earth would make him leave London until the trial was over. You may be sure that nothing will: he is quite insane on the subject . . . If W[ilde] was released, Bosie would do anything he asked, and no entreaty from you or his mother would weigh with him.

But W[ilde] is humanly speaking, sure to be imprisoned. I told Bosie so; and he agreed that it was almost certain . . .

Whatever is proved, it is common knowledge in London that there was a sort of secret society around the man Taylor.

Wilde was removed from Bow Street to Holloway Prison, where he remained in custody from the date of his first remand until he was eventually released on bail on the jury's failure to reach a verdict after his first trial nearly a month later. During this period he was deserted by almost all his friends, with the conspicuous exception of Lord Alfred Douglas. In the case of a number of them, however, it must be admitted that their desertion was enforced since, fearing for their own skins, they crossed in a troupe to the Continent, there to stay until the trials were over and they judged it safe to return. As for Douglas, he visited Wilde at Holloway every day down to the eve of the first trial, when, in response to a request from Sir Edward Clarke, who considered that his continued presence in London was prejudicial to his client, he too withdrew to France.

On 13 April, W. E. Henley wrote to Charles Whibley, in characteristic language, thus repaying the sympathy shown him by Wilde at the time of his daughter's death:

Yes: Oscar at bay was on the whole a pleasing sight. The air is alive with rumours, of course; but I believe no new arrests will be made, and that morality will be satisfied if Oscar gets two years; as, of course, he will. Why he didn't stay at Monte Carlo, once he got there, God alone knows. Seeing that . . . he returned to face the music, and play the roman fool to Caesar's Destiny, I can only conjecture that, what between personal and professional vanity, he was stark mad. Be that as it may, he is mad no more. Holloway

[8] These young men were nearly all accomplices and no evidence was given at the trials to show that Wilde had "ruined" any of them.

and Bow Street have taken his hair out of curl in more senses than one. And I am pretty sure that he is having a damn bad time . . . I hear that he is ill; and am very glad to hear it.

The position in which Wilde now found himself undoubtedly came as a great shock to him. He could not have believed it possible. "With what a crash this fell!" he wrote to his friend Ada Leverson, one of the very few who, with her husband, stood by him, on his third day in Holloway. "Why did the Sybil say fair things? [9] I thought but to defend him from his father; I thought of nothing else, and now—" And then, some days later: "My counsel seems to wish the case to be tried at once—I don't—nor does Bosie;—bail or no bail, I think we had better wait." About the same time he wrote to Robert Sherard: "I am ill—apathetic. Nothing but Alfred Douglas's daily visits quicken me into life, but even him I only see under humiliating and tragic conditions." Douglas has described these visits in his autobiography, how they sat facing each other in one of a long row of boxes and separated by a long corridor about a yard wide, which was patrolled throughout the interview by a warder. As Wilde was slightly deaf, he had considerable difficulty in hearing what his visitor said, owing to the confused babel of voices from the adjoining boxes, where similar interviews were taking place. As he looked at Douglas, and Douglas looked at him, the tears would roll down his cheeks. Although he finally agreed to his friend's departure to Calais, that event greatly depressed him. "I don't know what to do," he wrote at this time; "my life seems to have gone from me. I feel caught in a terrible net. I don't know where to turn. I care less when I think he is thinking of me—I think of nothing else."

The conduct of the press generally has already been noticed. One paper, in a shocking exhibition of bad taste, not to mention downright cruelty, described with glee an imaginary picture of the prisoner pacing up and down his cell at night like a caged beast. As Frank Harris wrote later, "his arrest was the signal for an orgy of Philistine rancour such as even London had never known before. The puritan middle class, which had always regarded Wilde with dislike as an artist and an intellectual scoffer, a mere parasite of the aristocracy, now gave free scope to their disgust and contempt, and everyone tried to outdo his neighbour in expressions of loathing and abhorrence." [10] Pamphlets attacking Wilde

[9] "The Sybil" was a fortune-teller named Mrs Robinson, whom Wilde and his wife had previously consulted. Constance Wilde wrote to her at this time (19 April 1895): "What is to become of my husband, who has so betrayed and deceived me and ruined the lives of my darling boys? . . . What a tragedy for him who is so gifted."

[10] A friend and fellow countryman of Wilde's, the late W. B. Yeats, with whom the present writer once discussed the subject, expressed himself in similar terms. He explained the unanimity of the mob by the fact that it had become hypnotized by a word or a notion, and showed the senseless behaviour of an individual under the effect of hypnotic suggestion. "The rage against Wilde," said Yeats, who was living in London at the time, "was also complicated by the Britisher's jealousy of art and the artist, which is generally dormant but is called into activity when the artist has got outside his field into publicity of an undesirable kind. This hatred is not due to any action of the artist or eminent man; it is merely the expression of an individual hatred and envy, become collective because circumstances have made it so."

and containing the more salacious portions of the evidence given at Bow Street Police Court were hawked for sale in the streets of the metropolis.

Another calamity the major catastrophe brought in its train was that his income immediately dried up at the source. His plays were taken off and the sale from his books practically ceased. Such of his books as were in print were struck out of the publishers' lists. *An Ideal Husband,* which had been transferred from the Haymarket to the Criterion Theatre under Charles Wyndham's management, was withdrawn after a fortnight. The author's name was pasted over on the bills advertising *The Importance of Being Earnest* at the St James's Theatre, prolonging the life of this play for a few weeks, but it too closed.[11] Sarah Bernhardt, the great French tragedienne, had some time ago agreed to produce *Salomé,* with herself in the name part, but on now being asked at Wilde's instance to advance some money on account of royalties, she ignored his request, although it was repeated several times.

A still worse blow fell when his creditors put the bailiffs into his house in Tite Street and he was sold up. The sale was conducted by the auctioneer under scandalous conditions. Valuable pictures and first editions were knocked down for trifling sums. For example, the artist Joseph Pennell boasted to Henley of how he had "bought a Whistler for a bob!" There were 246 lots in the sale, and they included such pathetic items as a rabbit hutch and "a quantity of toys" which belonged to Wilde's sons, Cyril and Vyvyan. Another item with a particularly sad provenance was the author's own signed copy of the large paper edition of *The Happy Prince,* used for reading to the boys at bedtime. Other possessions, including some of the author's original manuscripts, were actually pilfered on the spot, although Robert Ross did manage to rescue a few of them.[12]

[11] John Lane, Wilde's publisher, who was in New York on business at the time, wrote home to a colleague: "The London Theatres on Oscar are very amusing to me, retaining his plays and withdrawing his name! I might just as well have ripped out the title-pages and sold the books!" According to Lane's biographer, Lewis May, the publisher withdrew Wilde's books from his catalogue only under protest and in response to strong pressure exerted by six of the firm's leading authors: see J. Lewis May, *John Lane and the Nineties* (1936), p. 80. It may be added that Lane was extremely worried by the mention in the Queensberry trial of his employee Edward Shelley. So far as *The Importance of Being Earnest* is concerned, it is only fair to Sir George Alexander's memory to state the explanation of his action which has been given by his biographer, viz., that to help the author, whose financial condition he knew to be desperate, he hoped thereby to prolong the run of the play: see A. E. W. Mason, *Sir George Alexander and the St James's Theatre* (1935), p. 80.

[12] The stolen items included a draft of *A Florentine Tragedy,* of which the greater part was written during Wilde's visit to Florence with Alfred Douglas in 1894. It was long thought that the enlarged version of *The Portrait of Mr W.H.,* which John Lane had agreed to bring out with the assistance of Charles Ricketts and C. H. Shannon, had likewise been purloined, and Robert Ross afterwards searched in vain for it, since he wished to include it in the first Collected Edition of Wilde's works published under his editorship in 1908. Many years later it was discovered in the offices of Lane's publishing firm, The Bodley Head, in a drawer used by a member of the staff named George Chapman, who had died and had no doubt been engaged in preparing the work for publication at the time of Wilde's arrest. It was sold on behalf of Chapman's widow by the American antiquarian dealer Mitchell Kennerley to Dr W. S. Rosenbach and is now in the possession of the Rosenbach Foundation. The complete text was subsequently pub-

Since Wilde and Taylor were not committed for trial until 19 April, and as the next Old Bailey sessions were due to begin three days later, it would have been useless in point of time for their counsel to have applied for bail to a judge in chambers. However, Willie Mathews, on behalf of Wilde, did apply to Mr Justice Charles when the sessions opened, to ask for his client's trial to be postponed until the following sessions on the grounds that the defence had not had proper time in which to prepare their case and further that "in the state of popular feeling existing at the time Mr Wilde would not get a fair and impartial trial." The application was opposed by Charles Gill for the Crown, and in the circumstances the judge felt that he could not accede to it. As to the defendant's not having a fair trial, his lordship thought that "any suggestion such as that was groundless."

True bills having already been found by the grand jury against Wilde and Taylor, Mr. C. O. Humphreys, Wilde's solicitor, informed the press that his client intended to plead not guilty and that he would fight the case to the end.

3

Wilde's second appearance at the Old Bailey, his first in the dock, began on 26 April 1895. The presiding judge was Mr Justice Charles; Charles Gill, along with Horace Avory (later a well-known judge), and Arthur Gill appeared for the prosecution; Wilde was represented by the same three counsel as at the previous trial, while J. P. Grain appeared for Taylor, who was jointly indicted with Wilde. The case for the Crown took three days to complete, the greater part of the third day being occupied with the reading of the evidence given at the Queensberry trial. which was put in verbatim.

Wilde and Taylor were charged under a single indictment containing twenty-five counts and alleging: (a) the commission of acts of gross indecency by both men contrary to the Criminal Law Amendment Act, 1885, section 11; and (b) conspiracy to procure the commission of such acts by Wilde. There was a further charge against Taylor of having acted as a procurer for Wilde. The first nine counts in the indictment referred to misconduct with the two Parker brothers; the next three to Frederick Atkins; two more to incidents at the Savoy Hotel; two to the young man Sidney Mavor; three to charges of conspiracy; five to the blackmailer Alfred Wood; and the last to Wilde's conduct in regard to Edward Shelley. In regard to Taylor, the most serious counts in the indictment charged him with attempting to commit the felony of sodomy with both the Parkers. To all these counts the prisoners pleaded not guilty.

Charles Gill then opened the case for the prosecution in a restrained

lished by Kennerley in New York in a limited edition in 1921 and was republished in England with an introduction by Vyvyan Holland in 1958. Further details of this curious affair have been given by the present writer in *The Times Literary Supplement*, 5 December 1958.

speech to the jury. "I must beg you," he began, "to dismiss from your minds anything you may have heard or read about the prisoners and to abandon all prejudice towards either side, and to approach the case with absolutely open minds carefully and impartially." Unfortunately, the Crown counsel was asking the jury to do the impossible. The majority of the jurymen were no doubt already strongly prejudiced against both prisoners, and the details which Gill now gave them merely served to deepen these prejudices. More than anything else perhaps, they were influenced by the description of Taylor's rooms in Little College Street, with their heavily draped windows, candles burning on through the day, and the languorous atmosphere heavy with perfume.

"Here men met together," said Gill, "and here Wilde was introduced by Taylor to the youths who will give evidence in this case. Wilde did not hesitate, soon after his first introduction to Taylor, to explain to him to what purpose he wished to put their acquaintance. Taylor was familiar with a number of young men who were in the habit of giving their bodies, or selling them, to other men for the purpose of sodomy. It appears that there were a number of youths engaged in this abominable traffic, and that one and all of them were known to Taylor, who went about and sought out for them men of means who were willing to pay heavily for the indulgence of their favourite vice. It will be shown that Taylor himself was given to sodomy and that he has himself indulged in these filthy practices with the same youths as he agreed to procure for Wilde . . . The case of the two Parkers may be given as a sample of the others, on which I prefer to dwell with less minuteness. It will be shown that Taylor corrupted these lads and induced them to meet Wilde by assuring them that he was liberal in his payments."

Gill went on to describe the charges against Wilde as revealed in the course of the Queensberry trial and the subsequent proceedings at Bow Street Police Court, and he dealt in some detail with Wilde's alleged relations with Charles Parker, Atkins, Mavor, and Wood. Coming to the case of Atkins, he said: "This youth accompanied the prisoner Wilde to Paris, and there can be no doubt whatever that the prisoner endeavoured in the most systematic way to influence the young man's mind towards vicious courses and endeavoured to mould him to his own depraved will." Counsel then read out a note from Taylor to Mavor, in which the writer asked Mavor to "come at once and see Oscar at Tite Street." "The use of the Christian name of Wilde in so familiar a way," said Gill, "suggests the nature of the acquaintance which existed between Mavor and Wilde, who was old enough to be the boy's father." Finally counsel touched on the case of Shelley. "There is a difference about Wilde's acquaintance with Shelley, the lad whom he met in the shop of his publishers, Messrs Mathews and Lane, where he was employed. It was an acquaintance with a literary side, but it went through the same stages."

In his place in the dock beside Taylor, Wilde looked haggard and worn, his long hair dishevelled, and it was plain to the spectators in court that his confinement had begun to tell upon his physique. He appeared bored, too, by Gill's opening recitation, but immediately showed interest when the witnesses were called. The first of these was Charles Parker, a somewhat brash youth who stepped into the witness box with a jaunty air and gave his age as twenty-one.

In reply to Gill's questions, Parker said he had been employed as a valet to a gentleman, but at the beginning of 1893 was out of work. He remembered one day at that time being with his brother William in the bar of the St James's Restaurant. While they were there, Taylor came up and spoke to them. "He was an entire stranger," said Parker. "He passed the compliments of the day and asked us to have a drink. We got into conversation with him. He spoke about men."

"In what way?"

"He called attention to the prostitutes who frequented Piccadilly Circus and remarked, 'I can't understand sensible men wasting their money on painted trash like that. Many do, though. But there are a few who know better. Now, you could get money in a certain way easily enough if you cared to.' I understood to what Taylor alluded and made a coarse reply."

"I am obliged to ask you what it was you actually said."

"I do not like to say."

"You were less squeamish at the time, I dare say," Gill remarked to this witness. "I ask you for the words."

After a slight hesitation, Parker replied in a low voice, "I said that if any old gentleman with money took a fancy to me, I was agreeable. I *was* agreeable. I was terribly hard up."

"What did Taylor say?"

"He laughed and said that men far cleverer, richer, and better than I preferred things of that kind." Parker added that they parted after having given Taylor their address.

"Did Taylor mention the prisoner Wilde?"

"Not at that time."

Asked when he first met Wilde, Parker said that he and his brother met Taylor by invitation next day at his rooms in Little College Street, and Taylor told them he could introduce them to a man "who was good for plenty of money." For this purpose they arranged to meet Taylor the following evening at the St James's bar, which they did. Taylor then took them to a restaurant in Rupert Street, which Parker thought was the Solferino, and they were shown upstairs to a private room, where there was a dinner table laid for four. "After a while," Parker continued, "Wilde came in and I was formally introduced. I had never seen him before, but I had heard of him. We dined about eight o'clock. We all four sat down to dinner, Wilde sitting on my left."

"Who made the fourth?"

"My brother William Parker. I had promised Taylor that he should accompany me."

"Was the dinner a good dinner?" Gill went on.

"Yes," said Parker. "The table was lighted with red-shaded candles. We had plenty of champagne with our dinner and brandy and coffee afterwards. We all partook of it. Wilde paid for the dinner."

"Of what nature was the conversation?"

"General, at first. Nothing was then said as to the purpose for which we had come together."

"And then?"

"Subsequently Wilde said to me, 'That is the boy for me! Will you go to the Savoy Hotel with me?' I consented, and Wilde drove me in a cab to the hotel. Only he and I went, leaving my brother and Taylor behind. At the Savoy we went first to Wilde's sitting-room on the second floor."

"More drink was offered you there?"

"Yes, we had liqueurs. Wilde then asked me to go into his bedroom with him."

"Let us know what occurred there."

"He committed the act of sodomy upon me."

"With your consent?"

To this question the witness did not reply, and he was not pressed, since his consent was clearly implied by his behaviour. He went on to state that Wilde had given him £2 on this occasion, telling him to come back to the Savoy in a week. This the witness did, according to his story, one night about eleven o'clock, when they had a champagne supper, and Wilde afterwards committed the same acts as on the first occasion. This time Parker said he got £3.

Asked about his subsequent meetings with Wilde, Parker said that he had met him in Chapel Street when he (Parker) was staying there with Taylor, "and the same thing occurred as at the Savoy." Wilde also visited him, he said, when he was living in Park Walk. "I was asked by Wilde to imagine that I was a woman and that he was my lover. I had to keep up this illusion. I used to sit on his knees and he used to play with my privates as a man might amuse himself with a girl."

One night, Parker went on, Wilde visited him at Park Walk about half-past eleven or twelve. He came in a cab and drove away after staying about a quarter of an hour, having kept the cab waiting outside. In consequence of this incident, Parker admitted that his landlady had given him notice and he had left.

"Apart from money, did Wilde give you any presents?"

"Yes, he gave me a silver cigarette case and a gold ring. I don't suppose boys are different to girls in taking presents from them who are fond of them."

"You pawned the cigarette case and the ring?"

"Yes."

Asked about other visits, Parker said that Taylor had given him the address of Wilde's rooms in St James's Place, and that he had been there in the morning and to tea in the afternoon. Wilde had a bedroom and a sitting-room opening into each other. Speaking of the misconduct which he alleged had taken place there, Parker said that Wilde invariably began his "campaign" with indecencies. He used to require him to do what is vulgarly called "tossing him off," explained Parker quite unabashed, "and he would often do the same to me." Parker gave other details equally shocking and added, "He suggested two or three times that I would permit him to insert 'it' in my mouth, but I never allowed that."

"Where else have you been with Wilde?"

"To Kettner's Restaurant."

"What happened there?"

"We dined there. We always had a lot of wine. Wilde would talk of poetry and art during dinner, and of the old Roman days."

"On one occasion you proceeded from Kettner's to Wilde's house?" Gill prompted the witness's memory.

"Yes," said Parker. "We went to Tite Street. It was very late at night. Wilde let himself and me in with a latchkey. I remained the night, sleeping with the prisoner, and he himself let me out in the early morning before anyone was about."

"Where else have you visited this man?"

"At the Albemarle Hotel. The same thing happened there."

"Where did your last interview take place?"

"I last saw Mr. Wilde in Trafalgar Square about nine months ago. He was in a hansom and saw me. He alighted from the hansom and spoke to me."

"What did he say?"

"He asked me how I was and said, 'Well, you are looking as pretty as ever!' " Parker added that he did not ask him to go anywhere with him then.

The remainder of the examination-in-chief of this witness was concerned with the other prisoner. According to Parker, Taylor had told him, when Parker and his brother were staying in Little College Street and sleeping with Taylor, that he (Taylor) had gone through a form of marriage with a youth named Mason, that Taylor was in a woman's dress, and that they had a wedding breakfast.

"Who else did you meet at Little College Street?"

"Atkins, Wood, and Scarfe, amongst others."

"Did you continue your acquaintance with Taylor until a certain incident occurred last August? You were arrested in the course of a police raid on a certain house in Fitzroy Street?"

"Yes."

"Orgies of the most disgraceful kind used to happen there?"

"Yes."

This last exchange brought Taylor's counsel, J. P. Grain, to his feet. "My lord," he addressed the judge, "I must protest against the introduction of matter extraneous to the indictment. Surely I have enough to answer!"

The protest had its effect. The Crown counsel did not press the witness for details of what had gone on in the house in Fitzroy Street, but contented himself with explaining that he wished to show that Parker had ceased his acquaintance with Taylor after the incident of the raid. Then, continuing his examination, he asked Parker, "When did you cease your association with Taylor?"

"In August 1894 I went away into the country and took up another occupation."

"What was the occupation?" interposed the judge.

"I enlisted," Parker replied. He then went on to say that, while he was with his regiment, he was seen by Lord Queensberry's solicitor, who took down a statement from him.

"Until you became acquainted with Taylor, had you ever been mixed up with men in the commission of indecent acts?"

"No, never."

This concluded Gill's examination-in-chief of Charles Parker. His cross-examination by Sir Edward Clarke, which followed, was designed to show that not only was this witness a self-confessed accomplice in the offences he described but he also was a blackmailer and an associate of blackmailers. Clarke began by reminding him that he had admitted at Bow Street that he had received £30, part of moneys extorted from a gentleman with whom he had committed acts of indecency, not to say anything about the case.

"I don't ask the name of the gentleman from whom the money was extorted, but I do ask the names of the two men who got the money and gave you £30."

"Wood and Allen."

"You had had indecent behaviour with the gentleman in question?"

"Yes. But only on one occasion—at Camera Square, Chelsea."

"Where you were living?"

"Yes."

"Did the gentleman come to your room?"

"Yes."

"By your invitation?"

"He asked me if he could come."

"And you took him home with you?"

"Yes."

"How much did Wood and Allen tell you they got?"

"I can't remember."

"Try and remember!" Clarke pressed the witness.

There was a pause. Then Parker blurted out: "Three hundred pounds or four hundred."

"Was the £30 the first sum of money you received under circumstances of that kind?"

"Yes."

"What did you do with the £30?"

"Spent it."

"And then went into the army?"

"I spent it in about a couple of days."

"I'll leave that question. You say positively that Mr Wilde committed sodomy with you at the Savoy?"

"Yes."

"But you have been in the habit of accusing other gentlemen of the same offence?" Clarke again pressed the witness.

"Never," replied Parker, adding somewhat incautiously, "unless it has been done."

"I submit that you blackmail gentlemen."

"No, sir. I have accepted money, but it has been offered to me to pay for the offence. I have been solicited. I have never suggested this offence to gentlemen."

At counsel's request, the witness wrote down the name and address of his late employer, with whom he said he had been in service as a valet for nine or ten months. He added that he did not leave this place without a character.

"Did you not say that your employer had stated that you had stolen some clothes?"

"Yes."

"How did you know that he had said so?"

"He wrote and told me so, and asked me to send the things back, which I did. They were not clothes, they were shirts and collars."

"Well, I call them clothes," said Clarke. "Did you have a written character?"

"Yes."

"But was not that written before the robbery of the clothes was discovered?"

"Yes," Parker answered with obvious reluctance. "That is so."

"When Taylor asked you if you ever went with men and got money for it, did you understand what he meant?"

"Yes."

"You had heard of such things before?"

"Yes."

"Then it was with the intention of entering upon such practices that you called upon Taylor?"

"No."

"Then why did you call upon him?"

"Because he asked me to."

"You meant to go with men and get money?"

"Yes."

"You understood the practices you were going to enter upon?"

"Yes."

"When you allowed yourself to be introduced to Mr Wilde, you knew perfectly well the purpose for which the introduction was made?"

"Yes."

"At the dinner Mr Wilde was the principal conversationalist, I suppose?"

"Yes."

"And you found him a brilliant and amusing talker?"

"Yes. I told him that I wanted to get some employment on the stage. I knew that Mr Wilde was a dramatist and had much to do with theatres, and I suggested that he might help me. He showed curiosity about my family and affairs, and I told him my father was a horse dealer."

The rest of Clarke's cross-examination was mainly directed to showing that there was no attempt on Wilde's part to conceal any of the visits Parker paid to him at the Savoy and elsewhere. At the Savoy, for instance, Parker admitted that he gave his name, was shown up to Wilde's suite, and in going away did not attempt to avoid any of the servants.

"Were Mr Wilde's rooms on the ground floor of St James's Place very public ones?"

"Yes. There were menservants about. The sitting-room was a sort of library. There were a good many books about."

"Do you suggest that in rooms such as you have described and so situated this kind of conduct went on again and again?"

"Yes."

Finally, Parker admitted that he had heard that Wood had gone to America and that he had in his possession some letters written by Wilde. "I thought he had taken them away with him." The witness added that he had also heard—he could not remember from whom—that Wood got the letters out of some clothes which were given to him by Lord Alfred Douglas. "I never saw the letters," he said.

Asked by Gill in re-examination if he knew Lord Alfred Douglas, the witness replied that he did and that Taylor had introduced him. "I know that the letters referred to belonged to Lord Alfred Douglas," he went on. He added that until he met Taylor he also did not know Atkins, Wood, Allen, or Clibborn.

"When did you first make the acquaintance of Wood?"

"About six months before he went to America."

4

Charles Parker was followed into the witness box by his brother William, the groom who, it will be remembered, had made the fourth at the dinner given by Wilde in honour of Taylor's birthday. In corroborating the previous evidence that on this occasion Wilde had paid all his attention to his brother Charles, William Parker was able to add some interesting details to Charles's testimony. He stated that during the meal Wilde often fed his brother off his own fork or out of his own spoon, and that his brother accepted a preserved cherry from Wilde's own mouth. ("My brother took it into his, and this trick was repeated three or four times.") Charles then went off to the Savoy with Wilde, while he (William Parker) remained behind with Taylor, who remarked, "Your brother is lucky! Oscar does not care what he pays if he fancies a chap."

"What did you do after the dinner?" Clarke asked him in cross-examination.

"I went home after having had a drink or two."

"Hadn't you had enough at the dinner?"

"I know when I've had enough," replied the witness, who seemed rather put out by the question.

"Did you know when you went with your brother to the dinner that you were to be treated as women, and that you were to have money for it?"

"That was what I understood."

Four women now gave evidence in succession. Three of them were landladies who had let rooms to Taylor and Charles Parker at various dates; the fourth was a tenant of the house in Park Walk where Charles Parker had lodged for a time. Mrs Ellen Grant, landlady of the house at 13 Little College Street, stated that she had let Taylor four rooms, for which he paid £3 a month. She confirmed that he kept no servant and did his own cooking on a gas stove. The windows of his rooms were covered with strained art muslin and dark curtains and lace curtains, she said. They were furnished sumptuously, and were lighted by different-coloured lamps and candles. She swore that the windows were never opened or cleaned, and the daylight was never admitted. ("It could not come in, the curtains being always drawn.") There was no bedstead, she added, but there was a spring mattress on the floor of the bedroom.

"What have you seen in the rooms in the shape of apparel?" Gill asked her.

"I have seen a woman's wig and shoes and stockings. I never saw any dress."

"Was there any scent there?"

"Yes."

"Much of it?"

"Mr Taylor used to burn scent." In answer to another question, this witness said she noticed that her lodger's night-shirt was fastened by a gold brooch pin.

"Were Taylor's visitors, as a class, women or men?"

"Men, young men from sixteen to thirty . . . There were frequent tea parties."

"Who came to them—men or women?"

"Oh, always gentlemen." Answering further questions, Mrs Grant said that Taylor used to address his visitors by their Christian names—"Charlie, dear" and "Dear boy." She had heard Taylor talking to someone he called "Oscar," but she had never seen Wilde there. Once she tried the door, she said, and found it locked. She heard whispering and laughing and her suspicions were aroused, but she "did not like to take steps in the matter." Before Taylor left the rooms, in August 1893, a sergeant of police had called and she had shown him the rooms at the officer's request.

In cross-examination this witness confirmed that she had never seen Wilde in the house. She also stated that she understood that the wig and other things were used by her lodger for fancy dress. Another landlady, Mrs Lucy Rumsby, said she had let a bedroom to Charles Parker at 50 Park Walk, Chelsea, in 1893. When he had been there a fortnight, she gave him notice to quit in consequence of the complaint of another lodger. The lodger in question, Mrs Margery Bancroft, who was the next witness, said that late one night she heard a cab drive up and someone enter the house. Afterwards she heard someone going downstairs, and looking out of the window, she saw Wilde enter the cab accompanied by someone who might have been Parker. "I had my suspicions," this inquisitive lodger went on, "and complained to the landlady next morning." Asked how she knew the departing visitor was Wilde, she said he had previously been pointed out to her, when he was standing outside the Royal Academy "with two ladies."

The third landlady, Mrs Sophia Gray, stated that Taylor had lodged in her house at 3 Chapel Street, where he occupied two rooms, from August to December 1893. She had seen Parker there and also Oscar Wilde. Mr Wilde was only there on one occasion she could remember, when he stopped but a few minutes. But Parker stayed all night. Other young men called upon Taylor and were alone with him for a long time, she said, but he used to say they were clerks for whom he hoped to find employment. "I had no idea of the nature of what was going on," she added, causing loud laughter in court by this seemingly naïve remark.

Mrs Gray also stated that when Taylor went away he left behind a box of papers which she later handed over to Lord Queensberry's solicitor. She was followed in the witness box by Frederick Kearley, a retired detective-inspector who said he had examined the documents in question and amongst them he had found the piece of paper on which Charles Parker had written his address in the St James's Restaurant.

Next to go into the witness box was the blackmailer Alfred Wood, who was examined by Gill's junior counsel Horace Avory. He said he was formerly a clerk, but was out of work in January 1893 when he first met Taylor and stayed for about three weeks with him in Little College Street.

"Where did you sleep there?"

"In the same room with Taylor. There was only one bed there."

"When did you first know Wilde?"

"About a month after I made the acquaintance of Taylor."

"How did you come to know Wilde?"

"I was introduced to him by a gentleman at the Café Royal."

"Who was the gentleman?"

"Must I give his name?"

"Yes."

"Lord Alfred Douglas."

"What took place when you were introduced to Wilde?"

"I was introduced by telegram."

Here the judge interrupted the witness by remarking, "You would have led anyone to believe that you were personally introduced!"

After this reproof, the witness went on to relate how, in consequence of the telegram, he went to the Café Royal at nine o'clock one evening. Wilde spoke to him first and asked whether he was Alfred Wood. He then offered the witness a drink, which Wood accepted, and later invited him to dinner. Wood said he went with Wilde to the Florence Restaurant in Rupert Street and they dined in a private room.

"What kind of meal was it?" asked Avory.

"Very nice," replied Wood, "one of the best to be got."

"What wine did you have?"

"Champagne."

During dinner, the witness went on, Wilde would put his hand inside his (Wood's) trousers underneath the table and compel Wood to do the same to him. "Afterwards I lay on the sofa with him," Wood said. "It was a long time, however, before I would allow him to actually do the act of indecency." This, according to the witness, took place after the dinner in Tite Street, when Wilde brought him into a bedroom and they first drank hock and seltzer. Wood then swore that Wilde had used his influence to induce him to consent to the act. "He made me nearly drunk," he added by way of further explanation.

"Did he give you any money that night?"

"Yes, at the Florence. About £3, I think it was. He said he thought I must need some money to buy things with."

"Did he give you this money before any suggestion was made about going to Tite Street?"

"Yes."

Describing further meetings between them, Wood related how on one occasion Wilde called on him in the room in Langham Street where he was living, took him out to tea, and bought him half a dozen shirts, some collars and handkerchiefs, and a silver watch and chain, all of which gifts the witness apparently accepted gratefully at the time.

Asked about the letters he found in the old suit of clothes which Lord Alfred Douglas had given him, Wood said he could not remember how many there were, nor did he remember giving them back to Wilde after he had got the £30 to go to America with. "I might have put them on the table," he added. He confirmed that he saw Wilde again next day at the Florence, where Wilde had invited him to lunch.

"What sort of lunch was it?"

"Very nice lunch. We had champagne." While at lunch, he went on, his host said to him, "Thirty pounds is very little to go to America with, and I will send you £5." This he did by messenger, and Wood went off to America two or three days afterwards.

Wood was still in the witness box when the court rose at the end of the first day of the trial. Next morning he was cross-examined by Sir Edward Clarke, to whom he admitted that he had represented to Wilde in 1893 that he wished to get away from "a certain class of people" he was connected with, and it was by means of this representation that he obtained the £30 from Wilde.

"What have you been doing since your return from America?"

"Well, I have not done much."

"Have you done anything?"

"I have had no regular employment."

"I thought not," commented Clarke.

"I could not get anything to do," replied Wood.

"As a matter of fact, you have had no respectable work for over three years?"

"Well, no."

"Charles Parker has told us that you and a man named Allen obtained £300 or £400 from a gentleman and that you gave Parker £30." Clarke went on to ask, "Is that true?"

"I didn't get the money," the witness answered after some hesitation. "It wasn't paid to me."

"Well, tell us," Clarke pressed, "did you get £300 from a gentleman?"

"Not me," said Wood. "Allen did." It may be noted here that the witness's answers were not always clearly heard, as he appeared to be chewing something all the time.

"You were a party to it?"

"I was there, yes."

"Do you mean by that that you came into the room whilst the gentleman was there with Parker?"

"I did not. Allen went in first."

"At all events Allen and you got £300 or £400 from the gentleman?"

"Yes."

"And you gave Parker £30?"

"I did not. Allen might have done." The witness added that he did not know the exact amount Parker got.

"How much did you get?"

"One hundred and seventy-five pounds."

"What for?"

"Well, it was given me by Allen."

"Then Mr Wilde's giving you £30 to get away from this class of person did not have a very satisfactory result?"

"I was in employment all the time I was in America."

"How did you live when you came back?"

"On some money left me by my father. I was not twenty-one when I went to America."

"Was that before you had the £175?"

"No."

Asked about the Wilde-Douglas letters, the witness said that they came into his possession between January and March 1893, when he was at Oxford. They lay about his rooms for a long time.

"To your knowledge, had one of those letters been copied?"

"I don't know," Wood replied at first. Then he corrected himself and added, "No. Not to my knowledge was one copied."

"When you gave the letters back, or left them on the table, or whatever it was you did with them, did you know that there was one which you did not give back?"

"Yes."

"Where was that one?"

"Allen had it."

"Did you give it to him?"

"No. He took it out of my pocket."

"Did it remain in Allen's possession?"

"I don't know. I didn't want to have it back."

"Since you came back from America, have you ever visited Charles Parker?"

"Yes, at Camera Square."

"Have you stayed there?"

"No."

Asked by Gill in re-examination whether the people he wanted to get away from when he went to America were people whose names had been mentioned in this case, Wood replied that some of them were, but there were others.

"Whom did you mean by the class of people you had been mixed up with?"

"I meant not only Wilde and Taylor but several others whose names have not been mentioned here."

Wood was followed in the witness box by a waiter, Thomas Price, who said he was employed at a private hotel at 10 St James's Place, where Wilde had rooms from October 1893 to April 1894. He recognized Taylor, whom he remembered calling there on one occasion. A number of other young men "of quite inferior station," including Charles Parker, Atkins, and Scarfe, also called to see Wilde there, as well as a young man named Harry Barford, whose name was introduced for the first time. "Mr Wilde had a latchkey, but never slept there more than a dozen times," said the waiter. "He generally arrived about eleven o'clock in the morning, did some literary work, went out to lunch, and returned in the afternoon."

5

"What is your business?" Avory for the Crown asked the next witness, twenty-year-old Fred Atkins.

"I have been a billiard marker," the youth answered. "I have also been a bookmaker's clerk and a comedian."

"You are doing nothing now?"

"No."

"Who introduced you to the prisoners?"

"I was introduced to Taylor by a young fellow named Schwabe in November 1892, and afterwards by Taylor to Mr Wilde."

"Have you met Lord Alfred Douglas?"

"I have. I dined with him and Mr Wilde at the Florence."

"What happened at dinner?"

"Mr Wilde kissed the waiter."

After this unexpected answer, the witness went on to say that Wilde had invited him to go to Paris with him. "We were seated at the table, and he put his arm round me and said he liked me. I arranged to meet him two days afterwards at Victoria Station, and went to Paris with him as his private secretary." He added that they stayed at 29 Boulevard des Capucines, and had two rooms there, a bed-sitting-room and a bedroom, one leading into the other. The day after their arrival, Atkins said he did some copying for Wilde. "Afterwards I lunched at the Café Julien with him. We went for a drive in the afternoon. Next day we went to a hair-dresser's and I had my hair cut."

"Did you tell him to curl it?"

"No. He did it on his own account."

"Mr Wilde was there?"

"Yes, he was having his hair cut and was talking to the man in French all the time."

Atkins then described how on their second day in Paris he went to the Moulin Rouge. "Mr Wilde told me not to go, but I went. I had to pay to go in. I had some money Mr Wilde had given me."

"What did Mr Wilde tell you?" the judge interposed at this point.

"Mr Wilde told me not to go to see those women, as women were the ruin of young fellows. Mr Wilde spoke several times about the same subject, and always to the same effect."

Replying to further questioning Atkins said he got back very late to the hotel from the Moulin Rouge, went into Wilde's bedroom, and dis-covered him in bed with a young man he recognized as Schwabe. He then went to bed by himself. Next morning, while he was still in bed, Wilde came into his room and talked about the Moulin Rouge. Then, according to Atkins, Wilde said, "Shall I come into bed with you?" Atkins said he replied that it was time to get up and Wilde did not get into bed with him. He later returned to London with Wilde, who gave him money and a silver cigarette case. Asked about other meetings, Atkins said he had visited Wilde at Tite Street and once at St James's Place. Wilde had also called on him once at Osnaburgh Street, where he was living; on this occasion Harry Barford was also present.

Clarke's cross-examination of this witness had the object of exposing Atkins as a blackmailer.

"Have you ever lived with a man named Burton?"

"Yes, at Osnaburgh Street, Tachbrook Street, and other places."

"What was he?"

"A bookmaker. I acted as his clerk when he went to the races." Then, as if slightly ashamed of this occupation, Atkins added, "I have also ap-peared at music halls."

"Have you also been engaged in the business of blackmailing?" Clarke asked, eyeing the witness sternly.

"I don't remember."

"Think."

"I never got money in that way."

"Has Burton not obtained money from persons on the ground that they have committed acts of an indecent nature with you?"

"No, sir."

After Atkins had persisted in this denial, Clarke observed, "That being your answer, I must particularize. On the ninth of June 1891, did you and Burton obtain a large sum of money from a Birmingham gentleman?"

"Certainly not."

"What names have you gone by?"

"I have a professional name. I have sometimes called myself Denny."

Clarke then wrote a name on a piece of paper, which was handed up to the witness.

"Do you know that name?"

"No."

"Do you know anything about a Birmingham gentleman?"

"No."

"Where were you living on the ninth June 1891?"

"In Lennox Gardens, Chelsea."

"On that date did a Birmingham gentleman come with you to the rooms you were living at, and did Burton come in, and did you and he get a large sum of money from that gentleman?"

"Certainly not," said Atkins emphatically. "Nothing of the kind ever took place."

"Now I am going to ask you a direct question," said Clarke, "and I ask you to be careful in your reply. Were you and Burton ever taken to Rochester Row Police Station?"

"No."

"Well, was Burton?"

"I think not. At least, not that I know of."

The witness went on to deny that he had taken the gentleman home. Nor had Burton come in and threatened him, nor had he taken the gentleman's wristwatch and chain and given it to Burton.

"And were you taken to the police station the following night, and did you there and then give up the watch and chain?"

"No, never."

"Did not that gentleman give Burton a cheque for £200 made out in the name of St Denis or Denny, which he supposed to be your name?"

"No. I swear the thing never happened."

As he sat down, Clarke turned to one of his junior counsel and whispered something to him. The junior in turn spoke to one of his instructing solicitor's clerks, who immediately left the court.

The next witness was a woman, Mrs Mary Applegate, who said she was the housekeeper at the house in Osnaburgh Street where Atkins had lodged until about a month before. She said that Wilde visited the house at least twice in one week to her knowledge, when Atkins was there. He came about five in the afternoon and left at seven. One of the housemaids came to her and complained of the state of the sheets on the bed in which Atkins slept after Wilde's first visit. "The sheets were stained in a peculiar way," she added.

Mrs Applegate was followed into the witness box by Sidney Mavor, a youth of some education and better breeding than the others who had so far given evidence. It will be remembered that, when he was questioned during the Queensberry trial about his relations with Mavor, Wilde had admitted that this witness had once spent the night with him as his guest at the Albemarle Hotel.

In his evidence-in-chief Mavor said he was in partnership with a friend in business in the city. He first met Taylor at the Gaiety Theatre in 1892, when Taylor had introduced himself and was "very civil and friendly." Taylor invited him to Little College Street and he went there to tea several times; he also admitted to having slept there with Taylor. One day Taylor said to him, "I know a man in an influential position who could be of great use to you, Mavor. He likes young men when they're modest and nice in appearance. I'll introduce you." It was arranged that they should dine at Kettner's Restaurant the next evening. Mavor called for Taylor to keep the appointment, and Taylor said, "I'm glad you've made yourself pretty. Mr Wilde likes nice clean boys!" This was the first time Wilde's name was mentioned, according to Mavor. On arriving at the restaurant, they were shown into a private room, where they were joined shortly afterwards by Wilde, Schwabe, and another gentleman, whom Mavor believed to be Lord Alfred Douglas. "I thought the conversation at dinner peculiar," Mavor went on, "but I knew Mr Wilde was a Bohemian, and the talk therefore did not seem strange. I was placed next to Mr Wilde, who used occasionally to pull my ear or chuck me under the chin, but he did nothing that was actually objectionable."

According to the witness, Wilde said to Taylor at the dinner, "Our little lad has pleasing manners. We must see more of him." Mavor added that before they parted Wilde took his address, and soon afterwards he received a silver cigarette case. On opening it, he found it inscribed, "Sidney from O.W. October 1892." "It was quite a surprise to me!" Mavor said, with an air of innocence.

At this point, in spite of the injunction in *The Importance of Being Earnest* that it is "a very ungentlemanly thing to read a private cigarette case," the one given by Wilde to Mavor was produced and handed up to the judge on the bench. It was then passed round the jury box, where each juryman examined it with great interest.

Mavor went on to describe the night he spent with Wilde in the Albemarle Hotel and was quite definite that no misconduct occurred between them on that occasion. He confirmed this when Clarke cross-examined him and even went further in his denials. "No impropriety has ever taken place between me and Mr Wilde," he said, "and Mr Wilde has never given me any money. I was always glad of Mr Wilde's friendship."

This statement followed the evidence which Mavor gave at Bow Street Police Court, when he had made a similar denial, although this denial came as a surprise to the prosecution, since it was directly contrary to what Mavor had previously told the police. According to him, it was Lord Alfred Douglas who was responsible for this sudden change of front. Douglas happened to meet Mavor in the corridor of the Police Court while he was waiting to go into the witness box with the other Crown witnesses. "Surely you are not going to give evidence against Oscar?" said Douglas. "Well, what can I do?" answered Mavor, looking round in a frightened manner. "I daren't refuse to give evidence now. They got a statement out of me." "For God's sake," said Douglas, "remember you are a gentleman and a public school boy. Don't put yourself on a level with scum like Wood and Parker. When counsel asks you the questions, deny the whole thing, and say you made the statement because you were frightened by the police. They can't do anything to you." "All right," said Mavor, grabbing Douglas's hand, "I'll do what you say."

Next to go into the witness box was Edward Shelley, the young man who had been employed in the office of Wilde's publishers. He described the night he had spent with Wilde at the Albemarle Hotel, and how his host had kissed him and invited him to come into his bedroom. "I felt insulted, degraded, and objected vigorously," Shelley said. Wilde saw him next day and again kissed him "and there was a repetition of the previous night's performance." He went on to say that Wilde had given him inscribed copies of *The Picture of Dorian Gray* and other examples of his works, but he had torn out the pages with the inscriptions after he had heard of the charges suggested by Lord Queensberry. He also explained how he wrote to Wilde, saying that he could not have anything more to do with a man of his morality and he would break off the acquaintance.

"If such a thing as you allege happened, you must have resented the outrage upon you?" Clarke asked him in cross-examination.

"Yes, I did."

"Then why did you go and dine with him the very next day?"

"I suppose I was a young fool. I tried to think the best of him."

Asked why he had left the firm of publishers where he worked, Shelley said that his fellow clerks chaffed him about his friendship with Wilde.

"In what way?"

"They implied scandalous things. They called me 'Mrs Wilde' and 'Miss Oscar.' "

"So you left?"

"I resolved to put an end to an intolerable situation."

"You were in bad odour at home too, I think?"

"Yes, a little."

"I put it to you that your father requested you to leave his house?"

"Yes. He strongly objected to my friendship with Mr Wilde. But the difference between us was made up again."

"Were you arrested for an assault upon your father?"

"Yes, I was."

"Were you quite in your sound mind when you assaulted your father?"

"No, I couldn't have been."

"Where were you taken?"

"To Fulham Police Station."

"Did you send to Mr Wilde and ask him to bail you out?"

"Yes."

"What happened?"

"In an hour my father went to the station and I was liberated. My father withdrew the charge and the case was dismissed."

As soon as Shelley had left the witness box, Sir Edward Clarke asked for Atkins to be recalled. At the same time, counsel handed up a folded document to the judge. It contained a record of the charge sheet at Rochester Row Police Station, and on reading it Mr Justice Charles assumed a grave expression.

"Now," said Clarke to Atkins, "I warn you to attend and to be very careful. I am going to ask you a question. Think before you reply!"

"Just be careful now, Atkins," the judge added.

"On the tenth of June 1891, you were living at Tachbrook Street?"

"Yes."

"James Burton was living there with you?"

"He was."

"Were you both taken by two constables 369A and 500A—you have probably forgotten the officers' numbers—to Rochester Row Police Station and charged with demanding money from a gentleman with menaces?"

The witness looked taken aback. Then he answered in a husky voice, "I was not charged with that." Asked what he was charged with, Atkins said it was with hitting a gentleman, whom he had met the same night at the Alhambra Music Hall and taken home to his room in Tachbrook Street for a game of cards.

"Did the landlady give you and Burton into custody?"

"No, nobody did."

"Some persons must have done. Who did?"

"All I can say is, I did not hear anybody."

At this point Sir Edward Clarke called Police Constable 369A into court. The officer took up his position close to the witness box, where Atkins began to eye him uneasily.

"Now I ask you in the presence of this officer, was the statement made at the police station that you and the gentleman had been in bed together?"

"I don't think so."

"Think before you speak," Clarke thundered. "It will be better for you. Did not the landlady actually come into the room and see you and the gentleman naked on or in the bed together?"

"I don't remember that she did."

"You may as well tell us about it, you know. Was that statement made?"

"Well, yes, it was." The truth came out at last.

"You had endeavoured to force money out of this gentleman?"

"I asked him for some money."

"At the police station the gentleman refused to prosecute?"

"Yes."

"And you and Burton were liberated?"

"Yes."

"About two hours ago, Atkins, I asked you these questions," said Clarke, "and you swore upon your oath that you had not been in custody at all, and had never been taken to Rochester Row. How came you to tell me those lies?"

"I did not remember it" was all Atkins would reply.

The judge turned to the witness. "Leave the box," he said sternly, and Atkins slunk out of court, to face a charge of perjury.

The remaining four witnesses that day were relatively unimportant. There was Elkin Mathews, a former partner in Wilde's firm of publishers, who said that Shelley was asked to leave the firm's employ when it was discovered that Wilde was writing to him. The owner of the Albemarle Hotel said that, owing to the number of young men who called to see Wilde when he was staying in the hotel, he came to the conclusion that it would be better if Wilde did not come to the hotel again, and he accordingly issued a writ for the payment of an outstanding bill. A member of a firm of jewellers in Bond Street gave evidence that he had supplied Wilde with silver cigarette cases and other articles, including the one with the inscription to Mavor, which he had instructions to engrave. Finally, the bookkeeper at the Savoy Hotel stated that Wilde had stayed there in March 1893, and had occupied rooms 361 and 362 and afterwards 353 and 346.

The case for the prosecution was continued on the third day. The first witness to be called was Antonio Migge, who described himself as a "professor of massage" and said that he attended the hotel "to massage patients," including Wilde. On entering Wilde's bedroom one morning, after knocking, he said he saw someone in bed whom he first took to be a lady but later recognized as a young man. At the time Wilde was dressing, and according to this witness, Wilde told him that he felt so much better and was also very busy, so that he could not stay to have the treatment. The masseur said he never attended Wilde again.

"Was the door of the bedroom locked?" Clarke asked in cross-examination.

"No, the door was not locked."

"And when you opened the door, Mr Wilde was dressing?"

"Yes."

"In what part of the room was he?"

"At the washstand."

The masseur's evidence was confirmed by a chambermaid, Jane Cotter, who said she saw a boy of sixteen, with close-cropped hair and a sallow complexion, in Wilde's bed. At this time Lord Alfred Douglas, she said, occupied the adjoining room. She went on to say that she found it necessary to draw the housekeeper's attention to Wilde's bed sheets, which were also "stained in a peculiar way." This latter statement was confirmed by the housekeeper, Annie Perkins, who said she remembered the incident and "gave instructions accordingly." The stains appeared to have been caused by grease and Vaseline.

After formal evidence had been given of the arrest of Wilde and Taylor, Gill put in the transcript of Wilde's cross-examination at the Queensberry trial. The reading of this evidence, followed by Sir Edward Clarke's re-examination, occupied the rest of the day. It also concluded the case for the Crown.

The general impression, now that the halfway mark in the trial had been reached, was that Clarke had and would continue to put up an admirable fight for his client. But, as Gill remarked, "only a miracle can save him."

6

As soon as the judge had taken his place on the Bench for the fourth day of the trial, Charles Gill rose and announced the prosecution's decision to drop the conspiracy charges. This caused considerable surprise among the spectators in court. It also brought Sir Edward Clarke to his feet in protest. "My lord," he said, "if those counts had been withdrawn in the first instance, I should have made an application to your lordship for the charges against the two prisoners to be heard separately." But he agreed, nevertheless, that Crown counsel had a perfect legal right to withdraw the counts at any stage of the case. The judge likewise agreed. "After the evidence had been given," he observed, "it occurred to my own mind that the counts for conspiracy were really unnecessary counts altogether." The result of Gill's action, in the event of Wilde and his fellow prisoner going into the witness box, was to remove all restrictions on the evidence they might wish to give.[13]

Sir Edward Clarke then opened his defence and addressed the jury at some length. "I am going to call Mr Wilde as a witness," he began. "That decision to call him as a witness has not been arrived at in conse-

[13] The inclusion of the conspiracy counts in the indictment was an anomaly, since (as the law then was) an accused could not give evidence in respect of such counts, although he could do so on the indecency counts by virtue of the Criminal Law Amendment Act, 1885. The arbitrary distinction as to the competency of witnesses in criminal trials was abolished by the Criminal Evidence Act, 1898, which provided that, subject to certain qualifications, every person charged with an offence should be a competent witness for the defence at every stage of the proceedings.

quence of the statement just made by Mr Gill—but I certainly felt strengthened in my resolution to call Mr Wilde by the fact of this tardy withdrawal of charges which, if they were not intended to be proceeded with, ought never to have been put in the indictment."

Wilde's counsel went on to discuss what he called the literary part of the case. "The case has been commented on by a large section of the press in a way that I think is disgraceful," he said. "Such conduct is calculated to imperil the administration of justice and is in the highest degree prejudicial to the interests of the prisoners. Mr Gill has asked you to dismiss from your minds anything you may have seen in the newspapers. Mr Gill, in saying that, was quite fair. But I do not think it was quite fair of Mr Gill to have insisted upon reading the cross-examination of Mr Wilde on his writings which you have heard. It is not fair to judge a man by his books. Coleridge said long ago: 'Judge no man by his books. A man is better, higher than his books.' Hidden meanings have been most unjustly read into the poetical and prose works of my client, and it seems that an endeavour, though a futile one, is being made to convict Mr Wilde because of a prurient construction which has been placed by his enemies upon certain of his works. I allude particularly to *The Picture of Dorian Gray.*"

What he described as "the strange unfairness in this case," said Clarke, was that an attempt had been made—and repeated by the reading of Wilde's cross-examination at the Queensberry trial—not to judge Wilde by his own books but by books which he did not write, and to judge him by a story ("The Priest and the Acolyte") which he did not write and which he repudiated as horrible and disgusting. "There was a pretence for such conditions in the former trial, when the question was one as to whether Mr Wilde was 'posing' or not, but in the present case there is no such excuse." Clarke reminded the jury that his client had been most indignant when he saw his name on the title page of a publication which contained such a disgraceful story as "The Priest and the Acolyte." Yet he had been cross-examined on it, and it had been sought to attach stigma to him in that connection. "Faint and far off as was the justification for the cross-examination with reference to *Dorian Gray,* for that with reference to "The Priest and the Acolyte" there was no justification whatever. As to Mr Carson's cross-examination of Mr Wilde on the French work *À Rebours,* it was grossly unfair and a violent misadministration of every canon of justice. The question of the literature is, therefore, an entirely different question from that which you have now to determine."

Dealing with the circumstances of the previous trial, Clarke emphasized that it was entirely his client's act in charging Lord Queensberry with criminal libel which had brought the matter before the public and placed Wilde in his present position of peril. "Men who have been charged with the offences alleged against Mr Wilde shrink from an investigation," he said, "and in my submission the fact of Mr Wilde taking the initiative of a public trial is evidence of his innocence. Nor is that all. A few days before the first trial, notice was given of certain charges made against him with names and dates. On the thirtieth of March Mr Wilde knew the catalogue of accusations which were contained in Lord Queensberry's written plea of justification. Gentlemen of the jury, do you believe that had he been guilty he would have stayed in England and faced those accusations? Men guilty of such offences suffer from a species of insanity. What then would you think of a man who, knowing himself to be guilty and that evidence would be forthcoming from half a dozen different places, insisted on bringing his case before the world? Insane would hardly be the word for it, if Mr Wilde really had been guilty and yet faced the investigation."

Clarke concluded his opening speech to the jury by underlining what he called the remarkable fact that there was only one statement in his client's evidence at the first trial which the prosecution had called an independent witness, who was not an admitted accomplice, to contradict—namely, the statement that Wilde had never been to see Charles Parker at Park Walk. "To my mind that is most significant," said Clarke, "and I hope that if any doubt remains in your minds as to whether it is possible for you to convict the defendant upon such evidence as you have heard, the doubt will be at once removed when you hear Mr Wilde deny upon oath that there is any truth whatever in the allegations made on the part of the prosecution."

Wilde now left the dock and stepped up into the witness box. He answered his counsel's questions quietly and deliberately, and made no attempt to show off, as he had done at the previous trial. After he had been taken through the details of his career as an author and dramatist, he said that since the time of his marriage in 1884 he had lived with his wife in Tite Street. "I have also occupied for a time some rooms in St James's Place, which I took for the purpose of my literary work," he added, "it being quite out of the question to secure quiet and mental repose at my own house when my two young sons were at home."

"Was the evidence you gave at the Queensberry trial absolutely and in all respects true?"

"Entirely true evidence."

"Is there any truth in any of the allegations of indecent behaviour made against you in the evidence in the present case?"

"There is no truth whatever in any one of the allegations, no truth whatsoever."

Charles Gill then rose to cross-examine the witness. "You are acquainted with a publication entitled *The Chameleon?*" he began.

"Very well indeed," Wilde answered with a wry smile.

"I believe that Lord Alfred Douglas was a frequent contributor?"

"Hardly that, I think. He wrote some verses occasionally, and indeed for other papers."

"The poems in question were somewhat peculiar, were they not?"

"They certainly were not mere commonplaces, like so much that is labelled poetry."

"The tone of them met with your critical approval?"

"It was not for me to approve or disapprove. I left that to the reviews."

"At the last trial you described them as beautiful poems."

"I said something tantamount to that. The verses were original in theme and construction, and I admired them."

Here Sir Edward Clarke broke in. "I do not want to make any difficulty," he said, "but I understood from my learned friend that he was willing to confine himself to the specific charges made here."

"This is cross-examination as to credit," said Gill, as his opponent turned towards the judge.

"I do not see how I can interfere," Mr Justice Charles observed. "Questions which the learned counsel thinks should go to credit he is entitled to put."

"Listen, Mr Wilde," Gill continued. "I shall not keep you very long in the witness box." Counsel then picked up a copy of *The Chameleon*, with its distinctive green cover, from which he proceeded to read out the poem entitled "In Praise of Shame."

> Last night unto my bed methought there came
> Our lady of strange dreams, and from an urn
> She poured live fire, so that mine eyes did burn
> At sight of it. Anon the floating flame
> Took many shapes, and one cried: "I am Shame
> That walks with Love, I am most wise to turn
> Cold lips and limbs to fire; therefore discern
> And see my loveliness, and praise my name."
>
> And afterwards, in radiant garments dressed
> With sound of flutes and laughing of glad lips
> A pomp of all the passions passed along
> All the night through; till the white phantom ships
> Of dawn sailed in. Whereat I said this song,
> "Of all sweet passions Shame is loveliest."

"Is that one of the beautiful poems?" Gill asked the witness.

"That is not one of Mr Wilde's," Clarke commented.

"I am not aware that I said it was," said Gill.

"I thought you would be glad to say it was not!" Clarke snapped back.

At this point the judge intervened. "I understand that was a poem by Lord Alfred Douglas."

"Yes, my lord," said Gill, adding in tones of heavy sarcasm, "and one which the witness described as a beautiful poem. The other beautiful poem is the one that follows immediately, and precedes 'The Priest and the Acolyte.' "

Wilde made as if to speak. "May I—" he began. But Gill cut him short with, "No! Kindly answer my questions."

"Certainly," said Wilde.

"If you have any explanation to add to your answer, you may do so," Mr Justice Charles said, addressing the witness.

"I will merely say this, my lord," Wilde replied. "It is not for me to explain the work of anybody else. It does not belong to me. But the word 'shame' in that poem is a word used in the sense of 'modesty.' I mean that I was anxious to point out that 'Shame that turns cold lips to fire'—I forget the line exactly—is a quickened sense of modesty."

"Your view, Mr Wilde," continued Gill, "is that the 'shame' mentioned here is that shame which is a sense of modesty?"

"That was the explanation given to me by the person who wrote it. The sonnet seemed to me obscure."

"During 1893 and 1894 you were a great deal in the company of Lord Alfred Douglas?"

"Oh, yes."

"Did he read that poem to you?"

"Yes."

"You can perhaps understand that such verses as these would not be acceptable to the reader with an ordinary balanced mind?"

"I am not prepared to say," Wilde answered. "It appears to me to be a question of taste, temperament, and individuality. I should say that one man's poetry is another man's poison!"

"I daresay!" commented Gill dryly, when the laughter had subsided. "The next poem is one described as 'Two Loves.' It contains these lines:

> Sweet youth,
> Tell me why, sad and sighing, dost thou rove
> These pleasant realms? I pray thee tell me sooth,
> What is thy name? He said: "My name is Love,"
> Then straight the first did turn himself to me,
> And cried: "He lieth, for his name is Shame.
> But I am Love, and I was wont to be
> Alone in this fair garden, till he came
> Unasked by night; I am true Love, I fill
> The hearts of boy and girl with mutual flame."
> Then sighing said the other: "Have thy will;
> I am the Love that dare not speak its name."

"Was that poem explained to you?"

"I think that is clear."

"There is no question as to what it means?"

"Most certainly not."

"Is it not clear that the love described relates to natural love and unnatural love?"

"No."

"What is the 'Love that dare not speak its name'?" Gill now asked.

" 'The Love that dare not speak its name' in this century is such a great affection of an elder for a younger man as there was between David and Jonathan, such as Plato made the very basis of his philosophy, and such as you find in the sonnets of Michelangelo and Shakespeare. It is that deep, spiritual affection that is as pure as it is perfect. It dictates and pervades great works of art like those of Shakespeare and Michelangelo, and those two letters of mine, such as they are. It is in this century misunderstood, so much misunderstood that it may be described as the 'Love that dare not speak its name,' and on account of it I am placed where I am now. It is beautiful, it is fine, it is the noblest form of affection. There is nothing unnatural about it. It is intellectual, and it repeatedly exists between an elder and a younger man, where the elder has intellect and the younger man has all the joy, hope, and glamour of life before him. That it should be so, the world does not understand. The world mocks at it and sometimes puts one in the pillory for it."

Wilde's words produced a spontaneous outburst of applause from the public gallery, mingled with some hisses, which moved the judge to say he would have the court cleared if there were any further manifestation of feeling. There is no doubt, however, that what Wilde said made an unforgettable impression on all those who heard him, not least the jury. The incident also seemed to give Wilde renewed self-confidence in the witness box.[14]

"I wish to call your attention to the style of your correspondence with Lord Alfred Douglas," Gill went on.

"I am ready," Wilde replied. "I am never ashamed of the style of my writings."

"You are fortunate, or shall I say shameless?" was Gill's neat rejoinder. "I refer to passages in two letters in particular."

"Kindly quote them."

"In letter number one you use the expression 'Your slim gilt soul' and you refer to Lord Alfred's 'red rose lips.' The second letter contains the words 'You are the divine thing I want' and describes Lord Alfred's letter as being 'delightful, red and yellow wine to me.' Do you think an ordinarily constituted being would address such expressions to a younger man?"

"I am not, happily, I think, an ordinarily constituted being."

"It is agreeable to be able to agree with you," said Gill, as he bowed ironically to the witness, who continued his explanation of the controversial correspondence.

"There is nothing, I assure you, in either letter of which I need be ashamed. The first letter is really a prose poem, and the second more of a literary answer to one Lord Alfred Douglas had sent me."

Gill then turned to the specific charges in the case, beginning with the incidents alleged against Wilde at the Savoy Hotel. "Are you prepared to contradict the evidence of the hotel servants?" he asked.

[14] "Oscar was quite superb," wrote Max Beerbohm, who attended the trial. "Here was this man, who had been for a month in prison and loaded with insults and crushed and buffeted, perfectly self-possessed, dominating the Old Bailey with his fine presence and musical voice. He has never had so great a triumph, I am sure, as when the gallery burst into applause—I am sure it affected the gallery." Max Beerbohm, *Letters to Reggie Turner*, ed. Rupert Hart-Davis (1964), p. 102.

"It is entirely untrue," Wilde declared with some emphasis. "Can I answer for what hotel servants say years after I have left the hotel? It is childish. I am not responsible for hotel servants. I have stayed at the hotel and been there constantly since."

"There is no possibility of mistake? There was no woman with you?"

"Certainly not."

Equally emphatically, Wilde denied all the incidents of indecent conduct alleged by Shelley, Charles Parker, Atkins, and Wood, on which prosecuting counsel catechized him. "These witnesses have, you say, lied throughout?" Gill asked, after he had dealt with each individually.

"Their evidence as to my association with them, as to the dinners taking place and the small presents I gave them, is mostly true," said Wilde. "But there is not a particle of truth in that part of the evidence which alleged improper behaviour."

"Why did you take up with these youths?"

"I am a lover of youth!"

"You exalt youth as a sort of god?"

"I like to study the young in everything. There is something fascinating in youthfulness."

"So you would prefer puppies to dogs and kittens to cats?"

"I think so," Wilde answered after a slight pause. "I should enjoy, for instance, the society of a beardless, briefless barrister quite as much as the most accomplished Q.C." Loud laughter followed this remark.

"I hope the former, whom I represent in large numbers, will appreciate the compliment," rejoined Gill amid renewed laughter. "These youths were much inferior to you in station?"

"I never inquired, nor did I care, what station they occupied. I found them, for the most part, bright and entertaining. I found their conversation a change. It acted as a kind of mental tonic."

"Why did you go to Taylor's rooms?"

"Because I used to meet actors and singers of many kinds there."

"Did it strike you that this place was at all peculiar?"

"Not at all."

"Not the sort of street you would usually visit in? You had no other friends there?"

"No. This was merely a bachelor's place."

"Rather a rough neighbourhood, isn't it?"

"That I don't know. I know it is near the Houses of Parliament."

"What did you go there for?"

"To amuse myself sometimes; to smoke a cigarette; for music, chatting, and nonsense of that kind; to while an hour away."

"You never suspected the relations that might exist between Taylor and his young friends?"

"I had no need to suspect anything. Taylor's relations with his friends appeared to me to be quite normal."

"You have attended to the evidence of the witness Mavor?"

"I have."

"Is it true or false?"

"It is mainly true, but false inferences have been drawn from it as from most of the evidence." Then, as if his old self again, Wilde added, to the accompaniment of some mirth, especially from the barristers' seats: "Truth may be found, I believe, at the bottom of a well. It is, apparently, difficult to find it in a court of law!"

"Nevertheless we endeavour to extract it," retorted Gill, who had his own brand of dry humour.

"Did the witness Mavor write to you expressing a wish to break off the acquaintance?"

"I received a rather unaccountable and impertinent letter from him, for which he afterwards expressed great regret."

"Why should he have written to you, if your conduct had been altogether blameless?"

"I do not profess to be able to explain the conduct of most of the witnesses. Mavor may have been told some falsehood about me. His father was greatly incensed at his conduct at the time and, I believe, attributed his son's erratic course to his friendship with me. I do not think Mavor altogether to blame. Pressure was brought to bear on him."

"What do you say about Alphonse Conway?"

"I met him on the beach at Worthing. He was such a bright happy boy that it was a pleasure to talk to him. I bought him a walking-stick, a suit of clothes, and a hat with a bright ribbon—but I was not responsible for the ribbon!"

"You made handsome presents to all these young fellows?"

"Pardon me, I differ. I gave two or three of them a cigarette case. Boys of that class smoke a good deal of cigarettes. I have a weakness for presenting my acquaintances with cigarette cases."

"Rather an expensive habit, if indulged in indiscriminately, isn't it?"

"Less extravagant than giving jewelled garters to ladies!"

This final piece of repartee, which virtually concluded the cross-examination, went down particularly well with counsel, as Gill had a reputation of being a great ladies' man.

Sir Edward Clarke re-examined his client very briefly, confining himself mainly to the letters to Lord Alfred Douglas which Wood had misappropriated. "Wood gave me three letters back," Wilde said. "They were not what I should call matters of great consequence, but no one likes to have his private letters read. They contained some slighting allusions to other people which I should not have liked made public. Then I received an anonymous letter saying that Wood had other letters and intended to try and extort money by means of them. I did not give any money for them at all, but I gave Wood some money to enable him to go to America."

"Had you anything to do with the publication of the two poems by Lord Alfred Douglas in *The Chameleon?*"

"No, nothing whatever."

7

Since Clarke called no other witnesses besides his client, Wilde was immediately followed into the witness box by his fellow prisoner, whose testimony occupied the remainder of the morning. Answering his counsel, J. P. Grain, Alfred Taylor said he was thirty-three years old and the son of a cocoa manufacturer whose business was now being carried on by a limited liability company, his father having died in 1874. He was educated at Marlborough School, which he left when he was about seventeen to go to a private tutor. His intention had always been to go into the army, which in fact he entered through the militia, serving for a short time in the City of London Regiment. But on coming of age in 1883 he had inherited a fortune of £45,000 and since then he had had no occupation but had lived a life of pleasure. All the allegations of misconduct made against him, he said, were absolutely untrue.

Cross-examined by Gill, Taylor denied that he was expelled from his public school for being caught in a compromising situation with a small boy in the lavatory. He admitted, however, that he used to have a number of young men living in his rooms and sleeping in the same bed. He had never gone through a mock marriage with a youth named Charles Mason, but he admitted to having a woman's dress, "an Eastern costume," in his rooms, including a woman's wig and stockings.

"At the time you were living in Chapel Street, were you in serious money difficulties?"

"I had just gone through the Bankruptcy Court."

"Have you not actually made a living since your bankruptcy by procuring lads and young men for rich gentlemen whom you knew to be given to this vice?"

"No."

"Did you know Mr Wilde well?"

"Yes."

"Did you tell certain lads that he was fond of boys?"

"No, never."

"Did you know that he is?"

"I believe he is fond of young people."

"Why did you introduce Charles Parker to Mr Wilde?"

"I thought Mr Wilde might use his influence to obtain for him some work on the stage."

"Why did you burn incense in your rooms?"

"Because I liked it."

Re-examined by his counsel, Taylor explained that the woman's dress which had been found by the police in his rooms was an Oriental dress which he had got in order to go to a fancy-dress ball at Covent Garden. "It came from Constantinople," he said, "and I bought it from a lady."

The remainder of the fourth day of the trial was taken up with the counsel's closing speeches to the jury. Sir Edward Clarke began his immediately after the luncheon adjournment and spoke with great power and emotion for nearly two hours. At the outset, he attacked the prosecution for their conduct over the conspiracy counts which were later withdrawn. If there was not sufficient evidence to substantiate these charges, why were they included in the indictment in the first place?

"Counsel for the Crown ought to have made up their minds on that point at the outset," said Clarke. "A cruel hardship has in consequence been inflicted on Mr Wilde. With whatever anxiety you may seek to separate the evidence in your minds, you will hardly be able to do so. The evidence of literature which has been called against Mr Wilde is not evidence against Taylor, nor is the case of Shelley. At the same time, the character of the young men who frequented Taylor's rooms is not evidence against Mr Wilde. His lordship will tell you that the conversation alleged to have taken place between Taylor and the Parkers at the St James's Restaurant, when they first met, is not evidence against Mr Wilde." ("It is evidence against Taylor only," the judge added at this point.) "In disentangling the evidence, therefore, you will be in a terrible position of responsibility."

Turning to the question of literature, Clarke castigated Gill for having devoted so much of his cross-examination to interrogating Wilde about two poems of which he was not the author.

"The two poems were written by Lord Alfred Douglas, and with them Mr Wilde had no more to do than I have, or you have, gentlemen. What can be said about the morality of our poets if we are to measure it by the writings, not of themselves, but of others? A poet is no more responsible for what others may have said than an artist is guilty of murder when he paints a picture depicting the murder of Rizzio at the feet of Mary Queen of Scots!

"As to the affection which Mr Wilde has expressed in the letters which have been put in," Clarke continued, "he has himself described it as a pure and true affection, absolutely unconnected with, alien to, irreconcilable with the filthy practices which this band of blackmailers you have heard has been narrating. Again, if Mr Wilde were guilty, would he not have recoiled from being put in the witness box? Yet he has gone into the witness box fearless as to what might be produced against him. Mr Wilde is not an ordinary man. He is a man who has written poetry and prose, brilliant drama, charming essays; a man who from his youth has been trained in the study of the literature of the world, not of this England of ours alone, but of those empires whose glories are to us only a name. He writes letters in a tone which to others may seem highflown, inflated, exaggerated, absurd. But he is not ashamed or afraid to produce these letters. He goes into the witness box and says that they speak of pure love, and when he says so, is he not to be believed?"

Finally, in a most memorable peroration, Clarke brought tears to the eyes of at least one person who heard his final words:

"I know with what extreme difficulty it is that juries are able to efface from their recollection things which bias their judgement, and to address themselves only to that evidence which is sound and true. Before you deal with this case, therefore, I implore you to make the effort, and let your judgement be affected only by those witnesses with regard to whom you can say with a clear conscience that you, as honourable men, are entitled to be guided by true and honest and honourable testimony. Fix your minds firmly on the tests that ought to be applied to evidence before you can condemn a fellow man on a charge like this. If you guard yourself from these prejudices which have floated about—they have been dissipated to some extent by the incidents of the last few days, but from them all it is impossible that the atmosphere should be absolutely clear—then I trust that the result of your deliberations will be to gratify those thousands of hopes which are hanging upon your decision, and will clear from this fearful imputation one of our most renowned and accomplished men of letters of today and, in clearing him, will clear society from a stain."

A murmur of appreciation went round the court as Clarke sat down. Of all who heard this superb example of Victorian advocacy, the most grateful was the advocate's client. As he wiped a tear from his cheek, Wilde took a piece of paper and wrote a few lines expressing his gratitude to Clarke for the great effort he had put forward on his behalf. The note was handed down to counsel, who read it and nodded his thanks to the figure in the dock.

Taylor's counsel, J. P. Grain, who addressed the jury next, had a most difficult task in the face of the evidence he had to meet, but he did his best for his client in the circumstances. An endeavour had been made, he said, to prove that Taylor was in the habit of introducing youths to Wilde whom his client knew to be amenable to Wilde's practices and that he got paid for this degrading work; but the attempt to establish this disgusting association had completely broken down. It was true, he admitted, that Taylor was acquainted with the Parkers, Wood, and Atkins. He had seen them constantly in restaurants and music halls, and they had at first forced themselves upon him and thus got acquainted with a man whom they hoped to blackmail. Counsel went on to point out that the Parkers were the only two witnesses who claimed to have been introduced by Taylor to Wilde, and all the resources of the Crown and the solicitors employed by Lord Queensberry had been unable to produce any corroboration of the charges of misconduct made by those witnesses. If Taylor had been employed by Wilde, where was the proof of any kind of payment? Not a farthing piece, in money or in value, Grain submitted, had passed between the two. As for his client's means of livelihood, he had been living on a small allowance from his late father's firm.

The final speech of the day was made by Charles Gill for the prosecution. "It has been argued by my learned friend Sir Edward Clarke," he began, "that no man conscious of guilt would have dared to set the criminal law in motion against Lord Queensberry. As to that, I say you cannot tell what was upon the defendant Wilde's mind, or how he was misled by the expectation that the case would take an entirely different course. The fact remains that from the first Lord Queensberry undertook to justify the libel . . . Sir Edward Clarke has made a courageous and brilliant defence of the prisoner Wilde, and incidentally has made an admission—of which I now take full advantage—that he was in part at least responsible for the course taken on Mr Wilde's behalf at the previous trial, and that in part at least it was due to that circumstance that he—my learned friend—is now appearing on behalf of the accused. So far as the original charge made by Lord Queensberry goes, I have not found it necessary to cross-examine the defendant Wilde, since Mr Wilde's own counsel admitted that the justification was proved and that it was for the public interest that the libel was published."

Dealing with the particular case of Sidney Mavor, Gill argued that it was clear that Wilde had in some way continued to disgust this youth. "Some acts of Mr Wilde, either towards himself or towards others, have offended him," he said. "Is not the letter which Mavor addressed to the prisoner, desiring the cessation of their friendship, corroboration?"

At this point the judge interrupted Gill's speech with an observation which was to have a significant result. "Although the evidence of this witness is clearly of importance," said Mr Justice Charles, "yet he has denied that the defendant Wilde has been guilty of impropriety. I do not think, therefore, that the counts in reference to Mavor can stand." Accordingly, after some further discussion, the judge directed the two counts alleging the commission of acts of indecency with Mavor to be struck out of the indictment.

"At all events," counsel for the prosecution continued, "there is nothing to support the suggestion of my learned friend that Shelley, who has shown himself to be an absolutely respectable and trustworthy witness, was in a disordered state of mind; while as to those witnesses who have been described as blackmailers, they can have no conceivable object in bringing these accusations against the accused, unless the charges they have made are true in substance and in fact."

Gill concluded his speech with these words: "It is your duty, gentlemen, to express your verdict without fear or favour. You owe a duty to society, however sorry you may feel yourselves at the moral downfall of an eminent man, to protect society from such scandals by removing from its heart a sore which cannot fail in time to corrupt and taint it all."

8

It is not necessary to follow the judge into the details of his analysis of the evidence in his summing-up. Wherever there might be a doubt in the minds of the jury, the judge invariably urged the jury to give the prisoners the benefit of it. He began by reminding them that Wilde had given evidence under oath, and that it was a point in his favour that he had himself challenged inquiry into the accusations originally made against him by Lord Queensberry. The judge also took care to point out to the jury that they ought not to base any unfavourable opinion on the fact that Wilde was the author of *The Picture of Dorian Gray*. "If an imaginative writer puts into his novel some consummate villain, and puts into the mouth of that man sentiments revolting to humanity, it must not be supposed that he shares them . . . While some of our most distinguished and noble-minded writers have passed long lives in producing on the whole wholesome literature—such as, for instance, Sir Walter Scott and Charles Dickens, who never wrote, so far as I know, a single offensive line—it is unfortunately true to say that other great writers, who were perfectly noble-minded men themselves, have some-how or other given to the world, especially in the eighteenth century, works which it is painful for persons of ordinary modesty and decency to read. It would be unfair, therefore, when you are trying a man, to allow yourselves to be unfavourably influenced against him by the circum-stances that he has written a book of which you, in so far as you have read any extracts from it, may disapprove."

On the subject of the two letters to Douglas, of which so much had been made, especially at the Queensberry trial, Mr Justice Charles put the most favourable construction on them he could. "I question if Mr Carson was right in regarding these letters as of a horrible or indecent character," he said. "Mr Wilde himself has said that he is not in any sense ashamed of either of these two letters, and that, although they breathe the language of affection and passion, it is not an impure or un-natural passion . . . Furthermore, there is this to be said about the first letter of sufficient importance undoubtedly to be worthy of your atten-tion. It was produced by Mr Wilde himself in his examination-in-chief, which took place here last session; and so it was said on his behalf by his counsel, 'give him credit for not being ashamed.' "

The judge similarly advised the jury to treat with caution the evi-dence of the prosecution witnesses, particularly the chambermaid Jane Cotter and the masseur Migge from the Savoy Hotel. "To my mind it seems strange that, if what the hotel servants alleged is true, there was so little attempt at concealment," he said. "However, if the hotel ser-vants were telling the truth, then Wilde's denial that boys had ever been in his bed at the Savoy must be untrue. It is for you to say on which side the balance of credibility lies.

"I do not wish to enlarge upon this most unpleasant part of this most unpleasant case," the judge went on, "but it is necessary for me to remind you as discreetly as I can that, according to the evidence of Mary Applegate, the housekeeper at Osnaburgh Street, where Atkins used to lodge, the housemaid objected to making the bed on several occasions after Wilde and Atkins had been in the bedroom together. There were, she affirmed, indications on the sheets that conduct of the grossest kind had been indulged in. I think it my duty to remind you that there may be an innocent explanation of these stains, though the evidence of Jane Cotter certainly affords a kind of corroboration of these charges and of Atkins's own story."

Having gone through all the evidence, the judge concluded by saying that he had summed up the case with some minuteness because of its importance to the community at large and its gravity to the accused. "It is important that, if you think that the practices alleged have been proved, you should fearlessly say so," he declared; "but, on the other hand, it is of vast importance that people should not be convicted of acts which they have not committed. The prisoner Wilde has the right to ask you to remember that he is a man of highly intellectual gifts, a person whom people would suppose to be incapable of such acts as are alleged. Taylor, though nothing has been said about his abilities, has been well brought up, and he too belongs to a class of people in whom it is difficult to imagine such an offence. At the same time, you must deal with the evidence fearlessly, remembering the prisoners' position on the one hand and your duty to the public on the other. If you feel you cannot act on the evidence of the witnesses, you should say so; but if you feel constrained to believe that evidence, you must also fearlessly say so."

Before the jury retired to consider their verdict, Mr Justice Charles put four questions to them which he then wrote down and handed to the foreman:

1. Do you think that Wilde committed indecent acts with Edward Shelley and Alfred Wood and with a person or persons unknown at the Savoy Hotel, or with Charles Parker?
2. Did Taylor procure or attempt to procure the commission of these acts or any of them?
3. Did Wilde and Taylor or either of them attempt to get Atkins to commit indecencies?
4. Did Taylor commit indecent acts with Charles Parker or William Parker?

The jury then withdrew, and at the foreman's request the judge ordered that they should be provided with a reasonable amount of food and drink to sustain them during their deliberations. It was just after half-past one when they filed out into the jury room. They returned to court at a quarter-past five, having sent a message to the judge that they had arrived at a negative finding in regard to the third question above, but they disagreed about the remainder.

"Gentlemen of the jury," the judge addressed them when they had taken their places in the jury box, "I have received a communication from you to the effect that, with the exception of the minor question which I put to you in regard to Atkins, you are unable to arrive at an agreement."

"That is so, my lord," the foreman replied. "We cannot agree upon three of the questions you submitted to us."

"Is there any prospect that if you retire to your room—you have not been inconvenienced, you know, because I ordered what you asked—and continued your deliberations a little longer, you would be able to come to an agreement at least on some of the questions?"

"I put that also to my fellow jurymen," answered the foreman. "We have considered the question for three hours and the only result we have come to is that we cannot agree."

"Is there anything which you desire to ask me with reference to the case which you think would assist you in further deliberating upon your verdict?"

"It would be useless, my lord. We cannot agree on any of the subdivisions of questions 1 and 4.

"I am very unwilling to do anything at any time which should look like compelling a jury to deliver a verdict," Mr Justice Charles now observed. "You have been very long in deliberation over this matter, and no doubt you have done your very best to arrive at agreement on the questions. On the other hand, the inconveniences of another trial are very great, and if you thought there was any prospect of agreement after deliberating further, I would ask you to do so."

"My lord," said the foreman, "I fear there is no chance of agreement."

"That being so, I do not feel justified in detaining you any longer."

Before they left the box, the jury returned a formal verdict of "Not guilty" on the counts relating to Atkins, and also on those concerning Mavor, which had been struck out of the indictment on the judge's directions for lack of evidence, as well as the conspiracy counts, which had been withdrawn by the prosecution. This disposed of nine counts in all, out of a total of twenty-five in the indictment which the prisoners had to answer.

Looking back on this trial, at which the jury disagreed, it must be admitted that, in spite of the judge's honest attempt at impartiality, the scales were unquestionably weighted against Wilde. The evidence against Taylor, though technically not evidence against his fellow prisoner, was in the circumstances bound to influence the jury's minds against Wilde. Taylor had managed to run through a fortune of £45,000, dissipating most of it on various forms of loose living; he was known to be a habitual associate of youths of the lowest class; his rooms had been under police observation for some time; and he had actually been arrested during a police raid on an undesirable house in Fitzroy Street where he had been among those found on the premises. The bracketing of Wilde's name with that of Taylor was a great misfortune for Wilde, both in this trial, when he was tried jointly with him, and (as will be seen) in the subsequent trial, when, though tried separately, his case was heard immediately after Taylor's. In the former trial the prisoners should also have been tried separately. Had this been so, and had the jurors' minds not been impregnated with prejudicial press comments, there is a chance that on the evidence offered by the prosecution Wilde would have been acquitted on all the counts with which he was charged. That the jury disagreed was, in the circumstances, a considerable tribute to Clarke's advocacy.

As soon as the jury had been discharged, Clarke applied for Wilde to be released on bail pending his re-trial. Mr Justice Charles felt bound to refuse the application, but intimated that he could not object to its renewal before a judge in chambers. Accordingly, next day, 3 May, Willie Mathews made application to Baron Pollock, submitting that in cases of misdemeanour the judge had no option but was bound to grant bail by virtue of a statute of Charles II. Mathews offered two sureties in the sum of £1,000 each, but Baron Pollock, having consulted with Mr Justice Charles, fixed the total amount at £5,000, directing that Wilde must give his personal security for £2,500 and find two sureties in the sum of £1,250 each. In due course this was done, the sureties to come forward being the Marquess of Queensberry's eldest surviving son, Lord Douglas of Hawick, and the Rev. Stewart Headlam, a Church of England clergyman who, while almost unknown to Wilde, had admired his bearing during the trial and sympathized with him for his treatment by the press and public generally. For his generous action this kind-hearted parson was threatened with stoning by a furious mob outside his house in Bloomsbury.[15] "I became bail for Mr Oscar Wilde on public grounds," the Rev. Stewart Headlam declared afterwards. "I felt that the action of a large section of the press, of the theatrical managers at whose houses his plays were running, and of his publisher, was calculated to prejudice his case before his trial had even begun. I was a surety, not for his character, but for his appearance in court to stand his trial. I had very little personal knowledge of him at the time; I think I had only met him twice; but my confidence in his honour and manliness has been fully justified by the fact that (if rumour be correct), notwithstanding a strong inducement to the contrary, he stayed in England and faced his trial."

Max Beerbohm described his impressions of the closing stages of the trial to Reggie Turner, who, like other friends of Wilde, had deemed it prudent to go abroad for the time being. "Ned Clarke has done splendidly," wrote Max.

> Hoscar stood very upright when he was brought up to hear the verdict and looked most leonine and sphinx-like. I pitied poor little Alfred Taylor—nobody remembered his existence, and Grain made a very poor speech and he himself a poor witness. Hoscar is thinner and consequently finer to look at . . .
>
> It was horrible leaving the court day after day and having to pass through a knot of renters (the younger Parker wearing Her Majesty's uniform—another form of female attire) who were allowed to hang around after giving their evidence and to wink at likely persons.
>
> Trelawny [Backhouse] is raising money for the conduct of the case. Leverson has done a great deal. Clarke and Humphreys are going to take no fees . . . Rothenstein is most sympathetic and goes about the minor clubs insulting everyone who does not happen to be clamouring for Hoscar's instant release.

Some further delay was occasioned by the need for the police to make the customary inquiries about the sureties, but eventually, on the formal

[15] Further details about Stewart Headlam (1847–1924) will be found in his biography by F. G. Bettany (1926). He was an early member of the Fabian Society and a vigourous pioneer of elementary education. Asked by a heckler at a London School Board election meeting whether he was not "the man that went bail for the notorious convict Wilde," Headlam replied amid cheers: "Yes, I am the man, and by the laws of England everyone is reckoned innocent until he is proved guilty."

application of Travers Humphreys to the Bow Street magistrate on 7 May, Wilde was released in the bail agreed. He had been in custody in Holloway for just over a month, "bored and sick to death of this place." "Oh," he exclaimed, "I hope all will come well, and that I can go back to Art and Life." In fact, he had less than three weeks of freedom ahead of him.

7 / The Third Trial

From Bow Street Police Court, where the formalities for bail were completed, Wilde drove with Lord Douglas of Hawick to the Midland Hotel, St Pancras, where two rooms had been reserved for him. He stayed there for several hours and was about to sit down to dinner with Lord Douglas when the manager burst into their sitting-room. "You are Oscar Wilde, I believe." On Wilde admitting his identity, the manager told him he must leave at once. He now realized that the implacable Queensberry was on his trail again. The Marquess had hired a gang of roughs and instructed them to follow Wilde and see that he did not secure admittance to any hotel in town. They did indeed hunt Wilde from hotel to hotel, and managed to achieve their object even in the suburban localities of Kilburn and Notting Hill, where their unfortunate quarry imagined he would not be known. Towards midnight, however, they lost sight of him. At this time Wilde's mother was living with Willie in Oakley Street, Chelsea, and it was to the door of their house that Wilde at length staggered in a state of complete physical exhaustion. "Give me shelter, Willie," he gasped as his astonished brother opened the door. "Let me lie on the floor, or I shall die in the streets." With these words he collapsed across the threshold, as Willie Wilde put it, "like a wounded stag."

Oscar Wilde remained in Oakley Street for the next few days, feeling ill and miserable. The family atmosphere had the worst possible psychological effect on him. Both his eccentric mother and his drunken brother kept telling him that he must behave like an Irish gentleman and face the music. "This house is depressing," he complained. "Willie makes such a merit of giving me shelter. He means well, I suppose, but it is all dreadful." Robert Sherard, who came over from Paris to see him at this time, found the wretched man lying on a camp bed in a poorly furnished room, in which everything was in great disorder. His face was flushed and swollen and his voice broken. He also showed signs of heavy drinking.[1] "Why have you brought me no poison from Paris?" he kept repeating. Willie Wilde seemed incapable of understanding his brother. "Oscar was not a bad character," he naïvely told Bernard Shaw. "You could have trusted him with a woman anywhere."

The news of Wilde's misadventures was now becoming generally known, and had even passed beyond the Channel. On 15 May, Lord Alfred Douglas wrote from his enforced exile in Paris: "The proprietor is very nice and most sympathetic; he asked after you at once and expressed his regret and indignation at the treatment you had received." But it was for two ladies to show the greatest feeling of kindness towards the fallen writer. One of these good samaritans, Adela Schuster, who had heard of his threatened bankruptcy, sent him a cheque for £1,000. The other was Ada Leverson. She and her husband offered him the hospitality of their comfortable home in Courtfield Gardens, where he could rest and be quiet until the beginning of the next trial.

Meanwhile, in the Treasury offices in Whitehall preparations were going ahead for the new prosecution. It had already leaked out that this would be led, not by Charles Gill, as at the previous trial, but by Sir Frank Lockwood, the Solicitor-General. Thus it appeared as if the Crown was now determined to make every effort towards securing a conviction. To one member of the Bar at least, such a course did not commend itself. This was Edward Carson, who had defended Queensberry at the first trial but who had refused to have anything to do with the subsequent proceedings against Wilde. The great Irish advocate went to Lockwood. "Cannot you let up on the fellow now?" he said. "He has suffered a great deal."

"I would," replied Lockwood, "but we cannot: we dare not: it would at once be said, both in England and abroad, that owing to the names mentioned in Queensberry's letters we were forced to abandon it."

The Solicitor-General might have added that the name of his wife's nephew had also cropped up more than once in the two previous trials as having been one of Taylor's notorious circle of acquaintances. The circumstances were extremely unfortunate for Wilde. Indeed, but for their existence, the Crown might conceivably have abandoned the prosecution in the face of the jury's recent disagreement, while at the same time a strong semi-official hint might have been given to Wilde that he should leave the country for a time.

As it was, Wilde was pressed by most of his friends to "jump" his bail and go abroad. Lord Douglas of Hawick told his co-surety, the Rev. Stewart Headlam, that he would hold himself liable for the whole amount and that he hoped Wilde would bolt. "It will practically ruin

---

[1] W. E. Henley wrote to Charles Whibley at this time: "As for Hosker [sic] the news is that he lives with his brother, and is all day steeping himself in liquor and moaning for Boasy [sic] . . . They say he has lost all nerve, all pose, all everything; and is just now so much the ordinary drunkard that he hasn't even the energy to kill himself."

me if I lose all that money at the present moment," he said, "but if there is a chance even of a conviction, for God's sake, let him go." Frank Harris is said to have made arrangements for getting him away in a private yacht. Wilde's kind hostess Ada Leverson, added her voice to the others, and even the unfortunate Constance Wilde came round to Court-field Gardens and pleaded with her husband in tears. But their entreaties were all in vain. Wilde obstinately refused to budge. He would not "run away" and "hide" and "let down" his sureties. "I could not bear life if I were to flee," he said. "I cannot see myself slinking about the Continent, a fugitive from justice." More than once he remarked to Headlam, "I have given my word to you and to my mother, and that is enough." To Lord Alfred Douglas, who had been the unwitting cause of his misfortunes, he wrote: "A dishonoured name, a hunted life, are not for me to whom you have been revealed on that high hill where beautiful things are transfigured." And besides that, he considered he had, as he put it, "a good chance of being acquitted."

One day, when Wilde was still at his brother's house in Oakley Street, Frank Harris called in a hansom and persuaded him to come out to lunch. They avoided his old haunts like the Café Royal, where he might have been recognized and insulted, going instead to a quiet restaurant in Great Portland Street. Over coffee the two men discussed the way the trial had gone. Harris put forward the view that an English jury with normal healthy instincts could be expected not to convict a man solely on the sworn statements of proved blackmailers. The evidence which Harris felt weighed most with them was that of the youth Shelley and the various Savoy Hotel employees, particularly the chambermaid Cotter, since these witnesses were none of them connected with the blackmailers' loathsome business.

To Harris's intense surprise, Wilde declared that the testimony of the hotel employees was wrong. "They are mistaken, Frank," he said. "It was not I they spoke about at the Savoy. *It was Bosie Douglas. I was never bold enough. I went to see Bosie in the morning in his room.*"

"Thank God," exclaimed Harris, "but why didn't Sir Edward Clarke bring that out?"

"He wanted to, but I would not let him. I told him he must not. I must be true to Bosie. I could not let him."

"But he must," said Harris. "At any rate, if he does not, I will. I have three weeks, and in that three weeks I am going to find the chambermaid. I am going to get a plan of your room and Bosie's room, and I am going to make her understand that she was mistaken. She probably remembered you because of your size. She mistook you for the guilty person."

"But what good is it, Frank? What good is it?" asked Wilde. "Even if you convinced the chambermaid and she retracted, there would still be Shelley, and the judge laid stress on Shelley's evidence as untainted."

Harris observed that Shelley appeared in the witness box as an accomplice, and that his testimony consequently required corroboration. There was not a particle of corroboration, he went on. Sir Edward Clarke might have succeeded in having this part of the case withdrawn from the jury like the counts concerning Mavor, had not the issue been complicated by the conspiracy charges. "You'll see," he added reassuringly, "Shelley's evidence too will be ruled out at the next trial."

"Oh, Frank!" cried Wilde. "You talk with passion and conviction, as if I were innocent."

"But you are innocent, aren't you?" asked Harris in amazement.

"No, Frank," replied Wilde. "I thought you knew that all along." [2]

2

The secret of Wilde's stay with the Leversons was well kept. All the servants who were asked gladly agreed to look after him, excepting only the coachman, who was not told but sent away instead on a holiday lest he might talk in the neighbouring public houses. On this occasion Wilde certainly seems to have behaved like a model guest, remaining in his rooms upstairs all day, and only coming down for dinner in the evening with the rest of the household.

He remained at 2 Courtfield Gardens until 20 May, the date on which he was due to surrender to his bail at the Old Bailey. For the duration of the trial he returned to his brother's house in Oakley Street. Among his visitors during this brief interlude of freedom was the brilliant French painter Count Henri de Toulouse-Lautrec, who at a single sitting was able to sketch against a foggy background of Big Ben and the River Thames a most vivid Impressionist portrait. [3]

Since no fresh indictments had been preferred, it was unnecessary for the case to go before a grand jury a second time, although (as we have seen) several counts had been dropped from the original indictment in addition to those charging Wilde and Taylor with conspiracy, on all of which verdicts of not guilty had been returned by the jury at the previous trial. By special arrangement, the cases of the two defendants were called on the opening day of the sessions. The presiding judge was the seventy-seven-year-old Sir Alfred Wills, a person of considerable and varied attainments, being a well-known mountaineer, a scholar in classics and mathematics as well as in law, and the editor of a learned work

---

[2] This incident was later described by Harris in the original American edition of his book on Wilde, but the passages italicized above were omitted from the account given in the English edition since Douglas was still alive at the time and could and no doubt would have successfully sued Harris for libel had the passage been retained. Hesketh Pearson rejects the story in his biography; but, since its substance was confirmed by Wilde himself in the suppressed part of *De Profundis* as well as by R. H. Sherard, I feel it is entitled to belief.

[3] The portrait was used later, in the form of a lithograph reproduction, as part of the programme when *Salomé* was first performed in Paris in 1896, while Wilde was still in prison.

on circumstantial evidence. The Solicitor-General, Sir Frank Lockwood, Q.C., M.P., along with Charles Gill and Horace Avory, appeared for the prosecution. Wilde and Taylor were represented by the same counsel as at the preceding trial.

As soon as the defendants had taken their places in the dock and their pleas of not guilty had been formally recorded, Sir Edward Clarke applied to the judge that they should be tried separately. He pointed out that, since the conspiracy charges had been withdrawn, there was no single count standing in the indictment on which both prisoners could be convicted together. Although strenuously opposed by the Solicitor-General, Clarke's application was granted by the Bench. Lockwood thereupon intimated his intention of taking Taylor's case first. It was now Clarke's turn to protest. He urged upon the judge that his client's case should have priority since his name stood first on the indictment and the first count was directed against him. "There are reasons, I am sure, present to your lordship's mind," he went on, "why it would be unjust to Mr Wilde that his case should be tried after, and immediately after, the other defendant." Lockwood again intervened, and, in spite of Clarke's protests, Mr Justice Wills ruled that the prosecution could please itself in the matter. His lordship added that he was sure both the jury and himself would take care that the one trial should have no influence on the other. "If there should be an acquittal, so much the better for the other prisoner." He agreed, however, that while Taylor was being tried, Wilde should again be released on bail. Some hours elapsed before the sureties could be found, and Wilde did not leave the building until later in the afternoon.

The point of Clarke's remarks soon became painfully clear. Both Taylor and his defending counsel put up a good showing in the face of severe and, as Grain thought, unfair tactics on the part of the Solicitor-General; but his guilt was plain almost from the beginning. Besides the sworn statements of the Crown witnesses, the inferences to be drawn by the jury from the prisoner's own admission that a series of low-class youths had stayed in his rooms and that they had shared the same bed together were quite inescapable. For instance, Charles Parker swore that Taylor kept him in his rooms for a whole week, during which time they rarely went out, calling him "Darling" and referring to him as his "little wife." According to Parker, when he left, Taylor paid him some money. "He said I should never want for cash," Parker declared, "and that he would introduce me to men prepared to pay for that kind of thing."

Perhaps the most damaging corroboration of the prosecution's charges was a letter addressed to Taylor from a young man named Charles Mason, with whom, it will be remembered, Taylor at the previous trial had denied going through a mock marriage ceremony. The letter had been discovered by the police in a hat-box which Taylor had left behind in his rooms in Chapel Street. According to Taylor, Mason was "connected with a newspaper" in the sense of being a shareholder and was "a very busy man"; Taylor said he was a very old friend whom he had known since boyhood. The letter appears to have been written from the newspaper offices, although this was not disclosed in court.[4]

144 Fleet Street, E.C.
Nov. 30, '91

My dear Alfred,

Soon as you can afford to let me have some money, I shall be pleased and obliged. I would not ask you if I could get any myself, you know. Business is not so easy as one would think. There is a lot of trouble attached to it. I have not met anyone yet.

Come home soon dear and let us go out sometimes together. Have very little news. Going to a dance on Monday with the Goolds and to St J[ames's] Theatre tonight.

With much love,

Yours always,
CHARLIE

"I ask you, Taylor, for an explanation," said the Solicitor-General after he had read out the letter in the course of his cross-examination, "for it requires one, of the use of the words 'Come home soon dear,' as between two men."

"I don't see anything in it," the witness replied with a nervous laugh.

"Nothing in it?"

"Well, anyhow, I am not responsible for the expressions of another."

"You allowed yourself to be addressed in this strain?"

"It's the way you read it."

"Then read it yourself, sir," thundered the Solicitor-General, "and tell me if that is the kind of language you exchange with the men who were on such intimate terms with you that they slept in your bed?"

"I don't see anything in that" was all Taylor could answer.

At this point Sir Edward Clarke made as if to rise in his seat, and said something which was inaudible to those in court. As he did so, the Solicitor-General waved him down. "You are not engaged in this case!" he reminded him.

Then, turning to the witness, Lockwood continued: "Do you call it a proper letter?"

"I think it is a perfectly proper letter, seeing the very long friendship which had existed between us," Taylor replied. "But, remember, I did not write the letter."

Here Mr Justice Wills intervened. "In this letter written to you by Mason," the judge asked, "how do you explain the passage 'I have not met anyone yet'?"

"He had been expecting someone to help him to get work," the witness lamely explained.

"You are an old public school boy?" the Solicitor-General continued.

"Yes."

---

[4] This letter was among the documents intended to be put in evidence by Queensberry's solicitors at the first trial and sent by them to the Director of Public Prosecutions.

"Was it not repugnant to your public school ideas, this habit of sleeping with men?"

"Not to me," said Taylor. "Where there is no harm done, I see nothing repugnant in it."

Taylor was specifically charged with indecent behaviour with the two Parker brothers and also with procuring them and Wood for Wilde. So far as the indecency charges were concerned, Mr Justice Wills observed in his summing-up that, up to the point where indecency was alleged, the greater part of the Crown evidence had been admitted by the prisoner Taylor. "It is evidence that shows an association between men of education and position with uneducated menservants," said the judge, "and this is certainly remarkable. The two Parkers have declared that improper conduct took place, and in my opinion there is sufficient corroboration to warrant the case going to the jury." As for the charge of procuring, there was no doubt that the Parkers were introduced to Wilde by Taylor, but the judge warned the jury that unless they were satisfied that the introduction led to the consequences alleged, then it was nothing. "God forbid," the judge went on, "that I should for a moment entertain the thought that for a man to give another a supper— no matter how greatly removed socially they are—is sufficient ground for suspicion; nay, not even though the one gave money to the other." On the other hand, the judge directed that the counts charging Taylor with procuring Wood for Wilde must fail, as it had been shown that Wood's introduction to Wilde did not take place through Taylor, notwithstanding that Wilde and Wood subsequently met in Taylor's rooms. "If you have any reasonable doubt as to the prisoner's guilt, he is entitled to the benefit of it," Mr Justice Wills concluded. "If, on the other hand, you believe that the charges against the prisoner have been satisfactorily proved, you have but one duty, though it is a sad one, to perform."

After an absence of three-quarters of an hour, the jury returned to court and the foreman informed the judge that they could not agree on the counts charging the prisoner with procuring but that they were agreed on the other counts. Mr Justice Wills observed that in that case he thought it would be sufficient to take the jury's verdict on the counts alleging indecent behaviour with Charles and William Parker, to which course the Solicitor-General assented. The jury thereupon returned the verdict, which had been generally expected, of guilty on both these principal counts. The judge then announced that he would postpone sentence until after the charges against Wilde had been heard.

Some discussion followed as to whether the next trial should begin immediately. Clarke said he was quite ready if the Crown wished to go on, but, of course, with a different jury. Mr Justice Wills agreed that there should be a fresh jury, and on further consideration the Solicitor-General informed the Bench that he thought perhaps, as it was past four o'clock in the afternoon, it would be better to begin the next trial the following morning.

"Very well," said the judge, turning to the jury. "I may repeat what I said yesterday, that I am most anxious to keep these two cases separate, and in these circumstances, gentlemen, having heard the evidence in this case, I think it is most proper, in the interest of securing a fair trial, that you should not try the next case, and that it should be heard by a jury from the next court who have heard nothing in this case at all."

Wilde, who had been waiting in another part of the building with his sureties for most of the day, was at last able to leave, when he learned of the court's decision not to proceed with his case until the next day.

Meanwhile, the town was placarded with Wilde's name as the accused was preparing for the final judicial ordeal. "Well," his friend Sherard remarked to him, "you have got your name before the public at least."

Wilde laughed. "Yes," he said. "Nobody can pretend now not to have heard of it."

3

Wilde entered the dock at the Old Bailey to stand trial for the second time on 22 May 1895. There were certain noticeable differences from the previous occasion. The defendant no longer had to meet any charges of conspiracy. The counts relating to Atkins and Mavor had likewise disappeared from the indictment, and with them the testimony of these two youths—Atkins, because he had perjured himself in the witness box, and Mavor, because he had persisted in denying that any indecencies had ever taken place between himself and Wilde. Nevertheless, the accused still had a formidable series of eight counts to meet. Four of these charged him with committing acts of gross indecency with Charles Parker at the Savoy Hotel, St James's Place, and elsewhere; two counts charged him with committing similar offences with unknown persons in the Savoy Hotel; one count related to alleged indecency with Wood in Tite Street; and the final count concerned Shelley. In addition, as we have seen, the Solicitor-General led for the prosecution instead of Charles Gill. This meant that the Crown had a decided advantage, since Lockwood as a Law Officer was entitled to the "last word" in addressing the jury.

When the Solicitor-General had announced that Taylor would be tried first, Sir Edward Clarke had applied to have his client's trial stood over to the next sessions, since he felt that, notwithstanding the presence of a fresh jury, Wilde's position must be adversely affected if he were tried immediately after Taylor. Mr Justice Wills suggested that Clarke should renew his application at the end of Taylor's trial, but when the time came, he decided that it would be fruitless to do so in view of a letter he had received from the judge in the meantime. "I doubt myself if any earthly purpose can be answered by postponing your case," the judge had written to Clarke. "Every man in the kingdom will know, or does now, the outlines of the evidence in this case, and my experience is very much in favour of juries as to mere matters of prejudice in criminal trials. If anything could make the prospect of Wilde's trial tolerable to me or anyone else, it is the fact that you will conduct the defence."

Since a fresh jury had been empanelled, it was necessary for the prosecution to present its case in detail and to recapitulate much of the evidence given at Taylor's trial and at the two previous trials. However, in view of Mr Justice Charles's remarks in his summing-up as to the probative value of those portions of Wilde's publications which had been quoted by Carson and Gill at the two previous trials, the Solicitor-General wisely made no reference in his opening speech to what had come to be known as the literary part of the case, although the two letters to Lord Alfred Douglas were once more to be used against Wilde with damaging effect.

The first witness called by the prosecution was Edward Shelley, for whose story the Solicitor-General had claimed that there was independent corroboration, although it did not go to the length of describing the actual commission of the offences alleged to have been committed with Shelley. "Acts like those alleged are not committed in the light of day," Lockwood told the jury, "but as far as possible with strictest secrecy and concealment."

After he had repeated the evidence-in-chief he had given at the previous trial, Shelley was severely cross-examined by Clarke on his letters to Wilde: in these he expressed the most fulsome gratitude to Wilde for past kindnesses, although, according to his story, Wilde had forced him to commit indecencies with him on two separate occasions. "I am most anxious to see you," Shelley wrote in one letter. "I would have called on you this evening but I am suffering from nervousness, the result of insomnia, and am obliged to remain at home. I have longed to see you all through the week. I have much to tell you. Do not think me forgetful in not coming before, because I shall never forget your kindness to me and am conscious that I can never sufficiently express my thankfulness to you."

"Now, Mr Shelley," Clarke asked the witness, "do you mean to tell the jury that, having in your mind that this man had behaved disgracefully towards you, you wrote this letter?"

"Yes," Shelley replied, "because after these two occurrences he treated me very well. He seemed really sorry for what he had done."

Other letters written by Shelley to Wilde and quoted by Clarke showed the witness to have been constantly complaining about his health. He was "weak and ill" or "so nervous and ill" or "so thin, they think me strange." He admitted that when he attacked his father and was arrested he was not in his right mind. "I certainly could not have been sane to assault my father," he said.

"Was your mental health getting worse and worse?" Clarke asked.

"I made myself ill with studying," answered Shelley.

"Were you worse than you are today?"

"There is nothing the matter with me now."

"You are sure of that?" Clarke asked in tones of great disbelief.

"Quite sure."

The remainder of the day was mostly taken up with Alfred Wood's evidence. He repeated what he had said at the previous trials in his examination-in-chief; and, although cross-examined at length by Clarke, no new facts emerged from his testimony. It was only when he was re-examined by the Solicitor-General—his examination-in-chief had been conducted by Gill—that he said he had seen Wilde and Douglas together in the Savoy Hotel, a fact he had not mentioned before. "On what terms did Lord Alfred and Mr Wilde appear to be?" the Solicitor-General asked Wood. At this Clarke jumped up and objected to the question. His objection was immediately upheld by the judge and the re-examination concluded.

Next morning Clarke made a similarly successful objection, for what it was worth, when, in the course of re-examining William Parker, the Solicitor-General asked him what Taylor had said to him at the dinner after his brother and Wilde had gone off together to the Savoy Hotel. This evidence had in fact been given at the previous trial, when it was admissible, since on that occasion Taylor was being jointly tried with Wilde.

Having, as he felt, successfully disposed of Shelley's evidence, Clarke tried to do the same with the Savoy Hotel servants. Realizing that this was a weak part of its case, the prosecution had brought in two additional witnesses from that establishment, another chambermaid and a waiter. Clarke first dealt with Jane Cotter, the chambermaid who had appeared at the previous trial. On this occasion Clarke noticed that she was wearing spectacles.

"Why do you wear eyeglasses?" Clarke asked her.

"Because my sight is bad."

"Do you use them when you go about your work?"

"Oh dear, no!"

"Why do you wear them today?"

"Because I thought I might have to recognize somebody."

"Then you did not wear them when you say you saw the boy in Mr Wilde's room?"

"No."

"And you had to put them on if you wanted to recognize anybody today?"

"Yes."

Jane Cotter, whose evidence-in-chief had been rendered largely worthless by this courteously brief but devastating cross-examination, was followed into the witness box by her fellow servant, Alice Saunders. The latter stated that her attention had been drawn by the previous witness to the condition of the sheets in Wilde's bedroom at the hotel.

Clarke put one question only. "When were you first asked to give evidence in this case?"

"Last Friday."

The next witness was Antonio Migge, the hotel masseur. Again, answering Clarke, this witness said he had no idea whether the door of Wilde's bedroom was locked or not on the morning he called. Clarke then reminded him that at the last trial he had sworn that the door was not locked. Clarke's next question also emphasized the witness's faulty memory.

"Was the boy you saw there fair or dark?"

"I cannot remember."

The waiter, Émile Becker, said he remembered Wilde and Douglas staying in the hotel in March 1893. After Douglas had left, he had taken champagne and whiskies to Wilde's bedroom, and he remembered seeing several young men there, about five in all. He also said he had served a supper of cold fowl and champagne to Wilde and a dark young man in Wilde's sitting-room. The bill was 16s.

"I suppose you read the accounts of the previous trial?" Clarke asked the waiter in cross-examination.

"Oh, yes."

"You saw it stated that Parker said he had had chicken and champagne?"

"I think I saw it on Monday."

"Had you not seen it before?" the judge broke in.

"No," replied the waiter.

"It was a matter of considerable interest to everybody at the Savoy Hotel?" Clarke continued.

"Yes, it was," the witness agreed.

"How many rooms had you to look after?"

"Seven sitting-rooms."

"Plenty of suppers in such a busy place?"

"Not many upstairs."

"Have you seen Charles Parker?"

"Yes, he was pointed out to me."

"You did not recognize him?"

"No."

"When were you asked to give evidence at this trial?"

"Last Friday. I was seen by an inspector from Scotland Yard."

After the other Crown witnesses had given their testimony and the evidence at the Queensberry trial had been read out a second time, Sir Edward Clarke rose to make a number of submissions to the judge. In the first place, he submitted that, in regard to the counts alleging indecent practices at the Savoy Hotel, there was no case to go to the jury. "Parker has sworn that he left the hotel on both occasions after midnight," said Clarke; "and he cannot, therefore, be identified with the boys whom the hotel servants declared they saw there in the morning."

"The condition of the rooms furnishes a certain amount of corroboration of the charges of misconduct," Mr Justice Wills remarked. "The very fact that a man in such a position in life as the prisoner is found with a boy in his bedroom seems to me so utterly unusual that very little additional evidence would make the case go to the jury. On the other hand, it has been sworn to by the chambermaid that whatever happened there was reported to the housekeeper, and it is a very strange thing that she should have done nothing about it. I do not know what sort of a person she can have been to take no steps in the matter at once."

"It might have been," the Solicitor-General intervened to say, "that the hotel authorities were anxious to avoid the publication of a scandal that would be prejudicial to their establishment."

"In my submission," said Wilde's counsel, "there is no evidence whatever to support the charge that Mr Wilde and a boy were in bed together."

Clarke went on to submit that there was no corroboration with regard to Shelley, and that his evidence ought likewise to be withdrawn from the jury. "The letters of Shelley point to the inference that he may have been the victim of delusions," argued Wilde's counsel, "and, judging from his conduct in the witness box, he appears to have a peculiar sort of exaltation in and for himself."

Lockwood, on the other hand, maintained that Shelley's evidence was corroborated as far as it possibly could be. "What are the relations of these two men of such unequal ages? I shall invite the jury to say that Shelley is a young man who was fascinated by the literary culture of Wilde and brought within Wilde's control and domination—that he was 'entrapped,' as Shelley put it, and that he was not so much an accomplice as a victim. There is, after all, a certain amount of corroboration—evidence of opportunity."

"I must confess that Shelley's letters have left on my mind a notion of disturbed intellect," said the judge. "It would be a terrible thing for society at large if it were to be considered unnatural for a man to ask a younger man of good character to dine with him."

"I would remind your lordship of the letter in which Shelley wrote, 'Let God judge of the past,' the Solicitor-General rejoined, "and also of the fact that Shelley is not in the position of an accomplice."

"With regard to Shelley, I am very clearly of the opinion that he must be treated, on his own evidence, on the footing of an accomplice, and that his evidence should be corroborated," Mr Justice Wills remarked. "It seems to me there is nothing of the kind here. Shelley's own letters to Wilde are rather against the supposition. After a most careful consideration of the point, I adhere to the view, which I had already formed, that there is no corroboration of the nature required by law to warrant conviction, and therefore I feel justified in withdrawing this part of the case from the consideration of the jury."

This judicial ruling from the Bench, which necessarily involved the acquittal of the prisoner on an important count in the indictment— indeed the only one charging him with an offence against a youth of good education and character—created a great impression, and a buzz of excitement ran round the court.

Finally, Wilde's counsel referred to the case of Wood, submitting that there was no corroboration of any sort or kind of his evidence that he had been to Tite Street.

"My lord," said the Solicitor-General, addressing the Bench, "I must protest against any decision being given on these questions other than by a verdict of the jury. In my opinion the case of the man Wood cannot be withheld from the jury. I submit that there is every element of strong corroboration of Wood's story, having regard especially to the strange and suspicious circumstances under which Mr Wilde and Wood became acquainted. There is also corroboration on the payment by Mr Wilde of the money which enabled Wood to go to America." The Solicitor-General went on to quote authorities to show that, although Mr Justice Wills had rightly stated the rule of practice, it was not a rule of law, and that it was the duty of a judge to tell the jury that they might, if they so pleased, act on the unconfirmed testimony of an accomplice.

This brought Clarke to his feet. "It is cruel to suggest," he said, "that the generous action of a man in giving a lad the means of getting away from bad companions to begin a new life in another country is a corroboration of his own misconduct." The judge eventually resolved the matter by saying that he thought that the counts affecting Wood ought to go to the jury. "I think that this case is slightly different from that of Shelley," he said. "It seems to me, after hearing the cross-examination of Mr Wilde in the Queensberry case, that the relations of the two men form a question which the jury ought to consider."

4

Sir Edward Clarke opened his defence on the third morning of the trial. "I shall call Mr Wilde into the witness box again to state on his oath for the third time in this court that there is no truth whatever in the accusations which are made against him," he told the jury, "and to face for the third time in this court, and now with a new assailant, that cross-examination which may be administered to him in regard to these accusations." After relating how the conspiracy charges had been withdrawn in the previous trial, and how the jury had disagreed upon a verdict as to the remaining counts, Clarke said he could not imagine any reason "of logic or fairness" which could be suggested for the course which was adopted of trying Taylor first. In Taylor's trial, moreover, the jury had been unable to agree on the issue referring to Wilde, and they had been discharged without giving a verdict as to that issue. "Practically, this is the third time that this issue has been placed before a jury," said Clarke. "There can be no cause of complaint against me if I feel a little soreness at the treatment Mr Wilde has received."

Wilde's counsel then spoke of the Crown evidence and emphasized that at the previous trial his client had made only one statement contradicted by an independent witness, namely, that he had never been to Charles Parker's lodgings in Park Walk. "I ask you to remember that in relation to the question with which you have to deal," he said. "It is not enough to discredit the evidence of the accused. The Crown must persuade you to believe the evidence of their witnesses, if their case is to be established. The action of Mr Wilde has not been in the least inconsistent with that of a man who, conscious of innocence, is prepared to face the charges of blackmailers. I ask you to believe that a guilty man could not undergo the terrible ordeal of examination and cross-examination in the witness box on three different occasions . . . Mr Wilde has heroically fought against the accusations made against him, accusations that have broken down piece by piece."

As the case had been whittled down, Clarke went on, so the efforts of the prosecution had been redoubled. Instead of Gill—"of the tone of whose conduct of the last case I had never for a moment to complain"—down came a Law Officer of the Crown armed with a strange and invidious privilege, "which I myself when Solicitor-General never once exercised and will not exercise if ever I fill that distinguished position again," of overriding the usual practice of the court. "Whether the defendant calls witnesses or not, the Solicitor-General enjoys the right—though why he should enjoy it I cannot imagine—of the last word with the jury. But for this, I might have relied upon the reading of the defendant's evidence at the last trial. Reckoning with this, the defendant, broken as he is now, as anyone who saw him at the last trial must see he is, by being kept in prison without bail—contrary to practice and, as I believe, contrary to law—will submit himself again to the indignity and pain of going into the witness box. Unfit as he is after the ordeal he has gone through, he will repeat on oath his denial of the charges which have been made against him."

It was only when Wilde had taken his place in the box and had begun to answer his counsel's questions that the full force of Clarke's remarks became apparent. He looked haggard; his hair, usually so neatly dressed, was in disorder; and his voice sounded hollow and husky. At his counsel's request, he was allowed to remain seated while giving evidence. But, if his customary sparkle and verve seemed largely to have deserted him, he certainly answered Clarke's final question in the examination-in-chief with marked determination.

"Is there any truth in the accusations made against you in this indictment?"

"None whatever."

When the Solicitor-General began to cross-examine, it was evident that Clarke's remonstrance had exercised some salutary effect, since the tone of his questions was relatively moderate. Lockwood began by asking the witness about his association with Douglas.

"Was he in London at the time of the trial of the Marquess of Queensberry?"

"Yes, for about three weeks. He went away to France at my wish before the first trial on these counts came on."

"Of course," said Lockwood, "you have been in communication with him?"

"Certainly," answered Wilde. "These charges are founded on sand. Our friendship is founded on rock. There has been no need to cancel the acquaintance."

"What did you do when you learned that the Marquess of Queensberry objected to your friendship with his son?"

"I said I was perfectly ready to cease the acquaintance, if it would make peace between him and his father. But he preferred to do otherwise."

"And the intervention of his father had no effect?"

"No."

The Solicitor-General then proceeded to read out the now notorious "prose poem" letter. He also referred to the second letter, which had been written from the Savoy Hotel.

"Are these a sample of the style in which you addressed Lord Alfred Douglas?"

"No! I do not think I should say a sample," Wilde replied. "No! The letter written from Torquay was intended to be a kind of prose poem, in answer to a poem Lord Alfred had written to me. It was written under circumstances of great feeling."

"Why did you choose the words 'My own Boy' as a mode of address?"

"I adopted them because Lord Alfred Douglas is so much younger than myself. The letter was a fantastic, extravagant way of writing to a young man. As I said at the first trial, it does not seem to me to be a question of whether a thing is right or proper, but of literary expression. It was like a little sonnet of Shakespeare."

"I did not use the word proper or right," said Lockwood. "Was it decent?"

"Oh, decent?" Wilde replied. "Of course. There is nothing indecent in it."

"Do you think that was a decent way for a man of your age to address a young man of his?"

"It was a beautiful way for an artist to address a young man of culture and charm. Decency does not enter into it."

"Doesn't it?" said Lockwood sharply. "Do you understand the meaning of the word, sir?"

"Yes," Wilde replied, keeping his temper under control.

" 'It is a marvel that those red rose-leaf lips of yours should have been made no less for music of song than for madness of kisses.' And do you consider that decent?"

"It was an attempt to write a prose poem in beautiful phraseology."

"Did you consider it decent phraseology?" Lockwood pressed.

"Oh, yes, yes," Wilde answered with a touch of impatience.

"Then do you consider that a decent mode of addressing a young man?"

"I can only give you the same answer, that it is a literary mode of writing what is intended to be a prose poem."

" 'Your slim gilt soul walks between passion and poetry . . . Hyacinthus, whom Apollo loved so madly, was you in Greek days.' You were speaking of love between men?"

"What I meant by the phrase was that he was a poet, and Hyacinthus was a poet."

" 'Always, with undying love'?" Lockwood went on quoting.

"It was not a sensual love."

"Is that again poetic imagery, or an expression of your feelings?"

"That is an expression of my feelings," said Wilde, rising from his seat in the witness box and bowing with a smile to the Solicitor-General.

Lockwood then read the letter from the Savoy Hotel. When he came to the passage "My bill here is £49," he broke off. "That, I suppose, is true? That is not poetic?" he asked the witness in his most sarcastic tone of voice.

"Oh, no, no!" Wilde replied good-humouredly. "That is prose of the most sordid kind!"

Asked about Alphonse Conway and when he had last seen him, Wilde said he had seen him outside the court two days previously. Lockwood was going on to inquire about the "moral effects" of taking a lad in Conway's position on an outing to Brighton and spending a night with him in a hotel there, when Lord Queensberry suddenly entered the court. Being unable to find a seat, he remained standing at the back for some time, sucking the brim of his hat and staring at the witness. This unwelcome apparition had a most disconcerting effect upon the man in the witness box, who was seen to take frequent sips of water from a glass by his side.[5]

The Solicitor-General's concluding questions concerned Wilde's stay in the Savoy Hotel.

"In reference to the Savoy Hotel evidence, is it true that the masseur and the chambermaid saw the boys in your room?"

"Entirely untrue. No one was there."

"There was no one there, man or woman?"

"No."

"You answer also that the chambermaid's statement is untrue?"

"Absolutely."

"You deny that the bed linen was marked in the way described?"

"I do not examine bed linen when I arise. I am not a housemaid."

"Were the stains there, sir?"

"If they were, they were not caused by the way the prosecution has most filthily suggested."

5

"This trial seems to be operating as an act of indemnity for all the blackmailers of London," Sir Edward Clarke declared in his final speech

---

[5] Wilde later wrote to Lord Alfred Douglas from prison, in the suppressed part of *De Profundis:* "I used to feel bitterly the irony and ignominy of my position when in the course of my three trials, beginning at the Police Court, I used to see your father bustling in and out in the hopes of attracting public attention, as if anyone could fail to note or remember the stableman's gait and dress, the bowed legs, the twitching hands, the hanging lower lip, the bestial and half-witted grin. Even when he was not there, or was out of sight, I used to feel conscious of his presence, and the blank dreary walls of the great courtroom, the very air itself, seemed to me at times to be hung with multitudinous masks of that apelike face."

to the jury. "Wood and Parker, in giving evidence, have established for themselves a sort of statute of limitations. In testifying on behalf of the Crown, they have secured immunity for past rogueries and indecencies. It is on the evidence of Parker and Wood that you are asked to condemn Mr Wilde. And Mr Wilde knew nothing of the characters of these men. They were introduced to him, and it was his love of admiration that caused him to be in their society. The positions should really be changed. It is these men who ought to be the accused, not the accusers. It is true that Charles Parker and Wood never made any charge against Mr Wilde before the plea of justification in the libel case was put in. But what a powerful piece of evidence that is in favour of Mr Wilde! For if Charles Parker and Wood thought they had material for making a charge against Mr Wilde before that date, do you not think, gentlemen, they would have made it? Do you think that they would have remained year after year without trying to get something from him? But Charles Parker and Wood previously made no charge against Mr Wilde, nor did they attempt to get money from him—and that circumstance is one among other cogent proofs to be found in the case that there is no truth whatever in the accusations against Mr Wilde."

Clarke then repeated in detail and at some length his already familiar arguments that neither the evidence of Charles Parker nor that of Wood could be relied upon, and that there was no corroboration of it. He likewise submitted that there was nothing to support the counts charging the prisoner with having committed the acts which had been alleged with unknown persons in the Savoy Hotel. As the prosecution had produced two additional witnesses from the Savoy, including a second chambermaid, who bore out the testimony previously given by her fellow servant as to the state of the sheets on Wilde's bed after he had slept in them, Clarke was obliged to deal with this aspect of the case, which he did as briefly and as delicately as he could. There was a perfectly innocent explanation of the stains on the sheets, he suggested. His client had been suffering from attacks of diarrhoea at the time.

"You must not act upon suspicion or prejudice, but upon an examination of the facts, gentlemen," he concluded in a peroration which moved his listeners to a round of applause when he had finished, "and on the facts I respectfully urge that Mr Wilde is entitled to claim from you a verdict of acquittal. If upon an examination of the evidence you therefore feel it your duty to say that the charges against the prisoner have not been proved, then I am sure that you will be glad that the brilliant promise which has been clouded by these accusations, and the bright reputation which was so nearly quenched in the torrent of prejudice which a few weeks ago was sweeping through the press, have been saved by your verdict from absolute ruin; and that it leaves him, a distinguished man of letters and a brilliant Irishman, to live among us a life of honour and repute, and to give in the maturity of his genius gifts to our literature of which he has given only the promise in his early youth."

In his closing speech for the prosecution, Sir Frank Lockwood took the utmost advantage of his exclusive right to the last word with the jury. It was certainly an address of great power, and in it the Solicitor-General showed few signs of the comparatively restrained line he had taken in cross-examining Wilde.

As he listened to this damning recitation of his delinquencies, the man in the dock appeared stunned. Afterwards he was to recall the effect which such oratory had upon him at the time.

I remember as I was sitting in the dock on the occasion of my last trial, listening to Lockwood's appalling denunciation of me [he wrote in *De Profundis*]—like a thing out of Tacitus, like a passage in Dante, like one of Savanarola's indictments of the Popes at Rome—and being sickened with horror at what I heard. Suddenly it occurred to me: *"How splendid it would be if I was saying all this about myself!"* I saw then at once that what is said of a man is nothing. The point is, who says it. A man's very highest moment is, I have no doubt at all, when he kneels in the dust, and beats his breast, and tells all the sins of his life.

"Whatever may be the guilt or innocence of the accused," Mr Justice Wills remarked to the jury at the beginning of his summing-up, "it is clear that Mr Wilde has been obliged, from the result of the Queensberry trial, to confess that his conduct, especially with regard to Lord Alfred Douglas, has been such that Lord Queensberry was justified in applying to him the words of the original libel. It is in my opinion impossible, therefore, for twelve intelligent, impartial, and honest gentlemen to say there was no good ground for an indignant father, a loving and affectionate parent, to charge Mr Wilde with having posed as the Marquess of Queensberry has suggested."

As befitted an authority on circumstantial evidence, Mr Justice Wills summed up the evidence in this trial in a manner which, while it cannot be said that it was actually unfair to the prisoner, was much less favourable to him than Mr Justice Charles's summing-up in the previous trial, particularly on the subject of the two letters to Lord Alfred Douglas. "Is the language of those letters calculated to calm and keep down the passions which in a young man need no stimulus?" Mr Justice Wills asked the jury. "It is strange that it should not occur to a gentleman capable of writing such letters that any young man to whom they were addressed must suffer in the estimation of everybody, if it were known. Lord Queensberry has drawn from these letters the conclusion that most fathers would draw, although he seems to have taken a course of action in his method of interfering which I think no gentleman should have taken, whatever motives he had, in leaving at the defendant's club a card containing a most offensive expression. This was a message which left the defendant no alternative but to prosecute or else be branded publicly as a man who could not deny a foul charge."

Unlike the previous judge, Mr Justice Wills made no reference to the hostile and vindictive press campaign against Wilde, which had tended to prejudge the issue. However, he deprecated the joining of the charges with those against Taylor at the first trial, which he felt justified the disagreement of the jury on that occasion. "As to the present trial," he went on, "I would have preferred to try the prisoners in a different order; but, on the other hand, I do not think that the defendant has suffered by the course taken by the Solicitor-General, nor do I think that the fact that Taylor's case has been heard first has in any way prejudiced the case of Mr Wilde. Whatever your verdict may be, gentlemen, it cannot leave things precisely as they were before this trial."

Coming to the evidence, the judge dealt first with the case of Wood, remarking that it was impossible for him to do this without also dealing with that of Lord Alfred Douglas. "Now, Lord Alfred Douglas is not present and is not a party to these proceedings," he said, "and it must be remembered in his favour that, if neither side called him, he could not volunteer himself as a witness. Anything, therefore, which I shall have to say to Lord Alfred Douglas's prejudice arises simply out of the facts which have transpired in the course of the evidence you have heard. I am anxious, too, to say nothing, in the case of a young man like this who is just on the threshold of life, which might to a great extent blast his career. I do not desire to comment more than I can help either about Lord Alfred Douglas or the Marquess of Queensberry, but I must say that the whole of this lamentable inquiry has arisen through the defendant's association with Lord Alfred Douglas. It is true that Lord Alfred's family seems to be a house divided against itself. But even if there was nothing but hatred between father and son, what father would not try to save his own son from the associations suggested by the two letters which you have seen from the prisoner to Lord Alfred Douglas? I will avoid saying whether these letters seem to point to actual criminal conduct or not. But they must be considered in relation to the other evidence in the case, and it is for you to say whether their contents lend any colour to Wood's story."

Describing what he called the "ill-assorted friendship" between Wood and Douglas, by whom Wood was introduced to Wilde and from whom he received a suit of clothes, the pockets of which contained the compromising letters, the judge remarked that he found it more understandable that a lad like Wood should be given cast-off clothes than cigarette cases. "Now, Lord Alfred Douglas, who was on terms of intimacy with Wood, had just previously to that received a letter from the prisoner, of which it is difficult for me to speak with calmness, as addressed from one man to another," Mr Justice Wills continued. "It is for you, however, to consider whether or not that letter is an indication of unclean sentiments and unclean appetites on both sides. It is to my mind a letter upon which ordinary people would be very liable to put an uncomfortable construction." As for the other letters which Wood had got possession of and returned to Wilde, the judge asked why, if they were really harmless, Wilde had not kept them instead of destroying them. From the value which the blackmailers had put upon them, Wilde must have known that they would be useful in answer to any charge which might be brought against him in respect of the two letters which had been produced. "But I doubt very much," said the judge, "whether the letters were harmless and trivial."

In refusing to withdraw the case of Wood from the jury earlier in the trial, it will be remembered that Mr Justice Wills had undertaken to explain the reason for his so doing and in what direction he found corroboration. "In my opinion," he now said, "the stress of the case with regard to Wood depends upon the character of the original introduction of Wood to Mr Wilde. Do you believe that Mr Wilde was actuated by charitable motives or by improper motives? On the question of corroboration, you are not expected—because corroboration in cases of such a kind as this is difficult to obtain—to be satisfied with less corroboration than you would be if it were easy to obtain. Unless you feel that Wood's evidence is corroborated, you must not act upon it, because Wood is a blackmailer, a person who belongs to the vilest type of men which great cities produce and which society is pestered with."

At this point the foreman of the jury rose from his place in the jury box and put a question to the judge: "In view of the intimacy between Lord Alfred Douglas and Mr Wilde, was a warrant ever issued for the apprehension of Lord Alfred Douglas?"

"I should think not," Mr Justice Wills replied. "We have not heard of it."

"Was it ever contemplated?" the foreman went on to ask.

"Not to my knowledge," said the judge, "A warrant would in any case not be issued without evidence of some fact, of something more than intimacy. I cannot tell, nor need we discuss that, because Lord Alfred Douglas may yet have to answer a charge. He was not called. There may be a thousand considerations of which we may know nothing that might prevent his appearance in the witness box. I think you should deal with the matter upon the evidence before you."

"But it seems to us," the foreman persisted, "that if we are to consider these letters as evidence of guilt, and if we adduce any guilt from these letters, it applies as much to Lord Alfred Douglas as to the defendant."

"Quite so," remarked the judge somewhat testily. "But how does that relieve the defendant? Our present inquiry is whether guilt is brought home to the man in the dock. We have got the testimony of *his* guilt to deal with now. I believe that to be the recipient of such letters and to continue the intimacy is as fatal to the reputation of the recipient as to the sender, but you have really nothing to do with that at present.

"There is a natural disposition to ask," Mr. Justice Wills continued, indicating the prisoner by a motion of the hand, "why should this man stand in the dock and not Lord Alfred Douglas? But, gentlemen of the jury, the supposition that Lord Alfred Douglas will be spared because he is Lord Alfred Douglas is one of the wildest injustice. The thing is utterly and hopelessly impossible! I must remind you that anything that can be said for or against Lord Alfred Douglas must not be allowed to prejudice the prisoner, and you must remember that no prosecution would be possible on the mere production of Mr Wilde's letters to Lord Alfred Douglas. Lord Alfred Douglas, as you know, went to Paris at the request of the defendant, and there he has stayed, and I know absolutely nothing more about him. I am as ignorant in this respect as you are. It may be that there is no evidence against Lord Alfred Douglas. But even about that I know nothing. It is a thing we cannot discuss, and to entertain any such consideration as I have mentioned would be a prejudice of the worst possible kind.

"There is some truth in the aphorism that a man must be judged by the company he keeps," the judge went on. "Gentlemen, you have seen the Parkers, as you have seen Wood, and the same question must arise in your minds. Are these the kind of young men with whom you yourselves would care to sit down to dine? Are they the sort of persons you would expect to find in the company of men of education?" What was more, these young men had frequented Taylor's rooms and Taylor had admitted that they had shared his bed. Indeed, the jury knew that Taylor had just been convicted of indecencies with both the Parkers, although the judge naturally did not allude to this. "Now, gentlemen, you must not presume that the mere fact of two men sleeping together is something to be punished. Poverty and misery frequently compel this to happen, and drive even men and women to sleep together promiscuously. God forbid that I should say that that in itself is a serious crime! But when we come to a man who is spending £40 or £50 a week [as Taylor was doing], it seems astonishing to me that he should not get at least the whole use of a bed for his money, and it is natural to ask why he did not offer another room to his guest."

Still on the subject of Charles Parker, the judge mentioned the evidence of the Savoy Hotel waiter who, it will be remembered, had testified to having served a supper of chicken and champagne to Wilde and a guest in a private sitting-room. Although it might conceivably constitute corroboration, the judge told the jury that it was a very long time ago for a waiter to remember. "The sums too which appeared on the bill are high for such a supper," the judge added. "I know nothing about the Savoy but I must say that in my view 'Chicken and salad for two. 16s.' is very high! I am afraid I shall never have supper there myself."

In going on to deal with what the other Savoy Hotel servants had stated in the witness box, the judge expressed regret that medical evidence had not been called for. "It is a loathsome subject," he said, "but I make a point of never shrinking from details that are absolutely necessary. The medical evidence would have thrown light on what has been alluded to as marks of grease or Vaseline smears. Then, with reference to the condition of the bed, there was the diarrhoea line of defence. That story, I must say, I am not able to appreciate. I have tried many similar cases, but I have never heard that before. It did strike me as being possible; but more than anything else it impressed me with the importance of medical evidence in such a case, which evidence unfortunately we have not had. The worst state of the sheets was not alleged on the date the boy was said to have been seen in the bed by the chambermaid Cotter. There was the same sort of thing, said the woman, but not so bad."

But of course, the evidence of the Savoy Hotel servants after a long lapse of time must not be entirely relied upon. If a servant noticed anything wrong and said nothing about it for two years, then I would not consider that as evidence on which I would hang a dog. It is, in my opinion, a strange thing that this should not be made a matter of inquiry until two years afterwards. The evidence of Migge, the masseur, is remarkable but here again it is not safe to rely on it. The evidence of the woman, Jane Cotter, is no less extraordinary, no matter from what point it is viewed. The thing that strikes me as most remarkable about her story is that, though the housekeeper was acquainted with what had been seen, absolutely no notice was taken of the circumstance. Why, Mrs Perkins, the housekeeper, became an accomplice in the whole affair, and—without saying she is as bad as any of them—I do say it was a very great breach of her sense of right in these matters. She herself has admitted that Cotter, the chambermaid, had made communications to her, and I consider that if the housekeeper was informed of the condition of the room and of the boy having been seen in the bed, and if she yet took no steps to prevent such a thing in the future, she was liable to become an accessory before the fact in the event of it being repeated.

It is a condition of things one shudders to contemplate in a first-class hotel. If it can be assumed that such practices could be tolerated with a man who was running up a bill of £50 a week, then it will look as if we are coming to a state of society when it will be possible to have a magnificently built place of accommodation on the Thames Embankment!

Having delivered himself of this homily, Mr Justice Wills once more went through the evidence, this time briefly, and concluded by telling the jury that the question they must answer was whether there was evidence of guilt or of suspicion only. Finally, he thanked the jury for the patience they had displayed throughout the prolonged hearing. It was just 3:30 p.m. by the courtroom clock when the jury retired to consider their verdict. The judge withdrew to his room and the prisoner was taken to a room below the dock.

Then began the agonizing period of waiting. One hour passed, then two hours, and still there was no word from the jury room. People were beginning to wonder whether there would be another disagreement, when suddenly an usher was seen bearing a note from the jury room to the judge's room.

"That means an acquittal!" said one of the Treasury counsel. "You'll dine your man in Paris tomorrow," Lockwood remarked to Clarke.

But the great advocate who had put up such a brilliant defence of his client was not so sanguine. He shook his head uneasily as they made their way into the dingy old courtroom.

6

The question which the jury asked the judge turned out to be of relatively minor interest. "My lord," said the foreman, "would you read your notes of the evidence of Thomas Price, the waiter, as to the alleged visits of Charles Parker to the prisoner's rooms at 10 St James's Place?"

"There is evidence as to only one of the counts in reference to St. James's Place," replied Mr Justice Wills. The judge then read over his notes of Price's evidence, adding a few words which seemed to imply that this part of the case was not vitally important.

The jury again retired, but were out for only a few minutes. When they filed back to the jury box for the second time, it was clear that they had arrived at a decision.

"Gentlemen," the Clerk of Arraigns addressed them, "have you agreed upon your verdict?"

"We have," the foreman replied.

"Do you find the prisoner at the Bar guilty or not guilty of an act of gross indecency with Charles Parker at the Savoy Hotel on the night of his first introduction to him?"

"Guilty."

"Do you find him guilty or not guilty of a similar offence a week later?"

"Guilty."

"Do you find him guilty or not guilty of a similar offence at St James's Place?"

"Guilty."

"Do you find him guilty or not guilty of a similar offence about the same period?"

"Guilty."

"Do you find him guilty or not guilty of an act of gross indecency with Alfred Wood at Tite Street?"

"Guilty."

"Do you find him guilty or not guilty of an act of gross indecency with a male person unknown in room 362 of the Savoy Hotel?"

"Guilty."

"Do you find him guilty or not guilty of a similar offence in room 346 of the Savoy Hotel?"

"Guilty."

"Do you find him guilty on all counts in the indictment except that relating to Edward Shelley?"

"Yes. Not guilty on that count."

"And is that the verdict of you all?"

"It is."

The prisoner appeared to be dazed by these terrible exchanges, and he only recovered himself when he was joined a minute or two later in the dock by Taylor, whom the judge had directed to be brought up for sentencing along with Wilde. Meanwhile, Sir Edward Clarke was on his feet in a last desperate attempt to save his client, arguing that on technical legal grounds the indictment was bad owing to the joining of the conspiracy counts.

"Of the correctness of the indictment I have myself no doubt," said Mr Justice Wills, thus dashing Clarke's final forlorn hope. "In any case, my passing sentence will not interfere with the arguing of the point raised, and I think it my duty to pass sentence at once. It is not a matter about which I entertain any doubt, and to pass sentence now will in no sense prejudice the result of the inquiry. I think it may be well to complete the proceedings here on the other counts."

The judge then turned to the two prisoners in the dock and continued:

Oscar Wilde and Alfred Taylor, the crime of which you have been convicted is so bad that one has to put stern restraint upon oneself to prevent oneself from describing, in language which I would rather not use, the sentiments which must rise to the breast of every man of honour who has heard the details of these two terrible trials. That the jury have arrived at a correct verdict in this case, I cannot persuade myself to entertain the shadow of a doubt; and I hope, at all events, that those who sometimes imagine that a judge is half-hearted in the cause of decency and morality, because he takes care no prejudice shall enter into the case, may see that that is consistent at least with the utmost sense of indignation at the horrible charges brought home to both of you.

It is no use for me to address you. People who can do these things must be dead to all sense of shame, and one cannot hope to produce any effect upon them. It is the worst case I have ever tried. That you, Taylor, kept a kind of male brothel it is impossible to doubt. And that you, Wilde, have been the centre of a circle of extensive corruption of the most hideous kind among young men, it is equally impossible to doubt.

I shall, under such circumstances, be expected to pass the severest sentence that the law allows. In my judgment it is totally inadequate for such a case as this. The sentence of the Court is that each of you be imprisoned and kept to hard labour for two years.

There were a few murmurs of "Oh!" and "Shame!" since the harsh words employed by the judge in passing the maximum sentence had contrasted strongly with the comparatively moderate language of his summing-up. But the protests were quickly drowned in a hum of approval from the majority of the spectators in the gallery. Meanwhile, all eyes were focused on the dock. There Taylor heard his sentence with seeming indifference, but the other frock-coated figure swayed slightly, his face suffused with horror, and tried to utter a few words. "And I?" he began. "May I say nothing, my lord?" But Mr Justice Wills made no reply beyond a wave of the hand to the warders in attendance, who touched the prisoners on the shoulder and hurried them out of sight to the cells below, there to await the Black Maria to take them to Pentonville Prison.

There is no need to dwell upon the final scene. Among those present in court who witnessed it were two young men who had known Wilde in his heyday. Seymour Hicks, the actor, and Max Beerbohm, the writer and caricaturist. On both of them the scene made an unforgettable impression, as indeed they were to tell the present writer many years later. "I have seen many awful happenings at the Old Bailey," said Seymour

Hicks, "but to me no death sentence has ever seemed so terrible as the one which Mr Justice Wills delivered when his duty called upon him to destroy and take from the world the man who had given it so much." [6]

Meanwhile, in the streets outside the Old Bailey, the verdict was received with sundry marks of popular approval. A few people literally danced with joy, and some prostitutes were seen to kick up their skirts with glee at the news. " 'E'll 'ave 'is 'air cut reglar now!" shouted one of them. This sally provoked a loud chorus of laughter from others on the pavement.

[6] Sir Seymour Hicks told the present writer in the course of a warm tribute to Wilde for his kindness and help to a young and struggling actor that he used to drive home with him alone in a hansom cab after the theatre, but that Wilde never by as much as a hint made a single improper advance to him. The side of Wilde's life which was revealed at the trials came, he said, as a complete shock to him.

SIR WILLIAM WILDE
". . . a wide reputation as one of the most popular writers of the age on Irish subjects"

LADY WILDE ("SPERANZA")
after a portrait by Mulrenin
"I don't think that age has dimmed the fire and enthusiasm of that pen which set the Young Irelanders in a blaze"

OSCAR WILDE (AGE TWO)
"He is to be called Oscar Fingal Wilde. Is not that grand, misty and Ossianic?"

THE UNDERGRADUATE
"I was the happiest man in the world when I entered Magdalen"

HIS COLLEGE SITTING-ROOM
Wilde's room on Kitchen Staircase in Magdalen College, as it was in 1930, when occupied by Montgomery Hyde, unchanged since Wilde's time (1876–8) except for the furniture

Detail from W. P. Frith's painting, *The Private View of the Academy* (1881), showing young Oscar Wilde in the center with a catalogue

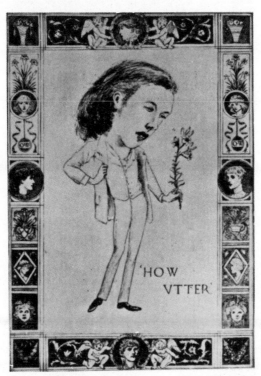

'HOW
VTTER'

Wilde the aesthete ("How Utter"),
in an 1881 cartoon

Culver Picture

In America for lecture tour, 1882,
Wilde posed in New York for these
five photographs by Sarony, the top
theatrical photographer

Culver Pictures

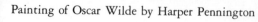
Painting of Oscar Wilde by Harper Pennington

The house at 16 Tite Street, Chelsea, restored and redecorated by E. W. Godwin, where Oscar and Constance Wilde lived with their two sons from 1884 to 1895

Constance Lloyd Wilde
The Wilde sons, Cyril (left) and Vyvyan (right)

Oscar Wilde and Lord Alfred Douglas at Oxford in 1893

Robert Ross and Reginald Turner

William Rothenstein and Max Beerbohm as
Oxford undergraduates

Robert Sherard

Richard Le Gallienne

Caricatures of Wilde by Sir William Rothenstein (above) and Sir Max Beerbohm (below)

The leading actors of *The Importance of Being Earnest*, George Alexander (left) and Allan Aynsworth (right), of whom Wilde said, "You are neither of you my favorite actor"

ST. JAMES'S THEATRE.

SOLE LESSEE AND PROPRIETOR · · MR. GEORGE ALEXANDER.

PRODUCED THURSDAY, FEBRUARY 14th, 1895.

Every Evening at 9,

The Importance of being Earnest,

A TRIVIAL COMEDY FOR SERIOUS PEOPLE

BY OSCAR WILDE.

John Worthing, J.P. { of the Manor House, Woolton, Hertfordshire }		Mr. GEORGE ALEXANDER
Algernon Moncrieffe	. (his Friend) .	Mr. ALLAN AYNESWORTH
Rev. Canon Chasuble, D.D.	. (Rector of Woolton) .	Mr. H. H. VINCENT
Merriman	. (Butler to Mr. Worthing)	. Mr. FRANK DYALL
Lane	. (Mr. Moncrieffe's Man-servant)	. Mr. F. KINSEY PEILE
Lady Bracknell	. . . . .	Miss ROSE LECLERCQ (By permission of Mr. J. COMYNS CARR.)
Hon. Gwendolen Fairfax	. (her Daughter) .	Miss IRENE VANBRUGH
Cecily Cardew	. (John Worthing's Ward) .	Miss VIOLET LYSTER
Miss Prism	. (her Governess) .	Mrs GEORGE CANNINGE

The cast of the play

Oscar Wilde at the height of his success

John Sholto Douglas, ninth Marquess of Queensberry

ward Carson, who appeared for Lord
eensberry in the first trial

Sir Edward Clarke, who appeared for Wilde in all
three trials

CHARLES PARKER.

MARGERY BANCROFT.

WILLIAM PARKER.

Wilde's fellow-defendant, Alfred Taylor, and some

ALFRED WOOD.

ALFRED TAYLOR.

MRS. GRANT.

prosecution witnesses sketched at the second trial

Reading Gaol

Wilde's cell (C.3.3.) and his cell block

The opening page of *De Profundis*, Wilde's 50-page letter to Lord Alfred Douglas written at Reading. It was presented to the British Museum by Robert Ross on condition that it be kept sealed for fifty years, and was opened on January 1, 1960

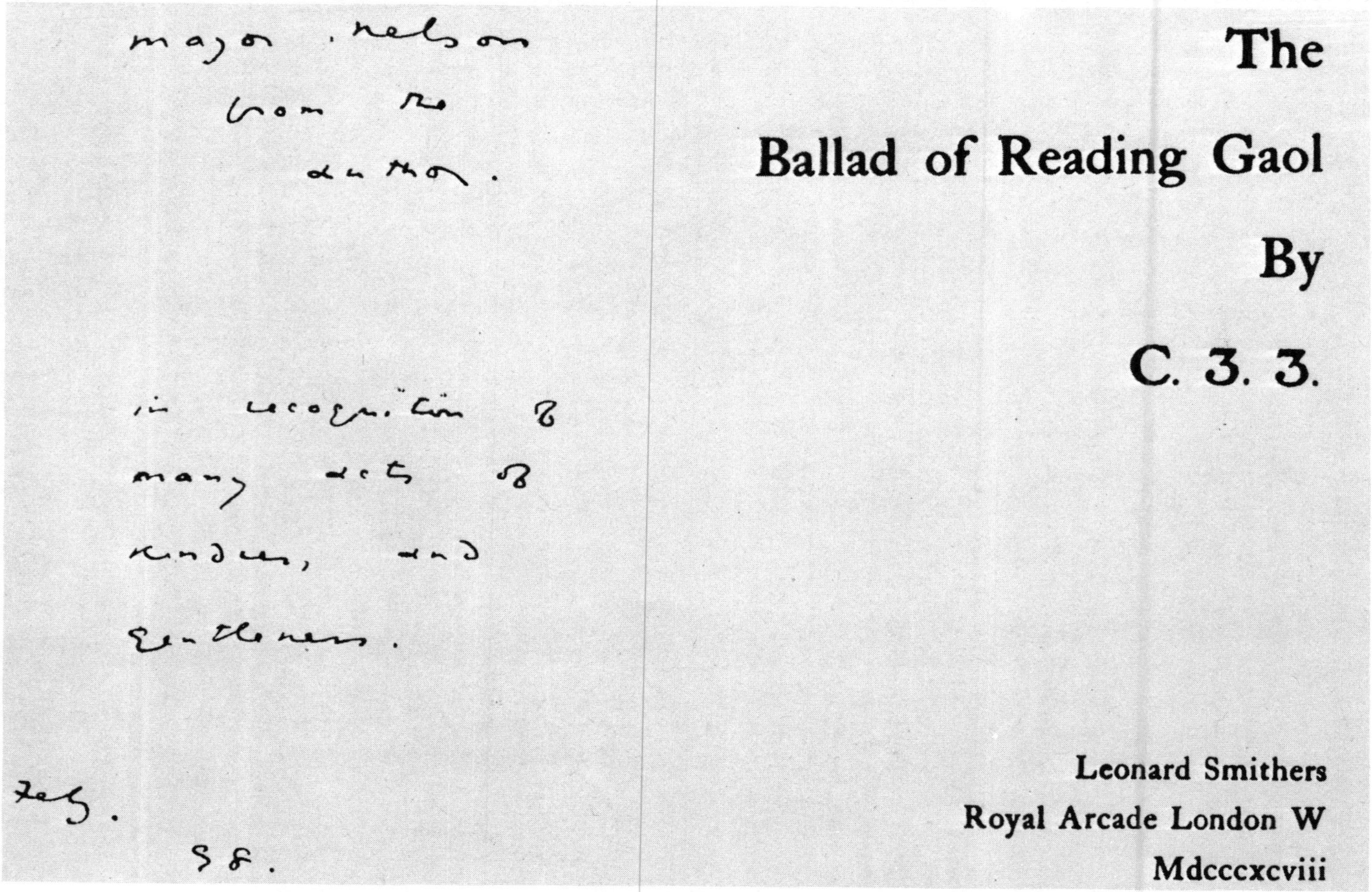

The
Ballad of Reading Gaol

By

C. 3. 3.

Leonard Smithers
Royal Arcade London W
Mdcccxcviii

major nelson
from the
author.

in recognition of
many acts of
kindness, and
Gentleness.

Feby.
98.

A copy of his poem inscribed by Wilde to Major Nelson, Governor of Reading Gaol, "in recognition of many acts of kindness, and gentleness"

Wilde after his release from prison, in a photograph taken outside the royal palace in Naples in 1897. He inscribed himself as "a young unmitred bishop *in partibus*" for his friend Reggie Turner

Ada Leverson ("The Sphinx")

Leonard Smithers, "The most learned erotomaniac in Europe. He is also a delightful companion and a dear fellow, very kind to me"

Frank Harris

Wilde and Douglas together in Naples in 1897; they took photos of each other

Hôtel d'Alsace in Paris, where Wilde lived intermittently
from March 1898 until his death in November 1900

The writing-table in Wilde's room in the hotel,
subsequently acquired by Richard Le Gallienne

The last photograph of Wilde, taken with Wilde's own
camera (presumably by Robert Ross) in 1900

The tomb by Jacob Epstein in Père Lachaise

The plaque on the Tite Street house, unveiled by Sir Compton
Mackenzie on Wilde's centenary, 16 October 1954

8 / The Prisoner

I

The punishment which Wilde faced, although by reason of his age and physical condition he was to escape some of its worst features, was still one of terrible severity. Evidence given by a variety of witnesses before a recent Home Office Committee on Prisons had shown that two years' imprisonment with hard labour, involving solitary cell confinement with its attendant laborious and largely useless work in the shape of the tread-wheel, the crank, and oakum picking, which had to be performed on a poor and inadequate diet, were calculated to break a man in body and spirit. Indeed, old offenders greatly preferred penal servitude, which could not be imposed for less than three years, in a convict prison such as Dartmoor or Portland, since the prison labour was largely carried on in the open air and there was always the chance of being released on "ticket-of-leave" before expiration of the sentence. With a sentence of imprisonment, on the other hand, the various forms of "hard labour" were mainly conducted indoors, usually in the prisoner's cell, and there was no provision for remitting any portion of the sentence for good conduct.

The cells in which hard labour prisoners were confined for twenty-three out of the twenty-four hours in the day were badly ventilated, and the sanitary conditions were primitive. The plank bed on which the prisoner was condemned to lie at night was an instrument of torture, which inevitably produced insomnia. Visitors (for twenty minutes each) and the writing and receiving of letters were allowed only once every three months, save in exceptional circumstances. Letters written by prisoners were censored by prison officials for complaints, as well as for "slang or improper expressions," and on at least one occasion Wilde was to have a passage from one of his letters to Robert Ross excised by the governor's scissors. According to the current regulations, "the permission to write and receive letters is given to prisoners for the purpose of enabling them to keep up a connection with their respectable friends and not that they may be kept informed of public events." Later on, Wilde was to urge strongly that prisoners be allowed the privilege of both letters and visitors once a month. "One of the tragedies of prison life is that it turns a man's heart to stone," he wrote after his release. "The feelings of natural affection, like all other feelings, require to be fed. They die easily of inanition. A brief letter, four times a year, is not enough to keep alive the gentler and more humane affections by which ultimately the nature is kept sensitive to any fine or beautiful influences that may heal a wrecked or ruined life." [1]

During the first three months of his imprisonment, the prisoner was allowed no books to read, except a Bible, a prayer-book, and a hymn-book. Thereafter he was allowed one book a week from the prison library, whose stock consisted chiefly of third-rate theological works selected by the prison chaplain. The first work given to Wilde to read by the chaplain, who had evidently chosen it for its high moral tone, was John Bunyan's *Pilgrim's Progress.* "The prison chaplains are entirely useless," Wilde wrote afterwards. "They are, as a class, well-meaning, but foolish, indeed silly men. They are no help to any prisoner. Once every six weeks or so the key turns in the lock of one's cell door, and the chaplain enters. One stands, of course, at attention. He asks one whether one has been reading the Bible. One answers 'Yes' or 'No,' as the case may be. He then quotes a few texts, and goes out, and locks the door. Sometimes he leaves a tract." The chaplain at Pentonville appears to have been a typical example of his kind. "Did you have morning prayers in your house?" he asked Wilde on the occasion of their first meeting. "I am sorry," the prisoner replied, "I fear not." To which the chaplain rejoined, "You see where you are now!"

Wilde's first experience of Pentonville Prison was thoroughly disagreeable, and he always remembered it. After he had gone through the reception office, where his particulars were entered in the prison records, he was weighed and measured and he handed over his personal belongings.[2] He was then taken to the baths and told to strip, after which he was made to get into a filthy bath, into which may other prisoners had preceded him. There followed a medical examination, as a result of which he was certified as "fit for light labour," which meant that he could be put to such tasks as oakum picking and sewing mailbags. He then put on the coarse prison dress with its distinguishing broad arrow marks, and followed a warder to a cell where he was locked in for the night. "At first it was a fiendish nightmare," he told Frank Harris;

---

[1] Fuller details of Wilde's imprisonment than it is possible to give here can be found in *Oscar Wilde: The Aftermath* (1963) by the present writer, who was the first member of the public allowed access to the relevant Home Office papers.

[2] The Nominal Register with these particulars is still preserved at Pentonville. It shows that Wilde's weight on reception was just under fourteen stone and his height six feet.

"more horrible than anything I had ever dreamed of: from the first evening when they made me undress before them and get into some filthy
water they called a bath and dry myself with a damp brown rag and put
on this livery of shame. The cell was appalling: I could hardly breathe in
it, and the food turned my stomach; the smell and sight of it were
enough: I did not eat anything for days and days, I could not even
swallow the bread; and the rest of the food was uneatable; I lay on the
so-called bed and shivered all night long . . . After some days I got so
hungry I had to eat a little, nibble at the outside of the bread, and drink
some of the liquid; whether it was tea, coffee, or gruel, I could not tell.
As soon as I really ate anything it produced violent diarrhoea and I was
ill all day and all night. From the beginning I could not sleep, I grew
weak and had wild delusions . . . The hunger made you weak but the
inhumanity was the worst of it. What devilish creatures men are! I had
never known anything about them. I had never dreamt of such cruel-
ties."

A rumour that Wilde had become insane during his first few weeks in
Pentonville (the prison barber was supposed to have realized his condition) got into the press. As a result the Home Secretary, Mr Asquith,
ordered a special medical examination of the prisoner, but this merely
revealed that, with the exception of a slightly relaxed throat, he was "in
good health and perfectly sane." But the truth was that he was far from
well, as subsequent events were to show, and Wilde held a low opinion
of the doctor who made this diagnosis. As we have seen, Wilde's father
had been a distinguished surgeon, and from earliest youth Wilde had
always regarded medicine as by far the most humane profession in the
country. But his gaol experiences caused him to make a striking exception in the case of prison doctors. At that period, they nearly all had a
large private practice and held appointments in other institutions. "The
consequence is that the health of the prisoners is entirely neglected,"
wrote Wilde later, "and the sanitary conditions entirely overlooked." As
for the doctors themselves, they were, "as far as I came across them, and
from what I saw of them in hospital and elsewhere, brutal in manner,
coarse in temperament, and utterly indifferent to the health of the prisoners or their comfort." [3]

The cell in which Wilde found himself at Pentonville, and which was
copied by most of the other English prisons at the time, was thirteen
feet long, seven feet wide, and nine feet high. This was supposed to be
adequate for strictly separate confinement with cell labour. The stone or
brick wall surface and ceiling were lime-washed. The door was solidly
lined with sheet iron to prevent tampering by ingenious prisoners, and
in the middle was a small glass peep-hole, covered by a moveable shut-
ter, to enable the interior of the cell to be observed by patrolling warders. Artificial illumination was provided by flaring gas jets let into the
corridor outside. These cast a pale glare through a glazed opening in the

[3] Letter to the *Daily Chronicle*, 24 March 1898.

cell wall above the door. In daytime, only a relatively small amount of natural light penetrated through the cell window, which consisted of fourteen small opaque panes of glass situated at a height of six feet nine inches above floor level, shutting out even a glimpse of the sky. Ventilation was provided partly by a ventilator in the window and partly by gratings. But Wilde found that the window ventilator was too small and so badly constructed that it did not admit enough fresh air, while the gratings were usually choked up. The result, in his experience, was that for most of the day and night prisoners were breathing the foulest possible air. He was later to describe it in *The Ballad of Reading Gaol.*

> Each narrow cell in which we dwell
> Is a foul and dark latrine,
> And the fetid breath of living Death
> Chokes up each grated screen,
> And all, but Lust, is turned to Dust
> In humanity's machine.

The cell was indeed as bare and repellent as it was possible to make it. The only articles of furniture permitted were the plank bed, blanket, hard pillow, and a small table for the prisoner's toilet and feeding utensils. Nothing else was allowed in the way of personal possessions, not even a photograph of the prisoner's wife and children, which might break the monotony of the cell wall or help to keep alive any feeling of family affection. A daily cell inspection was carried out, at which each prisoner had to exhibit the contents of his cell, such as they were, in the prescribed order. These official visits became a nightmare for Wilde, and in consequence he developed a nervous habit, which his friends noticed when he came out of prison, of always arranging objects in front of him symmetrically. "I had to keep everything in my cell in its exact place," he said, "and if I neglected this even in the slightest, I was punished. The punishment was so horrible that I often started up in my sleep to feel if each thing was where the regulations would have it, and not an inch either to right or to the left." In time, however, he was to learn to do this correctly. One of the warders who had him in his charge for a time has described how Wilde, when he had arranged all his tins as should be, "would step back and view them with an air of childlike complacency."

At one time each cell was equipped with a form of latrine, but the closets were later removed because the drainpipes made unauthorized communications between prisoners easier. In place of the old latrine, the prisoner was supplied with a small tin chamber pot. This he was allowed to empty three times a day. But he was not allowed to have access to the prison lavatories, except during one hour when he was at exercise. And after locking-up time, between five o'clock in the afternoon and five the following morning, the prisoner was forbidden to leave his cell under any pretence or for any reason; anyhow, the warder on night duty had no key. The prison diet, consisting mostly of weak gruel—so-called stir-about made of coarse Indian meal—suet, water, and greasy cocoa, was a frequent cause of diarrhoea, and the miseries and tortures which sufferers from this endemic prison complaint underwent, especially at night, can be imagined. It was no uncommon thing for warders, when they came on duty in the morning out of the fresh air to open and inspect the cells, to be violently sick. Wilde himself witnessed this on a number of occasions, and several warders went out of their way to mention it to him as "one of the disgusting things which their office entails on them." At certain times in the day the warders would serve out astringent medicines. But after a comparatively short time, usually about a week, the medicine produced no effect at all. In Wilde's words: "The wretched prisoner is then left a prey to the most weakening, depressing, and humiliating malady that can be conceived; and if, as often happens, he fails, from physical weakness, to complete the required revolutions on the crank or the mill he is reported for idleness and punished with the greatest severity and brutality."

Wilde's prison routine was as follows. He got up at 6 a.m. and cleaned out his cell. At seven he had breakfast, consisting of cocoa and brown bread. He was then taken out with other prisoners for exercise, which lasted an hour. On returning to his cell, he picked oakum until midday, when dinner was brought round. This meal consisted of greasy bacon and beans or soup; on one day a week he had cold meat. At 12:30 p.m. oakum-picking was resumed and he was expected to continue with this occupation until 6 p.m. He then had tea, and at seven lights were turned out and he went to bed. A newspaper report accurately described his life at this time: "He is compelled to pick a certain quantity of oakum per day, is not allowed to converse with anyone, and with the exception of an hour's exercise is kept in solitary confinement in his cell." [4]

> With midnight always in one's heart,
>   And twilight in one's cell,
> We turn the crank or tear the rope,
>   Each in his separate Hell,
> And the silence is more awful far
>   Than the sound of a brazen bell.
>
> And never a human voice comes near
>   To speak a gentle word:
> And the eye that watches through the door
>   Is pitiless and hard:
> And by all forgot, we rot and rot,
>   With soul and body marred.

The lesson which Wilde set himself to learn in prison was that of humility. From the outset he found it very hard, since he began each day by going down on his knees and washing the floor of his cell. "For

[4] *The Morning*, 6 June 1895.

prison life with its endless privations and restrictions makes one rebel-
lious. The most terrible thing about it is not that it breaks one's heart—
hearts are made to be broken—but that it turns one's heart to stone.
One sometimes feels that it is only with a front of brass and a lip of
scorn that one can get through the day at all." To succeed, he felt that
he must overcome this mood of rebellion, which "closes up the channels
of the soul and shuts out the airs of heaven." His achievement he was to
epitomize in the composition of the work known as *De Profundis,* which
he completed in his prison cell eighteen months later. "The plank bed,
the loathsome food, the hard ropes shredded into oakum until one's
fingertips grew dull with pain, the menial offices with which each day
begins and finishes, the harsh orders that routine seems to necessitate,
the dreadful dress that makes sorrow grotesque to look at, the silence,
the solitude, the shame—each and all of these things I had to transform
into a spiritual experience."

2

The first person to give Wilde any feeling of hope in prison was his
first visitor from the outside world. This was the Liberal Member of Parliament and lawyer R. B. Haldane, later Lord Haldane, who had been a
member of the Home Office Committee under the chairmanship of Lord
Gladstone, which had recently reviewed in searching terms the whole
range of prison administration in England. According to Haldane, he
used to meet Wilde in the days of his social success, and although he
had not known him well, he was "haunted by the idea of what this
highly sensitive man was probably suffering under ordinary prison treatment." As a member of the Gladstone Committee, Haldane had a warrant which enabled him to go to any prison at any hour and call on the
governor to produce any prisoner he liked. Haldane's visit to Pentonville
was probably also prompted by the alarming accounts which had been
appearing in the *Daily Chronicle* and other newspapers about Wilde's
mental condition.

Before he saw Wilde, the visitor met the prison chaplain in the governor's room in the prison. This reverend gentleman told Haldane he was
glad he had come, since he had "failed to make any way" with the prisoner, which, in view of his remarks to Wilde at their first meeting, was
hardly surprising. The visitor then saw Wilde alone in a special room.
"At first he refused to speak," noted Haldane afterwards. "I put my
hand on his prison-dress-clad shoulder and said that I used to know him
and that I had come to say something about himself. He had not fully
used his great literary gift, and the reason was that he had lived a life of
pleasure and had not made any great subject his own. Now misfortune
might prove a blessing for his career, for he had got a great subject."
Haldane added that he would try to obtain for him the privileges of
books and writing materials, so that in due course he would be "free to
produce."

Wilde was so overcome by this prospect that he immediately burst into tears. Nevertheless, he promised to make the attempt. For books he asked eagerly, saying that all he had to read was *Pilgrim's Progress,* and that work, in Haldane's words, "did not satisfy him." Among others he asked for Flaubert's works, particularly *Madame Bovary.* To this latter request Haldane replied that the dedication by the author to his advocate, who had successfully defended him on a charge of obscene publication, made such a work as *Madame Bovary* unlikely to be sanctioned. At this remark, according to Haldane, the prisoner began to laugh and immediately became cheerful. After some discussion, they settled on the writings of St Augustine, several books by Cardinal Newman, Pascal's *Pensées,* and Walter Pater's work on the Renaissance. These Haldane succeeded in procuring for him, and they accompanied him to his next prison when he moved, although the governor of Pentonville objected to several of them as being "of a controversial character" and consequently not in conformity with the Local Prison Code.[5]

One day, about a year after Wilde's release, Haldane received a small anonymous parcel. When he opened it, he found a copy of *The Ballad of Reading Gaol.* "It was the redemption of his promise to me," wrote Haldane afterwards.

Haldane had promised to get in touch with Wilde's wife and family and give them news of the prisoner. He failed to see Constance Wilde and the two children, as they had gone abroad, but he called at Oakley Street and saw Lady Wilde and Willie, also Willie's second wife, a kindhearted woman from Dublin whom Willie had married recently and whom Oscar seems to have known fairly well. This visit prompted Mrs Willie Wilde to write to the governor of Pentonville asking him to give "my unhappy brother-in-law" her "fondest love" and to say "how often I think of him and long to see him; also, what perhaps will give him the most pleasure, that his mother is wonderfully well." This the governor seems to have done.

Wilde's next visitor brought less pleasant news. He was a clerk from the Marquess of Queensberry's solicitors who came down to Pentonville to serve the prisoner with a bankruptcy notice. On 21 June 1895, Queensberry had filed a petition in the Bankruptcy Court asking for a receiving order to be made against Wilde. The sum claimed was £677, being the amount of the petitioner's taxed costs in the disastrous action for criminal libel which Wilde had brought against Queensberry. This news came as a cruel blow to Wilde and it made him feel very bitter for a long time. At the time of the trial he had received definite assurances from Lord Alfred Douglas that the various members of the Queensberry family who hated its titular head, particularly Douglas's elder brother Lord Douglas of Hawick, would be responsible for the costs of the libel prosecution into which, as we have seen, Alfred Douglas had vigorously egged Wilde on. This was a subject to which Wilde in his prison corre-

[5] Haldane later added ten more volumes of Pater and other books. At Haldane's request, the collection was later presented to the Wandsworth Prison Library.

spondence was to revert bitterly again and again. "I feel most strongly that these costs should have been borne by your family," he told Douglas. "You had taken personally on yourself the responsibility of stating that your family would do so. It was that which made the solicitor take up the case the way he did. You were absolutely responsible. Even irrespective of your engagement on your family's behalf, you should have felt that, as you had brought the whole ruin on me, the least that could have been done was to spare me the additional ignominy of bankruptcy for an absolutely contemptible sum of money, less than half of what I spent on you in three brief summer months at Goring."

In what seems to have been an attempt to stave off the bankruptcy proceedings, Wilde's solicitors applied to the Home Office for permission to see their client "with reference to the translation and publication of some of his works." The request was made towards the end of June, but it was not until several weeks later that permission was granted. The delay was possibly due to the change in Home Secretaries consequent upon the fall of the Liberal government of Lord Rosebery, and also perhaps to a misunderstanding of the nature of the publications contemplated. Because Wilde had been convicted of indecent practices, it was assumed by at least one senior Home Office official that the publications might also be indecent. "Let them see him in the ordinary course as his solicitors to take his instructions in regard to property and business matters," this official wrote on the relevant file. "If they publish anything objectionable it will be their look-out, and the Law can intervene."

When the solicitors received the necessary order and were ready to see their client, they learned that he had been transferred from Pentonville to Wandsworth. What determined the Prison Commissioners on this change, which occurred on 4 July 1895, is not clear. It was possibly due to Haldane, who may have wished to bring Wilde under the influence of the Wandsworth prison chaplain, the Rev. W. D. Morrison, an unusually enlightened clergyman who could be relied upon to keep a particular eye on him. However, we do know that Wilde was even more unhappy at Wandsworth, where he found the food worse than at Pentonville. "It even smelt bad. It was not fit for dogs. . . . At Wandsworth I thought I should go mad," he admitted afterwards. He became more and more mentally depressed and longed to die. "I was dreadfully unhappy, so utterly miserable that I wanted to kill myself," he told André Gide after his release. "But what kept me from doing so was looking at the others, and seeing that they were as unhappy as I was, and feeling sorry for them." From one fellow prisoner he received a touching expression of sympathy, which was to land him in trouble. One day at exercise in the prison yard, a prisoner whispered in the hoarse voice men get from long and compulsory silence, "I am sorry for you. It is harder for the likes of you than it is for the likes of us!" This kindness brought tears to Wilde's eyes. "No, my friend," he replied. "We all suffer alike." He had not learned to speak like other prisoners, without moving his lips. Therefore, he was punished for talking, and, as he told the governor that it was he who had begun the conversation, he received double punishment.[6]

The visit of Wilde's solicitors was memorable because it brought the first message which the prisoner received from Lord Alfred Douglas, with whom the solicitors had been in touch in the forlorn hope of receiving some financial help. The firm had sent down one of their clerks to Wandsworth, accompanied by a Commissioner for Oaths, in order to take the necessary depositions from their client to file with his Statement of Affairs in connection with his pending bankruptcy, and the interview took place in the presence of the customary warder. Suddenly the clerk leaned across the table and, having consulted a piece of paper which he pulled out of his pocket, said in a low voice, "Prince Fleur de Lys wishes to be remembered to you!" Wilde stared at him. The clerk repeated the message, adding mysteriously, "The gentleman is abroad at present." Suddenly the meaning flashed on the prisoner and he laughed bitterly. "In that laugh was all the scorn of the world," he wrote later to Douglas, recalling the incident. "You were, no doubt, quite right to communicate with me under an assumed name. I myself, at that time, had no name at all. In the great prison where I was then incarcerated, I was merely the figure and letter of a little cell in a long gallery, one of a thousand lifeless numbers as of a thousand lifeless lives. But surely there were many real names in real history which would have suited you much better, and by which I would have had no difficulty at all in recognising you at once? I did not look for you behind the spangles of a tinsel vizard only suitable for an amusing masquerade . . ."

The first meeting of Wilde's creditors, under the Receiving Order which had been made, took place before the Official Receiver in London on 26 August 1895. According to the Official Receiver, the debtor's accounts showed unsecured liabilities of £2,676 and partly secured debts of £915, disclosing a total deficiency of £3,591. Travers Humphreys, who had appeared as Wilde's junior counsel in the three trials and at the preliminary police-court proceedings, represented the debtor. He stated that, although every effort had been made, Wilde was not in a position to submit any offer to his creditors. For this reason it had not been considered necessary for the debtor to attend the meeting. In these circumstances it only remained to pass a resolution that he be adjudged bankrupt and to appoint a trustee. This was accordingly done, on the motion of Lord Queensberry, and the Official Receiver was appointed trustee. At the same time, the date of the debtor's public examination was fixed for four weeks later.

Having completed the first three months of his sentence, Wilde was now entitled under the prison regulations to receive and send one letter, and also to have a visit from a friend. Feeling that he had to reserve his

---

[6] Gide attributes this incident to Reading, but Wilde states in *De Profundis* that it took place in Wandsworth. The punishment for this breach of regulations was confinement in a dark cell for up to three days on a diet of bread and water.

first letter for the subject of "family business," Wilde accepted his first letter from his brother-in-law, Otho Holland Lloyd, in preference to a letter from Alfred Douglas, who had applied for permission to write to him. What his brother-in-law told him on this occasion was that, if he would only write once to his wife, she would in all probability, for his sake and the sake of the children, take no action for a divorce, as she was being pressed by Sir George Lewis and other family advisers to do. In these circumstances, Wilde not unnaturally felt it his duty to send his first letter to her. Surprising as it seemed to some of his friends, he was really very fond of his wife and felt extremely sorry for her, although he was aware that she could not understand him, and on his own admission he had been "bored to death with married life."

The text of Wilde's letter to his wife has not survived. But whatever he wrote to her must have touched her deeply. At this time Constance Wilde was staying with friends on the Continent, and she accordingly applied to the governor of Wandsworth for a visiting order, as she had an opportunity of travelling to England with a friend who had promised to look after her on the journey. The governor replied that her husband had just received a visit—this was from Robert Sherard—and that he was not due for another visit under the rules for a considerable time, and he advised her to make application to the Prison Commissioners. She did so, and as a result a special visit was authorized. This visit took place on 21 September 1895, under the most painful and humiliating conditions.

"It was indeed awful, more so than I had any conception it could be," she told Sherard afterwards. "I could not see him and I could not touch him. I scarcely spoke . . . When I go again I am to get at the Home Secretary through Mr Haldane and try to get a room to see him in and touch him again. He has been mad these last three years, and he says that if he saw Alfred Douglas he would kill him. So he had better keep away and be satisfied with having marred a fine life. Few people can boast of so much."

Three days later Wilde underwent a further ordeal, this time in the Bankruptcy Court, to which he was brought in the custody of two policemen for his public examination. A considerable crowd had collected in Carey Street in anticipation of an entertaining spectacle. But, although they caught a glimpse of the prisoner in handcuffs, they were largely disappointed. Pending an application for an adjournment, which was made by counsel on his behalf, Wilde waited with the policemen in an adjoining room. Later he was to pay a warm tribute to these two members of the metropolitan force, "who, in their homely, rough way, strove to comfort me in my journeys to and from the Bankruptcy Court under conditions of terrible mental distress."

It appeared that several of Wilde's friends had subscribed various sums of money, and with others, which were expected to be forthcoming, there was every reason to believe, said counsel, that there would be sufficient to pay all the creditors twenty shillings in the pound. Since no creditor appeared to oppose the application, the registrar adjourned the examination for seven weeks. Meanwhile, one of the friends in question, Robert Ross, was waiting in the long dreary corridor outside the courtroom so that, as Wilde put it in a memorable passage in *De Profundis,* "before the whole crowd, whom an action so sweet and simple hushed into silence, he might gravely raise his hat to me, as handcuffed and with bowed head I passed him by."

Wilde was now approaching a complete physical and nervous breakdown. He had already lost nearly thirty pounds in weight, and his prison clothes hung loosely on his emaciated frame. One morning, about ten days after his visit to Carey Street, he felt so ill that he could get up and dress himself only with the greatest effort, having previously been accused of malingering by the prison doctor. While he was dressing, he fell and bruised one of his ears badly on the stone floor of his cell. He then went with the other prisoners to the prison chapel for prayers, where he immediately fainted. When he recovered consciousness, he found himself in hospital where he was kept for several weeks and seems to have been well treated, given special food, and nursed back to strength. During this period, he was examined on the Home Secretary's instructions by two mental specialists from Broadmoor Criminal Lunatic Asylum. In due course, the specialists reported that they could discover no evidence of any mental disease in the prisoner, whom they were first able to observe through a spy-hole in one of the doors leading to the hospital. There they saw Wilde, apparently in excellent spirits, the centre of a group of prisoners whom he was holding entranced by his talk. In their report the doctors recommended that Wilde be transferred to a country prison where there would be an opportunity for healthy exercise and employment on garden work, "with a view of a more wholesome state of his tissues being induced and his mind being thereby roused to more healthy action so far as the subjects of his thoughts are concerned."

On 12 November 1895, Wilde was considered to have sufficiently recovered to attend his adjourned public examination in Carey Street. Up to the last moment his solicitors hoped that the need for this further trial would be obviated by the subscription of a sufficient sum of money by Wilde's friends to enable his creditors to be paid in full. A certain amount was indeed subscribed, but the balance was not forthcoming. Thus the public examination took place. It was conducted in open court by the Official Receiver.

"Step by step with the Bankruptcy Receiver," Wilde wrote afterwards, "I had to go over every item in my life. It was horrible." He had never kept any books or accounts, he told the Official Receiver, but he estimated that his expenditure during the two or three years preceding the receiving order was close on £3,000 a year. Much of this, he admitted, had gone to the entertainment of Lord Alfred Douglas, as he was subsequently to remind that young man in several stinging passages in *De Profundis.* Between the autumn of 1892 and the date of his arrest, he reckoned he had spent over £5,000 on Douglas. In a single week in

Paris, for instance, he spent £150, which besides their own costs included the expenses of Douglas's Italian servant, while in the summer of 1893 he took a house ("The Cottage") for three months at Goring-on-Thames at a total cost of £1,340. "Though it may seem strange to you that one in the terrible position in which I am situated should find a difference between one disgrace and another," he wrote to Douglas from prison, "still I frankly admit that the folly of throwing all this money on you, and letting you squander my fortune to your own hurt as well as mine, gives to me and in my eyes a note of common profligacy to my bankruptcy that makes me doubly ashamed of it.

"You may be interested to know," he added, "that your father openly said in the Orleans Club that if it had cost him £20,000 he would have considered the money thoroughly well spent, he had extracted such enjoyment and delight and triumph out of it all. The fact that he was able not merely to put me into prison for two years but to take me out for an afternoon and make me a public bankrupt was an extra refinement of pleasure that he had not expected. It was the crowning point of my humiliation and of his complete and perfect victory."

3

A few days after Wilde's public examination in Carey Street, the Chairman of the Prison Commission, Evelyn Ruggles-Brise, informed the Home Secretary that, since the bankruptcy proceedings had come to an end, Wilde would be transferred to Reading Prison, where "suitable occupation in the way of gardening and bookbinding and library work may be found for him." Ruggles-Brise, it may be noted here, had been appointed earlier in the year by Asquith, with Haldane's support, and he was perhaps the most enlightened and humane prison administrator so far to be in charge of the service.[7] The betterment of Wilde's lot which took place at this time was largely due to Ruggles-Brise, although it was possible to mitigate the harsher features of the system only gradually. The conditions under which the prisoner was removed from Wandsworth to Reading was one of those features.

· The transfer was later described by Wilde in De Profundis in a passage which has often been quoted and which caught the attention of the critics and the public possibly more than any other when that work was first published in a considerably expurgated edition ten years later. The transfer took place on 20 November 1895.[8]

From two o'clock till half past two on that day I had to stand on the centre platform at Clapham Junction in convict dress and handcuffed, for the world to look at. I had been taken out of the hospital ward without a moment's notice being given to me. Of all possible objects I was the most

---

[7] Sir Evelyn Ruggles-Brise (1857–1935) was Chairman of the Prison Commission from 1895 to his retirement in 1921. He founded the Borstal system for juvenile offenders.

[8] Wilde mistakenly gave the date in De Profundis as 13 November.

grotesque. When people saw me they laughed. Each train as it came in swelled the audience. Nothing could exceed their amusement. That was, of course, before they knew who I was. As soon as they had been informed they laughed still more. For half an hour I stood there in the grey November rain surrounded by a jeering mob.

No wonder that for a year afterwards Wilde, as he confessed, was to weep every day at the same hour and for the same space of time. According to Sherard, Wilde's initial recognition on the station platform was accompanied by a particularly revolting exhibition of philistinism and cruelty. A man who had been staring at the handcuffed figure for some minutes suddenly exclaimed for the benefit of the other onlookers: "My God, that's Oscar Wilde!" He then stepped up to him and spat in his face.

Reading Gaol, which has become famous as the place where Wilde was to serve the remainder of his sentence, was one of the smaller county prisons built on the Pentonville model. During Wilde's time its prison population averaged 150, including a number of soldiers who had come from the nearby barracks at Windsor. The governor, Major Henry Isaacson, was a military despot, under whose harsh rule Wilde was to suffer for the next eight months. He was "tall and not unlike the headmaster of a public school," according to Robert Ross, who was not unfavourably impressed by him on the occasion of their first meeting. But to Frank Harris, a fairly acute observer, to whom the governor boasted that he was "knocking the nonsense out of Wilde," Major Isaacson seemed "almost inhuman." Wilde himself has put on record that under him the prison system was carried out with the greatest harshness and stupidity, because, as he subsequently told André Gide, "he was entirely lacking in imagination." As for the chaplain, he was kindly enough but ineffective, while the prison doctor, with his greasy white beard, reminded Robert Ross of a bullying director of a sham city company.

At Reading, Wilde was allocated Cell 3 on the third landing of Gallery C, so that his prison number, by which he was officially known, was C.3.3. It was with this number as pseudonym that *The Ballad of Reading Gaol* was originally published.

Meanwhile, a group of Wilde's friends headed by More Adey had prepared a petition to the Home Secretary asking for Wilde's early release. This document was largely the work of Bernard Shaw, who, although he had never been at all friendly with his fellow Irishman, felt that he had already been more than sufficiently punished and that confinement for the full term of his sentence under the harsh prison regulations which then prevailed would make him incapable of further literary work. The difficulty was to find supporters of the petition whose names would carry some weight with the authorities. Bernard Shaw told Willie Wilde at this time that, while he himself and the Rev. Stewart Headlam, who had gone bail for Wilde after his first trial, were quite ready to sign the petition, "that would be no use, as we were two notorious cranks and our names would by themselves reduce the petition to absurdity and do Oscar more harm than good." Willie Wilde replied that he did not think that signatures would be obtainable, and events speedily proved him right.

The only prominent individual whom Adey could persuade to sign the petition was York Powell, Regius Professor of Modern History at Oxford. Several other signatures of influential persons were promised; but, when the time came, they were not forthcoming. Most people who were approached were afraid to sign. But some refused on moral grounds. Among the latter was Holman Hunt, the Pre-Raphaelite artist and painter of religious pictures, of which the best known is "The Light of the World." "I must repeat my opinion that the law treated him with exceeding leniency," Hunt wrote to Adey in his letter of refusal, "and state that further consideration of the facts convinces me that in justice to criminals belonging to other classes of society, I should have to join in the cry for doing away with all personal responsibility, if I took any part in appealing for his liberation before the completion of his term of imprisonment. While such a course might seem benevolent to malefactors, it would scarcely be so to the self-restrained and orderly members of society." As Wilde's younger son was to put it in his autobiography, it is only fair to suppose that Holman Hunt, when he wrote this letter, had forgotten the quotation which inspired his celebrated painting, now in the Tate Gallery.[9] In these circumstances the project of the petition had to be abandoned.

Shortly after her son's arrival at Reading, Lady Wilde became seriously ill with bronchitis. Feeling that her end was near, she asked that Oscar might be allowed to come and see her for the last time. Naturally enough, this request was refused. When they brought her the news in bed, she said, "May the prison help him!" She thereupon turned her face to the wall and died.

Like many of the Irish, Wilde was superstitious, and he also liked to think that he possessed certain psychic qualities. After he came out of prison, he told Vincent O'Sullivan, the Irish-American writer whom he met in Paris, that on the night of his mother's death (3 February 1896) she appeared to him in his cell. She was dressed in outdoor clothes, and he asked her to take off her hat and cloak and sit down. But she shook her head sadly and vanished. It was then, he said, that he knew that she was dead.

Wilde had always been deeply devoted to his mother, and he was very proud of her achievements in Irish politics and literature. Even his profligate brother Willie, between whom and Oscar there was little love lost, had to admit that "despite all his faults and follies, he was always a good son to her." The tribute which Oscar paid to her memory, along with that of his father, is one of the most striking passages in De Profundis. "Her death was so terrible to me," he wrote, "that I, once a lord of

[9] "I expect to pass through this world but once. Any good, therefore, that I can do, or any kindness that I can show to any fellow creature, let me do it now. Let me not defer or neglect it, for I shall not pass this way again."

language, have no words in which to express my anguish and my shame
. . . She and my father had bequeathed to me a name they had made
noble and honoured, not merely in Literature, Art, Archaeology, and
Science, but in the public history of our country in its evolution as a nation. I had disgraced that name eternally. I had made it a low byword
among low people. I had dragged it through the mire. I had given it to
brutes that they might make it brutal, and to fools that they might turn
it into a synonym for folly. What I suffered then, and still suffer, is not
for pen to write or paper to record."

It was from his wife ("at that time kind and gentle to me") that
Wilde learned the news of his mother's death. Rather than that he
should hear it from "indifferent or alien lips," Constance Wilde travelled
from Genoa to Reading to break "the tidings of so irreparable, so irre-
deemable a loss." They also discussed the future of their two children,
and Wilde advised her to enlist the help of a guardian if she could not
manage their future upbringing alone. He begged her not to spoil them,
particularly Cyril, the elder, as Lady Queensberry had done with Lord
Alfred Douglas. Later Wilde told Robert Ross how kind his wife had
been to him on this occasion. Unfortunately, it was to be the last time
that Wilde ever saw his wife, although unknown to him she is believed
to have caught a glimpse of her husband in prison on one other occasion.
They became estranged because of the well-meant but ill-judged action
by some of Wilde's friends in acquiring a half share of his interest under
his marriage settlement from the Official Receiver. Although Wilde
himself was opposed to this action, he was blamed for it by his wife and
her advisers. Owing to various difficulties, they were never able to meet
after his release.

One encouraging piece of news reached the prisoner at this time. On
10 February 1896, his play *Salomé,* which the Lord Chamberlain had
banned in England, received its first public performance in Paris, where
it was produced at Théâtre de l'Oeuvre by the well-known French actor-
manager Aurélien Lugné-Poe, who also played the part of Herod.
"Please write to Stuart Merrill in Paris or Robert Sherard to say how
gratified I was at the performance of my play and have my thanks conveyed to Lugné-Poe" Wilde wrote to Ross when he was able to send his
next letter from Reading. "It is something that at a time of disgrace and
shame I should still be regarded as an artist. I wish I could feel more
pleasure, but I seem dead to all emotions except those of anguish and
despair. However, please let Lugné-Poe know that I am sensible of the
honour he has done me. He is a poet himself." Indeed, Wilde attributed
the change which followed at Reading to this event. "The production of
Salomé was the thing that turned the scale in my favour, as far as my
treatment in prison by the Government was concerned," he later told
Lord Alfred Douglas, "and I am deeply grateful to all concerned in it."

About this time Wilde received a visit from Frank Harris, to whom
he appears to have complained about his treatment. "The governor loves
to punish," he told Harris, "and he punishes by taking my books from

me. It is perfectly awful to let the mind grind itself away between the upper and nether millstones of regret and remorse without respite. With books my life would be livable—any life."

Harris promised to try to get him more books and also writing materials, of which Wilde was deprived. Wilde repeated these requests in a long petition, which he drafted to the Home Secretary, pointing out that he was allowed only two books a week from the extremely small and poor prison library. Wilde further complained that the abscess which had formed in his ear after his fall at Wandsworth was giving him trouble, and that his eyesight had suffered very much from enforced living in a whitewashed cell with a flaring gas jet at night.

These representations had some effect, as the Prison Commissioners ordered that the rule as to two books a week should be relaxed, that he should send in a list of requests for books which could be purchased, provided that the total cost did not exceed £10, and that he should be provided with foolscap paper, ink, and pen "for use in his leisure moments, in his cell." The prison doctor was also directed to watch his general health with care and to call in a second opinion if necessary.

At their meeting Harris had urged Wilde to write something about his prison experiences, or at least to use them for a future literary work. Wilde did not seem particularly enthusiastic about the idea. However, the fact remains that during the summer of 1896 the incident occurred which inspired the composition of his best-known poetic work. This, at Robert Ross's suggestion, was to be called *The Ballad of Reading Gaol*, and it described the last days and execution of a young Guards soldier who was said "to have cut his wife's throat in a very determined manner, she having excited his jealousy and (so far as the evidence went) greatly annoyed him." [10]

> The man had killed the thing he loved,
> And so he had to die.

Harris always claimed it was as a result of the report which he made to Ruggles-Brise after seeing Wilde that a change of governors took place at Reading. However that may be, in July 1896 Isaacson was transferred to another post in the service and his place was taken by Major J. O. Nelson, a very different type. While Isaacson, according to Wilde, was unable to enjoy his breakfast unless someone was punished before he ate it, Nelson was "the most Christlike man" he had ever met. "The present Governor of Reading is a man of gentle and humane character, greatly liked and respected by all the prisoners," wrote Wilde at the time of his release. "Though he cannot alter the rules of the prison system, he has altered the spirit in which they used to be carried out by his predecessor. He is very popular with the prisoners and the warders. Indeed he has quite altered the whole tone of prison life." It was under

[10] *Reading Mercury*, 10 July 1896.

Major Nelson's kindly dispensation that Wilde served out the remaining ten months of his sentence, and that he was able to make use of his privilege of writing materials by composing the work which was first given to the world in considerably abbreviated form under the title *De Profundis.*

At the same time he had another most painful experience. This was the handing over of his children by an order of the High Court to the joint guardianship of his wife and her cousin Adrian Hope, while he was to be restrained from attempting to remove them from their mother's custody or otherwise "interfering" with them. For their father this was an appalling blow. "My two children are taken from me by legal procedure," he wrote shortly afterwards in *De Profundis*. "That is and always will remain to me a source of infinite distress, of infinite pain, of grief without end or limit. That the law should decide and take upon itself to decide that I am one unfit to be with my own children is something quite horrible to me. The disgrace of prison is as nothing compared with it. I envy the other men who tread the yard along with me. I am sure that their children wait for them, look for their coming, will be sweet to them."

Eventually, after a lengthy correspondence between Constance Wilde's solicitors and the solicitors employed by Ross and Adey on Wilde's behalf, Wilde's wife agreed to make him an allowance of £150 a year, provided that the contingent interest in his marriage settlement which Ross and Adey had bought in for him from the Official Receiver was surrendered and furthermore that Wilde did nothing which would entitle his wife to a divorce or judicial separation and was not guilty of any moral misconduct and did not "notoriously consort with evil or disreputable persons." This agreement was embodied in a Deed of Arrangement, which was signed by Wilde in the presence of the respective solicitors a few days before his release.

On this occasion Constance Wilde is stated to have accompanied her solicitor to Reading and to have waited in the corridor outside the "solicitors' room," a pathetic, tearful figure dressed in black. In response to her request to have "one glimpse of my husband," the warder on duty in the corridor stepped back silently so as to enable her to look through the glass peep-hole in the door. In the warder's words: "Mrs Wilde cast one long lingering glance inside and saw the convict-poet, who, in deep mental distress himself, was totally unconscious that any eyes save those of the stern lawyer and myself witnessed his degradation." At that precise moment Wilde was in the act of putting his signature to the deed. She drew back, "apparently labouring under deep emotion," and a few minutes later left the prison with her solicitor, still unseen by Wilde. She never saw him again. To the warder it remained the saddest story he knew of the prisoner.[11]

---

[11] *Evening News,* 2 March 1905.

4

About two months before Wilde was due to be released, a new warder was appointed to the prison. He was a young man of thirty named Tom Martin, a native of Belfast who had spent some years in the army before transferring to the prison service. On his arrival at Reading he was put in charge of Gallery C, in which Wilde was confined, so that Wilde saw him constantly. They immediately became friends, for Martin was unlike many other warders in the service. "I was struck by the singular kindness and humanity of the way in which he spoke to me and to the other prisoners," Wilde wrote of him after his release. "Kind words are much in prison, and a pleasant 'Good-morning' or 'Good-evening' will make one as happy as one can be in prison. He was always gentle and considerate." More than that, Martin consistently broke the prison rules to give Wilde and the other prisoners in Gallery C some unexpected relaxations. Every day, for instance, he used to smuggle a copy of the *Daily Chronicle* into the prison for Wilde, an action which was of course a most serious breach of the regulations. He would also bring him and the others little delicacies of food. It was this conduct which ultimately landed him in trouble and led to his dismissal.

Wilde was in the habit of writing him notes on the backs of envelopes and other odd scraps of paper, and pushing them under the cell door. Several of these have survived. This is the first:

My dear Friend,
    What have I to write about except that if you had been an officer in Reading Prison a year ago my life would have been much happier? Everyone tells me I am looking better and happier.
    That is because I have a good friend who gives me the *Chronicle* and *promises* me ginger biscuits!

O.W.

At the foot of this note Warder Martin wrote in pencil: "*Your ungrateful I done more than promise.*"

In another note, Wilde asked for the address of a fellow prisoner who was due for release and to whom he wished to send a sum of money to help him to get started again in life. "Of course I would not for worlds get such a friend as you are into *any danger*. I quite understand your feelings." Yet the kindly Warder Martin ran great risks to procure for Wilde the reading matter he wanted. On one occasion, when Wilde was reading the *Daily Chronicle* in his cell, he suddenly heard footsteps in the gallery outside and the key turned in the lock. He had no time to do more than fold up the paper and put it with his books on the trestle table where he worked. Then the governor walked in. Wilde immediately stood to attention in front of the table and remained in this position throughout the interview, which happened to be unusually long that day. Fortunately, Major Nelson did not see the incriminating newspaper or, if he did, he pretended not to notice it. But Wilde was not content with the *Daily Chronicle;* he persuaded the warder to get him the *Saturday Review* and other weekly periodicals, which presented much greater difficulties than the newspaper. "To give him the *Chronicle* to read was easy enough, as I had it delivered to me at the prison," Warder Martin afterwards told Sherard, "but what gave me a lot of trouble was getting him the weeklies that he wanted, because I could not have those sent to the prison, as that would have attracted attention. Prison warders don't read *Spectators* and *Saturday Reviews.* I had to go out into the town to fetch them, and was often anxious lest my absence might be noticed, and then there was always the risk of my being questioned as to what I had been to fetch and what it was for."

Wilde quickly responded to the actions of Martin and the other friendly warders at Reading. One of them, aware that he had a distinguished literary reputation, was constantly trying to improve his own mind with the prisoner's help.

"Excuse me, sir, but Charles Dickens, sir," asked the warder on one occasion, "would he be considered a great writer now, sir?"

"Oh, yes, a great writer indeed. You see he is no longer alive."

"Yes, I understand, sir. Being dead he would be a great writer, sir."

On another occasion, John Strange Winter was mentioned.

"Would you tell me what you think of him, sir?"

"A charming person," Wilde replied, "but a lady, you know, not a man. Not a great stylist, perhaps, but a good simple story-teller."

"Thank you, sir. I did not know he was a lady, sir."

On a third occasion the warder asked about another woman novelist.

"Excuse me, sir, but Marie Corelli. Would she be considered a great writer, sir?"

This, Wilde admitted in recounting the incident afterwards to the artist Will Rothenstein, was more than he could bear. Putting his hand on the warder's shoulder, he said to him gravely: "Now, don't think I've anything against her moral character, but from the way she writes she ought to be here!"

"You say so, sir, you say so," replied the amazed warder in wide-eyed belief.

A particularly kindhearted act of Martin, which is worthwhile describing in detail, had somewhat painful consequences for the warder, although all was well in the end. It happened on a certain bleak, raw morning in March, when Martin entered Cell C.3.3 and, to his surprise, found its occupant still in bed. "I have had a bad night," Wilde explained. "Pains in my inside, which I think must be cramp, and my head seems splitting." The warder asked whether he ought not to report sick. "No, not for anything," said Wilde. "I shall be better, perhaps, as the day advances. Come back in a few minutes, when I will be up." Martin returned to the cell a little later, and found the prisoner was up, but looking so ill that he again advised him to see the doctor. Wilde refused, saying he would be all right when he had had something warm to drink.

The warder knew that in the ordinary course of events Wilde would have nothing for at least another hour, so he resolved to find something to give him in the meanwhile himself. He hurried off and warmed up some beef tea, poured it into a bottle, placed the bottle inside his jacket, and returned towards Wilde's cell. While he was ascending the staircase to Gallery C, the bottle slipped down between his shirt and skin. It was very hot. Martin knew that there was an unoccupied cell in the next gallery, and he decided to go there and withdraw the bottle from its painful position. But at that moment a voice called out to him from the central hall below. Martin looked down and saw the Chief Warder, who beckoned him towards him. There was a discrepancy in the previous night's muster report and the Chief Warder wished to speak to him about it. Martin went back and tried to elucidate the mystery of two prisoners being in the prison who apparently had no claim on its hospitality. Meanwhile, the hot bottle burned into his skin like molten lead. "I could have cried out in my agony, but dared not," wrote Martin afterwards in his account of the incident. "The cold, damp beads of perspiration gathered on my brow; I writhed and twisted in all manner of ways to ease myself of the dreadful thing, but in vain. I could not shift that infernal bottle—try as I might . . . And the strange thing about it was the longer it lay the hotter it became. The Chief eyed me curiously. I believe he thought I had been drinking. I know I was incoherent enough for anything. At last he walked off, and left me, for which I was truly thankful."

Martin thereupon bounded up the iron stairs to Wilde's cell, where he pulled out the bottle and, "amid gasps and imprecations," related his awful experience. Wilde smiled when he heard the story and then, to Martin's surprised indignation, burst out laughing. The warder, who thought it a poor reward for all he had undergone, left the cell angrily, slamming the door with a bang.

A little later, when Martin brought his breakfast, Wilde looked a picture of contrition. He said he would not touch it unless the warder promised to forgive him. "Not even the cocoa," the prisoner replied, looking at it longingly. "Well, rather than starve you, I'll forgive you." "And supposing I laugh again," said Wilde with a smile. "Then I shan't forgive you again." Next day Martin received a charming written apology, full of subtle humour and characteristic epigrams. "Yesterday morning I laughed, which showed my perversity, for I felt really sorry for you," Wilde told Martin, after he had read the apology. "I didn't mean to laugh: I had vowed never to laugh again."

Martin developed a tremendous admiration for Wilde, whom he used to call "the Poet," and later on, when Sherard was writing Wilde's biography, he was to contribute an interesting chapter of reminiscences, a remarkable composition for a prison warder. Amongst others, he described the effect of the order issued by the Prison Commissioners, during the latter part of Wilde's time at Reading, that first offenders were to be kept apart from other prisoners. They were distinguished by two red stars, one worn on the jacket and the other on the cap—thus they were known as "star-class men." The order did not apply to Wilde, who was obliged to stand with his face to the wall when any of the "star-class" were passing nearby. "The framers of the order were, no doubt, actuated by the best of motives," wrote Warder Martin in the chapter alluded to, "but its too literal interpretation caused it to look rather ludicrous. I have seen the Poet having to stand with his face to the wall while a villainous-looking ruffian, who had been convicted of half killing his poor wife, passed him. In fact nearly every day he was forced to assume this undignified position, which might have been obviated but for the crass stupidity of officialdom."

5

Wilde's scribbled messages to Warder Martin are among the most convincing proofs of his essential kindness of heart and humanity. The following was written during the last week of his imprisonment:

> Please find out for me the name of A.2.11. Also the names of the children who are in for the rabbits, and the amount of the fine.
> Can I pay this and get them out? If so, I will get them out tomorrow. Please dear friend do this for me, I must get them out.
> Think what a thing for me it would be to be able to help these three little children. I would be delighted beyond words: if I can do this by paying the fine tell the children they are to be released tomorrow by a friend, and ask them to be happy and not to tell anyone.

Wilde had noticed A.2.11 for the first time among the other prisoners at exercise about three months previously. He was a young man who seemed to him to be silly or half-witted. "Every prison, of course, has its half-witted clients, who return again and again, and may be said to live in the prison," Wilde wrote after his release. "But this young man struck me as being more than usually half-witted on account of his silly grin and idiotic laughter to himself and the peculiar restlessness of his eternally twitching hands. He was noticed by all the other prisoners on account of the strangeness of his conduct." From time to time A.2.11 did not appear at exercise, which showed that he was being punished by being confined to his cell. Finally, Wilde discovered that he was under observation, and was being watched day and night by warders. "When he did appear at exercise, he always seemed hysterical, and used to walk round crying or laughing. At chapel he had to sit right under the observation of two warders, who carefully watched him all the time. Sometimes he would bury his head in his hands, an offence against the chapel regulations, and his head would be immediately struck up by a warder so that he should keep his eyes permanently in the direction of the Communion table. Sometimes he would cry—not making any disturbance—but with tears streaming down his face and an hysterical sobbing in his throat. He was on more than one occasion sent out of chapel to his cell, and of course he was continually punished." As the bench on which Wilde used to sit in chapel was directly behind the bench at the end of which this unfortunate young man was placed, he had full opportunity of observing him. "I also saw him, of course, at exercise continually," wrote Wilde, "and I saw that he was becoming insane and was being treated as if he was shamming."

On the Saturday before his release, Wilde was in his cell occupied in cleaning and polishing the tins he had been using for dinner. Suddenly he was startled by the most horrible and revolting shrieks, or rather howls, which broke the prison silence and made him think at first that some animal like a bull or a cow was being unskilfully slaughtered outside the prison walls. He soon realized, however, that the howls proceeded from the basement of the prison, and he knew that some wretched man was being flogged. "I need not say how hideous or terrible it was for me," Wilde observed, "and I began to wonder who it was who was being punished in this revolting manner. Suddenly it dawned on me that they might be flogging this unfortunate lunatic." They were. Wilde subsequently learned from another prisoner at exercise that the wretched creature had received twenty-four lashes in the cook-house, by order of the Visiting Justices on the report of the doctor.

The next day Wilde saw the poor fellow at exercise, his weak, ugly, wretched face bloated by tears and hysteria almost beyond recognition. "It was my last Sunday in prison, a perfectly lovely day, the finest day we had had the whole year," Wilde recalled later, "and there in the beautiful sunlight, walked this poor creature—made once in the image of God—grinning like an ape, and making with his hands the most fantastic gestures, as though he was playing in the air on some invisible stringed instrument, or arranging and dealing counters in some curious game. All the while these hysterical tears, without which none of us ever saw him, were making soiled runnels on his white swollen face. The hideous and deliberate grace of his gestures made him like an antic. He was a living grotesque. The other prisoners all watched him. Everybody knew what had happened to him, and that he was driven insane—was insane already."

From Warder Martin, in response to his note, Wilde learned that the man's name was Prince, that he was a soldier, and that he had been sentenced to six months for some military offence by a court-martial. "This man is undoubtedly becoming insane," Wilde wrote in a letter of protest which he sent to the *Daily Chronicle* a few days after leaving Reading. "The case is a special instance of the cruelty inseparable from a stupid system." As for the medical officer who passed the man as fit for punishment in these circumstances, Wilde was justly severe in his criticism:

Prison doctors have no knowledge of mental disease of any kind. They are as a class ignorant men. The pathology of the mind is unknown to them. When a man grows insane, they treat him as shamming. They have him punished again and again. Naturally the man becomes worse. When ordinary punishments are exhausted, the doctor reports the case to the justices. The result is flogging. Of course, the flogging is not done with a cat-of-nine tails. It is what is called birching . . . The result on the wretched half-witted man may be imagined . . . This man A.2.11 will, I have no doubt, be able to tell his name, the nature of his offence, the day of the month, the date of the beginning and expiration of his sentence, and answer any ordinary simple question; but that his mind is diseased admits of no doubt. At present it is a horrible duel between himself and the doctor. The doctor is fighting for a theory. The man is fighting for his life. I am anxious that the man should win. But let the whole case be examined into by experts who understand brain disease, and by people of humane feelings who have still some common sense and some pity. There is no reason that the sentimentalist should be asked to interfere. He always does harm.

On the subject of the half-witted Prince, it only remains to add that Wilde's protest does not seem to have had any effect on the authorities. The last that Wilde heard of him, some weeks after his own release, was that he had again been flogged.

As for the three children, about whom Wilde also wrote to Warder Martin, he was able to do more for them. They had been committed to prison for snaring rabbits. The magistrates who had convicted them had given them the option of paying fines. They, of course, had no money of their own, and their parents were unable to pay the fines for them. Wilde did so, and so secured their release. To the youngest of them, Warder Martin also performed an act of humanity—the child was crying with hunger and the warder gave him some biscuits—and for this kindness he was dismissed.

Wilde saw them for the first time just after they had been convicted. They were standing in a row in the central hall in their prison dress, carrying their sheets under their arms before being sent to the cells allotted to them. Wilde happened to be passing along one of the galleries on his way to the reception room, where he was to have an interview with his solicitor. The description of these children and of their treatment, in the form of a letter which he subsequently sent to the *Daily Chronicle,* is a vivid and moving example of his writing.

They were quite small children, the youngest—the one to whom the warder gave the biscuits—being a tiny little chap, for whom they had evidently been unable to find clothes small enough to fit. I had, of course, seen many children in prison during the two years during which I was myself confined. Wandsworth Prison especially contained always a large number of children. But the little child I saw on the afternoon of Monday the 17th, at Reading, was tinier than any of them. I need not say how utterly distressed I was to see these children at Reading, for I knew the treatment in store for them. The cruelty that is practised by day and night on children in English prisons is incredible, except to those that have witnessed it and are aware of the brutality of the system . . .

Of course no child under fourteen years of age should be sent to prison at all. It is an absurdity, and, like many absurdities, of absolutely tragic results. If, however, they are to be sent to prison, during the daytime they should be in a workshop or schoolroom with a warder. At night they should sleep in a dormitory, with a night-warder to look after them. They should be allowed exercise for at least three hours a day. The dark, badly ventilated ill-smelling prison cells are dreadful for a child, dreadful indeed for any one. One is always breathing bad air in prison. The food given to children should consist of tea and bread-and-butter and soup. Prison soup is very good and wholesome. A resolution of the House of Commons could settle the treatment of children in half an hour . . . The way that children are treated at present is really an outrage on humanity and common sense. It comes from stupidity.[12]

6

"I don't defend my conduct, I explain it." Thus wrote Wilde on the eve of his release from Reading Gaol to his friend and literary executor, Robert Ross. The explanation is to be found in a curious document, a mixture of apology, self-abasement, and violent recrimination, which Wilde composed during his last three months in prison. This document took the form of a long letter to Lord Alfred Douglas, and it was originally entrusted to Ross for the purpose of having copies made of it before its dispatch to Douglas. In 1905 Ross published parts of it—actually less than half—under the title De Profundis, to which a few other excerpts were added in a new edition which appeared four years later, but without any indication that it was really a letter to Douglas. In 1913, Lord Alfred Douglas brought an action for libel against Arthur Ransome, who had written a study of Wilde in which he described De Profundis as having been written to "a man to whom Wilde felt that he owed some at least of the public circumstances of his disgrace." In his plea of justification, the defendant put in substantial portions which had been "suppressed" by Ross in the published versions. These passages, which were read out in court, were far from complimentary to Douglas.[13] In this manner the public, including Douglas himself (so he said), learned for the first time the true nature of the work known as De Profundis. Meanwhile, Ross—who swore he had sent Douglas a copy and that Douglas had received it during Wilde's lifetime—presented the original manuscript to the British Museum, on condition that it should remain sealed up for fifty years. In accordance with this condition, the MS was opened to the public for the first time on 1 January 1960.[14]

[12] *Daily Chronicle,* 27 May 1897. The imprisonment of children was abolished by the Children Act, 1908, which also instituted juvenile courts.

[13] This libel action, which was tried before Mr Justice Darling in the King's Bench Division in April 1913, resulted in a verdict for Ransome: for details see *Cases That Changed the Law* (1951) by the present writer.

[14] Before handing over the original to the British Museum, Ross had fifteen copies hurriedly printed in the United States, of which two were deposited for copyright purposes in the Library of Congress, Washington, D.C.; only one was offered for sale, at what Ross considered to be the prohibitive price of $1,000, and was bought by an unknown purchaser at that figure. A page of the original was photographed at the same time lest the authenticity of the work should be doubted: it was reproduced by Mason in his bibliography of Wilde. For further details, see article in the *Sunday Times,* 3 January 1960, by the present writer.

It may well be asked what caused Wilde to turn so bitterly against his friend, particularly as Wilde had written to him in terms of deep affection whilst he was in Holloway on remand awaiting his first trial; after all, it was only at Wilde's earnest entreaty that Douglas, who was certainly ready to stand by him, had reluctantly consented to leave the country. From his chosen place of exile in France, Douglas had continued to write to the English press on Wilde's behalf, and he had even addressed a petition to Queen Victoria pleading for the exercise of royal clemency. "Most gracious lady," he wrote, "your heart is kind and tender, and even in these latter days the arm of the Queen is strong. Will you not save this man, who even if he be guilty has already been punished more, a thousand times more cruelly than he deserves, seeing that in addition to the ruin of his life, the destruction of his art and the loss of every worldly possession, he has been condemned to a sentence which the highest authorities have declared to be equivalent to a sentence of 'death or madness,' and which has been unanimously condemned as inhuman by the Prison Commission which has just recently laid its report before your Majesty's Court?" [15]

While he was in prison, Wilde had plenty of time to reflect upon the consequences of his unfortunate friendship with Douglas, which, as Mr Justice Wills had remarked in his summing-up at the last trial, had led to "the whole of this lamentable inquiry." We have already noticed the unfavourable impression which Douglas had made by his first message to Wilde from "Prince Fleur de Lys" and Wilde's reaction to it. But what really produced the most bitter feelings in Wilde was Douglas's intention (which Wilde first heard of from Sherard and which was later confirmed by the governor of Wandsworth when Douglas wrote to him) to include the Holloway letters in an article he had written for the French literary monthly *Mercure de France*—"the letters," as Wilde subsequently reproached Douglas, "that should have been to you of all things sacred and secret beyond anything in the whole world!"

No doubt Douglas had acted from the best of intentions. He honestly believed that, if it were published, the article would have the effect "of completely rehabilitating Oscar, at any rate in France." It is much more likely that the appearance of these letters in print, even in a French translation, would have done Wilde even more harm than the two compromising letters which had been quoted in the trials. Wilde himself seems to have realized this. But, as events turned out, he had alarmed himself unnecessarily. Sherard was already in touch with the editor of the *Mercure de France,* and although the article was already in type, the editor wrote to Douglas asking him to omit the letters. This Douglas refused to do, and in consequence the whole article was withdrawn. [16]

[15] The Queen never saw this petition, dated 25 June 1895; it was intercepted by her private secretary and forwarded to the Home Secretary, who rejected it immediately.

[16] Douglas has given his version of the affair in his autobiography (1929), chapter XXI. He refused to hand over the letters to Ross, who undertook to seal them up until Wilde came out of prison, and he subsequently destroyed them. However, it has been

Wilde was not allowed to send his letter to Douglas, surely one of the longest ever written—it runs to over thirty thousand words—but he was permitted to take it with him when he left Reading on his release. He was also allowed to write before his release to Ross, telling him the underlying reasons for its composition and giving directions for its copying, as he wished several copies to be made.

> Well, if you are to be my literary executor, you must be in possession of the only document that really gives any explanation of my extraordinary behaviour with regard to Queensberry and Alfred Douglas. When you have read the letter, you will see the psychological explanation of a course of conduct that from the outside seems a combination of absolute idiocy with vulgar bravado. Some day the truth will have to be known—not necessarily in my lifetime or in Douglas's. But I am not prepared to sit in the grotesque pillory they put me into for all time; for the simple reason that I inherited from my father and mother a name of high distinction in literature and art, and I cannot for eternity allow that name to be the shield and catspaw of the Queensberrys.

As for the mode of copying the document, Wilde felt that "the only thing is to be thoroughly modern and have it typewritten." He suggested that a girl from the agency where he had had his last play typed might be sent to More Adey's flat in London to do the work under Ross's supervision. ("Women are the most reliable, they have no memory for the important.") "I assure you," he wrote to Ross, "that the typewriting machine, when played with expression, is no more annoying than the piano when played by a sister or near relation. Indeed many among those most devoted to domesticity prefer it." He playfully suggested that the typist "might be fed through a lattice in the door, like the Cardinals when they elect a Pope, till she comes out on the balcony and can say to the world '*Habet mundus Epistolam';* for indeed it is an Encyclical letter, and as the Bulls of the Holy Father are named from their opening words, it may be spoken of as the *Epistola in Carcere et Vinculis.*"

In *De Profundis* Wilde showed how fully he realized that, but for his precipitate action with Queensberry, he would probably not have been writing as he was from Reading Gaol.

> Remember how and why I am here at this very moment. Do you think I am here on account of my relations with the witnesses at my trial? My relations, real or supposed, with people of that kind were matters of no interest to either the Government or Society. They knew nothing of them and cared less. I am here for having tried to put your father into prison. My attempt failed, of course. My own Counsel threw up their briefs. Your father completely turned the tables on me, and had *me* in prison, has me there still. That is why there is contempt felt for me. That is why people despise me.

possible to reconstruct the text from the French translation, which was later retranslated into English: see Hart-Davis, *Letters of Oscar Wilde,* pp. 393–4 and 396–8.

That is why I have to serve out every day, every hour, every minute of my dreadful imprisonment. That is why my petitions have been refused.[17]

Of the folly of his conduct Wilde had no illusions. "I became the spendthrift of my genius," he wrote, "and to waste an eternal youth gave me a curious joy. Tired of being on the heights, I deliberately went to the depths in search of a new sensation. What the paradox was to be in the sphere of thought, perversity became to me in the sphere of passion."

Not even during his imprisonment did the fact that he had been on intimate terms with the kind of individual who had testified against him at the Old Bailey fill Wilde with any conscious sense of shame. What disturbed him was the false role which he was consequently forced to play in the ensuing tragedy.

People thought it dreadful of me to have entertained at dinner the evil things of life, and to have found pleasure in their company. But they, from the point of view through which I, as an artist in life, approach them, were delightfully suggestive and stimulating. It was like feasting with panthers; the danger was half the excitement. I used to feel as a snake-charmer must feel when he lures the cobra to stir from the painted cloth or reed basket that holds it and makes it spead its hood at his bidding and sway to and fro in the air as a plant sways restfully in a stream. They were to me the brightest of gilded snakes. Their poison was part of their perfection. I did not know that when they were to strike at me it was to be at another's piping and at another's pay. I don't feel at all ashamed at having known them, they were intensely interesting; what I do feel ashamed of is the horrible Philistine atmosphere into which you brought me.

My business as an artist was with Ariel, you set me to wrestle with Caliban. Instead of making beautiful coloured musical things such as *Salomé* and the *Florentine Tragedy* and *La Sainte Courtisane,* I forced myself to send long lawyers' letters to your father and was constrained to appeal to the very things against which I had always protested. Clibborn and Atkins were wonderful in their infamous war against life. To entertain them was an astounding adventure; Dumas père, Cellini, Goya, Edgar Allan Poe, or Baudelaire would have done just the same. What is loathsome to me is the memory of interminable visits paid by me to the solicitor Humphreys, in your company, when in the ghastly glare of a bleak room you and I would sit with serious faces telling serious lies to a bald man till I really groaned and yawned with *ennui*. *There* is where I found myself after two years' friendship with you, right in the centre of Philistia, away from everything that was beautiful or brilliant or wonderful or daring. I had come forward on your behalf as the champion of respectability in conduct, of puritanism in life, and of morality in art.

The truth is that Oscar Wilde was amoral rather than immoral; and, in looking back upon the scandal of the trials in which he was involved,

---

[17] Wilde also reminded Douglas that he (Douglas) had laughed when, in the early days of their association, Wilde told him how Taylor ("that unfortunate young man who ultimately stood beside me in the dock") had warned Wilde more than once that Douglas would prove "far more fatal" in bringing Wilde to "utter destruction" than any of the "common lads" whom he was foolish enough to know.

the English public has an uneasy conscience about him. For a good deal of the mud thrown at the time has stuck. It is still thought in some quarters that Wilde was a debaucher of youth. In passing sentence upon him, Mr Justice Wills described Wilde as having been "the centre of a circle of extensive corruption of the most hideous kind among young men." Strictly speaking, this statement is not true; Wilde was never proved to have corrupted any youthful innocents. In respect of the charges relating to the only two young men of decent background with whom he was accused of immoral practices—Mavor and Shelley—he was acquitted. On the other hand, that he was guilty of the crimes of which he was accused is now beyond dispute. But, for the sake of English justice, it is regrettable that Wilde's guilt was not brought home to him, and to the world at large, beyond all reasonable doubt—in other words, with that measure of certainty in proof which the English law demands in criminal trials.

9 / The Exile

Although Wilde petitioned the Home Secretary to be released a little before the due date, so as to avoid unwelcome attentions by the press, this was not permitted and he was obliged to serve out the whole of his two-year sentence to the day. He was actually released from Pentonville early in the morning of 19 May 1897, having been brought up from Reading the previous evening, since the regulations in those days required that a prisoner be released from the same prison to which he had been originally committed. Fortunately, everything went off well. His friend More Adey and Stewart Headlam, the kindly clergyman who had gone bail for him, arrived at Pentonville in a brougham with the blinds drawn shortly after 6 a.m. and they were able to drive away unobserved to Headlam's house in Bloomsbury, where Wilde was able to change and have breakfast. "He was given the first cup of coffee after two years," his host noted. "How grateful he was!" He was later to leave for Dieppe, where Ross and Turner had arranged to meet him, having gone on ahead.

While he was still at breakfast, there was a ring at the door. It was Ernest Leverson and his wife, Ada, at whose house he had stayed when he was out on bail between his two trials. They were shown into the drawing-room, which Mrs Leverson was to remember as "full of Burne-Jones and Rossetti pictures, Morris wallpaper and curtains, in fact an example of the decoration of the early eighties, very beautiful in its way, and very like the aesthetic rooms Oscar had once loved." Both Mrs Leverson and her husband felt intensely nervous and embarrassed. ("We had the English fear of showing our feelings.") Presently Wilde entered the room, "with the dignity of a King returning from exile," and immediately put them both at their ease. According to Mrs Leverson, "he came in talking, laughing, smoking a cigarette, with waved hair and a flower in his button-hole, and he looked markedly better, slighter, and younger than he had two years previously." He greeted his friends characteristically. "Sphinx," he cried, "how marvellous of you to know exactly the right hat to wear at seven o'clock in the morning to meet a friend who has been away! You can't have got up, you must have sat up."

There was some discussion as to where Wilde was to go after Dieppe, and a projected driving tour with Frank Harris was mentioned. According to Headlam, Wilde said, "It would be like a perpetual football match to be with him." The conversation then got on to the subject of religion. Wilde remarked that he looked on all the different religions "as colleges in a great university" and that he regarded Roman Catholicism as "the greatest and most romantic of them." At length he said he would like to go into a retreat for six months, and he asked Headlam to send a message to this effect to one of the priests at the Jesuit church in Farm Street. His host obligingly wrote a letter and dispatched it by cab. Whilst waiting for the reply, Wilde walked up and down the drawing-room. He continued to talk gaily in response to his friend's enquiries about his life at Reading. "The dear governor," he exclaimed, "such a delightful man, and his wife is charming. I spent happy hours in their garden, and they asked me to spend the summer with them. They thought I was the gardener." He began to laugh. "Unusual, I think? But I don't feel I can. I feel I want a change of scene."

He chatted on. "Do you know one of the punishments that happen to people who have been 'away'? They are not allowed to read the *Daily Chronicle*." He explained that, on his journey in the train on the previous night, he had asked permission to read it. Apparently one of the warders had a copy. This was refused. Wilde then suggested that he might be allowed to read it upside down. "This they consented to allow," he added with a chuckle. "I read the *Daily Chronicle* upside down all the way, and never enjoyed it so much. It's really the only way to read newspapers."

The laughter suddenly died away with the return of the messenger from Farm Street. He handed Wilde a letter and the others looked aside while he read it. His face suddenly assumed a serious expression. Then he broke down and sobbed bitterly. The reply was in effect a polite refusal. It was intimated that he could not be accepted in the retreat on the impulse of the moment but must first consider the matter for at least a year.

The arrangement had been made that Wilde and Adey should cross together by the day boat from Newhaven to Dieppe. But Wilde talked for so long and seemed to be enjoying himself so much that no one liked to tell him when the time had come for him to leave. He had other visitors too besides the Leversons, a young couple whom he had befriended in happier days, when he had given the husband a cheque to enable him to get married. Anyhow, he and Adey missed the train. In the circumstances, the only thing to do was to go for the night boat, which they did. So it was the afternoon when they said goodbye to their generous host, "of whose care, charity and kindness," wrote Robert Ross, "it would be impossible to speak too highly." Wilde's visit made a vivid impression on Headlam. "I like to think of him as I knew him for those six hours on that spring morning," this kindhearted clergyman later recalled, "and to hope that somewhere and somehow the beauty of his character may be garnered and the follies and weaknesses burnt up."

Taking care to avoid Victoria Station, after being recognized in Hatchard's bookshop in Piccadilly, where they had called for a few minutes, Wilde and Adey went by cab to West Croydon, where they caught the Newhaven train. On reaching Newhaven, Wilde sent the following telegram to Ross at the Hotel Sandwich, Dieppe:

Arriving by night boat. Am so delighted at prospect of seeing you and Reggie. You must not mind one foolish unkind letter. More has been such a good friend to me and I am so grateful to you all I cannot find words to express my feelings. You must not dream of waiting up for us. In the morning we will meet. Please engage rooms for us at your hotel. When I see you I shall be quite happy. Indeed I am happy now to think I have such wonderful friendship shown to me.

SEBASTIAN MELMOTH

Ross and Turner were on the landing stage at Dieppe when the boat steamed into the harbour at half-past four in the morning. In the first rays of the dawn, Wilde's tall figure was easily discernible on deck, dominating the other passengers. As Ross and Turner began to run along the jetty, Wilde recognized them and waved smilingly. At this moment he made an unforgettable impression in appearance. "His face had lost all its coarseness," noted Ross afterwards, "and he looked as he must have looked at Oxford in the early days before I knew him and as he only looked again after death. A good many people, even friends, thought his appearance almost repulsive, but the upper part of his face was extraordinarily fine and intellectual."

There was the usual irritating delay, and then Wilde, with his odd elephantine gait which Ross had never seen in anyone else, stalked off the boat. He was holding in his hand a large sealed envelope. Inside it was the manuscript of *De Profundis*. "This, my dear Robbie, is the great MS about which you know," he exclaimed, coming down the gangway. He handed it to Ross to deal with according to his instructions. He then broke into what Ross called "a great Rabelaisian sort of laughter," as he went on to speak in a bantering tone about Adey: "More has behaved very badly about my luggage and was anxious to deprive me of the blessed bag which Reggie gave me." Their greetings over, Wilde handed Turner the keys of his luggage and his friend went off to open the suitcases for customs examination. On his return, he found Wilde in the buffet surrounded by other passengers, "sitting at the head of the buffet table drinking his coffee and dominating the whole seasick company." The four friends then made their way to the hotel, where "a feast of sandwiches" had been prepared for the travellers. Here Wilde broke down, but this did not prevent him from continuing to talk until nine o'clock, when Ross insisted on going to his room for some rest.

While the others were resting, Wilde went to his own room and wrote a note to Ada Leverson. The style was quite like the old Wilde, especially the characteristic postscript.

> Hotel Sandwich,
> Dieppe.

Dear Sphinx,

I was so charmed with seeing you yesterday morning that I must write a line to tell you how sweet and good it was of you to be the very first to greet me. When I think that Sphinxes are minions of the morn and that you got up early before dawn, I am filled with wonder and joy.

I often thought of you in the long black days and nights of my sad life, and to find you just as wonderful and dear as ever was no surprise; the beautiful are always beautiful.

It is my first day of real liberty, so I try to send you a line.

> Ever affectionately yours,
> OSCAR WILDE

I am stopping here as Sebastian Melmoth—not Esquire, but Monsieur Sebastian Melmoth.

Reggie Turner is staying here under the name "Robert Ross." Robbie under the name "Reginald Turner." It is better they should not use their own names.

The four men met again at midday for *déjeuner,* all of them exhausted except Wilde, according to Ross. In the afternoon they drove over to Arques-la-Bataille, and sat for a while on the ramparts of the old castle. Wilde enjoyed the trees and the grass and the country scents and sounds in a way Ross had never known him to do before, just as a city-bred child might enjoy his first day in the country. Ross remembered afterwards that he had a characteristic adjective for everything, such as "monstrous," "purple," "grotesque," "gorgeous," "curious," and "wonderful." During that day and for many days afterwards, he talked principally of Reading Gaol and his experiences there. According to Ross, it had already become for him a sort of enchanted castle of which Major Nelson was the presiding fairy; the prison's machicolated turrets were turned into minarets, the very warders were benevolent mamelukes, and his three companions were Paladins reclaiming him after his captivity. He mentioned the various warders by name, and of each one he had a good story to tell.

On this particular afternoon, Ross remembered asking him if he had met any Freemasons in prison, since he knew that Wilde belonged to the brotherhood. Ross, who was a particularly devout Catholic convert, had a great prejudice against the craft, particularly English Freemasonry, but he was bound to admit that Wilde rose to the occasion. "Yes, it was very terrible," he replied. "As I was walking round the yard one day, I noticed that one of the men awaiting trial was signalling to me by masonic sign. I paid no attention until he made me the sign of the widow's son, which no Mason can ignore. I found he was in on a charge of fraud of some kind and was anxious that I should get all my friends to petition for his release. He was quite mad, poor fellow. As he *would* carry on signalling, and I was afraid the warders would get to notice it, I persuaded Major Nelson to let me wear black goggles until he was convicted and sent to Portland."

Wilde and his friends made several other excursions through the surrounding countryside and along the coast, partly with the object of finding a quiet little hotel where Wilde could settle. Wilde and Turner usually drove, while Adey and Ross rode behind on bicycles. Ross did his best to persuade Wilde to take to a bicycle, but the experiment was not a success. As Wilde had occasion later to remind Ross, "even my leg remembers it." Eventually they discovered the Hôtel de la Plage at Berneval-sur-Mer, a few miles from Dieppe, and Wilde arranged to move in there.

Lugné-Poe, who had produced *Salomé* in Paris while Wilde was in prison, came through Dieppe on his way to London for a visit, and he breakfasted with Wilde, Ross, and Turner. Wilde was "quite charmed with him"; he had had no idea he was so young or so handsome, having expected "a *maladif* edition of the great poet whom America put to death on a clearly proved charge of having written poems entirely composed of those three wonderful things, Romance, Music and Sorrow." However, one aspect of this meeting troubled Wilde. The young French actor-manager had been asked by a newspaper to record his impressions of the newly released prisoner. "I earnestly impressed on him the importance of writing no interview, and giving no details of my strange name, my place of sojourn, my altered appearance, and the like," wrote Wilde after Lugné-Poe had departed, "but I know how tempted people are to write for their own pleasure about others, thoughtlessly and without care . . . . What I want him to say is how grateful I was and am to France for their recognition of me as an artist in the day of my humiliation, and how my better treatment in an English prison was due to the French men of letters."

After about a week Adey and Turner went back to London, while Ross remained a few days longer to see Wilde settled in at Berneval. On May 27, Wilde wrote to Turner from the Hôtel de la Plage: "This is my first day here. Robbie and I arrived last night: the dinner was excellent and we tried to eat enough for eight as we occupy so many rooms. However, we soon got tired. Only the imagination of man is limitless. The appetite seems curiously bounded. This is one of the many lessons I have learnt."

For the time being Wilde was tolerably contented, although he quickly realized what he called his "terrible position of isolation" as soon as Ross had left him. Any momentary feelings of annoyance he had felt with Adey and Ross had now disappeared, nor did he nourish any other hard feelings by reason of his imprisonment. "You will be pleased to know that I have not come out of prison an embittered or disappointed man," he told the artist William Rothenstein at this time. "On the contrary. In many ways I have gained much. I am not really ashamed of having been in prison: I often was in more shameful places: but I *am* really ashamed of having led a life unworthy of an artist. I don't say that Messalina is a better companion than Sporus, or that the one is all right and the other all wrong: I know simply that a life of studied materialism and a philosophy of appetite and cynicism, and a cult of sensual and senseless ease, are bad things for an artist: they narrow the imagination, and dull the more delicate susceptibilities. I was all wrong, my dear boy, in my life. I was not getting the best out of me. *Now*, I think that with good health and the friendship of a few good, simple nice fellows like yourself, and a quiet mode of living, with isolation for thought, and freedom from the endless hunger for pleasures that wreck the body and imprison the soul—well, I think I may do things yet that you may all like."

2

"The prison style is absolutely and entirely wrong," Wilde had written when he was at Reading. "I would give anything to be able to alter it when I go out. I intend to try." He began by writing a letter to the Liberal *Daily Chronicle* on the treatment of children in prison in the context of Warder Martin's dismissal, which appeared over his own name. Some months later he followed this up with a second letter to the editor on penal reform generally, inspired by the introduction into Parliament of legislation designed to effect such changes as the ability to earn remission of sentence by good conduct and the abolition of such barbaric and outmoded punishments as the crank and the treadmill. "I have tried to indicate in my letter a few of the reforms necessary to our English prison system," Wilde concluded. "They are simple, practical and humane. They are, of course, only a beginning. But it is time that a beginning should be made, and it can only be started by a strong pressure of public opinion formularised in your powerful paper, and fostered by it. But to make these reforms effectual much has to be done. And the first, and perhaps the most difficult task, is to humanise the governors of prisons, to civilise the warders and Christianise the chaplains." [1]

As soon as Ross and his other friends had left him towards the end of May to return to England, Wilde settled down at Berneval to write *The Ballad of Reading Gaol*. He had been reading *A Shropshire Lad* by A. E. Housman, and to some extent the metre he adopted, as well as the subject, was inspired by Housman's poem. On 1 June he wrote to Ross: "I have begun something that I think will be very good." A few days later, in order to secure quiet for his work, he made up his mind to move into a nearby house, the Châlet Bourgeât, which happened to be vacant and which had a large writing-room, though he continued to take his meals

[1] *Daily Chronicle*, 24 March 1898.

at the Hôtel de la Plage. "Don't be nervous," he reassured Ross, who was worried about the expense. "I have many irons and a huge fire. But to work I must be isolated . . . Overhead here is a lady with two children—perfect darlings—and their racket is appalling. There is no peace except in one's own home." Accordingly, he took the chalet and set to work. Here the first draft of the ballad was completed in about six weeks. "The poem is nearly finished," he wrote to Ross on 20 July. "Some of the verses are awfully good." But at other moments he had doubts. He read some of the verses to the young Irish-American poet Vincent O'Sullivan, who happened to be on a visit to Dieppe. His hearer noted that he did so with great modesty and hesitation, which seemed to O'Sullivan quite extraordinary for a person of his intellectual position in relation to a young man who had yet to make his way as a writer. "I feel quite sure you won't like it," said Wilde at the time. "I am not sure that I like it myself. But catastrophes in life bring about catastrophes in art."

While he was at Berneval, Wilde was popular with the local inhabitants of the little Normandy village. On 22 June, he celebrated Queen Victoria's Diamond Jubilee by giving a party in the garden of the Châlet Bourgeât for a dozen or so schoolchildren, who feasted on strawberries and cream, apricots, chocolates, cakes, and grenadine syrup, washed down with cider.

I had a huge iced cake with *Jubilé de la Reine Victoria* in pink sugar just rosetted with green, and a great wreath of red roses round it all. Every child was asked beforehand to choose his present: they all chose instruments of music!!!

> 6 accordions
> 5 trompettes
> 4 clairons

They sang the Marseillaise and other songs, and danced a *ronde,* and also played "God Save the Queen": they said it was "God Save the Queen," and I did not like to differ from them. They also all had flags which I gave them. They were most gay and sweet. I gave the health of *La Reine d'Angleterre,* and they cried "*Vive la Reine d'Angleterre*"!!!! Then I gave "*La France, mère de tout les artistes,*" and finally I gave *Le Président de la République:* I thought I had better do so. They cried out with one accord "*Vivent le Président de la République et Monsieur Melmoth*". . . So I found my name coupled with that of the President. It was an amusing experience as I am hardly more than a month out of gaol.

They stayed from 4:30 to seven o'clock and played games: on leaving I gave them each a basket with a jubilee cake frosted pink and inscribed, and *bonbons.*

They seem to have made a great demonstration in Berneval-le-Grande, and to have gone to the house of the Mayor and cried "*Vive Monsieur le Maire! Vive la Reine d'Angleterre. Vive Monsieur Melmoth.*" I tremble at my position.[2]

---

[2] One of the children, named Alin Caillas, then aged ten, was still living in 1971, in which year he published a small book, *Oscar Wilde tel que je l'ai connu,* recording his recollections of the occasion.

While working on his poem at Berneval, Wilde was relatively contented, since various friends paid him visits—André Gide and Vincent O'Sullivan from Paris, the poet Ernest Dowson, the composer and pianist Dalhousie Young, and the painters Will Rothenstein and Charles Conder from London, who found the beach at Dieppe congenial for their work.

On 3 June, Wilde reported to Ross: "Ernest Dowson, Conder and Dal Young came out here this afternoon to dine and sleep—at least I know they dine, but I believe they never sleep." They stayed up drinking and talking until three o'clock in the morning, "very bad for me but it was a delightful experience," noted Wilde afterwards. "Young is the best of fellows, and Ernest has a most interesting nature." Wilde had not previously met the musician, and the occasion enabled him to thank Young for his courage in publishing a pamphlet in his defence shortly after the last trial.[3] Young now offered to build Wilde a house at Berneval, so that he could have a permanent home, at a cost of £700. "This offer I declined," Wilde afterwards told Ross. "I thought it a piece of generous but quixotic enthusiasm. I hardly knew him at the time. I did not think it right to accept such an offer." Young then proposed to Wilde that he should write the libretto of a musical piece to be called *Daphnis and Chloë*, but nothing came of the idea, although Wilde seems to have accepted an advance of £100 from Young—"What I knew in my heart was meant half as gift, half as encouragement. He told me to take my own time about it. He said that all he wanted was that I should know he believed in me etc. etc."

One day he met Dowson at a café in Dieppe. According to W. B. Yeats, who claimed to have had the story from Dowson himself, Dowson kindly offered to conduct Wilde to a local brothel for the purpose of acquiring "a more wholesome taste." They managed to scrape up enough cash between them to defray the cost of the expedition, and thereupon set off together for the brothel, to which apparently Dowson was no stranger. Meanwhile, the news of the incident quickly became known in the neighbourhood and a small crowd began to collect round the entrance to the brothel, where Dowson was waiting. Presently Wilde emerged from the building, evidently disappointed by his experiences within. "The first these ten years," he said to Dowson in a low voice, "and it will be the last. It was like cold mutton!" And then, raising his voice so that the crowd could hear, he added, "But tell it in England, for it will entirely restore my character!"

Having completed the first draft of his poem, Wilde was now faced with the problem of finding a publisher for it. John Lane, who had published more of Wilde's writings than any other publisher, had struck his name out of the firm's list after his downfall. No other reputable publisher could be expected to touch anything of Wilde's after what had

---

[3] Young, who was a pupil of Paderewski, published his *Apologia pro Oscar Wilde* in June 1895. He was twenty-nine at the time. He died in 1921.

happened; the risk of injury to his business, if he did so, would be too great. According to Vincent O'Sullivan, it was Robert Ross who now thought of Leonard Smithers. During the course of the summer, this amazing Yorkshireman paid several visits to Dieppe in the company of Aubrey Beardsley and Vincent O'Sullivan, with whom Smithers had become friendly as publisher of the short-lived but brilliant periodical *The Savoy,* which was illustrated by Beardsley and to which O'Sullivan contributed. On 26 July, Wilde wrote to Ross: "I saw Aubrey at Dieppe . . . . Smithers, the publisher, was with him: very intoxicated but amusing."

Leonard Smithers, at this date in his middle thirties, was one of the most extraordinary men who ever ventured into the world of publishing. He originally came from Sheffield, where he had been admitted a solicitor. He already knew Wilde, since as a young practitioner of twenty-six in Sheffield he had written to the author congratulating him on the publication of *The Happy Prince,* which had first appeared in 1888. An amiable reply from Wilde had led to their becoming acquainted when Smithers migrated to London a few years later.

In London Smithers had gradually dropped the law for printing, publishing, and bookselling. His methods were daring and unorthodox. "I'll publish anything that the others are afraid of," he said to Vincent O'Sullivan on the occasion of their first meeting. For this reason he refused to advertise and hardly ever sent out review copies to the press. Nevertheless, some finely produced books had issued from his offices in the Royal Arcade, off Bond Street, including works of poets like Ernest Dowson and Vincent O'Sullivan and artists like Beardsley, Conder, and Max Beerbohm. He also ran a more or less surreptitious business in retailing pornography. There is a story that the widow of a famous High Court judge, finding after his death a large library of erotic books, sent for Smithers to "take them away," which the obliging bookseller quickly did, having already sold most of them to his late lordship at a handsome profit. Women were said to be irresistible to Smithers. He was also noticeably fond of the absinthe bottle. "Since I last wrote to you I have neglected absinthe, and have drunk whiskey and water," he wrote to Wilde in one of his letters, "but I have distinctly seen the error of my ways and have gone back to absinthe." Indeed, a combination of drink and drugs eventually killed him. But in the days of his success, he seems to have been a genial and generous friend, who on the whole treated his authors and artists well.

"I do not know if you know Smithers," wrote Wilde to Reggie Turner at this time. "He is usually in a large straw hat, has a blue tie delicately fastened with a diamond brooch of the impurest water, or perhaps wine, as he never touches water.—it goes to his head at once. His face, clean shaven as befits a priest who serves at the altar whose God is literature, is wasted and pale, not with poetry, but with poets, who, he says, have wrecked his life by insisting on publishing with him. He loves first editions, especially of women—little girls are his passion—he is the most learned erotomaniac in Europe. He is also a delightful companion, and a dear fellow, very kind to me."

Smithers had just sent Wilde a parcel of books, for which Wilde was most grateful. "How nice it is of you to give them to me," wrote Wilde to the publisher on 4 August. "I hope very much that some day I shall have something that you will like well enough to publish." Smithers's chance came about a fortnight later when he was in Dieppe. Wilde mentioned his poem, and in an expansive moment Smithers offered to publish it and give Wilde the whole profit. "This offer, I may say, was made before, not after dinner, at the Café Tribunaux," wrote Wilde, recalling the incident. "I said I would not agree to it, as I did not think it fair . . . but that I would take half the profits. This was agreed to."

On 24 August, Wilde wrote to Ross from Berneval:

My poem is still unfinished, but I have made up my mind to finish it this afternoon, and send it to be type-written. Once I see it—even type-written—I shall be able to correct it: *now* I am tired of the MS.

Do you think this verse good? I fear it is out of harmony, but wish you were here to talk about it . . .

> The Governor was strong upon
>   The Regulation Act,
> The Doctor said that Death was but
>   A scientific fact;
> And twice a day the Chaplain called
>   And left a little tract.

It is, of course, about the condemned man's life before his execution. I have got in "latrine"—it looks beautiful.

On the same day Wilde sent Smithers the first draft in manuscript with a request to have it typewritten for him. "I want it done on good brown paper—*not* tissue paper—and bound in a brown paper cover," wrote Wilde in his covering letter. "It is not yet finished, but I want to see it typewritten. I am sick of my MS." The manuscript was returned to the author, with the typed copy, ten days later. "I yesterday sent you back your poem," Smithers wrote to Wilde on 2 September. "I showed it to Aubrey [Beardsley] and he seemed to be much struck by it. He promised at once to do a frontispiece for it—in a manner which immediately convinced me he will never do it. He has got tired already of *Mlle de Maupin* and talks of *Casanova* instead. It seems hopeless to try and get any connected work out of him of any kind." At this time Beardsley was in an advanced stage of tuberculosis and had only a few months to live. Although he had provided the illustrations for *Salomé,* he had never much liked the author; he now made a point of avoiding him in Dieppe and only consented to edit a new magazine called *The Peacock* which Smithers planned to bring out, "if it is quite agreed that Oscar Wilde contributes nothing to the magazine anonymously, pseudonymously or otherwise." Wilde, as was his wont, bore no ill-will. "It was *lâche* of Aubrey" was his only comment on the Dieppe incident.

"I was greatly shocked to hear of poor Aubrey's death," he later wrote to Smithers, who had been Beardsley's close friend and whom the artist had begged on his deathbed to destroy all his obscene drawings. "Superbly premature as the flowering of his genius was, still he had immense development and had not sounded his last stop. There were great possibilities always in the cavern of his soul and there is something macabre and tragic in the fact that one who added another tenor to life should have died at the age of a flower." [4]

3

While Wilde was still in prison, his wife had changed her surname and the surnames of Cyril and Vyvyan by deed poll to Holland, as did her brother Otho, whose second name it was. This was done at the same time as she appointed Adrian Hope to be the children's guardian. On leaving England after her husband had been sentenced, Constance took the boys to a hotel at Glion above Montreux and the Lake of Geneva. Here she had registered herself and the boys in their proper surname. However, the hotel manager discovered who they were after they had been there for some weeks and he politely asked them to leave, "fearing for the good name of his house," as Vyvyan later put it. Fortunately, Constance had a good friend in Margaret Ranee of Sarawak, who was then living near Nervi on the Ligurian coast, a few miles from Genoa. Accordingly, the Ranee engaged rooms for them at the Hotel Nervi, where the manager was not so fussy. Nevertheless, the unhappy experience at Glion convinced Constance that her identity might again be discovered at any time and it was this possibility which induced her to change her and her children's surnames to Holland, which was a family name on her mother's side. [5] When her husband was released from Reading, Constance was staying with her brother Otho and his wife near Neuchâtel, so as to be near the boys, who were at school there. One of the first things Wilde did on settling in Berneval was to write his wife a letter which she described as being "full of penitence" and which she answered. The text of this letter has not survived, but it is clear from what she told their mutual friend Carlos Blacker, who was also in Switzerland at this time and with whom she was in touch, that Wilde wanted her to bring the two boys to see him in Dieppe or Berneval. [6] "I have heard

---

[4] Beardsley was only twenty-five when he died in Menton on 8 March 1898. He is buried in the cemetery at Roçquebrune above the town. Richard Le Gallienne, who was to survive both Beardsley and Wilde by nearly half a century, is also buried there.

[5] J. H. Lloyd's mother was a Miss Holland.

[6] Carlos Blacker (1859–1928) was an Englishman of independent means who lived mostly on the Continent. He was an excellent linguist, and in his old age he learned Hebrew, so that "if he went to Heaven he could talk to God in his own language." Wilde dedicated *The Happy Prince and Other Tales* to him. It is possible that he had a financial interest in the original production of *Lady Windermere's Fan*. Wilde's niece Dorothy (Dolly) Wilde met Blacker in Dinard in 1928 shortly before his death. "I met Carlos Blacker here," she wrote to a friend at the time, "a charming man—dying alas! but railing against religion and virtue in fine spirit. *Extremely* intelligent . . . He knew Oscar very well and all the interesting people of that time. Tried to prove to me that my dear scholastic grandmother had an affair with Oscar, King of Sweden, and indeed the resemblance *is* uncanny. Amusing, isn't it?"

from my wife," Wilde wrote to Ross at the end of May. "She sends me photographs of the boys—such lovely little fellows in Eton collars—but makes no promise to allow me to see them: she says *she* will see me twice a year, but I want my boys. It is a terrible punishment, dear Robbie, and oh! how well I deserve it. But it makes me feel disgraced and evil: and I don't want to feel that."

For some weeks thereafter, she wrote to him regularly, while Ross sent him a photograph of her for which he had asked. Then, towards the end of July, Blacker wrote to him with the shattering news that she was suffering from spinal paralysis. This was the delayed result of an accident shortly before she left Tite Street when she tripped over a loose stair rod and fell down a whole flight of stairs, injuring her spine and her right arm. Wilde replied immediately:

Dear Friend,

I am terribly distressed about what you tell me about Constance. I had no idea it was so serious.

Of course she could not come here. I see that. She would require the attendance of a maid, and I have only my man-servant, and the journey would be too much.

Do you think I should go and see her in about three weeks? I really think it would be better for her to see me, and have it over. I would only stay a couple of days. I think that she is afraid I am fearfully altered. I don't think I am in appearance. My friends say I am not. Just try and advise me.

I am so glad she is with you and your charming, brilliant wife.

For myself, I really am quite heart-broken. Nemesis seems endless.

With many thanks, dear old friend, ever yours

OSCAR

After talking it over with Constance, Blacker wrote again, putting him off, as Constance was about to return to Nervi, but holding out some hope that she might be able to see him there after she had got settled in. On 4 August, Wilde wrote back to Blacker:

My dear Friend,

I am simply heart-broken at what you tell me. I don't mind my life being wrecked—that is as it should be—but when I think of poor Constance I simply want to kill myself. But I suppose I must live through it all. I don't care. Nemesis has caught me in her net: to struggle is foolish. Why is it that one runs to one's ruin? Why has destruction such a fascination? Why, when one stands on a pinnacle, must one throw oneself down? No one knows, but things are so.

Of course I think it would be much better for Constance to see me, but you think not. Well, you are wiser. My life is spilt on the sand—red wine on the sand—and the sand drinks it because it is thirsty, for no other reason.

I wish I could see you. Where I shall be in September I don't know. I don't care. I fear we shall never see each other again. But all is right: the gods hold the world on their knees. I was made for destruction. My cradle was rocked by the Fates. Only in the mire can I know peace.

Ever yours,
OSCAR

Towards the end of August, when *The Ballad* was being typed, Wilde came to a fateful and unfortunate decision for himself. He had begun to feel very lonely at Berneval, he was tired of his Dieppe admirers, and he was out of patience with his wife, who for one reason or another had put off seeing him. Meanwhile, he had been in touch with Alfred Douglas. They had narrowly missed meeting at Berneval in June when Douglas was on the point of coming to stay at the Châlet Bourgeât and was put off at the last moment by Wilde, who had just received a letter from his solicitor repeating his previous warnings of the danger of such a visit. At that time, too, apparently Queensberry had dispatched a private detective to Berneval to report on Wilde's movements and visitors. Wilde now planned to meet his friend clandestinely at some spot between Dieppe and Paris, where Douglas was staying. By a coincidence—for there is no evidence that Constance knew anything of his intention—she wrote to him too late, saying that she would see him, as she had then got their children "out of the way." Wilde was so irritated at what he considered his wife's "extraordinary want of tact" that, contrary to the advice given by Ross and other friends, he refused to go to her, writing to the effect that he was "utterly lonely, treated like a pariah and worn out with her perpetual procrastination, and was therefore going to live with the only person ready to give him his companionship," namely, Alfred Douglas.

Wilde set out to meet his friend at Rouen on 4 September. Half an hour before he left he scribbled a note to Ross. "I have not yet finished my poem!" he wrote. "I have got in about the kiss of Caiaphas: it is very good." The reunion in Rouen was conclusive. Wilde cried at the station when Douglas met him, and they "walked about all day, arm in arm, or hand in hand, and were perfectly happy." Wilde returned to Berneval next day to pack his bags and prepared to join Douglas *en route* from Paris to Naples. Before he left, he was writing to Douglas in the old adoring strain: "I feel that my only hope of again doing beautiful work in Art is being with you. It was not so in the old days, but now it is different, and you can really re-create in me that energy and sense of joyous power on which Art depends. Everyone is furious with me for going back to you, but they don't understand us. I feel that it is only with you that I can do anything at all. Do remake my ruined life for me, and then our friendship and love will have a different meaning to the world. I wish that when we met at Rouen we had not parted at all."

"The weather has been so dreadful at Berneval that I have come here, where the weather is much worse," he wrote from Rouen to Carlos Blacker. "I cannot stay in the North of Europe: the climate kills me. I don't mind being alone where there is sunlight, and a *joie de vivre* all about me, but my last fortnight at Berneval has been black and dreadful, and quite suicidal. I have never been so unhappy. I am trying to get some money to go to Italy, and hope to be able to find my way to Sicily, but the expenses of travelling are frightening . . . I am greatly disappointed that Constance has not asked me to come and see the children. I don't suppose I shall ever see them."

When he reached Paris, which he did on 15 September, Wilde sent a note to Vincent O'Sullivan, who was then living in Paris, asking him if he could see him and suggesting he should come to his hotel next day about noon.[7] O'Sullivan went to the hotel at the appointed time and found that Wilde was expecting a homosexual friend named Rowland Strong.[8] After waiting about a quarter of an hour for Strong, who did not turn up, Wilde left a message for him. He and O'Sullivan then called a cab and went off to lunch in Montmartre. Afterwards O'Sullivan described the occasion in his *Aspects of Wilde:*

> In the cab, I asked him who was Rowland Strong? He said he was an English journalist, the Paris correspondent, I think he said, of some London paper, and, what he seemed to think more important, a descendant on his mother's side of Chateaubriand. He seemed in very good spirits and launched into a description of Strong's valet, an elderly man, who, he said, was the extreme type of the English well-trained servant. When Strong heard that Verlaine was dying, as he did not care to go himself to the mean street and the squalid abode, he sent his man to get the news. The valet returned imperturbable.
> "Well?" asked Strong.
> "I saw the gentleman, sir, and he died immediately."
> As Wilde finished this story we arrived at the restaurant, a restaurant chosen by himself, which still exists at the moment of writing [1935], up a flight of stairs over a passage giving on to the Boulevard Montmartre, having somehow survived the drastic overhauling of Paris since the war. It was a kind of restaurant where nobody would recognise Wilde, and he did not want to be recognised.

Towards the end of the meal, Wilde admitted that he was rather troubled and said he was "passing through a crisis." Some friends of his family in England, O'Sullivan gathered, wished him to go into a mountain village and write plays, "a most stupid suggestion," so it seemed to O'Sullivan. "What he required was to forget, to be stimulated, distracted from his black thoughts. How could he find that in a mountain village? It would have continued the penal cell." He went on to tell O'Sullivan that he was inclined to go to Italy and rejoin Douglas there, having "thought it all out." Finally he declared, "I shall go to Italy to-night. Or rather, I would go, but I am in an absurd position. I have no money."

O'Sullivan asked him how much he needed. When Wilde told him, they drove together to the bank where O'Sullivan had an account. "He stayed in the cab and I brought him out the sum he wanted," noted

[7] Vincent O'Sullivan (1868–1940) spent most of his life in France. His *Aspects of Wilde* (1936), in which he recorded his recollections of Wilde during his last years, was warmly praised by Bernard Shaw at the time of its publication.

[8] Rowland Strong (1865–1924) was the Paris correspondent of the *Morning Post* and the *Observer* and also of *The New York Times*. He wrote two books, *Where and How to Dine in Paris* (1900) and *Sensations of Paris* (1912), both of which had a considerable success. He was a younger brother of the Rt. Rev. Thomas Banks Strong, successively Dean of Christ Church, Oxford, Vice-Chancellor of Oxford, and Bishop of Oxford.

O'Sullivan afterwards. "It is one of the few things I look back on with satisfaction. It is not every day that one has the chance of relieving the anxiety of a genius and a hero. I think he left Paris the same evening; certainly very soon."

At Naples Wilde and Douglas were to spend most of the next two months together. "I love him and have always loved him," Wilde wrote to Reggie Turner shortly after his arrival. "He ruined my life, and for that reason I seem forced to love him more: and I think that now I shall do some lovely work. Bosie is himself a poet, far the best of all the young poets of England, an exquisite artist in lyric and ballad. It is to a poet that I am going back. So when people say how dreadful of me to return to Bosie, do say NO. Say that I love him, that he is a poet, and that, after all, whatever my life may have been ethically, it has always been *romantic*—and Bosie is my romance. My romance is a tragedy of course, but it is none the less a romance—and he loves me very dearly, more than he loves or can love anyone else, and without him my life was dreary."

After about a fortnight in the Hôtel Royal et des Étrangers at Naples, where they ran up a bill of £68, the two friends moved into a furnished villa at Posilipo. It was called the Villa Giudice, and was charmingly situated, overlooking the Bay of Naples, with a terrace and marble steps leading down to the sea. ("The French papers describe me as living broken down in health, in the lovely villa of the son of Lord Douglas.") There was, however, one initial disadvantage. The villa was infested with rats. These were eventually removed through the combined operation of an orthodox rat-catcher and a bearded old woman who had the reputation of being the local witch: she came and "burned odours" and muttered incantations which she assured the two friends that no rats could resist. Anyhow, the rats disappeared and the two friends were able to settle down to work. Here Wilde completed *The Ballad,* while Douglas wrote several sonnets.

On 14 October, Wilde triumphantly announced to Reggie Turner: "I have finished the great poem—600 lines now—I hope it will make a good effect. I like much of it myself—much is, I feel, for a harsher treatment than the languorous flute I love." A few days later he told this same friend that Smithers was letting him have twelve free copies of the published version of *The Ballad.* "Of course you are to have a presentation copy, and Robbie and More. The rest are for the Governor, Chaplain, warders and prisoners of Reading Gaol."

Two days later he told Turner that Smithers had sent the £20 he had asked for. "With it we go to Capri for three days. I want to lay a few simple flowers on the grave of Tiberius. As the tomb is of someone else really, I shall do it with deeper emotion."

Meanwhile, Constance Wilde had returned to Nervi, having left both the boys to spend the remainder of the holidays with Carlos Blacker and his wife at Freiburg in the Rhineland. "Not a sign of Oscar or a word from him," she wrote to Blacker on 25 September, "but I have an idea that he will turn up some day without writing." However, the very next day she had a letter from Oscar from Naples, in which he told her that he was going over to Capri and that he would come to stay with her in October, adding that if he came he must come as her husband. "The people who live here know my brother and know that I have no other," she had confided in Blacker. "Besides, I hate telling lies more than this terrible thing called life makes necessary. I look forward to nothing." Nevertheless, the feeling persisted with her that Oscar might turn up at any moment, and this induced her to rent part of a nearby villa, and to hurry on her preparations for moving in, even borrowing linen from her hotel.

On the other hand, the fact that her husband was in Naples and planning to visit Capri, always popular with homosexuals, aroused her suspicions that he was meeting "that dreadful person," as she called Douglas. ("No one goes to Naples at this time of year, so I see no other reason for his going, and I am unhappy.") Shortly afterwards her suspicions were confirmed by her husband's solicitor, A. D. Hansell, who by agreement with her advisers was acting as arbiter under the deed of arrangement. Hansell now informed her that in his opinion his client had violated the undertaking he had given not to keep bad company and that consequently he had forfeited his right to the allowance she was making him. "It grieves me to the heart that he should have behaved in this way," she told Blacker. "He is as weak as water."

"Women are so petty—and Constance has no imagination" was her husband's immediate reaction to Hansell's news. "For one's own solicitor this seems a little strong," he went on to tell Smithers. "Unluckily he has it in his power to stop my wretched allowance, and he is going to do so. And as I see that my poem is a very unsaleable affair, I simply have starvation or suicide before me—the latter, as I dislike pain from choice. Alfred Douglas has no money—not enough for his own wants—and cannot do anything, even temporarily, for me. I am anxious however to correct my proofs before retiring from a world of injustice, worry and annoyance, so do let me have them."

To More Adey, who had been concerned with the execution of the deed of arrangement, he wrote at the same time:

> I am quite ready to agree not to live in the same house with Bosie again. Of course to promise to cut him, or not to speak to him, or not to associate with him, would be absurd. He is the only friend with whom I can be in contact, and to live without some companion is impossible. I had silence and solitude for two years: to condemn me now to silence and solitude would be barbarous.
>
> It is not a matter of most importance, but I never wrote to my wife that I was going "to keep house with Alfred Douglas." I thought "keep house" was only a servant-girl's expression.
>
> My wife wrote me a very violent letter on September 29 last saying, "I *forbid* you to see Lord Alfred Douglas. I forbid you to return to your filthy, in-

sane life. I forbid you to live at Naples. I will not allow you to come to Genoa." I quote her words.

I wrote to her to say that I would never dream of coming to see her against her will, that the only reason that would induce me to come to see her was the prospect of a greeting of sympathy with me in my misfortunes, and affection and pity. That for the rest, I only desired peace, and to live my own life as best I could. That I could not live in London, or, as yet in Paris, and that I certainly hoped to winter at Naples. To this I received no answer.

"Had I received this letter a year ago I should have minded but not now," she wrote in forwarding it to Blacker. "I look upon it as the letter of a madman who has not even enough imagination to see how trifles affect children, or unselfishness enough to care for the welfare of his wife. It rouses all my bitterest feelings, and I am stubbornly bitter when my feelings are roused. I have latterly (God forgive me) an absolute repulsion to him."

Smithers duly sent the proofs, and Wilde worked hard at them for the next fortnight. He then wrote again to his publisher:

I wish you would start a Society for the Defence of Oppressed Personalities: at present there is a gross European concert headed by brutes and solicitors against us. It is really ridiculous that after my entire life has been wrecked by Society, people should still propose to exercise social tyranny over me, and try to force me to live in solitude—the one thing I can't stand. I lived in silence and solitude for two years in prison. I did not think that on my release my wife, my trustees, the guardians of my children, my few friends, such as they are, and my myriad enemies would combine to force me by starvation to live in silence and solitude again. After all in prison we had food of some kind: it was revolting, and made as loathsome as possible on purpose, and quite inadequate to sustain life in health. Still, there *was* food of some kind. The scheme now is that I am to live in silence and solitude and have no food at all. Really, the want of imagination in people is appalling. This scheme is put forward on moral grounds! It is proposed to leave me to die of starvation, or to blow my brains out in a Naples urinal. I never came across anyone in whom the moral sense was dominant who was not heartless, cruel, vindictive, log-stupid, and entirely lacking in the smallest sense of humanity. Moral people, as they are termed, are simply beasts. I would sooner have fifty unnatural vices, than one unnatural virtue. It is unnatural virtue that makes the world, for those who suffer, such a premature Hell.

All this has, of course, direct reference to my poem: and indeed is the usual way in which poets write to publishers.

Douglas now reconciled himself to the necessity of parting from his friend. "I do not know if, now that we are going to separate, there is any likelihood of my income being restored to me," Wilde wrote to Smithers. "I unluckily have no one to plead my cause aright. I have alienated all my friends, partly thro' my own fault and partly thro' theirs. The Paris *Journal* has a sympathetic paragraph to say I am starving at Naples—but French people subscribe nothing but sonnets when one is alive and statues when one is not." Wilde's nervous condition was as bad as his financial state. "My handwriting once Greek and gracious is now illegible," he told Smithers. "I am very sorry, but I really am a wreck of nerves. I don't eat or sleep, I live on cigarettes."

Early in December, Douglas departed for Paris, leaving Wilde alone in the villa. In a letter which he sent shortly afterwards to Ross, Wilde explained what had happened between them. "The facts of Naples are very bald and brief," he wrote. "Bosie for four months, by endless letters, offered me a home. He offered me love, affection and care, and promised that I should never want for anything. After four months I accepted his offer, but when we met at Aix on our way to Naples, I found he had no money, no plans, and had forgotten all his promises. His one idea was that I should raise money for us both; I did so to the extent of £120. On this Bosie lived quite happily. When it came to his having to repay his own *share*, he became terribly unkind and penurious, except where his own pleasures were concerned, and when my allowance ceased, he left . . . The bald fact is that I accepted the offer of the home, and found that I was expected to provide the money, and when I could no longer do so I was left to my own devices. It is, of course, the most bitter experience of a bitter life. It is a blow quite awful and paralysing. But it had to come, and I know it is better that I should never see him again. I don't want to, he fills me with horror."

It must be admitted that, when he wrote this letter, Wilde did considerably less than justice to his friend, since Lady Queensberry, who was making an allowance of about £8 a week to her son, had threatened to cut this off if he continued to live with Wilde. Douglas consequently agreed to separate and furthermore undertook never to sleep again under the same roof as Wilde, if his mother would pay Wilde the "debt of honour" which Wilde considered was due to him from the Queensberry family. Lady Queensberry could not apparently manage the whole sum, but she promised to let Wilde have £200. This she sent Wilde in two instalments through More Adey. About the same time she also sent her son some money, with which he was to settle the hotel bill in Naples which had remained unpaid when he and Wilde moved into the villa, and also to pay three months' rent of the villa in advance for Wilde before he left. There would appear, therefore, to be some justification for Douglas describing Wilde's letter about him as "one of the most astonishing products that the history of literature has ever recorded."

Wilde's conduct seems to be a good illustration of the line about all men killing the thing they love, which occurs so frequently in *The Ballad*. Incidentally, when they were together in Naples, Douglas asked Wilde what exactly he meant by this line. Wilde replied, "It's a mistake to ask a poet what he means by any obscure phrase in a poem, because he may mean one thing or several things. The answer is that it means just what it says in the poem." On another occasion Douglas repeated the question, and this time Wilde said, "*You* should know." This reply gave Douglas the clue he wanted, namely that "if one loves anyone very much, one creates an image of the beloved in one's mind and then is apt gradually and inevitably to destroy it."

Wilde did not remain for long in the villa after Douglas had left. About the middle of December he accepted an invitation from an elderly Russian ("He is very cultivated and of advanced years") whom he had met in Italy to spend a week or two as his guest at Taormina. Unfortunately, during his absence the servant whom he left in charge at the villa stole all his clothes and some other belongings, including the portrait William Rothenstein had painted of him in Paris and probably the MS of the first draft of *The Ballad.*

On his return to Naples at the beginning of the new year, Wilde found a long letter from Smithers dealing with various printer's corrections to *The Ballad* "by C.3.3." and enclosing a further proof of the title page, with which Wilde had been dissatisfied on the ground that the publisher's name appeared too large. "I trust the 'Leonard Smithers' is now small enough to satisfactorily show that I am not the author of the poem but only that humble person, its introducer to the public," wrote the publisher. Wilde did not stay in the villa again, although the rent had been paid until the end of February.

> 51 Santa Lucia, Naples.
> January 9, 1898.

. . . As regards America, I think it would be better to publish there *without* my name. I see that it is my *name that* terrifies. I hope an edition of some kind will appear. I cannot advise what should be done, but it seems to me that the withdrawal of my name is essential in America as elsewhere, and the public likes an open secret. Half the success of Marie Corelli is due to the no doubt unfounded rumour that she is a woman. In other respects pray do as you like about America, but do see that there is some edition.

I have had misfortune since I wrote to you: influenza, the robbery during my absence in Sicily, of *all* my clothes, etc. by a servant whom I left in the villa, ill-health, loneliness, and general *ennui* with a tragi-comedy of an existence. But I want to see my poem out . . .

The only newspaper in America which showed any interest in the poem was a Sunday publication, the New York *Journal.* Smithers asked the agent, Miss Marbury, to arrange for publication on 13 February, which was a Sunday. Unfortunately, the best offer Miss Marbury could persuade the New York *Journal* to make was only $100. This offer was refused and Smithers contented himself with asking Miss Marbury to secure the American copyright, while adhering to 13 February as the date of publication of the book in England. Meanwhile, Wilde had left Naples for Paris, where he put up in the Hôtel de Nice, a small hotel in the Rue des Beaux Arts, the street in the Latin Quarter where he was to die not quite two years later. From here he continued to bombard the publisher with anxious and at times pathetic letters. "Is the book out?" he asked Smithers. "Tell me and send me a few copies. Give my address to B[osie] and beseech him to write to me, for I simply long to hear from my old friends. I am so lonely and poor. What is the end to be?"

To this appeal Smithers replied, stating that *The Ballad* was with the binder, and sending Wilde samples of the binding together with twenty copies of the title sheet. He requested Wilde to inscribe them to those to whom he wished author's presentation copies to be sent, and to return the sheets to be bound up with the rest of the text. "I would send you a sample copy of the book, which I have received today from the binder," Smithers added, "but as it is not yet in a complete state, with its white and cinnamon back on it, I must remember the old proverb, which says that children should never see things half finished. So I will hold it back until it has got its binding on it."

Apart from what he considered one blemish, Wilde was delighted with the appearance of *The Ballad* when he received the first bound copy. "I am really charmed with the book," he wrote to Smithers. "The cover is very nice and the paper excellent. The title page is a master-piece, one of the best I have ever seen." But he was disappointed with the sales methods adopted by his unorthodox publisher. "Smithers is absurd," he wrote to Ross, "only printing 400 copies to begin with, and not advertising. I fear he has missed a popular 'rush.' He is so fond of 'suppressed' books that he suppresses his own." As a result of Wilde's protest, Smithers increased the initial printing to eight hundred copies.

4

The date of publication of *The Ballad,* originally intended to coincide with its appearance in New York, which never materialized, was 13 February 1898. Since this was a Sunday, it was not until the following day that copies were on sale to the English public. Despite the previous lack of advertising and the fact that very few review copies had been sent out, there was an immediate rush to buy the book, such as Wilde had indeed anticipated. Fifty copies were sold at one bookshop the morning after it was published, and by the end of the week the whole of the first edition, including most of the de luxe copies printed on Japanese vellum, was sold out. Among its purchasers was Wilde's defender at the Old Bailey, Sir Edward Clarke, who is said to have bought a dozen copies. Smithers was completely taken by surprise at this unexpected demand. Some delay in reprinting was inevitable, and although the publisher announced on the Saturday following publication that a second edition would be "ready next week," the delay proved damaging.

Nor could the press notices be regarded as satisfactory. "I fear that the Press will boycott the work," Wilde wrote apprehensively to Ross on publication day. "It is very bitter and unfair, and I have not much hope of recognition." His fears were to a great extent justified, but as much by reason of the small review list as by any personal animus towards the anonymous author, whose identity was soon generally recognized. The only national "daily" to notice it was the *Daily Telegraph,* which described the poem as "a moving piece of work, without doubt, despite its tone" and as having "already had a certain vogue, not merely for the reason that it is a strikingly vivid and realistic description of prison life, but also because everyone is ready with a suggestion as to whom the anonymous author really is." Next day Wilde wrote to Smithers on the subject of this review: "The *D.T.* by the influence of Reggie Turner has been forced to notice the book, but grudgingly and badly."

Henley wrote a bitter, unsigned review in a journal called *The Outlook*. "I have read Henley," commented Wilde. "It is very coarse and vulgar—so entirely lacking in literary or gentlemanly conduct." To some extent Henley's production was offset by a friendly appreciation from Arthur Symons, whom Frank Harris got to review it for the *Saturday Review,* which he now edited. This greatly pleased Wilde. "I don't think I should answer Henley," he told Smithers. "I think it would be vulgar—what does it matter? He is simply jealous. He made his scrofula into 'vers libre,' and is furious because I have made a sonnet out of 'skilly.' [9] Besides, there are only two forms of writers in England, the unread and the unreadable. Henley belongs to the former class."

A second impression of one thousand copies was on sale towards the end of February 1898. During the next few weeks, as a result of the demand for the poem, the second printing was augmented by three more printings amounting to 3,200 copies in all, thus bringing the total number of the ordinary edition to five thousand, all printed on hand-made paper. "Such is the public!" was Henley's uncharitable comment when he heard that some three thousand copies had been sold in three weeks. Smithers put what Wilde called "a flaming advertisement" of these sale figures into *The Athenaeum.* "When I read it," said Wilde, "I feel like Lipton's tea." After this the demand began to fall off. However, the poem continued to sell steadily and most of the remaining twelve hundred copies were disposed of during the succeeding twelve months. In addition, there was a limited edition of ninety-nine copies numbered and signed by the author, and specially bound in purple and white. This so-called third edition or "Author's Edition," as Wilde described it, was also distinguished by a leaf design embossed in gilt on the front which was the work of Charles Ricketts. The possibility of printing a popular six-penny edition, with "a prison reform preface" by Michael Davitt or John Burns, was also discussed, but nothing came of this idea. Later Smithers wrote to Wilde that he was proposing to print some more copies and asked him whether he had any objection to his name appearing on the title page, underneath the "C.3.3." in a parenthesis. "I think the time has now come when you should own *The Ballad*," he added. Wilde had no objection, and accordingly two thousand copies were printed of this new edition, with the author's name on the title page. This was the last English edition to appear in Wilde's lifetime.[10]

---

[9] In referring to Henley's verse, Wilde was thinking of the *In Hospital* poems, of which the best known begins "Out of the night that covered me." The staple prison diet in those days was a kind of thin, watery porridge or gruel, made from oatmeal and known as "skilly."

[10] After Wilde's death, Smithers, who claimed to have purchased the copyright from Wilde, brought out a number of unauthorized editions. These pirated editions are easily distinguishable from the authorized version by the fact that the publisher's address does not appear on the title page; the printing of "C.3.3" is also different. After Smithers's

Among those to whom Wilde asked the publisher to send complimentary copies of the first edition was Constance. She was so touched by this gesture that she relented on the subject of the forfeited allowance, which she now proposed to restore at the slightly reduced rate of £10 a month, subject to receiving a satisfactory report on him from Carlos Blacker, who was going to Paris. "If you do see him," she wrote to Blacker, "tell him that I think the *Ballad* exquisite, and I hope that the great success it has had in London at all events will urge him on to write more." To Blacker's wife she wrote the following day, asking whether her husband would like a copy of the poem. "I hear that Burne-Jones thinks it wonderful," she added, "and indeed I think that everyone does that." She further asked Blacker to get her a copy of the *Mercure de France,* in which she understood that a French translation of the poem by Henry Davray was shortly to appear. "Also I wonder if you could get hold of for me a copy of the French translation of *Dorian Gray?* I had one but I lent it, and like most things one lends, one rarely sees them again!"

As soon as he heard that Blacker had arrived in Paris, Wilde wrote suggesting he should come to his hotel:

> I am living here quite alone; in one room, I need hardly say, but there is an armchair for you. I have not seen Alfred Douglas for three months: he is I believe on the Riviera . . . The fact is that if he is ever with me again he loses £10 a month of his allowance, and as he has only £400 a year he has adopted the wise and prudent course of conduct . . .
>
> I am so glad my poem has had a success in England. I have had for some weeks a copy for you—of the first edition—by me, which I long to present to you.
>
> It appears with a French translation in the *Mercure de France* for April, and I hope to have it published in book form also in Paris, in a limited edition of course, but it is my *chant de cygne,* and I am sorry to leave with a cry of pain—a song of Marsyas, not a song of Apollo; but Life, that I have loved so much—too much—has torn me like a tiger, so when you come and see me, you will see the ruin and wreck of what was once wonderful and brilliant, and terribly improbable. But the French men of letters and artists are kind to me, so I spend my evenings reading the *Tentation* by Flaubert. I don't think I shall ever write again: *la joie de vivre* is gone, and that, with will-power, is the basis of art.
>
> When you come ask for Monsieur Melmoth.

At their meeting, which took place next day, Wilde borrowed some money from Blacker in order to pay his hotel bill. "I don't know what to do, and I have pawned everything I had," he wrote to Blacker a few days later. "It was very kind of you writing to my wife, but I have a sort of idea she really wants me to be dead. It is a horrible and persistent thought, and I daresay she would be relieved to hear you had recognised me at the Morgue."

death in 1907 his heirs attempted without success to claim the copyright, when about one thousand "pirated" copies were seized by the authority of Wilde's literary executor.

After she had heard from Blacker that he had seen her husband, Constance went ahead with her plan to restore his allowance. "I am putting a codicil in my will so that the allowance may continue after my death," she told Mrs. Blacker.

This will, I think, be an advantage to the boys as they will not be called upon to pay anything themselves. I cannot, and do not intend to, make myself at all responsible for his debts. It may interest your husband and disgusted me that A[lfred] D[ouglas] is received in society by the embassy at Rome and by private persons at Nice. So much it is with a bourgeois nation to be of the aristocracy.

At the same time she wrote to Vyvyan, who was now at school in Monaco: "Try not to feel harshly about your father; remember that he is your father and that he loves you. All his troubles arose from the hatred of a son for his father, and whatever he has done he has suffered bitterly for."

Throughout the spring and summer of 1898, and indeed until his death, Wilde experienced an inability to produce anything in the way of sustained writing. "I don't think I shall ever really write again," he told Ross at this time. "Something is killed in me. I feel no desire to write. I am unconscious of power. Of course my first year in prison destroyed me body and soul. It could not have been otherwise." Amongst his literary plans never carried out was a work on prison life and penal reform. "I have no doubt we shall win," he told the criminologist George Ives shortly after the publication of *The Ballad,* "but the road is long, and red with monstrous martyrdoms. Nothing but the repeal of the Criminal Law Amendment Act would do any good. That is essential. It is not so much public opinion as public officials that need educating." He collected some books and pamphlets on the subject of prison, including John Howard's celebrated treatise, and these were found among his few effects after his death. But apart from the two letters to the *Daily Chronicle* on the case of Warder Martin and the Prisons Bill of 1898, he completed nothing on this, or indeed any other subject, after the publication of *The Ballad.* Judging by the *Daily Chronicle* letters, it is a pity that he did not do so. Many of his friends considered he should make the attempt, and even his wife thought so after she had read the second letter in the *Daily Chronicle.* "I think that Oscar had better write a book on the present prison system, which I am sure would sell," she wrote to Carlos Blacker, "as people know exceedingly little about it and they always want to know those sort of things."

The letter in which Constance Wilde expressed this opinion was written on 30 March 1898 and was one of the last, if not the very last, she wrote. A few days later she went into a nursing home in Genoa for an operation to relieve the pressure on her spine which was now causing her unbearable pain. A week later she was dead. Both her brother Otho and her friend the Ranee of Sarawak afterwards told her son Vyvyan that she had no suspicion that she might die from the effect of the operation.

"But I can only think, from the contents of her last letter to me," wrote Vyvyan later, "that she knew in her heart that her sorrows would soon be over."

By this time Wilde had moved to the Hôtel d'Alsace in the same street ("much cleaner") from which he had written to Blacker on 28 March 1898 that he had had "a horrid accident in a fiacre three days ago, and cut my mouth terribly."

What happened to me was simply that through the horse coming down I was thrown almost through the front window of a fiacre, and cut my lower lip almost in two. It was quite dreadful, and, of course, a hideous shock to my nerves. It is so horrible to have no one, or to see no one, when one is cooped up in a wretched hotel. I hope to go out tomorrow.

"I had a very nice letter from Constance yesterday," he added. The next news he had of Constance overwhelmed him with grief. "It is really awful," he told Carlos Blacker, who came to offer his condolences. "I don't know what to do. If we had only met once, and kissed each other. It is too late. How awful life is."

However, he seems to have recovered fairly quickly, as Robert Ross, whom he asked to come over from London and comfort him in his grief, wrote to Smithers on his arrival in Paris, where Douglas had also turned up:

You will have heard of Mrs Wilde's death. Oscar of course did not feel it at all. It is rather appalling for him as his allowance ceases and I do not expect his wife's trustees will continue it.[11] He is in very good spirits and does not consume too many . . . . Oscar has only seen Douglas once. I went to see his lordship. He is less interested in other people than ever before, especially Oscar. So I think that alliance will die a natural death.

Oscar is very amusing as usual but is very abstracted at times. He says that *The Ballad of Reading Gaol* doesn't describe his prison life, but his life at Naples with Bosie and that all the best stanzas were the immediate result of his existence there . . .

Oscar says he will give me full leave to write *your* biography.

It was only when he was alone in his hotel room that Wilde felt depressed and miserable. When he was with his friends, he brightened up and was soon quite like his old self. Nor had he lost the gift of epigram. "A man's face is his autobiography," he told Ross when they met and talked over recent happenings. "A woman's face is her work of fiction."

With some of his old French acquaintances, he was not so much at his ease. Once at this period he was sitting alone outside a café in one of the boulevards and happened to see André Gide walking along with a companion. He hailed them and they came over. Gide purposely took a chair facing Wilde, that is, with his back to the passers-by, whom he was afraid might see him in such company. "Oh, sit here, near me," said Wilde, pointing to a chair next to him. "I am so alone these days."

---

[11] The codicil to Constance's will was admitted as valid by her executors and the allowance continued to be paid through Ross until Wilde's death.

Gide noted that Wilde was still well dressed, but his hat was no longer so glossy, his collar was the same shape but it was no longer so clean, and the sleeves of his frock-coat were slightly frayed. Also, Wilde's gaiety was rather forced. However, he insisted on paying for the round of drinks he had ordered, and as Gide rose to go he took him aside and said to him in a low voice, "Look, you've got to know—I'm absolutely broke." It was to be his constant complaint for the next two years.

5

In his old age Lord Alfred Douglas assured the present writer as an "absolute fact" that it was Robert Ross who "dragged" Wilde back to homosexual practices when they were staying together at Berneval. "Oscar told me this himself one night after dinner in Paris when he had had a great many drinks," Douglas claimed. "I did not mention it in my autobiography because I thought everyone would think I was inventing it to get even with Ross. Also, the idea was so revolting that I preferred not to say anything about it." As for Wilde's last years in Paris, Douglas went on, "the manner of his life there was notorious and he was quite open about it."

> He was hand in glove with all the little boys on the Boulevard. He never attempted to conceal it. Oscar believed, as many other eminent people do, that he had a perfect right to indulge his own tastes. He would not thank you for trying to make people believe it was otherwise. In fact, nothing irritated him more than to meet—as he occasionally did—admirers who refused to believe that he was addicted to the vices for which he was condemned. This used to infuriate him.

When Douglas said this, he had become a sincere convert to the Roman Catholic faith and in consequence had forsworn his former homosexual activities. Otherwise his statement might be regarded as a case of the pot calling the kettle black. In fact, when Douglas arrived in Paris and took a flat in the Avenue Kléber, which Wilde helped him to furnish, he was just as much attracted by the Boulevard boys as Wilde was. For example, Wilde wrote of Douglas in a letter to Ross dated 11 May 1898:

> He is devoted to a dreadful little ruffian aged fourteen, whom he loved because at night, in the scanty intervals he can steal from an arduous criminal profession, he sells bunches of purple violets in front of the Café de la Paix. Also every time he goes home with Bosie he tries to rent him. This, of course, adds to his terrible fascination. We call him the *"Florifer,"* a lovely name. He also keeps another boy aged twelve! whom Bosie wishes to know, but the wise "Florifer" declines.

A few days later, Wilde again wrote to Ross from the Hôtel d'Alsace:

> I hope the £10 for May will arrive soon. I have had to pay my washerwoman and my doctor and some money Bosie lent me.
> Bosie is now furious with me, because when Davray, who is or wishes to

be most respectable, invited me to a café to meet a poet who desired to know me, Bosie turned up ten minutes after my arrival with *Gaston!* of all people, and placed him at Davray's table, where he gabbled about bicycles and was generally offensive. Davray was much annoyed, and so was I. Bosie cannot understand the smallest idea of social tact, and does not see that to thrust "Giton, the boy-paederast" into a literary reunion, without being invited, is vulgar.[12] So life goes on.

Vallette (of the *Mercure*) has ultimately arranged to bring out my poem in volume form at two francs. I fear my only profit will be looking at the daffodil paper cover. They never pay for translations of poems . . .

Wilde and Douglas continued to meet from time to time, but the old spell was broken and they never resumed their former intimacy. Wilde also commented unfavourably on Douglas's peculiar sense of humour. "Bosie has no real enjoyment of a joke unless he thinks there is a good chance of the other person being pained or annoyed," he told Ross at this time. "It is an entirely English trait, the English type and symbol of a joke being the jug on the half-opened door, or the distribution of orange peel on the pavement of a crowded thoroughfare."

After the incident in the café with Davray, Wilde and Douglas made up, and in the following month they spent a week or so together in "a little inn where poor poets go" at Nogent-sur-Marne, since, as Wilde told Smithers, "I dare not go back to my hotel, and at Nogent I have credit." He also told Ross, "It is a lovely place, and we have had some charming days, but Bosie goes up to Paris daily, and only returns for dinner. He goes and sits in his rooms. He says it is absurd to have rooms and not to sit in them."

Although the final break between them did not come for another two years, it is convenient to mention it here. Lord Queensberry died in January 1900 and his third son immediately inherited £8,000 from his estate with the prospect of a further £6,000 to come. "Bosie is over here with his brother," Wilde wrote shortly afterwards from the Hôtel d'Alsace. "They are in deep mourning and the highest spirits. The English are like that." Wilde thought that, in view of everything that had happened, Douglas should now give him a substantial sum, particularly as he had recently had two good wins on the racecourse. What happened when Wilde broached the subject one night after dining with Douglas he described in a letter to Ross:

I asked Bosie what you suggested—without naming any sum at all—after dinner. He had just won £400 at the races, and £800 a few days before, so he was in high spirits. When I spoke to him he went into paroxysms of rage, followed by satirical laughter, and said it was the most monstrous suggestion that he had ever heard, that he would do nothing of the kind, and that he was astounded at my suggesting such a thing, that he did not recognise I had any claim of any kind on him. He was really revolting: I was quite disgusted . . .

It is a most horrible and really heart-breaking affair. When I remember

---

[12] Giton, presumably a pun on Gaston, was the catamite in the *Satyricon* of Petronius.

his letters at Dieppe, his assurances of eternal devotion, his entreaties that I should always live with him, his incessant offers of all his life and belongings, his desire to atone in some way for the ruin he and his family brought on me—well, it sickens me, it gives me nausea.

The affair occurred in the Café de la Paix, so, of course, I made no scene. I said that if he did not recognise my claim there was nothing more to be said . . .

"I can't afford to spend anything except on myself" was one of his observations.

"Bosie I have not seen for a week," wrote Wilde to Ross at the end of June 1900, evidently referring to their dinner at the Café de la Paix. "I feel sure he will do nothing. Boys, brandy, and betting monopolise his soul. He is really a miser: but his method of hoarding is spending: a new type." It was about this time that Ross, who was anxious to obtain Wilde's discharge from bankruptcy, offered Douglas a half share in all future Wilde royalties in return for £800, the sum required to pay off all the remaining creditors in full. But Douglas, to his subsequent regret, refused, possibly because he considered he had contributed and was contributing all he felt he could afford. In fact, as the statements from his bank account show (reproduced in the appendix to his autobiography), Douglas had already given Wilde over £200 since the beginning of the year, and he was to give him nearly £200 more between 30 June and 15 November 1900, the final payment being made during Wilde's last illness. They did not meet again after the argument in the Café de la Paix, since Douglas crossed to England shortly afterwards and did not return to Paris until his erstwhile friend's funeral, the expenses of which, incidentally, he paid.

It should also be mentioned that Wilde's occasional meetings with Douglas after Constance's death, particularly when they stayed together at Nogent-sur-Marne, were one of the factors that caused the breakup of his long-standing friendship with Carlos Blacker. On 27 June 1898, Wilde wrote to Ross from Nogent:

> C. Blacker has behaved like a hypocritical ass to me . . . The comic thing about him is the moral attitude he takes up. To be either a Puritan, a prig, or a preacher is a bad thing. To be all three at once reminds one of the worst excesses of the French Revolution . . . He came down to see me about a fortnight ago, inquired affectionately into my financial position, actually wept floods of tears, begged me to let him pay the balance of my hotel bill—a request that I did not think it right to refuse—and left me with violent protestations of devotion.
>
> A week later he wrote me a Nonconformist conscience letter in which he said that as he did not approve of my knowing Bosie he thought it would be morally wrong of him to help me in any way except by advice! He also added that his wife disapproved of my knowing Bosie!!
>
> So Tartuffe goes out of my life.[13]

---

[13] This passage from the original letter in the Clark Library and another from Wilde's next letter to Ross, quoted below from the same source, in the context of Wilde's relations with Blacker at this time, are omitted by Rupert Hart-Davis in his edition of *The*

Another cause of difference between them arose out of Blacker's interest in the Dreyfus case. In 1894 Captain Alfred Dreyfus had been convicted of betraying military secrets to Germany in the form of a *bordereau* or schedule of documents which he was alleged to have communicated to the German military attaché, Colonel Max von Schwarzkoppen, who ran the German espionage network in France. Unfortunately, the handwriting of the *bordereau* resembled that of Dreyfus, and this largely contributed to his being sent to Devil's Island. Two years later an officer in the ministry, Georges Picquart, became possessed of the fragment of a letter which had been thrown into a wastepaper basket and which proved to have been written (but not sent) by Schwarzkoppen to another French officer, Major Count M. C. F. Walsin-Esterhazy, a dissolute character who was in fact a paid agent of Schwarzkoppen. The discovery was reported to the French General Staff, who hushed up the mistake about Dreyfus. Picquart was transferred to a distant overseas post, but before leaving France, he enlisted the help of a number of influential people including Joseph Reinach, who owned the newspaper *La Libre Parole*. Mathieu Dreyfus wrote to the War Minister accusing Esterhazy of the crime for which his brother had been condemned. As a result, in January 1898, Esterhazy was court-martialled and acquitted. Two days later, Émile Zola published his famous open letter, *J'Accuse*, denouncing the efforts being made to stifle the truth, for which he was sentenced to a year's imprisonment at the instigation of the War Ministry. Meanwhile, the public agitation to free Dreyfus as a victim of a terrible miscarriage of justice continued to be carried on by his supporters, known as the Dreyfusards.

Blacker's connection with the case is somewhat obscure. According to Wilde, he was employed by the Dreyfusards as intermediary between Reinach and Schwarzkoppen, presumably for the purpose of collecting further evidence against Esterhazy. However, it appears that he fell foul of Reinach, since some allegedly discreditable details about his private life appeared in *La Libre Parole* and in another Paris journal. Blacker thought that Wilde had been responsible for supplying the paper with these particulars, but Wilde strongly rebutted this charge. "I need hardly say I never read the paper or saw the attack, and that I never write anonymous attacks on people anywhere," he told Ross. He added that he "was so angry" that he had written Blacker "a very strong letter." At all events, that ended their friendship. The attack also irreparably damaged Blacker's reputation in France.

Shortly after Esterhazy's acquittal, Wilde met him at dinner. "The Commandant was astonishing," he noted afterwards. "Of course he talked of nothing but Dreyfus *et Cie*." Wilde later told Henry Davray that Esterhazy had admitted to being the author of the *bordereau*. "Esterhazy is much more interesting than Dreyfus who is innocent," he

Letters of Oscar Wilde. The careful use made of them by the present writer should not in his opinion cause pain to Blacker's close descendants, the possibility of which led Hart-Davis to omit them.

commented. "One is always wrong to be innocent. To be guilty, one needs imagination and courage . . . But it is a pity that Esterhazy has never gone to prison." Some months later, Wilde dined with the journalist Rowland Strong to meet Esterhazy again, this time with his mistress Marguerite Pays, a registered prostitute known as "Fourfingered Margaret" whom Esterhazy had picked up one night at the Moulin Rouge—"a most charming woman," Wilde called her, "very clever and handsome." Like Esterhazy, she had also been tried and acquitted for lack of evidence. "I am to dine with her and the *Commandant* on Thursday," Wilde added.

About a month later, Rowland Strong published an article in *The Observer* in which he reported that Esterhazy was in London and ready to make startling disclosures, and a week after that he published a long confession in which Esterhazy admitted that he had written the *bordereau*. This was republished in a French version by two of the leading Paris newspapers, *Le Temps* and *Le Figaro*. "Great rows here over Strong's selling Esterhazy's confession," Wilde wrote to Ross at the time. "He is violently attacked by his old *confrères,* and Robert Sherard writes terrific diatribes." Finally, Esterhazy denied everything and threatened *The Observer* with a libel action, which the paper avoided by paying him £500.

Wilde's old friend Sherard had expressed strong anti-Semitic views during the Dreyfus controversy. He had recently created "a horrible scene" at a bar frequented by Wilde and Douglas by shouting *"À bas les juifs"* and insulting and assaulting one of the customers, who he said was a Jew. "The fight continued in the street," Wilde so described the scene to Ross, "and Robert tried to create an Anti-Semite, Anti-Dreyfus demonstration. He succeeded, and was ultimately felled to the ground by the Jew!"

Bosie and I met him at Campbell's [Bar] by chance next day. Campbell told him that the only reason he would consent to serve him was that Bosie and I had shaken hands with him! This rather amused me, when I remember Robert's monstrous moralising about us, and how nobody should know us. Robert looked quite dreadful, all covered with cigar-ash, stains of spilt whiskey, and mud. He was unshaven, and his face in a dreadful state. He had no money, and borrowed a franc from Bosie.

Yesterday he turned up again, and had to receive a rather insolent lecture from Campbell, who told him he preferred Jews to drunkards in his bar. He was much depressed, so of course I gave him drinks and cigarettes and all he wanted. To show his gratitude he insisted on reciting *The Ballad of Reading Gaol* at the top of his voice, and assuring me that I was *"le plus grand maître de la littérature moderne, et le plus grand homme du monde."* At the end he got very tedious, and lest I might love my poem less than I wish to, I went away. Poor Robert, he really is quite insane, and unbearable, except to very old friends who bear much.

"I saw Robert Sherard last night," Wilde wrote to Ross about a year later. "He was very insane and sentimental: wept over a friendship of seventeen years; upon the other hand abused all my friends in the foulest way. I had to stop him in the most peremptory manner. Three times he parted from me, and three times I found him following me to other places. He and Strong have each other on the brain. They think of nothing else. It is a great bore. Robert has lost all his good looks. He was dreadful of aspect last night: quite dreadful." So far as is known, they never met again. At this time Sherard was in somewhat straitened circumstances and was living at Catford, where he had befriended the poet Ernest Dowson, who died in his house. "Poor wounded wonderful fellow that he was," wrote Wilde when he heard the news of Dowson, "a tragic reproduction of all tragic poetry, like a symbol, or a scene. I hope bay-leaves will be placed on his tomb, and rue, and myrtle too, for he knew what love is."

Toward the middle of December 1898, Frank Harris, who had just sold the *Saturday Review* and had acquired a luxury hotel in Monte Carlo, invited Wilde to accompany him to the Riviera. However, Wilde was not accommodated at the Cesari Palace ("I won't go to the Palace because it would not be good for your hotel for me to be seen there") but in a much smaller establishment at Napoule near Cannes. "Frank insists on my being always at high intellectual pressure," he wrote to Ross before leaving Paris. "It is most exhausting; but when we arrive at Napoule I am going to break the news to him—now an open secret—that I have softening of the brain, and cannot always be a genius." He did not see much of Harris, who was busy with his new hotel business, but he saw a good deal of a wealthy young man, named Harold Mellor, who was wintering with his mother in Cannes. According to Wilde, Mellor had been "sent away from Harrow at the age of fourteen for being loved by the captain of the cricket eleven"; he was now about twenty-six, but looked younger. "He has a pretty Italian boy with him," Wilde wrote to Ross on 27 December. "They stayed last night at Napoule, and we had plum-pudding and Mellor ordered Pommery-Greno, so I kept Christmas pleasantly, and Christmas improves by being kept a day. On the real Christmas I dined alone." He went on:

> The fishing population of the Riviera have the same freedom from morals as the Neapolitans have . . .
> I went to Nice the other day, for the afternoon. It was most pretty and gay. I met there a very nice boy whom I knew in Paris, one of the noble army of the Boulevard. He is eighteen, very elegant, and apparently a leader of fashion at Nice. At least he seemed to know everyone, and, on my leaving, accompanied me to the station and borrowed five francs.

Mellor also invited Wilde to Nice as his guest for the night and they went together to see Sarah Bernhardt in *La Tosca*. ("I went round to see Sarah and she embraced me and wept, and I wept, and the whole evening was wonderful.") "I wish to goodness you would come here," he wrote to Ross. "I need you immensely. As regards my marrying again, I am quite sure that you will want me to marry this time some sensible, practical, plain, middle-aged boy, and I don't like the idea at all. Besides I am practically engaged to a fisherman of extraordinary beauty." Incidentally, Mellor's boy was called Eolo, "his father, who sold him to Harold for 200 lire, having christened all his children—seventeen in number—out of the *Mythological Dictionary*. Harold is a nice fellow, but his boy bores him. It is dreadfully sad."

Frank Harris eventually appeared and spent a few days with Wilde at the Hôtel des Baines in Napoule. "Frank Harris is upstairs, thinking about Shakespeare at the top of his voice," Wilde wrote to Ross. "I am earnestly idling." And to Reggie Turner: "Life goes on very pleasantly here. Frank Harris is of course exhausting. After our literary talk in the evening I stagger to my room, bathed in perspiration. I believe he talks the Rugby game."

In February 1899, Harold Mellor took a villa at Gland, on the borders of the Lake of Geneva, bringing Eolo to wait at table and asking Wilde to stay there with him. In the same month, Leonard Smithers published *The Importance of Being Earnest* "by the author of *Lady Windermere's Fan*." It was dedicated "in appreciation in affection" to Robert Ross, whom the author described in his presentation copy to Ross as "the mirror of perfect friendship." Charles Wyndham also received an autographed copy, inscribed "gratefully, admiringly," because unlike George Alexander he had refused to cover up Wilde's name on the playbills of *An Ideal Husband* on its transfer to his theatre on the day after Wilde's arrest. Unfortunately, the appearance of the play in book form passed practically unnoticed by the reviewers. "I am sorry my play is boycotted by the press," Wilde told Ross at the time, "particularly for Smithers's sake; he has shown great pluck in bringing it out at all. However I hope some of the faithful, and all the elect, will buy copies. If you hear anything nice said about the play, write it to me: if not, invent it."

On his way to Mellor's villa in Switzerland, Wilde stopped at Genoa, "where," so he confessed to Reggie Turner, "I met a beautiful young actor, a Florentine, whom I wildly loved. He has the strange name of Didaco. He had the look of Romeo, without Romeo's sadness: a face chiselled for high romance. We spent three days together." He also paid a visit to Constance's grave in the local cemetery at Staglieno above the town, which he described in a letter to Robert Ross:

It is very pretty—a marble cross with dark ivy-leaves inlaid in a good pattern. The cemetery is a garden at the foot of the lovely hills that climb into the mountains that girdle Genoa. It was very tragic seeing her name carved on a tomb—her surname, my name, not mentioned of course—just "Constance Mary, daughter of Horatio Lloyd, Q.C." and a verse from *Revelations*.

The pilgrim had brought some flowers with him, which he laid on the grave. "I was deeply affected—with a sense, also, of the uselessness of all regrets. Nothing could have been otherwise, and Life is a very terrible thing."

6

Wilde suffered another personal loss at this time, although he did not feel it so much as Constance's death. His brother Willie died in London on 13 March 1899, largely as a result of excessive drinking. The news was contained in a telegram from Ross. "I suppose it had been expected for some time," wrote Wilde in thanking Ross for his thoughtfulness in letting him know so promptly. "I am very sorry for his wife, who, I suppose, has little left to live on. Between him and me there had been, as you know, wide chasms for many years. *Requiescat in Pace.*" Until she married Alexander Texeira de Mattos eighteen months later, Lily Wilde was very poor and could not bring up her daughter Dolly without help. "One has always sad memories of what Willie might have been," she wrote to her brother-in-law, "instead of dying practically unknown and leaving his child to be supported by my sister. She is well and happy and I think will have a good share of the family brains."

Wilde spent a month at Gland, but he soon became bored with the place and irritated by his host's meanness. "The villa is pretty and on the borders of the Lake of Geneva with pretty pines about . . . but I don't like Switzerland: it has produced nothing but theologians and waiters . . . I attribute it all to the lack of physical beauty in the race: they are shapeless, colourless: grey of texture, and without form." As for his host, "Mellor is tedious, lacks conversation: also he gives me Swiss wine to drink: it is horrid: he occupies himself with small economies, and mean domestic interests. So I suffer very much. *Ennui* is the enemy." Eventually he left for Genoa at the beginning of April. "It is impossible for me to go to Paris," he told Smithers: "I have not enough money."

I am going to try and find a place near Genoa, where I can live for ten francs a day (boy *compris*). The chastity of Switzerland has got on my nerves. Neither Sporus nor Ganymede treads these fields of snow, and Mellor is too repulsive for anything. When I got your fiver, I had no money at all, and asked him to lend me three francs to go into Geneva with. He declined, on the ground that he made it a rule never *to lend money* to anyone! I had to get my railway fare from the cook! On my return, to a dreary dinner with Swiss beer, he told me that he did not like people borrowing money from his servants!

On the other hand, when I told him I was going away, he went into floods of tears, and said that all his friends deserted him!

Mellor literally wept at Wilde's departure, apologized, and implored him to stay, but Wilde refused. "However, we parted amicably on my side, and on his with protestations of admiration and remorse." After what he called "the chill virginity of Swiss Alps and snow," Wilde longed for "the red flowers of life that stain the feet of summer in Italy." But all he found was a room above a small restaurant at Santa Margherita, a few miles beyond Nervi on the Ligurian coast where Constance had stayed, and where he soon felt ill and lonely. "Whatever I do is wrong, because my life is not on a right basis," he appealed to Ross. "In Paris I am bad: here I am bored. The last state is the worse. I wish I could see you. A few days with you would be a tonic." Ross responded by coming to Genoa and taking him back to Paris. He afterwards told their mutual friend Adela Schuster that he noticed that Wilde was now drinking more alcohol than was good for him, although he never bore outward signs of it. "In fact owing to his extraordinary constitution he was able (unfortunately perhaps) to take a great deal too much without being affected . . . When I was with him in Genoa in the spring of 1899, just after his brother's death, I managed to frighten him so much on the subject that he quite reformed for six months. Had circumstances permitted me to be with him more than I was, I might have done something with him as he liked being ordered about by people whom he knew were fond of him."

Wilde did not immediately return to the Hôtel d'Alsace, possibly because his old room there was not available. He spent a somewhat aimless summer in various other small hotels in Paris, and when his credit ran out there he moved to La Varenne on the Marne and later to Le Havre and other places on the Normandy coast in search no doubt of congenial company. In August he was back in the Hôtel d'Alsace, begging Smithers to let him have £10, the amount of his next month's allowance. "Robbie cannot himself advance it, and I have no money at all. I am in a dreadful state, as all my clothes are at the Hôtel Marsollier, where I owe a bill. I am really in the gutter . . . Since Sunday I have only had seven francs to live on." It was Jean Dupoirier, the kindhearted *patron* of the Hôtel d'Alsace, who paid Wilde's bill at the other hotel and enabled him to recover his clothes. "Dear Monsieur Melmoth," Dupoirier would say, "he tells such wonderful stories—and always has a pleasant word for one."

Wilde got a little more money from his eccentric publisher Smithers on the publication of *An Ideal Husband* in July 1899. This was dedicated to Frank Harris as "a slight tribute to his power and distinction as an artist, his chivalry and nobility as a friend." In seeking Harris's permission to do this, Wilde wrote to him: "I look back with joy and regret to the lovely sunlight of the Riviera, and the charming winter you so generously and kindly gave me: it was most good of you; nor can it ever be forgotten by me." What he really thought of Harris was more accurately reflected by what he wrote about him as the editor of the *Saturday Review:* "Frank Harris has no feelings. It is the secret of his success. Just as the fact that he thinks other people have none is the secret of the failure that lies in wait for him somewhere on the way of Life."

Except for a few days in hospital and about two months the following spring when he revisited Italy and Switzerland with Harold Mellor, to whom he had become reconciled, the Hôtel d'Alsace was to be Wilde's last earthly home. Here he had a room on the first floor, reached by a spiral staircase and overlooking the small courtyard at the back, where Wilde would sometimes sit reading Balzac and sipping absinthe or *fine à l'eau*. Besides the large bed, which was said to be a few inches too small for him, the bedroom furniture consisted of a mirror into which he rarely looked, a threadbare sofa, some built-in bookshelves, and a small table on which he used to write.[14] On the mantelpiece stood a clock of metal and marble ornamented by the figure of a crouching lion, and the wallpaper had a motif of large magenta flowers. "Decidedly one of us will have to go," he said on one occasion.

Few people came to see him here. But one of them was his old friend Robert Sherard, who was now in as bad a financial way as Wilde. Seeing writing materials on the table during one of his visits, Sherard congratulated Wilde on taking up literary work again. But he only wrote letters now, said Wilde. "One has to do something . . . It is a penance for me; but, as was said of torture, it always helps to pass an hour or two." A Radley schoolboy named Louis Wilkinson had started a correspondence with him at this time by pretending to dramatize *Dorian Gray*. "His photograph, which he has sent me, and sends me constantly, is most beautiful," Wilde told Reggie Turner. "He seems to read nothing but my books, and says his one desire is to 'follow in my footsteps'! But I have told him that they lead to terrible places."

In one letter which he wrote to Wilkinson from the Hôtel d'Alsace in January 1900, Wilde explained how he had come to use the name Sebastian Melmoth, after he had heard that Wilkinson might be coming to Paris after he left school:

> So you are coming abroad. I think it is an admirable idea. Radley had nothing left to teach you, though you could have taught it much: did so, no doubt.
>
> I fear you would not like my hotel. I live here because I have no money ever. It is an absurd place: it is not a background: the only really nice thing in the whole hotel is your own photograph: but one cannot, or one should not, play Narcissus to a photograph: even water is horribly treacherous: the eyes of one who loves one are the only mirror.
>
> You asked me about "Melmoth": of course I have not changed my name: in Paris I am as well known as in London: it would be childish. But to prevent postmen having fits I sometimes have my letters inscribed by the name of a curious novel by my grand-uncle Maturin: a novel that was part of the romantic revival of the early century, and though imperfect, a pioneer: it is still read in France and Germany: Bentley republished it some years ago. I laugh at it, but it thrilled Europe, and is played as a play in modern Spain.

Wilde's health now began to show signs of deterioration, although he remained on the whole in good spirits, judging by his letters. He had only celebrated his forty-fifth birthday the previous October. An illness which he had in February, and for which he spent ten days in hospital, he attributed to food poisoning. "I am very ill and the doctor is making

[14] At a sale of some of the hotel effects shortly before the First World War, the table was bought by Richard Le Gallienne, who happened to be passing along the Rue des Beaux Arts at the time. Le Gallienne showed it to the present writer in his apartment at Menton shortly before his death in 1947. Its present whereabouts are unknown.

all kinds of experiments," he told Ross, who had invited him to stay with him in Rome. "My throat is a lime kiln, my brain a furnace and my nerves a coil of angry adders." He went on to explain that for the last four months he had been a neurasthenic, "quite unable to get out of bed till the afternoon, and quite unable to write letters of any kind."

My doctor has been trying to cure me with arsenic and strychnine but without much success, as I became poisoned through eating mussels, so you see what an exacting and tragic life I am leading. Poisoning by mussels is very painful and when one has one's bath one looks like a leopard. Pray never eat mussels.

The skin rash which was a symptom of Wilde's illness has been regarded as a manifestation of his syphilis, but according to the latest informed medical opinion it is much more likely to have been an allergy or a dermatitis secondary to a vitamin deficiency as the result of his drinking. It was to recur intermittently until his death.

During his illness he was visited by an Anglo-French youth, named Maurice Gilbert, who saw a lot of him at this period. "I've shared all my medicines with him, shown him what little hospitality I can," wrote Wilde. Gilbert also acted as part-time secretary to Rowland Strong. When Wilde was recovering, Gilbert went to spend a few days with Reggie Turner in London, so as to see Queen Victoria driving through cheering crowds celebrating the relief of Ladysmith, which had been besieged by the Boers. "I suppose Maurice has by this time arrived," Wilde, who was still in bed, wrote to Turner early in March. "Of course his place was by my side, as I am very ill, but he longed to see the Queen, so I gave in. He has been most sweet and kind to me, quite a darling boy, and looked after me in every way." He added in his old lighthearted vein: "I hear you volunteered for the front at 5 a.m. at the [Hôtel] Cecil, intoxicated by Bosie and Perrier-Jouet '89, but subsequently felt that duty called you to stay in the Fleet Street Kopje. Quite right—the pen is more dangerous than the sword."

He had recovered by the middle of March, since he told Charles Wyndham, to whom he wrote for an advance on a play he hoped to write for him, that he was anxious to get away from his hotel "as soon as I can pay them, and go into the country." Fortunately, Harold Mellor reappeared at this point, with what result he gleefully told Ross:

Mellor, with whom I am friends (below zero of course) has invited me to go to Italy to the extent of £50! When that gives out I shall have to walk home, but as I want to see you I have consented to go, and hope to be in Rome in about ten days. It will be delightful to be together again, and this time I really must become a Catholic, though I fear that if I went before the Holy Father with a blossoming rod it would turn at once into an umbrella or something dreadful of that kind. It is absurd to say that the age of miracles is past. It has not yet begun.

From Paris they went directly to Palermo, where they spent eight days, making frequent visits to the cathedral and cloisters of Monreale, where Wilde picked up a fifteen-year-old seminarist named Giuseppe Loverde. Asked by Wilde why he was entering the Church, Giuseppe gave a "singularly medieval" reason. "My father is a cook and most poor," he said, "and we are many at home, so it seemed to me a good thing that there should be in so small a house as ours one mouth less to feed, for, though I am slim, I eat much: too much, alas, I fear."

I told him to be comforted, because God used poverty as a means of bringing people to Him, and used riches never, or but rarely. So Giuseppe was comforted, and I gave him a little book of devotion, very pretty, and with far more pictures than prayers in it; so of great service to Giuseppe, whose eyes are beautiful. I also gave him many *lire,* and prophesied for him a Cardinal's hat, if he remained very good and never forgot me. He said he never would: and indeed I don't think he will, for every day I kissed him behind the high altar.

The letter to Ross, from which the foregoing is an extract, was written from Rome on Easter Monday 1900. In it Wilde went on:

At Naples we stopped three days. Most of my friends are, as you know, in prison, but I met some of nice memory, and fell in love with a Sea-God, who for some extraordinary reason is at the Regia Marina school instead of being with a Triton.

We came to Rome on Holy Thursday. H[arold] M[ellor] left on Saturday for Gland, and yesterday, to the terror of Grissell [the Papal Chamberlain] and all the Papal Court, I appeared in the front rank of the pilgrims in the Vatican, and got the blessing of the Holy Father [Pope Leo XIII]—a blessing they would have denied me.

He was wonderful, as he was carried past me on his throne, not of flesh and blood, but a white soul robed in white, and an artist as well as a saint— the only instance in History, if the newspapers are to be believed.

I have seen nothing like the extraordinary grace of his gesture, as he rose, from moment to moment, to bless—possibly the pilgrims, but certainly me . . .

How did I get a ticket? By a miracle, of course, I thought it was hopeless, and made no effort of any kind. On Saturday afternoon at five o'clock Harold and I went to have tea at the Hôtel de l'Europe. Suddenly, as I was eating buttered toast, a man, or what seemed to be one, dressed like a hotel porter, entered and asked me would I like to see the Pope on Easter Day. I bowed my head humbly and said *"Non sum dignus,"* or words to that effect. He at once produced a ticket!

When I tell you that his countenance was of supernatural ugliness, and that the price of the ticket was thirty pieces of silver, I need say no more.

"By the way, did I tell you that on Easter Sunday I was completely cured of my mussel-poisoning?" he wrote to Ross in a later letter. "It is true, and I always knew I would be. Five months under a Jewish physician at Paris not merely did not heal me but made me worse: the blessing of the Vicar of Christ made me whole."

Ross could manage only a few days with Wilde in Rome ("Do you observe that I have fallen in love with you again? Our Indian winter"), as he could not leave his mother for long. Wilde talked to his friend about becoming a Catholic, but Ross, who was himself a Catholic, told him that he should never attempt his conversion until he thought he was serious, the difficulty being that Wilde was never quite sure himself where and when he was serious. Furthermore, Ross did not know any priest in Rome sufficiently well "for a rather grave intellectual conflict," since Wilde was well equipped for controversy, being deeply read in Catholic philosophy. Later Ross reproached himself for not making the effort to find a suitable priest to undertake his conversion, but he did not think Wilde was "quite serious" and he dreaded a relapse, since he had known many people under the influence of sudden impulse, aesthetic or other emotion, becoming converts and then causing grave scandal by lapsing. "I need hardly say," Ross afterwards told Adela Schuster, "he made a good story out of his stay with me in Rome, and told people that whenever he wanted to be a Catholic I stood at the door with a flaming sword which only turned in *one* direction and prevented him from entering." At the same time, Wilde explained how he stood to More Adey: "My position is curious: I am not a Catholic: I am simply a violent Papist. No one could be more 'black' than I am. I have given up bowing to the King. I need say no more."

He wrote to Adey from a tiny café in front of the Fontana Trevi: "The sound of the waters is wonderful: it soothes: it has *catharsis*. Robbie left me a legacy of a youthful guide, who knows nothing about Rome. Omero is his name, and I am showing him Rome."

Omero was succeeded in Wilde's affections by Dario, "a new friend," whom Wilde presented with a ticket to see the Pope. "I like his name so much," he told Ross: "it was the first time he had ever seen the Pope: and he transferred to me his adoration of the successor of Peter: would I fear have kissed me on leaving the Bronze Gateway had I not sternly repelled him. I have become very cruel to boys, and no longer let them kiss me in public."

When he left the Eternal City, Ross gave Wilde a cheque which enabled him to stay on there for several weeks. Wilde had recently taken up photography as a hobby, and it is to this that we owe the interesting snapshots taken of him in Naples and Rome at this time and reproduced in this book. On 21 April, he wrote to Ross from Rome with an account of his doings since Ross's departure:

> I have not seen the Holy Father since Thursday, but am bearing up wonderfully well. I am sorry to say he has approved of a dreadful handkerchief, with a portrait of himself in the middle, and basilicas at the corners. It is very curious the connection between Faith and bad art: I feel it myself . . .
>
> I have been three times to see the great Velásquez of the Pamfili Pope: it is quite the grandest portrait in the world. The entire man is there.[15] I also go to look at that voluptuous marble boy I went to worship with you at the Museo Nazionale. What a lovely thing it is!
>
> I have given up Armando, a very smart elegant young Sporus. He was

[15] Giovanni Battista Pamfili, whose pontificate as Pope Innocent X lasted from 1644 until his death in 1655. His portrait by Velásquez is in the Doria Palace in Rome.

beautiful, but his requests for neckties and raiment were incessant: he really bayed for boots, as a dog moonwards. I now like Arnaldo: he was Armando's greatest friend, but the friendship is over. Armando is *un invidioso* apparently, and is suspected of having stolen a lovely covert-coat in which he patrols the Corso. The coat is so delightful, and he looks so handsome in it, that, although the coat wasn't mine, I have forgiven him the theft . . .

Rome is burning with heat: really terrible: but at 4:30 I am going to the Borghese [Gardens], to look at daisies, and drink milk: the Borghese milk is as wonderful as the Borghese daisies. I also intend to photograph Arnaldo. By the way, can you photograph cows well? I did one of the cows in the Borghese so marvellous that I destroyed it: I was afraid of being called the modern Paul Potter. Cows are very fond of being photographed, and, unlike architecture, don't move.

I propose to go to Orvieto tomorrow: I have never seen it, and I must revisit Tivoli. How long I shall stay here I don't know—a fortnight perhaps.

At the same time, he wrote to Mellor in Gland proposing himself for a visit. Mellor replied on 24 April: "Thanks for your words from the wicked little café . . . You shall come here when you leave Italy and stay for a fortnight before going to Paris . . . My new big house is quite delightful. Eolo is very naughty. And you I suppose are and always will be both."

On 14 May, Wilde wrote again to Ross to say that he was leaving next day for Naples, "thence by boat to Genoa, thence to Chambéry, where Harold Mellor awaits me, or should do, with his automobile— and so to Paris. I suppose one of us will arrive safely; I hope it will be me." He went on:

Rome has quite absorbed me. I must winter here; it is the only city of the soul. I have been to Albano, and Nemi, and Tivoli, and seen much of the French painter Armand Point, who is really a dear fellow, gay and romantic, simple and intellectually subtle, with an inordinate passion for beauty in its most complete expression, and an inordinate love of life.

My photographs are now so good that in my moments of mental depression (alas! not rare) I think that I was intended to be a photographer. But I shake off the mood, and know that I was made for more terrible things of which colour is an element.

Today I bade goodbye, with tears and one kiss, to the beautiful Greek boy who was found in my garden—I mean Nero's garden. He is the nicest boy you ever introduced to me.

In the mortal sphere I have fallen in and out of love, and fluttered hawks and doves alike. How evil it is to buy Love, and how evil to sell it! And yet what purple hours one can snatch from that grey slowly-moving thing we call Time! My mouth is twisted with kissing, and I feed on fevers. The Cloister or the Café—there is my future. I tried the Hearth, but it was a failure.

7

Wilde reached Switzerland safely, and after spending ten days at Gland he and Mellor motored to Paris. "The automobile was delightful, but, of course, it broke down," he reported to Ross on his arrival. "They, like all machines, are more wilful than animals—nervous, irritable, strange things." He added that he was going to write an article on "nerves in the inorganic world."

Wilde now resumed his old life on the boulevards, enlivened by the company of Frank Harris and other old English friends who had come over to see the great Exhibition which had opened near the Eiffel Tower and was attracting masses of visitors that summer.

> Frank Harris is very wonderful and really very good and *sympathique.* He always comes two hours late for meals, but in spite of that is delightful. He keeps Bosie in order: clearly the age of miracles is not over. The only ugly thing at the Exhibition is the public. The most beautiful modern picture is Shannon's picture of himself.[16] I have gone several times to see it.

When he was on his own, he would stroll along the quais, stopping at a little restaurant in the Rue Jacob for a meal. ("Nothing is so fattening as a dinner at 1 fr. 50," he used to say.) [17] Afterwards he would walk on to the Cours-la-Reine entrance to the Exhibition; this was surmounted by a gigantic statue of a Parisienne which reminded him of Sarah Bernhardt, "that serpent of the old Nile, older than the Pyramids." Inside, he particularly liked the Café de l'Égypte, where "a slim brown Egyptian, rather like a handsome bamboo walking stick," served him with drinks.

He wrote again to Ross about the end of June:

> Smithers appeared here with his new mistress. She is quite clean and charmingly dressed. We went to the Exhibition one night. Mellor was with me. He doesn't like Mellor . . . he [Smithers] is a pleasant, plausible *ruffiano:* and one touch of comedy sends morality and moralising sky-high . . .
>
> I dined with Vincent O'Sullivan last night: he was really very pleasant for one who treats life from the standpoint of the tomb. He was much amused at my asking him where Walter Pollock was "taking" the whiskies and waters now.[18]

Maurice Gilbert also turned up again and they spent two evenings together at the Exhibition. "He was pale, and sweet, and gentle," Wilde told Ross. "He now forms part of a *ménage à trois:* none of the members sleep: the girl—a rose-like thing I hope—lies in the middle, and knows the pleasure and insecurity of the *Via Media.* Maurice won't tell me the name of the other partner, but admits he has a slight mous-

---

[16] The self-portrait known as "A Man in a Black Shirt" was painted in 1897 and is now in the National Portrait Gallery.

[17] The restaurant at 42 Rue Jacob was kept by a couple named Bechet, and "Monsieur Sebastien," as Wilde was known to the *patron* and his wife, had a special table reserved for him with the other regular clients who ate on the first floor. A pathetic incident occurred when Wilde was asked by a child whom his parents had brought to the restaurant whether he had any boys, and replied in French that they did not come with him "because they were too far away," after which he broke down and sobbed in English, "Oh, my poor dear boys!"

[18] W. H. Pollock (1850–1928), author, poet, and journalist, edited the *Saturday Review* for eleven years before it was taken over by Frank Harris in 1894.

tache. He does odd jobs for Strong and quarrels with him incessantly. I find I am very fond of Maurice still. He is a dear fellow."

To honour the sixty-year-old sculptor Auguste Rodin, the city of Paris erected at its own expense a special pavilion near one of the entrances to the Exhibition, in which almost all the artist's works were displayed, including the incomplete "Portal of Hell." Wilde was entranced by "all his great dreams in marble," and described Rodin as "by far the greatest poet in France," who had, "as I was glad to tell myself, completely outshone Victor Hugo," whose celebrated etching by Rodin was also on view. In spite of the public, Wilde found the Exhibition "very delightful" and all the old works of art "quite wonderful."

It was during one of these visits to the Exhibition that Wilde was recognized in the American pavilion, where one of the stands was devoted to the inventions of Thomas Edison. One of these inventions was the "phonograph or speaking machine," and Wilde was asked to say something into the horn of the recording mechanism. He responded by reciting Part VI of *The Ballad of Reading Gaol,* which consists of the last three stanzas of the poem, and identifying it with his name at the end. The recording, which lasted a little more than two minutes, was made on a wax cylinder. Fortunately, it survived along with other Edison memorabilia and to it we owe the preservation of the only recording ever made of Wilde's voice. To anyone hearing it for the first time, the result is unexpected. The voice is plummy and somewhat affected, but with no trace of an Irish brogue, though with unmistakeable Irish inflexions, of which the most marked is the tendency to accentuate the final syllable of words in contrast to the English habit of stressing the first or penultimate syllable, and also to raise the pitch when pronouncing the final word of a line or verse.

More than most of Wilde's contemporaries at this time, Vincent O'Sullivan had opportunities of observing Wilde during the last two or three years of his life. His short *Aspects of Wilde,* which he was to publish many years later, is one of the most perceptive pieces of writing on Wilde at this period and indeed is indispensable for all students of Wilde's life. In this work O'Sullivan points out that Wilde suffered from loneliness—not so much from physical as from moral loneliness, which in turn was the result of Wilde's habit of keeping disreputable company in disreputable places.

Physical loneliness he could not stand, and so to avoid it he seized any measures that offered. So did he take to frequenting a little bar on the Boulevard des Italiens with the absurd name Kalisaya—a place he would never have dreamed of entering in his best days. There he could always find someone to talk to, were it only the bar-tender, and there he did often find a clever and erratic journalist named Ernest La Jeunesse.[19] Wilde's resorting to

---

[19] Ernest La Jeunesse (1874–1917) was a dedicated boulevardier who dressed in bohemian style and had once been Anatole France's secretary. In 1899, he published a book on Napoleon which "greatly fascinated" Wilde. He also published some brief recollections of Wilde in the *Revue Blanche* (15 December 1900) and in his book *Cinq Ans chez les Sauvages* (1901).

this place did him harm with the censorious: they accused him of lack of dignity and counted up the number of whiskeys-and-sodas he absorbed daily.

But what was he to do? The censorious took care not to invite him to their houses, took care, in fact, not to show any interest in him whatever save a malevolent interest. He went to places like the Kalisaya driven by the instinct of self-preservation. He knew he would go mad if he sat alone with his bitter thoughts. Besides, where was he to sit? In the little room of his hotel with the thousand horrible noises of the cheap hotel? As well be back in his prison cell. Nobody would have come to see him there; he would be as one who had gone down among the dead . . .

But for his moral loneliness there was no remedy bad or good. Except Frank Harris, who did not see him very often or for long spells, there was nobody to whom he could talk of the people and things in his past life which really interested him. Of the other English he saw, some like Leonard Smithers were in a different sphere of life and would not have understood, others were too young—not of his own period . . .

This moral loneliness of his I did not think of at all at the time, but I have since come to realise that it must have been heavy. Practically all the French who considered themselves important, young or old or middle-aged, avoided him.

After the publication of his book in 1936, O'Sullivan was consulted by A. J. A. Symons, who himself was planning to write a biography of Wilde, a project which never progressed beyond a couple of chapters. In particular, Symons asked about a statement he had come across in one of Smithers's letters which suggested that something Smithers had heard from O'Sullivan about Wilde's way of life at this time was slanderous. O'Sullivan provided Symons with an explanation in the form of a letter, which should be read as supplementing the account given above. The letter, hitherto unpublished, bears no date, but it was probably written in 1938, when Symons was beginning his researches.[20]

> . . . Wilde, as you know, if you have read André Gide's book or Lemonnier's, was shunned in his last days by all his erstwhile French friends.[21] Pierre Louÿs, Retté, Henri de Régnier, Stuart Merrill, Marcel Schwob, André Gide, even Jean Lorrain who was known to have the same vice as himself—all avoided him. As for the general public, Lemonnier is right in saying that he was only tolerated in Paris; he was never welcomed there.
>
> Several of those I have mentioned were willing to see Wilde and even to help him on condition that he would live discreetly in a retired way in Paris or in the country. He could not live in a provincial town; the town authorities would not have had him at any price. Schwob, Merrill and some others were constantly begging me to get Wilde's English friends to make him realise that he was ruining what sympathy was left for him by showing himself drunk on the Boulevards in such a place as the Kalisaya Bar with sodomist outcasts, who were sometimes even dangerous in other ways.[22]

[20] The original is in the Clark Library.

[21] André Gide's *In Memoriam* was originally published in 1901 (English translation, 1905). Léon Lemonnier's *Vie d'Oscar Wilde* appeared in 1931 but has not been translated.

[22] "Kalisaya, the American Bar near the Crédit Lyonnais, is now the literary resort of myself and my friends," Wilde wrote to Ross in December 1898: "and we all gather there at 5 o'clock—Moréas, and La Jeunesse, and all the young poets. One beautiful boy of bad character—of the name of Georges—goes there too, but he is so like An-

Although I refrained as much as possible from expressing any opinion about Wilde's mode of life, I perhaps did mention what Merrill and the others had said when I was talking to Smithers, and he was a kind of man who would call it a "slander." He knew nothing whatever of the higher life of Paris; he hardly spoke French and knew no more about Paris than a Margate tripper who goes to Paris on a week-end ticket. In his visits to Paris, which never extended to more than 3 or 4 days, he never saw anybody capable of giving him the general opinion of the better people about Wilde. You may think Dowson could have done so; but Dowson was by that time in too degraded a state himself and lived in too squalid a way (Wilde was *never* squalid) to realise anything else. Besides he hardly ever saw Wilde, and was as indifferent to Wilde's mode of life as I was myself. We were both too young to speak to Wilde personally on the subject even if we had wanted to.

"Smithers was not a man to see anything particularly objectionable in some of Wilde's actions in Paris in his last days," O'Sullivan added in a postscript to this letter. "It was hard for him to understand *why* the young Frenchmen should object. I think myself they were rather priggish; but then they had their careers to make and Wilde knew his career was over." Jean Lorrain, for example, was told by the morning newspaper for which he wrote, and from which he derived a good income, that he would be discharged if he published a single line in defence of Wilde. And it was Lorrain who some years previously had refused to shake hands with Wilde when they met at Stéphane Mallarmé's. "You are not one of my friends," said Lorrain on that occasion. "Ah, my dear Jean, you are right," Wilde replied. "When one leads the life that you and I lead, one no longer has friends—one only has lovers!" The attitude of the others, as O'Sullivan put it, was described in the phrase of one of them: *"Je ne fréquente pas les forçats."*

Some of the English who came to Paris at this time actually accused Wilde of extravagance. "He can't be badly off," they would say. "Look what he spends on drink. And he always takes cabs." It was further said that he was always well dressed, and this is certainly borne out by his photographs.

"It is sorrowful to dwell on such disgusting charges" was O'Sullivan's comment. "Wilde was not a man to be slovenly if he could avoid it. It is a matter of temperament. By all accounts Edgar Allan Poe and Baudelaire in their most desperate hours were always neat. As for his drinking, if he had drunk fifty times as much as he did, who would grudge it to him if it relieved even for an hour the pressure of his misery? He was obliged to take cabs because he suffered from a painful malady. This he did not tell me himself: he never, so far as I know, complained of the state of his health. In that and some other matters he had the style of the

tinous, and so smart, that he is allowed to talk to poets. One of the poets was the intimate friend of Émile Henry, the young anarchist who was guillotined under Carnot, and he has told me wonderful things about him and his life." Henry and a confederate were condemned for throwing a bomb into the Chamber of Deputies when it was sitting. In revenge another anarchist, an Italian named Cesario, assassinated President Carnot in 1894.

eighteenth century." O'Sullivan sometimes wondered why he did not stay in Italy and "by what reasoning he persuaded himself to come back to Paris. One reason, no doubt, was that it was easier for close friends such as Ross to see him in Paris. But in Italy he would have lived longer, and, I should think, happier . . . Wilde endured too much cruelty in the Paris of his time; he received too many wounds, hardly ever resented them openly, but finally died of them."

Sometimes he was recognized by visiting Englishmen with unhappy results. Once, after he had been shaved in a barber's shop on the Boulevards and had vacated his chair, the barber cried, "Next, please." The next customer, who happened to be English, said to the barber in a loud voice, so that all the other waiting customers could plainly hear, "If you wish to shave me, you must give me another chair, for I won't sit in the same place as that fellow who has just got up. That is Oscar Wilde!" Describing the incident to Robert Sherard afterwards, Wilde told him, "I staggered as though I had been shot, and I went reeling out into the street like a drunken man."

Some old friends whom Wilde had known in England deliberately sought him out and invited him to lunch or dinner. But these occasions were not invariably happy ones. Laurence Housman, who has recaptured Wilde's table talk in his *Echo de Paris,* describes a meeting outside a restaurant near the Place de l'Opéra in September 1899 at which Ross and Henry Davray were also present. The other invited guest, whose real name Housman does not reveal, was unaware that Wilde was going to be there until he recognized him in the distance; he then abruptly departed, unnoticed by anyone else except Wilde himself, who eventually followed suit.

In the same month Will Rothenstein visited Paris with his wife, Charles Conder, and Augustus John, then barely twenty-one. Wilde dined several times with Rothenstein and the others, including young John, who found it difficult to say much in the presence of "the Master," remembering Wilde's quip that "little boys should be obscene and not heard." On the last occasion Wilde proposed dining in an open-air restaurant. He chose a table near the musicians; he liked being near the music, he said. But during dinner it was plain to his host that he was less interested in the music than in one of the players. Rothenstein was annoyed and resolved not to see him again. "I have heard nothing from you, so I suppose you are busy," Wilde wrote a week or so later from the Kalisaya Bar. "Do let us meet before you leave. My kindest regards to your dear wife, and also to the charming Celtic poet in colour," as he called young John.

They do not appear to have met again during this visit. Nor did Rothenstein let Wilde know when he and his wife next came to Paris, which was for the Exhibition the following summer. But on their very first evening, they met Wilde on the Boulevards. "I saw at once that he knew we had meant to avoid him," Rothenstein afterwards recalled. "The look he gave us was tragic, and he seemed ill, and was shabby and down at heel. Of course we asked him to join us. He came in a chastened mood, and made himself very charming, but his gaiety no longer convinced; there was a stricken look in his eyes, and he plainly depended on drink to sustain his wit." Describing Wilde's appearance many years later to Harold Nicolson, Rothenstein also recalled that he had a red face, grey lips, and very bad teeth. "He was so ashamed of his teeth that he used to put his hand over them when he spoke, giving an odd furtive expression to his jokes."

"I have been with Harold Mellor at Gland," Wilde reported to Ross at the end of August. "He is almost as neurasthenic as I am: but there was the automobile. I had to consult a specialist before I left Paris, I was so ill: but it seems that not 'mussels' but neurasthenia were the cause of my illness, which had returned with renewed violence." A few days later, on 1 September, he wrote again, thanking Ross for a cheque and going on:

> Your letter is very maddening: nothing about yourself: no details, and yet you know I love middle-class tragedies, and the little squabbles that build up family life in England . . .
> The "Mellor" cure was dull, but I got better. He is now in Paris with his slave Eolo, who like all slaves is most tyrannical. He and I, however, are great friends. I think Harold is on the verge of acute melancholia. At present he has almost arrived at total abstinence—drinks and talks mineral waters. I like people who talk wine.[23]
> So Bosie is in London: where is he staying? Do you think he has really spent all his money? It is a great pity if he has. How is dear More? And Reggie? Paris is full of second-rate tourists. German and American are the only languages one hears. It is dreadful.

Wilde was by no means as poor as he liked to make out. He had received about £500 since the beginning of the year over and above his monthly allowance of £12 10s paid by his wife's trustees through Ross—£400 from Douglas and £100 from George Alexander in respect of fees from theatrical performances. He may also have had something from Tree, who wrote to him about fees from a performance of *A Woman of No Importance,* saying that he had asked Alexander to send on other fees. "I am indeed glad, and we shall all be, to know that you are determined to resume your dramatic work," Tree added in his kind letter, "for no one did such distinguished work as you. It has been rumoured that you had already finished some play, but I suppose that was not true. I do most sincerely hope that good luck may come to you and that your splendid talents may shine forth again. I have a lively remembrance of your many acts of kindness and courtesy and was one of those who devoutly hoped that misfortune would not submerge you."

At the time of Wilde's bankruptcy, Alexander had been able to acquire the performing rights to *Lady Windermere's Fan* and *The Importance of Being Earnest* for a small sum. Although he knew that he could not put them on with any chance of a satisfactory return for some time, he

[23] Mellor eventually committed suicide in his villa at Cannes, aged fifty-seven, in 1925.

also realized that he had two potentially valuable properties which were bound to appreciate in value if he kept them long enough. He felt too that he should make Wilde some voluntary payments on account of them, although there was no legal obligation upon him to do so. No doubt it was at Ross's suggestion that these payments should be made monthly for the next twelve months, through Ross instead of in a lump sum, as indeed he told Wilde when they met in Paris during the summer of 1900. Afterwards Wilde wrote from the Hôtel d'Alsace to Alexander, whom he was delighted to see "so well and so unchanged."

> It was really a great pleasure to see you again, and to receive your friendly grasp of the hand after so many years. Nor shall I forget your dear wife's charming and affectionate greeting of me. I know how to value things like that.
> With regard to your proposal to spread the payment for the plays over a certain time, I know it was dictated by sheer kindness and the thoughtfulness of an old friend.
> If you would send Robert Ross £20 on the first of every month for me it would be a great boon. He would send it to me, as he looks after all my affairs . . . I would then have a year free from worry, and perhaps may do something you would like. Could you do this for me?

Nevertheless, Wilde continued to write his friends begging letters, pleading poverty. For instance, he wrote to George Ives on 6 September asking for the loan of £10 against his next month's allowance: "I am in great worry and annoyance over money, the price of my rooms has been doubled owing to the Exhibition, and my landlord presses me." Ives promptly obliged by sending notes in a registered letter, as Wilde asked. (It is almost certain that the price of his room was not doubled, nor was the patient Dupoirier pressing him unduly.) Three days after getting the money from Ives, he wrote in a similar strain to Frank Harris: "My *propriétaire* is worrying me to distraction to pay my bill, or part of it. Could you send me £20? I am quite without a sou, and I must give the landlord £15. I suppose this is a great bore to you, but really I don't know what to do."

It will be recalled that during the summer of 1894, when he was staying with his family at Worthing, Wilde had written the scenario for a play which he provisionally entitled *Mr and Mrs Daventry*. He had been unable to write any of the play before his imprisonment, but after his release his thoughts reverted to the subject, and although he wrote little if any of it, he was able to raise money on the scenario from various people, including Tree, Alexander, Ada Rehan, Leonard Smithers, and Frank Harris. With Harris he apparently went further than with the others, since he told him that he could write it himself if he wished. This Harris proceeded to do, and by the early autumn of 1900 he had made plans to put it on at the Royalty Theatre, London, with Mrs Patrick Campbell in the part of Mrs Daventry.[24] When Wilde heard of

---

[24] The script of *Mr and Mrs Daventry* could not be traced for many years; even the copy in the Lord Chamberlain's office had disappeared. Eventually the present writer discovered Mrs Patrick Campbell's acting version in the Gabriel Enthoven collection in the

this, he asked Harris for some more money on account of the royalties, and Harris crossed over from London to see Wilde, in order to conclude the matter. They met towards the end of September, when Harris gave Wilde £25 in cash as an advance, with the promise of a further £175 to be paid within a week in addition to one quarter share of the profits from the production, in return for Wilde's assigning "the entire rights in the plot and scenario." According to Wilde, Harris was unable to pay the balance of the agreed advance of £200 on the spot as he had forgotten to bring his cheque book with him from London, an excuse which Wilde claimed to see through and for which he later reproached him. "It is difficult to imagine you living in Paris, in the style and luxury that you are accustomed to, without a cheque book! I don't suppose you are like President Kruger and travel with bullion."

It was not long before Harris discovered that Wilde had sold the scenario to the others, who had to be paid off in the sum of £100 each before the production could begin. Thus he sent Wilde only £50 instead of the agreed balance of £175. This time it was Wilde's turn to feel aggrieved. However, when Ross told him that he was bound to get something more for himself after the play had been put on, Wilde replied characteristically: "Frank has deprived me of a source of income by taking a play on which I could always have raised £100."

8

That summer Wilde had a premonition that he would die before the end of the year. "My time is short, my work is done," he told his mother's old friend Anna Comtesse de Brémont, whom he met by chance on the river-boat which went down the Seine to St Cloud. He added, "When I cease to live, that work will begin to live—my work will be my great monument." As they parted, he said to her, "Contessa, don't sorrow for me, but watch and pray—it will not be for long." Then, as the boat grated against the landing pier, he repeated, "Watch and pray." When she looked for him to say goodbye, he had gone.[25] About the same time, he saw the Paris correspondent of the *Daily Chronicle* and spoke to him about his religious feelings. "Much of my moral obliquity is due to the fact that my father would not allow me to become a Catholic," he confided to the journalist. "The artistic side of the Church would have cured my degeneracies. I intend to be received before long."

Victoria and Albert Museum. This enabled him to publish it in 1956 with a full introduction giving the history of the whole matter.

[25] Anna Comtesse de Brémont, *née* Dunphy, of Cincinnati, was an American singer, poetess, and journalist who married a titled French doctor in New York. She was a friend of Lady Wilde and wrote an indifferent memoir of her and her younger son. "Don't read an appalling production by the Comtesse de Brémont called *Oscar Wilde and His Mother*," Christopher Millard wrote to Walter Ledger at the time of its publication in 1911. "It out Sherards Sherard." She is said to have died penniless in London in 1922.

The day after his meeting with Frank Harris, Wilde was kept in bed by a recurrence of the ear trouble from which he had suffered intermittently since his accident in prison when he had fallen in his cell and injured the middle ear. This now caused him increasing pain. Dr Tucker, the British embassy doctor—"a silly, kind, excellent man," so Ross described him—was summoned; he called in a specialist named Hobean, who recommended an operation. This was carried out by the specialist on 10 October. A wire was sent to Ross in Wilde's name, probably by the faithful Maurice Gilbert, asking him to come over as soon as possible, since Wilde was "terribly weak." The exact nature of the operation is not known. It could have been for a mastoid infection; certainly the prolonged daily dressing which was afterwards necessary suggests that there was an open wound as a result of the operation. A surgeon who has made a study of Wilde's last illness, on the basis of the evidence available, has remarked that "it would indeed be ironic if he had submitted to the then fashionable incision for mastoid infection, a procedure introduced by and called after his father." [26]

Ross arrived in Paris on the seventeenth and went to see his friend that morning, staying for two hours. "He was in very good spirits," noted Ross; "and though he assured me his sufferings were dreadful, at the same time he shouted with laughter and told many stories against the doctors and himself." He also discussed his money troubles with Harris over *Mr and Mrs Daventry*. Ross did his best to reassure him. Reggie Turner turned up about the same time, and for the next few weeks, while Wilde was in bed, they had lunch or dinner with him in his room, food and champagne being sent in from an outside restaurant, since no cooking was possible in the hotel. On the twenty-fifth, Ross's brother Alec came to see him with Wilde's sister-in-law, Lily, who was on her honeymoon with her new husband, Alexander Teixeira de Mattos. On this occasion, Ross noted that the sick man was in particularly good form, saying that he was "dying beyond his means," and repeating that he would never outlive the century. "The English people would not stand him," according to Ross. "He was responsible for the failure of the Exhibition, the English people having gone away when they saw him there so well-dressed and happy . . . all the French people knew this too, and would not stand him any more."

About a fortnight after the operation, the doctor said Wilde might get up, but at first he refused to do so and stayed in bed. However, he did get up on 29 October and after dinner in the evening insisted on going out, assuring Ross that Dr Tucker had said he might do so. "We went to a small café in the Latin Quarter, where he insisted on drinking absinthe," Ross later recalled. "He walked there and back with some difficulty, but seemed fairly well. Only I thought he had suddenly aged in the face, and remarked to Reggie Turner next day how different he looked when up and dressed. He appeared *comparatively* well in bed."

[26] See Terence Cawthorne, FRCS, "The Last Illness of Oscar Wilde": *Proceedings of the Royal Society of Medicine*, vol. 52, February 1959.

Ross noticed for the first time that his hair was slightly tinged with grey—it had previously retained its soft brown tone even when he was in prison.

Next day Ross was not surprised to find that Wilde had a cold and was also suffering great pain in his ear. However, the doctor said he might go out again, and as it was a very mild day, Ross took him for a drive in the Bois. Wilde seemed much better but complained of giddiness. When he made his usual call at the Hôtel d'Alsace a few days later, Ross happened to encounter Hennion, the male nurse who came every day to dress Wilde's ear. The nurse assured Ross that Wilde's general condition was "very serious," that he could not live for more than a few months unless he moderated his drinking habits, and that Ross ought to speak to Dr Tucker, who, he said, did not realize the patient's serious state, adding that in his opinion "the ear trouble was not of much importance in itself, but a grave symptom." To Reggie Turner, who remonstrated with him about his drinking, Wilde protested: "You are qualifying for a doctor. When you can refuse bread to the hungry and drink to the thirsty, you may apply for your Diploma."

Ross had two meetings with Tucker during the next few days. Although he endorsed Hennion's opinion to the extent of agreeing that Wilde should stop drinking alcohol in the quantities he did, at the same time he expressed the view that Wilde was "getting well now." On going to see Wilde later in the day, Ross found him very agitated. "He said he did not want to know what the doctor had told me," Ross noted. "He said he did not care if he had only a short time to live, and then went off on to the subject of his debts, which I gather amounted to something more than £400. He asked me to see that at all events some of them were paid if I was in a position to do so after he was dead; he suffered remorse about some of his creditors."

Much to Ross's relief, Reggie Turner came in shortly afterwards. Wilde then told them that he had had a horrible dream the previous night. "I dreamed I was supping with the dead." Whereupon Turner rose to the occasion with a typical response: "My dear Oscar, you were probably the life and soul of the party." This quip delighted Wilde, who, in Ross's words, "became high-spirited again, almost hysterical." Ross, who was a good Catholic, happened to mention that he had been to Père Lachaise cemetery on All Souls' Day. Wilde was much interested and asked Ross if he had chosen a place for his tomb. "He discussed epitaphs in a lighthearted way," noted Ross, "and I never dreamt he was so near death."

That night Ross wrote to Douglas telling him that he was obliged to leave Paris so as to be with his mother, and adding "that the doctor thought Oscar very ill, that Frank Harris ought to pay some of his bills as they worried him very much, and the matter was retarding his recovery—a great point made by Dr Tucker." Indeed, Wilde had already managed with an effort to write a few lines to Harris:

The operation I have had to undergo was a most terrible one. The surgeon's fee is 1500 francs (£60). This, by the aid of my doctor, I reduced to 750 francs. I was obliged to give a *post-dated* cheque for next Monday. I also have to have a hospital male nurse all day, and a doctor to sleep at night in the room. I then have to pay my own doctor who comes daily and the hotel for another room; and the chemist's bill is about £20 already. I entered on these expenses as I have your signed agreement to send me £175. You send me £25! It is really too monstrous.

Meanwhile, *Mr and Mrs Daventry* had opened at the Royalty Theatre in London and was doing quite good business, although it was a comparatively small theatre. In a later letter, the last entirely in his own handwriting, Wilde told Harris that he ought to have a weekly account of the takings so as to know what royalties were due to him under their agreement. "From *A Woman of No Importance* at the Haymarket I used to draw £170 to nearly £200 a week. I hope you will do your best to make Mrs Campbell try and get hold of a smart West-end theatre, if one can be got. The Royalty is useless as far as author's fees go."

On 12 November, Ross called at the Hôtel d'Alsace to say goodbye, as he was leaving for the Riviera next day. It was in the evening after dinner and Reggie Turner came with him. Wilde knew Ross was coming, but when he entered the room his friend paid little attention to him and addressed all his remarks to Turner, which Ross considered rather strange. Wilde had had a letter from Harris about Smithers's claim to be repaid £100 for his interest in the scenario of *Mr and Mrs Daventry*, which was complicated by the fact that the publisher had just been declared bankrupt. Wilde appeared upset and his speech seemed a little thick, but Ross attributed this to the fact of his having been given morphia and also having drunk too much champagne during the day. While they were talking about Wilde's financial troubles, a letter arrived from Alfred Douglas with a cheque, partly the result no doubt of Ross's having written to him. Ross noted that Wilde wept a little, but soon recovered himself. About 10:30 Ross and Turner got up to go. Wilde then asked Turner and the nurse to leave the room for a few minutes as he wished to say goodbye to Ross alone.

When the other two had left the room, Wilde rambled on for a little about his debts, and then implored Ross not to go away because he felt that a great change had come over him during the past few days. Ross was rather stern with him, as he thought that Wilde was "simply hysterical," although he knew that he was genuinely upset by his imminent departure. Suddenly Wilde broke into violent sobbing and said he would never see his friend again because he felt that "everything was at an end." Looking back afterwards, Ross felt that he did not respond to Wilde's emotional outburst as he should have done and really did not attach much importance to his farewell, especially as Wilde asked him as he was leaving the room, "Look out for some little cup in the hills near Nice where I can go when I am better, and where you can come and see me often." These were the last articulate words that Wilde ever spoke to him.

Before leaving Paris, Ross asked Turner to look after Wilde in his absence and send him regular bulletins on his condition. This Turner did, visiting Wilde every day and writing briefly every other day. Wilde got up on most days during the next fortnight and several times went out driving with Turner, seemingly much better. On 20 November he was able to dictate a long letter to Frank Harris. It was taken down by Maurice Gilbert and signed by Wilde, who wrote the last few lines in his own hand: "I rely on receiving the £150 you owe me. Sincerely yours." In this letter Wilde stated that the expenses of his illness amounted to close on £200 and he begged Harris to send him the money immediately. "I need not say how distressed I am that things should have turned out in this manner between us," he added, "but you must remember that the fault is in no sense mine."

> Had you kept your word to me, fulfilled your agreement and sent me the money that was due to me and for which I gave you a receipt which you still hold, all would have been well; and indeed I myself would have perfectly recovered two weeks ago, had it not been for the state of mental anxiety which your conduct kept me in all day long, with its accompanying sleeplessness at night, a sleeplessness over which none of the opiates the doctors dared to order me seemed to have any effect.

During the second week an abscess developed in the ear which had been operated upon, and the doctor called in another specialist named Kleiss, since it was feared that Wilde had contracted meningitis. Unfortunately, this proved to be the case. Until the twenty-fifth he was able to laugh and talk, but complained of giddiness and in the evening became quite lightheaded. On 26 November, Turner wrote to Ross:

> At the consultation yesterday the doctors gave very little hope of Oscar's recovery, and Tucker was very anxious that you should be sent for . . . As for Oscar, he knows nothing of what they say, but he is beyond taking notice, his mind wanders and he sleeps. That is I think partly the result of the morphine they inject into him, but now that is forbidden, so they are going only to pretend to inject. He welcomed me today and was pleased to see me, and we had a moment's lucid conversation, but he then relapsed into drowsiness and when he did speak seemed to wander. Of course this may be the result of drugs. I myself cannot help thinking he may yet live to furnish Frank Harris with another plot, but I may be quite wrong. What they fear is, I think, that the disease should go to the brain.

Turner was wrong, and what the doctors feared came to pass. Wilde soon became delirious, displaying all the symptoms of cerebral meningitis. Turner now rarely left his bedside, sitting with him throughout the night until 5:30 in the morning of the twenty-eighth. After Turner had been holding an ice pack on his head for three-quarters of an hour, Wilde suddenly said to him, "You dear little Jew, don't you think that is enough?" He then talked about *Mr and Mrs Daventry,* "saying it was worth fifty centimes." He also raved about the packet-boat on the Kingstown-Holyhead route, adding that "one steamboat was very like another."

"Maurice Gilbert came this morning but does not like being in the room," Turner wrote to Ross later the same day. "I am having a special nurse tonight, though they say it is not any good . . . I think everything is being done for him that can be. An operation is out of the question as is set out in the doctor's statement. He takes no nourishment or hardly any. By turning the lights out and substituting milk for water I deceived him into drinking three glasses last night."

In the late afternoon, since there was no improvement, Turner sent Ross a wire: ALMOST HOPELESS. Ross just caught the Paris express the same evening.

9

Ross reached the Hôtel d'Alsace soon after ten o'clock the morning of 28 November. Dr Tucker and Dr Kleiss were both there, and they informed him that Wilde could not live for more than two days. "His appearance was very painful, he had become quite thin, the flesh was livid, the breathing heavy. He was trying to speak. He was conscious that people were in the room, and raised his hand when I asked him whether he understood. He pressed our hands." Ross then went in search of a priest who could come at once and administer the sacraments of Baptism and Extreme Unction, with Holy Communion if possible. "You know, I had always promised to bring a priest to Oscar when he was dying," Ross afterwards told Adela Schuster, "and I felt rather guilty that I had so often dissuaded him from becoming a Catholic, but you know my reasons for doing so." After considerable difficulty, Ross found Father Cuthbert Dunne, an Irish priest from Dublin who was attached to the Passionist Church of St Joseph in the Avenue Hoche. On being asked to come quickly to attend a dying man, Father Dunne immediately accompanied Ross back to the hotel. Ross knelt by the bedside and assisted the priest as best he could, while Father Dunne administered conditional Baptism, afterwards answering the responses as the priest gave Extreme Unction to the prostrate man and recited the prayers for the dying. On account of Wilde's semi-comatose condition, the priest did not attempt to administer the Viaticum. According to the record which Father Dunne made of the occasion, the dying man when roused gave signs of being inwardly conscious:

He made brave efforts to speak, and would even continue for a time trying to talk, though he could not utter articulate words. Indeed I was fully satisfied that he understood me when I told him that I was about to receive him into the Catholic Church and give him the Last Sacraments. From the signs he gave as well as from his attempted words, I was satisfied as to his full consent. And when I repeated close to his ear the Holy Names, the Acts of Contrition, Faith, Hope and Charity, with acts of humble recognition to the Will of God he tried all through to say the words after me.

Father Dunne returned later the same day to pray by the bedside and give the dying man Absolution. The priest noticed on this occasion that there were two leeches on either side of Wilde's head above the forehead, "put there to relieve the pressure on the brain." The priest was further convinced of Wilde's "inward consciousness" when one of the nurses offered him a cigarette which "he took in his fingers and raised to his face, although, in the attempt to put it to his lips, he failed."

Ross and Turner both stayed the night in the hotel, but their sleep was twice interrupted by the nurse, who summoned them in the belief that Wilde was dying. Ross described the final scene next day, 30 November, to More Adey:

> About 5:30 in the morning a complete change came over him, the lines of the face altered, and I believe what is called the death rattle began, but I had never heard anything like it before; it sounded like the horrible turning of a crank, and it never ceased until the end. His eyes did not respond to the light test any longer. Foam and blood came from his mouth, and had to be wiped away by someone standing by him all the time. At 12 o'clock I went out to get some food, Reggie mounting guard. He went out at 12:30. From 1 o'clock we did not leave the room; the painful noise from the throat became louder and louder. Reggie and myself destroyed letters to keep ourselves from breaking down. The two nurses were out, and the proprietor of the hotel had come up to take their place; at 1:45 the time of his breathing altered. I went to the bedside and held his hand, his pulse began to flutter. He heaved a deep sigh, the only natural one I had heard since I arrived, the limbs seemed to stretch involuntarily, the breathing came fainter; he passed at 10 minutes to 2 p.m. exactly.[27]

After washing and winding the body, and "removing the appalling débris which had to be burnt," Ross and Turner and the hotel proprietor went off to the Mairie to make the official declaration of death.[28] "The excellent Dupoirier lost his head, and complicated matters by making a mystery over Oscar's name," Ross's narrative continues, "though there was a difficulty, as Oscar was registered under the name of Melmoth at the hotel, and it is contrary to the French law to be under an assumed name at your hotel." After hanging about the offices of the Mairie and the Commissaire de Police for an hour and a half, Ross got angry and went off to find the British embassy undertaker, whose name was Gesling and who had been recommended by Father Dunne. Gesling prom-

---

[27] On the fiftieth anniversary of Wilde's death in Paris, marked by a ceremony at the graveside in Pére Lachaise, the present writer took Mrs Margery Ross, Robert Ross's niece, and Mrs Vyvyan Holland to the Hôtel d'Alsace, where Jean Dupoirier's daughter, who then ran the hotel, showed us the clock which had been in Wilde's room and which according to her stopped at the exact time of his death.

[28] The latest medical opinion expressed by Terence Cawthorne FRCS is that the cause of death was an intercranial complication of suppurative *otis media,* or middle ear disease complicated by an abscess in the left lobe. In addition, the doctors who attended Wilde in his final illness diagnosed cerebral meningitis, and this is confirmed by his persistently wild delirium. As he afterwards told Arthur Ransome, Ross thought that the meningitis was "the legacy of an attack of tertiary syphilis." But it is practically certain that neurosyphilis was in no way responsible for his terminal illness.

ised to come to the hotel at eight next morning, whereupon Ross went to find some nuns to watch the body. "I thought that in Paris of all places this would be quite easy, but it was only after incredible difficulties that I got two Franciscan sisters." That he was eventually able to do so was largely due to Father Dunne. "He [Wilde] was particularly devoted to St Francis," Ross wrote, thanking the priest, "and deeply read in all his life and literature, so it is very appropriate."

The undertaker had warned Ross that owing to Wilde's assumed name the authorities might insist on his body being taken to the morgue, and it was to avoid this "final touch of horror" that Ross and the undertaker spent the whole of the following morning seeing various officials, while Turner stayed at the hotel interviewing journalists and "clamorous creditors." The district doctor called in the afternoon and asked if the dead man had committed suicide or been murdered; he would not look at the certificates which Kleiss and Tucker had signed. "After examining the body, and indeed, everybody in the hotel, and after a series of drinks and unseasonable jests, and a liberal fee, the District Doctor consented to sign the permission for burial. Then arrived some other revolting official; he asked how many collars Oscar had, and the value of his umbrella. (This is quite true, and not a mere exaggeration of mine.) Then various poets and literary people called . . . and various English people who gave assumed names, together with two veiled women. They were all allowed to see the body when they signed their names."

Ross told More Adey afterwards that he was glad to say that "dear Oscar looked calm and dignified, just as he did when he came out of prison, and there was nothing at all horrible about the body after it had been washed." Around his neck was a blessed rosary which Adey had given Ross some time before, and on the breast a Franciscan medal given him by one of the nuns, together with a few flowers placed there by Ross and "an anonymous friend," probably Carlos Blacker, "who had brought some on behalf of the children, though I do not suppose the children know that their father is dead." In addition, there were the usual crucifix, candles, and holy water.

As Ross told Adela Schuster, the French authorities "could not understand the absence of relatives or legal representatives," and this was why Wilde's remains barely escaped being taken to the morgue.

> By great efforts and kind assistance of others I was able to prevent such a ghastly contingency. Mr Hope, the guardian of the children, for some reason or other did not communicate with me, although I wired to him directly I arrived in Paris asking for instructions in the case of death . . .
>
> I blame Mr Hope very much, but I dare say he acted according to his view and of course could not be expected to take much interest in the matter. He communicated with me after everything was over and all difficulties overcome, through *my solicitor*. I think on the children's account he might have taken a little more interest, at all events when he knew Mr Wilde was dead. But on the other hand he had every reason to distrust me as a friend of the

father, and suspected my motives at all times since the difficulty about the annuity. He highly disapproved of *Mrs Wilde* corresponding with me as she did, after her husband's release.

The undertaker advised Ross to have the remains placed in the coffin at once, as decomposition would begin very rapidly. Before this was done, Maurice Gilbert, at Ross's request, took a photograph of the body in bed, but it was not very successful owing to the flashbulb not working properly. The last person to view the body before the undertaker's men arrived in the evening to screw down the lid was Henry Davray, who had translated *The Ballad*. It had previously been glimpsed by Frank Harris's secretary Tom Bell, whom Harris had sent over from London with some money in response to Wilde's last appeal. According to Bell, he handed the money over to Ross, although Ross does not mention this. Next day, 2 December, Alfred Douglas arrived in response to Ross's telegram and agreed to pay for the funeral expenses. The funeral itself started from the hotel on the following morning at nine o'clock, Ross and the other principal mourners following the hearse on foot to the nearby church of St-Germain-des-Prés, where a low Mass was said by one of the *vicaires* at the altar behind the sanctuary, after which Father Cuthbert Dunne read the burial service. Although Ross had sent out no official notices, "being anxious to keep the funeral quiet," there were over fifty in the church for the service, some of whom afterwards made the long drive to the cemetery at Bagneux, where Ross had hired a temporary concession until he could arrange to have the remains transferred to a permanent resting place. "I have not yet decided what to do, or the nature of the monument."

There were altogether twenty-four wreaths, some sent anonymously. The proprietor of the hotel supplied "a pathetic bead trophy," inscribed *"à mon locataire,"* and there was another of the same kind from the *"service de l'hôtel."* The remaining twenty-two were of real flowers, coming, among others, from Douglas, Turner, Adey, Adela Schuster, Alexander and Lily Texeira de Mattos, Louis Wilkinson, Maurice Gilbert, and *Mercure de France,* Wilde's French publishers. At the head of the coffin, Ross placed a wreath of laurels inscribed, "A tribute to his literary achievements and distinction," and setting out inside the wreath the names of those who had shown kindness to Wilde during or after his imprisonment, including Max Beerbohm, Charles Ricketts, C. H. Shannon, Charles Conder, Ada Leverson, Frank Harris, Harold Mellor, Rowland Strong, and Will and Alice Rothenstein, and by special request a friend who wished to be known as "C.B.," presumably Carlos Blacker. Afterwards Rothenstein wrote: "Ross told me he had added my name, and my wife's, to the few he had written on the wreath he laid on Oscar's grave; I was glad he had done so."

"I can scarcely speak of the magnanimity, humanity and charity of Dupoirier, the proprietor of the Hôtel d'Alsace," Ross stated in his letter to Adey at the time. "Just before I left Paris Oscar told me he owed him over £190 . . . Dr Tucker is also owed a large sum of money. He was most kind and attentive, although I think he entirely misunderstood Oscar's case." Ross also wrote of Dupoirier's kindness in the account he gave Miss Schuster:

> I may say here that the proprietor of the Alsace was a most charitable and humane man, that he never spoke to Mr Wilde on the subject of his debt from the time of the operation, paid *himself* for luxuries and necessities ordered by the physicians, and never even spoke to me about it until after the funeral, while all the other creditors of course flocked round directly they heard the case was hopeless. I trust Mr Harris will be able to settle the proprietor's bill at all events, as he has promised to do. I merely mention this point because there is an *unfounded* report which has been reproduced in the newspapers that Mr Wilde died in a sort of neglected and sordid way. Of course the hotel is rather a shabby little place compared to what he would have liked to stay in, but it is perfectly comfortable as I know by staying there often, and Mr Wilde wanted for *nothing* in the last weeks of his life. He had a special nurse, food sent in from a restaurant, the Embassy doctor Tucker; Hobean, a well-known specialist, operated, and Mr Turner and myself had in a brain specialist Dr Kleiss, when meningitis declared itself. As long as he was allowed champagne, he had it *throughout* his illness.

"Reggie Turner had the worst time of all in many ways," Ross concluded, "—he experienced all the horrible uncertainty and the appalling responsibility, of which he did not know the extent. It will always be a source of satisfaction to those who were fond of Oscar that he had someone like Reggie near him during his last days while he was articulate and sensible of kindness and attention."

Postscript: Full Circle

I n the account of Wilde's last days which Robert Ross wrote to Adela Schuster, Ross truly remarked that "though everyone who knew him well enough to *appreciate* his wonderful power and the sumptuous endowment of his intellect will regret his death, apart from personal affection the terrible commonplace 'it was for the best' is really true in his case." Ross went on to indicate the existence, completely out of character, that Wilde had led since his release from Reading in terms which later received independent confirmation from Vincent O'Sullivan, as expressed in the letter to A. J. A. Symons already quoted. In his perceptive assessment, Ross also touched on how he considered Wilde's literary work was likely to be regarded in the light of his unique personality:

Two things were absolutely necessary for him, contact with comely things, as Pater says, and social position. Comely things meant for him a certain standard of living, and this, since his release, he *was able to have* except for a few weeks at a time, or perhaps months. Social position he realised after five months he could not have. Many people were kind to him, but he was too proud, or too vain, to be forgiven by those whom he regarded as social and intellectual inferiors. It galled him to have to appear grateful to those whom he did not, or would not have regarded, before the downfall. You who knew him so well in former years will understand what others will never understand I suppose. He chose therefore a Bohemian existence, entirely out of note with his genius and temperament. There was no use arguing or exhorting him. The temporary deprivation of his annuity produced no result. You cannot ask a man who started on the top rung of the ladder to suddenly start again from the lowest rung of all. Among his many fine qualities he showed in his later years was that he never blamed anyone but himself for his own disasters. He never bore any ill-will to anybody, and in a characteristic way was really surprised that anyone should bear any resentment against him. For example he really did not understand how cruel he was to his wife, but I never expect anyone to believe that.

I was not surprised by the silence of the press. Journalists could hardly say very much, and it was better to be silent than point a moral. Later on I think everyone will recognise his achievements; his plays and essays will endure. Of course you may think with others that his personality and conversation were far more wonderful than anything he wrote, so that his written works give only a pale reflection of his power. Perhaps that is so, and of course it will be impossible to reproduce what is gone for ever. I am not alas a Boswell, as some friends have kindly suggested I should become. But I only met him in '86 and only became intimate with him when he was writing *Lady Windermere*, but there were long intervals when I never saw him, and he never corresponded with me regularly until after the downfall.

"I suppose really it was better that Oscar should die," Max Beerbohm wrote to Reggie Turner from London at this time. "If he had lived to be an old man he would have become unhappy. Those whom the gods, etc. And the gods *did* love Oscar, with all his faults . . . Poor Oscar! I wish he were here, alive and superb—the Oscar before the fall."

A year later, many of Wilde's Paris debts were still unpaid. However, Dupoirier had received half of what was owing to him, and it appears from Ross's correspondence with Miss Schuster that she was good enough to send him a cheque for the balance. "I must tell you that I have been *promised* assistance for paying the Paris debts from George Alexander," Ross wrote to her again on 3 January 1902, "but I do not like to rely any further on promises as Douglas, Harris and others have failed me in that respect for no fault of their own. Alexander now owns the dramatic rights in perpetuity of two of the plays and is putting on *Earnest* next week at the St James's so he may shortly redeem his promise to some extent."

As Wilde's literary executor, Ross was engaged in protracted negotiations with the Official Receiver in regard to the copyright in Wilde's books and plays, complicated by the fact that seven or eight different publishers, one of whom (Leonard Smithers) had been declared bankrupt, possessed an interest in the copyright of the books. In the same letter to Miss Schuster, Ross wrote:

> I have been able to secure the support of Mr Adrian Hope who as trustee of Mr Wilde's estate is one of the principal creditors and would have to be consulted by the Official Receiver before he sold the copyrights . . . It is arranged that if obtainable the rights shall be purchased by *me,* and Mr Hope was kind enough to say that they would prefer that I should possess them. If ever there is any remuneration I would of course hand it over to Mr Hope for the benefit of the children if the Paris debts were by that time cleared off and I notified my intention to Mr Hope, but he would not permit me to write any promise to that effect as he says the children must not have any official benefit from their father's works, as the names are changed and it would only handicap them in life. I suppose this is best though it seems rather sad . . .

It would be tedious to tell you the various ramifications of the copyrights.

Someone has been pirating a good many of the books in private editions but I hope to stop them.[1]

In 1901, when Wilde's creditors had received about three shillings in the pound sterling, "a kind-hearted official at the Court of Bankruptcy" assured Ross that the debtor's works were "of no value, and would never command any interest whatsoever." As Ross had recalled, "It was a less kind successor who, with more enthusiasm," relieved him of the first £1,000 produced by *De Profundis* on its publication four years later. But it was the royalties from the German translations of his books and the receipts from the production of his plays in Germany, particularly after Richard Strauss had produced his operatic version of *Salomé* in Dresden in December 1905, that made Wilde's estate solvent and put it in credit.[2] By the middle of the following year, Ross was able to declare that all the English creditors had been paid in full, and there was a surplus available to satisfy the French creditors in accordance with Wilde's last wishes. The fact that Wilde's literary rehabilitation should have begun in so pronounced a manner in Germany would certainly have surprised the author, who was inclined to deride the Germans for being so serious-minded and lacking a sense of humour. Thus, while Wilde's books were virtually unobtainable in England, except surreptitiously in pirated editions, and his plays were banned in the London theatres—they were occasionally performed in the provinces without his name—the German public took to them eagerly, particularly *Salomé,* which had been produced as a play by Max Reinhardt in Berlin as early as November 1902. One of the remarkable facts about Wilde which emerges strongly from *De Profundis,* and which Ross pointed out at the time of its original publication in February 1905, is that while he was alive the author should have exaggerated his lost contemporary position in England, whilst showing no idea of his European reputation after his death. The original publication of *De Profundis* took place in Germany in a translation by Dr Max Meyerfeld, and it was the interest shown in this event which prompted Ross to consider bringing out the first English edition. This was due to the enterprise of Methuen & Co., the English publishers, who took a risk in doing so, since their action was bound to provoke hostile criticism. However, although *De Profundis* was denounced by the Rev. H. C. Beeching, Canon of Westminster, as "a doctrine of devils" in a sermon which he preached in Westminster Abbey, the book had an immediate success, going into five editions in a year.

[1] Leonard Smithers and Charles Carrington in Paris were responsible for most of these piracies. Particulars of forty-three are given by Stuart Mason in his *Bibliography.* In 1910 over five thousand copies of an unauthorized edition of *De Profundis* were seized, as a result of which two printers and a bookseller were sentenced to imprisonment at the Guildhall in London. This effectively stopped the piracies.

[2] *Salomé* had its first operatic performance at the Royal Opera House in Dresden on 9 December 1905. It was also produced by Strauss at the Metropolitan Opera in New York on 22 January 1907, and later the same year in Brussels and Paris.

"Its reception seems to me remarkable—unprophesiable five or six years ago," Laurence Housman wrote to Ross at the time. "Perhaps before we die a tablet will be put up in Tite Street on the house where he used to live." Housman's words came true just fifty years later as regards himself, though not as regards Ross.

The success of *De Profundis* encouraged Ross and Methuen to bring out the first collected edition of Wilde's writings. This was issued in 1908 in fourteen volumes, edited by Robert Ross. The event was appropriately celebrated by a complimentary dinner given to Ross by his friends and admirers in the Savoy Hotel at which two hundred were present. Sir Martin Conway, later Lord Conway of Alington, was in the chair, and Ross's health was proposed by H. G. Wells and William Rothenstein. In his reply, Ross was able to inform those present that Wilde's plays were now performed in every European language, including Yiddish in the Jewish quarter of New York, while Chinese and Russian translations of *The Soul of Man under Socialism* were on sale in the bazaars of Nijni Novgorod. He was also able to announce that a donor "with cowardly generosity characteristic of anonymity" had just sent him £2,000 to place a suitable monument to Wilde at Père Lachaise.[3] "The condition of the gift is not one to which I have certainly any objection," he added. The condition was that the work should be carried out by "the brilliant young sculptor" Jacob Epstein. "May I take that generous gift and your hospitality this evening," Ross concluded his speech, "as symbols that in after years it will by my privilege to boast that I was the occasion, though never the cause, of giving back to Oscar Wilde's children the laurels of their distinguished father untarnished save by tears?"

On 19 July 1909, Wilde's remains were removed from Bagneux cemetery to their present resting place at Père Lachaise in the presence of Wilde's younger son Vyvyan Holland, Robert Ross, and Sir Coleridge Kennard. The latter, a contemporary of Vyvyan Holland, had recently entered the diplomatic service, and he may have been asked by the Foreign Office or the Paris embassy to attend as an unofficial observer. In order to identify the remains, it was necessary for the gravediggers to open the coffin before transferring them to a new one which Ross had had made with a fresh inscription. At the time of Wilde's death, the doctors had told Ross that he should be buried in quicklime. This, they said, would consume the flesh and leave the skeleton bones of the body intact, so that they could be easily placed in another coffin for removal when the temporary concession at Bagneux had expired. To Ross's surprise, the quicklime, instead of destroying the flesh, was found to have preserved it. The face was clearly recognizable, although the hair and beard had grown quite long. According to Reggie Turner, Ross claimed

---

[3] The anonymous donor was Mrs James Carew, widow of Hugh Kennard and mother of Sir Coleridge Kennard, Bart. Ross dedicated Volume XIII (*Reviews*) of the collected edition of Wilde's works to her, also *Intentions* in the second collected edition.

to have descended into the grave and actually moved the remains with his own hands into the new coffin "in loving reverence." [4]

Epstein now went to work on a solid block of stone weighing twenty tons which he discovered in the Hopton Wood quarries in Derbyshire. His task proved a difficult one, since he found it impossible to please everyone concerned or interested. Wilde's more enthusiastic admirers would have liked a Greek youth standing by a broken column, or some scene from his works, such as "The Young King," which was suggested many times. On the other hand, the artist had to bear in mind that cemetery sculpture was expected to conform to certain fixed canons, and in Latin countries like France there was a definite "cult of the dead," so that anything at all original would be bound to give offence, as indeed occurred in this instance, in spite of the fact that Epstein's motif was restrained enough. The sculptor conceived a vast winged figure in the guise of a messenger swiftly moving with vertical wings, thus giving the impression of forward flight. "It was of course purely symbolical, the conception of a poet as a messenger," Epstein afterwards recalled, "but many people tried to read into it a portrait of Oscar Wilde."

The work took Epstein three years to complete. During the summer of 1912, it was exhibited in a nearly finished state for a month in his London studio when such notices as it received in the press were generally favourable, not always the case in England with Epstein's masterpieces. It was then transported to Père Lachaise and erected over Wilde's remains, thus actually constituting a tomb and not merely a graveside monument. On the back were carved the following lines from *The Ballad of Reading Gaol:*

> And alien tears will fill for him
> Pity's long broken urn
> For his mourners will be outcast men,
> And outcasts always mourn.

One morning, when Epstein arrived at Père Lachaise to put some finishing touches to his work, he found the sculpture covered with a tarpaulin and a gendarme standing beside it. The gendarme informed Epstein that the tomb was banned and he would not be allowed to do any more work on it. Apparently the reason was that the *conservateur* considered the sculpture indecent and had informed the police, who imposed the ban. Thereafter Epstein could carry on his work only under considerable difficulties by bribing the gendarme to let him work while he looked the other way. Several artists and writers whom Epstein invited to inspect his work, such as Remy de Gourmont and Raymonde de la Tailhade, wrote protests to the French press. But to no avail. The tar-

---

[4] This would not appear to accord with Sir Coleridge Kennard's recollection, since he is stated to have been under the impression that the physical transfer of the remains was carried out by the gravediggers. See Frank Harris and Lord Alfred Douglas, *New Preface to "The Life and Confessions of Oscar Wilde"* (1925), p. 16.

paulin stayed in place. A petition inspired by Ada Leverson was organized by Lytton Strachey and signed by Bernard Shaw, H. G. Wells, Robert Ross, and Léon Bakst, who had recently produced *Salomé* in Paris, to remit the £110 duty, which the sculptor had been charged by the French customs. It likewise failed.

Eventually, Epstein bowed to the storm and agreed to a significant alteration to the tomb. Robert Ross consequently had a large plaque modelled and cast in bronze; this was fitted to the sculptured figure like a fig leaf. At the same time, Ross with his customary wit wrote to *The Pall Mall Gazette* (28 September 1912):

> I regard the arrest of the monument by the French authorities as a graceful outcome of the Entente Cordiale and a symptom on the part of our allies to prove themselves worthy of political union with our great nation, which, rightly or wrongly, they think has always put Propriety before everything. I hesitate to say that the rest lies in the lap of the gods, but that is precisely the part of the statue to which exception is taken.

The tomb remained covered until the outbreak of the First World War, when the tarpaulin was removed without comment from the critics. In 1922, it had to be fenced off temporarily so as to protect it from the unwelcome attentions of the students of the neighbouring *lycée,* who used to invade the cemetery at night and assault the tomb, in the words of one of Dolly Wilde's friends, "hacking at it intimately until its significance had been almost chiselled away"—this included tearing away the bronze plaque which served as a fig leaf. Shortly afterwards a young man appeared in the Café Royal wearing the plaque suspended from his neck and, approaching Epstein, who happened to be there, asked him to explain its significance.

Fortunately for Wilde's two children, their guardian's desire that they should not benefit from their father's literary estate had been frustrated by the death of Adrian Hope, which occurred in 1904, when Cyril and Vyvyan were still minors. Five years later Alexander revived *The Importance of Being Earnest* for the second time at the St James's Theatre with conspicuous success. "We had splendid houses yesterday and turned away money from the *'pit and gallery,' "* he wrote to Ross on 5 December 1909, "—how this would have pleased him!" From then onwards, Wilde's rehabilitation proceeded apace, although there were occasional setbacks and there were some countries where Wilde's writings were specially popular which had no copyright arrangements with Britain. After a visit to Russia, Ross wrote to Vyvyan Holland on 7 October 1913:

> Some day you must really go to Russia where you will be fêted even more than I was. I returned from Moscow last night. Your father is regarded there as a sort of hero and he is one of the few authors who is admired both by the intellectuals and by the Ultra-Tory party. One of the papers, which is called *The Faith of Russia*—a sort of combination of the *Church Times,* the *Family Herald* and the *Spectator*—which circulates among the clericals, has issued the

complete works at 2½d a copy. Unhappily, as you know, there is no copyright in Russia, so we do not benefit by this.

So long as he was alive, Adrian Hope insisted on keeping the Wilde children at arm's length from Robert Ross, no doubt acting in what he considered to be their best interests and having every reason to be suspicious of Ross, as indeed the latter realized. Consequently, it was only after their guardian's death that Cyril and Vyvyan got to know Ross at all well and to appreciate what he had done and was continuing to do for them and their father's memory. This was also appreciated, among others, by George Alexander, who wrote to Ross at this time: "No one knows better than I do what a heroic role you have played in the Wilde drama, and what your unselfish devotion has done for his memory, and for his children."

In due course, Ross was able to tell Vyvyan—Cyril had been killed in action during the First World War—that he had inherited the rights in his father's two most valuable literary properties which Alexander possessed at the time of his death in 1918. It so happened that this news coincided with the sensational trial for criminal libel of an eccentric Independent Member of Parliament named Noel Pemberton Billing. The prosecution was a private one brought by the actress Maud Allen, who had recently played the name part in a performance of *Salomé*. Homosexuality was the dominant theme, and for reasons into which it is unnecessary to enter here, the trial was in effect a trial of Wilde and his works. One of the successful defendant's so-called expert witnesses was Lord Alfred Douglas, who bitterly attacked his former friend's memory and works in the course of his evidence. Ross, who had himself been driven to prosecute Douglas for criminally libelling him as a practising homosexual four years previously, was now in failing health, and a feeling of depression may have led him to attribute more weight to the Billing trial in the context of Wilde's reputation than the facts warranted.[5]

On 9 June 1918, four months before his death, Ross wrote to Vyvyan Holland:

> Alexander has fulfilled his promise and bequeathed to you *Earnest* and *Lady Windermere's Fan*. I fear it will prove but a barren legacy. The Billing case has ruined the Wilde Estate. Douglas, having ruined your father twice, has now effectually ruined the property on which he always cast greedy eyes. His chief hatred of me was due to the fact that he had ignored my belief in the commercial possibilities of the estate and refused my sporting offer in 1900.[6]

Ross's pessimistic assessment turned out to be misjudged. The Billing case, a deplorable example of wartime public hysteria, was soon forgot-

---

[5] The Billing case, known at the time as "The Black Book Trial," has been fully described by the present writer in his *Cases That Changed the Law* (1951), pp. 182–9. In his evidence Douglas described Wilde as being in his opinion "the greatest force for evil that has appeared in Europe during the last 350 years." He intensely regretted having met him, he said, and having helped him with the translation of *Salomé*, which he now regarded as "a most pernicious and abominable piece of work."

[6] See above, p. 349.

ten, and its effect on the Wilde estate in the long term proved negligible. Vyvyan Holland enjoyed a comfortable income from the royalties on his father's works for the next thirty years, until (with the exception of the posthumously published *De Profundis*) they fell into public domain in 1950 under the Copyright Act.[7]

In 1950, the fiftieth anniversary of Wilde's death was appropriately marked in Paris by a simple graveside ceremony at Père Lachaise and literary reunions of the few who had known Wilde in his last years, like the fencing champion Jean-Joseph Renaud and the poet Tristan Klingsor, as well as admirers and writers like Natalie Clifford Barney and Guillot de Saix. The principal oration in Père Lachaise on 30 November—a bright cold winter's morning—was made by M. Renaud. Others present who spoke or delivered messages included Mrs Margery Ross, Mrs Vyvyan Holland, the present writer, and M. Guillot de Saix, who organized the arrangements. Robert Ross had expressed the wish that his ashes might eventually be placed beside those of Wilde, and the occasion was taken to have the tomb opened so that Mrs Ross, who had brought them over from Kensal Green cemetery in London, could carry out her uncle's wishes. Later in the day, the present writer accompanied Mrs Ross and Mrs Holland to the Hôtel d'Alsace, where the former patron Jean Dupoirier's daughter was then running the hotel. She produced a fine linen shirt with the initials of Wilde's pseudonym Sebastian Melmoth embroidered on it which she presented to Mrs Holland as a relic of the dead poet, whom she recalled. Her father had given it to her and she had carefully treasured it over the years.[8]

With the approach of the centenary of Wilde's birth in 1954, a committee was formed with the object of suitably commemorating the event in London. The Centenary Committee consisted of Mr and Mrs Vyvyan Holland; Lord Alfred Douglas's nephew Lord Cecil Douglas; the present writer; and Eric Barton, an antiquarian bookseller, and his wife, Irene, who acted as secretary of the committee. It was largely due to the persistent prodding of the London County Council by Mr and Mrs Barton that the council eventually agreed to the committee's suggestion that a blue and white plaque should be erected on the outside wall of the house in Tite Street (formerly No. 16, now 34) where the "wit and dramatist" had lived between 1884 and 1895 and where he had done much of his best work. It was hoped that Sir Max Beerbohm would perform the unveiling ceremony on the actual date of the centenary (14 October 1954), but he was in too frail health to make the journey from his home in Rapallo. However, he sent an appropriate message, as did two of Wilde's other surviving friends, Laurence Housman, author of the evoca-

[7] Vyvyan Holland told the present writer that these royalties averaged £10,000 a year.

[8] In 1963, the hotel was bought by a former French actor, M. Guy Louis Duboucheron, who largely rebuilt it with the aid of an American architect, Robin Westbrook, and converted it into a luxury hotel. Now known simply as L'Hôtel, it is one of the most expensive establishments of its kind in Paris, the charge for Wilde's old room when available being 40,000 francs a night. The charge in Wilde's time was three francs a night, about 2s 6d at the then rate of exchange.

tive *Écho de Paris,* and Allan Aynsworth, the actor who had played a
leading part in *The Importance of Being Earnest* on its first performance
nearly sixty years before. The unveiling was performed by Sir Compton
Mackenzie at Vyvyan Holland's request in the presence of a large gathering of spectators who crowded the street. The present writer, then an
Ulster Unionist M.P., presided on an improvised platform and introduced Sir Compton and the other principal speakers, Guy Edmiston,
the Mayor of Chelsea, and his mayoral predecessor, Basil Marsden-
Smedley. As the *Manchester Guardian* observed in its account of the proceedings; "In a sense the Mayor was the most notable person present.
The verdict of art has long been given to Wilde; civic recognition is the
latest tribute to his work. The presence on Saturday of the Mayor and of
Mr Fiske, chairman of the L.C.C.'s Town Planning Committee, deserves
to be celebrated."

Besides Vyvyan Holland, there were at least two others present who
had known Wilde, an artist and an artist's widow, namely Augustus
John and Lady Rothenstein. The latter, who had in her time been a
talented actress and now witnessed the proceedings from a wheelchair,
could vividly recall having tea with the Wildes in the house. Literature
was represented by, among others, T. S. Eliot, Sacheverell Sitwell, Alec
Waugh, and Lady Cynthia Asquith (for the P.E.N. Club), and the theatre
by Dame Edith Evans, Peggy Ashcroft, Isobel Jeans, Margaret Rawl-
ings, Esmé Percy, Michael Redgrave, and Michael MacLiammoir. Trinity College, Dublin, sent its provost and Magdalen College, Oxford, one
of its dons, while the Irish government was represented by its Ambassador in London, and the French and West German governments by
their cultural attachés. Indeed, Wilde would have been surprised and
gratified by such an impressive turnout, considering that he had died an
exile and an outcast just over half a century before.

Max Beerbohm's tribute was the first to be read out. In it the man of
whom Wilde had once remarked that the gods had bestowed upon him
the perpetual gift of old age stated that he had had the privilege of listening to many other masters of table-talk, such as Meredith, Swinburne, Edmund Gosse, Henry James, Augustine Birell, Arthur Balfour,
and others, all of them splendid in their own way. "But assuredly Oscar
in *his* own way was the greatest of them all—the most spontaneous and
yet the most polished, the most soothing and yet the most surprising."

> That this talk was mostly a monologue was not his own fault. His man-
> ners were very good; he was careful to give his guests or his fellow-guests
> many a conversational opening, but seldom did anyone respond with more
> than a few words. Nobody was willing to interrupt the music of so magnifi-
> cent a virtuoso. To have heard him consoled me for not having heard Dr
> Johnson or Edmund Burke, Lord Brougham or Sydney Smith.

Like Max Beerbohm, Laurence Housman, who was then in his nineti-
eth year, felt unable to face the chilly October weather. After confirming
in his message that Wilde was "incomparably the best talker" he had

ever met, of which Housman had himself given a brilliant example in his *Écho de Paris,* he went on to say that he was not only the best talker but "he was also the most courteous and the most charming."

His unhappy fate has done the world a signal service in defeating the blind obscurantists; it has made people think. Far more people of intelligence think differently today because of him. And when he wrote his *Ballad of Reading Gaol,* he not only gave the world a beautiful poem but a much-needed lesson in good will, pity, pardon, and understanding for the down and out.

Sir Compton Mackenzie took his cue from Housman's theme. He recalled the public auction which had taken place "in the house behind me" at the time of Wilde's arrest in April 1895 in the scandalous circumstances which have already been described. But he did not think that the dreadful story of that action could be repeated now, when he felt that there was more generosity and humanity than existed in Wilde's time. "I think today we are better," he said, "and I think we have had a great lesson." The present writer had previously shown the speaker the catalogue of the sale, of which the last two lots were "a rabbit hutch and a quantity of toys," and Sir Compton referred to them in passing. With Vyvyan Holland standing beside him, one of the two little boys at the time to whom the rabbit hutch and the toys belonged, Sir Compton was momentarily overcome with emotion and unable to proceed with his speech. However, he eventually did so, and when he came forward to perform the unveiling a few minutes later, this act was greeted with wet eyes as well as loud cheers.

As the London correspondent of the *Irish Times* reported, "Sir Compton Mackenzie did the unveiling to perfection, to everyone's absolute satisfaction." With one conspicuous exception, the national press commented favourably on the ceremony. The exception was "Peterborough" in the *Daily Telegraph,* who provided what Sir Compton subsequently described in a private letter to the columnist as "the *only* sneer throughout the Press." Sir Compton added: "It was a vicious paragraph because it was obviously intended to wound Vyvyan Holland who is a dear friend of mine." This was all the more extraordinary since the well-known Peterborough column had been started by Wilde's close friend, Reggie Turner, who had nursed him with such unselfish devotion during his final illness. However, the account by Peterborough was evidently premeditated on the part of the individual who wrote it, since Sir Compton Mackenzie had been told on the previous day that there was likely to be an offensive reference to the ceremony in the column. "Presumably this was editorial policy," Sir Compton subsequently wrote to the editor, "and the curious coincidence becomes curiouser and curiouser."

The unveiling of the plaque in Tite Street was followed by a commemoration luncheon at the Savoy Hotel, at which the present writer was likewise in the chair. The coincidence there was proof, if any additional proof were needed, that the wheel had come full circle, since it was in the Savoy that Wilde's activities had called down upon him such severe strictures by the judge in the last trial. But this was rightly forgotten in the laudatory speeches which were delivered at the luncheon. The Irish Ambassador (F. H. Boland) gave a vivid sketch of Wilde's Irish origins and of his special debt to his mother, "known to us in Ireland as Speranza." The French Cultural Counsellor (M. Boyer) spoke of Wilde's association with André Gide and communicated a tribute from André Maurois. The German Cultural Secretary (Eugen Gurster) shamed a British audience by saying that not a week passed without one of Wilde's plays being performed somewhere in Germany. ("His plays belong to the very foundation of the German Repertory Theatre.") Sir Compton Mackenzie added a further tribute to the morning's ceremony when he described the excitement he had experienced as a teenager in his discovering the sophistications in Wilde's writing. ("We felt that the world was coming to life again after the long, long sleep of the later Victorian age.") Finally, Louis Wilkinson, better known by his pen name, Louis Marlow, told of the generosity with which Wilde during his exile in France and Switzerland had conducted a correspondence with him while he was a schoolboy at Radley.

The centenary was also appropriately marked in Dublin and Paris. In the Irish capital the playwright Lennox Robinson unveiled a plaque at 21 Westland Row, where Wilde was born. "Had Wilde been alive twenty-five years ago when the Irish Academy was founded," said Robinson, "he would indubitably have been one of its foundation members." An exhibition of Wilde's books and manuscripts was also put on in the library of Trinity College. Meanwhile, in Paris messages of homage were read at Père Lachaise from members of the French Academy and from Jean Cocteau, while an exhibition of Wilde memorabilia was opened at the Hôtel d'Alsace. The centenary was also marked by a public meeting at the Sorbonne where extracts from his works were read.

A few days after the ceremony in Tite Street, some hooligans daubed the plaque with black paint and tar, completely obliterating the inscription. Fortunately, the damage turned out to be only superficial, and since then the plaque has been left alone, unlike some other London memorials. As Robert Ross wrote to Wilde's son Vyvyan Holland at the time of the infamous Pemberton Billing trial in 1918: "I only hope dear Vyvyan that you don't mind. Oscar's works have now stood the shock of ages, and his permanent position in English drama and literature must compensate for all the rest."

Had Bernard Shaw been alive at the time of the Wilde centenary, he could undoubtedly have been relied upon to send a characteristically Shavian message to mark the occasion. As it is, the final word may well be left with him. "Please let us hear no more of the tragedy of Oscar Wilde," he wrote in his preface to the English edition of Frank Harris's controversial biography in 1938. "Oscar was no tragedian. He was the superb comedian of his century, one to whom misfortune, disgrace, imprisonment were external and traumatic. His gaiety of soul was invulnerable: it shines through the blackest pages of *De Profundis* as clearly as his funniest epigrams. Even on his deathbed he found in himself no pity for himself, playing for the laugh with his last breath, and getting it with as sure a stroke as in his palmiest prime."

Bibliography

Manuscript Sources

The largest and most important collection of Wilde manuscripts, autograph letters, and Wildeana was bought at public auction in Dulau's sale rooms in London in 1929 by the American collector William Andrews Clark, Jr, and is now in the Clark Memorial Library at the University of California, Los Angeles. "This is in my belief the last large collection of Wilde material likely to come on the market," the bibliographer Seymour de Ricci wrote at the time. "The gathering of it took many years and the addition of it to the W. A. Clark, Jr, library completes the latter in a most remarkable way." Only two comparable collections, both assembled by Americans, had previously come on the market and they had been dispersed mostly among private purchasers. The first, which belonged to Richard Butler Glaenzer, was sold in New York in 1911, and the second, the property of John B. Stetson, Jr, was also sold in New York, in 1922.

The greater part of the collection purchased by Clark had belonged to Wilde's close friend and literary executor, Robert Ross, who died in 1918, and included more than 120 letters and telegrams from Oscar Wilde to Ross, among them the remarkable letters written from Reading Gaol, as well as letters from both Wilde's parents to him. The Ross collection was inherited by Wilde's younger son, Vyvyan Holland, who similarly acquired the collection of Wilde's industrious bibliographer Christopher Sclater Millard (Stuart Mason) after the latter's death in 1927. The core of the Clark collection consists of Lots 1 to 67 as described in the published Dulau Catalogue 161 (*A Collection of Original Manuscripts, Letters and Books of Oscar Wilde*), together with some later items which include fifty-nine volumes of press cuttings (Lot 218). A checklist of the manuscript portion of the Clark collection, consisting of nearly three thousand items and taking into account those acquired subsequently to the Dulau sale, such as upwards of ninety letters from Adela Schuster to More Adey, has been compiled by J. C. Finzi and published by UCLA under the title *Oscar Wilde and His Literary Circle* (Los Angeles, 1957).

After the Clark, the most comprehensive Wilde collection is in private hands. The bulk of it was assembled by the present writer between 1930 and 1962, and it now belongs to the distinguished American collector Mary Hyde, whose interest in Wilde and that of her husband, the late Donald F. Hyde, was originally inspired by their acquisition of Wilde's letters to Reginald Turner. No catalogue or checklist of the Hyde collection has been published, but the present writer has given an account of its principal contents in *Four Oaks Library*, edited by Gabriel Austin (Somerville, N.J., 1967). The manuscripts of Wilde's writings in the Hyde collection include seven poems, including *The Sphinx*, portions of his two blank-verse plays *The Duchess of Padua* and *A Florentine Tragedy*, his lecture on "The Irish Poets of '48," part of an unpublished essay on "Hellenism," and the important critical study "The Critic as Artist" published in *Intentions*. There are approximately 150 letters from Wilde to a wide range of correspondents as well as a few letters from his wife to him. The Wildeana include the architect E. W. Godwin's specifications and drawings for the alteration and redecoration of the Wildes' house in Tite Street.

Elsewhere, Oscar Wilde's holograph or autograph letters are dispersed among more than twenty institutions and about seventy-five private collections. Their locations are given with the text of each letter by Sir Rupert Hart-Davis in his admirable edition of the *Letters of Oscar Wilde* (London and New York, 1962). The whereabouts of the manuscripts or drafts of Wilde's writings where known are also indicated in footnotes to the text. With the exception of *The Picture of Dorian Gray* and *Salomé*, the most important are in the British Museum, to which they were presented by Robert Ross. They consist of the final autograph draft of *The Sphinx*, early autograph drafts of the whole of *Lady Windermere's Fan*, *A Woman of No Importance*, *An Ideal Husband*, and of Acts III and IV of the original four-act version of *The Importance of Being Earnest*, and the autograph manuscript of *De Profundis*. Acts I and II of *The Importance of Being Earnest* are in the Arents collection in the New York Public Library.

The Clark Library has the original typescript with the author's autograph corrections and emendations of *The Picture of Dorian Gray*, from which the text of the published book was taken; also the autograph MS of Chapter III. Also in the Clark Library are the following: an early MS draft of *Vera;* the original typescript with the author's autograph corrections and emendations of *A Woman of No Importance;* the MS of ninety stanzas of *The Sphinx;* and the original MS draft of *An Ideal Husband*, together with a typescript corrected in the author's hand.

The corrected typescript of *Lady Windermere's Fan* is in the University of Texas. Of the three known MS versions of *Salomé*, the first is in the Bodmer Library in Geneva, the second is in the University of Texas, and the third, with corrections by Pierre Louÿs, is in the Rosenbach Foundation Museum in Philadelphia. Also in the latter is the enlarged version of *The Portrait of Mr W.H.* The Bodmer Library also contains the MS of "The Fisherman and His Soul" dedicated to Princess Alice of Monaco and originally published in *A House of Pomegranates*.

Besides the letters from Sir William and Lady Wilde in the Clark Library, there are others of importance in the collections of Sir John Gilbert and Sir Thomas Larcom in the National Library of Ireland.

The MS of "Oscar Wilde: An Oxford Reminiscence," by Wilde's college friend and contemporary William Ward, is preserved along with Wilde's letters to Ward in the library of Magdalen College, Oxford.

The diaries and correspondence of Charles Ricketts and Charles Shannon, consisting of thirty-four volumes, are in the British Museum Add. MSS 58085–580118.

Also in the British Museum is a small correspondence between Frank Harris's secretary T. H. Bell and Reginald Turner, Lord Alfred Douglas, and Frank Harris, mostly concerning Bell's visit to Paris at the time of Wilde's death (Add. MSS 58079b).

The MS of Bell's unpublished work *Oscar Wilde without Whitewash* is in the Clark Library.

The typescript of R. H. Sherard's last work on Wilde and himself, *Ultima Verba,* which was never published, is in the Hyde collection.

The diaries and letters of Laura Troubridge, who married Adrian Hope, the guardian of the Wilde children, including those portions referring to Oscar and Constance Wilde not reproduced in *Life amongst the Troubridges* by Laura Troubridge (London, 1966), are in the possession of her grandson Mr Felix Hope-Nicholson.

The curious memoirs of the eccentric English baronet and Chinese scholar Sir Edmund Trelawny Backhouse, of which the first part, entitled "The Dead Past," contains detailed references to Wilde and descriptions of his activities mainly of a scandalous and unpublishable character, are in the Bodleian Library, Oxford. The memoirs, unpublished as well as unpublishable, were written by Backhouse in his old age in Peking half a century or more after the events they purport to describe, and insofar as they concern Wilde and his contemporaries they should be regarded with considerable caution.

The plea of justification filed by the defence in *Regina (Wilde)* v *Queensberry* in 1895 and published by the present writer in *The Trials of Oscar Wilde* (London, 1948) is kept in the records of the Central Criminal Court. The file relating to this trial is in the Public Record Office: Crim 1/41. The manuscript of the unpublished recollections of Sir Edward Clarke, Wilde's leading counsel in all three trials, is in the possession of Clarke's grandson Judge Edward Clarke. The extensive official correspondence and other papers concerning Wilde's imprisonment, amounting to 108 files, is in the Home Office: the file numbers are A 56887/1–25 of the Secretary of State, and 13629/1–83 of the Prison Commissioners respectively. This material, which is still subject to restriction, has been fully used by the present writer in his *Oscar Wilde: The Aftermath* (London and New York, 1963).

The papers of Father Cuthbert Dunne C.P. and his account of his reception of Wilde into the Roman Catholic Church and his administration of the last rites are in the University of Texas. They were used by Father Edmund Burke C.P. in his account ("Oscar Wilde: The Final Scene") in *The London Magazine,* May 1961, and by Rupert Croft-Cooke in his account ("Oscar Wilde Discoveries") in *Books and Bookmen,* February 1974.

Robert Ross's letters to the Wilde collector and bibliographer Walter Ledger, written between 1902 and 1918, are in the Robert Ross Memorial Collection in the Bodleian Library. Also in this collection are copies of letters from Wilde, Louis Wilkinson, and Ross dated 1898–1914, as well as about 150 letters from C. S. Millard (Stuart Mason) to Walter Ledger on details of Wilde's bibliography; these cover the years 1904 to 1918. Ross's letters to Vyvyan Holland are in the Hyde collection. Ross's correspondence with Jacob Epstein and other persons relating to the monument at Wilde's grave in Père Lachaise are in the British Museum.

Published Sources

The largest individual collection of printed works, consisting of more than a thousand volumes, was formed by Walter Ledger and bequeathed by him to University College, Oxford. In 1932, it was placed on permanent deposit in the Bodleian, where it is known as the Robert Ross Memorial Collection. However, although more comprehensive, it is not so rich in association and author's presentation copies as other collections like the Clark and the Hyde. The Clark collection has been minutely described in the five volumes of *The Library of William Andrews Clark Jr: Wilde and Wildeana* (San Francisco, 1922–31), and the Hyde collection more briefly by the present writer in *Four Oaks Library,* as already noted.

The Bibliography of Oscar Wilde by Stuart Mason (London, 1914), which took the author most of ten years to compile, is an indispensable printed source, as is his earlier *Bibliography of the Poems of Oscar Wilde* (London, 1907). The former was reprinted in a facsimile edition with an introduction by Timothy d'Arch Smith in 1967. While the introduction gives a useful short biographical sketch of Millard, it indicates only a few minor omissions from the bibliography and notices nothing published after 1914 except the Dulau catalogue in 1928 and the bibliographical study of *The Ballad of Reading Gaol* by Abraham Horodisch (New York, 1954). Nor does it mention the fact that Mason (Millard) was working on a second and enlarged edition of the bibliography at the time of his death and that his own copiously annotated and amended copy of the original edition is now in the Clark Library.

Although it does not claim to be exhaustive, the following is a list of the principal printed sources consulted in the preparation of this book:

Atkinson, G. T. "Oscar Wilde at Oxford." *Cornhill Magazine,* London, May 1929.

Beardsley, Aubrey. *Last Letters.* London, 1904.

—— *Letters to Leonard Smithers.* London, 1937.

Beddington, Mrs Claude. *All That I Have Met.* London, 1929.

Beerbohm, Max. *Letters to Reggie Turner.* Edited by Rupert Hart-Davis. London, 1964.

—— *A Peep into the Past and other prose pieces.* Collected and introduced by Rupert Hart-Davis. London, 1972.

Bell, T. H. "Oscar Wilde's Unwritten Play." *The Bookman.* New York, April–May 1930.

Benson, E. F. *As We Were.* London, 1930.

Benson, Sir Frank. *My Memoirs.* London, 1930.

Bettany, F. G. *Stewart Headlam.* London, 1926.

Birnbaum, Martin. *Oscar Wilde. Fragments and Memories.* London, 1920.

Biron, Sir Chartres. *Without Prejudice. Impressions of Life and Law.* London, 1936.

Blanche, Jacques-Emile. *Portraits of a Lifetime.* London, 1937.

Blei, Franz. See La Jeunesse, Ernest.

Blunt, Wilfrid Scawen. *My Diaries.* 2 vols. London, 1932.

Brasol, Boris. *Oscar Wilde: The Man—The Artist.* London, 1938.

Brémont, Anna Comtesse de. *Oscar Wilde and His Mother.* London, 1911.

Broad, Lewis. *The Friendships and Follies of Oscar Wilde.* London, 1954.

Brome, Vincent. *Frank Harris.* London, 1959.

Brown, W. Sorley. *The Life and Genius of T. W. H. Crosland.* London, 1928.

Burdett, Osbert. *Memory and Imagination.* London, 1935.

Burke, Rev. Edmund, C.P. "Oscar Wilde: The Final Scene." *The London Magazine,* New Series, May 1961.

Byrne, Patrick. *The Wildes of Merrion Square.* London, 1953.

Caillas, Alin. *Oscar Wilde tel que je l'ai connu.* Paris, 1971.

Carrington, Charles. *The Trial of Oscar Wilde.* Paris, 1906.

Cawthorne, Terence. "The Last Illness of Oscar Wilde." *Proceedings of the Royal Society of Medicine,* Vol. 52, London, February 1959.

Cecil, Lord David. *Max.* London, 1964.

Charteris, Evan. *The Life and Letters of Sir Edmund Gosse.* London, 1931.

Choisy, L. F. *Oscar Wilde.* Paris, 1927.

Clark, William Andrews. *The Library of William Andrews Clark Jr: Wilde and Wildeana.* 5 vols. San Francisco, 1922–31.

Connell, John. *W. E. Henley.* London, 1949.

Croft-Cooke, Rupert. *Bosie.* London, 1963.

—— *The Unrecorded Life of Oscar Wilde.* London, 1972.

—— "Oscar Wilde Discoveries." *Books and Bookmen,* February, 1974.

Davray, Henry D. *Oscar Wilde. La Tragédie Finale.* Paris, 1928.

Douglas, Lord Alfred. *Sonnets.* London, 1909.

—— *Oscar Wilde and Myself.* London, 1914.

—— *Collected Satires.* London, 1926.

—— *Autobiography.* London, 1929. New edition. London, 1931.

—— *Without Apology.* London, 1938.

—— *Oscar Wilde: A Summing Up.* London, 1950.

See also Harris, Frank.

Dulau & Co. Ltd. *A Collection of Original Manuscripts Letters and Books of Oscar Wilde including his Letters written to Robert Ross from Reading Gaol and Unpublished Letters Poems and Plays formerly in the possession of Robert Ross, C. S. Millard (Stuart Mason) and the younger son of Oscar Wilde.* London, 1928.

Ellmann, Richard. *Oscar Wilde: A Collection of Critical Essays.* Edited by Richard Ellmann. Englewood Cliffs, 1969.

Epstein, Jacob. *The Sculptor Speaks.* London, 1931.

—— *An Autobiography.* London, 1955.

Ervine, St John. *Oscar Wilde: A Present Time Appraisal.* London, 1951.

Fido, Martin. *Oscar Wilde.* London, 1973.

Fish, Arthur. "Oscar Wilde as Editor." *Harper's Weekly,* New York, 4 October 1913.

—— "Memories of Oscar Wilde." *Cassell's Weekly,* London, 2 May 1923.

Gaunt, William. *The Aesthetic Adventure.* London, 1945.

Gerson, Noel B. *Lillie Langtry.* London, 1972.

Gide, André. *Oscar Wilde.* London, 1951.

See also La Jeunesse, Ernest.

Girouard, Mark. "Chelsea's Bohemian Studio Houses." *Country Life,* 23 November 1972.

Glaenzer, Richard Butler. *The Library of Richard Butler Glaenzer. A Remarkable Assemblage of Manuscripts, Autograph Letters, Presentation Copies and Rare Editions of Oscar Wilde.* New York, 1911.

Goncourt, Charles and Edmond de. *Pages from the Goncourt Journal.* Edited, Translated and Introduced by Robert Baldick. London, 1962.

Gower, Lord Ronald. *My Reminiscences.* London, 1884.

Green, Roger Lancelyn. *A. E. W. Mason.* London, 1952.

Grosskurth, Phyllis. *John Addington Symonds.* London, 1964.

Haldane, R. B., Viscount. *Autobiography.* London, 1929.

Hamilton, William. *The Aesthetic Movement in England.* London, 1882.

Harbron, Dudley. *The Conscious Stone.* London, 1949.

Harris, Frank. *The Life and Confessions of Oscar Wilde.* 2 vols. New York, 1918. New edition with a Preface by Bernard Shaw. London, 1928.

—— and Lord Alfred Douglas. *New Preface to "The Life and Confessions of Oscar Wilde."* London, 1925.

—— *My Life and Loves.* 4 vols. Privately printed, 1925–30. New edition with introduction by John F. Gallagher. London, 1964.

—— *Mr and Mrs Daventry.* Edited with an introduction by H. Montgomery Hyde, London, 1956.

Hichens, Robert. *The Green Carnation.* London, 1894. New edition, with introduction by the author. London, 1949.

Hicks, Seymour. *Between Ourselves.* London, 1930.

Holland, Vyvyan. *Son of Oscar Wilde.* London, 1954.
—— *Time Remembered after Père Lachaise.* London, 1956.
—— *Pictorial Biography of Oscar Wilde.* London, 1960.
Holroyd, Michael. *Lytton Strachey.* Vol. II. *The Years of Achievement.* London, 1968.
Hopkins, R. Thurston. *Oscar Wilde. A Story of the Man and His Work.* London, 1913.
Humphreys, Sir Travers. *Criminal Days.* London, 1946.
—— *A Book of Trials.* London, 1953.
Hunter Blair, Rt. Rev. Sir David. *In Victorian Days.* London, 1939.
Hyde, H. Montgomery. *The Trials of Oscar Wilde.* With an introduction by Sir Travers Humphreys. London, 1948. New and enlarged edition. London, 1962; New York, 1973.
—— *Cases That Changed the Law.* London, 1951.
—— *Carson. The Life of Sir Edward Carson, Lord Carson of Duncairn.* London, 1953.
—— "Some Unpublished Recollections [of Oscar Wilde] by Stuart Merrill." *Adam International Review,* Nos. 241–3, London, 1954.
—— "An Afternoon with Max." *The Spectator,* 5 October 1956.
—— "The Portrait of Mr W.H." *The Times Literary Supplement,* 5 December 1958.
—— "New Light on the Oscar Wilde Tragedy." *Waterloo Review,* Vol. 2, No. 1, Summer 1959.
—— "The De Profundis Affair." *Sunday Times,* 3 January 1960.
—— *Oscar Wilde: The Aftermath.* London, 1963.
—— Introduction to *Teleny.* London, 1966.
—— "Oscar Wilde." *Four Oaks Library.* Edited by Gabriel Austin. Somerville, New Jersey, 1967.
—— *The Other Love.* London, 1970.
Ingleby, Leonard Cresswell. *Oscar Wilde.* London, 1907. New edition. London, 1912.
John, Augustus. *Chiaroscuro.* London, 1952.
Jopling, Louise. *Twenty Years of My Life, 1867 to 1887.* London, 1925.
Jullian, Philippe. *Oscar Wilde.* Translated by Violet Wyndham. London, 1969.
Kenilworth, Walter Winston. *A Study of Oscar Wilde.* New York, 1912.
Kernahan, Coulson. *In Good Company.* London, 1917.
Kingsmill, Hugh. *Frank Harris.* London, 1932.
La Jeunesse, Ernest; Gide, André; and Blei, Franz. *In Memoriam Oscar Wilde.* Translation and introduction by Perceval Pollard. Greenwich, Connecticut, 1951.
Lambert, Eric. *Mad with Much Heart. A Life of the Parents of Oscar Wilde.* London, 1967.
Langtry, Lillie. *The Days I Knew.* London, 1925.
Laver, James. *Oscar Wilde.* London, 1954.
Le Gallienne, Richard. *The Romantic Nineties.* London, 1926. New edition with introduction by H. Montgomery Hyde. London, 1951.
Lemonnier, Léon. *Vie d'Oscar Wilde.* Paris, 1931.
Leslie, Shane. *Sir Evelyn Ruggles-Brise.* London, 1938.
Leverton, W. H. *Through the Box Office Window.* London, 1932.
Lewis, Lloyd, and Smith, Henry Justin. *Oscar Wilde Discovers America.* New York, 1936.
Lutyens, Lady Emily. *A Blessed Girl.* London, 1953.
Mahaffy, Rev. J. P. *Social Life in Greece from Homer to Menander.* London, 1874.
Marjoribanks, Edward. *Life of Lord Carson.* Vol. I. London, 1932.

Marlow, Louis (Louis Wilkinson). *Seven Friends.* London, 1953.

Mason, A. E. W. *Sir George Alexander and the St James's Theatre.* London, 1935.

Mason, Stuart. *Oscar Wilde. A Study.* Oxford, 1905.

—— *Bibliography of the Poems of Oscar Wilde.* London, 1907.

—— *The Oscar Wilde Calendar.* London, 1910.

—— *Oscar Wilde: Art and Morality.* London, 1912.

—— *Oscar Wilde Three Times Tried.* London, 1912.

—— *Bibliography of Oscar Wilde.* London, 1914. Facsimile edition with introduction by Timothy d'Arch Smith. London, 1967.

Maxwell, W. B. *Time Gathered.* London, 1937.

May, J. Lewis. *John Lane and the '90s.* London, 1936.

Merle, Robert. *Oscar Wilde.* Paris, 1948.

—— *Oscar Wilde ou la destinée de l'homosexuel.* Paris, 1955.

Millard, Christopher. See Mason, Stuart.

Mix, Katherine Lyon. *A Study in Yellow.* Lawrence, Kansas and London, 1960.

Neilson, Julia. *This for Remembrance.* London, 1940.

Newbolt, Sir Henry. *Memoirs.* Vol. I. London, 1932.

Nordau, Max. *Degeneration.* London, 1894.

Nowell-Smith, Simon. *Letters to Macmillan.* London, 1967.

O'Sullivan, Vincent. *Aspects of Wilde.* London, 1936.

—— *Opinions.* With an introduction by Alan Anderson. London, 1959.

Pearson, Hesketh. *Modern Men and Mummers.* London, 1921.

—— *Oscar Wilde.* London, 1946.

—— *Beerbohm Tree.* London, 1956.

Pennell, E. R. and J. *The Life of James McNeill Whistler.* 2 vols. London, 1908.

Pullar, Philippa. *Frank Harris.* London, 1975.

Queensberry, Marquess of, and Cohen, Percy. *Oscar Wilde and the Black Douglas.* London, 1949.

Raffalovich, André. *L'Affaire Oscar Wilde.* Lyons, 1895.

—— *Uranisme et Unisexualité.* Lyons, 1895.

Ransome, Arthur. *Oscar Wilde: A Critical Study.* London, 1912.

—— "Oscar Wilde in Paris." *The Bookman,* New York, May 1911.

Renier, G. J. *Oscar Wilde.* London, 1933.

Ricketts, Charles. *Recollections of Oscar Wilde.* London, 1932.

—— *Self-Portrait. Letters and Journals of Charles Ricketts.* Collected and compiled by T. Sturges Moore, edited by Cecil Lewis. London, 1939.

Robertson, Graham. *Time Was.* London, 1931.

Rodd, Sir James Rennell. *Social and Diplomatic Memories.* Vol. I, London, 1922.

Rose, Kenneth. *Superior Person.* London, 1969.

Ross, Robert. *Robert Ross. Friend of Friends. Letters to Robert Ross, Art Critic and Writer, together with extracts from his published articles.* Edited by Margery Ross. London, 1952.

Rothenstein, John. *The Life and Death of Conder.* London, 1938.

Rothenstein, William. *Men and Memories.* Vol. I. London, 1931.

Ryskamp, Charles. *Wilde and the Nineties. An Essay and an Exhibition.* Richard Ellmann, E. D. H. Johnson, and Alfred C. Bush. Edited by Charles Ryskamp. Princeton, 1966.

Saltus, Edgar. *Oscar Wilde: An Idler's Impression.* Chicago, 1917.

Sherard, Robert Harborough. *Oscar Wilde. The Story of an Unhappy Friendship.* Privately printed, 1902. London, 1905.

—— *Twenty Years in Paris.* London, 1905.

—— *Life of Oscar Wilde.* London, 1906.

—— *The Real Oscar Wilde.* London, 1911.

—— *Oscar Wilde Twice Defended.* Calvi, 1934.

Sherard, Robert Harborough. *Bernard Shaw, Frank Harris and Oscar Wilde*. London, 1937.

Sickert, W. R. *A Free House! The Writings of Walter Richard Sickert*. Edited by Sir Osbert Sitwell. London, 1947.

Sitwell, Osbert. *Noble Essences*. London, 1950.

Sitwell, Sacheverell. *For Want of the Golden City*. London, 1973.

Sladen, Douglas. *Twenty Years of My Life*. London, 1915.

Smithers, Jack. *The Early Life and Vicissitudes of Jack Smithers*. London, 1939.

Speaight, Robert. *William Rothenstein*. London, 1962.

Stanford, W. B., and McDowell, R. B. *Mahaffy*. London, 1971.

Stetson, John B. *The Oscar Wilde Collection of John B. Stetson, Jr.* New York, 1920.

Swanwick, H. M. *I Have Been Young*. London, 1935.

Symons, A. J. A. "The Diner Out," "Wilde at Oxford," and other draft chapters of unfinished biography. *Horizon*, Vol. III, 1944.

Symons, Arthur. *A Study of Oscar Wilde*. London, 1930.

Terry, Ellen. *Memoirs*. London, 1933.

Tobin, A. I., and Gertz, E. *Frank Harris*. Chicago, 1931.

Trinity College, Dublin. *Catalogue of an Exhibition of Books and Manuscripts in Commemoration of the Centenary of the Birth of Oscar Wilde*. Dublin, 1954.

Troubridge, Laura. *Life amongst the Troubridges*. Edited by Jacqueline Hope-Nicholson. London, 1966.

Walford, L. B. *Memories of Victorian London*. London, 1912.

Walker-Smith, Derek, and Clarke, Edward. *The Life of Sir Edward Clarke*. London, 1939.

Weintraub, Stanley. *Reggie. A Portrait of Reginald Turner*. New York, 1965.

Whistler, James McNeill. *The Gentle Art of Making Enemies*. London, 1890.

White, Terence de Vere. *The Parents of Oscar Wilde*. London, 1967.

Whittington-Egan, Richard, and Smerdon, Geoffrey. *The Quest of the "Golden Boy": Life and Letters of Richard Le Gallienne*. London, 1960.

Whyte, Frederic. *William Heinemann*. London, 1928.

Wilde, Oscar. *Impressions of America*. Edited with an introduction by Stuart Mason. Sunderland, 1906.

—— *Decorative Art in America*. Edited with an introduction by Richard Butler Glaenzer. New York, 1906.

—— *Works*. First Collected Edition. Edited by Robert Ross. 14 vols. London, 1908.

—— *Essays and Lectures*. London, 1909.

—— *The Portrait of Mr W.H.* London and New York, 1921.

—— *After Reading. Letters of Oscar Wilde to Robert Ross*. Edited by Stuart Mason. London, 1921.

—— *After Berneval. Letters of Oscar Wilde to Robert Ross*. Edited by More Adey. London, 1922.

—— *Some Letters from Oscar Wilde to Alfred Douglas 1892–1897*. With illustrative notes by Arthur C. Dennison, Jr, and Harrison Post, and an essay by A. S. W. Rosenbach, Ph.D. San Francisco, 1924.

—— *Letzte Briefe*. Translated with notes by Dr Max Meyerfeld. Berlin, 1925.

—— *Letters to the Sphinx from Oscar Wilde*. With reminiscences of the author by Ada Leverson, and introduction by Robert Ross. London, 1930.

—— *Sixteen Letters from Oscar Wilde to William Rothenstein*. Edited by John Rothenstein, London, 1930.

—— *De Profundis. The Complete Text*. With an introduction by Vyvyan Holland. London, 1949.

—— *The Epigrams of Oscar Wilde*. An Anthology by Alvin Redman. With an introduction by Vyvyan Holland. London, 1952.

—— *The Importance of Being Earnest . . . in Four Acts as originally written.* With an introduction by Sarah Augusta Dickson. 2 vols. New York, 1956.

—— *Letters of Oscar Wilde.* Edited by Rupert Hart-Davis. London and New York, 1962.

—— *Literary Criticism of Oscar Wilde.* Edited by Stanley Weintraub. Lincoln, Nebraska, 1968.

—— *The Artist as Critic. Critical Writings of Oscar Wilde.* Edited by Richard Ellmann. London, 1970.

—— *Irish Poets and Poetry of the Nineteenth Century.* Edited by Robert D. Pepper. San Francisco, 1972.

—— *The Picture of Dorian Gray.* Edited with an introduction by Isobel Murray. London, 1974.

Wilde, Dorothy (Dolly). *"Oscaria." In Memory of Dorothy Ierne Wilde.* With an introduction and epilogue by Natalie Clifford Barney. Paris, 1951.

Wilde, Sir William R. *Lough Corrib.* Dublin, 1872.

Wilkinson, Louis. See Marlow, Louis.

Wilson, T. G. *Victorian Doctor.* London, 1942.

Winwar, Francis. *Oscar Wilde and the Yellow Nineties.* New York, 1940.

Wyndham, Horace. *Speranza.* London, 1951.

Wyndham, Violet. *The Sphinx and Her Circle. A Biographical Sketch of Ada Leverson.* London, 1963.

Yeats, W. B. *The Trembling of the Veil.* London, 1926.

—— *Letters of W. B. Yeats.* Edited by Allen Wade. London, 1956.

—— *Memoirs.* Edited by Denis Donoghue. London, 1972.

Young, Dalhousie. *Apologia pro Oscar Wilde.* London, 1895.

Index

HOTEL D'ALSACE
J. DUPOIRIER
13, Rue des Beaux-Arts, 13

DÉJEUNERS & DINERS - SERVICE A VOLONTÉ
APPARTEMENTS & CHAMBRES MEUBLÉS
SONNERIE ÉLECTRIQUE

M⁻ Melmoth.   Doit

PARIS le 2 X^bre 1900

			Timbre...	0	10
		Chambre 1 mois	90	
		chambre du domestique au 6e	20	
9^e	23	1 bouillon d'une poule	5	
		riz et pain		40
		linge de lit d'échange en plus	1	50
		41 thé pain et beurre	16	80
		11 lit de lait supérieur 0.70	7	70
		2 œufs 0.25		50
		3 b. de limonade 1.f	3	
		3 lit de citronade	2	40
		1 chocolat complet		70
		5 socs de charbon le 4.50	22	50
		2 paniers de bois	4	
		6 fois service de table et pain	1	50
		3 cafés cognac 0.60	1	80
		4 fois glace	2	
		Total	**180**	**40**